THE REVOLUTIONARY CITY

The Revolutionary City

URBANIZATION AND THE GLOBAL
TRANSFORMATION OF REBELLION

MARK R. BEISSINGER

PRINCETON UNIVERSITY PRESS
PRINCETON & OXFORD

Copyright © 2022 by Princeton University Press

Princeton University Press is committed to the protection of copyright and the intellectual property our authors entrust to us. Copyright promotes the progress and integrity of knowledge. Thank you for supporting free speech and the global exchange of ideas by purchasing an authorized edition of this book. If you wish to reproduce or distribute any part of it in any form, please obtain permission.

Requests for permission to reproduce material from this work should be sent to permissions@press.princeton.edu

Published by Princeton University Press
41 William Street, Princeton, New Jersey 08540
99 Banbury Road, Oxford OX2 6JX

press.princeton.edu

All Rights Reserved

Library of Congress Cataloging-in-Publication Data

Names: Beissinger, Mark R. author.
Title: The revolutionary city : urbanization and the global transformation of rebellion / Mark R. Beissinger.
Description: Princeton, New Jersey : Princeton University Press, [2022] | Includes bibliographical references and index.
Identifiers: LCCN 2021029315 (print) | LCCN 2021029316 (ebook) | ISBN 9780691224749 (paperback) | ISBN 9780691224763 (hardback) | ISBN 9780691224756 (ebook)
Subjects: LCSH: Revolutions. | Sociology, Urban. | Urbanization—Political aspects. | Regime change.
Classification: LCC HM876 .B46 2022 (print) | LCC HM876 (ebook) | DDC 307.76—dc23
LC record available at https://lccn.loc.gov/2021029315
LC ebook record available at https://lccn.loc.gov/2021029316

British Library Cataloging-in-Publication Data is available

Editorial: Bridget Flannery-McCoy and Alena Chekanov
Production Editorial: Mark Bellis
Cover Design: Lauren Smith and Kimberly Castañeda
Production: Erin Suydam
Publicity: Kate Hensley and Charlotte Coyne

Cover Credit: Aerial view of Maidan Nezalezhnosti (Independence Square) crowded by supporters of EU integration during a rally in central Kiev, December 8, 2013. REUTERS/Inna Sokolovska

This book has been composed in Arno

10 9 8 7 6 5 4 3 2 1

For my father, and for all who dream of a better life.

CONTENTS

List of Illustrations ix
List of Tables xv
Preface xvii

	Introduction. Revolution and the City	1
1	A Spatial Theory of Revolution	19
2	The Growth and Urbanization of Revolution	56
3	The Urban Civic Revolutionary Moment	103
4	The Repression–Disruption Trade-off and the Shifting Odds of Success	151
5	Revolutionary Contingency and the City	198
6	Public Space and Urban Revolution	236
7	The Individual and Collective Action in Urban Civic Revolution	271
8	The Pacification of Revolution	319
9	The Evolving Impact of Revolution	359
10	The City and the Future of Revolution	417

Appendix 1. Construction of Cross-National Data on Revolutionary Episodes 435
Appendix 2. Revolutionary Episodes, 1900–2014 441
Appendix 3. Data Sources Used in Statistical Analyses 461

Appendix 4. Choices of Statistical Models 469

References 497

Index 547

ILLUSTRATIONS

1.1. The relationship of revolution to other forms of politics. 28
1.2. Exposure to regime repression, disruptive efficiency, and proximity to centers of power. 39
1.3a. Revolutionary episodes, 1900–2014: locations. 50
1.3b. Revolutionary episodes, 1900–2014: tactics. 50
1.3c. Revolutionary episodes, 1900–2014: goals. 51
1.3d. Revolutionary episodes, 1900–2014: outcomes. 51
2.1. The yearly onset of new revolutionary episodes, 1900–2014. 58
2.2. The number of ongoing revolutionary episodes per year, 1900–2014. 59
2.3. The average duration of revolutionary episodes, by onset year. 60
2.4. The yearly hazard rate of the materialization of a revolutionary episode across 158 fixed territorial units around the world. 61
2.5. Revolutionary episodes and attempted military coups, 1945–2014. 62
2.6. The onset of new social revolutionary episodes, 1900–2014. 63
2.7. The onset of urban civic and other urban revolutionary episodes, 1900–2014. 64
2.8. Time and the incidence of new revolutionary episodes. 65
2.9. Land concentration and the probability of onset of social revolutionary episodes. 66
2.10. Percentage of global population that is urban/rural, 1800–2050. 67
2.11. Average level of urbanization of societies experiencing new revolutionary episodes, 1900–2014. 71
2.12. Percentage of revolutionary episodes occurring primarily in a rural or an urban setting. 72

2.13. The onset of rural and urban social revolutionary episodes, 1900–2014.   73

2.14. Class and occupational participation in revolutionary episodes, by time period.   83

2.15. The probability that a particular media form was used, by urban/rural location of revolutionary episode.   87

2.16. State capacity by location and type of revolution (Hanson/Sigman state capacity index).   92

3.1. The probability of onset of urban civic and social revolutionary episodes, by Polity score (t−1).   109

3.2. The probability of onset of urban civic and social revolutionary episodes, by longevity of incumbent leader in power.   111

3.3. The probability of onset of urban civic and social revolutionary episodes, by GDP per capita (t−1).   113

3.4. The probability of onset of urban civic and social revolutionary episodes, by rates of economic growth (t−1).   114

3.5. Predicted probabilities for an urban civic revolutionary episode in Tunisia, 1960–2014.   124

3.6. Predicted probabilities for an urban civic revolutionary episode in Serbia, 1960–2014.   127

3.7. Predicted probabilities for an urban civic revolutionary episode in Myanmar, 1960–2014.   128

3.8. Predicted probabilities for an urban civic revolutionary episode in Ukraine, 1992–2014.   131

3.9. Predicted probabilities for an urban civic revolutionary episode in South Korea, 1960–2014.   135

3.10. Predicted probabilities for an urban civic revolutionary episode in Czechoslovakia, 1960–2014.   137

3.11. Predicted probabilities for an urban civic revolutionary episode in Indonesia, 1960–2014.   138

3.12. Predicted probabilities for an urban civic revolutionary episode in the Philippines, 1960–2014.   140

3.13. Predicted probabilities for an urban civic revolutionary episode in Mexico, 1960–2014.   145

3.14. Predicted probabilities for an urban civic revolutionary episode in Malaysia, 1960–2014.   147

4.1.	Successful and failed revolutionary episodes over time, 1900–2014.	154
4.2.	Percentage of successful revolutionary episodes over time, 1900–2014.	155
4.3.	Marginal probability of revolutionary success by episode type, controlling for the effects of time.	156
4.4.	Polity scores and the mean probability of opposition success, by rural, urban, and urban civic episodes.	158
4.5.	Military expenditure per soldier (deciles) and revolutionary outcomes, with and without civil war.	165
4.6a.	ROC curves based on regime features (rural vs urban episodes), complete-case analysis.	174
4.6b.	ROC curves based on regime features (rural vs urban episodes), multiple-imputation analysis.	175
4.7.	Peak participation and the marginal probability of opposition success.	180
4.8.	Peak participation and the average probability of opposition success in urban, rural, urban civic, and other urban revolutionary episodes.	183
4.9.	Violence and the probability of opposition victory, rural vs urban context.	186
4.10a.	ROC curves based on opposition features (rural vs urban episodes), complete-case sample.	191
4.10b.	ROC curves based on opposition features (rural vs urban episodes), multiple imputation.	192
6.1.	Khreshchatyk and Duma Square in 1918, as seen from a German aerial photo.	238
6.2.	Khreshchatyk and Independence Square in 2017.	240
6.3.	Distance from seat of government, by outcome.	258
6.4.	Mean concentration of populations in capital cities, 1900–2014.	260
7.1.	Behavioral categories in the Orange and Euromaidan revolutions.	280
7.2.	Behavioral categories in the Tunisian and Egyptian revolutions.	282
7.3.	The probability of participating in revolutionary protests, by gender.	289

7.4. The probability of participating in revolutionary protests, by age category. 290

7.5. Occupations of participants in revolutionary protests (percentage of participants), relative to percentage of occupation in society as a whole. 293

7.6. The probability of participating in revolutionary protests, by income quintiles. 295

7.7. The probability of participating in revolutionary protests, by consumer goods ownership. 296

7.8. The probability of participating in revolutionary protests, by level of education. 297

7.9. Probability of participation in, support of, or opposition to revolution, by whether respondent speaks Ukrainian at home (Orange and Euromaidan revolutions). 299

7.10. Probability of participation, support, or opposition to revolution, by level of religiosity among Muslims (Egyptian and Tunisian revolutions). 301

7.11. Political self-identification among participants, supporters, and opponents of revolution (Orange and Euromaidan revolutions). 303

7.12a. Profile plots for three-cluster model of revolution participants: Orange Revolution. 306

7.12b. Profile plots for three-cluster model of revolution participants: Euromaidan Revolution. 306

7.13. Probability of participation in revolutionary protests, by participation of friends and family and the use of internet as the primary source of information about the revolution (Egyptian and Tunisian revolutions). 315

8.1. Average predicted deaths (thousands) per revolutionary episode involving civil war, by year of episode onset. 326

8.2. The probability of a revolutionary episode involving civil war, by year of episode onset. 334

8.3. Average predicted deaths per revolutionary episode without civil wars, by year of episode onset. 340

9.1. Conceptualizing the impact of revolution. 367

9.2. Survival functions for regimes after social and urban civic revolutionary episodes. 369

9.3. Survival functions for post-revolutionary regimes, by length of revolutionary episode. 371

9.4a. Growth in GDP per capita for failed revolutions, relative to matched cases. 380

9.4b. Growth in GDP per capita for successful revolutions, relative to matched cases. 381

9.5a. Growth in GDP per capita for successful social revolutions, relative to matched cases. 383

9.5b. Growth in GDP per capita for failed social revolutions, relative to matched cases. 384

9.6a. Growth in GDP per capita for successful urban civic revolutions, relative to matched cases. 385

9.6b. Growth in GDP per capita for failed urban civic revolutions, relative to matched cases. 386

9.7a. V-Dem political corruption index for urban civic revolutionary episodes, failed vs successful episodes. 390

9.7b. V-Dem political corruption index for social revolutionary episodes, failed vs successful episodes. 391

9.8a. V-Dem equal distribution of resources index for successful social revolutions, relative to matched cases. 397

9.8b. V-Dem equal distribution of resources index for successful urban civic revolutions, relative to matched cases. 398

9.9a. Income inequality (Gini index) for social revolutions (successful vs failed revolutions). 400

9.9b. Income inequality (Gini index) for urban civic revolutions (successful vs failed revolutions). 401

9.10a. V-Dem political killing index for successful social revolutions, relative to matched cases. 404

9.10b. V-Dem political killing index for successful urban civic revolutions, relative to matched cases. 405

9.11a. V-Dem political civil liberties index for successful social revolutions, relative to matched cases. 407

9.11b. V-Dem political civil liberties index for successful urban civic revolutions, relative to matched cases. 408

9.12a. V-Dem private civil liberties index for successful social revolutions, relative to matched cases. 409

9.12b. V-Dem private civil liberties index for successful urban civic revolutions, relative to matched cases. 410

9.13a. V-Dem rule of law index for successful social revolutions, relative to matched cases. 411

9.13b. V-Dem rule of law index for successful urban civic revolutions, relative to matched cases. 412

9.14a. V-Dem government accountability index for successful social revolutions, relative to matched cases. 413

9.14b. V-Dem government accountability index for successful urban civic revolutions, relative to matched cases. 414

TABLES

3.1. A probabilistic model of the onset of urban civic revolutionary contention. 116
3.2. A comparison of factors associated with the onset of revolutionary contention and military coup attempts. 120
4.1. Incumbent regime characteristics and the likelihood of opposition victory in revolutionary contention. 170
4.2. Opposition characteristics and the likelihood of opposition victory in revolutionary contention. 177
4.3. Combined models of regime and opposition characteristics and the likelihood of opposition victory in revolutionary contention. 194
8.1. Number of deaths in revolutionary episodes, by period of onset. 322
8.2. Estimated impact of changing conditions of contention on deaths in revolutionary civil wars, Cold War vs post–Cold War periods. 329
8.3. Estimated impact of selection processes into or away from civil war on deaths in revolutions in the Cold War and post–Cold War periods. 336
8.4. Estimated impact of changing conditions of contention on deaths in episodes without civil wars, first half of the twentieth century vs post–Cold War period. 341
A2.1. Revolutionary episodes, 1900–2014. 442
A3.1. Cross-sectional data, means and distributions. 467
A4.1. Multiple imputation for panel data, summary statistics. 472
A4.2. Multiple imputation for cross-sectional data, summary statistics. 479
A4.3. Covariate balances before and after matching. 494

PREFACE

> History is a forest of a million trees. Wild beasts run through it, vines hide its branches, strange birds sing in its upper reaches, and wildflowers burst out in its clearings.... We can explain its particular features, discover recurrent causal mechanisms in its evolution, and provide overall accounts of its changes. But woe to the ecologist or historian who seeks to catalog, reconstruct, vivisect, and explain every niche, every creature, every change of a particular forest; madness lies that way.
>
> CHARLES TILLY, *POPULAR CONTENTION IN GREAT BRITAIN, 1758–1834* (1995)[1]

THERE ARE CERTAIN TOPICS to which scholars knowledgeable about Russia and the former Soviet Union are naturally drawn. Revolution is one, for obvious reasons. But specialists on the region gravitate to the topic not only because of the Russian Revolution of 1917 and its outsized influence on global history. The Russian, East European, and Eurasian region has been the site of repeated outbursts of revolutionary contention over the twentieth and twenty-first centuries. It still remains one of the world regions most susceptible to revolutionary upheaval. Among the chief reasons for this is its long-standing record of pernicious governance, which unfortunately persists to this day.

Work on this book began in 2010, when historian Steven Pincus invited me to a workshop at Yale on "blank spots" in our knowledge of revolutions. Having written on protest and violence during the Soviet collapse, the spread of the color revolutions, and the Orange Revolution in particular, I was asked to address the evolving relationship of violence to revolution. Like many scholars, I had strong priors that revolutions had been growing less lethal over time. But this was merely an impression based on folk wisdom and the cases I knew best. While data existed on deaths in civil wars, there were no data on deaths in revolutions more broadly to be able to test the proposition in a systematic

---

1. Tilly 1995b, 340.

way or identify the factors responsible for trends. I decided to spend some time in Princeton's Firestone Library exploring how difficult it would be to gather such information. What I discovered convinced me of the promise of such an approach and what a knowledge of evolving global patterns of revolution might teach us. Eventually, what I observed brought me to the city. This was not my original purpose. I first had to wander the forest before I could see how the growth of the city had changed it. But evidence, logic, and the questions I received from others pushed me toward my ultimate destination.

This book embraces Charles Tilly's entreaty to "build concrete and historical analyses of the big structures and large processes that shape our era,"[2] while trying to remain sensitive to history's wild beasts, strange birds, and wildflowers. Its scope—encompassing the impact of urbanization on revolution over more than a century—will strike some as audacious. While I have relied heavily on their work and have striven to remain attentive to the specifics of individual cases, historians may disapprove of my understanding of revolution, take issue with my classification of particular cases, or shudder over my efforts to generalize across such a broad expanse of time. My approach (which in part uses statistical inference to identify patterns across cases that would be difficult to discern if focused on a single case only, and then examines how specific cases do or do not conform to these patterns) may seem an alien language to some. The use of statistical inference to study revolutions has lagged far behind our knowledge of individual cases. For the sake of readability, I have tried to keep statistical jargon to a minimum in the text, to present results visually, and to put more detailed discussions in the footnotes and appendices.[3] My approach is meant to interrogate the ways in which the overall patterning of cases has evolved over time and the large-scale structural factors associated with this; statistics are merely a tool for accomplishing these goals reliably and methodically. But as readers will see, I also pay great attention to the details of individual cases and how they unfold, and my multi-method approach leaves ample sway for agency, interaction, emotion, ambiguity, and error. It is not as foreign to the craft of the historian as it may superficially seem.

I have also adopted a multidisciplinary approach in this study that draws on work from political science, sociology, history, economics, geography, anthropology, and urban design. Disciplinary boundaries have always been artificial in the study of revolution, though their guardians are legion. Given the historical, spatial, political, social, and economic dimensions involved, any study of the ways in which urbanization has transformed revolution must necessarily

2. Tilly 1984, 14.

3. Those who wish to know more can also consult the results files and robustness tests available from the author.

reflect a variety of disciplinary perspectives. Within my own discipline, current trends lean heavily toward the micro and toward fine-grained studies of causal identification. Many questions, however, cannot be answered at a micro-level, and no matter how hard one tries, it is impossible to replicate the stakes and risks involved in revolution in a laboratory setting or survey experiment. Revolutions are rare events, and the historical conditions under which they occur have changed dramatically. Countries and people cannot be assigned to revolution randomly, and the complexity of the interactions involved renders simplistic theories hollow. All this challenges our abilities to pin down causal identification with surgical precision. That does not mean that micro-foundations are unimportant for understanding revolutions, or that analyses should not be conducted with rigor. On the contrary, I have attacked my subject at multiple levels of analysis—from the global to the episodic to the individual—bringing to bear new forms of evidence at each level with the goal of generating novel perspectives. But in the study of revolutions (like many important topics) we must necessarily be content with plausible, logically coherent, empirically backed explanations that remain sensitive to variation and to temporal and spatial contexts. That is how I have approached my subject.

I could not have written this book without the assistance and advice of many. I am extremely grateful to the John Simon Guggenheim Memorial Foundation, which provided support during much of the writing. Nuffield College at Oxford afforded me a comfortable and stimulating environment in which to work. I obviously owe a huge debt of gratitude to Princeton, where I carried out most of the research, enjoyed the university's considerable funding, and benefited from the advice of colleagues. In particular, I want to thank the Mamdouha S. Bobst Center for Peace and Justice for organizing a book conference, during which I received outstanding feedback and suggestions. I also want to thank the Princeton Institute for International and Regional Studies, which provided a wonderful multidisciplinary venue from which to learn from colleagues.

The ideas and analyses in this book received excellent input during presentations at Yale University, Harvard University, the University of Oxford, the University of Wisconsin, Brown University, the University of Toronto, the CUNY Graduate Center, George Washington University, New York University, the London School of Economics, the University of Edinburgh, the University of Manchester, Uppsala University, Sciences Po, the Centre on Social Movement Studies of the Scuola normale superiore in Florence, Bremen International Graduate School of Social Sciences, the Center for East European and International Studies (ZOiS) in Berlin, Korea University in Seoul, Panteion University in Athens, and the Brazilian School of Public and Business Administration at the Getúlio Vargas Foundation (FGV) in Rio de Janeiro, as well as at various meetings of the American Political Science Association, the

International Studies Association, the Association for the Study of Nationalities, and the International Conference on Europeanists. I also thank the Institute of Sociology of the Ukrainian Academy of Sciences, the Kyiv International Institute of Sociology, and the Arab Barometer Survey for providing me with the survey data used in chapter 7. Portions of chapter 7 were previously published in the *American Political Science Review* and *Comparative Politics*.[4]

In compiling the cross-national data on revolutionary episodes used in this book, I benefited significantly from the research assistance of Valarie Hansen, Brittany Holom, Daniel Johnson, Seongcheol Kim, Reid Knabe, and Alexander Powell. Mia Katz provided additional support throughout the project. Raymond Hicks at the Niehaus Center for Globalization and Governance, Gordon Arsenoff at the Bobst Center, and Oscar Torres-Reyna of Princeton's Data and Statistical Services provided excellent advice concerning statistical modeling. Needless to say, they bear no responsibility for my mistakes.

I owe a special debt to Carles Boix, Valerie Bunce, Killian Clarke, Jack Goldstone, and Lucan Way (as well as an anonymous reviewer), who read my draft manuscript in its entirety and provided outstanding suggestions for revision. At Princeton I have benefited from an excellent group of former and current students—Chantal Berman, Killian Clarke, Ben Crisman, Sarah El-Kazaz, Kevin Mazur, and Bryn Rosenfeld—who have worked with me on related topics, commented on my work, and exercised an important impact on my thinking. Students from my seminars will be familiar with many of the arguments. Excellent comments on portions of the manuscript were also provided by Chris Achen, Nancy Bermeo, Perry Carter, Rafaela Dancygier, Atul Kohli, Amaney Jamal, Grigore Pop-Eleches, Nicholas Rush Smith, Rory Truex, Jacob Tucker, Manuel Vogt, Jennifer Widner, Andreas Wiedemann, and Deborah Yashar. Stathis Kalyvas, Neil Ketchley, Charles Kurzman, Olga Onuch, Gwendolyn Sasse, and Andreas Wimmer also contributed critical conversations or support. I also thank Marc Lynch, who provided opportunities to test some of my ideas on the Project on Middle East Politics (POMEPS) network.

Despite the pretensions of authors, books are also written by families. My great fortune in this regard has been the most important factor in my life and a source of endless happiness, for which—my dearest Margaret, Jonathan, and Rebecca—I am eternally grateful.

Finally, I dedicate this book to my father, who fled Nazi Germany as a boy with his family in search of a better life, and to all who dream of a better life. Quite literally, this book could not have been written without you.

4. Beissinger 2013; Beissinger, Jamal, and Mazur 2015; Beissinger 2017.

THE REVOLUTIONARY CITY

Introduction

Revolution and the City

> He has shown the strength of his arm,
> he has scattered the proud in their conceit.
> He has cast down the mighty from their thrones,
> and has lifted up the lowly.
>
> LUKE 1:51–52

TWO UPRISINGS in the city of Kyiv, separated by almost a century, tell the basic story of this book. Like much of the rest of the Russian Empire in 1905, Kyiv—then a multicultural industrial center of three hundred thousand and the empire's third most important city—seethed with revolutionary activity. Unrest began with worker strikes in sympathy with the victims of Bloody Sunday (January 22) in St. Petersburg. By May, massive waves of peasant rebellion had unfolded in the surrounding countryside. They would persist for another two years. After ten months of turmoil, Tsar Nicholas II issued his October Manifesto recognizing political freedoms and the limited authority of a Duma. Angry that the monarch had not abdicated, crowds gathered the following day on Khreshchatyk, Kyiv's commercial boulevard. Students burst into the university and destroyed portraits of the tsar. A crowd of twenty thousand assembled at Duma Square (today known as Independence Square, a.k.a. Maidan) to listen to revolutionary speeches. After participants refused orders to disperse, mounted Cossacks with drawn sabers charged the gathering, and soldiers fired into the crowd. The protestors rioted, and in the tumult twelve demonstrators and ten soldiers were killed. That same evening, pogroms unfolded against the city's Jewish population, leaving forty-seven dead and four hundred wounded. A Soviet of Workers' Deputies was established and, with an arsenal of revolvers, hunting guns, and garden spades, began preparations for an armed uprising. On November 18, soldiers from the Kyiv garrison mutinied over social conditions in the army and paraded through the city. Their numbers increased as workers spontaneously joined the rebellion. Troops loyal to the regime surrounded the rebels and opened fire, killing forty and wounding two hundred. Martial law was declared, and the city was temporarily pacified. But on December 12, in solidarity with an armed rebellion that had broken out in Moscow, the Kyiv Soviet mounted an insurrection in the working-class neighborhood of Shuliavka. It armed workers and proclaimed an independent Shuliavska Republic, declaring it the sole authority in the city. The uprising lasted four days before it was crushed.[1]

Contrast Kyiv in November 1905 with Kyiv in November 2004. By 2004, Kyiv was a major metropolitan center of 2.5 million—more than eight times its population in 1905—and the capital of an independent Ukraine. Whereas in 1905 78 percent of Ukraine's population consisted of peasants, by 2004 only 6 percent of the country's workforce was employed in agriculture, rendering peasant rebellion in the surrounding areas of Kyiv unthinkable. Not only had socialist collectivization (and post-socialist transition) transformed property relations in the countryside, but the majority of the population in outlying districts now lived in urban areas.

The Orange Revolution began when two hundred thousand citizens—ten times the number who participated in demonstrations on the same site a century before—descended on Independence Square to protest electoral fraud and support opposition candidate Viktor Yushchenko. Despite frigid temperatures, in the ensuing days the number of protestors climbed to almost a million as people from all over Ukraine converged on the square. There was no Soviet of Workers Deputies during the Orange Revolution. But two competing centers of authority existed: Yushchenko was hastily sworn in as president on the Maidan in front of a large crowd of onlookers, even before the fraudulent electoral results declaring pro-incumbent candidate Viktor Yanukovych the winner had been formally announced. In 2004, no Cossacks with sabers drawn charged the massive crowds. After initially contemplating a crackdown, the regime backed off—fearful of what might ensue were violence perpetrated against such an enormous gathering. No mutinous soldiers roamed Kyiv's streets with their weapons, though cadets from the Interior Ministry academy did march into the square wearing orange to show their support for Yushchenko, and some members of the army and security services declared their loyalty to the Yushchenko camp. In all, the unrest associated with the 1905 revolution in Kyiv dragged on for several years and involved hundreds of deaths, with the revolutionary opposition eventually losing. In 2004, after seventeen days of round-the-clock protest that

---

1. Edelman 2016; Heywood 2005; Hamm 1993; Khiterer 1992; Ascher 2004.

shut down the government and paralyzed the country, the authorities caved in. Only one person died during the Orange Revolution—apparently of a heart attack.

This book is about political revolutions—though truth be told, all revolutions are political. Understood as a mass siege of an established government by its own population with the goals of bringing about regime-change and effecting substantive political or social change, revolutions are, in Foucauldian terms, exceptional moments of "chance reversal"[2]—when the ongoing trajectory of a political order is ruptured and potentially altered in fundamental ways by those subject to it. As Trotsky put it, revolutions involve "the forcible entry of the masses in the realm of rulership over their own destiny";[3] they are political projects of mass collective agency in the remaking of government and society. Ordinarily, social and political life is heavily constrained by the regimes to which we are subject and the orderliness they impose, as well as by the exigencies of everyday life. Revolutions, by contrast, are extraordinary moments when populations attempt to force regime-change from below and fashion new regimes in their stead. In the words of political philosopher John Dunn, "Revolution raises in the most acute and painful form the two most fundamental questions in political understanding: how free ever are we to shape our own lives together on the scale of a political community; and how far do we ever understand what we are doing in politics, or what, in failing to act, we are contributing decisively to bringing about."[4]

But the frequency of these extraordinary moments, the ways in which populations go about the business of regime-change from below, the reasons they engage in such action, and the locations and social forces that mobilize in revolution have changed dramatically over the last century. This study is about that transformation—and in particular about the impact of the concentration of people, power, and wealth in cities on the incidence, practice, and consequences of political revolutions.

It is sometimes said that the age of revolutions is over. Certainly this is true with respect to one type of revolution—social revolutions, which Theda Skocpol defined as "rapid, basic transformations of a society's state and class structures that are accompanied and in part carried through by mass based revolts from below."[5] The study of social revolutions once dominated the

---

2. Lemert and Gillan 1982, 4.

3. Trotsky 1932, vol. 1, xvii. Sewell (1996, 851) similarly refers to revolution as "a self-conscious attempt by the people to impose by force its sovereign will."

4. Dunn 2008, 19.

5. Skocpol 1994, 5.

scholarly literature on revolutions—and for good reason: social revolutions were often spectacular explosions of class upheaval, violence, and mobilization that exercised deep impacts on the societies that experienced them. But in recent decades, social revolutions aimed at transforming the class structures of society have largely vanished. A number of movements attacking class inequalities have been elected at the ballot box, and a number continue to press revolutionary struggles on the ground. But since the overthrow of Nicaraguan dictator Anastasio Somoza by the Sandinista National Liberation Front in July 1979, no movements openly seeking to transform their society's class structure have gained power through revolutionary means, anywhere in the world. Moreover, since the mid-1990s no new revolutionary seizures of power have started that involved at least a thousand civilian participants and articulated goals of class transformation.[6]

Yet, there has never been a shortage of political revolutions. By my counting, from 1985 to 2014 there were approximately fifty-six revolutions worldwide involving mobilizations of at least a thousand civilian participants that successfully displaced incumbent rulers; there were also another sixty-seven attempted revolutions during this period that involved mobilizations of at least a thousand civilian participants but failed to gain power. Two-thirds (eighty-two) of these "successful" and "failed" revolutionary episodes since 1985 occurred primarily in cities—compared to only 45 percent of revolutionary episodes from 1900 to 1984. In the late twentieth and early twenty-first centuries, revolution became a predominantly urban phenomenon.

The contrast between these new urban revolutions and the social revolutions that long dominated theorizing about revolution could scarcely be sharper. From the late eighteenth through the early twentieth century, revolution had been largely an urban affair, manifesting itself primarily as armed insurrections in capital cities.[7] This was, after all, where the nerve centers of government were located, and where the social forces interested in revolutionary regime-change were concentrated. As William Sewell noted, these cities were

---

6. The most recent were the Chiapas Rebellion of 1994 and the Nepalese civil war of 1996. I use the peak number of direct participants in revolutionary mobilization as a way of identifying the mass character of revolutionary contention and differentiating revolutions from terrorist attacks and other small-scale actions aimed at seizing power. See Appendix 1 for further justification.

7. Many revolutions from the seventeenth to the early nineteenth century (the English Civil War and wars of independence in the Americas) did not follow this pattern, but rather involved conventional armies pitted against one another. The Haitian Revolution, as a slave revolt, was also not an urban armed affair but consisted of uprisings on plantations, subsequently morphing into irregular and conventional civil war.

characterized by "a particularly flammable combination. Not only did they have densely built poor neighborhoods whose labyrinthine streets were susceptible to barricades, but these working-class quarters were within easy striking distance of the neighborhoods of the rich and of the grand public squares of the ceremonial city."[8] The urban revolts that broke out in Europe from the late eighteenth through the early twentieth century generally aimed at a combination of curbing monarchical power and transforming class relations in society. They assumed the form of street fighting and used the built environment of the city as cover for armed attacks, with the hope that armed revolt would catalyze a mass uprising and stoke mutiny within the armed forces. Although the main locus of these revolts was cities, almost all of them occurred in societies that were overwhelmingly rural. And like the Russian Revolution of 1905, they were often accompanied by significant peasant disorders.

But the old-fashioned way of making revolution through urban armed revolt generally had a low rate of success. As I will explore in more detail, proximity to command centers of power and commerce maximized the disruptive capabilities of revolutionary oppositions, but did so at the expense of their exposure to a regime's repressive capacities. As the state's repressive capacity and firepower grew, its strategic superiority over armed rebels in urban centers became overwhelming. Engels already recognized the stacked odds against urban armed revolts by the end of the nineteenth century: "Rebellion in the old style, street fighting with barricades, which decided the issue everywhere up to 1848, had become largely outdated. Let us have no illusions about it: a real victory of insurrection over the military in street fighting, a victory as between two armies, is one of the rarest exceptions."[9] Beginning in the 1920s, and especially during the Cold War years, a ruralization of social revolution took place, as social revolutionaries migrated to the countryside, where rebels used distance from government centers and rough terrain as safe zones from which to hide from government retaliation. Revolutionaries still sought the ultimate prize of capturing power in cities. But cities had become too dangerous for them, given the imbalance in power between regimes and oppositions. Essentially, revolutionaries traded off capacity to disrupt for safety from government repression. As a result of this relocation to the countryside, peasants—once thought to be reactionary and irrevocably focused on local issues of access to land—became the new social force underpinning social revolution.

As Skocpol observed in her classic work *States and Social Revolutions*, social revolutions were characteristic of a particular type of society—an

---

8. Sewell 2001, 62.
9. Marx and Engels 1990, 517.

"agrarian-bureaucratic society," which she defined as a social formation in which control over and extraction of resources from peasants depended on a coordination and division of labor between a semi-bureaucratic state and a landed upper class.[10] Most theories of social revolution revolved around some aspect of this agrarian-bureaucratic society and the conditions under which it produced revolution—irrespective of whether social revolution primarily unfolded in an urban or a rural setting.

However, by the late twentieth and early twenty-first centuries, agrarian-bureaucratic society was rapidly fading. Land inequality had not vanished.[11] But over the prior century there had been a growing concentration of people, power, and wealth in cities, as states proliferated and consolidated, urban economies developed, and the proportion of the global population living in urban areas rose from 13 percent in 1900 to 52 percent by 2010.[12] In 1900, there were sixteen cities in the world (located in nine countries) that had more than a million inhabitants.[13] By 2016, there were 519 such cities located in 125 countries.[14] In Latin America, for instance, the conditions that had once led Che Guevara to view the countryside as a hotbed of revolution have disappeared, as "capitals and industrial centers have swallowed up what were once independent towns," and "ranch land and farmland have been turned into airports and highways."[15]

Cities also functioned as the main spatial sites for the heightened connectedness and concentration of wealth characteristic of globalization in the late twentieth and early twenty-first centuries. According to the McKinsey Global Institute, six hundred cities around the world (representing 22 percent of the world's population) are responsible for over 60 percent of the world's economy.[16] As a United Nations report concludes, "global forces are centered in cities," where their effects are most acutely felt.[17] Modern communications and transportation connect the world's urban centers into an integrated global network that penetrates deeply into the fabric of contemporary society.[18]

---

10. Skocpol 1979. See also Eisenstadt 1963; Moore 1966.

11. See Frankema 2010.

12. For data on world urbanization since 1950 as reported by the United Nations, see http://esa.un.org/wup2009/unup/index.asp?panel=1.

13. Chandler 1987, 492.

14. Cox 2017. Twenty countries had five or more cities with at least a million inhabitants.

15. Rosenthal 2000, 37.

16. Dobbs et al. 2011.

17. United Nations Center for Human Settlements 2001, xxxi.

18. Castells 1996, 380.

Urban culture and modes of consumption have become increasingly available to rural populations, greatly affecting the countryside as well.[19]

All this has left a profound impact on revolutionary regime-change. As population, power, and wealth shifted to cities, so too did the phenomenon of revolution. In the world described by Skocpol (prior to the publication of her book in 1979), 60 percent of revolutionary episodes involved peasants. In the world since the publication of Skocpol's book, only 34 percent have. There are rare instances in overwhelmingly rural societies in which peasants from the surrounding countryside descend on the city and constitute the majority of participants in urban revolutionary protests. This occurred, for example, during the April 2006 revolution in Nepal—a society that, at the time, was one of the least urbanized on the planet, with only 16 percent of its population living in cities.[20] But for the most part the growth of contemporary urban revolutions has been associated with a different set of social forces. Not peasants, but the urban middle class (professionals, the technical intelligentsia, shopkeepers, and public and private sector employees) have participated disproportionately, usually with sizeable contingents of other urban groups: skilled workers, manual laborers, clerical workers, craftsmen, small-business owners, and the so-called de-commodified (individuals who occupy no niche on the labor market, such as students, pensioners, housewives, and the unemployed).[21]

Even though class has been an extremely important phenomenon in the societies experiencing urban revolutions in the late twentieth and early twenty-first centuries, structuring life chances and the practice of everyday life, and though class, as we will see, has certainly not been absent in these revolutions, unlike social revolutions the political cleavages animating these new urban revolutionary mobilizations have tended to revolve less around social class and more around hostility toward the political class—a civic reclaiming of the state that, to varying degrees, cuts across urban class divides. This multi-class urban coalition (with the middle class disproportionately represented) becomes possible precisely because the state is most physically present in cities, where its dysfunctions are most directly felt, and where populations are most capable of learning about them. Government itself—not social class—has increasingly become the axis around which revolutionary cleavages have formed.[22]

The most common form that these new urban revolutions have assumed is what I call in this book the "urban civic" revolution—that is, uprisings like the

---

19. Clark 1996, 117–19.
20. Routledge 2010, 1290.
21. Offe 1985; Esping-Andersen 1990.
22. Farhi 1990, 18. See also Goodwin 2001.

Orange Revolution that seek to overthrow abusive government by mobilizing as many people as possible in central urban spaces, paralyzing commerce, administration, and society through the power of numbers rather than relying primarily on armed rebellion, street-fighting, strikes, or urban rioting. Since 1985, urban civic revolutions have constituted almost two-fifths (forty-seven) of all revolutionary episodes around the world (and nearly three-fifths of all urban revolutions). Some refer to them as "democratic" revolutions,[23] and they generally do articulate broadly liberal aims of containing the abuses of predatory and unaccountable government, among other goals. I prefer to call them "urban civic," for several reasons.

For one thing, a significant number of revolutions have articulated goals of establishing democratic government, but have not utilized urban civic tactics of concentrating large numbers of unarmed protestors in central urban spaces. Certainly this was true of liberal revolutions of the late eighteenth and nineteenth centuries, which used a combination of conventional civil warfare, irregular civil warfare, urban riots, and urban street-fighting to challenge incumbent regimes.[24] But a significant number of later cases also did not rely on urban civic tactics. The 1974 Carnation Revolution in Portugal, for example, was largely a military mutiny accompanied by demonstrations and strikes. The 1980 Solidarity uprising in Poland was primarily based on strikes rather than demonstrations. In the 1989 Romanian Revolution, demonstrations and riots morphed into violent armed combat. There have also been a number of revolutionary civil wars that produced democratic arrangements of varying degrees that could also be interpreted as "democratic" revolutions, even though democracy may not have originally been a goal.[25]

While urban civic revolutions are focused against repressive and abusive governments, as we will see, there is a great variety of motives impelling people to participate in these revolts, and democratic purposes and values often rank low among them or are prioritized only by a minority of participants. Framing these revolutions as "democratic" can thus obscure the diversity of motivations underpinning them. Indeed, in some cases, a democratic moniker has been imposed on these revolutions by outsiders, or has been used strategically by movement entrepreneurs seeking external validation or support. And for reasons that will be explored, the democratizing effects of successful urban civic revolutions, while substantial in some areas, usually fall well short of the

23. See, for instance, Thompson 2004.
24. Palmer 2014; Sperber 2005; Weyland 2014.
25. See Wood 2000; Wantchekon and Neeman 2002; Gurses and Mason 2008; Fortna and Huang 2012; Huang 2016.

standards of the average electoral democracy—especially as regards the rule of law and corruption. Moreover, these achievements are often quite precarious. In this sense, such revolutions might be better understood as revolutions *against* repressive and abusive regimes rather than revolutions *for* democracy. They are more about what people are struggling against than what they are struggling for. Nevertheless, these revolutions do seek to reclaim power in the name of citizens suffocating from lawless, corrupt, and oppressive government. They have generated some extraordinary displays of civic activism. And the setting of the city is critical to the social forces underpinning them and the mobilizational politics that they involve.

According to the *Oxford English Dictionary*, the word "civic" means "of, belonging to, or relating to a citizen or citizens." It also means "of, belonging to, or relating to a city, town, borough, or other community of citizens."[26] Notions of city and citizen have been intimately intertwined since Greek and Roman times. The very term "citizen" derives from the Latin word for city (*civitas*) and historically was used largely to refer to urban dwellers.[27] As Anthony Giddens notes, only after sovereignty had been turned into a territorial principle of government did citizenship come to be widely applied beyond the confines of cities.[28] Modern ideas about inclusive citizenship first emerged in European and American cities in the eighteenth and nineteenth centuries—the product of a series of revolutions and incorporating reforms from above.[29] In the late twentieth and early twenty-first centuries, in an era of massive urbanization and growth in the size, power, and wealth of cities, the two meanings of "civic" have once again converged to produce numerous eruptions of large-scale urban revolt around the world, in which millions have mobilized to reclaim control from corrupt and despotic governments in the name of those to whom these states theoretically belong—their citizens.[30] Saskia Sassen has written of "the return of the city" as a site for the making of political and civic change and observes that urban revolts have become a "source for an expanded civicness" by opening up possibilities for remaking the political.[31] This book is about that transformation—about the return of

26. Both meanings relate to the Latin word *civicus*.
27. Riesenberg 1992, 3–84. On the nature of citizenship in medieval European cities, see Weber 1958, 91–120.
28. Giddens 1987, vol. 2, 94.
29. Riesenberg 1992, 203–66.
30. Mona El-Ghobashy pointed to the "genius" of the 2011 Egyptian Revolution as "its methodical restoration of the public weal.... It revalued the people, revealing them in all their complexity—neither heroes nor saints, but citizens." El-Ghobashy 2012, 39.
31. Sassen 2011, 575, 579.

the city as a site for revolution, and about the urban civic revolts that have been situated at the center of this development.

Social revolutions in the twentieth century were dominated by grievances over poverty, redistribution of wealth, and land inequality. By contrast, government repression, corruption, and misrule have been the main grievances of urban civic revolutions, though economic despair and the absence of civil liberties are often prominent complaints as well. As societies urbanized and moved into closer proximity to where state power was most concentrated, and as states proliferated and consolidated, the state came to matter more in people's lives. In cities, populations came into more regular contact with the state, including the state's unequaled capacities for predation and oppression. Urban civic revolutions have generally occurred in countries in which the political class has become a law unto itself, a mafia-like organization displaying an arrogance and venality that has pitted it against the bulk of the population it governs.

This does not mean that economics are unimportant in urban civic revolutions. On the contrary, they matter deeply. Urban civic uprisings have predominantly been a phenomenon of the era of neoliberalism, in which rapid private-sector growth has been considered the principal source of societal prosperity, while public sectors have been pressured to contract. Neoliberal economic growth was accompanied by a massive expansion of cities. It fostered the emergence of a new global middle class, especially in developing and emerging economies. The term "middle class" is often used loosely to refer to those who are neither rich nor poor, while others define it mainly by reference to consumption patterns. I use the term in this book in the sociological sense, as encompassing a particular range of occupations between those of the bourgeoisie and the working class.[32] These groups primarily contribute to economic growth not through investment of their capital, but through their skills and the services that they provide. They are likely to be better educated than other citizens and to enjoy an above-average income and standard of living. But they should not be confused with the bourgeoisie, which today is usually closely enmeshed with ruling regimes and for the most part is not supportive of revolution (though sometimes switches allegiance as revolutionary challenges multiply).[33]

---

32. Wright 1980.

33. In Marxist theory, bourgeois revolutions were oriented against the political power of landed elites and sought to establish the political predominance of capital. By contrast, urban civic revolutions are aimed against the predatory and repressive powers of the state in a world in which capital already predominates.

Levels of income and consumption among the urban middle class can vary substantially within and across societies. Urban civic revolutions have sometimes occurred in a context of fiscal austerity, downward mobility, and declining levels of urban subsistence—motivated by what Asef Bayat terms the contractual norms of urban life:

> Modern urbanity generates particular needs, such as access to cash to conduct exchange instead of relying on trust and reciprocity, as was practiced in traditional village life; urbanites need to learn work discipline instead of enjoying flexibility and self-arrangement; they need to behave in their urban life according to certain set contracts instead of relying on negotiations or customary norms. In addition, while modern urbanity engenders certain desires and demands (like paid jobs, regular pay, particular norms of consumption), it simultaneously inculcates among urbanites a set of entitlements and rights, for instance, the right to have optimum urban services such as roads, schools, police, and broadly what the city can offer. . . . If states are expected but are unable or unwilling to fulfill those demands, or if they are seen to violate those entitlements, urbanites are likely to feel and express moral outrage at the public authorities.[34]

Middle-class youth unemployment, taxes on essential services, and the removal of government subsidies on fuel, food, or transportation in the context of widespread enrichment by the political elite have been common catalysts for urban civic revolt in the late twentieth and early twenty-first centuries.

This was largely the pattern exhibited in the Arab Spring, as well as in a number of urban uprisings in Latin America, Africa, and Southeast Asia. But it is not the only pattern. Urban civic revolutions have at times transpired in the absence of economic distress (what Bryn Rosenfeld calls "protests of the 'want-mores' rather than protests of the 'have-nots'")[35]—rooted in a broader frustration over the suffocating predation of government on society. The Orange Revolution in Ukraine, for instance, occurred in the context of a growing rather than a shrinking economy, but a society that was nevertheless deeply discontented over the pervasive graft and corruption of its political elite. Urban dwellers have shown particular concern about government corruption. World Values Survey data show, for instance, that city dwellers around the world are less likely to believe that it is justifiable to accept a bribe from someone in the course of official duties than are inhabitants of rural areas. This relationship is especially strong for inhabitants of large cities (with populations

---

34. Bayat 2017, 131.
35. Rosenfeld 2017, 643.

over five hundred thousand).[36] Studies also show that in middle- and lower-income countries, the middle class is more likely than the poor and less educated to perceive widespread corruption.[37] Whether this is due to different class experiences with the state, differential access to media, different time horizons or marginal utilities, or class differences in oppositional identity is not clear. Nevertheless, middle-class intolerance for corruption and clientelism has been well documented.[38]

These two faces of neoliberal development—the rapid growth of urban middle-class populations frustrated by corrupt and repressive regimes, and the contraction of public goods provision and subsidies to many of these same urban groups—lie at the center of much of the animus fueling contemporary urban revolutions. But other factors can be at play as well. Some urban civic revolutions (the Orange Revolution, for example) have tapped into cultural difference, harnessing grievances over the relationship between culture and the state.[39] Looked at across countries and world regions, the individuals participating in urban civic revolutions have relatively little in common other than their desire to reclaim the public sphere from predatory and repressive government. As we will see, they display diverse grievances and ideologies—both within and across revolutions.

As the locations, social forces, and grievances involved in revolution have shifted, so too has the organization and technology of revolt. In his famous pamphlet *What is to Be Done*, Lenin emphasized the need to organize revolution around a vanguard party—a disciplined group of professional revolutionaries who could provide organizational and ideological coherence to revolt. He also devoted a significant portion of his treatise to the need for a newspaper to function as the main means for Russian revolutionaries, then primarily in exile abroad, to recruit workers by surreptitiously smuggling copies into the Russian Empire. Most social revolutions were organized around vanguard parties, and would-be social revolutionaries relied primarily upon the printed word or face-to-face agitation to spread their message. Today, the vanguard

---

36. For large cities, statistically significant at the .001 level. Results based on Wave 6 of the World Values Survey (47 countries), controlling for age, gender, and fixed country effects (with robust standard errors). The surveys also showed that in the seven Middle Eastern countries in which the question was asked, residents of large cities were more likely than rural dwellers to believe that their governments were corrupt. See Inglehart et al. 2014.

37. Maeda and Ziegfeld 2015. The study also found, however, that in higher-income countries, the middle class is less likely than the poor and less educated to perceive widespread corruption.

38. Stokes 2009.

39. Beissinger 2013.

party is as obsolete as the typewriter—part of a technology of rebellion appropriate for a completely different historical era. It has been replaced by the loose revolutionary coalition—a rapidly assembled and highly fragmented alliance of opposition movements, bloggers, and political figures united only by their common hostility to the incumbent regime. This trend has been further amplified by the rise of the internet as a medium for coordinating revolt: it dilutes the role of leadership within revolutionary movements and accentuates the speed with which diverse oppositional groups can be convened.[40]

In 1917, Lenin learned of the events of Russia's February Revolution on the day that the revolution ended; he was forced to rely on newspaper dispatches published with a several-day lag, or on word of mouth within the small Russian émigré community in Zurich. As he wrote to Alexandra Kollontai at the time, "Just imagine thinking about 'directives' from here, when news is exceptionally meagre."[41] By contrast, in 2010 the large Tunisian diaspora abroad (10 percent of the country's population) was one of the driving forces behind the Tunisian Revolution.[42] Many of the informational sites utilized during the revolution were managed overseas, and through the magic of cellphones, Facebook, and video-archiving sites abroad, urban Tunisians and the rest of the world could witness revolutionary protests and acts of government repression practically in real time. Today, most participants in revolutions do not even read newspapers.[43] Rather, television, Facebook, and Twitter have reconfigured the enterprise of revolution in fundamental ways, rendering visual representation and simultaneity increasingly integral to revolutionary processes and transcending international borders with speed and relative ease. These technologies and modes of organization are ideal for gathering large numbers quickly. They are most appropriate precisely where large numbers are concentrated: cities.

Essentially, the movement of hundreds of millions of people into cities over the past century rendered possible new urban repertoires for challenging regimes on the basis of the power of numbers rather than the power of arms. The population of Kyiv in 1905 could not have carried out the kind of massive mobilizations characteristic of the Orange Revolution a century later. As I will show, the city in 1905 was simply too small to generate the kind of numbers

40. Bennett and Segerberg 2013.
41. Lenin 1981, 287, 406; Lenin 1980, 297.
42. Graziano 2012, 9–10.
43. In the Euromaidan Revolution in Ukraine in 2014, only 44 percent of revolution participants reported reading a newspaper in the previous week, while 83 percent reported watching television. Only 2 percent of participants in the Egyptian Revolution, and no participants in the Tunisian Revolution, said that they primarily used newspapers to follow the events of these revolutions. On the sources for these data, see Chapter 7.

necessary for protecting protestors against government repression and exerting leverage over a regime through unarmed crowds. Governments at the beginning of the twentieth century were also significantly more likely than governments today to shoot into unarmed crowds, making unarmed rebellion in cities a risky affair. And technologies for coordinating large crowds in the early twentieth century were primitive and severely limited in their reach. But by the late twentieth and early twenty-first centuries, the proliferation of large, resourced, and highly networked populations in close proximity to the state's command centers altered the possibilities for making urban revolution, tilting the relationship between exposure to government repression and the ability to exert disruption in favor of urban oppositions.

Contrary to the belief in some circles that the age of revolution is over, as the world has urbanized and people, power, and wealth have shifted to cities, revolution as a mass political project of regime-change from below has actually become a more frequent affair. The historian Hugh Seton-Watson declared in 1951 that "the first half of the twentieth century is richer than any previous period of human history in the activities of revolutionary movements."[44] This may have been true in 1951. But revolutionary episodes occurred at a significantly greater pace in the late twentieth and early twenty-first centuries than at *any* prior time in history—greater than during the first half of the twentieth century, and greater than during the Cold War. As we will see, this growth in revolutionary activity was driven by the multiplication of urban civic revolutions and was the product of a variety of factors—political, demographic, social, economic, spatial, technological, and geopolitical—that magnified the grievances, opportunities, and possibilities underpinning mass revolt in cities. Rather than disappearing, revolution as a mode of regime-change proliferated even as it urbanized. It evolved rather than evaporated—altering in its spatial location, the purposes to which it is put, the forms it has assumed, the social forces and organizational structures sustaining it, and the outcomes it involves. This book is about that transformation—about how the concentration of people, power, and wealth in cities has altered the frequency, character, and consequences of revolution.

Plan of the Book and Key Arguments

Travelers who are about to embark upon a long journey deserve to know where they are headed. Essentially, the analysis that follows begins at the global level, progressively drills downward to the level of the episode and the individual,

---

44. Seton-Watson 1951, 251. Martin Malia has argued (2006, 1) that, together with global war, revolution was "the defining characteristic of the twentieth century."

and then broadens back to the global. In chapter 1, I define revolution and lay out a theory about how spatial location influences revolutionary processes, outlining what I call the repression–disruption trade-off in revolution and the "proximity dilemma" that all revolutionaries face. In essence, that trade-off emerges from the fact that cities are where the state is strongest, and therefore urban revolutionaries are more directly exposed than rural revolutionaries to the repressive capacities of the state. But cities are also where the nerve centers of government that revolutionaries seek to capture are located, and therefore where regimes are most directly vulnerable to disruption. Thus, proximity to centers of power involves both opportunities and dangers for revolutionaries. A basic dilemma facing revolutionary movements is how to manage this repression–disruption trade-off—that is, how to leverage their disruptive power to induce regime collapse while warding off regime repression.

Several factors affect the nature of this trade-off. One is the spatial location of rebellion. By moving further from centers of power, revolutionaries can gain safety at the cost of disruptive capacity; by moving closer, they can gain disruptive capacity at the cost of safety. Tactical learning and innovation by revolutionaries and regimes also affect the trade-off, as each side seeks to take advantage of its opponent's weaknesses within particular spatial contexts. Finally, long-term social structural and technological changes have greatly influenced the possibilities and effectiveness of particular tactical repertoires within spatial locations. Chief among these has been urbanization, which has concentrated large numbers in cities and thereby rendered repertoires relying on the power of numbers increasingly effective for warding off repression. The proximity dilemma not only helps us to understand the starkly different characters of urban and rural revolutionary processes. It also provides a framework for explaining why the locations of revolutionary challenges have shifted over time and how large-scale urbanization has altered the character and outcomes of revolutionary contention. In chapter 1 I also review my approach to analyzing revolution that centers on the revolutionary episode as a unit of analysis, the ways in which I classify episodes, and the empirical research on which the book is based.

Chapter 2 examines the shifting frequency and character of revolutionary episodes around the world since 1900. It shows that revolutionary contention has been growing more frequent over time despite a marked decline in the incidence of social revolutions. This increase is largely due to the urbanization of revolution and the proliferation of urban civic revolutionary episodes at the end of the twentieth and beginning of the twenty-first centuries. I show that the growth of urban revolutions derives from many of the long-term structural trends that are also responsible for the decline of social revolutions: the end of agrarian-bureaucratic society, large-scale urbanization, the shift of power to cities, the proliferation and consolidation of national states, and changes in the global geopolitical and economic order in the wake of the Cold War.

Chapter 3 explores the factors associated with the outbreak of urban civic revolutionary contention. It develops a probabilistic model of the onset of urban civic revolutionary contention, identifying the structural conditions associated with the materialization of an urban civic revolutionary episode. It shows that these conditions are not associated with the onset of social revolutions, other types of revolutions, or attempted military coups. The outbreak of urban civic revolutions is more sensitive to the features of political regimes, whereas the outbreak of social revolutionary contention is more closely associated with inequality, poverty, and underdevelopment. I then use the model's predictions of structural risk as a baseline for analyzing the actual emergence (or absence) of urban civic contention in specific cases, engaging in case studies of how episodes materialized in order to understand why the model's predictions proved accurate or inaccurate in particular cases. The analysis points to the critical processes that render urban civic revolutionary contention more similar to the emergence of hurricanes than to the outbreak of wildfires or earthquakes. Though clearly related to conducive structural conditions, they nonetheless develop tentatively and with uncertainty out of interactions between regimes and oppositions.

Chapter 4 explores revolutionary "success" in a minimalist sense—that is, whether revolutionary oppositions are able to overthrow incumbent regimes once revolutionary contention has materialized. It shows that, in general, the chances of revolutionary success have substantially increased over time. I show that these increased odds of opposition victory are rooted in several factors: the urbanization of revolution and the strategic advantages that proximity to the state provides for disrupting and toppling regimes; the increased vulnerability of regimes to disruption from urban mass revolt after the Cold War; and a revolutionary repertoire that effectively leverages these advantages.

Even taking these factors into consideration, revolutionary success is considerably less predictable, by the factors identified in the statistical model, than revolutionary failure. Chapter 5 shifts the focus downward to the eventful and "playful" processes in urban revolutionary contention. I argue that the speed, intensity, and compactness of urban revolutionary contention—themselves the products of proximity to governmental centers of power—create significant information problems for both regimes and oppositions and heighten the impact of contingency and miscalculation on revolutionary outcomes. The consequences of these problems are also acutely magnified in urban revolutions by the proximity of contention to nerve centers of state power, which leaves little margin for error.

Chapter 6 focuses on contention over public space in urban revolutions. As states have proliferated and consolidated, and as urbanization has proceeded, large open spaces in proximity to the command centers of power have spread throughout the world, especially in capital cities. These spaces have been particularly important in urban civic revolutions, which rely on a strategy of rapidly concentrating large numbers in the spaces between buildings rather than using the built environment of the city as cover for armed attack. I explore how the shape, location, availability, and symbolic value of public space affect the manner in which urban civic revolutions unfold and how incumbent regimes attempt to forestall or undermine urban civic revolutionary challenges through regulation and control of public space.

Chapter 7 addresses urban civic revolutions at the level of the individual, using nationally representative surveys from four such revolutions to show that those who participate in them are highly diverse—more diverse, in fact, than either supporters or opponents of revolution in society at large. Urban civic revolutionaries harbor fundamental disagreements over major policy issues even while they are united by their intense disaffection vis-à-vis their regimes. This, I argue, is the product of urban civic revolutionary tactics that maximize numbers in a concentrated period of time. I also show that the social composition of participants has differed significantly across urban civic revolutions, even while in general the urban middle class has been over-represented. Despite the democratic master-narratives of these revolutions, most participants display weak commitment to democratic values. Thus, urban civic revolutions are better understood not as revolutions for democracy, but as revolutions against repressive, corrupt, and predatory government.

Chapter 8 examines changing patterns of mortality within revolutionary contention over the past century. The number of revolutionary episodes has grown; even so, many fewer people are dying in revolution. Much of this has to do with the declining incidence and lethality of revolutionary civil wars. But there has also been a decline in lethal violence in revolutionary episodes that have not involved civil war. As I show, urbanization and the shift of revolutionary contention to cities are among the factors associated with this pacification of revolution. To alleviate the controversy and likelihood of backlash mobilizations and defections associated with lethal violence in urban revolts, regimes over the past century have increasingly countered urban revolutionary challenges with less lethal technologies of crowd control. This has greatly reduced revolutionary fatalities and has lowered the risks involved in participation in urban revolution. Ironically, the weaponry used to counter rural rebellions has moved in the opposite direction—toward increasing lethality. I explore this paradox and the reasons behind it.

Chapter 9 turns to the substantive impact of revolution. It compares the effects of urban civic revolutions with those of social revolutions in the years immediately following each type in terms of the outcomes that we ultimately care about: political order, economic growth, inequality, political freedoms, and government accountability. As I show, new regimes that result from successful urban civic revolutions last in power for significantly less time than those emerging from successful social revolutions. This fragility is largely the product of the compact, coalitional character of the urban civic repertoire. Urban civic revolutions generally bring a substantial increase in political freedoms in their wake. But on many dimensions of liberal democracy, they fall well short of what one finds in most electoral democracies (i.e., democracies defined in a minimalist sense). This is largely because they inherit the state, with its embedded relationships of corruption, intact from the old regime, limiting the ability of post-revolutionary governments to enact political and social change and contributing to an emerging crisis of economic stagnation.

The concluding chapter speculates about the future of revolutions. That future will undoubtedly be urban, given the continuing concentration of people, power, and wealth in cities. But one should expect that, just as revolutions in the early twenty-first century differ in fundamental respects from those of the past, revolution will continue to evolve in response to the structural forces long affecting it: changing patterns of political and economic power; altered social structures and the concentration of people into cities; new technologies of rebellion and counterinsurgency; and shifting currents of geopolitics. I suggest that the urban civic repertoire is likely to come under stress in the future, as governments find new ways of countering the power of numbers in cities and geopolitics shifts in new directions. Still, new patterns of rebellion—perhaps already visible—will emerge, overlapping with the old. Revolutionary regime-change is hardly likely to disappear. On the contrary, as the world urbanizes, revolutionary contention has been growing in frequency, even as it alters in its forms, purposes, and outcomes.

1

A Spatial Theory of Revolution

> Cities, like dreams, are made of desires and fears, even if the thread of their discourse is secret.
>
> ITALO CALVINO, *INVISIBLE CITIES* (1972)[1]

CONTRARY TO WHAT MANY BELIEVE, most states have experienced a significant episode of revolutionary contention at some point in their modern histories. Much of Europe and the Americas faced major revolutionary challenges from the seventeenth through the nineteenth century.[2] In the twentieth century, revolution spread still farther. Out of a sample of 166 countries, 79 percent (131) underwent at least one episode of revolutionary contention from 1900 to 2014, with 46 percent (76) experiencing more than one. Revolutionary oppositions were brought to power in 49 percent (81) of these countries during this period, and in 19 percent (31 countries) they were brought to power multiple times.

Nevertheless, revolutions remain rare occurrences. On average, only 2.6 revolutionary episodes occurred annually around the world from 1900 to 1985. But while revolutions have always been rare, at the end of the twentieth and beginning of the twenty-first century their frequency increased substantially. As subsequent chapters will show, this growth was closely associated with the proliferation of revolution in cities and with the rise of urban civic forms of revolution (i.e., unarmed revolutions that seek to overthrow abusive governments by mobilizing as many people as possible in central urban spaces).

In this chapter, I outline a theory that helps to explain the urbanization of revolution in the late twentieth and early twenty-first centuries, the consequences

---

1. Calvino 1972, 44.
2. Hobsbawm 1962; Palmer 2014; Klooster 2018; Polasky 2015; Weyland 2009.

of this move back to cities for revolution, and the emergence of the urban civic repertoire. While urban revolt has drawn attention in recent years, the most widely known theories have come not from the fields of history, sociology, or political science, but from geography and urban design. They have emphasized a collective "right to the city"—a popular sovereignty over urbanization and the wealthy interests that control urban development.[3] These theories are useful for understanding local conflicts within cities. But they have limited applicability for understanding revolutionary processes focused on national governments and aimed specifically at effecting regime-change.[4]

I lay the foundations for a theory of urban revolution instead on the differences between the spatial context of the countryside and that of the city, and how these spatial differences structure social control and revolutionary forms and processes. As William Sewell noted, "most studies of mobilization bring in spatial considerations only episodically," treating space as "an assumed and unproblematized background, not as a constituent aspect of contentious politics that must be conceptualized explicitly and probed systematically."[5] I focus on the city not only as a locus of high population densities, capitalist development, and elaborate built structures that set it apart from the countryside, but also as a site of the thickened presence of the state. Cities are where the nerve centers of the state are concentrated, and therefore control over the city is the ultimate goal of all revolutionary movements. But paradoxically, cities are where the state is most vulnerable to overthrow *and* where revolutionaries are most vulnerable to the repressive capacities of the state. I call this trade-off between exposure to regime repression and possibilities for oppositional disruption "the proximity dilemma" in revolution, and I use its implications to analyze how revolution has evolved over time as people, power, and wealth have concentrated in cities.

I begin by defining what revolution is, identifying it as a unique form of regime-change and relating it to other forms of politics. I then turn to how the city has been treated in the vast theoretical literature on revolution. Nineteenth-century theorists such as de Tocqueville and Marx placed the city centrally into their analyses of revolution. But subsequent theories dropped the city from their purview, particularly as social revolution—revolution's most

---

3. Lefebvre 2003; Harvey 2013.

4. For a critique of the "right to the city" literature on this score, see Uitermark, Loopmans, and Nicholls 2012.

5. Sewell 2001, 51. In his study of the storming of the Bastille, Sewell (1996, 876–77) pointed to the uneven character of space as it affects collective action. He noted how spatial concentration made possible acts of "collective effervescence," and how action taken in some locations "has only a local scope, while the scope of other actions is much wider . . . because some locations are central nodes in social practices of wide extent."

theorized form—migrated to the countryside in the middle of the twentieth century. In the late twentieth and early twenty-first centuries, the marked growth in urban revolutions has pushed the city back onto the agenda of scholarly analyses of revolution.

I elaborate a theory of how spatial location influences revolution, outlining the logic of the proximity dilemma and some of its observable implications for revolutionary politics. Due to the proximity dilemma, urban revolutions tend to be extremely compact in time, creating significant information problems for both regimes and oppositions and heightening the impact of interaction, contingency, and error on urban revolutionary processes. I explain why armed rebellion tends to be less effective in cities but more effective in a rural context. I show how unarmed rebellion is more effective in large cities, where oppositions can rely on the power of numbers and regimes fear the potential effects of backlash mobilizations and defections in close proximity to government nerve centers. The repression–disruption trade-off also establishes the features of states and societies associated with revolutions within particular spatial contexts. Urban revolutions, for example, are much more affected by the character of the political regimes that they confront than are rural revolutions. I also illustrate how the nature of the repression–disruption trade-off can be altered through tactical innovation and large-scale structural change. In particular, the concentration of people, power, and wealth in cities over the last century rendered regimes more vulnerable to disruption through the power of numbers and helped give rise to the urban civic repertoire. The urban civic tactic of concentrating large numbers in central urban spaces has led in turn to a different type of spatial politics in revolutionary contention revolving around control over public space. It also bears significant consequences for revolutionary processes and outcomes and for what occurs in the aftermath of revolution.

In short, location matters enormously in revolution. It is, of course, not the only thing that matters. The ideologies and substantive goals of revolutionary oppositions, the resources available to governments, and the choices made by regimes and oppositions in interaction with one another are also critically important. But the spatial dimensions of revolution merit far greater attention than they have hitherto attracted.

What Revolution Is, and What It Is Not

Any analysis of revolution must confront what is undoubtedly the most contentious issue within the study of revolution: the definition of revolution itself. Some argue that the concept should be reserved solely for social revolutions—instances of violent, rapid change from below aimed at transforming the class structure of society. According to these accounts, there have only been two dozen or so "real" revolutions throughout history, with revolutions having been characteristic of a particular era stretching from the Enlightenment to the mid-twentieth century, but no longer occurring due to the exhaustion of revolutionary ideologies.[6] From this perspective, some revolutions have been more "revolutionary" (i.e., more rapid, total, and violent) than others. A handful of paradigmatic cases (the so-called Great Revolutions—the French Revolution of 1789, the Mexican Revolution of 1910, the October Revolution of 1917, and the Chinese Revolution of 1949) represent the essence of revolutionary phenomena, constituting a core around which theoretical and empirical inquiry should revolve. Due to the limited number of such upheavals, empirical analyses under this definition have been reduced methodologically to comparative historical studies of paradigmatic cases (usually with significant issues of case selection and sampling on the dependent variable).[7]

But social revolutions always represented only one of the many faces of revolution in the modern world. Indeed, when one looks at the origins of modern revolutions, it is clear that revolution began as a fundamentally political phenomenon. The word initially had an astronomical meaning, referring to the regular motion of the stars in the sky, with the original Latin literally meaning a rolling back, return, or restoration. It was first applied to politics in England in 1688 to describe the overthrow of King James II. After widespread mass disorders over James's attempts to favor Catholicism and usurp the powers of parliament, a foreign invasion placed William and Mary on the throne. The new monarchs had to sign a Bill of Rights that introduced freedom of speech, limited royal power, and committed them not to suspend laws or levy taxes without parliamentary approval, thus signifying what was viewed as a return to the sovereign rights of parliament vis-à-vis the monarchy.[8] In its early modern usages (including the Glorious Revolution and the American Revolution), "revolution" implied a restoration of what were seen as usurped natural rights (at the time, usually imagined as belonging only to white, male property owners)—not the creation of a completely new society or transformation of society's class structure. The infusion of the social into revolution was largely the product of the French Revolution. Although the French Revolution was primarily a political revolution that claimed the state on behalf of the Third Estate, it awakened the politics of class in a new way, and goals of transforming

---

6. For various lists of revolutions that qualify by this definition, see Goodwin 2001, 4; Foran 2005; Lachapelle et al. 2020.

7. Goldstone 2003; Skocpol 1979. For an excellent critique of the failure of systematic comparison in the study of revolution, see Beck 2018. Occasionally, medium-n studies have been carried out using Boolean logic (see Foran 2005).

8. Pincus 2014. See also Arendt 1965; Koselleck 2004, 43–71.

society's class structure became a growing component of revolutionary politics in its wake. This social element increasingly dominated revolutionary discourse over the nineteenth and early twentieth centuries, as industrialization concentrated large numbers of impoverished proletarians into cities and posed the class question more sharply.

Revolutions have occurred for a wide variety of reasons. Social revolutionary contention seeking to transform the class structure of society has constituted less than a quarter (23 percent) of revolutionary episodes since the beginning of the twentieth century. About 8 percent of revolutionary episodes since 1900 have been constitutional revolutions, aiming to transform monarchies into republics. Other revolutionary episodes aspired to liberation from colonial rule (15 percent) or independence from a multinational state (20 percent). Still others have been liberal revolutions, aiming to attain civil liberties, establish a democracy, or contain the abuses of a despotic regime (25 percent), while others have aimed to substitute a religiously based political order in place of a secular one (9 percent), or invert a dominant ethnic or racial order (16 percent). It is quite common for these various purposes to overlap and interpenetrate within particular revolutions. Any attempt to restrict the notion of revolution to social revolutions not only misses this key variation in the purposes to which revolution has been put, but also consigns the notion of revolution to history books, overlooking one of the central aspects of the history of modern revolution: its continual evolution and adaptation to multiple purposes and situations.[9] As Skocpol observed, "the likelihood and forms of revolutions tend to change over world time," rendering any truly generalizable theory of the causes of revolutions problematic.[10]

Widespread death and destruction may be associated with certain types of revolutions, but they are not necessary attributes of revolution in general. Some revolutions have led to very large numbers of deaths, earning revolution's reputation as one of the major sources of large-scale political violence around the world. Others have involved surprisingly little violence. The revolutions that overthrew communism in eastern Europe in 1989 were accomplished largely without widespread lethal violence in most places, though the transformations introduced by these revolutions were monumental. In the so-called Bulldozer Revolution in Serbia that overthrew dictator Slobodan Milošević in 2000, two people died—one from a heart attack, and one from being hit by a car.

---

9. As Lawson (2005, 4) noted, "there is no theoretical reason to suggest that revolution cannot take a contemporary form in keeping with an era of globalization and heteronomy."

10. Skocpol 1979, 288. See also Skocpol 1994, 242; Goodwin 2001, 8; Goldstone 2001. Goldstone (2001, 140) suggests, the study of revolution may be "overwhelmed by the variety of cases and concepts it seeks to encompass."

Certainly, little in political life is riskier than revolution. Because the state, in Weberian terms, is a repository of coercive power, and because revolutionaries aim to overthrow those who control the state, some element of violence (or at a minimum, the threat of violence) is an inherent part of all revolutions. Even in so-called nonviolent uprisings, participants face the possibility of death, injury, or arrest, and the violence visited upon participants can sometimes be horrific. Still, widespread lethal violence is not an inherent quality of revolution. It is rather a variable outcome to be explained.

Nor can revolutions be defined simply by the degree of change that they introduce. As Hannah Arendt rightly noted, revolutions are attempts at new beginnings involving the desire to bring about a rupture with an existing order and the introduction of new modes of rule.[11] But the extent to which they actually succeed in achieving something qualitatively different from the old (and how long those changes last) has varied considerably. All revolutions have two goals—to achieve power and to bring about substantive change. In order to achieve the second, one must have previously achieved the first. But even in the most minimalist sense of gaining power, there are many more "failed" revolutions than "successful" ones.

The record of those revolutionary movements that have managed to gain power in achieving their substantive goals has been decidedly mixed, with some introducing sweeping, lasting change, while others have effected only minor change or change that proved to be short-lived. The Orange Revolution in Ukraine was spectacularly successful in mobilizing millions of citizens in the streets to evict a corrupt and criminal regime; but it was spectacularly unsuccessful in institutionalizing substantive change in its wake. Once it gained power, the coalition underpinning the revolution unraveled and its leaders became engulfed in factional squabbles, quickly leading to its breakup. Within two years of the revolution, those whom it had evicted from power had won their way back to political office through the ballot box, undermining any sense that a revolution had ever occurred in the first place. In this particular instance, the failure of the original revolution to achieve substantive change precipitated a second revolution less than ten years later.

In few revolutions are the substantive changes introduced by revolution truly lasting—and sometimes what lasts is not necessarily what revolutionaries aimed to achieve. Only twenty-four years after the onset of revolution, many of the major institutional changes introduced by the French Revolution were overturned with the fall of Napoleon. The monarchy was restored, as was the prestige of the nobility and role of the Catholic Church. Yet, we do not consider

---

11. Arendt 1965, 21.

the French Revolution as any less of a revolution because of this. The government introduced by the American Revolution in 1781 failed completely and had to be invented anew only a few years after its adoption. But the effects of the American Revolution tend to be judged not by the Articles of Confederation (its original government) but by the political order that was put into effect after their failure. In short, the course of post-revolutionary governance has never been straight. Many of the actual consequences of revolutions are completely unanticipated by revolutionaries, and the path to substantive change in the wake of revolution is always difficult and circuitous. The desire to bring about substantive change is the main reason that people participate in revolutions. But the extent to which revolutions are actually able to introduce change in their wake is a question that merits serious empirical investigation rather than summary consignment to the definition of "revolution" itself.[12]

I define a revolution as a mass siege of an established government by its own population with the goals of bringing about regime-change and effecting substantive political or social change.[13] As such, I understand revolutions as a distinct mode of regime-change that differs in fundamental respects from other modes such as military coups, electoral turnovers in competitive authoritarian regimes, government-initiated political reform from above, or foreign invasions aimed at regime-change. They differ from military coups and foreign invasions aimed at regime-change in the large number of civilian (i.e., not military or police) actors involved. They differ as well from electoral turnovers in competitive authoritarian regimes and political reform from above in the specifically extra-institutional siege of government that they entail.

By its dictionary definition, a siege is "the surrounding and blockading of a city, town, or fortress by an army attempting to capture it." In the case of revolution, a government is laid siege to not by a foreign army or its own military, but by its civilian population. I view revolution as a mass siege of an established government for several reasons. For one thing, a siege implies forceful change[14]—change that is imposed on government against its will. In this respect, the notion of a mass siege places armed and unarmed revolutionary

12. As Tilly (1991, 4–5) wrote, "A broad definition [of revolution] has two important advantages over a narrow one: it permits examination of change and variation over a considerable range of time and place; second, it turns the relationship between social transformation and transfer of state power into an empirical problem."

13. For similar approaches, see Trotsky 1932; Tilly 1978; Tilly 1993; Aya 1979; Dix 1983; Goldstone 2001; Goldstone 2014. This definition bears similarity to Goodwin's (2001, 9) definition: "any and all instances in which a state or political regime is overthrown and thereby transformed by a popular movement in an irregular, extraconstitutional, and/or violent fashion."

14. Lawson 2005, 52.

action within a single analytical field—something long overdue in the study of revolution.[15] Among other decisions, revolutionary oppositions face a choice as to whether to embark upon armed or unarmed rebellion. This choice needs to be thought of holistically, as unarmed revolt can evolve into armed rebellion (and vice versa), and revolutionary oppositions can engage simultaneously in both. Moreover, nonviolent resistance is widely understood by its practitioners as a form of asymmetric warfare.[16] Unarmed crowds in revolutions engage in the "surrounding and blockading" of ruling regimes by occupying city centers, obstructing city streets, seizing control of symbolic spaces, and assailing government command posts. It is as much a siege of government as is an assault by an armed regiment and is frequently talked about in those terms.[17]

The notion of siege is also meant to signal a resolve and commitment to compelling regime-change that differentiates revolution from quasi-revolutionary protests (such as occasional mass actions that articulate demands for a leader's resignation). The 2011–12 electoral protests in Russia over widespread electoral fraud were the largest manifestations of civic activism in Russia since the collapse of the Soviet Union, involving up to a hundred thousand participants in Moscow alone. While the ruling United Russia Party was branded at the demonstrations as "the party of swindlers and thieves," and calls were raised for Vladimir Putin's resignation, no overt effort was made to impose regime-change. Rather, protestors gathered in a public square that had been agreed upon beforehand with the government, voiced their demands, and then dispersed, reassembling intermittently over the following months. The movement even went into abeyance over the summer so that activists could go on their summer vacations. I refer to such protests as "quasi-revolutionary" in that they articulate demands for regime-change, and thereby bear some resemblance to revolution, but fall short of revolution in that a mass siege aimed at compelling regime-change never materializes.[18] Quasi-revolutionary protests are in fact quite common—much more common than revolution. But they are to a greater extent purely expressive in their purposes and lack the resolve, commitment, and effort to impose regime-change that are inherent elements of a revolutionary siege of power.

---

15. For a critique of the artificial division between the literatures on revolution and civil war, see McAdam, Tarrow, and Tilly 2001.

16. Sharp 2012; Chenoweth and Stephan 2011; Nepstad 2011; Zunes 1994.

17. Helvey 1984.

18. Mather (1974, 115–16) uses the term "semi-revolutionary" to describe the General Strike of 1842 in Britain—perhaps the closest that Britain came in the nineteenth century to a revolutionary episode. As Mather notes, "the state's monopoly of power was not in imminent danger of being overthrown."

A mass siege, when it is aimed at displacing an established government, inherently raises issues of sovereignty, which has long been understood to lie at the center of modern revolution. As Trotsky, Tilly, and others have noted, revolutions are characterized by situations of competing sovereignties—when the right of an incumbent regime to rule is rejected and rival claims for control over the same state are made.[19] In some cases (for example, the October Revolution in Russia in 1917), a clear alternative center claiming sovereignty emerges before or during the course of revolutionary events. In other cases (for instance, the 1989 East German Revolution), no clear alternative center emerges, even though the incumbent regime is subjected to a mass siege that aims at regime displacement. Subjecting a regime to a state of siege in order to displace it is a sufficient indicator of rejection of its right to rule, even without a formal declaration of sovereignty by an alternative center of power.

There are many types of contentious episodes that are non-revolutionary in that they fail to articulate clear demands for regime displacement. Before 1800, participants in peasant uprisings in Europe "never thought of defending or furthering their interests by ensuring representation at the center."[20] The authors of the Twelve Demands in the 1525 German Peasants' War condemned the power of the clergy, the exploitation of peasants, and the feudal rights of the aristocracy, but they never called for the seizure of political power or questioned the right of princes to rule over them.[21] In the Moldovan Peasant Revolt of 1907, landless peasants attacked the properties of landowners, burning their houses to the ground and destroying crops; but they articulated no demands for overthrow of the government, instead directing their ire against local landlords and their Jewish middlemen.[22] In a more recent example, the Occupy Wall Street Movement engaged in a mass siege of Wall Street and articulated demands for a redistribution of wealth, but it never aimed at displacing the American government in Washington. Rather than a revolution, it was in some ways the modern urban equivalent of a peasant revolt.[23]

Figure 1.1 provides a 2 × 3 summary of the relationship of revolution to a number of other modes of politics. It classifies forms of politics by three criteria: whether they involve significant mass mobilization; whether they involve a mass siege of government; and whether they aim at displacement of an incumbent regime. It highlights the distinctiveness of revolution as a mode of

19. Trotsky 1932; Tilly 1978.
20. Sabean 1976, 355. See also Desai and Eckstein 1990, 454.
21. Engels 1956.
22. Chirot and Ragin 1975.
23. For a similar opinion on the radical but non-revolutionary character of Occupy, see Mitchell 2013, 95.

| | Aimed at regime displacement ||
	No	Yes
Mass mobilization — No mass mobilization	conventional institutional politics	military coups, foreign invasions, political reform from above
Mass mobilization — Mass mobilization without siege of government	election campaigns, peasant revolts, urban riots, social movements, "revolutions-from-above"	electoral turnovers in hybrid regimes, quasi-revolutionary protests
Mass mobilization — Mass mobilization with siege of government	non-revolutionary siege of government	revolutions

FIGURE 1.1. The relationship of revolution to other forms of politics.

regime-change. It also shows how revolution shares a number of features with other phenomena. Whereas military coups, foreign imposed regime-change, and political reform from above aim at regime displacement, they contain little mass mobilization. Whereas electoral turnovers in competitive authoritarian regimes and quasi-revolutionary protests involve mass mobilization and aim at regime-change, they do not subject government to a mass siege. Social movements seek to bring about changes in government policies or in the attitudes and behaviors of groups in society. On some occasions, social movements engage in a mass siege of government without articulating demands for regime-change—what I call (for want of a better term) "non-revolutionary sieges of government." Examples include the 2005 Cedar Revolution in Lebanon, the February 20 Movement in Morocco during the Arab Spring, the 2011 Indignados Movement in Spain, and the 2014 Sunflower Student Movement in Taiwan. In each of these cases, movements clearly subjected governments to a mass siege, but they sought to compel reforms or policy changes without demanding regime-change.[24] Social movements can become revolutionary. But they only become revolutionary when they engage in a mass siege of government *and* articulate demands for regime-change.

---

24. Major rebellions that aimed at defending local autonomy but never articulated demands for state independence also fall into this category. Examples include the 1964 Montagnard Rebellion, the 1979 Kurdish Rebellion in Iraq, and the 2004 Houthi Rebellion in Yemen.

So-called revolutions-from-above (such as Stalin's collectivization campaign, the Shah's White Revolution in Iran, or Mao's Cultural Revolution) are attempts by incumbent rulers to mobilize populations against rivals and to accomplish rapid social change through mass mobilization. Revolutions-from-above have sometimes been lumped together with revolutions—largely because they utilize mass mobilization to accomplish their goals.[25] But regime-change is the last thing that rulers enacting revolutions-from-above have in mind, and they should therefore be treated as analytically distinct from revolution.

Revolutions can develop out of other forms of contentious politics. Social movements and revolutions, for instance, can originate in similar processes but evolve toward different outcomes.[26] Often failed repression pushes social movements along a revolutionary path. But revolution can also hybridize with other modes of regime-change, such as electoral turnovers in authoritarian regimes (e.g., the 2000 Bulldozer Revolution in Serbia, the 2002 Madagascar Electoral Revolution, and the 2004 Orange Revolution in Ukraine)[27] or political reform from above (the June Uprising in South Korea in 1987, the Estonian Singing Revolution of 1987–91, and the Beninese Revolution of 1989–90).[28] Maoist revolutions have sought to harness peasant revolt to purposes of revolution, while urban armed revolts (such as the October Revolution in Russia in 1917) have tended to combine elements of urban riots with military insurrections. Most revolutions pull on elements of other modes of politics as they target specific social groups or particular weaknesses of the regimes they challenge.

A number of revolutions have assumed the form of a "coupvolution"—that is, a mass siege of government aimed at regime-change that precipitates a military coup in support of revolution, or an attempted military coup accompanied by mass protests in support of regime-change.[29] Trotsky observed that

---

25. In Trimberger's (1978) conceptualization of revolution-from-above (which includes the Meiji Restoration, the Turkish War of Independence, and the Valasco coup in Peru), military bureaucrats impose social change on society, but there is little mass mobilization involved.

26. On the ways in which social movements and revolutions can relate to one another, see Goldstone 1998a; McAdam, Tarrow, and Tilly 2001.

27. On stolen elections as occasions for revolution, see Thompson 2004; Tucker 2007; Bunce and Wolchik 2011.

28. On reform as an occasion for revolution, see Tocqueville 2011, 157.

29. The term is a play on Timothy Garton Ash's (1990) expression "refolution," which referred to a mixture of reform from above and revolutionary pressure from below that characterized the collapse of communism in Poland and Hungary. Holmes (2019) employs a similar notion for what she calls "coups from below."

"the first task of every insurrection is to bring the troops over to its side."[30] Coupvolutions go one step further: not only does the military defect to the side of the opposition in the face of a mass uprising; it also attempts to seize power in support of revolution. The Xinhai Revolution in China in 1911 that overthrew the Qing dynasty was led by revolutionary groups that had penetrated into China's "new army."[31] In the Guatemalan Revolution of 1944, dissident elements in the military seized power in the wake of massive demonstrations seeking to oust the regime of General Jorge Ubico.[32] In Burkina Faso in 2014, in response to President Blaise Compaoré's attempts to amend the constitution to allow him to extend his twenty-seven years in office, large-scale demonstrations led by the opposition Movement of People for Progress were eventually joined by soldiers, precipitating a military coup that led to a return to civilian rule.[33] Since 1900, about 12 percent of revolutionary episodes have taken the form of a coupvolution involving a mass uprising accompanied by an attempted military coup, though coupvolutions have been becoming less frequent over time.[34]

The City in the Study of Revolution

There is of course a vast theoretical literature on revolutions, stretching back to the nineteenth-century classics of de Tocqueville and Marx.[35] The city was not ignored in it, and for good reason: the city was the primary location of most revolutionary contention up through the early twentieth century. De Tocqueville, for instance, wrote of the enormous concentration of power, people, and industry in Paris during the eighteenth century, which, he believed, explained why Paris so dominated the events of the French Revolution.[36] For Marx, "the essential life of man could take place only in cities, where the classes confront each other [and] where men in the mass demonstrate the nature and destiny of mankind."[37] In Marx's writings, the city was

---

30. Trotsky 1932, vol. 3, 181. See also Chorley 1973; Barany 2016.
31. Rhoads 1975; Fung 1980.
32. Grieb 1976.
33. Frère and Englebert 2015.
34. Despite a number of prominent cases (the 1985 Sudanese Revolution, the 1986 People Power Revolution in the Philippines, the 2002 Anti-Chavez Revolt in Venezuela, and the 2013 Egyptian Counter-Revolution), the probability of a revolutionary episode also involving a military coup or rebellion halved during the post–Cold War years (from .15 to .07).
35. Of course, even earlier, revolution had played an important role in political thought extending from Aristotle through Burke.
36. Tocqueville 2011, 71–75.
37. Trilling 1972, 20.

the site for all revolutions—both bourgeois and proletarian—and the grievances and social processes that were to produce socialist revolution were deeply ingrained in the logic of the capitalist city.

Yet, over the course of the twentieth century, as social revolution increasingly shifted from the city to the countryside, the city as a locus of revolution came to be de-emphasized within the study of revolution. With much simplification, scholars have divided theoretical work on revolutions into four generations of thought: 1) a so-called natural history approach; 2) a functionalist or disequilibrium approach; 3) a structural approach; and 4) a processual or agential approach.[38]

The natural history approach dominated early scholarship on revolution. It drew heavily on Gustave Le Bon's crowd psychology, which posited that individuals in the context of crowds were subject to heightened suggestibility. In Le Bon's view, subversive ideas spread by suggestion and contagion, manifesting themselves in revolution when the moment grew ripe.[39] First-generation thinkers feared the unsuppressed instincts of the masses that revolutions were said to unleash. They envisaged a set of phases through which revolutions naturally progressed—best exemplified in the writings of Crane Brinton.[40] Like Le Bon, Brinton saw revolution as a kind of fever through which the sickened body politic proceeded, culminating in the moment of delirium (terror), when the fever broke and society experienced convalescence, leading to the re-emergence of pre-revolutionary habits and behaviors. Brinton placed particular emphasis on the centrality of class antagonisms, the alienation of intellectuals, a decline in self-confidence among ruling elites, and the inefficiency and fiscal crisis of the state as key conditions setting societies on a revolutionary path.[41] But what generally pushed societies along this path, in Brinton's account, were the radical revolutionary intellectuals and the fire of ideology with which they were consumed.[42] They manipulated mass grievances and class antagonisms and whipped up the passions of the crowd to the point of fanaticism. Although a number of the revolutions examined by Brinton had their origins in cities, and most of the social forces he

---

38. For synthetic reviews of the theoretical literature, see Goldstone 1980; Goldstone 2001; Foran 2005; Lawson 2019. The review that follows hardly does justice to the breadth and variety of scholarly writings on revolution.

39. Le Bon 1913. For Le Bon, discontent alone was never enough to cause a revolution. Rather, revolutions required leaders to exaggerate discontent and "persuade the discontented that the government is the sole cause of all the trouble" (15).

40. Brinton 1965. See also Sorokin 1925; Hopper 1950.

41. Brinton 1965.

42. For a somewhat analogous argument, see Billington 1980.

described were urban, the setting of the city played little role in his arguments. Much the same could be said of Le Bon. The growth of cities provoked the problematic that crowd theory sought to address. But the city itself was incidental to the theory.

A second generation of scholarship—adopting a functionalist or disequilibrium approach—was prevalent from the late 1950s through the early 1970s. It viewed revolution as a manifestation of social strain and the breakdown of norms and institutions, often precipitated by modernization and rapid social change. Authors such as William Kornhauser and Chalmers Johnson analyzed revolution as a response to a disequilibrated social system and the deterioration of social structures and societal values, leading to a loss of elite authority and to revolt by alienated and anomic individuals.[43] Others, such as Samuel Huntington, described revolution as the product of rapid modernization and the increased demands for participation to which it gave rise, particularly when these could not be adequately channeled into existing institutions.[44] Still others, such as James Davies and Ted Robert Gurr, saw revolutions as caused by high levels of anger and frustration brought on by the disequilibrating effects of relative deprivation.[45] The appeal of second-generation theories faded by the 1980s, as scholars realized that high rates of modernization and relative deprivation were much more common phenomena than revolution, and that these theories suffered from issues of internal inconsistency and difficulties in measuring key concepts.[46]

The city was not overlooked in second-generation scholarship. The rapid growth of cities was commonly treated as a cause or indicator of dislocation and social strain, feeding into the conditions that generated social breakdown. Among second-generation scholars, Huntington provided the most detailed account of the role that cities played in revolution. He viewed the city as "the center of opposition" in countries undergoing rapid modernization, with the middle class (rather than the urban poor or working class) constituting "the focus of opposition." For Huntington, the intelligentsia was the most revolutionary sector of the middle class, though, according to him, as the middle class grew larger, it also became more conservative. But to make a revolution, Huntington argued, the intelligentsia needed to forge an alliance with peasants:

---

43. Kornhauser 1959; Smelser 1963; Johnson 1982; Hagopian 1974.
44. Huntington 1968.
45. Davies 1962; Gurr 1970; Feierabend, Feierabend, and Gurr 1972.
46. For discussions of the decline of second-generation theories, see Goldstone 1980; Brush 1996.

As modernization progresses, the middle class and other groups in the city emerge as political actors challenging the existing system. Their successful overthrow of the system, however, depends upon their ability to win rural allies, that is, to win the support of the peasants against the traditional oligarchy. The ability of the political system to survive and of its government to remain stable depends upon its capacity to counter this revolutionary appeal and to bring the peasants into politics on the side of the system. As political participation expands, those groups dominant in the political system must shift their basis of support within the countryside and win the allegiance of the peasants.

As Huntington put it, "opposition within the city is disturbing but not lethal. Opposition within the countryside, however, is fatal. He who controls the countryside controls the country."[47] In Huntington's view, the city was not the primary site where revolutions unfolded, and urban opposition was insufficient on its own to bring about revolution. For second-generation scholars such as Huntington, the pace of urbanization and the disruptions it wrought on traditional social structures were generally more important in conditioning revolutions than the city per se.

Third-generation scholars focused their attention on social revolutions, and drew much of their inspiration from Marxist theory. But whereas Marx had emphasized the city as the locus of revolutions, third-generation scholarship largely abandoned the city and pointed instead to class relations in the countryside as key to explaining social revolutions. This abandonment of the city paralleled broader patterns of social revolution during the Cold War, which, as we will see, also shifted from city to countryside. Authors in this tradition concentrated their attention on factors such as patterns of land tenure, the commercialization of agriculture, village social structures, rapid population growth in the countryside, and relations between landed aristocracies and the state.[48] For Jeffrey Paige, for instance, patterns of quiescence and revolt were largely the product of the ways in which rural labor was organized and the degree to which cultivators were dependent on upper-class non-cultivators within the agricultural production process. Revolutionary challenges were most likely to develop when non-cultivators were dependent on income from land and cultivators were dependent on wages. In these circumstances, rural cultivators tended to form strong, radical, and cohesive political organizations,

---

47. Huntington 1968, 289–92.
48. For examples, see Paige 1975; Wolf 1969; Migdal 1974; Scott 1977; Goldstone 1980; Goldstone 1991.

and non-cultivators were incapable of granting concessions that might quell revolutionary impulses.[49]

Third-generation theories were known for their structural determinism, whereby revolution depended not on the choices or actions of individuals, but on relatively given factors of the social order. As Skocpol, quoting Wendell Phillips, put it, "revolutions are not made; they come."[50] They come when all the necessary structural conditions that render them inevitable align. Skocpol argued that social revolutions only occurred in agrarian-bureaucratic societies, in which the resources extracted from peasants were shared between a semi-bureaucratic state and a landed upper class. As states modernized, conflicts emerged between the central state and the landed elite over division of the surplus generated by peasants, peasants came to constitute a vast sea of discontent, and the surplus that supported both the government and the landed aristocracy could not be easily increased due to the limits of agricultural production. As Skocpol recognized, these weaknesses were present in all agrarian-bureaucratic societies, though only a subset experienced revolution. Her theory outlined the conditions that rendered social revolution in agrarian-bureaucratic societies unavoidable.

One important factor was pressure due to international competition, military defeat abroad, or foreign commitments. This stretched the resources of the state, intensified contradictions between the state and its landed elite, and facilitated a breakdown in the government's ability to repress internal opponents. A second factor was the degree to which the government bureaucracy was recruited from landed elites and was therefore unable to assert its autonomy from them. This, Skocpol argued, determined whether conflicts between landlords and the government for control over peasant resources emerged, and the extent to which governments were able to engage in reforms. Finally, she argued that massive peasant uprisings were critical to transforming these revolutions into social revolutions. In particular, three conditions in the countryside facilitated peasant rebellion: first, the degree of solidarity of peasant communities; second, the degree of autonomy of peasants from day-to-day supervision and control by the landed elite; and third, relaxation of the state's coercive control over peasants, often as a result of war.[51]

Skocpol observed that all successful social revolutions "occurred in one or another sort of agrarian state, and nothing is to be gained by ignoring this fact."

49. Paige 1975.
50. Skocpol 1979, 17.
51. Skocpol 1979; Skocpol 1994.

She maintained that "the most politically significant popular revolts" in social revolutions "were grounded in village communities."[52] Third-generation theories were in significant part theories of this rural society. They largely ignored the city and seriously underplayed its role in several of the social revolutions that they analyzed. For example, despite Skocpol's focus on peasant communities, the key events of the French and Russian revolutions unfolded in cities, not in the countryside. To be sure, these were overwhelmingly peasant societies, and peasant unrest contributed mightily to the disorder surrounding these upheavals. But the critical supporters of both revolutions were urban, and in both cases, large numbers of peasants were lined up against these urban revolutionary forces.[53] Third-generation scholars correctly identified many of the political and societal characteristics associated with social revolutions. But the actual events that made up these revolutions were mostly ignored in favor of a focus on the structural conditions that supposedly made the onset and outcome of social revolution unavoidable.

A fourth generation in the study of revolution developed in the 1990s and early 2000s. It derived its inspiration from social movement theory, rational choice analysis, and the cultural turn in the social sciences, placing particular emphasis on agency and the roles that incentives, organization, networks, framing, culture, and emotions play in revolutionary processes.[54] As Jack Goldstone noted, fourth generation theories rejected the structuralist orientation of third generation scholarship and sought instead to "treat stability as problematic, see a wide range of factors and conditions as producing departures from stability, and recognize that the processes and outcomes of revolutions are mediated by group identification, networks, and coalitions; leadership and competing

---

52. Skocpol 1994, 113, 245.

53. The Bolsheviks, for instance, received their main support from urban workers and soldiers weary of the regime's war effort, while peasants had their grain confiscated at gunpoint by the Bolsheviks in order to feed the cities, ultimately generating a sea of peasant hostility to Soviet power. In the French Revolution, large numbers of peasants rebelled against the revolution and the urban elites it represented, defending traditional authority. This differed fundamentally from mid-twentieth century peasant-based social revolutions like the Chinese, in which peasant mobilization *was* the revolution. See Gill 1979; Retish 2008; Tilly 1964; Mayer 2000. Skocpol recognized that peasants played relatively little part in the 1979 Iranian Revolution, which she instead ascribed to autonomous urban enclaves rooted among bazaar merchants and the mosque. But the case did not fit her theory well. See Skocpol 1994, 247–50.

54. Goldstone 2001; Foran 2005; Lawson 2016. For examples, see Tilly 1978; Lohmann 1994; Sewell 1996; Kuran 1997; Goldstone 1998a; Goldstone 2001; Goodwin 2001; McAdam, Tarrow, and Tilly 2001; Beissinger 2002; Kurzman 2004; Goldstone 2013.

ideologies; and the interplay among rulers, elites, popular groups, and foreign powers in response to ongoing conflicts."[55]

In many ways, the "fourth-generation" label has merely been a category of convenience, as these arguments encompassed an eclectic variety of theories united largely by their rejection of the structural determinism of third-generation scholarship and their focus on revolutionary processes. In refocusing attention on these less "given" and more evanescent aspects of revolutionary contention, fourth-generation scholars at times introduced a radical indeterminacy into the study of revolution. Some saw fundamental similarities between what occurs within mobilizational cycles and what happens within revolutions—the difference being that revolutions develop into efforts to overthrow a regime out of the interactions between regimes and oppositions.[56] Rational choice analyses utilized collective-action, social choice, and coordination frameworks to explicate the roles played by leadership and information within revolutions and the significance of tactical choice.[57] Other rational choice scholars, such as Timur Kuran, argued that revolutions were fundamentally unpredictable because of the ways in which the expression of falsified preferences over regime-change was interdependent across individuals.[58] Some fourth-generation scholars pointed to the ways in which revolutionary movements influenced one another across boundaries.[59] Others directed attention to the critical roles of networks, culture, ideologies, narratives, and individual agency in shaping revolutionary outcomes.[60]

The first three generations of scholarship concentrated mainly on social revolutions and had little to say about the city as a site of rebellion. Fourth-generation theorists, by contrast, recognized that a shift had taken place in the character of revolutions and included the urban revolutions that were spreading in the late twentieth and early twenty-first centuries in their purview. But fourth-generation studies largely failed to make broader analytical sense of the explosion of revolutions that they encountered; they were, as several synthetic reviews noted, "overwhelmed" by the variety of cases that they confronted.[61] Nor did they, for the most part, attempt to theorize the city as a particular

55. Goldstone 2001, 172.
56. Tilly 1978; Goldstone 1998a; Tarrow 1998; McAdam, Tarrow, and Tilly 2001.
57. Tullock 1971; Popkin 1979; DeNardo 1985; Taylor 1988; Lichbach 1998; Bueno de Mesquita 2010.
58. Kuran 1997.
59. Katz 1999; Beissinger 2002; Beissinger 2007; Kurzman 2008; Weyland 2009; Beck 2011; Weyland 2014.
60. See, for example, Gould 1995; Zhao 2004; Sewell 1996; Wood 2003; Selbin 2010.
61. Goldstone 2001; Lawson 2016; Beck 2018; Allinson 2019.

spatial locus for revolt, or to provide an explanation for why social revolution had gone into decline in the late twentieth century and urban revolutions had proliferated. Indeed, they generally eschewed the kind of structural thinking that would have been necessary to account for this evolution, neglecting bigger, slower moving, less proximate processes of change.[62] The "givens" that structured revolutionary situations were often overlooked in favor of more immediate and dynamic processes.

This book is profoundly influenced by fourth-generation thinking on revolutions—particularly its focus on regime–opposition interactions and the contingencies that this injects into revolutionary contention. My own writing has been squarely within this tradition, and much of the book incorporates this perspective. But this book differs from most fourth-generation scholarship in two respects.

First, it attempts to put structural explanation back squarely into the study of revolutions by embedding revolutionary processes and interactions within the structural factors that condition, facilitate, or constrain them. It positions large-scale structural factors like urbanization, geopolitics, and technological change at the center of an understanding of how revolution has evolved over time and integrates structure and agency into a broader, probabilistic approach to revolutionary contention.[63] In doing so, it abstains from the kind of deterministic structural thinking characteristic of third-generation theorizing, while rejecting the tendency to downplay structural explanation exhibited in many fourth-generation studies. It also rejects the notion that all types of revolutions can be explained by the same set of causal factors, embracing the fourth-generation understanding of the diversity of purposes to which revolution has been put. In a probabilistic structural approach, there is no set of necessary or sufficient conditions that unequivocally produces revolution— only conditions that make certain kinds of revolutionary contention more or less likely to break out or succeed. These conditions can occur in a variety of combinations, and the weakness of any one condition does not necessarily preclude revolution in the presence of others; it simply makes it harder. A probabilistic approach distinguishes between the structural risk associated with revolt based on the law of averages and the actual materialization of revolt in any particular case. Structure leaves its traces primarily through the

---

62. Pierson 2003. For a critique as applied to the social movement field, see Walder 2009. For exceptions, see Tilly 1978; Gould 1995; Traugott 2010. For calls for a fifth generation of research aimed at re-synthesis of the field, see Allinson 2019; Bayat 2017; Ritter 2015; Della Porta 2016; Lawson 2016; Lawson 2019.

63. See Ritter (2015) for another study that has sought to explain the evolving character of revolutions over time, focusing in particular on the influence of the liberal international order.

patterning of action it produces across multiple contexts, not by precluding action or rendering action inevitable in any particular context. Revolution is not a matter of lining up a set of conditions, winding them up, and sitting back and watching the result. Outcomes are conditioned, facilitated, and constrained by structural factors, but outcomes emerge from the ways in which actors take advantage of the structural conditions that confront them.

Secondly, this book is distinct from much of fourth-generation thinking in its attempt to theorize the city as a political and spatial site for revolt and the ways in which spatial location structures political action. I argue that the spatial dimensions of power are central to an understanding of revolutionary politics. In doing so, I direct particular attention to how the spatial context of the city shapes mobilizational processes and the opportunities and resources that governments and oppositions command for achieving their ends.

Spatial Location and the Proximity Dilemma

Central to the arguments of this book is the notion that revolutionary processes in cities—with their proximity to centers of power, concentrated populations, diverse and abundant networks, robust communication systems, and built environments—differ in fundamental respects from revolutionary processes in the countryside, where population density is low, networks revolve around kinship and locality, and topography frequently presents a barrier to the penetration of state power.

Cities present certain advantages and disadvantages to those who would challenge regimes through revolution. Lewis Mumford defined the city as the "point of maximum concentration for the power and culture of a community."[64] Indeed, as empirical studies have shown, measures of state capacity such as law enforcement or service delivery tend to decline as distance from cities grows.[65] This thickened presence of the state in cities exercises a profound effect on the character of urban rebellion. It changes the risks involved in revolution, alters the rhythm of revolutionary contention, and shapes the nature of the revolutionary playing field, advantaging certain tactics over others. Urban revolts take place where the coercive capacity of the state is strongest,

---

64. Mumford 1938, 3.

65. Wibbels 2019, 3. Despite the concentration of state power in cities, there can of course be pockets in cities in which state infrastructural power remains weak. Only rarely, however, have these formed the basis for revolutionary threats to regimes. See Soifer and vom Hau 2008, 222.

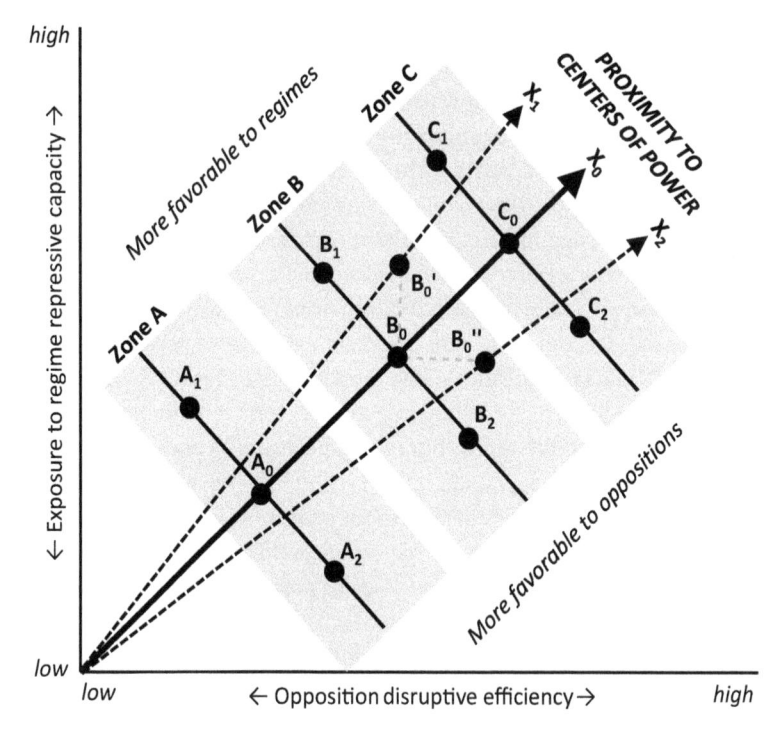

FIGURE 1.2. Exposure to regime repression, disruptive efficiency, and proximity to centers of power.

rendering them highly vulnerable to repression. But the strategic advantages of regimes in cities due to heightened repressive capacity are partially offset by the strategic advantages that accrue to oppositions due to their proximity to command centers of power—the ultimate targets of revolutionary regime-change. Because of this proximity, urban revolts can potentially threaten and disrupt a regime more effectively and directly than rural revolts, occurring at a distance, generally are able to. Thus, proximity to centers of state power not only magnifies the stakes and risks involved in revolution for rebels; it also magnifies the stakes and risks involved for regimes.

I refer to this as the "proximity dilemma" in revolution (displayed in Figure 1.2). Rural revolutions may be able to fend off repression by hiding in places distant from government forces. But they do so at the cost of their ability to exert pressure on regimes directly through disruption. Essentially, the closer a revolutionary opposition is to centers of power (movement from Zone A to Zone B, or from Zone B to Zone C in Figure 1.2), the more capable it is of influencing a ruling regime directly through its disruptive actions, but the more exposed it is to a regime's repressive capacities. A basic dilemma facing all revolutionary movements is how to manage this repression–disruption trade-off—that is, how to leverage their disruptive power to induce regime collapse while warding off regime repression.

An analogous trade-off exists within evolutionary biology—the so-called growth versus predation-risk trade-off, whereby organisms thrive in particular habitats and engage in activities that provide "enough food to grow and reproduce while trying not to become someone else's dinner."[66] More frequent foraging in food-rich habitats provides individual organisms with greater opportunities to thrive, but at the risk of greater exposure to predators, who also congregate in these same locations. The most efficient sites for foraging and the most dangerous locations for falling to predators tend to coincide. Individuals navigate this trade-off differently. But over time, learning and natural selection lead toward adjustments in habitat selection and foraging behaviors to balance the risks and rewards. To reduce the risk of predation, organisms may, for example, alter where and for how long they forage or the timing of foraging, engage in herding or migratory behaviors, or devote a portion of their foraging time to vigilance rather than feeding. Natural selection can also lead toward the development of special camouflage or escape capabilities among species.

Like the growth versus predation-risk trade-off in nature, the repression–disruption trade-off in revolution can similarly be managed by spatial relocation—that is, by moving closer to or farther away from centers of power along the repression–disruption trade-off function (X_0). By moving further away from centers of power (from C_0 to B_0 or from B_0 to A_0), a revolutionary opposition can better avoid government repression, but at the expense of its disruptive capabilities. By moving closer to centers of power (from A_0 to B_0 or from B_0 to C_0), it can increase its ability to pressure a regime, but at the cost of increased exposure to the regime's repressive capabilities.

Like the growth versus predation-risk trade-off, the repression–disruption trade-off in revolution can also be managed within spatial contexts through learning behavior—specifically, through tactical choice by regimes and oppositions. Holding spatial context and other factors constant, opposition tactics that increase the degree of disruptive efficiency against a regime or decrease exposure to a regime's repressive capacity are likely to be more effective at inducing regime-change (i.e., from the point of view of revolutionary oppositions, a preference for point C_0 over C_1 and for C_2 over both C_0 and C_1). By contrast, government tactics that increase opposition exposure to a regime's repressive

---

66. McPeek 2004, E88. See also Brown 1988; Camp et al. 2012. For a study that views revolution through a predator-versus-prey lens, see Tsebelis and Sprague 1989.

capacity or decrease the degree of an opposition's disruptive efficiency are likely to be more effective in repressing revolutionary challenges (from the point of view of regimes, a preference for point C_0 over C_2 and for C_1 over both C_0 and C_2). Thus, in general, tactics that move toward the lower right-hand region in Figure 1.2 are more favorable to oppositions, while those that move toward the upper left-hand region are more favorable to regimes.

Finally, the slope of the repression–disruption trade-off function itself can be affected by structural changes in the environment that push it in a direction more favorable either to regimes or to oppositions (changes that operate similarly to the ways that climate change affects natural selection). Under trade-off function X_1, for instance, oppositions must endure more exposure to regime repression in order to achieve the same amount of disruptive efficiency within roughly the same spatial location (point B_0' versus B_0) than they would under trade-off function X_0, while under function X_2 oppositions gain more disruptive efficiency for the same degree of exposure to repression within roughly the same spatial location (point B_0'' versus point B_0). This type of structural change in the slope of the repression–disruption trade-off function can occur as a result of shifts in the nature of political or economic power, alterations in social structures or the character of networks, new technologies of communication, rebellion, or counter-rebellion, or changing currents of geopolitics that render oppositions more exposed to regime repression or regimes more vulnerable to opposition disruption. For example, new technologies of surveillance (facial recognition, for instance) could increase an opposition's exposure to government repression in cities. Alternatively, new technologies of communication (mobile phones, for example) could render regimes more vulnerable to disruption from oppositions in cities. These structural changes alter the advantages available to regimes and oppositions within particular spatial contexts, shaping the evolving character of revolutionary contention over time. They are often most intensely felt in cities, where governments and oppositions are more directly exposed to innovations in technologies and forms of communication, changes in government, and global political and economic forces. When they do occur, they provide advantages to one side or the other by tilting the repression–disruption trade-off function in a particular direction. Typically, those adversely affected attempt to adapt by adjusting their tactics as well, in the hope of countering the increased structural disadvantage they are experiencing.

As I detail throughout this book, the proximity dilemma shapes revolutionary processes in profound ways. For one thing, because it renders urban revolution a high-risk/high-stakes endeavor for all involved, revolutions in cities tend to be extremely compact in time. As we will see, this quickened pace of revolutionary contention creates significant information problems for both regimes and oppositions and heightens the role of contingency and error in urban revolutionary processes. By contrast, because of their distance from centers of power, rural revolutions tend to unfold over longer periods of time, with the hope of eventually being able to move closer to centers of power as those centers gradually weaken. In revolutionary contention, distance is not only about the compression of time for oppositions and regimes due to direct exposure to the actions of one's opponents and the speed of interactions that this creates. It is also about the ability to recover from mistakes. While contingency and error also play roles in rural revolutions, the physical distance that separates revolutionaries and regimes means that both are often able to recover from mistakes by taking advantage of the cushion that distance and remoteness afford. No such cushion exists in urban revolutions. Mistakes are more likely to be fatal when their consequences are immediately felt.

The proximity dilemma also affects many of the factors associated with the onset and outcomes of particular types of revolutions. It would be reasonable to assume, for instance, that because urban revolutionary oppositions are more directly exposed to a regime's repressive capacities, urban revolutionary processes will be more sensitive to regime-type and the degree of openness/closedness of a regime. Conversely, regime-type and the openness/closedness of regimes should matter less in rural revolutions, as distance from centers of power buffers rural oppositions from exposure to government repression. As city-based oppositions are more directly exposed to the repressive capacities of regimes, political opportunities revolving around the opening of regimes should play a larger role in shaping urban revolutions than in shaping rural ones. By contrast, one should expect the infrastructural strength or weakness of the state (i.e., the ability of a state to penetrate its territory) to matter more for rural than for urban revolutions. Infrastructural weakness allows rural revolutionaries to operate without fearing government repression but has little effect on revolutionary challengers in cities, where the coercive capacity of the state is stronger. As we will see in subsequent chapters, these intuitions do indeed hold true.

Spatial context also shapes the availability and effectiveness of tactics for managing the proximity dilemma. Different spatial locations are associated with different physical structures within which revolutionary contention must be played out—various types of built environments, open spaces, and physical terrains. Spatial locations are also associated with different population densities, social forces, types of networks, forms of communication, and connections to the outside world. These also strongly affect the ways in which revolutionaries are able to manage the repression–disruption trade-off. Rough terrain in rural areas, for instance, aids the ability of revolutionaries to hide from government repression, while low population densities in the countryside and distance from centers of power render tactics that rely on the power of numbers ineffective for pressuring regimes, leaving oppositions exposed to government repression. Consequently, in rural areas, armed rebellion should be a more effective tactic than unarmed rebellion. But for rural revolutionaries to be victorious, they must eventually bring their rebellion closer to cities and their ultimate targets of rebellion. In urban contexts, by contrast, the opposite is true. Armed insurrections in close proximity to centers of power expose revolutionaries to the full repressive capacity of the state, as armed rebels in cities tend to be outnumbered and outmatched by government forces.[67] In cities, rebels are directly exposed to this asymmetry—unbuffered by distance or terrain. Unarmed rebellions in cities are also highly exposed to the repressive capacity of the state; but in the presence of very large populations, urban revolutionaries can potentially exploit the power of numbers as a strategy for protecting themselves from government repression while exerting disruptive pressure on government. Governments are often reluctant to shoot into large, unarmed crowds—either out of moral compunction or because of the ways in which this can provoke backlash mobilizations and defections in close proximity to centers of power. Thus, in contrast to the countryside, in cities unarmed tactics that utilize the power of numbers tend to be more effective than armed tactics against regimes. However, as we will see, exploiting this vulnerability generally requires the mobilization of very large numbers, and only under conditions of massive urbanization is this widely feasible.

As cities represent intensified centers of control over political, economic, and social life, over time people have tended to "concentrate at the control points . . . because all sorts of resources and opportunities concentrate at those locations."[68] This aggregation of people in cities has been driven by multiple factors: industrialization and the development of urban economies; administrative centralization and the growth of the modern state; war and political violence; and poverty, famine, dispossession, and mechanization in the countryside. Over the past century, urbanization has transformed the physiognomy of societies. This concentration of people, power, and wealth in cities has altered the repression–disruption function. The presence of large, well-resourced, and highly networked populations in cities has given rise to new repertoires of revolutionary challenge that rely on the power of numbers rather than the force of arms. The growth of robust systems of communication

---

67. As Traugott (2010, 206) observed, in urban armed warfare "[s]upremacy in armament and equipment, complemented by the discipline and hierarchical coordination that are the hallmarks of military organization, normally confer upon government troops an insuperable advantage over irregular forces, however highly motivated."

68. Tilly 1974, 3. See also Pierskalla, Schultz, and Wibbels 2017.

in urban centers has enhanced the ability of challengers to mobilize urban populations, and the increased presence of foreign populations, foreign commerce, and contacts with the outside world has afforded further opportunities to leverage international connections in seeking to undermine regimes. Indeed, because cities are more exposed to the outside world, transnational waves of revolution matter more within an urban than a rural environment. Over the past century, as urban populations have multiplied, and as regimes have grown more hybrid and less outwardly autocratic, more dependent on fostering economic growth for their legitimation, and more integrated into global economic, normative, and informational orders, governments have also grown increasingly vulnerable to urban revolution.

Urban civic revolutionary tactics have sought to leverage the strategic advantages of large cities for revolutionary challengers while minimizing vulnerability to repression. As we will see, urban civic revolutions have demonstrated an extraordinarily high rate of success compared to other forms of revolutionary contention. This high rate of success is largely due to the ways in which the urban civic repertoire effectively utilizes the revolutionary advantages of large cities: proximity to centers of power and commerce; the presence of large numbers; highly networked and well-resourced populations; heightened visibility and robust communications networks; and thickened connections to the outside world. In contrast to rural rebellions, which take advantage of distance and the rough terrain of the countryside to hide from state repression, and in contrast to urban armed revolts, which treat the cityscape as if it were rough terrain (providing protection from government attack), urban civic revolutions attempt to take advantage of the spaces between buildings[69]—the empty space of the public square and the boulevard—to mobilize large numbers as a strategy for disrupting political, commercial, and everyday life. They do not hide from government repression; indeed, they occur in full view of the nation and the world (and of the police), in centrally located public spaces in close proximity to centers of power. Visibility is one of the key features of the urban environment that such revolts seek to exploit as a tool for increasing pressure on regimes and staying the hand of regime repression. By making repression visible, urban civic revolutionaries seek to exploit the power of moral shocks to mobilize large numbers and induce defections from a regime.[70]

As those involved in rural counterinsurgency efforts have come to learn, for revolts that break out in sparsely populated areas "the key terrain . . . is not a

---

69. The term belongs to Gehl (2011).

70. As Jasper (1999, 76) notes, cities, with their dense populations and communications networks, are conducive environments for large-scale mobilization through moral shocks.

physical space, but the political loyalty of the people who inhabit that space"[71]—what has sometimes been referred to as control over "hearts and minds." For revolts that break out in cities, by contrast, it is not control over hearts and minds that determines outcomes, but control over public space—particularly, public space in close proximity to nerve centers of government. Urban civic revolutionary oppositions seek to reappropriate public space and use it as a site for mobilization and disruption. As we will see, the closer they come to the nerve centers of political power, the more likely they are to leverage success. Regimes attempt to contain these threats and to gain advantage over oppositions by regulating and controlling who can and cannot utilize public space, and for what purposes. They are particularly concerned to ensure that opposition actions remain distant from regime nerve centers. Urban design and spatial control have always been important tools in regime efforts to counter urban revolutionary challenges. Ironically, the very measures that regimes took to mitigate the risks of urban armed revolt (such as removing densely settled districts with narrow, winding alleys and creating broad boulevards and open public spaces in city centers) increased their vulnerability to urban civic revolutionary tactics based on the power of numbers[72]—particularly in monumental spaces in close proximity to governmental centers of power.

To maximize numbers in a concentrated period of time, urban civic revolutions typically forge a broad negative coalition in a makeshift manner, pulling in all who favor the removal of the incumbent regime, irrespective of purpose. They rely on hastily assembled coalitional leaderships (and sometimes, no leadership), an inclusive civic nationalism, and broadly "civic" minimalist demands for the reclaiming of state power from corrupt and abusive regimes—a least common denominator that can attract as many participants as possible. In the 2011 Egyptian Revolution, for instance, the opposition "cleverly" chose demands "from the bubbling stew of modern Egyptian grievances, settling on a short list of core issues that would resonate widely across society."[73] In the Tunisian Revolution, "activists were willing to absorb any issue, from the plight of unemployed miners to internet freedom, that challenged the dominance of the Ben Ali regime."[74] Since the goal is to deploy numbers rapidly, there is neither the desire nor the ability in urban civic revolutions to filter or socialize participants, as usually happens in the more prolonged and hierarchically organized contention typical of rural revolutions. But the consequences

71. Nagl 2006, ix.
72. See Hobsbawm 2005, 4.
73. Khalil 2011, 135.
74. Chomiak 2014, 37.

of this approach often return to haunt these revolutions after they come to power. While revolutions have increased in frequency, and the odds in favor of attaining power have grown, successful urban civic revolutions have found it difficult to bring about lasting substantive change in their wake. As we will see, this has much to do with the urban civic repertoire, the ways in which these revolts are organized, and the politics that this sets in motion.

The Revolutionary Episode as Unit of Analysis

In this study, I take the revolutionary episode as my main unit of analysis. Charles Tilly introduced the important distinction between "revolutionary situations" and "successful revolutions." To paraphrase Tilly, revolutionary situations are instances in which demands for regime displacement become the basis for a mass siege of government, while successful revolutions (in a minimalist sense) are revolutionary situations in which the opposition is able to gain power.[75] What I call a "revolutionary episode" is roughly analogous to Tilly's revolutionary situation.

In placing the revolutionary episode at the center of my analysis, I draw on McAdam, Tarrow, and Tilly's concept of contentious episodes, which they define as "continuous streams of contention including collective claims making that bears on other parties' interests." They called on researchers to treat streams of contentious actions as an episode and "to think through the similarities and differences with conflict streams that have occurred elsewhere or in the same system in different historical moments."[76] I define an episode as a stream of related events, with a roughly identifiable beginning and end, that is itself part of a broader series of analogous and related streams. In drama and literature, an episode is a story embedded within a larger story—an integral but extractable part of a broader narrative whole.[77] I understand the revolutionary episode similarly, as a narrative (i.e., an account of a connected stream of events) associated with an attempt to bring about revolution that is embedded within the larger story of revolutionary phenomena more generally.

Revolutionary episodes are examples of what philosophers refer to as "occurrences"—things that happen, as distinct from objects that occupy space across time.[78] As Sewell noted, occurrences have a fractal character—that is, they are themselves composed of occurrences, which in turn can be broken

---

75. Tilly 1978.
76. McAdam, Tarrow, and Tilly 2001, 29, 34.
77. Similar use of the notion of episode as an analytical unit can be found in psychology, medicine, and ecology.
78. Davidson 1980, 176.

down further into sub-occurrences.[79] I understand revolutionary episodes as composed of numerous actions and reactions that impart a particular character to each episode and move it toward its specific outcome. Revolutionary episodes are eventful narratives; they consist of connected streams of events (and the actions and reactions associated with them) that tell the story of revolutionary challenge and are part of a broader series of analogous and related streams around the world.

Revolutionary episodes are obviously connected with what precedes and follows them, and they are rooted in the deeper structural and conjunctural conditions that help to provoke them into being. Some degree of ambiguity is unavoidable in establishing their beginnings and ends, since they are flows of action, not clearly bounded things. But I roughly identify their beginnings by a multiplication of open challenges leading to a mass siege of power aimed at regime-change, and their endings by either a transfer of power or the end of significant challenge.[80] They begin as a thickening series of challenges leading to a mass siege of power demanding regime-change. They end when challenges grow marginalized (because they are repressed, suffer military defeat, or exhaust themselves); when the opposition gains control over the state (through resignation or flight of the incumbent government, or direct seizure of power); when a third force such as the military or a foreign state seizes control of the state; or when compromises are reached that demobilize the opposition (which may or may not lead to regime-change).

Defined in this way, revolutionary episodes are relatively rare occurrences—certainly much rarer than other forms of collective action. But the frequency of revolutionary episodes is not much different from that of other modes of regime-change such as attempted military coups, foreign-imposed regime-change, or electoral turnovers in mixed authoritarian regimes. Powell and Thyne have identified 454 military coup attempts from 1950 to 2008, 50 percent of which (225) were successful in gaining power.[81] For this same period, Downes and Monten identified only twenty-six cases of successful foreign-imposed regime-change, though the number of failed attempts is difficult to assess.[82] Electoral turnovers in competitive authoritarian regimes are also

---

79. Sewell 1996, 878.

80. Amann (1962, 39) used similar criteria, arguing that a revolution begins "when the state's monopoly of power is effectively challenged and persists until a monopoly of power is re-established."

81. Powell and Thyne 2011.

82. Downes and Monten 2013. Owen (2010, 19–21) identifies thirty-four instances of what he calls "forcible regime-change" from 1950 to 2003. To give some idea of the frequency of attempts by foreign governments to impose regime-change, data gathered by Pearson and

quite rare; according to Geddes, Wright, and Frantz, only twenty-nine such incidents occurred from 1950 to 2008.[83] By contrast, for the 1950–2008 period covered in these other data sources, I have identified 189 revolutionary episodes involving mobilizations of at least a thousand civilian participants, with the opposition successfully gaining power in eighty (42 percent) of these cases. Thus, historically, successful military coups have been approximately three times more frequent than successful revolutions,[84] while successful revolutions have been approximately three times more frequent than foreign-imposed regime-change or electoral turnovers in mixed authoritarian regimes. However, this situation is rapidly changing. As we will see, revolutionary episodes have been gradually increasing in frequency, while the frequency of military coups has dramatically declined, so that revolution has gained greater importance over time within the broader politics of regime-change.

This book brings to bear a number of novel sources and approaches to the study of revolution. For one thing, it utilizes a new dataset of 345 revolutionary episodes from 1900 to 2014 to examine how and why the character of revolution has changed over time.[85] The study of revolution has been dominated by case comparisons. Yet, there have been sufficient attempts at revolution by the definition used in this book to render large-n strategies not only feasible but also insightful. As British statistician George Box famously observed, all statistical models are limited and are at best approximations.[86] Large-n data omit critical aspects of reality in order to highlight others; but they can provide important evidence in relation to questions whose answers can only be guessed at in the absence of such information. Without systematic data we could not possibly know with any confidence whether revolutions have been growing more or less frequent over time, how their success rate has changed, or whether revolution has been becoming more or less violent. I use large-n

---

Bauman (1993) and Kisangani and Pickering (2008) include ninety-six episodes over the 1950–2005 period in which foreign states intervened militarily to oppose a government or to support rebels or the opposition. These figures are calculated from the merged datasets of these two studies and count an intervention only once if it involved multiple states.

83. Geddes, Wright, and Franz 2014.

84. Svolik (2012) similarly finds that authoritarian leaders were six times more likely to be forced out of office by a military coup than by a popular uprising.

85. Two episodes—the Dervish Rebellion in British-controlled Somalia and the Philippine–American War in the American-occupied Philippines—began in 1899 and continued into the twentieth century. They were included in analyses of ongoing episodes since 1900 but excluded from the analysis of episodes that began since 1900.

86. Box and Draper 1987, 74, 424.

cross-national comparisons to identify systematic trends, relationships, and structural patterns that otherwise would remain concealed to the observer.

There are numerous cross-national datasets on civil wars. When I began this study, there were no datasets on revolutions as a mode of regime-change. The data had to be created from scratch, with the help of a team of assistants. After scouring hundreds of sources to identify episodes that might qualify as revolutionary by my definition, and sorting out those that did, information about each episode was gathered and coded from secondary sources. I collected and recorded information on a wide variety of topics for each episode. Details about the data and how they were constructed are provided in Appendix 1. Further information about these regimes and societies was added from other data sources to form the data files used for the book's statistical analyses.[87]

Throughout the book, I refer to revolutionary episodes by their location, tactics, substantive goals, and outcomes. Appendix 2 provides classifications for each episode along these four dimensions. Any classification scheme involves acts of interpretation. I fully expect some readers to disagree with the ways in which I have coded specific cases. That is inherent to an enterprise like this (though as historians well know, stark differences in interpretation would be inevitable even in a book that dealt with a single revolution). The important thing is transparency: readers should know how I classified episodes and why I classified them in the way that I did. These justifications are included in my full dataset, available online. I also used a classification scheme that was flexible enough to allow cases to fit into multiple categories and to assume mixed forms when appropriate, thereby remaining attentive to the complexities of the historical record.

A summary of the distribution of episodes across categories is displayed in Figures 1.3a–d. The heart of my argument is that location matters: whether a revolutionary opposition is primarily concentrated in the countryside or in the city profoundly alters the nature of the revolution "game." The qualification "primarily" means that I do not exclude the possibility that rural rebels have urban supporters, or that urban revolutions find reflections in the countryside. Castro's guerrilla engagements against the Batista regime from his bases in the Sierra Maestra mountains, for instance, found middle-class allies in the Havana underground,[88] while the 2011 Egyptian Revolution, though

---

87. Sources for these other data can be found in Appendix 3. All statistical analyses were carried out using Stata (version 14.2). All Stata data files used in the statistical analyses (as well as the Stata do-files used to produce the output, the output files, and robustness test files) are available from the author.

88. Sweig 2002.

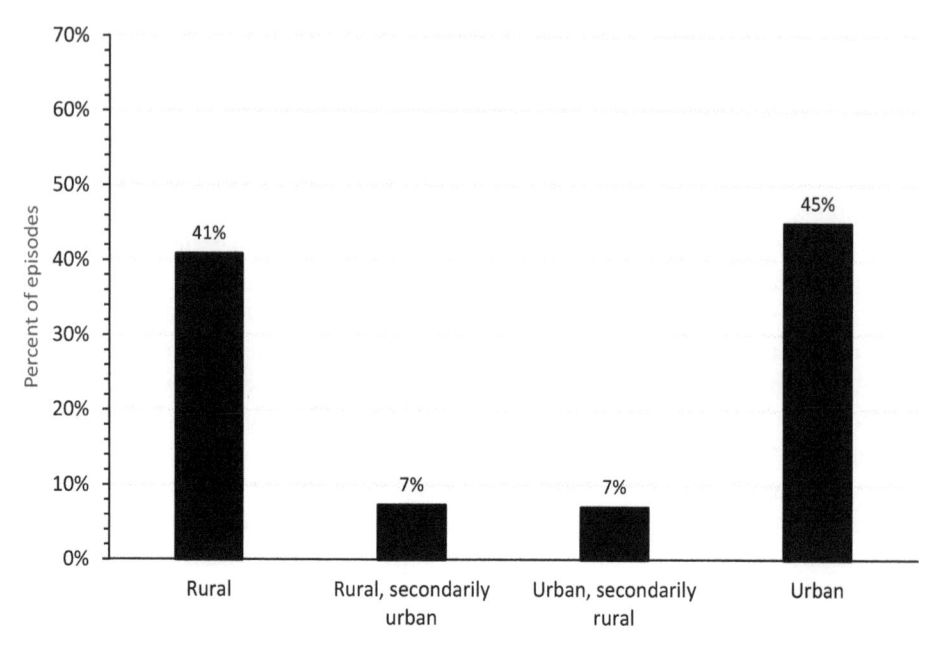

FIGURE 1.3A. Revolutionary episodes, 1900–2014: locations.

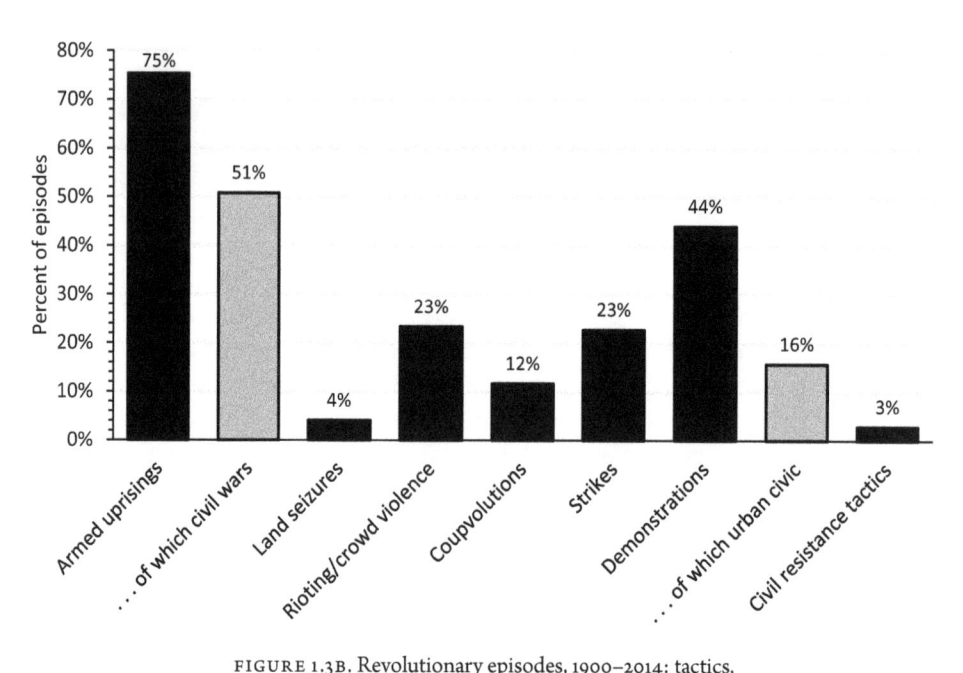

FIGURE 1.3B. Revolutionary episodes, 1900–2014: tactics.

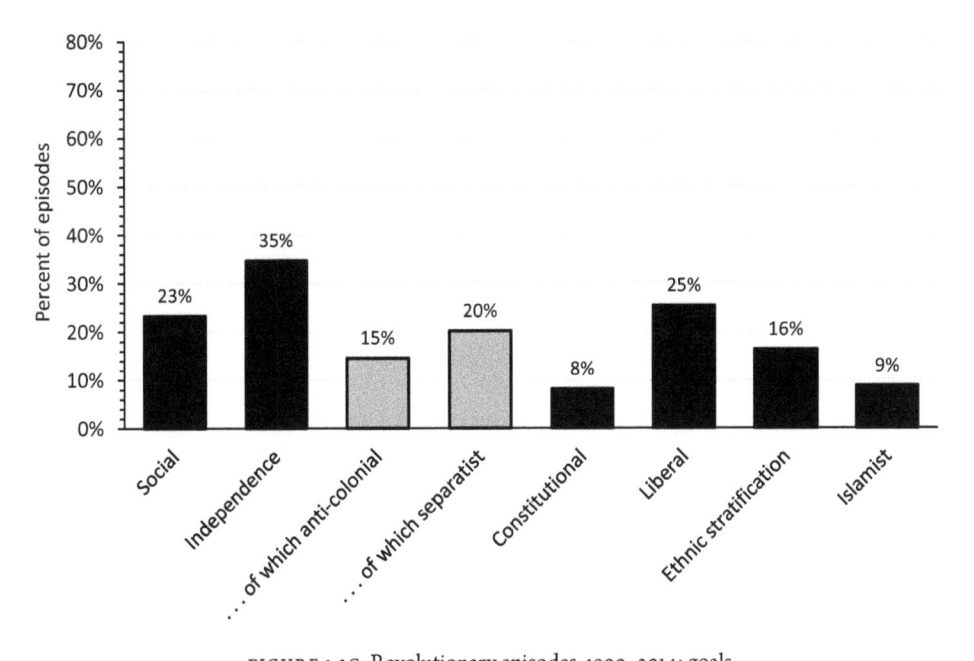

FIGURE 1.3C. Revolutionary episodes, 1900–2014: goals.

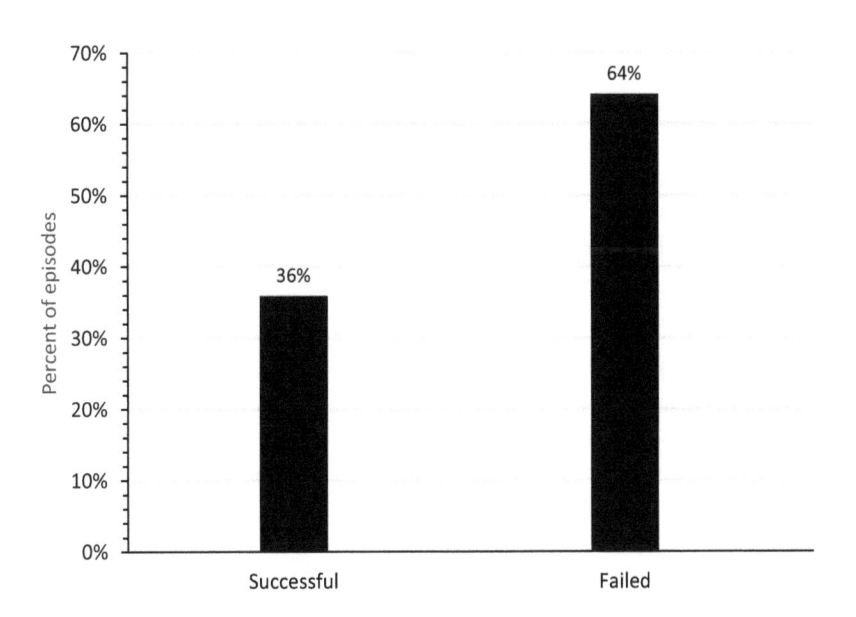

FIGURE 1.3D. Revolutionary episodes, 1900–2014: outcomes.

overwhelmingly urban, had some supporters in the Egyptian countryside.[89] But my concern with location revolves around the *main* locus of revolutionary contention, which, I argue, shapes the nature of the revolutionary process. In the vast majority of episodes (86 percent), revolutionaries choose to concentrate their challenge in *either* the city *or* the countryside. My classification scheme allowed for the possibility that a revolution was primarily urban with a secondary rural component (for example, the Bolshevik Revolution), or primarily rural with a secondary urban component (for example, the Cuban Revolution). In statistical analyses I treated these mixed forms according to their primary locations, reserving analysis of their mixed dimension for robustness checks.

Within these locations, revolutionary oppositions can select from a variety of tactics. From descriptions in secondary sources, I identified whether revolutionary contention involved an armed uprising (and if so, whether it involved civil war), land seizures, rioting or other forms of crowd violence,[90] strikes, civil resistance tactics (such as boycotts), or demonstrations (and whether demonstrations followed an urban civic pattern of concentrating large numbers in central urban spaces).[91] These categorizations were not exclusive. Half of all revolutionary episodes involved the use of multiple tactics. This was far more common in urban revolutions (76 percent) than in rural revolutions (20 percent). Indeed, practically all rural revolutionary episodes in the sample (99 percent) were armed uprisings, as oppositions in rural environments possess few unarmed means for exerting leverage over government, given population densities and distance from centers of power.[92] Moreover, 88 percent of rural episodes involved civil war, which I define as sustained armed combat between a revolutionary opposition and an incumbent regime.[93] By contrast, half of all urban revolutionary episodes since 1900 involved armed uprisings, with only 17 percent involving civil wars. Thus, as revolutionary contention has urbanized, it has also grown less likely to be armed and to involve prolonged armed combat—with profound

---

89. Abu-Lughod 2012.

90. Riots usually were lightly armed with stones, sticks, shields, or Molotov cocktails. See Kadivar and Ketchley 2018.

91. I did not classify cases according to whether they were "violent" or "nonviolent," as some studies do, preferring instead to classify them by whether tactics were armed or unarmed and to measure the actual number of deaths involved.

92. Oppositions in rurally based revolutions still face tactical choices over what type of armed rebellion to pursue: whether to embark upon civil war, fight through guerrilla tactics, organize conventional armies, etc.

93. For more on this definition, see chapter 8.

implications for the number of people dying in revolutions. In all, 16 percent of episodes since 1900 employed urban civic tactics, though urban civic tactics have been utilized in 38 percent of episodes since 1985.

In classifying revolutionary episodes by their substantive aims or goals (social, liberal, state independence, constitutional/anti-monarchical, Islamist, inversion of an ethnic order, or other), I again allowed episodes to be classified into multiple categories, as aims often overlap in revolutions. In all, 37 percent of episodes were classified in more than one category. There tends to be an elective affinity between locations and tactics on the one hand, and substantive goals and social forces on the other. Certain substantive goals are highly divisive and ambitious and are more likely to elicit violent opposition (for instance, transformation of the class structure of society), while other goals are minimalist and more likely to unite rather than divide (for instance, transforming a monarchy into a republic). Substantive goals also appeal to different social groups located within particular spatial settings. Over time, goals of state independence and class transformation have declined dramatically, dropping from 42 percent and 34 percent of new revolutionary episodes respectively during the 1900–1984 period to 22 percent and 1 percent of new episodes from 1985 to 2014. At the same time, episodes espousing liberal goals of attaining civil liberties, establishing a democracy, or containing the abuses of a despotic regime rose from 15 percent of new episodes from 1900 to 1984 to 44 percent of new episodes from 1985 to 2014. Whereas 72 percent of episodes for state independence and 56 percent of episodes for class transformation were largely centered in the countryside, 95 percent of revolutions espousing liberal goals occurred primarily in cities. Thus, the urbanization of revolution was associated with a marked shift in the substantive goals of revolution.

Finally, I classified revolutionary episodes by their outcomes. As noted earlier, revolutionary episodes can end in a variety of ways. Rebellion can be repressed or defeated in civil war, incumbent leaders can be forced to resign or flee, revolution can be cut short by foreign invasion, or compromise agreements can be reached. Sometimes the military seizes power in a coupvolution—either keeping it for themselves or turning it over to the opposition. I kept track of these outcomes, but also kept track of whether or not the opposition was brought to power at the end of revolutionary contention. I labeled episodes in which the opposition gained power at the end of revolutionary contention as "successful" (again, in a minimalist sense), and those in which it did not as "failed."

Skocpol argued that a truly generalizable theory of the causes and consequences of revolution is impossible, due to the diversity of purposes and social forces involved in revolutions and the evolving character of revolutionary contention across historical time. I agree with this, and will show it in fact to be true. But while a unified theory of the causes of revolutions may be unattainable, theories explaining the causes of different types of revolutions, how and why the character of revolution has changed over time, and how spatial context shapes revolutionary contention are certainly feasible. This is what I seek to establish. To do so, I compare the incidence and outcomes of different types of revolutionary episodes and their general effects. I also compare societies that experienced revolt with those that did not in an attempt to understand the distinctive dynamics involved.

Many of these comparisons naturally take place at the level of the episode. But my analysis also drills down to the events and interactions within episodes, the spaces in which episodes unfold, and the individuals who participate in order to understand what transpires within revolutionary episodes that imbues them with particular qualities or outcomes. For each episode in the dataset, I composed a short narrative based on secondary sources that described the major events of the episode, how it unfolded, and how it ended.[94] These narratives and the sources on which they were based are used throughout the book to illustrate patterns and trends and to analyze the choices, events, and interactions within revolutionary episodes. Thus, a qualitative strategy was consciously embedded within a quantitative strategy and forms the basis for a deepened analysis of what takes place within revolutionary contention.

This study also utilizes a series of highly unusual nationally representative public opinion surveys probing individual-level participation in four revolutions: the Orange Revolution, the Tunisian Revolution, the Egyptian Revolution, and the Euromaidan Revolution. These revolutions represent examples of the urban civic repertoire that has come to be more commonly deployed in recent decades. It is rare to have a detailed, systematic record of the attitudes, behaviors, and backgrounds of those participating in a revolution. It is even rarer to be able to analyze them across multiple revolutions—and still rarer to be able to compare participants with other members of society who aided or supported revolution but did not participate themselves, opposed revolution, or mobilized against it. Yet this is what these surveys allow us to do, making them unique records in the study of revolution. I use them to understand the social cleavages that fed into mobilization, individual preferences and behaviors, the character of social ties, and the nature of coalitions within these revolutions.

---

94. Many of these sources are not listed in the References section of the book, but all sources used to compose the data are referenced in the full dataset available from the author.

Thus, this study unfolds at multiple levels of analysis: the global and cross-national; the narrative and episodic; the chronological and eventful; and the granular and the individual. Throughout, I pay particular attention to the spatial dimension of revolutionary politics—especially to the ways in which urban location shapes revolutionary processes and how the struggle for control over space lies at the center of urban revolutionary contention. By unpacking revolutions at different levels and in different registers, I seek to gain a multifaceted understanding of the dynamics of revolution as a mode of regime-change, the forces that have shaped its evolution over time, and the consequences of those changes for the societies that experienced them.

2

The Growth and Urbanization of Revolution

> Man's course begins in a garden, but it ends in a city.
> ALEXANDER MACLAREN, *THE SECRET OF POWER AND OTHER SERMONS* (1902)[1]

ATTEMPTS AT revolutionary regime-change have always been rare. But in the late twentieth century, a profound change occurred in the incidence and character of political revolutions. The frequency of revolutionary episodes increased, and their form, location, and content changed. The social revolutions that had dominated most theorizing about revolution became marginalized. At the same time, rural revolutions declined in number, and urban revolutions proliferated. This growth in urban revolutions was driven almost entirely by a rising incidence in urban civic revolutionary contention—revolutions that aimed to mobilize as many people as possible in central urban spaces, seeking to overturn repressive governments through the power of numbers rather than through armed rebellion, urban rioting, or other means.

In this chapter, I establish these global patterns and identify some of the broader causes underlying them. I develop a structural explanation for the decline of social revolutions and the proliferation of urban civic revolutions in the late twentieth and early twenty-first centuries. That explanation unfolds on three levels: society, state, and the international system.

At the societal level, I show that the global decrease in social revolutions and the rise in urban civic revolutions were related phenomena. Both were rooted in the massive shift of people, power, and wealth to cities that

---

1. Maclaren 1902, 327.

accelerated during the latter part of the twentieth century. This transformation concentrated more than half of the world's population in cities and fueled the decline of what Skocpol called "agrarian-bureaucratic society." The revolutionary potential of peasants eroded in the late twentieth century under the impact of urbanization, development, and reform. But the decline of agrarian-bureaucratic society and the ensuing concentration of people, power, and wealth in cities also gave rise to new urban social forces, spaces, networks, and connections that were central to the proliferation of urban civic revolutionary forms.

At the state level, I show that the proliferation of urban revolution after the Cold War was associated with the multiplication and consolidation of states. Whereas rural revolts and peasant revolutions were closely linked with struggles for state independence, urban and urban civic revolutions have instead occurred in established states. Rural revolutions rely on an infrastructurally weak state that is incapable of penetrating and enforcing policies throughout its territory.[2] Urban revolutions, by contrast, occur precisely where state power is most acutely felt—in cities. As states proliferated and consolidated and populations concentrated in proximity to centers of state power, the infrastructural power of the state came to matter less for revolutionary processes, while the state's despotic and predatory powers came to matter more.

Finally, I show that the decline of social revolution and the growth of urban and urban civic revolution were facilitated by international and transnational factors—in particular, the decline of inter-state warfare, the collapse of the Soviet Union, the emergence of unilateral American power, globalization, and the rise of the neoliberal economic order. In this respect, the international and transnational have been deeply implicated in the changing fabric of revolutionary practice.[3]

The Growth and Shifting Character of Revolution after the Cold War

Figure 2.1 presents data on the onset of 343 revolutionary episodes involving mobilizations of at least a thousand civilian participants that began during the years 1900–2014. Unsurprisingly, revolutionary episodes over this period clustered in familiar waves: the republican and communist revolutions after World War I; the anti-colonial and communist revolutions that followed World War II;

2. Mann 1986.
3. Lawson 2016.

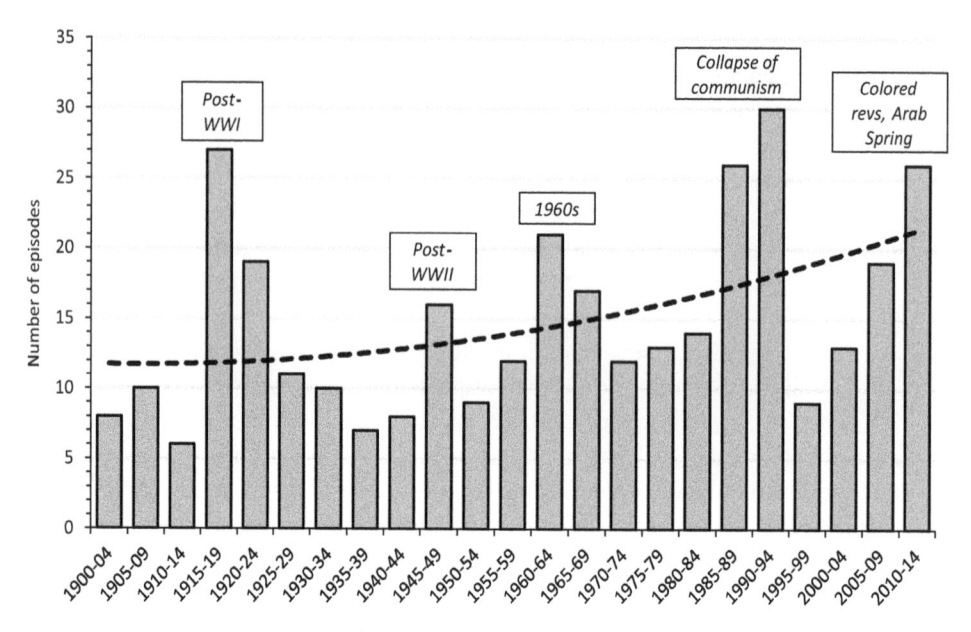

FIGURE 2.1. The yearly onset of new revolutionary episodes, 1900–2014.

the revolutionary upsurge of the 1960s; the revolutions associated with the collapse of communism; the color revolutions of the mid-2000s; and the Arab Spring upheavals of the early 2010s. Overall, there were significantly more new revolutionary episodes per year in the late twentieth and early twenty-first centuries than in either the first half of the twentieth century or the Cold War, and the trend over time has generally sloped upward. If new revolutionary episodes appeared at a pace of 2.44 per year during the first half of the twentieth century (1900–49) and at a pace of 2.80 per year during the Cold War (1950–84), during the post–Cold War period (1985–2014) they transpired at a rate of 4.10 per year—that is, between one and two additional outbreaks of revolutionary contention per year than had previously occurred. Averaged over five-year periods, six more revolutionary episodes occurred in a five-year span during the post–Cold War period than during the Cold War, and eight more than during the first half of the twentieth century.[4]

4. Using an autoregressive (AR2) time series count model, the incidence rate of revolutionary episodes per year was 60 percent greater in the post–Cold War era than during the 1900–84 period (statistically significant at the .001 level). Even if one excludes the unusual burst of revolutionary activity associated with the collapse of communism, the post–Cold War period still registered a significantly greater number of revolutionary episodes (3.5 per year) compared to

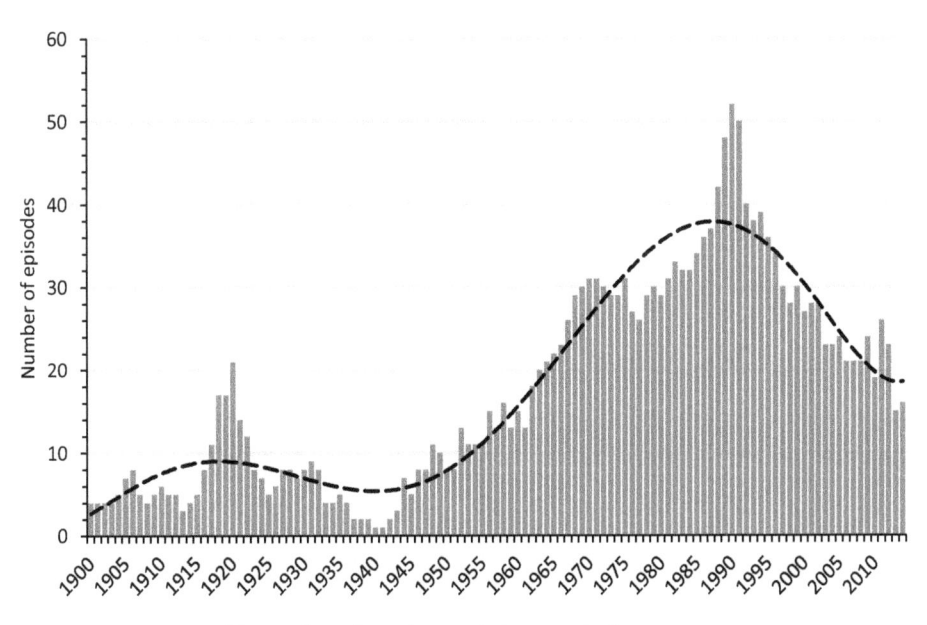

FIGURE 2.2. The number of ongoing revolutionary episodes per year, 1900–2014.

Another way of looking at the same information is to examine how many revolutionary episodes were ongoing anywhere in the world in a particular year—depicted in Figure 2.2. Again, by this criterion the late twentieth and early twenty-first centuries exhibited a higher incidence of revolutionary contention than the first half of the twentieth century or the Cold War period. On average, from 1900 to 1949 there were 6.6 ongoing revolutionary episodes per year throughout the world (with a maximum of twenty-one and a minimum of one), while the 1950 to 1984 period averaged 22.5 ongoing revolutionary episodes per year (with a maximum of thirty-three and a minimum of eight). From 1985 to 2014, by contrast, there was an average of 30.4 ongoing revolutionary episodes per year (with a maximum of fifty-two and minimum of fifteen). The number of ongoing revolutionary episodes per year began to climb during the Cold War, flattening out in the 1970s at a rate considerably higher than the highest peak during the first half of the twentieth century (i.e., 1917–22). It then exploded in the late 1980s and early 1990s, reaching its peak in 1990 at fifty-two, declining in the late 1990s and 2000s. It eventually leveled off,

---

the first half of the twentieth century or the Cold War, with an incidence rate per year that was 38 percent higher than the 1900–84 period (statistically significant at the .01 level). See Appendix 4A on the statistical model.

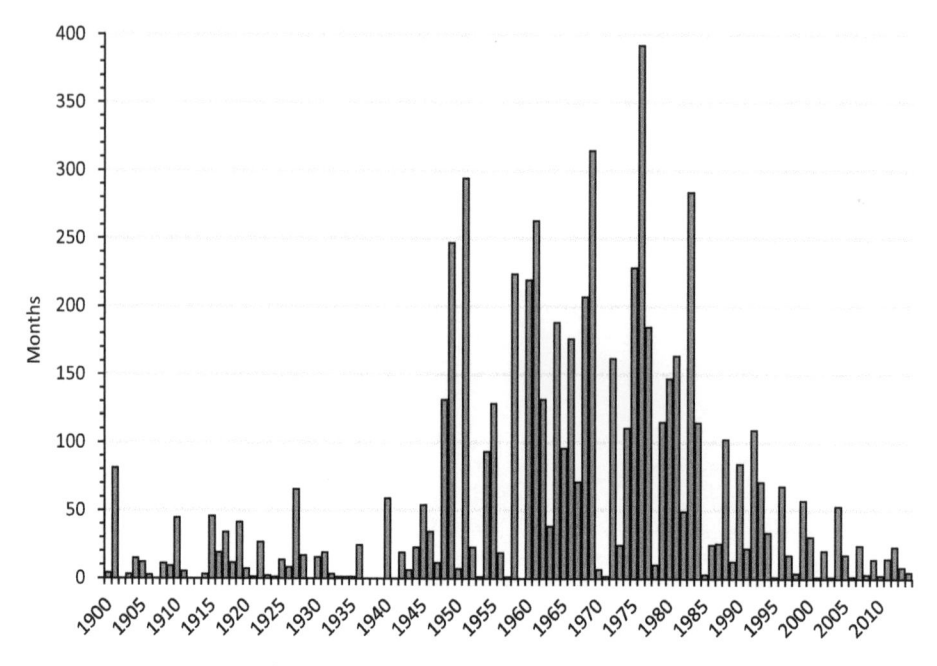

FIGURE 2.3. The average duration of revolutionary episodes, by onset year.

remaining significantly higher than for the first half of the twentieth century (and roughly akin to patterns in the late 1960s and early 1970s—the highest years of the Cold War).[5]

The number of ongoing revolutionary episodes per year is partially a function of their duration: when episodes last longer, this boosts the number ongoing in any particular year. When one takes this into account, the growth of revolutionary activity in the post–Cold War period is all the more impressive. As Figure 2.3 shows, revolutionary episodes that began during the Cold War lasted much longer than those that began during the first half of the twentieth century or the post–Cold War period. The median revolutionary episode that began during the Cold War lasted fifty-one months; the median revolutionary episode during the first half of the twentieth century and the post–Cold War period lasted only six months. As we will see, this was primarily driven by the

---

5. Again, even if one excludes cases connected with the collapse of communism, the average number of ongoing episodes per year during the post–Cold War era (28.5) was still significantly greater than the average number of ongoing episodes per year during the Cold War (22.5), with an incidence rate per year that was 316 percent greater than the first half of the twentieth century (statistically significant at the .001 level).

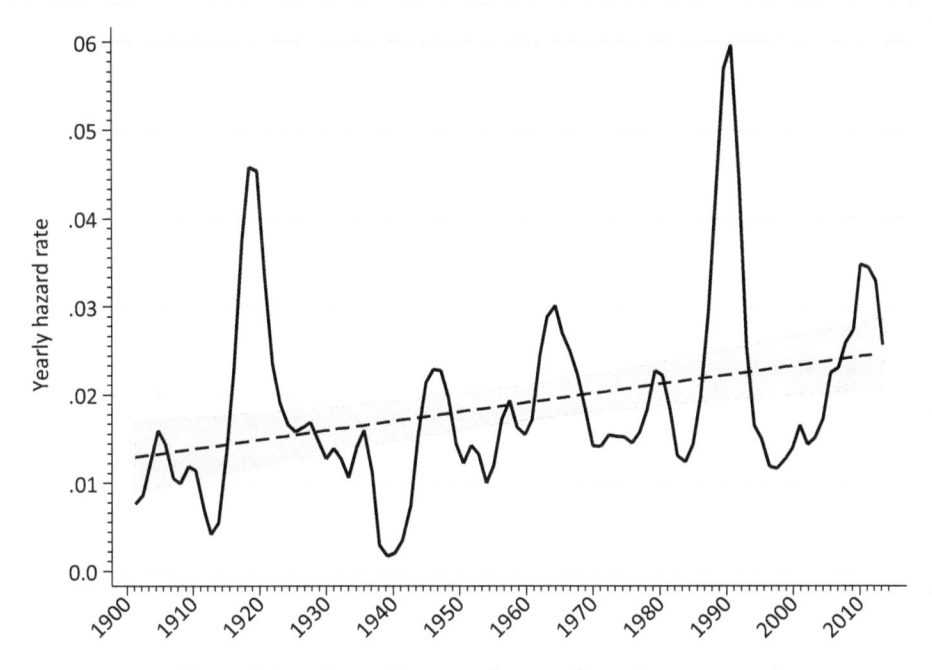

FIGURE 2.4. The yearly hazard rate of the materialization of a revolutionary episode across 158 fixed territorial units around the world (with 95 percent confidence intervals).

location of revolutions—the countryside or the city—as urban revolutions are much more temporally compact than rural revolutions. But geopolitical competition during the Cold War also fueled longer bouts of revolutionary contention, largely in the form of civil wars sustained through external aid from competing superpowers.

A third way of looking at the growth of revolutionary contention over the past century is to examine how the risk of experiencing revolutionary contention within a fixed territory has changed over time. That risk has always been quite low, but it has generally been increasing. Dividing the planet up into fixed territorial units that roughly correspond to the boundaries of the state system in 2001, the risk of a unit experiencing a revolutionary episode in any single year roughly doubled over the 1900–2014 period, from about .013 to approximately .025 (Figure 2.4).[6] In the early 1900s, one out of every seventy-seven

6. The data on revolutionary episodes include anti-colonial revolts aimed at state independence. The sampling frame for this analysis is an adaptation of the "From Empire to Nation-State" dataset created by Wimmer and Min 2006. I computed the monthly hazard rate of a revolutionary episode across 158 fixed territorial units from 1900 to 2014. The monthly hazard rate was then smoothed over a twelve-month period and transformed from a monthly rate to a yearly

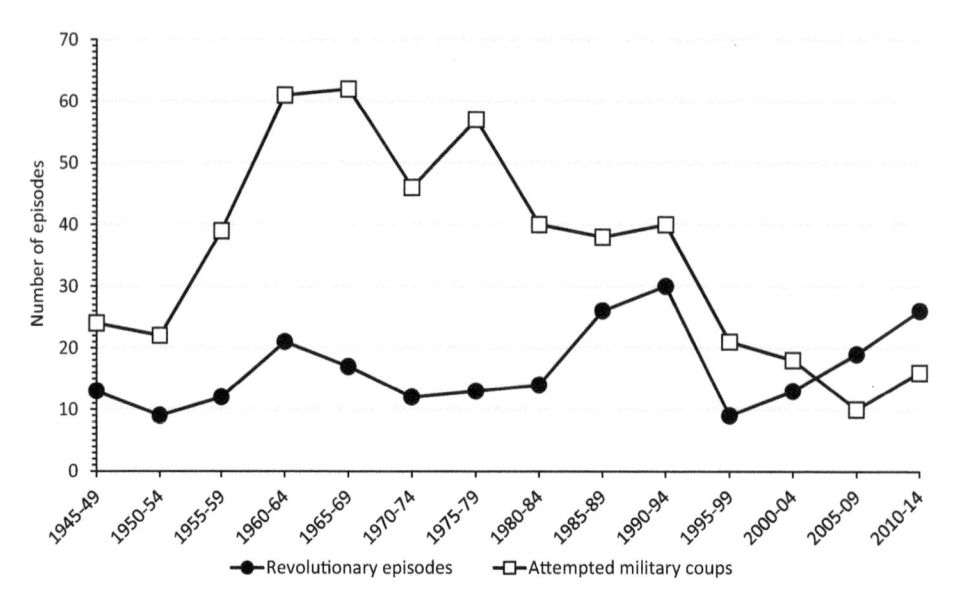

FIGURE 2.5. Revolutionary episodes and attempted military coups, 1945–2014.

territories experienced revolutionary contention in a given year. By the twenty-first century that rate had risen to one out of every forty.

Thus, looked at from multiple angles, the evidence for the global growth in the incidence of revolutionary contention over the past century is strong. In fact, as Figure 2.5 shows, by the early 2000s revolution had become the most common form of attempted extra-institutional regime-change in the world. The Cold War era was associated with a veritable explosion in the number of attempted military coups. American foreign policy prioritized the prevention of communist insurgency over the promotion of democracy during the Cold War and was tolerant of (and at times, actively promoted) military seizures of power as a way of containing popular unrest (the so-called "praetorian" model identified by Huntington and others).[7] A wave of military coups also swept across highly unstable, newly decolonized states—where colonialism left behind weak states, deep poverty, intense ethnic competition, and poorly professionalized militaries.[8] However, as the Cold War waned in the 1980s,

---

rate. Not only is the slope of the linear fit positive, but there is a statistically significant difference (at the .05 level) between the risk of revolution in the early twentieth and the risk in the early twenty-first century. The relationship remains significant even if one drops cases associated with the collapse of communism.

7. Huntington 1968; Nordlinger 1977; Perlmutter 1969; Thyne 2010.
8. Decalo 1976; Jackman et al. 1986; Collier and Hoeffler 2005.

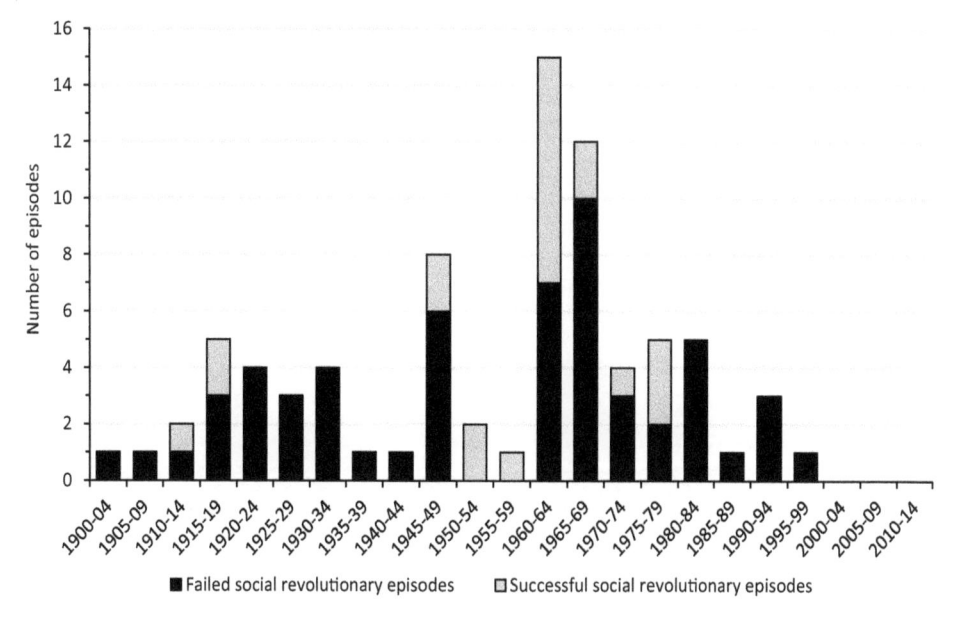

FIGURE 2.6. The onset of new social revolutionary episodes, 1900–2014.

attempted military coups declined sharply, even as the number of revolutionary episodes continued its long-term, gradual rise. By the early 2000s, revolutionary episodes were occurring at a faster pace than attempted military coups, though the number of successful revolutions and successful coups was approximately the same.[9]

The proliferation of revolutionary episodes in the late twentieth and early twenty-first centuries occurred at the very time that social revolutionary contention aimed at class transformation became marginalized on the historical stage. Figure 2.6 portrays the number of social revolutionary episodes (successful and failed) from 1900 to 2014. Most of these episodes were led by communist movements, but other cases (for example, the Mexican Revolution of 1910–19, the First APRA Rebellion in Peru in 1932, and the Iranian Revolution in 1979) also included significant elements seeking redistribution of property and wealth.[10]

9. Coups generally have a higher rate of success because the collective action problems involved are less acute and because the military already has at its disposal the force needed to evict a regime.

10. I classified the Iranian Revolution of 1978–79 as a social as well as an Islamist revolution. It contained a significant left-wing element that was subsequently sidelined, and the case is sometimes classified as a social revolution. Dropping the case does not affect any findings.

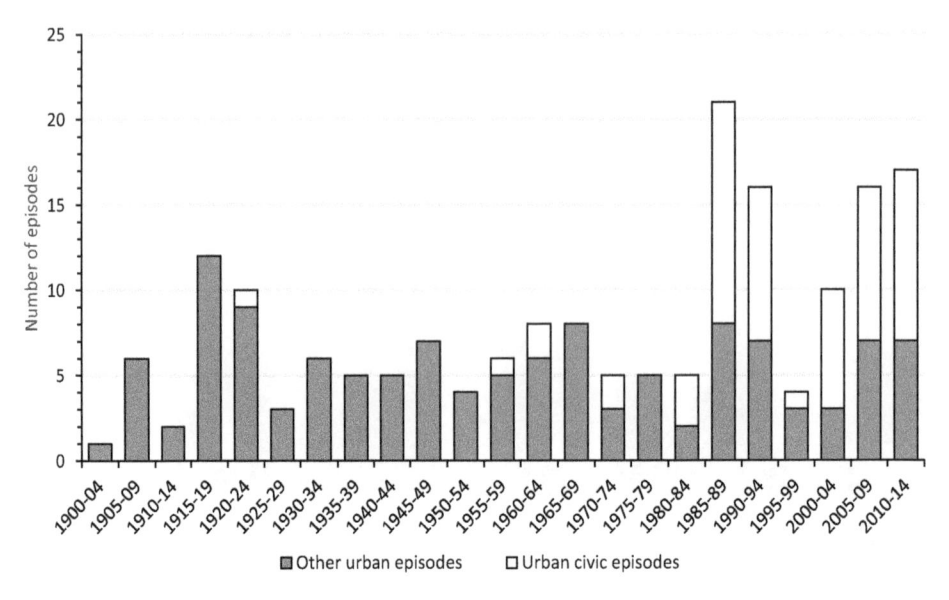

FIGURE 2.7. The onset of urban civic and other urban revolutionary episodes, 1900–2014.

As the Figure shows, the goal of class transformation was particularly conspicuous in revolutionary episodes in the mid-twentieth century. The Cold War period marked the height of success of social revolutionary challenges, but success rates dropped markedly from the 1980s onward, when the incidence of new social revolutionary episodes declined, disappearing by the 2000s.

Yet, as can be seen from Figure 2.7, at the very time when social revolutionary contention was declining, urban revolutions increased dramatically in number. This growth in urban revolutions was driven by a sharp increase in urban civic revolutionary contention. The spread of urban and urban civic revolutions in the late twentieth and early twenty-first centuries was largely responsible for the overall growth of revolutionary contention since 1900. Figure 2.8 reports the results of a simple statistical test to identify the effect of time (measured as the year in which a revolutionary episode began) on the yearly count of new revolutionary episodes. The effect is positive and statistically significant (at the .01 level) for all revolutionary episodes—a reflection of the general upward trend in new revolutionary episodes noted earlier. When social revolutionary episodes are excluded from sample, the result remains positive and statistically significant, as social revolutionary contention had a negative (though statistically insignificant) relationship with time (Figure 2.6 actually suggests an inverted-U relationship that peaked in the 1960s). Urban episodes, by contrast, are positively related with time, and the relationship of urban civic episodes with time is even stronger (both are statistically

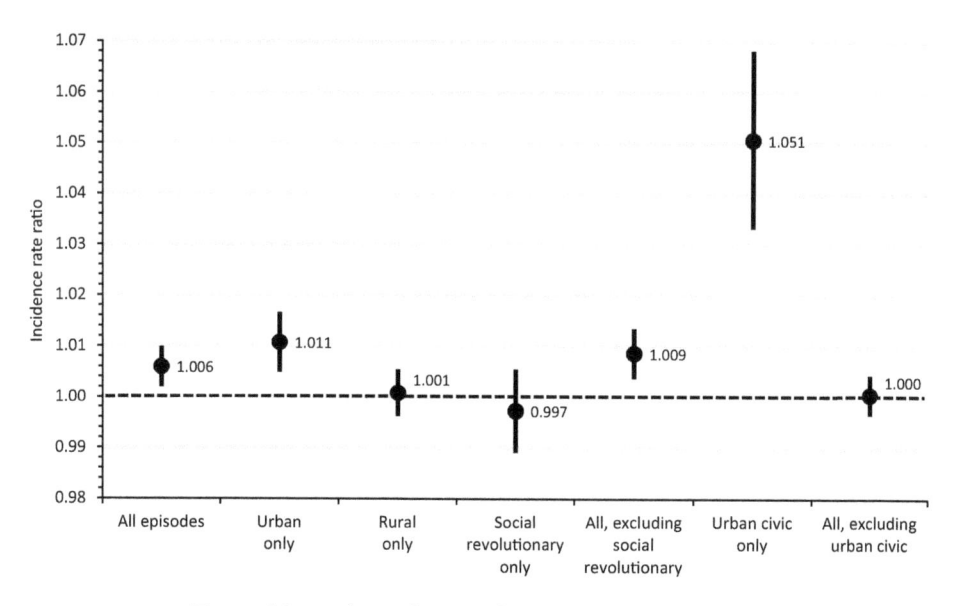

FIGURE 2.8. Time and the incidence of new revolutionary episodes. Poisson time-series count model (incidence rate ratios, with 95 percent confidence intervals).

significant at the .001 level). However, when urban or urban civic revolutionary episodes are excluded from the analysis, no relationship exists between revolutionary contention and time. Essentially, without the growth in urban and urban civic revolutionary contention, there would have been no worldwide increase in revolutionary contention over the last century.

On the surface, these trends could be interpreted as a challenge to "third-generation" theories of revolution (see chapter 1, "The City in the Study of Revolution"). Third-generation theories focused on explaining social revolutions, highlighting social relations in the countryside as a key cause and largely ignoring developments in cities. But as I will show, third-generation theorists were partially correct: the decline of social revolution in the post–Cold War period occurred in large part due to the weakening of many of the structural factors that they identified as fueling social revolutions in the first place. What third-generation scholars failed to anticipate, however, was that many of these same conditions, in their transcendence, might create conditions conducive to urban revolution.

The Decline of Agrarian-Bureaucratic Society and Revolution's Return to the City

The timing of the decline of social revolutions and the proliferation of urban civic revolutions suggests a linkage, and indeed, there are multiple ways in which the two trends were connected. Much of the attention of

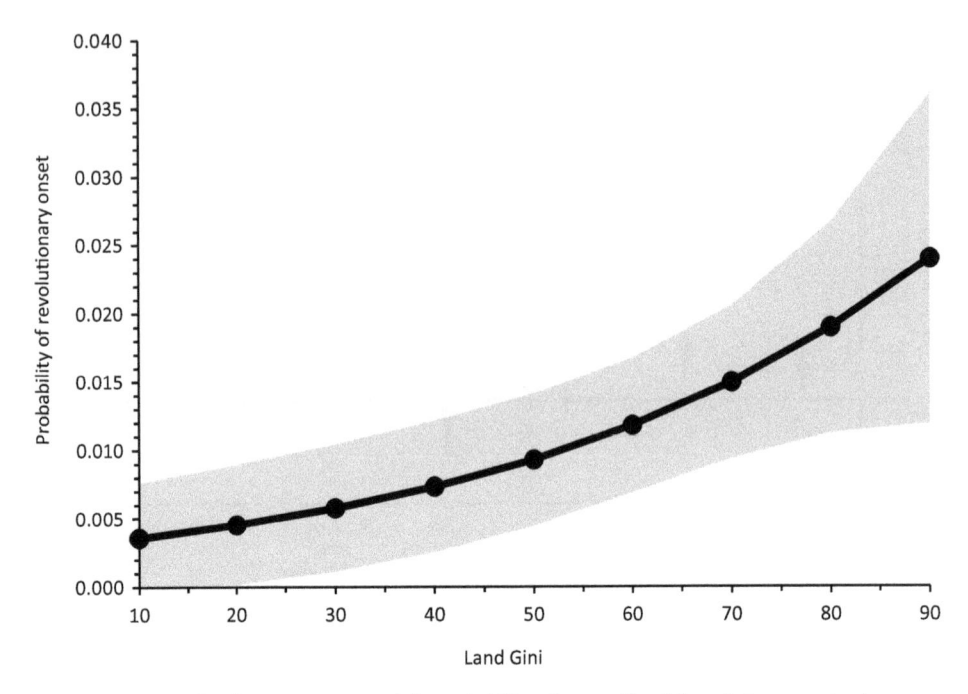

FIGURE 2.9. Land concentration and the probability of onset of social revolutionary episodes. Random effects complementary log-log panel regression with robust standard errors, controlling for the effects of time dependence (n = 6,634, with data on land Ginis available for 136 countries).

third-generation scholars was directed toward class relationships in the countryside, with forms of land tenure, the commercialization of agriculture, and the political power of landed aristocracies playing central roles in the outbreak and success of social revolutions.[11] Many second-generation theorists, too, pointed to land inequality (exacerbated by rapid rural population growth) as a cause of peasant revolution.[12] Indeed, inequality of land ownership was an important structural factor associated with social revolutions. As Figure 2.9 shows, there is a positive and statistically significant relationship between the degree to which land ownership was concentrated (as measured by land Gini scores) and the onset of social revolutionary contention over the 1900–2014 period.[13] Nearly all societies that experienced successful social

11. Paige 1975; Wolf 1969; Migdal 1974; Scott 1977; Moore 1966; Skocpol 1979.
12. Russett 1964; Huntington 1968; Midlarsky 1982.
13. Results statistically significant at the .01 level. By contrast, there is no statistically significant relationship between land inequality and the onset of either urban or rural revolutionary

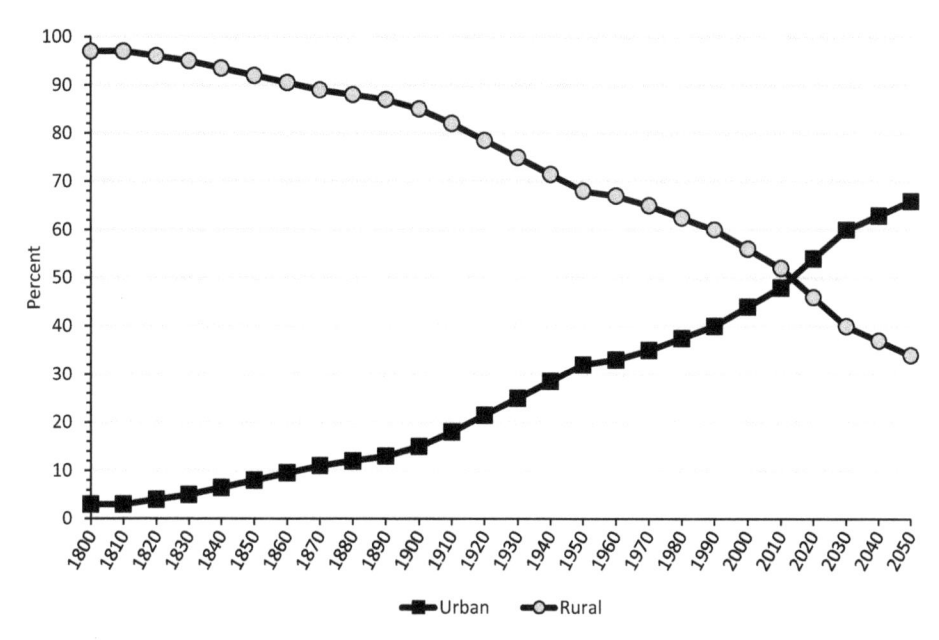

FIGURE 2.10. Percentage of global population that is urban/rural, 1800–2050. (Sources: United Nations Department of Economic and Social Affairs, Population Division 2014; Malpezzi 2006.)

revolutions—Russia, Mexico, Vietnam, Algeria, Cuba, Nicaragua, and others—had extremely unequal concentrations of land ownership.

Land inequality was a reflection of the political, social, and economic power of landed elites, who dominated peasants through control over land and patronage relationships. But over the course of the twentieth century the hold of the agrarian-bureaucratic world that Skocpol identified as the source of social revolution gradually dissipated under the impact of urbanization, development, and political change. In many places around the world, massive urbanization shifted the bulk of the population to urban settings (Figure 2.10). If only 3 percent of the world's population was urban in 1800, 13 percent by 1900, and 33 percent by 1960, by 2014, 54 percent of the world's population was urban, and by 2050 that proportion is expected to rise to 66 percent. Whereas the transition to a majority urban society occurred by the 1920s and 1930s in North America, western Europe, and portions of the southern cone of South

---

episodes in general, and a negative and statistically significant relationship between land inequality and the onset of urban civic revolutionary contention.

America, in the rest of Latin America and eastern Europe it occurred in the 1950s, 1960s, and 1970s. A majority urban society has not yet materialized in many low-income countries of Asia and Africa. Still, the largest cities in the world are located in less developed countries, and the total number of people living in cities in the less developed world is more than three times the number living in cities in the developed world.[14] The pace of urbanization in less developed countries is expected to accelerate in coming years, with the urban population of these countries anticipated to rocket from 2.9 billion in 2014 to 5.2 billion by 2050, while the rural population will decline marginally from 3.1 billion to 2.9 billion.[15] Whereas peasants and rural dwellers once represented the overwhelming majority of the earth's inhabitants, they have now become the minority.

Certainly, land inequality remains a cause of considerable conflict.[16] But the revolutionary potential of peasants has been eroding under the impact of migration, economic change, and reform. Urban migration is driven by rural poverty and the prospect of economic opportunity in cities. It has tended to drain the countryside of young male adults seeking to support their families, leaving behind a rural population consisting disproportionately of women, children, and older adults less capable of mounting revolt.[17] In many places, rural families are supported through remittances sent back by household members who have migrated to cities. Rural subsistence, which once depended entirely on peasant access to land, has come to rely increasingly on household access to urban jobs and the affordability of food in the context of the migration of family members to cities. Access to land no longer plays the exclusive role it once did within rural livelihoods, and rural populations have rather come to depend more on economic conditions within cities.

Goldstone argued that in largely agrarian states, population growth in excess of increases in land productivity played a significant role in precipitating revolts by creating pressure on resources, feeding inflation, and forcing states to expand taxation, thereby straining relationships between the state and key social groups.[18] Others have contended that youth bulges place heightened demands on the state and constitute a key condition for revolt, particularly

---

14. Malpezzi 2006, 61–62.

15. United Nations Department of Economic and Social Affairs, Population Division 2014.

16. Thomson 2016. See also Boone 2014; Albertus, Brambor, and Ceneviva 2018. Throughout the second half of the twentieth century, there remained a correlation between moderately high levels of land concentration and civil war.

17. United Nations Department of Economic and Social Affairs, Population Division 2006.

18. Goldstone 1991.

under conditions of low economic growth.[19] But with industrialization, the growth of trade and commerce, new technologies multiplying agricultural productivity, and the global decline in female fertility, population growth and youth bulges are no longer as significant in instigating revolutionary challenges as they once were. Statistical analysis shows that for the first half of the twentieth century and the Cold War period there was indeed a positive and statistically significant relationship (at the .001 level) between the share of youth within the adult population (measured as the proportion of population between the ages of fifteen and twenty-four) and the onset of a revolutionary episode—as youth bulge theories would predict. But for the post–Cold War period there is actually a *negative* and statistically significant relationship (at the .05 level) between youth bulges and the onset of revolutionary contention.[20] The location of revolutionary contention matters greatly in this regard. Thus, controlling for population size, the proportion of youth within the adult population is strongly associated with the onset of rural revolutions (statistically significant at the .001 level), but has no relationship to the onset of urban revolutionary contention.[21] In short, high birth rates, which continue to be concentrated in the countryside, no longer drive revolutionary processes in the ways they once did.

Land reform, often conducted under the threat of social revolution, has also played an important role in pre-empting social revolution in many parts of the world.[22] Roughly one-third of all countries have engaged in a major land redistribution program over the last century, and since the 1980s, a massive land titling effort has swept through the developing world. In Latin America, for example, 14 percent of all land in the region was redistributed through land reform between 1930 and 2008 (though Latin America still has very high levels of land inequality).[23] Michael Albertus's data on land reform around the world from 1900 to 2009 show that the height of land reform efforts globally occurred during the Cold War, when the threat of social revolution was at its greatest, and tapered off significantly in the 1990s, as the threat of social

---

19. Urdal 2006.

20. Based on a complementary log-log panel model with robust standard errors and controls for time dependence (n = 10,158 country-years across 160 countries). Results hold even when controlling for population size, level of economic development, and economic growth. Analogous (though statistically insignificant) results occur when measuring youth bulges by the proportion of population under the age of fifteen. On the choice of statistical models, see Appendix 4B.

21. Based on a complementary log-log panel model with robust standard errors and controls for time dependence and population size (n = 10,158 country-years across 160 countries).

22. Binswanger, Deininger, and Feder 1995.

23. Albertus 2015, 306.

revolution receded. Still, land redistribution muted tendencies toward social revolution, and in some cases transformed the character of the countryside. Vanhanen's data on the percent of family farms across societies show, for example, that among fifty-nine countries whose level of urbanization was below the global average in 1968, the percentage of family farms increased from 29 percent in 1968 to 50 percent by 1998—a major shift toward greater land equality.[24] Thus, social revolution played a role in its own demise: the threat of social revolution often led to the introduction of land reforms that undercut conditions for social revolution to occur.

As Barrington Moore observed, the power of landed elites once represented a major obstacle to capitalist economic development.[25] Democratization, communism, and state-led development, however, played critical roles in breaking the power of landed elites. In communist and post-communist societies (about a quarter of the world's population), landed elites were swept aside by force, with their lands either collectivized or redistributed into smallholdings. In other cases, colonialism reconfigured the power of local landholders and paved the way for eventual state-led development.[26] Historically, landed elites resisted democratization for fear that democratic government would come under strong pressures to redistribute, threatening their control over peasants and the wealth that flowed from this.[27] The introduction of the secret ballot also played an important role in undermining the control of landed elites over rural workers.[28] The mechanization of agriculture meanwhile reduced the need for labor in the countryside.[29] Altogether, with democratization, urbanization, development, and land reform, the center of gravity of political life, political power, and clientelist networks shifted markedly toward cities.[30]

Again, the extent and impact of these changes should not be exaggerated. The most severe poverty in the world still remains concentrated in the countryside, and the degree of change varies enormously by country and world region. But there are clear structural reasons for the marginalization of social revolution that are related to urbanization, the shift of power to cities, and the

24. For further evidence of a global decline in land inequality, see Erickson and Vollrath 2004.

25. Moore 1966.

26. Kohli 2004.

27. Boix 2003; Acemoglu and Robinson 2006.

28. Baland and Robinson 2008.

29. Samuels and Thomson 2019.

30. In most of Africa, landed elites never held significant political power, though urban bias in post-colonial governments was nevertheless widespread. See Bates 1981.

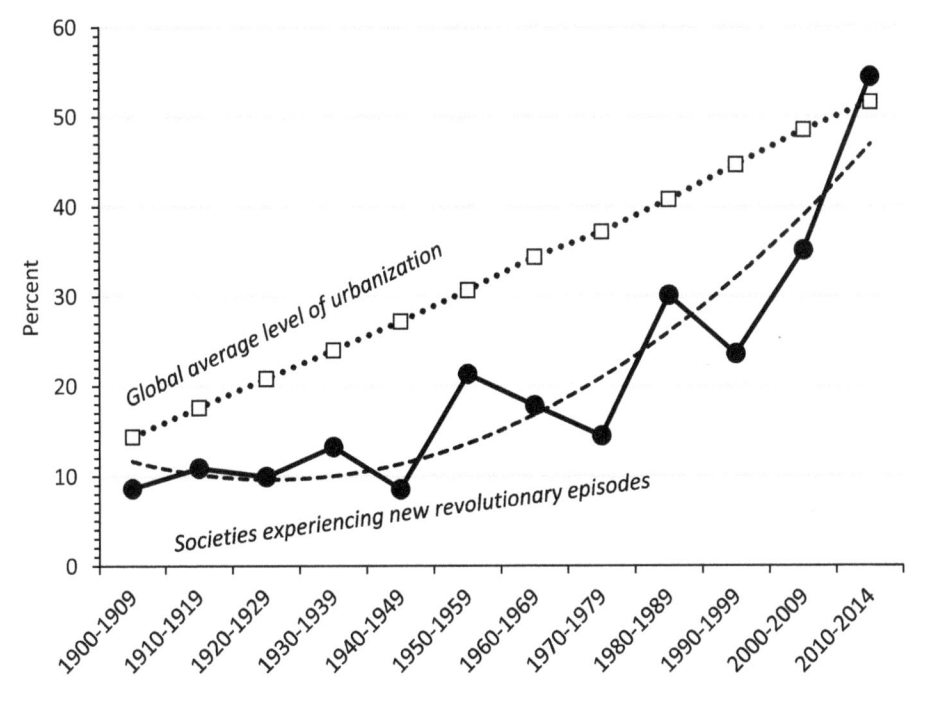

FIGURE 2.11. Average level of urbanization of societies experiencing new revolutionary episodes, 1900–2014.

weakening of the rural conditions and social forces that "third-generation" scholars identified as lying at the heart of social revolutions. Agrarian-bureaucratic society has faded, and with it the prospects for social revolution.

As the world's population migrated to cities, so too did the phenomenon of revolution. Figure 2.11 provides data on the average level of urbanization of societies that have experienced new revolutionary episodes since 1900, by decade. The level rose only by a total of about 10 percentage points from 1900 to 1980, such that the societies experiencing revolutionary contention in the 1970s were barely different in their level of urbanization than those experiencing revolutionary contention in the 1910s (on average, still less than 20 percent urban). Throughout this period, the societies undergoing revolutionary challenges were predominantly rural and lagged well behind the average level of urbanization in the rest of the world. But beginning in the 1980s, the level of urbanization of the societies experiencing revolutionary contention rose at an exponential rate—to the point that, by the 2010s, it exceeded 50 percent, approximating the global urban average.

Not only are the societies experiencing revolutionary episodes increasingly urban, but in contrast to the past, revolutionary episodes in the post–Cold War

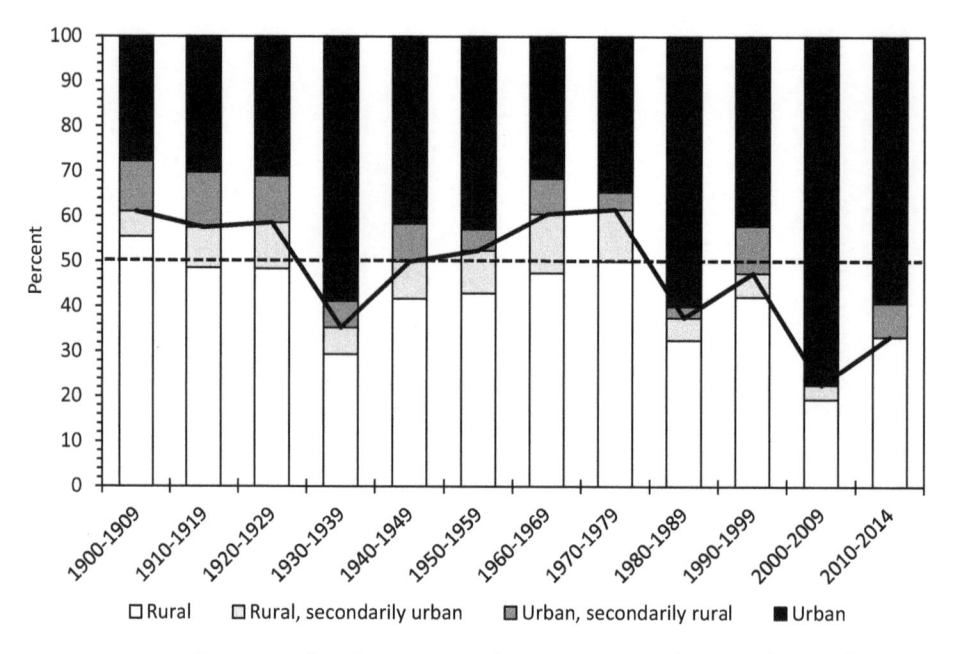

FIGURE 2.12. Percentage of revolutionary episodes occurring primarily in a rural or an urban setting.

era unfolded primarily in urban settings. For each episode I tracked whether revolutionary contention occurred primarily in a rural setting, in a rural setting with a secondary urban component, in an urban setting with a secondary rural component, or primarily in an urban setting. Some revolutions (for instance, the Bolshevik Revolution) occurred primarily in cities but included a secondary element of peasant revolt. Others, like the Cuban Revolution, occurred primarily in the countryside but included a secondary urban component. Social revolutionary contention was most prone to these mixed patterns, which occurred in 28 percent of all social revolutionary episodes since 1900 (but only 10 percent of other types of revolutions). As Figure 2.12 shows, with the sole exception of the 1930s, in every decade prior to the 1980s a majority of revolutionary episodes occurred primarily in the countryside. In connection with the Great Depression, the 1930s saw a short-term increase in urban revolutionary contention relative to rural revolutions.[31] But this soon faded, as rural revolutions multiplied. Mixed patterns were more prevalent before the 1980s, as a significant number of urban revolutionary episodes were still strongly influenced by the largely rural character of the societies in which they occurred.

---

31. Examples include the 1931 Chilean Revolution and the Cuban Revolution of 1933.

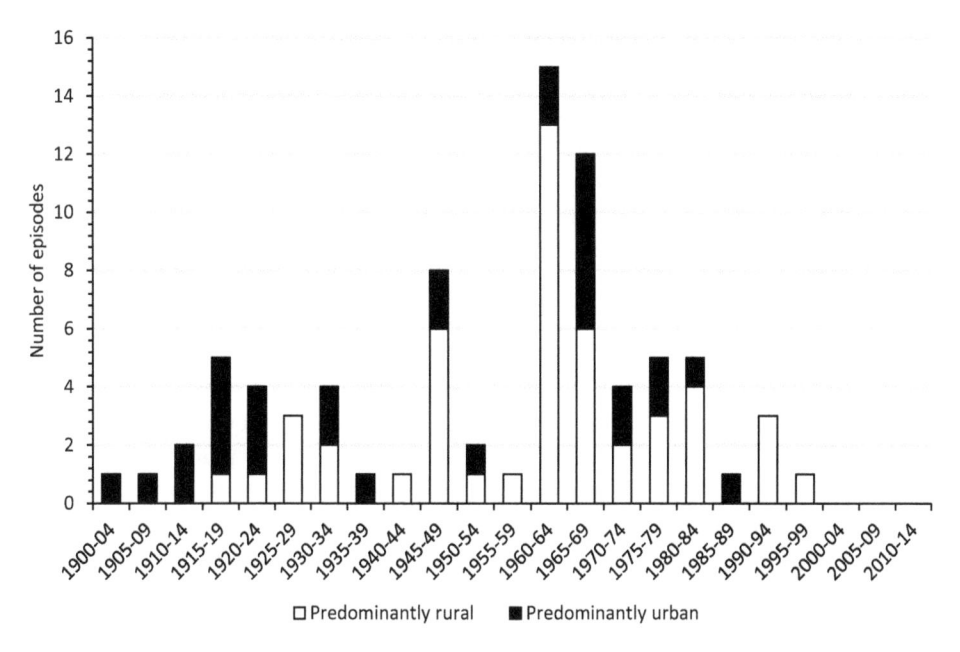

FIGURE 2.13. The onset of rural and urban social revolutionary episodes, 1900–2014.

Many of the rural revolutions of the first half of the twentieth century and Cold War period were anti-colonial revolts. Though typically led by urban elites, these revolutions tended to be based in the countryside, where indigenous populations were concentrated and colonial authority penetrated only weakly, with urban centers remaining under colonial control. But beginning in the late 1920s, social revolution began to migrate to the countryside. Figure 2.13 portrays this evolution. Social revolution had been a predominantly urban phenomenon in the nineteenth and early twentieth centuries, but it had become a predominantly rural phenomenon by World War II and remained predominantly rural throughout the Cold War. What Huntington called the "Eastern" model of revolution involved rurally based social revolutionaries mobilizing peasants to form alternative state institutions,[32] creating a parallel society that could serve as a base for rebels to capture urban centers through conventional or guerrilla warfare. Others identified a separate Latin American model, in which a relatively small guerrilla force took to the countryside, attacking regimes in a hit-and-run fashion.[33] Before 1925, 71 percent of social revolutionary episodes occurred predominantly in cities. After 1925, 62 percent

32. Huntington 1968.
33. Dix 1983; Wickham-Crowley 1992.

occurred predominantly in the countryside. Scattered incidents of urban social revolutionary contention occurred from the 1930s to the 1980s (for example, the 1970 Black Power Revolution in Trinidad, the Iranian Revolution, and the 1971 JVP Insurrection in Sri Lanka), and an unusual cluster emerged in the late 1960s.[34] But for the most part, over the course of the twentieth century social revolution abandoned the city for the countryside.

In all, prior to 1985, 55 percent of all revolutionary episodes occurred primarily within a rural setting. In the 1980s, this began to change. Since the end of the Cold War, 67 percent of revolutionary episodes have occurred primarily in cities. Moreover, mixed rural–urban patterns were progressively squeezed out from the 1980s onward. Unsurprisingly, there is a strong relationship between the overall level of urbanization in a society and whether a revolutionary episode, if one does occur, takes place primarily in an urban or a rural setting.[35] Moreover, controlling for population size, level of development, and degree of political openness, urbanization is positively associated with the onset of a city-based revolution and negatively associated with the onset of a rurally based one.[36] In short, urbanization played a substantial role in increasing the likelihood of urban revolt, returning revolution to the city and transforming it into a predominantly urban phenomenon.

Managing the Repression–Disruption Trade-Off in Cities

There are a number of ways in which the urbanization of revolution has fundamentally altered revolutionary contention. As noted in chapter 1, the physical topography of cities holds advantages and disadvantages for revolutionaries. The obvious advantage of rural rebellion is that revolutionary movements are able to retreat to areas of low population density, where government power is less capable of penetrating and where rebels are safer from government repression. The relationship between civil war and inaccessible terrain (mountains, forest, or jungle) is due in significant part to the ways in which rough terrain exacerbates state weakness, providing a barrier to state penetration and undermining the capacity of regimes to kill or capture rural rebels.[37] As Patrick

---

34. This included the Tupamaros in Uruguay, the Montoneros Rebellion in Argentina, May 1968 in France, and the Basque Separatist Movement in Spain.

35. Differences are statistically significant at the .001 level in a two-tailed t-test (t = −4.7257, with 244 degrees of freedom).

36. Results based on a complementary log-log model with robust standard errors and controls for time dependence (relationships statistically significant the .05 level).

37. Fearon and Laitin 2003; Goodwin 2001.

O'Sullivan puts it, the "effectiveness [of rural rebellions] increases with cover."[38] Rural rebellions rely on the presence of these "safe zones" where rebels are relatively protected from state repression and can develop support networks among local constituencies.[39]

Compared to rural rebellions, urban revolts are much more vulnerable to state repression. Cities are concentration points of state power, and the police and military are present in vastly higher numbers. Yet, as Gregory Ashworth noted, this same disadvantage can function as an advantage for urban insurgents, in that proximity to centers of power brings revolutionaries face to face with the ultimate targets of their insurgency, increasing the threat posed to regimes and the chances of disrupting them.[40] During rural revolts, life in cities can often function normally even in the midst of civil war, as disruptions due to revolt generally occur at a distance from where power and wealth are concentrated. In the Maoist civil war in Nepal in the late 1990s and early 2000s, for instance, "Kathmandu did not really suffer during the 10-year insurgency. Indeed, the capital's economy was booming at that time, favoring the Kathmandu establishment—that is, the business and media élites, the class and caste hierarchies, and the mainstream political party establishment."[41] By contrast, urban revolts occur where condensed clusters of transport, communications, production, and administration are located. As Ashworth observes, "attacks on, or disturbances around, such targets cannot be met with indifference [by government],"[42] for they impinge directly on its functioning and on the operation of the economy on which it depends.

In short, proximity to centers of power bears a dual character—what I refer to as the "repression–disruption trade-off." On the one hand, proximity renders rebellion more susceptible to government repression. On the other hand, it potentially allows for more effective disruption of commerce and administration. The logic of this situation has pushed urban revolutionaries toward tactics capable of countering the superiority of government forces in urban areas while taking advantage of the disruptive potential that proximity to state centers of power provides.

City-based social revolutions in the nineteenth and early twentieth centuries typically relied on a strategy of using the city to stage armed insurrection, street-fighting, the erection of barricades, and military mutinies.[43] They

---

38. O'Sullivan 1983, 147.
39. Bosi 2013.
40. Ashworth 1991, 88.
41. Quoted in Routledge 2010, 1284.
42. Ashworth 1991, 88.
43. Practically all social revolutionary episodes in cities over the past century were armed.

deployed the built environment of the city as cover for armed attacks, thinking of the cityscape as akin to rough terrain, much as rural rebels do in relation to the countryside. The hope was that armed revolt in cities would catalyze a mass uprising and stoke disaffection within the armed forces. Carlos Marighella, the Brazilian Marxist who, contradicting Che Guevara, championed armed struggle in cities, wrote of revolutionary struggle in the city as if the cityscape were analogous to the rough terrain of the countryside:

> The urban guerrilla's best ally is the terrain, and because this is so he must know it like the palm of his hand. To have the terrain as an ally means to know how to use with intelligence its unevenness, its high and low points, its turns, its irregularities, its fixed and secret passages, its abandoned areas, its thickets, etc., taking maximum advantage of all of this for the success of armed actions, escapes, retreats, covers, and hiding places. Impasses and narrow spots, gorges, streets under repair, police checkpoints, military zones and closed-off streets, the entrances and exits to tunnels and those that the enemy can close off, corners controlled or watched by the police, traffic lights and signals. . . . It is an impossible problem for the police, in the labyrinthine terrain of the urban guerrilla, to catch someone they cannot see, to repress someone they cannot catch, and to close in on someone they cannot find.[44]

Shortly after writing these words, Marighella was shot dead by the São Paolo police in an ambush.

Because they involved armed insurrection in close proximity to the state, urban social revolutionary episodes generally had a very low rate of success (23 percent), confirming Fidel Castro's observation that the city was the "graveyard of revolutionaries."[45] Unless they can bring the regime's military over to their side, and unless the state is extremely weak, armed revolutionaries are at a great disadvantage in cities. By the second half of the nineteenth century, artillery rendered it relatively easy to obliterate barricades,[46] and violent rebellion by urban insurgents invariably invited even more violent responses from incumbent regimes, who were usually in a far superior position in terms of arms, number of combatants, and quality of fighters.[47] Treating the

---

44. Marighella 2011, 35. For other cases of treating cityscapes as rough terrain, see Staniland 2010.

45. Quoted in Debray 1968, 67.

46. Traugott 2010.

47. As Marighella (2011, 11–12) recognized, "The urban guerrilla has to capture or steal weapons from the enemy to be able to fight. Because his weapons are not uniform—since what he has are expropriated or have fallen into his hands in various ways—the urban guerrilla faces the

cityscape as rough terrain was costly in terms of lives, property, and commerce and highly disruptive to civilian urban life, alienating the local populations on whom revolutionaries relied. The higher level of repressive capacity in cities also imposed severe limitations on the ability of urban armed rebels to hide. As Joerg Le Blanc observes, today "the operational repertoire of urban insurgent groups is largely limited to terrorist acts," as "close control of the incumbent state forces ... over the urban environment and the population hampers the development of a classical insurgency strategy. ... This control makes the urban insurgency a high loss game."[48]

A good illustration of the difficulties encountered by urban armed rebellion is the Irish Easter Uprising of 1916. Drawing an analogy between urban streets and rural glens and passes, James Connolly, one of the leaders of the revolt, had argued that the urban landscape was fundamentally similar to the countryside in its ability to function as cover for revolt.[49] During Easter week in 1916, Connolly and the Irish Republican Brotherhood organized an urban uprising against British rule, attacking and capturing a number of sites in Dublin with an armed force of 1,760 volunteers and declaring independence. Even though the British were involved in World War I at the time, they responded with overwhelming force, sending in twenty thousand troops, killing 450 in street battles, imprisoning over two thousand, and executing ninety (including Connolly).[50] It took the British one week to defeat the uprising.

Urban revolutionary episodes are much more compact temporally than rural revolutionary episodes, with most lasting two months or less. By contrast, the median rural revolt lasts fifty months. Rural revolts involve longer periods of contention because they typically entail civil wars fought at a distance from inaccessible areas. They must precipitate the collapse of the incumbent regime either by defeating its armies on the battlefield or by inflicting sufficient economic damage and military casualties to undermine its support. Urban revolutions are more difficult to sustain than rural revolts because of the costs and commitments involved and the concentrated presence of the military and police. Prolonged mobilization in urban revolutions is highly disruptive to urban economic life (including the livelihoods of the participants themselves) and requires a high level of emotional commitment. Eventually, exhaustion sets in and the character of urban revolutionary oppositions shifts, growing smaller and turning increasingly radical. Incumbent regimes often

---

problem of a variety of weapons and a shortage of ammunition. Moreover, he has no place in which to practice shooting and marksmanship."

48. Le Blanc 2013, 802 and 805.
49. O'Sullivan 1983, 147–48.
50. Foy and Barton 2011.

seek to suppress urban mobilizations precisely with such factors in mind, prolonging revolutionary contention in the hope that it will exhaust itself, oppositions will grow smaller, and opportunities will present themselves for repression of those who remain.

In the first decades of the twentieth century, most social revolutionary episodes (71 percent) occurred in cities, and most (80 percent) were armed insurrections. But as a result of the problems that they encountered due to the superior force of governments in cities, city-based social revolutions had begun to go into decline by the late 1920s, and social revolutionaries migrated to the countryside in search of safer bases from which to operate. The decimation of the Chinese Communist Party in Shanghai and other cities of southern China in 1927–28 and the party's subsequent migration to the countryside under Mao was the critical pivot in this regard in the history of twentieth-century social revolution.[51] It represented the beginning of the transition of social revolution from the built environment of the city to the rough terrain of the countryside.

The essential rationale for moving to the countryside for social revolutionaries was "to trade space for time,"[52] with the goal of slowly gnawing away at a regime's forces from the redoubts of safe spaces. As Che Guevara asserted, the purpose of moving to the countryside was to engage in revolutionary struggle "in places beyond the reach of the repressive forces," in "zones difficult to reach, either because of dense forests, steep mountains, impassable deserts, or marshes."[53] Timothy Wickham-Crowley observed that "guerrilla movements do not begin among peasants in the countryside but amongst urban-based intellectuals, especially in the twin milieus of universities and left-wing political parties."[54] The countryside afforded safety for urban intellectuals bent on revolution. They traded immediate disruptive capacity for safety from government repression, managing the proximity dilemma by spatial relocation.

This transition to the countryside vastly altered the tactics, support groups, and social networks on which revolutionaries relied. For the PKK in Turkey and the FLN/EZLN in Mexico—both Marxist revolutionary groups that developed among radicalized students in cities—the urban environment

---

51. Hofheinz 1977. There were social revolutionary episodes prior to the Chinese Revolution that were predominantly rural: the 1903 Ilinden Revolt in Ottoman-controlled Macedonia; the Mexican Revolution from 1910 to 1919; and the 1915 Jangal Rebellion in Iran. But these cases did not exercise the same influence on the ruralization of revolution as the Chinese Revolution (though the Mexican case did influence rebellions in neighboring Central America).

52. O'Sullivan 1983, 14.

53. Guevara 1961.

54. Wickham-Crowley 1992, 30. See also Huntington 1968.

presented enormous difficulties for mounting armed rebellion in the 1960s and 1970s. Not only was there significant competition from other Marxist groups, but these groups were limited to operating on university campuses in major urban centers, with new recruits almost entirely coming from the middle class rather than the social forces that rebels hoped to represent. State surveillance limited the extent to which these groups could engage in political action. And the clandestine cell structure that each was forced to adopt, while providing for greater security, came at the high price of isolation from the population at large.[55] In 1970, the FLN/EZLN relocated to Chiapas, and in 1976 the PKK transferred its center of activity to Kurdistan—transforming urban into rural rebellions. In both cases, the regions chosen as bases were selected because of their histories of revolt, their potentially receptive rural populations, the presence of rough terrain, and proximity to an international border. The moves allowed both movements to forge deeper connections with indigenous groups and with the social forces that they sought to represent while developing in relative isolation from state surveillance or competing rebel movements, helping them to mount armed rural rebellions by the 1990s.[56]

Prior to 1985, 70 percent of all revolutionary episodes in cities were armed. This was in part a reflection of the ideologies of revolutionary movements, as certain types of movements (social revolutionary movements among them) demonstrate a strong affinity with armed rebellion. But it was also very much a reflection of the ecology of cities in the first half of the twentieth century. The societies that experienced urban revolutionary contention in the first half of the twentieth century were overwhelmingly rural (88 percent, on average), and cities were considerably smaller than today's metropolises. The average size of the world's largest one hundred cities in 1900 was 607,000 inhabitants, and the median size was 389,000 (about the size of Wichita, Kansas in 2020).[57] The mean size of the capital cities of independent states in 1900 was 611,000, while the median size was 282,000 (approximately the size of Durham, North Carolina in 2020). By today's standards, most of these would be considered small to medium-sized cities. Essentially, in order to generate the massive crowds necessary for successful unarmed revolt (as we will see in chapter 4, generally in the hundreds of thousands), in most of these cities every man, woman, and child inhabitant would have had to have been mobilized

---

55. On this point more generally with regard to urban clandestine groups, see White and Falkenberg 1991, 126.

56. O'Connor and Oikonomakis 2015.

57. Data come from the 1905 *World Almanac*.

into revolutionary action. By contrast, the average population size of the world's one hundred largest cities in 2020 was 9.7 million, and the median size 7.3 million (almost nineteen times larger than the median in 1900).[58] The average size of capital cities of independent states was 3.2 million (with a median size of 1.5 million). In short, prior to the late twentieth century, the numbers necessary for mounting revolution in cities by relying on the power of numbers were simply absent in most parts of the world.[59]

There were other reasons too why urban rebellion tended to be armed prior to the second half of the twentieth century. For one thing, capabilities for coordinating large crowds in revolutionary action were severely limited. As loudspeakers only came to be used to amplify voices before crowds in the mid-1920s (and were first used for purposes of mass mobilization by the Nazis), the ability to communicate with participants in large crowds was severely constricted.[60] At the infamous Peterloo Massacre in Manchester in 1819, for instance, an estimated sixty thousand protestors gathered—one of the largest protests of first half of the nineteenth century in England. But protestors could only hear speakers at a distance of ten meters from the podium.[61] The kind of crowd coordination through sound amplification and mass communications characteristic of the late twentieth and early twenty-first centuries was completely absent. Communication about forthcoming protest actions in the early twentieth century relied primarily on word of mouth or print media. This greatly constricted the scope and speed with which revolutionary action could be coordinated across large numbers, forcing revolutionaries to rely heavily on localized networks and smaller crowds. Only with widespread application of radio and television in the mid-twentieth century did the kind of simultaneity of communications necessary for coordinating very large revolutionary mobilizations in cities come into being.

Moreover, prior to the mid-twentieth century, the strategic advantages of challenging regimes through unarmed crowds were quite modest. As we will see in chapter 8, regimes were much more willing to shoot into or ride over unarmed crowds than is the case today, making unarmed rebellion in cities a

---

58. Data come from https://www.macrotrends.net/cities/largest-cities-by-population.

59. Hobsbawm (2005) suggests that larger cities, with more than a million inhabitants, are less conducive to the use of riots and insurrections as a revolutionary tactic, since as cities grow, they transform from an integrated whole rooted in local networks into a loosely connected collection of communities, with central business and administrative centers physically distant from neighborhoods of the poor. He also notes that the development of mass transportation systems is conducive to the movement and congregation of large numbers.

60. Epping-Jäger 2011.

61. Read 1958, 134.

risky endeavor. The average number of deaths in unarmed rebellions in cities during the first half of the twentieth century was more than six times what it was during the post–Cold War period. Given the much smaller size of the crowds that could be generated, and the limited strategic advantages of unarmed rebellion, in the early twentieth century armed revolt, riots, or strikes were the main options available to urban revolutionaries. Contemporary forms of urban civic revolution were largely unimaginable. Indeed, from 1900 to 1949, only two revolutionary episodes in cities did not involve either armed rebellion or riots.[62]

Since 1985, by contrast, 79 percent of attempted urban revolutions have been unarmed. This decline in urban armed revolt reflects not only the difficulties of mounting armed insurrections in cities, but also the growing concentration of populations in cities, technological change, and the rise of the urban civic repertoire. Rather than treating the cityscape as rough terrain, the urban civic repertoire utilizes the large numbers that have concentrated in cities, the vulnerability of cities to disruption, technologies for coordinating large crowds, and the symbolic and strategic spaces between buildings to challenge incumbent regimes. What affords safety from government repression in urban civic revolutions is not arms, but numbers. In general, the larger the crowd, the less likely regimes are to apply force to break it up.[63] This safety in numbers is due to multiple factors: the general sense of illegitimacy that accompanies the naked use of force against unarmed civilians; the inability of the police or military to control large crowds; the fear that casualties in such situations can lead to massive backlash mobilizations, rioting, and disorders (even the storming of government offices); the greater media coverage accorded large protests,[64] potentially staying the hand of the regime; and the ways in which the use of force against crowds can become an occasion for defections of police and soldiers.

The modern cityscape—with its spacious public squares and broad boulevards—provides a propitious setting for such tactics. In Europe, design of the cityscape in the mid-nineteenth century consciously moved away from the narrow, circuitous streets that had aided urban armed insurrections and

62. These were the Persian Constitutional Revolution in 1905 and the Easter Crisis in Denmark in 1920.
63. For example, in 6,618 protest demonstrations in the Soviet Union during the glasnost period, repressive actions against demonstrators were negatively related to the number of participants in the demonstration (statistically significant at the .001 level). The probability that a demonstration would be repressed dropped by an inverse exponential rate after crowds reached twenty-five thousand participants.
64. McCarthy, McPhail, and Smith 1996.

instead gravitated toward the construction of large public squares and broad boulevards (what is famously known as "Haussmannization," after the rebuilding of Paris in the mid-nineteenth century under the direction of Baron Georges-Eugène Haussmann). Modernism further reinforced the trend toward monumental public spaces, and twentieth-century dictators often built such spaces as venues for officially sponsored spectacles celebrating and dramatizing their rule.[65] Seizing control of such spaces and declaring the illegitimacy of government is a statement of defiance and an open invitation to repression. Many of these urban public spaces hold significant symbolic value, helping to multiply numbers and challenging key myths of rule. Places associated with public punishment, repression, or previous uprisings are particularly thick with meaning in ways that naturally attract revolutionary challengers.[66] Urban civic revolutions occupy these urban spaces, mobilizing as many people as possible into them as a strategy for managing the repression–disruption trade-off. Through the protection afforded by overwhelming numbers, they seek to generate pressure to induce defections from a regime's coalition. As we will see, this affinity between tactics and the urban environment has rendered the urban civic repertoire a significantly more successful approach to capturing power than other forms of urban rebellion.

Social Forces, Networks, and Technologies in Rural and Urban Revolts

In addition to the modern city's numbers, proximity to centers of power, and open spaces, urban civic revolutions seek to exploit its other revolutionary advantages in terms of resources, networks, visibility, and diversity. As revolution has urbanized, the social forces involved in revolutions have changed. For each revolutionary episode in my dataset, I tracked the social groups mentioned in key secondary sources. Figure 2.14 reports the proportion of episodes in which particular class and occupational groups were mentioned, separated into time periods. In the first half of the twentieth century, three class groups dominated revolutions: peasants, workers, and the intelligentsia—as second- and third-generation theories of revolution argued. During the Cold War, youth (and in particular, students) came to occupy an increasingly visible role—fueled in particular by the growth of higher education in major urban centers within modernizing regimes. For example, the 1973 Thai Democracy Movement, which was led and carried out primarily by university students, was made

---

65. Scott 1990, 58–59.
66. Harison 2000.

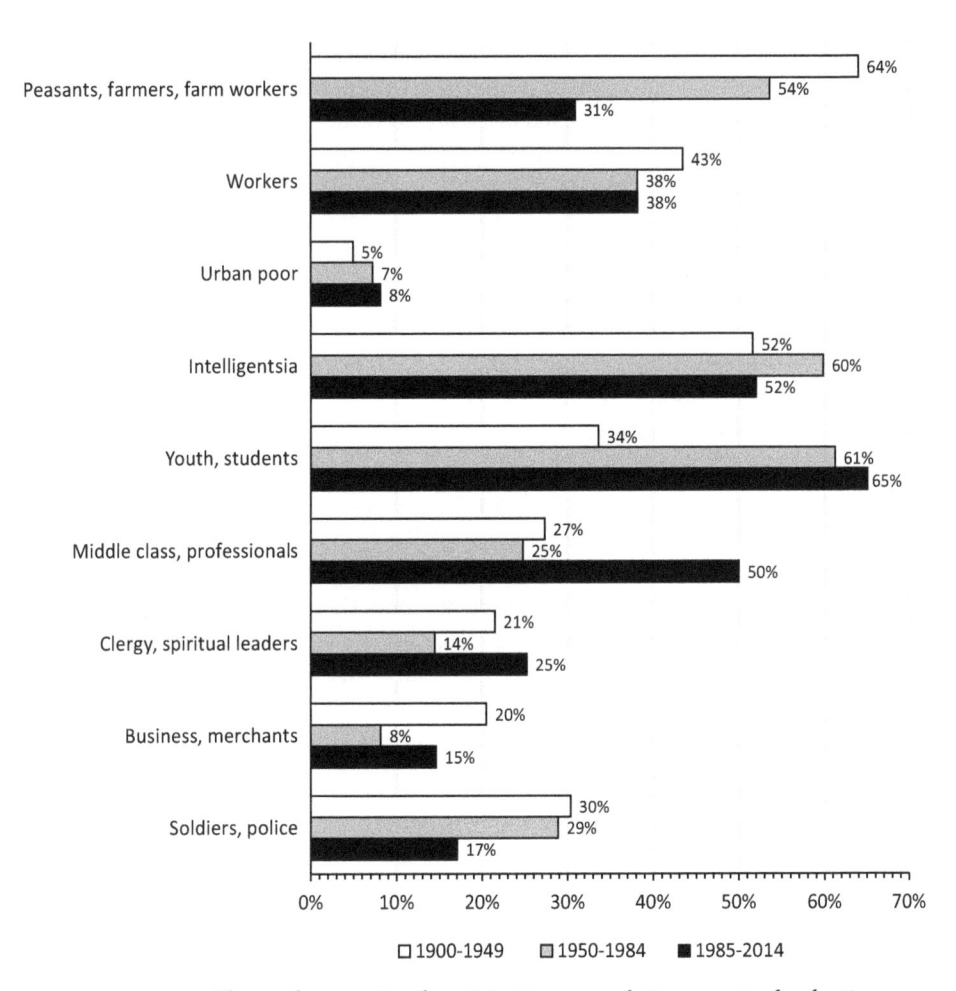

FIGURE 2.14. Class and occupational participation in revolutionary episodes, by time period.

possible in part by the extraordinary expansion of university enrollment in Thailand, from fifteen thousand in 1961 to ten times that number in 1972, with the number of universities increasing from five to seventeen during the same period.[67] Youth also played critical roles in anti-colonial revolts, and in the 1960s student groups were conspicuously represented among left-wing revolutionary movements. Soldiers played a significant role in a quarter to a third of episodes prior to 1985—either through mutinies or military coups. The

67. Kongkirati 2012.

urban poor have rarely been mentioned as participants in revolutions. There have only been two dozen revolts since 1900 in which the urban poor figured conspicuously (at least as reflected in the literature on these revolutions). Their absence has been the subject of much speculation and variably explained by the effects of clientelism, informality, lack of resources, the demands of daily survival, and alternative forms of everyday resistance.[68]

After the Cold War, the roles of peasants and mutinying soldiers diminished substantially. But the key change was the altered role played by the middle class. Since 1900, the middle class occupied a visible position in 35 percent of all revolutionary episodes, but 61 percent of urban and 89 percent of urban civic revolutionary episodes. Education and changes in occupational structure have long been thought to foster political participation (including protest participation) by providing critical skills and resources for participation in politics.[69] Due to their roles as centers of administration and commerce, cities contain high concentrations of middle-class citizens. These citizens are better educated and resourced than rural inhabitants or the urban poor, and therefore possess certain advantages for mounting collective action. Disproportionate participation by the educated and better-off in urban civic revolutions is confirmed in a number of public opinion surveys of revolutionary participation, including those examined later in this book.

Dissimilarities in the topography of revolt translate into very different network structures and modes of communication underpinning rural and urban revolts. In general, sustained high-risk activism like revolution is thought to require the presence of strong network ties (friendships, personal acquaintances, and face-to-face relationships) that pull individuals who otherwise might not have the resolve to participate into collective action.[70] Writing about partisan resistance to Soviet rule, Roger Petersen observed that strong, tight-knit communities constituted the backbone of recruitment for clandestine rural rebellion. Kinship and neighbor ties were particularly important. As he noted, "societies without strong communities may create passive forms of resistance, but they are unlikely to create the locally organized rebellion structures that would be able to spawn sustained violent action against a powerful regime."[71]

---

68. Huntington 1968; Cornelius 1975; Huntington and Nelson 1976; Stokes 1991; Bayat 2000; Holland 2017.

69. Lipset 1960; Verba, Nie, and Kim 1978; Verba, Schlozman, and Brady 1995; McCarthy and Zald 1977.

70. McAdam and Paulsen 1993.

71. Petersen 2001, 15.

Though it is not often recognized, strong ties also play important roles in urban revolutions. In the eighteenth and early nineteenth centuries, cities had higher population densities than the countryside but preserved many of the features of rural life, such as "gardens, orchards, grazing land, and heaths, and the sight and smell of animals of all kinds."[72] On the eve of the American Revolution, only five cities in the colonies had more than nine thousand inhabitants. Philadelphia had forty thousand residents, New York twenty-five thousand, and Boston fifteen thousand. In many ways these cities functioned like inflated villages. Their inhabitants lived in tightly packed housing in close proximity to waterways, often connected to one another through ties of religious congregation, commerce, and neighborhood tavern. These localized networks made the American Revolution possible by transforming colonial cities, in the context of imperial crisis, into epicenters of revolt.[73] Over the nineteenth and twentieth centuries, industrialization undermined this inflated-village model of cities by concentrating much larger numbers in urban centers and locating them in residentially segregated communities on the basis of class or ethnicity. But, as Roger Gould has described, throughout the nineteenth century, localized networks continued to play a critical role in revolutionary mobilizations, forming, for instance, the foundation for recruitment and solidarity among the Parisian National Guard in 1870.[74]

Extensive research has shown that, even in the large metropolitan centers of the late twentieth and early twenty-first centuries, inhabitants continue to be embedded in strong-tie networks, though the character of these ties is quite different from those in small communities.[75] Urban growth can occur in three ways: suburbanization, migration, and natural population growth. When urban growth results from swallowing the surrounding countryside, incorporating villages into metropolitan areas, it often leaves village networks intact on the urban periphery. Delhi in India and Manama in Bahrain represent examples of this pattern.[76] Settlement patterns in Syrian cities similarly produced dense kinship networks within compact urban quarters.[77] In these cases, the kinship ties of rural areas have been integrated into the fabric of the city and

72. Richardson 1992, 3.
73. Carp 2007.
74. Gould 1991, 719.
75. Piselli 2007, 869.
76. Mehra 2005; Ollamh and Lanthier 2016, 147. In the Tulip Revolution in Kyrgyzstan in March 2005, opposition supporters in the city of Jalalabad were able to mobilize up to ten thousand supporters quickly from nearby villages due to the presence of clan networks connecting the city to the surrounding countryside. See Khamidov 2002; Abdyrazakov 2005.
77. See Mazur 2017; Mazur 2021.

have at times become a basis for urban revolutionary mobilization—as occurred, for instance, in 2011 in Bahrain and Syria.

When urban growth results from mass migration to cities or from natural population growth, extended kinship ties typically contract, while those of friendship, neighborhood, school, workplace, and secondary associations expand. Given the housing, employment, and income constraints of urban life and the role played by women in the urban workforce, fertility rates normally decline for urban dwellers. This generally leads to a decline in the importance of extended kinship ties and focuses kin relationships on immediate family. Migrants from particular villages, regions, or countries also tend to concentrate in distinct neighborhoods, workplaces, and religious congregations, assimilating these ties into the fabric of urban life. And cities are where civil society thrives and where possibilities for association multiply. In short, cities contain more diverse populations than the countryside—networked together in a multiplicity of ways.[78] As critical mass theory tells us, sizeable, highly networked, and diverse populations are greatly advantaged in producing collective action, as such populations are more likely to contain resourced and networked minorities of citizens willing to act to obtain the provision of public goods.[79]

Thus, in cities, personal ties become increasingly variegated, functioning on a multiplicity of planes in ways that are not possible in rural population settings. As Claude Fischer observed, "the complex differentiation of urban society, especially in the division of labor, means that there are more distinct social contexts—in jobs, organizations, locales, and so forth—that people occupy. Given the way people build personal ties, this means that urbanites will have more varied and distinct social networks than residents of small communities."[80] Strong ties hardly disappear in cities; rather, they alter and diversify in character, constituting a mosaic of "little worlds" rather than a narrower, singular field of social influence, as tends to be the case in small-population settings. As we will see, the vast majority of participants in urban revolutions participate with friends, family, neighbors, or workplace colleagues—strong-tie networks that have repeatedly supplied the commitment and resolve necessary for sustained high-risk collective action.

As Goldstone argued, revolutionary mobilization is typically promoted by the presence of a multitude of strong-tie nodes connected by weak ties—the latter allowing rebellions to "scale up."[81] Mark Granovetter noted the importance

---

78. Wirth 1969, 156–58.
79. Marwell and Oliver 1993.
80. Fischer 1982, 11–12.
81. Goldstone 1994, 154.

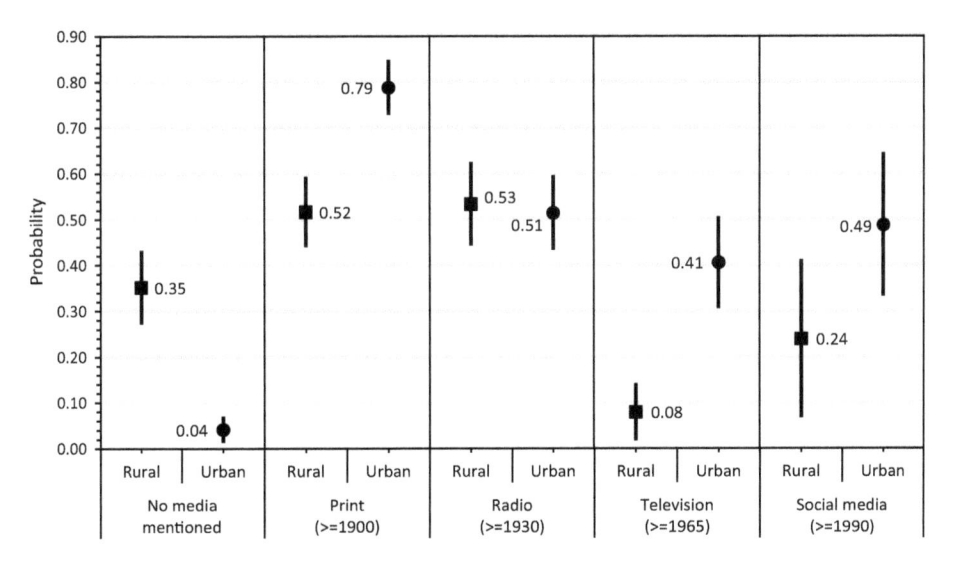

FIGURE 2.15. The probability that a particular media form was used, by urban/rural location of revolutionary episode. Point estimates, controlling for time (with 95 percent confidence intervals). The regressions for each communications medium were limited to the approximate years when it was potentially available for use (i.e., after mass application).

of weak ties between individuals for diffusing and spreading social behaviors.[82] Rural rebellions tend to "scale up" through cross-village ethnic or clan ties, the glue of rebel organization across village settings, or as a result of violence by the incumbent regime that drives villagers to seek rebel protection.[83] But scaling up in rural rebellions usually presents a significant challenge, given the less substantial nature of weak ties across village settings. This is one reason that rural revolutions tend to rely less on numbers and more on organizational cohesion and the force of arms for revolutionary success.

By contrast, urban settings are particularly conducive to scaling up, and not only because they constitute concentrated population centers. As Jeremy Wallace observes, "Cities bring together masses of people, improve communication links among them, and increase the ability of private grievances to accumulate and circulate."[84] Cities are characterized by robust networks of weak ties, which are multiplied by the denser presence of mass communication. I tracked the types of mass media utilized in revolutionary episodes over the last century, as mentioned in secondary sources (Figure 2.15). Urban

82. Granovetter 1973.
83. Kalyvas and Kocher 2007.
84. Wallace 2013, 632.

revolutionary episodes were much more likely than rural episodes to employ most media forms, and most mass media lend themselves better to mobilization in an urban than in a rural setting. Indeed, rural revolutionary episodes had a .35 probability of not using any forms of mass media (at least, as mentioned in secondary sources), compared to only a .04 probability for urban revolutionary episodes.

Print media have played a key role in revolutionary politics since the emergence of modern revolution in the seventeenth century.[85] However, rural populations have much lower levels of literacy than urban populations,[86] limiting the ability of revolutionaries working in rural settings to utilize newspapers and print media to scale up revolt. Radio is equally mentioned in sources on both urban and rural revolutionary episodes. Radios are inexpensive and often widespread in rural societies. Moreover, the technology for short-wave radio broadcasting is relatively cheap, and rebels have found it fairly easy to broadcast clandestinely from remote locations or across borders with impunity.

By contrast, television is a highly centralized medium that is more easily subject to governmental control due to the cost and complexity of broadcast technology. Since the emergence of television, television broadcasts or the seizure of television stations by revolutionary oppositions have played an important role in many urban revolutionary episodes. The proximity of television broadcast facilities to urban centers renders this possible, and the visuality and simultaneity of television lend themselves to the rapid mobilization of numbers characteristic of urban civic rebellion. But television has been a particularly poor way for revolutionaries to connect with rural populations. Rural revolutionaries are unlikely to gain access to television broadcasting facilities, and since 1965 (when television was first used as a communications medium in revolution) television ownership in societies experiencing rural revolutionary contention has been low (1,883 per hundred thousand) compared to societies experiencing urban revolutions (10,675 per hundred thousand).

Since 1990, social media have come to play an increasingly important role in urban revolutions. Societies experiencing rural revolutionary contention since 1990 have had a low level of internet penetration (on average, five users per hundred) compared to those experiencing urban revolutionary episodes

---

85. Eisenstein 1986.

86. For the 202 episodes for which data were available, societies experiencing rural revolutionary episodes were on average only 34 percent literate, while those experiencing urban revolts were on average 64 percent literate. Unsurprisingly, societies in which revolutionary contention predominantly occurs in the countryside have much lower levels of newspaper circulation (219 per ten thousand) than societies that experience urban revolutionary contention (1,093 per ten thousand).

(on average, sixteen users per hundred).[87] As a result, social media have been more than twice as likely to be utilized in urban as in rural revolutions. Social media are especially well suited for mobilization that depends upon the power of numbers; the simultaneity and visuality of digital communication are conducive to scaling up quickly, and the visibility afforded by social media has been critical to the ability to ward off regime repression. Indeed, since 1990, when internet-based media began to spread, 65 percent of urban civic revolutionary episodes have involved the use digital media.

Urban Revolution and State Power

Both urban and rural rebellions were common in the pre-modern world. But most pre-modern uprisings were localized affairs, reflecting the fragmented and disjointed character of pre-modern authority systems. As Tilly observed, modern revolution presupposes the presence (or at a minimum, the idea) of the national state.[88] It is closely connected with the notion of popular sovereignty—the idea that the state rightfully belongs, in a fundamental sense, to the broader community of the people. One factor accounting for the proliferation of revolutionary contention over the past century is simply the growth in the number of independent states in the world—from forty-two in 1900 to 195 in 2014. As a result of decolonization and the multiplication of states, the number of independent national governments at risk of experiencing revolutionary contention expanded enormously. These new national states provided a growing number of focal points around which revolutionary contention could coalesce. Indeed, there is a strong, statistically significant relationship between the number of new revolutionary episodes occurring in a year and the lagged number of states in existence in the world system.[89]

But the relationship between the growth in the number of states and the increased incidence of revolution is not so simple. For one thing, reverse causation has clearly been at work, as the growth in the number of states since 1900 has been in part a function of the incidence of revolution. The sample used here includes numerous anti-colonial revolts and independence movements that rebelled to establish independent states (35 percent of all revolutionary episodes from 1900 to 2014). During the first half of the twentieth century, 47 percent of revolutionary episodes sought independence from a colonial empire, overland empire, or

---

87. On the debate over whether mobile phone coverage in rural areas helps or hurts rural rebellion, see Pierskalla and Hollenbach 2013; Shapiro and Weidmann 2015.
88. Tilly 1978.
89. Statistically significant at the .01 level using an autoregressive (AR2) time series count model.

multinational state, and during the Cold War, 36 percent. That proportion dropped to 22 percent after the Cold War. But the fact remains: rather than being simply a by-product of the growth in the number of states, revolution has itself been responsible in significant part for the growth in the number of states.[90]

An alternative explanation for why the proliferation of states might be associated with an increased incidence of revolution is the political instability often associated with state independence. Independence frequently created a rupture in governance that, at least for several years following decolonization, increased the likelihood of political instability. For the first half of the twentieth century and the Cold War period, there is a negative and statistically significant relationship (at the .05 level) between the number of years after independence and the onset of revolutionary contention, with the first two years after independence displaying heightened vulnerability to revolution.[91] However, in the post–Cold War period, when revolutionary episodes increased at the most rapid pace, there was a positive (but statistically insignificant) relationship between the number of years since independence and the likelihood of onset of revolutionary contention.[92] Moreover, the revolutionary contention that followed political independence tended to be rural rather than urban.[93] All this casts strong doubt on the thesis that the disruptions associated with independence can explain the general increase in revolutionary contention in the late twentieth and early twenty-first centuries.

The goal of state independence was closely connected with rural revolution. Three-quarters of revolutions that sought to achieve state independence were

90. Wimmer 2012. The number of independent states in the world is perfectly correlated with time ($r = .97$), so that it could serve as a proxy for any number of temporally increasing factors (urbanization, levels of development, population growth, the growth of systems of communication, etc.). There is, for instance, a strong relationship (statistically significant at the .001 level) between the number of new revolutionary episodes occurring in a year and the lagged level of world urbanization. Not surprisingly, the number of states in the world is also perfectly correlated with the global level of urbanization ($r = .97$). It is impossible to sort out what these correlations mean at a global aggregate level of analysis.

91. Based on a complementary log-log panel model ($n = 7,367$ observations for 144 countries from 1900 to 1984), with cluster-robust standard errors and controls for time dependence.

92. Based on a complementary log-log panel model ($n = 4,601$ observations for 157 countries from 1985 to 2014), with cluster-robust standard errors and controls for time dependence.

93. There is a negative and statistically significant relationship (at the .05 level) between the number of years after independence and the onset of rural revolutionary contention, but a positive (though statistically insignificant) relationship between the number of years after independence and the onset of urban revolutionary contention. Based on a complementary log-log panel model ($n = 11,968$ observations for 158 countries from 1900 to 2014), with cluster-robust standard errors and controls for time dependence.

waged primarily from the countryside, constituting 53 percent of all rural revolutions since 1900. By contrast, most urban revolutions have occurred in states that were already independent, with only 18 percent of urban revolutions raising the issue of state independence. Thus, as independent states proliferated around the globe, one of the key rationales for rural revolution—attainment of state independence—weakened.

The types of states associated with rural revolutions have differed substantially from those associated with urban revolutions. Much of the literature on social revolutions attributed revolution to state weakness: states whose institutions were incoherent and could not effectively channel the increased demands for participation resulting from modernization;[94] states that were weakened by fiscal crisis or over-commitment in war;[95] states that were beholden to powerful landed elites, making them incapable of reforming themselves;[96] states with weak infrastructural power that were unable to penetrate their own territories, leaving areas where rebels could operate freely;[97] and states with weak militaries that could not adequately control their territories or police their borders.[98] As Skocpol argued, "before social revolutions could occur, the administrative and military power of these states had to break down."[99] Not oppression, but weakness, she said, fostered social revolutions.[100] The infrastructurally weak state has also been critical to the outbreak of rural revolutions, as it provided the basis for the "safe zones" on which rural revolutionaries heavily depended. Che Guevara is said to have chosen Bolivia as a site for launching social revolution, for instance, precisely because of its ineffective and poorly organized state.[101] Indeed, since 1900 there has been a strong and statistically significant relationship (at the .001 level) between the proportion of a state's territory over which it has effective control (as measured by the V-Dem measure for state authority over territory) and the outbreak of a rural revolution.[102] No such relationship exists for urban revolutions.

94. Huntington 1968.
95. Skocpol 1979, Goldstone 1991.
96. Skocpol 1979.
97. Goodwin 2001.
98. Wickham-Crowley 1992, 57.
99. Skocpol 1979, 285.
100. Skocpol 1994, 138.
101. Harris 2000, 89.
102. Based on a complementary log-log panel model (n = 11,358 observations for 162 independent countries from 1900 to 2014), with cluster-robust standard errors and controls for time dependence.

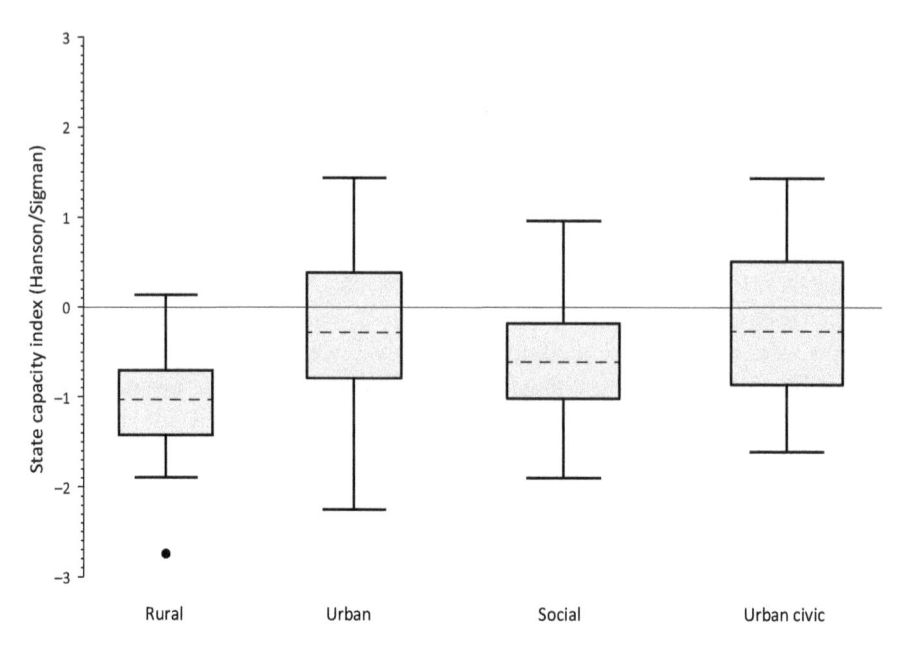

FIGURE 2.16. State capacity by location and type of revolution (Hanson/Sigman state capacity index). Dotted lines represent the median, the box—the 25th and 75th percentiles, and the whiskers—the lower and upper adjacent values.

Rather, urban revolutions have occurred in states with levels of state capacity considerably higher than in those where rural revolutions have occurred. State capacity is a notoriously difficult concept to measure, but one serious attempt to do so has been made by Jonathan Hanson and Rachel Sigman.[103] Using a large number of variables, their measure integrates three dimensions of state capacity (extractive, coercive, and administrative) for 173 countries from 1960 to 2009 and ranges roughly between −3 and 3, with an approximate mean of zero. Figure 2.16 presents a boxplot distribution comparing the Hanson/Sigman measure in states that experienced rural, urban, social, and urban civic revolutionary episodes. Rural revolutionary episodes have tended to occur in the bottom fifth of states in terms of state capacity (a mean of −1.01). By contrast, urban revolutionary episodes have occurred in states with only slightly below-average levels of state capacity (a mean of −0.17), with the differences between urban and rural episodes statistically significant at the .001

---

103. Hanson and Sigman 2013. I thank these authors for making their measure available for my use.

level.[104] Social revolutionary episodes have occurred in the bottom third of states (a mean of −0.57).[105] State capacity in societies experiencing city-based social revolutionary episodes has been higher (−0.37) than in those experiencing rurally based social revolutionary contention (−0.66). By contrast, urban civic revolts have occurred in states with only slightly below-average levels of state capacity (−0.23), distributionally straddling the global mean.

Urban revolutions occur precisely where the coercive capacity of the state is strongest. They do not seek to hide from state power. Rather, they confront state power directly. Urban revolutions are closely related to the coercive and predatory powers of the state as opposed to its infrastructural power.[106] Urban and urban civic revolutionary episodes have generally materialized against regimes that were more autocratic, more personalist, and more corrupt than regimes experiencing rural revolutions or other forms of revolutionary contention. The leaders of these regimes have generally been in office longer at the onset of revolutionary contention (8.3 and 12.0 years respectively) than the leaders of regimes experiencing rural (5.8 years) or social (6.9 years) revolutionary challenges. The Polity scale, which measures the degree to which governments are more closed and autocratic or more open and democratic, ranges from −10 to +10. The mean Polity score for regimes experiencing urban and urban civic revolutionary episodes has been considerably lower (−1.83 and −2.89 respectively) than for regimes experiencing rural (−0.99) or social (0.25) revolutionary episodes. Viewed in this light, it is hardly surprising that many of the grievances that permeate urban and urban civic revolutions revolve around reclaiming the public sphere from repressive, arbitrary government.

Urban and urban civic revolutions are less associated with the infrastructural weakness of the state than they are with dynamic political opportunities. Dynamic political opportunities are different from state weakness. They revolve around the temporal vulnerability of regimes to challenge rather than the ability of a state to penetrate its territory (which changes relatively slowly). Indeed, dynamic political opportunities can occur in states that have strong infrastructural capacity (the revolutions that overthrew European communism are prime examples). Sidney Tarrow identified a series of conditions that, if acted upon, increase the likelihood of movement success: the opening of access to participation for new actors; the initiation of political reforms; political realignment within the ruling group; the appearance of influential allies

---

104. In a two-tailed t-test, t=−5.41, with 119 degrees of freedom.

105. In a one-tailed t-test, the mean for social revolutionary episodes is significantly different from the global mean of zero at the .001 level (t=−4.6791, with 32 degrees of freedom).

106. Mann 1986; Levi 1981.

within a regime; the emergence of splits within a ruling elite; elections; and factors that undermine a regime's ability to repress.[107] Urban revolutions and urban civic revolutions are much more sensitive to the occurrence of elections and political reforms (occurring in 36 percent of urban and 61 percent of urban civic episodes) than are rural revolutions (14 percent of episodes) or social revolutions (15 percent of episodes). Because urban revolutions occur in proximity to centers of state power and are more exposed to the state's repressive capacity, dynamic political opportunities rather than weak infrastructural state capacity play more important roles within them.

Urban Revolution and the International System

Skocpol argued that "social revolutions cannot be explained without systematic reference to *inter*national structures and world historical development."[108] The marginalization of social revolution and growth of urban and urban civic revolts have been associated with deep changes in the international system—specifically, the decline of inter-state warfare, the collapse of the Soviet Union, the rise of American unipolar power, globalization, and neoliberal economic development.

For much of the past century, what Hannah Arendt called "the interrelationship of war and revolution"[109] played a central role in how scholars thought about revolution—especially social revolution. On the one hand, revolutions were thought to give birth to external wars by increasing uncertainty, heightening suspicions, and intensifying security competition among states.[110] On the other hand, as Skocpol and others argued, war, imperial ambition, and heated international competition among states played significant roles in precipitating social revolutions. The fiscal pressures created by war and the need to raise funds to support adventures abroad precipitated revolutionary crises. The enormous costs and burdens placed on civilian populations in order to fight wars abroad and to maintain empires was a significant grievance underpinning revolutions. Military defeat, war weariness, and declining morale during war played key roles in instigating instability. And the weakening of the state's repressive apparatus due to redeployment of military force to the war front was said to be a key condition for revolt.[111] Indeed, over much of the past century,

---

107. Tarrow 1998.
108. Skocpol 1979, 14. See also Lawson 2005; Lawson 2016; Gunitsky 2017.
109. Arendt 1965, 7.
110. Walt 1996.
111. Skocpol 1979.

there has been a statistically significant relationship between the number of battle deaths that a country experienced in external war and the outbreak of social revolutionary contention.[112] But as numerous studies have shown, inter-state warfare declined dramatically in the second half of the twentieth century, even while internal civil wars (often the product of revolution) multiplied.[113] The decline of major inter-state warfare from the 1950s onward severed the relationship between war and revolution and weakened one of the key structural conditions that underpinned social revolutions in the past.

The collapse of the Soviet Union, the breakdown of European communism, and the end of the Cold War were also central in altering patterns of revolutions around the world. They eliminated a major source of military and moral support for left-wing revolutionary movements and delegitimized Marxism-Leninism as a foundation for successful state-building. After 1945, the Soviet Union became the chief supplier of weapons and training to dozens of revolutionary movements, playing an important role in supporting attempted social revolutions in Asia, the Middle East, and Africa. Cold War competition increased the overall resources available to left-wing revolutionary movements. The collapse of the USSR not only brought an end to foreign support for left-wing movements and a decline in the appeal of left-wing ideologies. It also significantly weakened client states of the USSR and rendered them more vulnerable to revolutionary challenge.[114]

The subsequent emergence of a unipolar world order centered around American power was an important factor in fostering the growth of urban civic revolutions after the Cold War. For most of the Cold War, the United States assumed a counterrevolutionary position in world politics, seeking to undermine the spread of communism by shoring up local dictators and occasionally supporting right-wing anti-communist rebels. However, in the late 1970s the Carter administration shifted toward a new emphasis on human rights, and by the early 1980s the Reagan administration had embarked on an effort at democracy-promotion as part of its attempts to counter and roll back communism. In addition to providing moral support for dissident movements in the Soviet bloc, this included facilitating the resignation of dictators facing threats from democratizing mass movements from below in Latin America and the Philippines. With the collapse of European communism, America's democracy-promotion industry mushroomed, with over $700 million coming

112. Statistically significant at the .05 level, controlling for time dependence. Battle deaths were logged and lagged by one year. Colonies were excluded from the analysis.

113. Gleditsch et al. 2002; Sarkees, Wayman, and Singer 2003; Lacina, Gleditsch, and Russett 2006; Goldstein 2011; Pinker 2011.

114. Westad 2005.

to be spent annually by the late 1990s on promoting and consolidating democratic regimes.[115] Fueled by the ideological belief that democracy brought peace, prosperity, and stability, and no longer facing resistance from its superpower rival, in the 1990s and 2000s the United States launched a major effort to remake the world in its own image. As noted by Francis Fukuyama and Michael McFaul, "No country in the world has benefited more from the worldwide advance of democracy than the United States."[116]

But as progress toward democratization stalled and hybrid regimes multiplied, American democracy-promotion efforts began to spill over into encouragement of mobilized regime-change from below. Direct external financial and organizational aid from third-party countries or foreign NGOs was not a significant element in earlier third-wave democratizing revolutions such as the Portuguese Revolution, the "People Power" revolutions of East Asia, or the 1989 revolutions in eastern Europe. But in 1999, frustrated by the continuing carnage of the Balkan wars and the persistent grip on power of Serbian dictator Slobodan Milošević, the US turned toward actively aiding his overthrow by promoting electoral revolution. The American government spent over $41 million supporting anti-Milošević civil society groups such as Otpor—the student group that spearheaded the Serbian Bulldozer Revolution in 2000. The Clinton administration even erected a series of transmitters around the periphery of Serbia to provide alternative news coverage and established a special office in Budapest to coordinate assistance to Milošević's opponents. American NGOs played a similar role in the Rose Revolution in Georgia in 2003. The local Georgian branch of the Soros Foundation helped support Kmara (the Georgian version of Otpor) out of its $350,000 election support program, and Kmara and other opposition groups received significant financial and organizational aid from the National Democratic Institute. The United States spent $65 million promoting democracy in Ukraine in the years preceding the 2004 Orange Revolution—most of it channeled through NGOs such as Freedom House or the National Endowment for Democracy to Ukrainian NGOs and social movements that opposed the Kuchma regime.[117] In the larger scheme of things, these were not huge sums of money. But in resource-poor environments they provided oppositions with critical equipment, funds, and advice that helped tip the repression–disruption trade-off function in their direction.

A unipolar world dominated by the United States provided a conducive international opportunity structure for urban political entrepreneurs interested

115. Carothers 1999, 6–7.
116. Fukuyama and McFaul, 2007–8, 24.
117. Beissinger 2007.

in mobilizing populations against local autocrats, particularly when these autocrats were opposed to American interests.[118] Democracy-promotion and the politics of regime-change thus became closely fused. As Thomas Carothers explains,

> [A]lthough most external democracy activists may indeed be primarily interested in achieving free and fair elections, they also frequently hope that their efforts will increase the likelihood that autocrats will lose office. The motives of U.S. government agencies that fund (but do not specifically direct) many of the democracy groups are similarly complicated, ranging from the principled to the instrumental, depending on the country in question and the officials in charge. Not surprisingly, these subtleties are generally lost on the targets of democracy-promotion drives, who tend to view such efforts as concerted campaigns to oust them, instigated or at least backed by powerful Western governments, especially the United States.[119]

Eventually, a backlash materialized against democracy-promotion in many authoritarian regimes. In the wake of the color revolutions, Western NGOs began to be harassed or expelled in many authoritarian countries, restrictions were imposed on foreign funding of civil society groups, and greater limits were placed on political oppositions.[120] Many of the color revolutions were based on an "electoral model" that took advantage of the political opportunity presented by fraudulent elections in hybrid regimes to challenge them on the streets.[121] However, in the wake of the color revolutions, the growing repressiveness of threatened non-democracies and the imposition of restrictions on foreign aid to civil society groups greatly weakened the model.

The growth of urban and urban civic revolution in the post–Cold War period also strongly benefited from the heightened globalization of the late twentieth and twenty-first centuries. Giddens defined globalization as "the intensification of worldwide social relations which link distant localities in such a way that local happenings are shaped by events occurring many miles

---

118. Ritter (2015) points to the ways in which the liberal international order incentivized oppositions against authoritarian regimes. He argues that unarmed revolutions were more likely to succeed in cases in which authoritarian regimes were closely allied with Western democracies due to geopolitical pressure and the subtle influence of liberal discourse and human rights norms.
119. Carothers 2006, 61–62.
120. Carothers 2010, 64.
121. Bunce and Wolchik 2011.

away and vice versa."[122] Globalization is not new. But trade, travel, and communications intensified across the planet with the collapse of communism, the triumph of neoliberal economics, and the onset of the digital age.

Globalization in the late twentieth and early twenty-first centuries differed qualitatively from global connections of the past in three respects. First, the scope of global connections was far greater than during earlier periods, touching nearly everyone, penetrating remote areas, and encompassing multiple political, economic, social, cultural, demographic, and technological dimensions.[123] Second, the intensity of interactions across boundaries increased exponentially, as transnational relationships thickened and grew to become a normalized part of everyday life. Finally, in the late twentieth and early twenty-first centuries global connections came to function at accelerated speed, compressing time and space and mitigating the constraints upon both.[124] The instantaneous movement of capital and information across borders connected distant points on the planet in real time. Large-scale migration generated new transnational communities that complicated notions of territoriality and nationhood and altered the political field.[125] Globalization also greatly accelerated inequalities *within* states, becoming a significant factor conditioning economic grievance—even as it reduced inequalities *between* states.

All this profoundly affected revolutionary processes—particularly in cities. Because cities are globally connected through communication networks, trade, investment, government-to-government relations, and tourism,[126] urban revolts are better positioned than rural ones to take advantage of the external environment. Rural revolutionaries sometimes use porous state boundaries to hide from government repression or to acquire necessary weapons and materials from foreign sponsors. But urban revolts potentially have a much deeper connection with the outside world, given its immediate presence in cities. Cities have functioned as the main spatial sites for globalization, and globalization has facilitated the proliferation of urban revolutionary contention in multiple ways.

For one thing, uncontrolled global flows of capital, increasing levels of sovereign debt, and neoliberal economics precipitated economic and political crises that have at times become occasions for revolutionary challenges. In the past, external war was a major source of the fiscal crises that helped to trigger

---

122. Giddens 1990, 64.
123. United Nations Center for Human Settlements 2001, xxx.
124. Harvey 1990.
125. Appadurai 1996.
126. Sassen 2001.

social revolutions; today revolt is more likely to be connected with fiscal austerity measures in the face of excessive foreign debt or global economic crisis. The overthrow of Suharto in 1998 occurred in the wake of the 1997 Asian financial crisis, which brought about the collapse of the Indonesian currency and the imposition of an IMF structural adjustment program at the very time Suharto was running for re-election.[127] Massive foreign debt and an IMF austerity program limited the ability of the Argentinian state to respond to social needs, even while a banking and financial crisis in 2001 precipitated mass protests that ousted the regime of President Fernando de la Rúa.[128] In Madagascar, the unequal benefits of neoliberal economic growth became a grievance that helped fuel the overthrow of President Marc Ravalomanana in 2009, due to increased inequality, inflation, and the declining purchasing power of the lower and middle classes.[129] There is no consistent relationship between financial crisis and revolutionary contention. Only in about half of all instances of revolutionary contention around the world since 1900 has financial crisis played a role—including half of all urban civic revolutions. Financial crisis alone does not precipitate revolution, and urban civic revolts can occur under a variety of circumstances—financial crisis constituting one possible pathway. Nevertheless, financial stress has at times played an important role in helping to precipitate urban civic revolt, and compared to the past, financial crises became more common in the post–Cold War era due to globalization and the embracement of neoliberal development.[130]

Globalization also increased dependence on external trade, aid, and investment, providing foreign states with leverage. Ukraine's dependence on the outside world for energy and foreign aid became the context for an international tug-of-war during the Euromaidan Revolution of 2013–14. Russia heavily pressured Ukrainian president Viktor Yanukovych to crack down on protestors, threatening to raise gas prices to phenomenally high levels and to drive Ukraine into bankruptcy if he refused. When Yanukovych adopted a series of draconian measures at Russia's insistence, Europe and the United States threatened to cut off aid and impose trade sanctions. Greater foreign presence in urban centers has raised the visibility of urban oppositions and of acts of government repression against them, rendering it more difficult for states to quell rebellion

127. Pepinsky 2009.
128. Vilas 2006.
129. Maunganidze 2009.
130. Thus, of the sixty-eight countries covered by Reinhart and Rogoff (2009) in their data, periods of financial stress occurred in 35 percent of country-years during the first half of the twentieth century, in 39 percent of country-years during the Cold War, and 57 percent of country-years during the post–Cold War period.

without triggering a response from abroad. Urban revolutionaries today know that they are performing for a global audience, and this visibility is consciously used as a source of leverage on incumbent regimes. Many of the placards displayed at their protests are in English, the purpose being to influence international public opinion and generate pressure from foreign states on the protestors' government. Thanks to greater visibility, urban revolutionaries are better positioned than rural revolutionaries to leverage such pressures. The concentration of global trade, tourism, and investment in cities, meanwhile, renders these critical sources of government revenue vulnerable to disruption. All this tips the repression–disruption trade-off function further in favor of urban oppositions.

New communications technologies have also enabled émigré communities to remain in constant contact with their homelands. They have provided opportunities for diaspora groups to be directly involved in revolutionary processes from distant corners of the planet: to function as brokers of opposition information; to influence global media coverage of events; to lobby for international intervention; and to provide financial support to opposition movements. Take, for instance, the case of Iran. In the 1970s, when the Ayatollah Khomeini was in exile in Iraq, visitors would record his sermons on audiocassettes and smuggle them back into Iran, where they were distributed at bazaars and mosques. After Khomeini moved to Paris, two tape machines captured his every pronouncement; these recordings were then transmitted via landline telephone for re-recording in Iran and subsequent distribution.[131] Contrast this laborious and time-consuming process with the situation in Iran three decades later. Internet and satellite television broadcasts (some sponsored by foreign governments, others by émigré groups) had transformed the Iranian media landscape and the ability of diaspora groups to communicate directly with their homeland. As Marcus Michaelsen notes, "exile websites appeared even before the first online publications from within Iran."[132] As protest over falsified elections in 2009 escalated into violent clashes between protestors and the regime, the sizeable international media presence in Iran instantly relayed detailed stories and visual images around the world. The regime banned foreign press from the country in an attempt to control the flow of information. But the Iranian public could still rely on Iranian social media accounts shared by Iranian expatriates. When the shooting of twenty-six-year-old Neda Agha-Soltan at the hands of the authorities was captured by cellphone camera and posted on YouTube, it quickly became the iconic image of the uprising and

---

131. Rahaghi 2012.
132. Michaelsen 2015, 107–8.

was circulated on news networks around the world. The Iranian diaspora abroad engaged in numerous rallies pressuring their host governments to respond.[133]

Finally, globalization has enhanced processes of revolutionary diffusion—particularly, what scholars refer to as "non-relational" forms of diffusion in which mass communications function as a medium for inspiring action across spatially diverse contexts.[134] The rise of global television, the internet, and social media has enhanced the scope and speed of transnational diffusion.[135] Transnational waves of revolutionary contention have been growing more frequent over time,[136] brought on by the global intensification of communications and a growing sense of an interconnectedness across state boundaries formed by analogous institutions, histories, cultural affinities, or modes of domination. These similarities allow oppositions to read relevance into developments in spatially diverse contexts—and sometimes in locations far across the planet.[137] Cities in particular have been well positioned to take advantage of these processes, given the presence of denser communications networks. Controlling for the effect of time, urban revolutions are much more likely to occur within the context of a transnational revolutionary wave (a .65 probability) than rural revolutions (a .41 probability), and urban civic revolutions mostly occur within waves (a .82 probability).[138] These transnational waves have often been highly compact and have unfolded with startling speed.

Conclusion: The Structural Bases for Evolving Forms of Revolution

At the end of the twentieth and beginning of the twenty-first century, the frequency of revolutionary contention increased substantially, even while its forms and locations altered. Social revolutions became marginalized, while urban and urban civic revolutionary contention proliferated. What accounted for these patterns?

As I have argued, third-generation theorists of revolution were partially correct. The marginalization of social revolution in the post–Cold War period was in large part due to the diminution of many of the structural factors that third-generation scholars believed had fueled social revolutions in the first place: land

133. Alexanian 2011; Naghibi 2011; Rhoads and Chao 2009.
134. Givan, Roberts, and Soule 2010; Tarrow 2005.
135. Van Laer and Van Aelst 2010.
136. See Beck 2014.
137. Beissinger 2007.
138. All of these relationships are statistically significant at the .001 level.

inequality, rapid population growth, the political power of landed elites, external wars, and geopolitical competition. But what third-generation theorists failed to anticipate was that many of the processes that functioned to undermine the prospects for social revolution—massive movements of rural inhabitants to cities; land reform; increased agricultural productivity; declining female fertility; the shift of political power from landed elites to urban elites; the consolidation and proliferation of states; the diminishing role of external war in international affairs; the collapse of the Soviet Union; the rise of unipolar American power; globalization and the effects of neoliberalism—would also create conditions conducive to the multiplication of new forms of revolutionary contention centered in cities. These processes empowered new social forces in proximity to urban centers of power and commerce and facilitated collective action by concentrating diverse, well-resourced, and highly networked populations in increasingly populous urban areas. They connected oppositions transnationally and provided new opportunities for them to exert influence on their regimes from abroad. They created a communications environment favorable to visibility and scaling up, and an urban landscape vulnerable to disruption through massing large numbers in strategic and symbolic public spaces. Even while states were proliferating and consolidating, they grew increasingly vulnerable to a new repertoire of urban revolution. I turn now to examine the factors that structured the materialization of urban civic challenges and the extent to which they emerged in predictable patterns.

3

The Urban Civic Revolutionary Moment

> [W]e cannot predict revolutionary outcomes, only... revolutionary situations, and the factors we use to predict them are... the very defining elements of revolutionary situations! Tautology reigns.
>
> CHARLES TILLY, "THE BOURGEOIS GENTILSHOMMES OF REVOLUTIONARY THEORY" (1995)[1]

WHAT EVOKES the revolutionary moment? The question lies at the heart of much theorizing about revolutions. Two divergent positions stand out.

On one side are those who believe that the outbreak of revolutionary episodes is heavily determined. "Revolutions are not made," Skocpol approvingly quotes Wendell Phillips; "they come."[2] They arrive when all the necessary conditions align and sufficient pressure builds up, inexorably seeking release in a revolutionary explosion. As Goldstone put it,

> the causes of revolutions and major rebellions operate in ways that seem remarkably similar to the forces that build up to cause earthquakes.... [I]n the years before such a revolution or major rebellion, social pressures for change build. Yet the existing social and political structures for some time resist change (even though pressures and deformations may be visible). Suddenly, however, some response to the mounting pressure—a state bankruptcy, a regional rebellion—occurs which weakens that resistance (like a block breaking off along the fault). At that point, there is a sudden

---

1. Tilly 1995a, 140.
2. Skocpol 1979, 17.

release of the pent-up forces and a crumbling of the old social structures—a revolution or major rebellion.³

In this deeply structural and fatalistic view, events merely function as triggers for the release of built-up societal pressures, and had the specific event that triggered revolution never occurred, other events eventually would have transpired to cause revolution to materialize in any case. This of course is a counterfactual that can never be tested. But it lies at the heart of much structural thinking about revolution—particularly social revolution.

This determinist perspective stands in sharp contrast with the views of those who argue that the conditions under which revolutions emerge are inscrutable and indeterminate. Timur Kuran's work represents perhaps an extreme version of this view. He argued that individual preferences concerning regime-change are mostly falsified and concealed, so that revolutionary mobilizations burst upon us as a surprise, depending as they do on the interdependence of unknowable hidden preferences. Small shifts in hidden preferences—even arising from a single individual's interactions with a government bureaucrat—can "make all the difference between a massive uprising and a latent bandwagon that never takes off."⁴ For Kuran, the key analogy is not the earthquake but the wildfire. A single ephemeral spark causes society to burst into flames, with the indecipherable structure of hidden preferences constituting the fuel on which the wildfire burns.⁵

Both perspectives have their flaws. The determinist approach exaggerates the extent to which revolutions are made unavoidable by structural conditions. It views the emergence of revolution as automatic, merely awaiting the arrival of a trigger; but any trigger will do, so long as it places a regime under some degree of stress. If one potential trigger fails to produce revolution, another will inevitably succeed. The failure of revolution to materialize can only be ascribed to the absence of conducive structural conditions—not to proximate actions taken by regimes or oppositions. A trigger that generates stress but fails to produce revolution in the presence of structurally conducive conditions would be inexplicable within the determinist perspective.

At the same time, the outbreak of revolution is not as shapeless and impenetrable as Kuran would have us believe. He indicates that "anything that shifts private opinion"⁶ is capable of bringing about a revolutionary cascade. But he never reveals which conditions make the underlying structure of preferences

---

3. Goldstone 1991, 35.
4. Kuran 1997, 255.
5. Kuran 1997, 253–54.
6. Kuran 1997, 252.

more likely to produce revolution or the extent to which these factors conditcustomtion revolt. Are some societies more susceptible to revolution than others? Kuran does not tell us. He implies structure's presence, but fails to specify which structural conditions matter or to interrogate their sway. Once the fire ignites, the extent of its spread depends on an inscrutable structure of hidden preferences. As in the determinist perspective, actions taken by regimes and oppositions to contain the spread or to fan the flames have little part to play in the theory.

It may be that social revolutions do unfold like earthquakes—with a suddenness and fury that merely awaits a trigger due to the build-up of structural pressure.[7] But this is not the way that many urban civic revolutions have unfolded. If natural analogies are to be drawn, rather than earthquakes or wildfires, urban civic revolutions develop more like hurricanes. Hurricanes begin as tropical disturbances that form zones of low pressure. Under conditions of low vertical wind shear, interactive processes between the warm ocean surface and the upper atmosphere can transform a tropical disturbance into a heat engine that begins to assume a circular motion. But most tropical disturbances dissipate. Only one in eight ever strengthens and transforms into a tropical depression (the name meteorologists give to a tropical cyclone with below-gale-force winds). Tropical depressions that continue to strengthen can grow into tropical storms (roughly one out of every ten tropical depressions grows into a tropical storm). However, too strong a wind shear can rip these depressions and storms apart. In all, about eighty tropical storms form around the world every year. Only 60 percent of these ever achieve hurricane strength.[8] There are many points at which tropical disturbances might fail to develop into hurricanes, and most never do. Moreover, many hurricanes never reach land: they die at sea. Others slam into coastal regions, causing enormous havoc. There are also so-called "bomb" cyclones that form suddenly—seemingly out of nowhere—when air near the earth's surface rises quickly and triggers a sharp drop in barometric pressure, setting off intense wind spirals that can take on the characteristics of hurricanes. While there is a seeming randomness to the emergence and trajectory of each storm, hurricanes are clearly structured by oceanic and atmospheric conditions, and over the long run distinct patterns have emerged in their formation and pathways. Indeed, hurricanes have been growing more frequent over time (particularly in the Atlantic Basin) due to the global warming of oceans, much as revolutions have been growing more

---

7. However, in a number of cases (particularly rural social revolutions) the emergence of social revolutionary contention was not sudden but protracted.

8. Montgomery and Farrell 1993.

frequent as the world urbanizes. Hurricane prediction today is carried out by extensive satellite observation and the world's most powerful computers. Yet there is still great uncertainty over whether a tropical disturbance will evolve into a hurricane, and once a hurricane emerges, what its intensity and trajectory will be.

This combination of structural conduciveness and uncertain development is akin to how urban civic revolutionary contention emerges. Urban civic revolutions are usually not explosions in response to a trigger, or wildfires that burst into flames under unknowable conditions. They develop—often tentatively and with uncertainty, but in most cases in places where we would expect them to be. Occasionally they materialize in places we would not expect them to be. Sometimes they fail to develop altogether—even in the presence of conducive structural conditions and potential triggers.

In this chapter, I adopt a probabilistic approach to thinking about the onset of urban civic revolutionary contention. The advantages of a probabilistic approach lie in its ability to contemplate the universe of cases and to integrate structure and agency into a single framework. The study of revolutions has been dominated by Millian inference, which endeavors to identify a set of necessary conditions based on a detailed comparison of a small number of cases. These have often been paradigmatic cases chosen for their historical importance; thus, many of the same cases have received exaggerated attention.[9] But most social phenomena occur probabilistically. They are facilitated and constrained, not dictated, by structure.[10] As Mill himself recognized, the principal difficulty in applying his method of agreement and difference is "the extensive and constant reaction of the effects upon their causes," rendering politics "a subject matter whose properties are changeable."[11] The actions of regimes or oppositions can undermine or expedite the outbreak of urban civic revolutionary contention: they constitute the wind shear that can transform a tropical disturbance into a raging heat engine or rip it apart.

A probabilistic approach provides for a more realistic understanding of the urban civic revolutionary moment. In a probabilistic structural approach, there is no exclusive set of conditions that must be present to produce revolutionary contention—only conditions that make revolutionary onset more or less likely to materialize. The conditions associated with revolutionary onset can occur in a variety of combinations, and the weakness of any one condition

---

9. Goldstone 2003; Beck 2018.
10. Humphreys 2014.
11. Mill 1950, 344. For a call to integrate both structure and agency into the study of revolution, see Ritter 2015, 16.

does not preclude the outbreak of revolution in the presence of others. In a probabilistic approach, the probability of revolutionary onset and the actual materialization of revolutionary onset in any particular case are two different things. Because the emergence of revolutionary contention involves not just structural conditions and triggering events, but agency as well, revolution might not materialize even when the risk is high (through, for example, a collective action failure on the part of oppositions, or because a government preempts it through reform). Revolution could even materialize when the risk—judging by the conditions associated with most other cases—is low (for instance, due to a provocative act of a government, or through processes of diffusion).[12] By the law of averages, these outcomes should not happen in most cases—otherwise a structural model is capable of explaining little. But in a probabilistic approach, structural conditions translate into chance and risk, not directly into behavior. It is only through human action that chance and risk become reality. Of course, when we are talking about a rare event like revolution, the risk of occurrence is normally quite low. But at certain times and under certain conditions, the risk of even such a rare event as a revolution breaking out increases well above the normal.

In this chapter, I explore the structural factors associated with the onset of urban civic revolutions and the limits of their explanatory power.[13] Skocpol argued that no universal theory of the causes of revolution is possible, simply because of the diversity of purposes to which revolution has been put, the varied social forces involved, and the changing world-historical circumstances under which revolutions have occurred.[14] Indeed, as I will show, the factors that map onto the outbreak of urban civic revolutionary contention do not map onto the outbreak of social revolutionary contention. Nor are these conditions associated with the outbreak of other types of revolutions—or even other forms of political instability such as military coups. Social revolutions represented a crisis of the social order. They attacked class inequalities and were products of agrarian societies dominated by landed elites. By contrast, urban civic revolutions represent a crisis of the political order. They are revolts against predatory and repressive government and generally occur under corrupt authoritarian regimes whose leaders have been in power for a long time. As opposed to social revolutions, which predominantly broke out in low-income countries and benefited from the Cold War international order, urban

---

12. On the latter, see Weyland 2009.
13. For an attempt to test the limits of structural models of nonviolent campaigns, see Chenoweth and Ulfelder 2015.
14. Skocpol 1979, 288.

civic revolutions have tended to occur in lower middle- and middle-income countries that lacked large oil resources and faced a globalized and unipolar international environment.

I develop a probabilistic model that reflects these conditions and is able to identify correctly above-average risk for the onset of urban civic revolutionary contention in most instances in which it actually occurred. But even in the most structurally determined situation, regimes and oppositions still have to make something out of the structural conditions that they face. After developing the probabilistic structural model, I use it to generate predictions of the risk of outbreak of urban civic revolutionary contention for specific cases, assessing the extent to which these cases actually conformed to the predictions of the model and why some cases deviated from them. It is here that Mill's warning about the challenges that human agency poses to structural theorizing becomes particularly relevant. As we will see, sometimes a regime under heightened structural risk (according to the factors associated with most urban civic revolutions) acted to prevent a revolutionary crisis from emerging. There were also times when a regime that was not under significant structural risk acted in such a way as to incite revolutionary challenge where it would otherwise have been unlikely to occur. Sometimes oppositions failed to take advantage of propitious structural conditions for urban civic revolt because they were divided and incapable of acting. And sometimes potential triggers failed to evoke revolution, even in structurally conducive circumstances. In short, by looking at revolution probabilistically and using that knowledge as a baseline for a deepened analysis of individual cases, we gain greater purchase on the ways in which structure and agency conspire to produce revolutionary moments.

A Probabilistic Model of Urban Civic Revolutionary Contention

Societies vulnerable to urban civic contention differ substantially from those vulnerable to social revolutions. This is most clearly evident in the realm of politics. The outbreak of urban civic revolutions is highly sensitive to the features of political regimes. Social revolutionary contention, by contrast, is not. As Figure 3.1 shows, social revolutionary contention bore no consistent relationship with regime openness or closedness. Social revolutionary episodes appeared at times in highly autocratic regimes (Russia in 1905, Cuba in 1956, and Nicaragua in 1978), in more open non-democratic regimes (Germany in 1918, the Philippines in 1946, and Nepal in 1996), and even in lower-quality democracies (Finland in 1918, India in 1967, and Sri Lanka in 1971). By contrast, urban civic contention has been strongly related to closed regimes, with the most

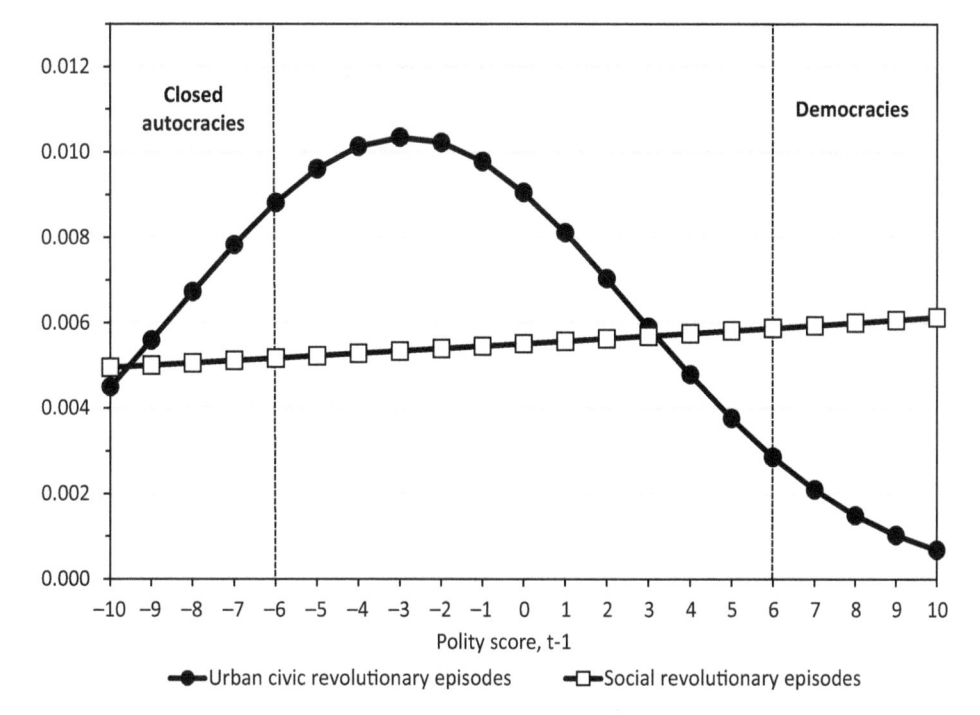

FIGURE 3.1. The probability of onset of urban civic and social revolutionary episodes, by Polity score (t−1). Complementary log-log panel model across 159 independent states from 1900 to 2014 (11,328 country-years), controlling for time dependence. Average marginal predictions, with confidence intervals omitted for readability.

vulnerable regimes centered over the autocratic end of the Polity scale (for example, the Philippines in 1986, Tunisia in 2010, and Egypt in 2011).[15] Even some highly closed autocracies (East Germany in 1989, Myanmar in 2007, and Iran in 2011) have been vulnerable to urban civic revolutionary contention—at least when compared with democracies and more open non-democracies.

Other regime features also affect the outbreak of urban civic revolutionary challenges. A number of studies have argued that in authoritarian regimes, the absence of parties or legislatures that can monitor potential opposition or engage in forms of power-sharing increases the likelihood of mass rebellion.[16] Military regimes tend to be short-lived in large part because they do not have such institutions, lack mass legitimation, and are ill suited

---

15. Statistically significant at the .01 level.
16. Gandhi and Przeworski 2006; Boix and Svolik 2013.

to running the machinery of the state.[17] Others argue that revolutionary situations are more likely to materialize in personalist regimes, as these regimes have difficulty creating coherent institutions, managing leadership succession, and preventing defections from ruling coalitions.[18] The Arab Spring also suggested to some that monarchies were less vulnerable to mass revolt than republican forms of government, due to their ability to co-opt and deflect demands for change.[19]

For social revolutions, these distinctions do not seem to matter: data on authoritarian regime-types (party, military, monarchical, and personalist) produced by Geddes, Wright, and Frantz[20] show that none of these regime-types had a consistent relationship with the onset of social revolutionary episodes. They are, however, strongly related to urban civic revolutionary contention. Military, personalist, and party non-democratic regimes had positive and statistically significant relationships with the onset of urban civic contention—with military and personalist regimes particularly vulnerable.[21] Monarchies, by contrast, have been the least vulnerable to outbreaks of urban civic contention relative to other non-democracies (and not statistically different from democracies).[22]

Some scholars maintain that the risk of mass challenges increases as a regime ages, particularly as personalism and corruption set in.[23] As Figure 3.2 shows, there is no consistent relationship between leader longevity and the outbreak of social revolutionary contention. There is, however, a strong and statistically significant relationship between how long an incumbent leader has been in power and the risk of experiencing an urban civic episode.[24] The risk particularly grows after fifteen years in office, continuing to rise in subsequent years (though is obviously limited by the physical mortality of leaders).

17. Magaloni 2008.
18. Goodwin 2001; Geddes, Wright, and Frantz 2014; Wright and Escribà-Folch 2012.
19. Yom and Gause 2012.
20. Geddes, Wright, and Frantz 2014.
21. Based on a complementary log-log panel model across 148 independent states from 1946–2010 (7,699 country-years), with cluster-robust standard errors and controlling for time dependence. Statistically significant at the .001 level for military and personalist regimes and at the .01 level for party regimes.
22. As Jack Goldstone rightly points out (personal communication), this finding could be time-dependent, as monarchy as a form of government had grown much rarer by the time urban civic revolutions proliferated. In the nineteenth and early twentieth centuries, when monarchies were the predominant form of government, they were highly vulnerable to social and republican revolutions.
23. Ulfelder 2005. For a contrary view, see Svolik 2012.
24. Statistically significant at the .001 level, controlling for time dependence and using cluster-robust standard errors.

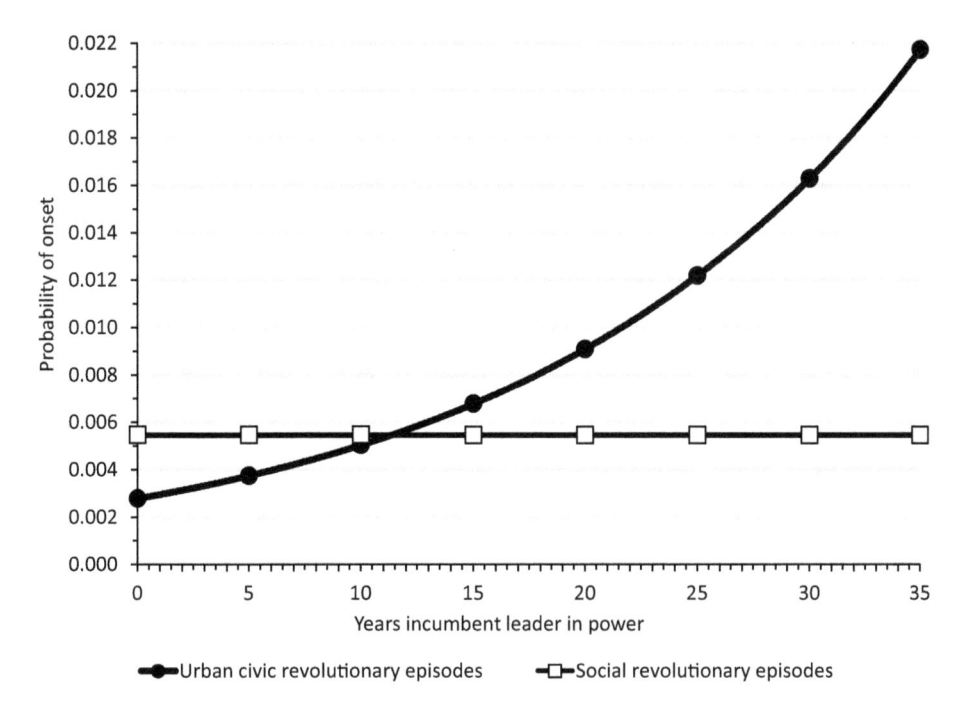

FIGURE 3.2. The probability of onset of urban civic and social revolutionary episodes, by longevity of incumbent leader in power. Complementary log-log panel model across 164 independent states from 1900 to 2014 (11,661 country-years), controlling for time dependence. Average marginal predictions, with confidence intervals omitted for readability.

Cases such as Didier Ratsiraka in Madagascar (in power for sixteen years before being overthrown by mass revolt in 1991), Mathieu Kérékou in Benin (in power for seventeen years before the Beninese Revolution in 1989), Erich Honecker in East Germany (in power for eighteen years before the East German Revolution in 1989), Ferdinand Marcos in the Philippines (in power for twenty-one years before the People Power Revolution in 1986), Hosni Mubarak in Egypt (in power for thirty years at the time of the Egyptian Revolution in 2011), and Suharto in Indonesia (in power for thirty-two years before succumbing to revolution in 1998) exemplify the pattern.

Regime corruption is also much more important as a factor conditioning the onset of urban civic revolutions than the onset of social revolutionary contention. According to V-Dem's executive corruption measure (on a scale from 0 to 1, with a global mean of .47 from 1900 to 2014),[25] executive corruption in countries experiencing urban civic contention was significantly higher on

25. See Coppedge et al. 2016.

average (.68) than in countries experiencing social revolutionary contention (.51).[26] Executive corruption is strongly related to the outbreak of urban civic revolutionary contention,[27] but there is no statistically significant relationship between executive corruption and the outbreak of social revolutionary contention. The top 10 percent of regimes in terms of executive corruption have had almost six times the risk of experiencing an urban civic episode in any given year compared to regimes in the bottom 10 percent. Examples of highly corrupt regimes that experienced urban civic revolutionary contention include the Philippines in 1986 (.90 on the V-Dem scale), Indonesia in 1998 (.94) Georgia in 2003 (.86), Ukraine in 2004 (.84) and 2013 (.83), Armenia in 2008 (.82), Egypt in 2011 (.93), and Venezuela in 2014 (.94).

Social revolutions revolved around class antagonisms and were associated with poverty and underdevelopment. Indeed, as Figure 3.3 shows, social revolutionary contention primarily broke out in low-income countries with a GDP per capita of less than $2,000 (in constant 1990 international dollars)—examples being Russia in 1905 ($1,348) and in 1917 ($1,517), China in 1927 ($560), and Nepal in 1996 ($919). By contrast, lower middle- and middle-income countries have been at greatest risk of experiencing urban civic revolt—specifically countries with a GDP per capita between $4,000 and $9,000 such as in South Korea in 1987 ($6,263), Tunisia in 2010 ($6,244), Egypt ($4,267) in 2011, and Ukraine in 2013 ($4,798).[28]

A number of studies have also identified economic contraction and fiscal austerity as key conditions leading to revolution. Economic contraction fosters grievances among affected groups and undermines the ability of governments to deliver expected services and co-opt opposition, while economic growth diminishes a sense of grievance and provides resources for governments to distribute, deflecting revolutionary sentiment.[29] At the same time, economic growth could facilitate the emergence of new social forces capable of challenging established elites. As Figure 3.4 shows, there was a sharply negative relationship (significant at the .001 level) between economic growth in the year prior to revolutionary onset and the probability of onset of a social revolutionary episode. The same, however, does not hold for urban civic episodes, for which the association between economic growth and the probability of

---

26. Statistically significant at the .001 level in a two-tailed t-test (t = -3.47, with 121 degrees of freedom).

27. Statistically significant at the .001 level, controlling for time dependence and using cluster-robust standard errors.

28. The relationship is linear for social revolutions (significant at the .05 level) and quadratic for urban civic episodes (significant at the .01 level).

29. Foran 2005; Ponticelli and Voth 2012; Knutsen 2014. See also Davies 1962; Gurr 1970.

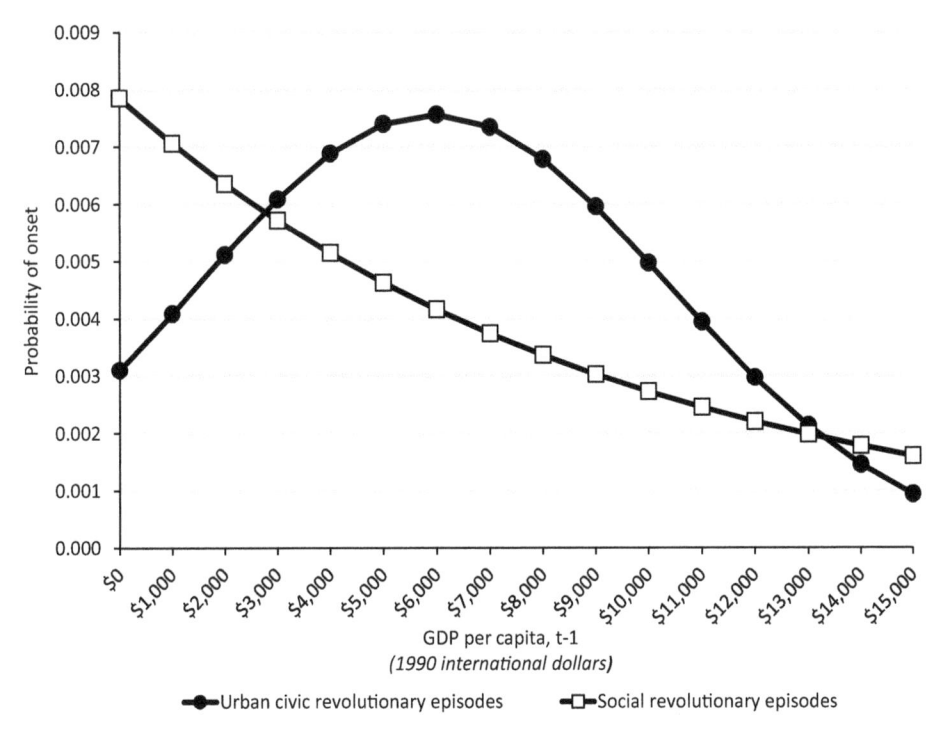

FIGURE 3.3. The probability of onset of urban civic and social revolutionary episodes, by GDP per capita (t−1). Complementary log-log panel model across 164 independent states from 1900 to 2014 (11,042 country-years), controlling for time dependence. Average marginal predictions, with confidence intervals omitted for readability.

onset is weakly positive but more or less flat, with the risk of revolt marginally changing as economic growth increases or decreases.[30]

The weakly positive relationship between economic growth and the onset of urban civic episodes reflects a great deal of heterogeneity. A variety of pathways of growth and contraction can lead to urban civic contention. Neoliberal development fostered the emergence of the new urban middle classes that have played a central role in organizing and participating in urban civic revolutions. In cases like the South Korean June Uprising in 1987, the Tiananmen Uprising in China in 1989, the Rose Revolution in Georgia in 2003, and the Orange Revolution in Ukraine in 2004, urban civic episodes developed in the wake of significant positive economic growth, as emergent middle classes

---

30. These relationships also hold using patterns of economic growth during the three years prior to onset.

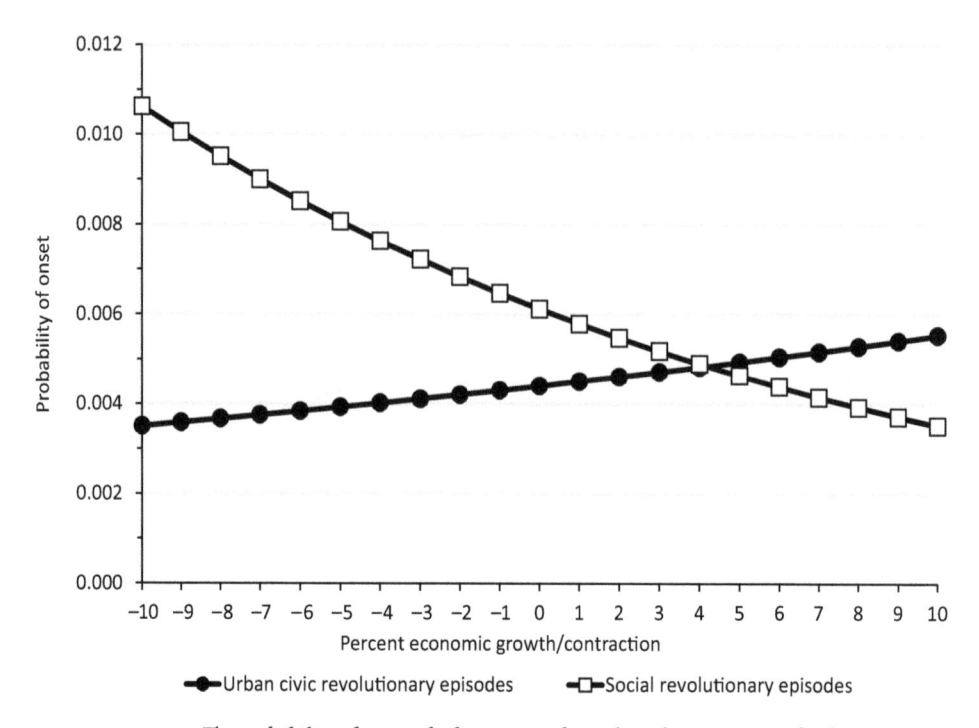

FIGURE 3.4. The probability of onset of urban civic and social revolutionary episodes, by rates of economic growth (t−1). Complementary log-log panel model across 164 independent states from 1900 to 2014 (10,980 country-years), controlling for time dependence. Average marginal predictions, with confidence intervals omitted for readability.

came to assert themselves in the political sphere against corrupt and repressive governments. But in other cases, neoliberal development led to increased societal inequalities and generated pressures on states for cutbacks in subsidies and public services. In a number of instances, urban civic contention broke out in the wake of significant economic contraction (the People Power Revolution in the Philippines in 1986, the Bulldozer Revolution in Serbia in 2000, and the 2014 protests in Venezuela aimed at ousting the regime of Nicolás Maduro) or in a context of declining employment opportunities, price increases on food or fuel, currency reforms, or cutbacks in state services forced by international indebtedness (the 8888 Uprising in Myanmar in 1988, the Beninese Revolution in 1989, the Indonesian Revolution in 1998, and the Tunisian Revolution in 2011).

On the basis of these relationships, I developed a multivariate statistical model for identifying the degree of structural risk for urban civic contention that countries experienced in a particular year. In addition to the degree of political openness or closedness of a regime, non-democratic regime-type, the number of years in which the incumbent leader had been in power, executive corruption, levels of development, and economic growth and contraction, I included variables for population size, oil production, and post–Cold War temporal location. A country's population size has long been shown in cross-national research to be positively related to contentious action.[31] The reasons have never been entirely transparent, but could reside in critical mass theory, which posits that population size facilitates mobilization by increasing the likelihood that a sufficient number of potential participants might have the requisite time, resources, and motivation to participate.[32] In the civil war literature, oil wealth has often been linked to rebellion through its capacity to stir regional separatism or facilitate easy enrichment among rebel groups.[33] But the rents collected from oil wealth can also help to prevent rebellion by funding the establishment of more effective military and police forces and providing resources to governments for buying off elites and populations.[34] Finally, as we saw in chapter 2, the post–Cold War international context strongly affected the incidence of urban civic revolutions. I included a dummy variable covering these years.[35]

A variety of models were estimated for both complete-case and multiple-imputation samples, as reported in Table 3.1.[36] As the table shows, all of the bivariate relationships found earlier to be associated with urban civic revolutionary contention held true when controlled for the influence of other factors, when subject to different methods of estimation, and when analyzing the twenty samples generated through multiple imputation. Middle-income nondemocracies with repressive, highly corrupt regimes whose leaders had been in power for a long time were particularly vulnerable to urban civic revolt, especially in the post–Cold War period (Model 4). Economic growth and

---

31. See, for instance, Hibbs 1973, 25. As is standard, I used the natural log of population.

32. Marwell and Oliver 1993. As applied to revolutions, see Kurzman 1996.

33. Fearon and Laitin 2003; Collier and Hoeffler 2004; Lujala, Gleditsch, and Gilmore 2005; Ross 2006.

34. Ross 2001; Haber and Menaldo 2011; Wright, Frantz, and Geddes 2015. I use the log of oil production to measure the extent to which a state generated oil revenues.

35. The inclusion of a dummy variable for the post–Cold War period obviated the need for further controls for time dependence. Not only were other time variables statistically insignificant when included with the post–Cold War dummy, but a likelihood ratio test (chi2(3) = 1.56, p =.67) demonstrated that their inclusion exercised no substantive effect on the coefficients of other variables.

36. See Appendix 4B for further details on the models used and on the multiple-imputation samples. I confined the analysis to independent states, as several key variables made no substantive sense in instances of colonial or foreign occupation or for territories that were part of another independent state.

TABLE 3.1. A probabilistic model of the onset of urban civic revolutionary contention[a]

	Discrete-time panel failure model[b,c]				Pooled models[b]		Multiple-imputation[f]	
	Model 1	Model 2	Model 3	Model 4	Cloglog[d]	Penalized[e]	Model 4	Penalized[e]
Ln (population), t–1	1.254 (2.46)*	1.244 (1.97)*	1.508 (4.23)***	1.519 (4.34)***	1.519 (3.87)***	1.524 (3.82)***	1.532 (4.73)***	1.534 (4.13)***
GDP per cap. ($ thousands), t–1	1.462 (3.44)***	1.436 (2.93)**	1.806 (4.65)***	1.824 (4.68)***	1.824 (4.32)***	1.745 (3.68)***	1.838 (4.71)***	1.761 (3.75)***
GDP per cap. ($ thousands squared), t–1	0.977 (–3.12)**	0.977 (–3.09)**	0.968 (–3.68)***	0.967 (–3.69)***	0.967 (–3.50)***	0.972 (–2.43)*	0.967 (–3.67)***	0.971 (–2.48)*
GDP growth, t–1	1.016 (1.59)		1.012 (0.81)					
Polity score, t–1	0.912 (–3.21)**		0.927 (–2.26)*	0.927 (–2.29)*	0.927 (–2.29)*	0.929 (–2.52)*	0.927 (–2.34)*	0.928 (–2.55)*
Polity score, t–1 (squared)	0.983 (–3.22)**		0.984 (–2.87)**	0.984 (–2.88)**	0.984 (–3.04)**	0.985 (–2.75)**	0.985 (–2.79)**	0.985 (–2.66)**
Party non-democracy, t–1		3.313 (2.13)*						
Military non-democracy, t–1		15.263 (4.53)***						
Monarchist non-democracy, t–1		2.727 (0.79)						
Personalist non-democracy, t–1		7.233 (3.64)***						

Years incumbent in power			1.033 (2.62)**	1.033 (2.67)**	1.033 (2.78)**	1.035 (2.46)*	1.035 (2.94)**	1.037 (2.68)**
Exec. corruption, t−1			5.073 (1.88)+	5.164 (1.92)+	5.164 (2.10)*	4.843 (2.36)*	5.224 (1.97)*	4.916 (2.39)*
Ln (oil production), t−1			0.879 (−4.42)***	0.878 (−4.41)***	0.878 (−3.84)***	0.879 (−3.52)***	0.877 (−4.48)***	0.878 (−3.59)***
Post–Cold War era	8.778 (5.28)***	7.823 (5.23)***	6.912 (4.38)***	6.900 (4.40)***	6.900 (4.58)***	6.524 (4.46)***	7.613 (4.72)***	7.194 (4.71)***
n	10611	7690	10494	10516	10516	10516	11742	11742
Number of countries	159	148	157	157	n.a.	n.a.	164	n.a.
Number of urban civic episodes	50	40	50	50	50	50	51	51
Log likelihood/penalized log likelihood	−273.7069	−215.6963	−263.4809	−263.6311	−263.631	−233.878	n.a.	n.a.
Wald chi-square/F-test[g]	94.29***	145.52***	83.36***	96.48***	74.72***	81.39***	11.60***	9.67***
Sigma_u	0.3360411	0.2431044	0.004072	0.0042712	n.a.	n.a.	0.006245	n.a.
Rho	0.0642393	0.0346823	0.0000101	0.0000111	n.a.	n.a.	0.000237	n.a.
Likeliood ratio test, rho = 0 [chibar²(1)]	0.07	0.01	0.00004	0.03	n.a.	n.a.	n.a.	n.a.
BIC on common sample (n = 10,494)	630.1353	n.a.	638.0646	629.0746	619.816	560.3099	n.a.	n.a.
AIC on common sample (n = 10,494)	564.8082	n.a.	550.9618	549.2305	547.2304	487.7243	n.a.	n.a.

(*Continued*)

TABLE 3.1. (*continued*)

	Discrete-time panel failure model[b,c]				Pooled models[b]		Multiple-imputation[f]	
	Model 1	Model 2	Model 3	Model 4	Cloglog[d]	Penalized[e]	Model 4	Penalized[e]
True positive rate (correctly predicted above-avg. risk)	.780	.775	.760	.760	.760	.800	0.765	0.843
False positive rate (falsely predicted above-avg. risk)	.256	.278	.234	.237	.237	.256	0.231	0.245
Area under the ROC curve	0.841	0.845	.856	0.857	0.857	0.856	0.866	0.865
Quadrature test	passed	passed	passed[h]	passed[h]	n.a.	n.a.	n.a.	n.a.

[a]Exponentiated coefficients, with z-scores in parentheses. Independent states only. [b]Complete case analysis. [c]Complementary log-log (discrete-time failure) random-effects model, with robust standard errors (complete cases only). [d]Pooled complementary log-log (discrete-time failure) model, with cluster-robust standard errors. [e]Pooled model using Firth penalized logistic regression. [f]Based on twenty imputed data sets using predictive mean matching (independent states only). [g]The multiple-imputation estimates produced an F-test rather than a Wald chi-square test. [h]Model estimated with 22 integration points rather than the default of 12.

+ $p < 0.10$, * $p < 0.05$, ** $p < 0.01$, *** $p < 0.001$

contraction were only marginally related to the outbreak of urban civic revolutionary contention (Models 1 and 3), and in a mildly positive direction. Military and personalist non-democracies were particularly vulnerable to urban civic revolutionary outbreaks, relative to monarchies and democracies, with party-based non-democracies subject to some degree of risk as well (Model 2). Like most other forms of contentious action, urban civic revolts were positively associated with a country's population size.[37] Oil production, while not related to revolutionary contention on its own, had a strongly negative effect on the outbreak of urban civic revolutionary contention when controlling for the effects population size, economic development, and regime-type (Models 3 and 4). And as expected, controlling for other factors, urban civic contention was much more likely to occur during the post–Cold War period than at other periods over the past century (Models 3 and 4).

I subjected the model to a large number of robustness tests to ensure its consistency and reliability. These tests are reported in Appendix 4B. The model proved robust to several methods of estimation, various combinations of variables and the inclusion and exclusion of each variable, both complete-case and multiple-imputation samples, the inclusion and exclusion of each country in the sample, regional fixed-effects, and the inclusion of eleven other variables that logically and theoretically might have been related to the onset of urban civic revolutionary contention but were not.[38]

As a test against the possibility that the model was simply a proxy for the conditions that cause all forms of political instability and was not specific to urban civic revolutionary contention, I used the multiple-imputation samples to test the same set of factors associated with urban civic contention on the onset of all revolutionary episodes, rural revolutionary episodes, all urban revolutionary episodes, social revolutionary episodes, other revolutionary episodes, and attempted military coups (The results are reported in Table 3.2).[39] These tests demonstrate that the factors associated with the onset of urban civic revolutionary contention map poorly onto these other forms of

---

37. The substantive effects, however, are small, with the risk of urban civic contention roughly doubling as a country's population increases from three million to a hundred million.

38. These were: military spending per soldier, military personnel per thousand population; average years of schooling; levels of urbanization; population density; youth as a proportion of the larger population; nominal trade as percentage of nominal GDP; the logged dollar exchange rate; the presence of financial crisis on the eve of revolution; child mortality under the age of five; and the age of the incumbent leader. None of these variables demonstrated a consistent relationship with the onset of urban civic revolt. Details can be found in Appendix 4B.

39. For these tests, I dropped the squared term for GDP per capita and included economic growth so as to better compare relationships across episode types.

TABLE 3.2. A comparison of factors associated with the onset of revolutionary contention and military coup attempts[a,b]

	All episodes	Rural	Urban	Social	Urban civic	All others	Coup attempts[c]
Ln (population), t–1	1.419 (7.32)***	1.401 (5.75)***	1.360 (4.42)***	1.430 (4.04)***	1.473 (3.79)***	1.384 (5.95)***	0.871 (–2.01)*
GDP per cap. ($ thousands), t–1	0.960 (–1.42)	0.693 (–3.54)***	1.049 (1.94)+	0.911 (–1.69)+	1.095 (2.42)*	0.89 (–2.20)*	0.871 (–2.73)**
GDP growth, t–1	0.974 (–3.15)**	0.967 (–3.41)***	0.989 (–0.92)	0.945 (–4.42)***	1.026 (2.17)*	0.978 (–1.86)+	0.983 (–1.89)+
Polity score, t–1	0.980 (–1.31)	1.006 (0.29)	0.961 (–1.77)+	1.043 (1.72)+	0.919 (–2.22)*	0.977 (–1.21)	0.965 (–2.32)*
Polity score, t–1 (squared)	0.990 (–3.81)***	0.997 (–0.98)	0.984 (–3.96)***	0.994 (–1.22)	0.985 (–2.51)*	0.990 (–2.66)**	0.988 (–4.74)***
Years incumbent in power	1.009 (1.30)	0.989 (–0.77)	1.023 (2.53)*	1.008 (0.54)	1.036 (2.78)**	0.991 (–0.66)	0.844 (–6.06)***
Exec. corruption, t–1	2.198 (2.69)**	2.318 (2.19)*	1.972 (1.52)	1.876 (1.29)	4.257 (1.72)+	2.198 (2.19)*	2.519 (2.45)*
Ln (oil production), t–1	0.991 (–0.50)	1.03 (1.09)	0.985 (–0.56)	1.028 (0.67)	0.924 (–2.43)*	1.014 (0.58)	1.06 (2.48)*

Post–Cold War era	1.009 (0.06)	0.749 (−1.65)+	1.432 (1.44)	0.078 (−5.01)***	8.512 (4.91)***	1.186 (0.97)	0.508 (−4.43)***
n	11742	11742	11742	11742	11742	11742	8934
Number of countries	164	164	164	164	164	164	163
Number of episodes	269	137	135	65	50	148	397
F-test	20.35***	14.77***	8.55***	9.82***	8.40***	12.32***	23.31***
Sigma_u	0.306816	0.270399	0.564936	0.315770	0.461103	0.334336	0.784445
Rho	0.054130	0.042557	0.162494	0.057153	0.114460	0.063630	0.272246

[a]Complementary log-log random-effects panel model, with cluster-robust standard errors (exponentiated coefficients, with t-statistics in parentheses). [b]Multiple imputation based on twenty imputed samples using predictive mean matching (independent states only). [c]Coup attempts cover the years 1946–2014 only.

+ $p < 0.10$, * $p < 0.05$, ** $p < 0.01$, *** $p < 0.001$

regime-change—a powerful warning to those who would attempt to develop a generic model of political instability or of revolutions more generally.

Like other forms of revolutionary contention, but unlike military coups (which occur more frequently in less populated countries), urban civic revolutions are positively related to population size. But whereas GDP per capita is negatively associated with the outbreak of other forms of revolutionary contention and military coups,[40] it is positively associated with the onset of urban civic revolutionary contention (and marginally related to all urban revolutionary episodes).[41] Lower economic growth is associated with revolutionary contention more generally (especially, rural and social revolutionary contention) and marginally related to attempted military coups.[42] But as noted earlier, the risk of urban civic revolutionary contention was positively related to economic growth. Military coups and other types of revolutionary episodes are distributed roughly across the Polity scale, with mixed regimes somewhat more vulnerable,[43] and Polity scores have no systematic relationship with the onset of social or rural revolutionary contention. Urban civic revolutionary episodes, however, tend to occur among regimes that are concentrated in the more autocratic portion of the Polity scale. The outbreak of social revolutionary and other types of revolutionary contention had no connection with incumbent leader longevity, and coup attempts have been more likely in countries where the leader has been in power for a shorter period of time. Urban civic revolutionary episodes, on the other hand, have been much more likely to occur in regimes in which the leader has been in office for a long time.[44] Oil production is positively related to coup attempts,[45] and has no relationship with the onset of social revolution or other forms of revolutionary contention; but it is negatively associated with the risk of urban civic contention. A number of forms of instability have some connection with regime corruption (less so, social revolutionary contention). But this relationship was twice as strong for urban civic revolutions as for other forms of regime-change. And unlike

40. For social revolutionary contention, the sign is negative but statistically insignificant. However, as noted in Figure 3.3, the bivariate relationship is negative and statistically significant. On the relationship between poverty and military coups, see Londregan and Poole 1990, 151.

41. When urban civic episodes are excluded, urban episodes are not related to GDP per capita.

42. For other studies that have identified an association between low economic growth and coups, see Collier and Hoeffler 2005; Kim 2016.

43. See, for instance, Powell 2012.

44. When urban civic episodes are excluded, leader longevity is not related to urban episodes.

45. For similar findings in other studies, see Collier and Hoeffler 2005; Mbaku 1994.

other forms of political instability, urban civic revolutions have been concentrated in the post–Cold War period.

In short, there is solid evidence that Skocpol was right: a general causal theory of revolution that could cover all its varieties across historical time is not possible, given that the structural conditions associated with one type of revolution differ sharply from those associated with others. The onset of urban civic revolutionary contention is associated with structural conditions significantly different from those linked with the onset of social revolutions, other types of revolutions, or military coups—a strong rationale for considering urban civic revolutions a distinct revolutionary form.

Illustrations of Correctly Predicted Cases

In the most accurate positive-predictive model in Table 3.1 (the pooled penalized model using multiple imputation), the variables noted earlier (population size, levels of economic development, the degree of political openness, the longevity in office of the incumbent leader, executive corruption, levels of oil production, and temporal location in the post–Cold War international order) correctly identify an above-average risk of revolt for 84 percent (forty-three out of fifty-one) of the country-years in which urban civic revolutionary episodes actually did break out. If the sample is restricted to the post–Cold War years alone (when urban civic episodes were more likely to occur), and the average risk for all states during this period is used to assess performance, the model correctly identifies above-average risk for 82 percent of cases (thirty-six out of forty-four). For a political phenomenon that has been labeled by some as fundamentally unpredictable, the ability to identify heightened risk in more than four-fifths of the cases in which revolution actually occurred is a relatively good rate of accuracy. Almost all of the best-known urban civic episodes since the 1980s are properly identified by the model as experiencing a heightened risk of revolt during the specific country-years of their actual occurrence. In short, urban civic revolutions clearly occurred in ordered patterns and are associated with an explicit set of identifiable structural conditions.

An elucidation of a few paradigmatic cases illustrates the strengths and limitations of the probabilistic model. As Figure 3.5 shows, according to the model, the probability of onset of an urban civic revolutionary episode in Tunisia had been gradually rising over the 1990s and 2000s, peaking in 2010 (the year of the outbreak of the Tunisian Revolution), when the model predicted a .058 probability of an urban civic revolutionary episode.[46] With rare events like

---

46. In 2010, Tunisia was a solidly middle-income country (GDP per capita of $6,244) and a slightly above-average oil producer, with a Polity score of −4 (i.e., on the autocratic side of

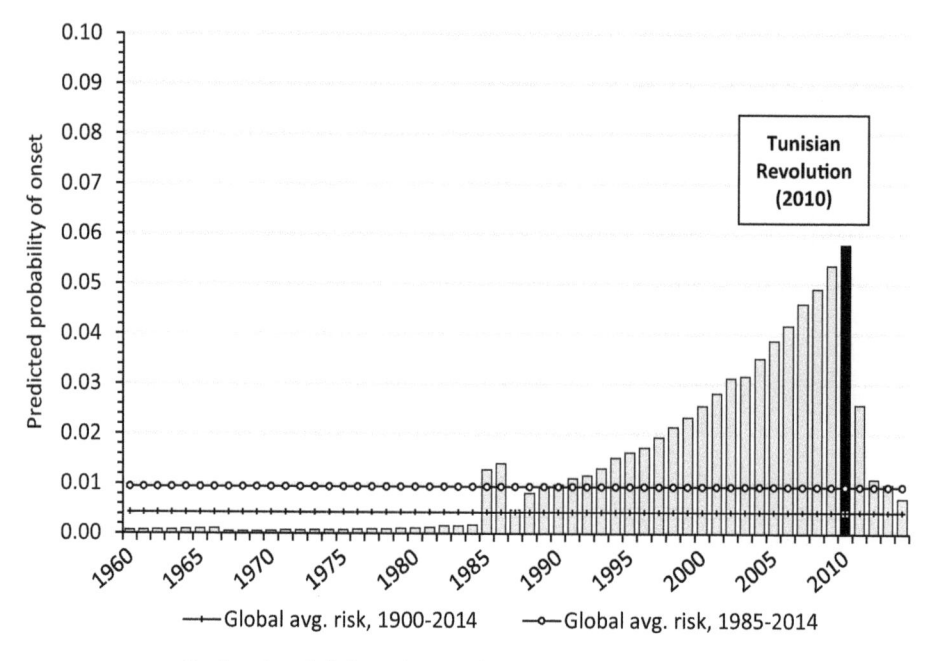

FIGURE 3.5. Predicted probabilities for an urban civic revolutionary episode in Tunisia, 1960–2014.

revolution, even strong predictions yield a low probability of onset in any given year. But Tunisia in 2010 had more than thirteen times the average risk of experiencing urban civic revolutionary contention in a particular country-year over the 1900–2014 period (.0043) and more than six times the average risk during the post–Cold War period (.0094).

Even under highly conducive structural conditions such as these, the materialization of revolution is still partially dependent on the actions and reactions of regimes and oppositions. Tunisian president Zine El Abidine Ben Ali, who had been in power for twenty-three years, had established a highly corrupt personal dictatorship, with a feared security apparatus that sought to extinguish all open expression of opposition. In 2002, he had orchestrated a referendum (supposedly receiving 99.5 percent approval) allowing him to continue in office without term limits, essentially ensuring his presidency for life. Ben Ali and his extended family came to control somewhere between 30

---

non-democracies), an executive corruption index of .76 (well above the global average of .47), a leader who had been in power for twenty-three years, and location in the post–Cold War international environment.

to 40 percent of the Tunisian economy.[47] His neoliberal economic policies resulted in a country characterized by sharply uneven regional development, high unemployment, food price inflation, and poor living conditions for much of the population—despite the World Bank's warm embrace. As one scholar notes, "middle class socio-economic status was sliding steadily, while the Trabelsi-Ben Ali business empire was devouring the traditional business class, alienating investors, and harassing entrepreneurs and small business owners," leading to a "breakdown of the social contract."[48] In July 2009, seventeen months before the events of the revolution began, the US Embassy summed up the situation in a classified cable to Washington:

> The problem is clear: Tunisia has been ruled by the same president for 22 years. He has no successor ... [and] he and his regime have lost touch with the Tunisian people. They tolerate no advice or criticism, whether domestic or international. Increasingly, they rely on the police for control and focus on preserving power. And corruption in the inner circle is growing. Even average Tunisians are now keenly aware of it, and the chorus of complaints is rising. Tunisians intensely dislike, even hate, First Lady Leila Trabelsi and her family. In private, regime opponents mock her; even those close to the government express dismay at her reported behavior. Meanwhile, anger is growing at Tunisia's high unemployment and regional inequities.[49]

In this case, the tropical disturbance that transformed into a hurricane, of course, was the self-immolation of street vendor Mohamed Bouazizi on December 17, 2010 in the small southern town of in Sidi Bouzid. Bouazizi was not the first to take his life in protest over the despair brought on by the Ben Ali regime. To name but one of many cases, Abdesslem Trimech had set himself ablaze in the town of Monastir on March 3 after facing bureaucratic hindrances to his work as a street vendor. Nor was it inevitable that the protests that Bouazizi's suicide provoked in Sidi Bouzid would spread. There had been, for instance, similar clashes between police and protesters in the town of Ben Guerdane, near the border with Libya, in August 2010 that did not lead to revolution.[50] In short, many events could have functioned as triggers for a Tunisian revolution but did not. What makes a trigger a trigger is not just structural

---

47. Lewis 2011.
48. Kaboub 2014, 2.
49. Godec 2009.
50. Ryan 2011.

conditions, but how people react to and take advantage of the trigger under structurally conducive conditions.

In this case, video footage of Bouazizi's suicide and the rioting it elicited in Sidi Bouzid were posted on the internet by a cousin, and when refracted through the circuits of the burgeoning social media sector, touched a deep chord among Tunisian youth. On December 18 two thousand police descended on Sidi Bouzid and successfully quashed the unrest. But almost a week later, on December 24, protests in solidarity with Sidi Bouzid spread to Kasserine, where demonstrations by lawyers and students were met with live ammunition from the police, killing one and wounding four (again, captured on the internet). On December 27, the first mass demonstration (involving a thousand participants) occurred in the capital, Tunis. Up to this point, the protests had largely been confined to the south, and it is conceivable that they might have remained contained had Ben Ali's ham-fisted and excessively violent responses not poured gasoline on the flames of the fire. In reaction to the repression, protests spread still further, inciting even more violent responses from the regime and ultimately leading to the massacre of protestors in Kasserine by special forces snipers on January 8. Once again, this was captured on the internet and shown to the entire nation. By this point, little could hold back the swirling storm that ultimately washed across Tunisia and eventually the rest of the Arab world.

The case of the Bulldozer Revolution in Serbia demonstrates a similar pattern of heightened structural risk (Figure 3.6) that could not have transformed into revolution without government missteps and organized opposition action. According to the predictions of the model, the probability of the outbreak of an urban civic revolutionary episode in Serbia increased gradually over the 1990s and peaked at .033 in 2000, when the Bulldozer Revolution broke out. This was more than seven times the average risk since 1900, and three-and-a-half times the average risk during the post–Cold War period.[51] Urban civic revolution in Serbia unfolded in a context markedly different from Tunisia. Led by strong civil society groups and enjoying American financial and political support, the Serbian opposition used the political opening afforded by an electoral campaign to challenge the Milošević regime. The Serbian president, who by 2000 had dominated the political arena for eleven

---

51. Serbia in 2000 was a solidly middle-income country (GDP per capita of $4,609), an average oil producer, with a Polity score of −6 (i.e., strongly on the autocratic side of non-democracies), an executive corruption index rating of .90 (in the top 10 percent of regimes), a leader who had been in power for eleven years, and location in the post–Cold War international environment. Prior to 1991, the variables used to compute revolutionary risk were for Yugoslavia as a whole.

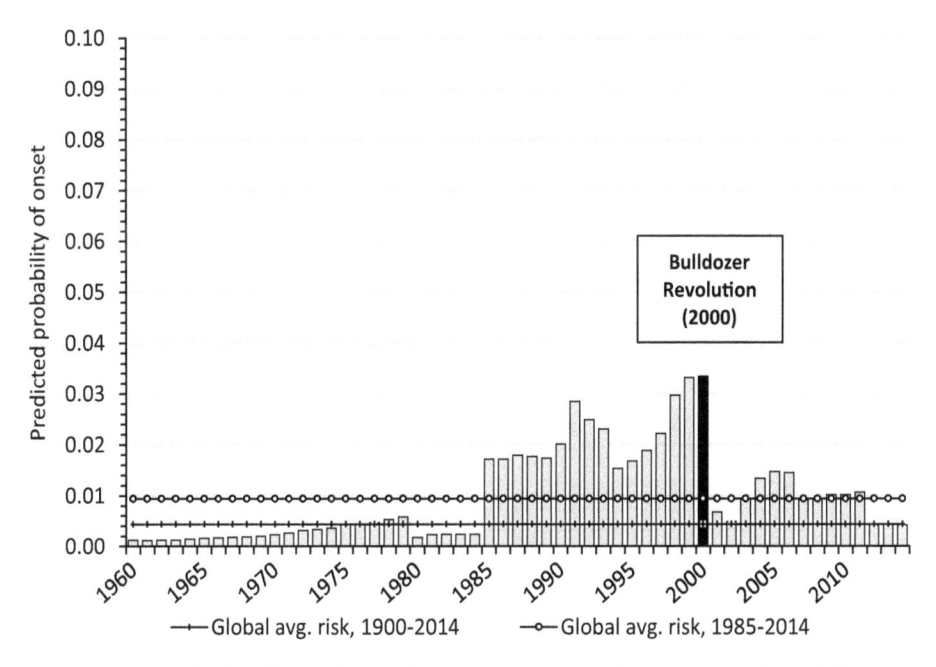

FIGURE 3.6. Predicted probabilities for an urban civic revolutionary episode in Serbia, 1960–2014.

years, had led Serbia (Yugoslavia) into several wars that had brought about the disintegration of the country and isolated it internationally. The living standards of average citizens had plummeted, while corruption blossomed, with billions of dollars of state-owned assets privatized into the hands of those close to the Milošević clan and the ruling Socialist Party.[52] While Milošević spent large sums on the country's secret police and military, unemployment climbed to 50 percent.

Opposition movements had led several failed campaigns in the early 1990s to contain Milošević, and a major movement emerged in 1996–97 over his use of fraud to control municipal elections. It managed to gain a small foothold for the opposition at the local level. But the country continued to be mired in war, corruption, political repression, and economic despair. As the end of his term approached, Milošević called early elections, thinking he would be able to catch the opposition off-guard and strengthen his position. But the antigovernment youth movement Otpor had been preparing the ground for

---

52. Smith 2000.

128 CHAPTER 3

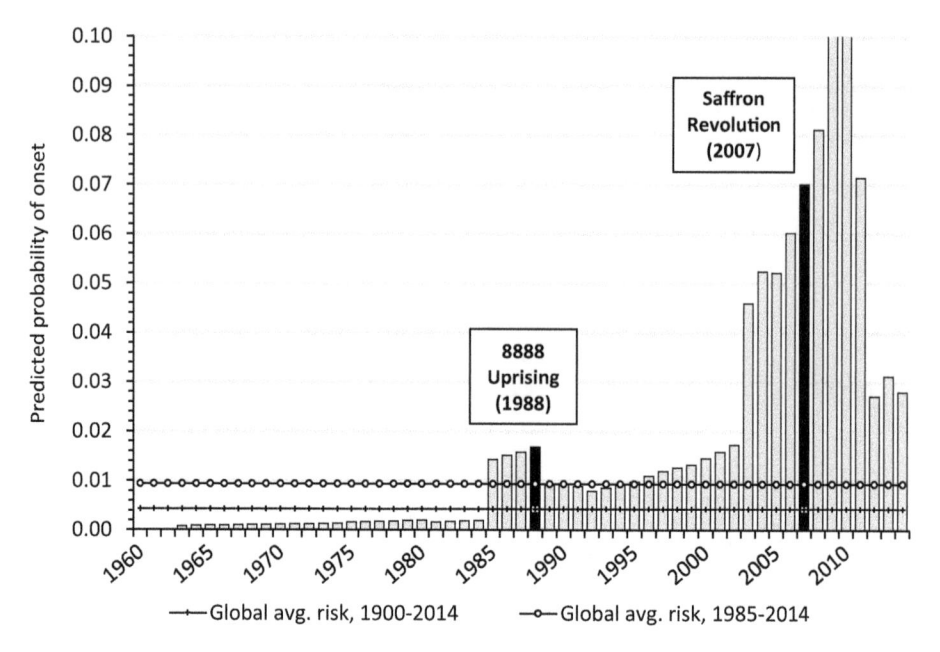

FIGURE 3.7. Predicted probabilities for an urban civic revolutionary episode in Myanmar, 1960–2014. Predicted probabilities for 2009–10 reduced for visibility.

challenging Milošević since 1998. It utilized the opening of the election to unite the opposition and undertake a concerted and well-planned civil resistance campaign to topple Milošević with the open support of the US government. The plan culminated on October 5, 2000 when several hundred thousand protesters from all over Serbia descended on Belgrade to occupy the parliament building in the wake of widespread electoral fraud by the regime.[53] One would be hard pressed to identify any particular trigger that set off the Bulldozer Revolution. It was a well-planned event timed to the political opportunity of elections—the result of concerted actions taken by a disciplined opposition in a society that, for structural reasons, was widely receptive to its message.

Myanmar provides an example of the repeated failure of urban civic challenges, in the 8888 Uprising and the Saffron Revolution, both of which occurred under conditions of above-average structural risk according to the statistical model (Figure 3.7).[54] In 1988, Myanmar had a probability of

53. Cohen 2001; Vejvoda 2009.

54. The predicted probabilities for an urban civic episode for 2009 and 2010 are truncated in Figure 3.7 for improved readability.

experiencing an urban civic revolutionary episode of .017—almost four times the average risk over the past century, and almost twice the average risk after the end of the Cold War.[55] Myanmar had been governed by a military junta since 1962, with the military regime evolving into a one-party state under the control of General Ne Win's Burma Socialist Program Party (BSSP) in 1974. By 1988, Ne Win had ruled over a closed and highly corrupt autocracy for twenty-six years. Moreover, the military character of the regime (not reflected in the statistical model but associated with heightened susceptibility to urban civic revolt) rendered it even more vulnerable than the predictions of the model indicated. In September 1987, the Ne Win government announced a currency reform to address its massive international indebtedness. Believing the number nine to be lucky, the superstitious Ne Win reissued the country's currency around denominations of nine, rendering half of the currency in circulation worthless. The prices received by farmers for their produce were lowered. Students were particularly incensed, as the change instantly wiped out family savings for tuition. The currency reform was an enormous misstep. But it did not set off an immediate explosion of revolt. Six months later, another trigger emerged. In March 1988, protests occurred over the release of the son of a BSSP official who had been involved in a brawl with students. Riot police were mobilized and successfully quashed the protest, one student being killed. It was the reaction to this act of repression that ultimately set off the protests that grew into the uprising. Protests continued to mount in the face of police brutality, becoming a daily occurrence and spreading widely. Eventually, in July, they forced the resignation of Ne Win, who was replaced by the widely despised Sein Lwin, otherwise known as the "Butcher of Rangoon" for his brutal suppression of successive student-led demonstrations. What eventually became known as the 8888 Uprising was so named for August 8, 1988—the date, considered auspicious according to folk superstition, that was chosen for launching large-scale protest action to force regime-change.[56] Thus, multiple triggers—largely created by regime missteps and regime–opposition interactions—pushed Myanmar along the path toward revolutionary contention over an eleven-month period.

By 2007, when the Saffron Revolution broke out, the structural conditions identified in the statistical model were even more pronounced, indicating a .070 probability of an urban civic episode (sixteen times the average risk since

---

55. In 1988, Myanmar was a poor country (GDP per capita of $867) and an above-average oil producer, with a Polity score of −8 (i.e., a closed autocracy), an executive corruption index rating of .90 (among the worst), a leader who had been in power for twenty-six years, and location in the post–Cold War international environment.

56. Maung 1999; Thompson 1999; Boudreau 2004; Katsiaficas 2013.

1900, and more than seven times the average risk after the Cold War).[57] Myanmar continued to be a highly corrupt, closed autocracy dominated by its military and led by General Than Shwe for the previous fifteen years. After the failed 8888 Uprising, the regime had allowed elections in 1990, though it rejected the results, keeping opposition leader Aung San Suu Kyi under house arrest. Human rights abuses were widespread, and the military functioned as a virtual state within a state, enjoying a relatively privileged lifestyle that was largely insulated from the economic insecurity experienced by the rest of the country. Myanmar remained isolated from the prevailing liberal international order, with continual tensions with the dominant American hegemon and heavy reliance on China as its main trade partner. The Burmese opposition had also been influenced by the cross-national wave of color revolutions that had unfolded in the post-communist region and had gained new tools as a result of the global growth of digital communications.[58] In late 2006, the cost of basic commodities rose sharply, and in August 2007 the government suddenly removed fuel subsidies, causing prices to rise by as much as 500 percent. When citizens protested the price increases, the government beat and arrested the demonstrators, drawing the condemnation of the United States. This in itself was not enough to provoke the storm. But when Buddhist monks further protested against the repression, soldiers fired warning shots into the crowd and beat and detained monks, whipping up enormous anger within the Buddhist community and leading to the revolutionary mobilizations of hundreds of thousands that followed.[59] Conducive structural conditions and price increases were central in conditioning the revolt. But the brutal response of the authorities is what ultimately transformed it into a swirling cyclone.

Ukraine on the eve of the 2004 Orange Revolution also exhibited heightened vulnerability to urban civic contention, according to the model. For 2004, the statistical model predicted a .039 probability of the outbreak of an urban civic revolt in Ukraine (Figure 3.8). This was nine times the average risk since 1900 and more than four times the average risk in the post–Cold War period.[60] By

---

57. By 2007, Myanmar's GDP per capita had grown to $2,711 (the upper end of poor countries), oil production had largely disappeared, the Polity score remained −8 (a closed autocracy), executive corruption had grown to .93, its leader had been in power for fifteen years, and it had a tensioned relationship with the post–Cold War international order.

58. Rosenberg 2011.

59. Fink 2009; Shen and Chan 2010.

60. In 2004, Ukraine was a lower middle-income country (GDP per capita of $3,547) with no oil of its own, stood at the open end of non-democracies (a Polity score of 6), had an executive corruption index of .83 (compared to the global average of .48), and a leader who had been in power for ten years.

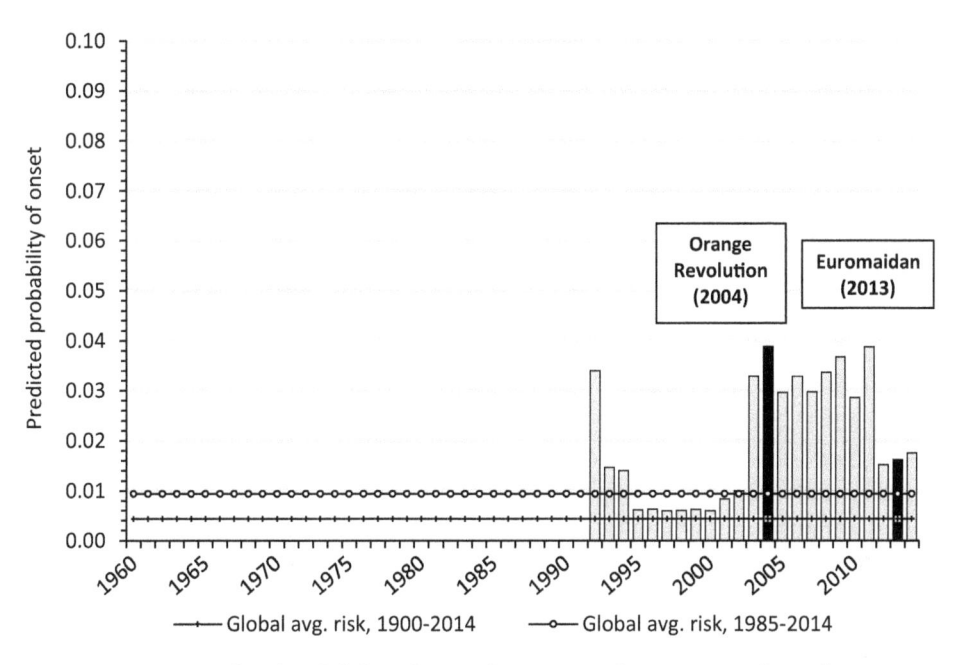

FIGURE 3.8. Predicted probabilities for an urban civic revolutionary episode in Ukraine, 1992–2014.

2004, Ukraine had been ruled by Leonid Kuchma for a decade—in part through widespread electoral fraud. Ukraine under Kuchma had a reputation as one of the most corrupt regimes on the planet. Pavlo Lazorenko, prime minister under Kuchma, was forced to flee the country in 1999 and was convicted of money-laundering in Switzerland, having stolen up to $700 million through "fraud, extortion, bribery, misappropriation, and embezzlement."[61] This, however, was only the tip of the iceberg of the tremendous organized graft and theft that typified the Kuchma regime.[62] While Ukraine remained a competitive authoritarian regime under Kuchma, in the late 1990s it took a decidedly authoritarian turn; Kuchma's power expanded to include the ability to appoint governors and heads of local government, informal control over major media (through ownership by various oligarchs affiliated with him), and use of the police and tax authorities to harass opponents. Opposition increased after 2000, when well-known journalist Georgy Gongadze disappeared; his headless body was found two months later. Tapes smuggled abroad by Kuchma's bodyguard showed that

61. Quoted in Wayne 2016.
62. Darden 2008.

Kuchma had given the order to eliminate Gongadze. A protest campaign dubbing itself "Ukraine Without Kuchma" demanded Kuchma's resignation but failed to exert sufficient leverage to force him from office. Nevertheless, civil society groups developed rapidly in the early 2000s, at times with American support and financing. Kuchma was barred constitutionally from running for a third term in 2004, so his hand-picked successor (Prime Minister Viktor Yanukovych) ran in his stead. Yanukovych was closely connected with the Donetsk political clan from eastern Ukraine and had a criminal past.

The immediate catalyst for the Orange Revolution was the attempt by the regime to fix the 2004 presidential elections in favor of Yanukovych. But these events functioned more as a focal point than a trigger.[63] Under the influence of the Bulldozer Revolution in Serbia and the Rose Revolution in Georgia, the opposition was well prepared to contest elections that they fully expected would be fraudulent.[64] Active preparations for the Maidan began at least a month and a half before the election. Tents, portable kitchens, sleeping bags, and toilets were procured ahead of time. Agreements were even reached with wholesale food companies to supply food to the protestors. But broader preparations had begun even earlier. In summer 2004, the Ukrainian youth movement Pora conducted summer camp training in civil disobedience for a campaign to prepare the way for the electoral defeat of the regime and to challenge its anticipated attempt to steal the election. All of this was part of a broader electoral model of revolution pioneered in Serbia and Georgia and shared across international borders.[65] The Orange Revolution was not triggered by an exogenous event, nor did it simply "come." It was engineered by the opposition at a moment anticipated well beforehand, albeit under structurally conducive conditions.

The statistical model performed less convincingly in anticipating the onset of the Euromaidan Revolution in 2013, identifying a probability of .016—almost four times the average risk since 1900, but only 70 percent greater than the average risk during the post–Cold War years, and lower than many of the surrounding years in Ukraine after the Orange Revolution. Little had changed in Ukrainian conditions after the Orange Revolution.[66] Indeed, anger and frustration over this motivated much of the revolutionary mobilization during Euromaidan—something that any statistical model would have difficulty capturing. By 2013, Viktor Yanukovych had become Ukraine's leader; he had been elected president in 2010, despite his history of electoral fraud. (The fact that

---

63. Tucker 2007.

64. Wilson 2005; Beissinger 2011.

65. Bunce and Wolchik 2011.

66. By 2013, Ukraine was still a middle-income country (GDP per capita of $4,798), the political system still ranked at the more open end of non-democracies (Polity score of 6), it was not a major oil producer, and its corruption was still "routine and expected."

he had been in power for only three years explains the model's prediction of moderate risk.) In the case of Euromaidan, the immediate cause of mobilization was the decision by Yanukovych, under pressure from Russia, not to sign an association agreement with the European Union. A case could be made that had Yanukovych decided to sign the association agreement, Euromaidan might have never materialized: the initial protests on Maidan on November 21 followed directly upon the regime's announcement of its intention not to sign. In the following days, the number of protestors grew to fifty thousand. They focused on lobbying the government to sign the agreement and did not aim at overthrowing the regime. On November 29, when the Yanukovych government failed to sign the agreement at the Vilnius summit with the European Union, demands shifted to Yanukovych's resignation. However, it was the regime's brutal repression of students camped out at Maidan on November 30, injuring fifty, that led to the explosion of protests that ensued. As a result of the repression, crowds swelled to eight hundred thousand in the following days, with the main grievance shifting from the association agreement to repression by the regime, accompanied by demands for its overthrow.[67]

Compared to other cases, the structural risk of urban civic contention in Ukraine at the time of Euromaidan was above average, but not extremely high.[68] It would be hard to maintain that Euromaidan was structurally determined, at least by the parameters associated with most other cases. Rather, Euromaidan emerged out of decisions made by the Yanukovych government and acts of brutal repression against the opposition. The polarization in Ukraine based on regional and cultural divisions was essential to shaping expectations about the government and its behavior and played an important role in structuring mobilization. This cultural element is poorly captured in the statistical model. But in a subset of cases (Ukraine in 2004 and 2014, Madagascar in 1991 and 2002, Bahrain in 1994 and 2011, Djibouti in 2011, Togo in 1991, and others), cultural difference has been critical in shaping the social forces involved in urban civic revolt.

Structural Vulnerability, Exogenous Events, and Regime–Opposition Interactions

As we have seen, structural vulnerability is important in conditioning the outbreak of urban civic revolt, and certainly urban civic revolt is made considerably harder in its absence. But structure alone is never enough to set

---

67. Wilson 2014.

68. At the same time, signing the agreement still could have set off rebellions in the Crimea and Donbas, with Russian support and instigation.

revolutionary contention in motion. Exogenous events (i.e., triggers) can also play a role in setting off urban civic contention. Indeed, four-fifths of urban civic episodes occurred within the context of a transnational revolutionary wave, in which revolutionary contention in another society became the occasion for oppositions to test the limits of the possible within their own. In other cases, externally induced financial crises, currency devaluations, or the collapse of commodity prices were directly implicated. But even in the presence of conducive structural conditions and exogenous triggers, revolutionary challenges still emerged out of interactions between regimes and oppositions. Half of all urban civic episodes, for instance, began with opposition demonstrations that were repressed by incumbent regimes and produced backlash mobilizations that set off revolutionary contention. Often, these acts of repression themselves became the central grievance underpinning revolt—as we saw earlier in the cases of Euromaidan and the Saffron Revolution. In other cases, sudden decisions by government leaders that violated widely held norms played key roles in instigating revolutionary mobilizations. These actions became focal points by heightening a sense of grievance, channeling mass emotions, and weakening authority.

The 1987 June Uprising in South Korea that led to South Korea's transition to democracy is a good example. According to the model, South Korea had a .14 probability of experiencing urban civic revolutionary contention in 1987—more than thirty-two times greater than the average risk over the 1900–2014 period, and almost fifteen times the average risk during the post–Cold War period.[69] Yet, the probabilistic model also identified extremely high probabilities for urban civic revolt in South Korea in 1985 (.11), 1986 (.12), and 1988 (.12) (Figure 3.9). Revolutionary mobilizations could have broken out in any of those years, and the precise timing of what ultimately became the 1987 June Uprising would have been difficult to identify simply from structural conditions alone. Instead, a confluence of exogenous events and government decisions provoked it into being.

Extensive government repression following the failed armed uprising against the regime in Kwangju in 1980 generated enormous hostility toward the government within South Korean society. But in 1983 the regime reversed course, allowing anti-regime professors and students to return to universities, withdrawing military police from campuses, and pardoning political prisoners.

---

69. On the eve of the revolt, South Korea had a GDP per capita of $6,230 (a middle-income country), a highly repressive regime (−5 on the Polity scale) whose leader (President Chun Doo Hwan, a former military general) had been in power for seven years, no major oil production, and a high level of executive corruption (.72).

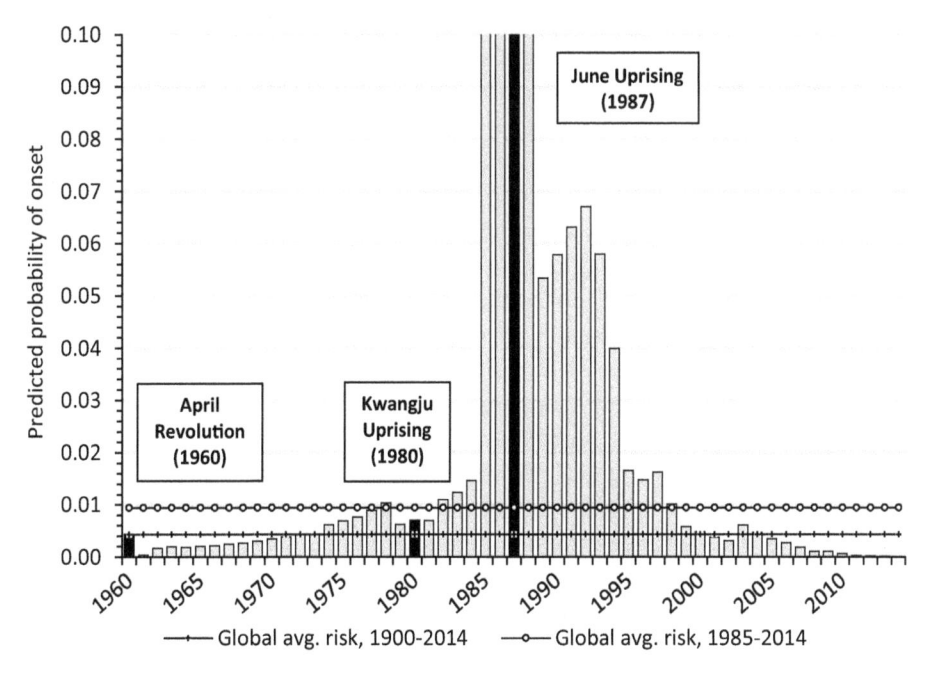

FIGURE 3.9. Predicted probabilities for an urban civic revolutionary episode in South Korea, 1960–2014. Predicted probabilities for 1985–88 reduced for visibility.

By 1984, student and labor groups had begun to organize civil society movements, and new political parties had emerged in support of democratization. The regime planned to open up the political system to competition gradually, and had that occurred, the June Uprising in 1987 might never have taken place. But the People Power Revolution in the Philippines in February 1986 radically changed the situation, exercising a major impact on South Korea's opposition and fostering a wave of student and worker protests pushing for reforms. In this context, on April 13, 1987 President Chun Doo Hwan suddenly announced that he would terminate public discussion of any constitutional revisions and instead pass power over to another military ruler. This decision elicited a chorus of protest, as tens of thousands demonstrated in major cities, and the opposition formed a National Movement Headquarters for a Democratic Constitution (NMHDC) to coordinate protests throughout the country. On June 9, a student was fatally injured by fragments of a tear gas grenade, and the next day forty thousand students began a continuous demonstration in Seoul. Chun decided to name General Roh Tae-woo as the presidential candidate of the ruling Democratic Justice Party (under existing rules, the next president). In response, the NMHDC organized a massive wave of rallies aimed at ending the dictatorship. This eventually forced the regime to compromise and announce far-reaching reforms, marking the transition to a democratic South Korea.[70] Despite heightened structural vulnerability over the course of several years and the impact of external events (the People Power Revolution), the regime's sudden reversal on constitutional reform, its clumsy attempts to fix the presidential transition, and backlash to regime repression against protestors all played critical roles in generating the revolutionary moment.

Another of the most highly determined urban civic episodes, according to the model, was the Velvet Revolution in Czechoslovakia. In 1989, Czechoslovakia had a predicted probability of urban civic revolt of .147 (thirty-four times the average risk over the last century, and fifteen times the post–Cold War average for country-years).[71] This was the highest prediction of structural risk from the model for any country-year during the entire 1900–2014 period. In this case, the earthquake analogy may well seem appropriate—a revolution simply awaiting the trigger of the collapse of communism elsewhere. Indeed, the model also identified extremely high probabilities of revolt in Czechoslovakia throughout the years 1985–88 (Figure 3.10), and the outbreak and timing of the Velvet Revolution was largely a matter of exogenous events. But even in this highly determined case, regime–opposition interactions played some role. After the Soviet invasion of 1968, Czechoslovakia was ruled by one of the most conservative communist leaderships within the Soviet bloc, though a vibrant dissident culture continued to thrive. Czechoslovakia remained largely unaffected by the waves of reform that had loosened politics inside the Soviet Union and had recently brought about reformist change in Poland and Hungary. On November 9, 1989, the Berlin Wall fell, and communist regimes collapsed in a number of neighboring Soviet satellite states. Shortly afterward, on November 17 (International Students' Day), riot police violently suppressed a student demonstration in Prague, sparking a series of backlash protests. False rumors spread that one of the students had been killed, and students and theaters declared a strike. On November 19, actors and members of the audience at a Prague theater led by Václav Havel and other members of the dissident group Charter 77 established the Civic Forum, an umbrella organization aimed at transcending communist rule. Protests quickly emerged on Prague's Wenceslas Square, spreading to Bratislava and other cities and eventually

---

70. Kim 2007; Katsiaficas 2012.

71. Czechoslovakia on the eve of its revolution had a fairly high GDP per capita ($8,709), a highly repressive government (−7 on the Polity scale), a leader who had been in power for twenty-one years, no oil production, and significantly above-average executive corruption (.63).

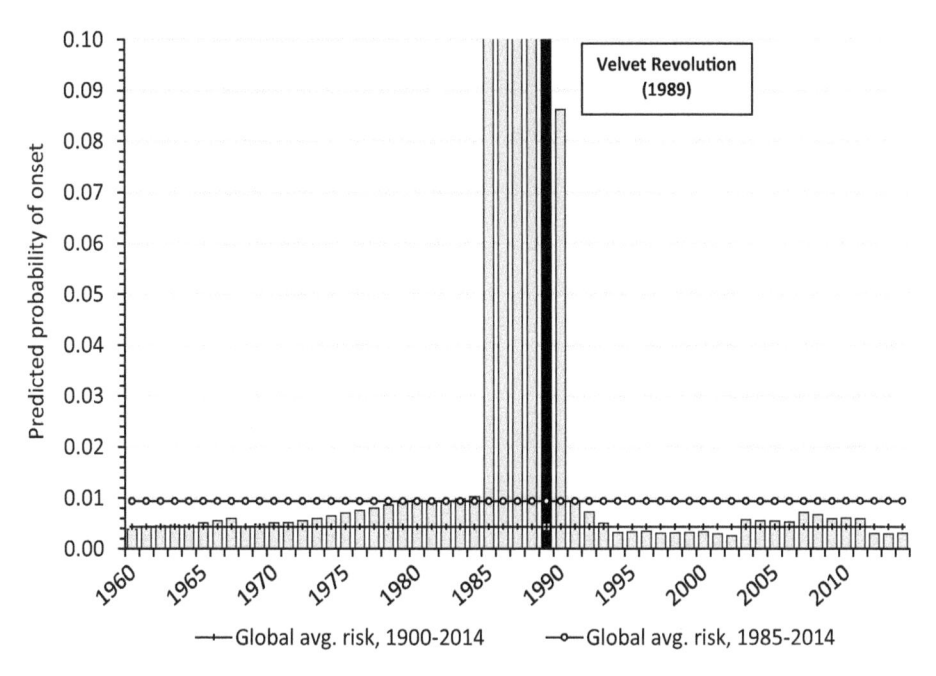

FIGURE 3.10. Predicted probabilities for an urban civic revolutionary episode in Czechoslovakia, 1960–2014. Predicted probabilities after 1991 are for the Czech Republic. Predicted probabilities for 1985–89 reduced for visibility.

forcing the Communist Party to relinquish power.[72] Given the general collapse of communist regimes in Europe and the structurally conducive conditions prevalent in Czechoslovakia at the time, there is probably little that the regime could have done to avert this outcome. But even here, regime–opposition interactions were an important part of the process.

Exogenous events and backlash against repression also played central roles in the emergence of the Indonesian Revolution in 1998. According to the model, Indonesia had a .093 probability of experiencing an urban civic revolutionary episode in 1998—almost twenty-two times the average risk since 1900, and almost ten times the average risk of country-years after the end of the Cold War.[73] Suharto came to power in a military coup in 1965, severely restricting civil liberties and effectively splitting power between his Golkar

72. Wheaton and Kavan 1992; Stokes 1993; Kenney 2003; Williams 2009.
73. In 1998, Indonesia had a GDP per capita of $3,704, a closed autocratic regime (−7 on the Polity scale), a leader in power for thirty-two years, and an extremely high level of executive corruption (.94)—though these factors were partially offset by significant oil production.

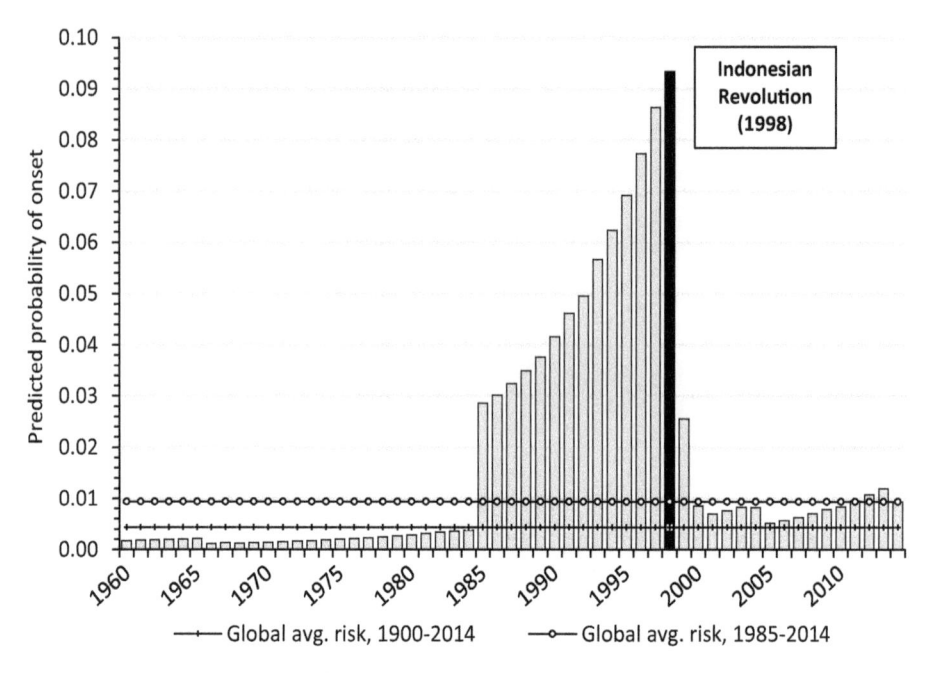

FIGURE 3.11. Predicted probabilities for an urban civic revolutionary episode in Indonesia, 1960–2014.

Party and the military. Corruption and crony capitalism flourished, with Suharto's ill-gotten fortune and family businesses placing him among the wealthiest individuals in the world.[74] But according to the predictions of the model, Indonesia had been under heightened risk of an urban civic revolutionary episode for at least the previous eight years (Figure 3.11). In 1994, Suharto had given indications that he was planning to step down in 1998 rather than run for re-election. But no clear successor emerged.

In the midst of this succession crisis, the July 1997 Asian financial crisis hit. It led to a collapse of Indonesia's currency and the imposition of a structural adjustment program by the International Monetary Fund. Suddenly, twenty-one million Indonesians were swept below the poverty line, and cuts in government subsidies led to the outbreak of food riots throughout the country. But rather than pass power on to a successor, which might have defused the situation, Suharto announced in January 1998 that he would stand for re-election for a seventh term—running unopposed, as in the past. Students began to organize a campaign of protest demanding his removal. It quickly grew to tens of thousands of participants. In early May 1998, the government

74. Katsiaficas 2013, 347.

announced increased fuel and electricity prices, inspiring larger numbers to join the student protests. When four students were killed in a clash with security forces at a demonstration on May 12, and the regime unleashed anti-Chinese riots to justify a lockdown, student demonstrators occupied radio stations and took over the legislature. Under threats of a crackdown in Jakarta, major protests broke out across the country, forcing Suharto's resignation.[75] To be sure, the Indonesian Revolution occurred because of heightened structural risk and the exogenous event of the Asian financial crisis. But its outbreak was also a product of the regime's mismanagement of the succession crisis and backlash against government repression.

Urban Civic Revolution under Adverse Structural Conditions

Despite the relative accuracy of the statistical model, approximately one out of every six urban civic episodes occurred in country-years with below-average levels of risk, according to the predictions of the probabilistic model.[76] These under-predicted cases either occurred prior to the post–Cold War era, were poorer or more democratic, had incumbent leaders in office for a relatively short period of time, or were less corrupt than most other cases. Nonetheless, the countries involved experienced urban civic revolutionary contention—something that the determinist perspective on revolution would have difficulty explaining. Why did revolutionary contention materialize when the structural conditions associated with most other cases were weaker?

A number of the under-predicted cases materialized out of crises that were suddenly imposed on society by leaders, often through the breaking of widely accepted norms—the "bomb cyclones" of revolutions that seemingly came out of nowhere. The Philippines provides contrasting examples in this regard. Figure 3.12 displays the predicted probabilities for the outbreak of urban civic contention in the Philippines from 1960 to 2014. As the Figure shows, the model accurately identified above-average risk of urban civic revolution at the time of the People Power Revolution in 1986 (a .040 probability—more than nine times the average risk since 1900, and more than four times the post–Cold War average), with the risk of revolution rising sharply in 1985.[77] Structural risk

---

75. Friend 2003; Boudreau 2004; Aspinall 2005; Pepinsky 2009.
76. For the post–Cold War years, the proportion of under-predicted cases was 18 percent.
77. In 1986, the Philippines had a GDP per capita of $1,997 and was an average oil producer, with a Polity score of −6, an extremely high corruption index of .90, and a leader who had been in power for twenty-one years.

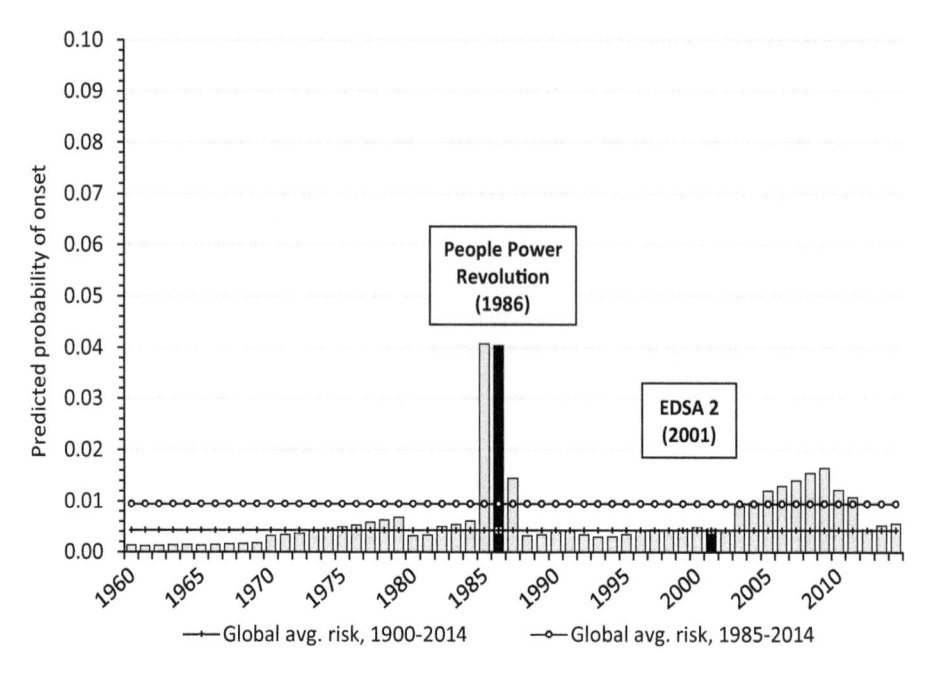

FIGURE 3.12. Predicted probabilities for an urban civic revolutionary episode in the Philippines, 1960–2014.

for urban civic contention in the Philippines had been building since 1972, when President Marcos declared martial law, suspended civil liberties, and arrested his political opponents. In 1983, he had the leader of the political opposition, Ninoy Aquino, assassinated. By the mid-1980s, the Philippine economy was bankrupt. Pressures from Marcos's chief ally, the United States, to improve the country's human rights image caused Marcos to announce a snap presidential election for February 7, 1986. Through extensive violence and electoral fraud, Marcos was declared the winner on February 15, though the opposition, led by Aquino's widow Corazon, contested the outcome. Computer technicians tasked with tallying the vote walked off the job in protest against the fraud, and the opposition planned a series of strikes and boycotts against businesses owned by Marcos's cronies. But all of this changed on February 22, when Marcos's defense minister Juan Ponce Enrile launched a military coup, setting off the events of the People Power Revolution.[78]

Contrast the more structured case of the People Power Revolution, however, with the EDSA 2 revolt fifteen years later, in 2001, when, according to the

78. Schock 2005; Mendoza 2009; Katsiaficas 2013.

statistical model, the Philippines had a risk of urban civic revolt (.0046) that was only slightly above the country-year average for the 1900–2014 period and below the country-year average for the post–Cold War period.[79] The EDSA 2 Revolution emerged quite suddenly when Philippine political institutions failed to hold President Joseph Estrada accountable for accepting millions of pesos in payoffs from illegal gambling. Estrada was impeached by the Philippine House of Representatives, and likely no revolution would have materialized had the impeachment process worked as it should have. But Estrada successfully thwarted his trial in the Senate when senators who were allied with him barred the introduction of key evidence.[80] This threw the country into chaos, causing all eleven prosecutors in the impeachment trial to resign and leading opposition representatives to walk out of the legislature. Large crowds of several hundred thousand gathered in front of the EDSA Shrine (built to commemorate the 1986 People Power Revolution), mobilized in part through SMS messaging and the encouragement of Jaime Cardinal Sin, archbishop of Manila, who called on Filipinos to protest until Estrada stepped down.[81] This episode was provoked by the actions of leaders despite structural conditions that, compared to other cases, were not particularly conducive to urban civic revolution.

Similarly, the Easter Crisis in Denmark in 1920, poorly predicted by the statistical model, emerged abruptly when King Christian X dismissed the Danish government for failing to support the reincorporation of Central Schleswig, triggering a constitutional crisis. Denmark at the time had an extremely low risk of revolution according to the statistical model (.0001), due to the fact that it was a democracy (Polity score of 10) with a leader who had been in power for only seven years, no oil resources, and hardly any executive corruption (a score of .03 on the executive corruption index), in a global era in which urban civic revolutionary contention was uncommon and was not facilitated by the international environment. The Danish monarchy had supposedly accepted parliamentary rule since 1901. But in 1920 the king claimed that, as monarch, he alone was the highest power in the country and had the sole authority to dismiss the government. The move sparked massive demonstrations in Copenhagen in support of greater democratization and an end to

---

79. In 2001, the Philippines was a lower middle-income country (a GDP per capita of $2,377) with a Polity score of 8 (i.e., a democracy), a leader in power for only three years, an executive corruption index of .58 (only slightly above average), and below-average oil production.

80. Similar actions during the first impeachment of Donald Trump in 2019 did not lead to mass revolt—also under unfavorable structural conditions for urban civic revolution.

81. Reid 2001; Rafael 2003; Abinales and Amoroso 2005.

the monarchy, but the risk of revolution was ultimately allayed through compromise, with the king accepting the role of ceremonial head of state.[82]

Likewise, according to the structural features associated with urban civic revolts elsewhere, Niger had a .005 risk of experiencing an urban civic revolutionary episode in 2009—slightly above the average for country-years from 1900 to 2014, but below the average for the post–Cold War era.[83] The Niger Constitutional Crisis of 2009 materialized suddenly when President Mamadou Tandja announced that he would seek a third term in office despite constitutional restrictions limiting him to two terms. Tandja called a referendum to scrap the constitution and dissolved the legislature, sending protesters onto the streets and triggering a general strike. In response, Tandja assumed emergency powers, provoking even larger demonstrations involving tens of thousands, who called for his overthrow. He eventually won the referendum and managed to survive the protests through repressive measures, though was later deposed in a military coup.[84]

In several under-predicted cases, urban civic revolutionary challenges materialized at the tail end of cross-national revolutionary waves. Albania, for instance, was the poorest of eastern European countries, and one of the last to shed communist rule. In 1991, it had a below-average probability (.002) of experiencing an urban civic revolutionary episode, according to the factors associated with other urban civic revolts.[85] But the collapse of communism elsewhere in eastern Europe severely challenged the continuation of the communist regime. As news of the events of 1989 trickled into what had been one of the most closed countries of the communist bloc, "a revolution of rising expectations . . . was beginning to grip the whole country,"[86] and the leadership of the ruling Party of Labor came to the conclusion that it needed to introduce radical reforms if it were to avoid a fate similar to its European communist cousins. The regime opened Albania's borders, engaged in market reforms, allowed religious freedoms, and eventually permitted the creation of independent political parties. Protests and student agitation multiplied (including the destruction of communist monuments and statues) in what later came to be known as the

---

82. Lidegaard 2009, 89–93.

83. In 2009, Niger was a poor country (GDP per capita of $514) with a Polity score of 6 (on the cusp of democracy), a leader who had been in power for ten years, no oil, and an above-average level of executive corruption (.73).

84. Baudais and Chauzal 2011; Mueller 2013.

85. In 1991, Albania had a GDP per capita of $2,499, with some small oil production, a Polity score of 1 (its political system had recently opened), a very low level of executive corruption (.17), and a leader who had been in power for only six years.

86. Vickers and Pettifer 1997, 24–25.

"time of dark forces." Hoping to be able to ride the storm, the regime held multi-party elections in March 1991 that resulted in a landslide victory for the ruling Party of Labor (though the opposition dominated in cities). It seemed as if the communists had succeeded in rebranding themselves and holding on to power—as occurred in a number of other parts of the communist world. But shortly after the election, four opposition activists were shot and killed at a demonstration outside the Party of Labor's headquarters. This sparked a major wave of unrest led by Albania's urban opposition and newly legalized trade unions, who called for an across-the-board wage hike and prosecution of those responsible for the killings. When the government refused to accede, a massive wave of protest ensued that forced the Party of Labor government out of office.[87]

Over-Prediction of Urban Civic Contention

In about a quarter of all country-years in the sample (spread across 135 countries) the probabilistic model over-predicted the outbreak of revolutionary contention, identifying above-average risk of urban civic revolt when no revolutionary contention occurred (i.e., false positives). Some of these countries did experience an urban civic revolutionary episode in a prior or subsequent year. But given that only forty-three countries ever experienced urban civic contention (ten having experienced it more than once), there is a significant number of countries which at one time exhibited the structural conditions associated with above-average risk but never experienced urban civic revolt.[88]

There were also many cases in which potential triggers—even under structurally conducive circumstances—might have set off urban civic revolutions but did not. For instance, of the country-years in the post–Cold War period that displayed an above-average risk of urban civic contention (i.e., greater than .0094), 36 percent suffered significant financial stress,[89] but only 2.7 percent of these country-years experienced urban civic contention.[90]

---

87. Vickers and Pettifer 1997.

88. Even if one includes urban civic quasi-revolutionary episodes that did not qualify for inclusion in the dataset, only fifty-five countries ever experienced an urban civic revolutionary or quasi-revolutionary episode, leaving over-predicted country-years in another seventy-three countries unexplained.

89. I considered a country to be under significant financial stress if it suffered from at least two of the stresses identified by Reinhart and Rogoff (2009) in the year in question or in the prior year.

90. Even if we use the mean level of risk associated with those cases that actually experienced an urban civic revolt during these years (.03), only 9 percent of high-risk country-years that also experienced financial stress saw the outbreak of an urban civic revolt.

Similarly, of the country-years that displayed an above-average risk of an urban civic revolution for the post–Cold years, 18 percent experienced an election that was not considered free and fair, but only 2.5 percent of these country-years witnessed an urban civic revolt.[91]

The determinist approach cannot explain these cases. Most potential triggers—even in structurally conducive circumstances—never generate urban civic revolutions. There is a tendency toward over-prediction inherent in all structural models of revolution—precisely because they overlook the ways in which regimes and oppositions act upon the structural conditions that they confront. Sometimes, regimes thwart the outbreak of revolt when conducive structural conditions are present, preventing a heightened risk of revolt from turning into a revolutionary crisis by engaging in reforms, co-opting opponents, repressing or disrupting oppositions, or buying off popular dissatisfaction. In other instances, oppositions fail to take advantage of favorable structural conditions because of an absence of political opportunity, factionalism or personal rivalries, mistakes by opposition leaders, or a preference for reform over risky mass revolt.

Mexico, for instance, represents a case in which an urban civic revolution should have broken out in the 1980s or 1990s, according to the structural conditions associated with urban civic episodes elsewhere. As can be seen in Figure 3.13, Mexico experienced heightened risk of urban civic contention from approximately 1986 through 1994 (coinciding with the de la Madrid and Salinas administrations).[92] The risk peaked in 1994 at .047—roughly eleven times the average risk since 1900, and five times the average risk after the Cold War. An above-average level of risk remained until 2000. But urban civic revolt never occurred during this period. Mexico did of course experience the Chiapas Rebellion in 1994—a rural leftist rebellion undertaken by poor Mayan peasants for land rights and against neoliberal reforms.[93] But this had more to do with the issues traditionally associated with social revolutions (poverty and land) than with the conditions associated with urban civic revolts. After its transition to democracy, Mexico also experienced large-scale protests by the political left in 2006 in the wake of a hotly contested election,

---

91. Again, even if we use the mean level of risk associated with those cases that actually experienced an urban civic revolt during these years, only 6 percent of high-risk country-years that experienced an election that was not free and fair witnessed the outbreak of an urban civic revolt.

92. In 1985, the Mexican political system lay on the autocratic side of the Polity scale (−3), Mexico was a middle-income country (GDP per capita of $6,162), and executive corruption was fairly high (.75 according to the V-Dem index).

93. A small-scale Maoist revolt led by the Popular Revolutionary Army (EPR) also emerged in 1996.

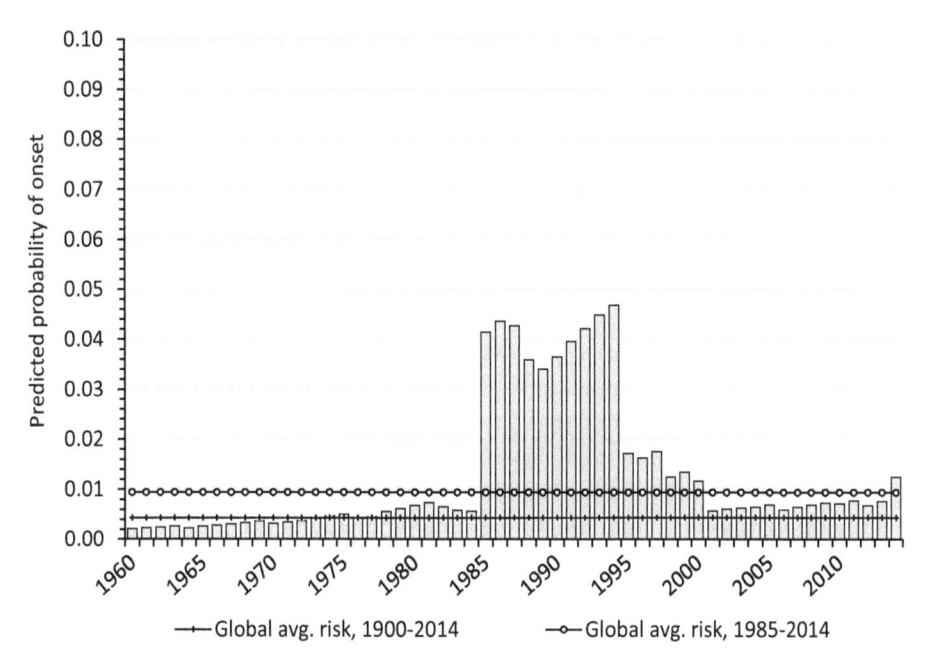

FIGURE 3.13. Predicted probabilities for an urban civic revolutionary episode in Mexico, 1960–2014.

amid accusations of electoral fraud; but this mobilization was largely unpredicted by the statistical model.[94]

There are a number of reasons why urban civic contention never materialized in Mexico during these years of heightened risk. For one thing, the country had some structural advantages of its own that helped to deflect attempts at urban civic revolution. Not only was it a major oil producer, but its six-year fixed presidential term effectively limited the tenure of incumbent leaders, allowing new forces to enter the political system on a regular basis and checking the degree to which leader longevity could act as a lightning rod for revolt. Still, the statistical model includes both of these factors in its calculations, and even taking them into account, it indicated a high level of risk of urban civic revolutionary contention in Mexico from 1985 to 1994.

---

94. Rather than a mass siege of power, the quasi-revolutionary 2006 protests in Mexico City in support of candidate Andrés Manuel López Obrador—involving up to a million citizens—simply called for a full re-count of the vote. In response, the electoral commission conducted a partial re-count of districts where irregularities were suspected. As a result of the re-count, Obrador's declining popularity, and the formal declaration of Filipe Calderon as the winner, the protests subsided. They did, however, lead to significant electoral reforms.

In the 1980s, the popularity of the ruling Institutional Revolutionary Party (PRI) declined as a result of economic recession, the growth of the urban middle class, and a devastating earthquake that had given rise to a host of popular movements due to the government's inept response.[95] After an initial attempt to introduce free and fair elections at the local level in 1983, and the rise of serious political opposition in the form of the conservative National Action Party (PAN) and the leftist National Democratic Front (FDN), the regime reversed course, using widespread electoral fraud in the 1988 presidential election to assure the election of its candidate Carlos Salinas. Not only did this cause serious splits within the PRI; it also sparked a series of protests calling for annulment of the elections. FDN candidate Cuauhtémoc Cárdenas proclaimed victory and refused to recognize the legitimacy of Salinas's election. In what might have turned into an electoral revolution, hundreds of thousands jammed into Constitution Plaza in central Mexico City to call for a re-count and the overturning of the result. But PAN refused to join in the protests, preferring instead to take advantage of its own legislative victories. As Beatriz Magaloni observes, "The outcome of the 1988 elections might have been quite different had the opposition parties opted to challenge the PRI in unison."[96] The inability of the opposition to cooperate in 1988 across the sharp left/right divide undermined the potential for a mobilizational effort that might have forced regime-change.[97]

A second opportunity presented itself at the time of presidential elections in 1994, when conditions for urban civic revolution once again were ripe, according to the probabilistic model. After his election, Salinas vigorously pursued economic liberalization, and confrontation with the political left continued throughout his years in office (as did PRI electoral fraud). But with the opposition controlling a significant portion of the legislature, the PRI began to loosen its grip over the electoral system. These changes (along with the Chiapas Rebellion and the assassination of PRI presidential candidate Luis Donaldo Colosio) led to the first largely fraud-free presidential election in Mexican history in August 1994. Under the administration of Ernesto Zedillo, electoral reforms were extended and eventually led to opposition control of the legislature in 1997 and of the presidency in 2000—sharply reducing the risk of urban civic revolt. In short, despite favorable structural conditions, and despite events that might have functioned as triggers, in the case of Mexico the outbreak of urban civic revolutionary contention was

---

95. Walker 2013; Camp 2016.
96. Magaloni 2006, 240.
97. See also Greene 2007.

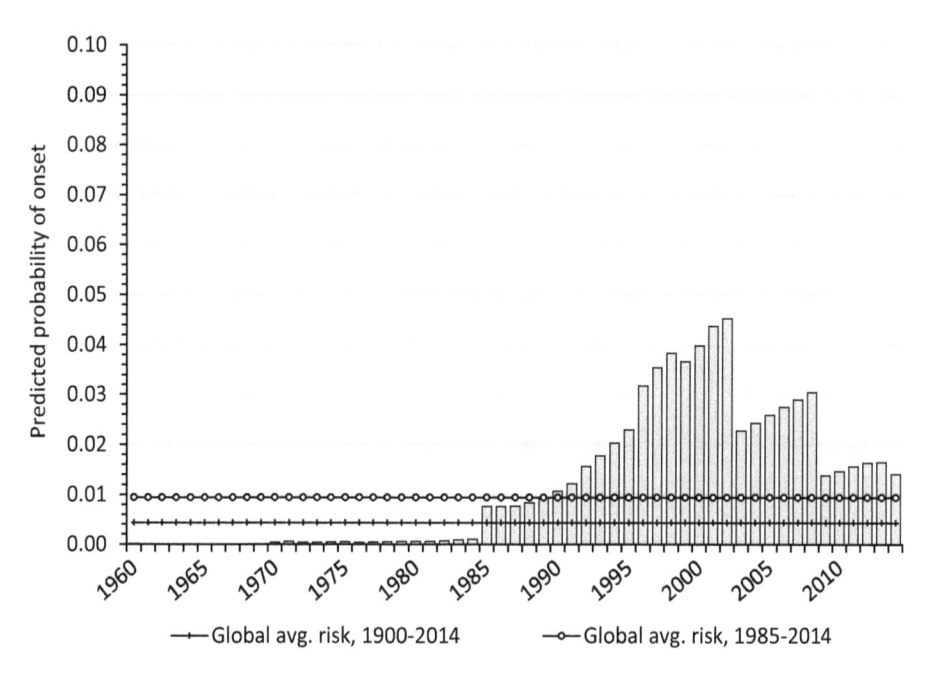

FIGURE 3.14. Predicted probabilities for an urban civic revolutionary episode in Malaysia, 1960–2014.

pre-empted by a failure of opposition coordination and by regime-initiated reforms from above.

Malaysia, similarly, is a country where, from 1992 through 2002, high levels of risk for urban civic revolution were identified by the statistical model (Figure 3.14). According to the model, over the 1990s the risk of urban civic revolt rose precipitously—driven by the growing repression, corruption, and tenure in office of Prime Minister Mahathir Mohamad, who had ruled the country since 1981. For 1998, the model identified the risk of urban civic revolt in Malaysia as .038—almost nine times the average risk since 1900, and four times the average risk after the Cold War. Potential triggers were plentiful. The Asian financial crisis plowed into Malaysia with even greater force than in Indonesia, causing a dramatic collapse of its currency and stock market.[98] As Dan Slater notes,

> For all its remarkable political stability throughout four decades of independence . . . , Malaysia suddenly seemed ripe for democratic transition by 1998. The Malaysian economy was suffering a crisis of unprecedented

98. Pepinsky 2009, 194.

proportions; long-serving Prime Minister Mahathir Mohamad had become increasingly perceived as despotic and incompetent; and Indonesia's dramatic authoritarian collapse in May raised the prospect of spillover to its ostensibly more liberal, pluralist Malaysian neighbor.[99]

Yet no such revolution occurred.[100]

A diminished echo of the Indonesian events rippled through Malaysia in connection with the firing of Deputy Prime Minister Anwar Ibrahim. A devout Muslim economist who embraced neoliberal reforms and possessed a relatively clean reputation, Anwar represented the aspirations of the emerging urban middle class for reining in the abuses of the Mahathir government. As Mahathir's heir apparent, he was fired from his position for seeking to supplant his mentor. This act led to a major outburst of protests and the emergence of the so-called *reformasi* movement, modeled on the changes introduced in neighboring Indonesia in the wake of its 1998 revolution. Pulling on a diverse coalition of opposition parties and Malay youth, the *reformasi* movement organized a series of quasi-revolutionary protests calling for the removal of Mahathir, though stopping short of a mass siege of power aimed at forcing regime-change.

The protests peaked in September 1998, when tens of thousands marched on the prime minister's residence. They were met with tear gas and water cannon.[101] In response, the regime arrested Anwar and sentenced him to prison on trumped-up charges of sodomy and corruption. For a while, the movement continued to hold intermittent rallies. But meeting consistent repression and plagued by divisions among its various factions, the protests never evolved into a revolutionary episode and petered out completely by November 1999, when the regime retained its two-thirds majority in parliamentary elections. In particular, Mahathir was able to rely on the loyalty of Chinese voters (then a quarter of the population) by raising the specter that *reformasi* might instigate the type of anti-Chinese riots that accompanied revolution in Indonesia. According to the probabilistic model, the risk of urban civic revolt remained high in Malaysia until 2003, when Mahathir resigned. It declined further after

---

99. Slater 2010, 111.

100. In 1998, corruption was "routine and expected" in both Malaysia and Indonesia, and both countries were significant oil producers. But Malaysia (GDP per capita of $8,139) was considerably wealthier than Indonesia ($3,704), its political system leaned to the open side of non-democracies (3 on the Polity scale) while Indonesia was a closed autocracy (−7 on the Polity scale), and Malaysia's leader Mahathir Mohamad had been in power seventeen years, compared to thirty-two years for Indonesia's Suharto.

101. Katsiaficas 2013, 356; Slater 2010, 216–17; Weiss 2006; Nair 2007.

elections in 2008. In short, the Malaysian regime was able to ride out a heightened risk of revolt and to marginalize opposition challenges through skillful deployment of repression, exploitation of divisions within the opposition, manipulation of communal tensions, and the continued cohesion of elite institutions.

Conclusion: The Power and Limits of Structural Explanation

Natural analogies abound in the study of revolutions. Do revolutions occur more like earthquakes, with pressure building beneath the surface of society until an inevitable trigger abruptly releases pent-up forces? Or do they occur more like wildfires, in which an arbitrary "spark" causes society to burst suddenly into flames, with an unknowable structure of hidden preferences constituting the fuel on which the fire burns?

In this chapter, I have offered a third perspective. Urban civic revolutionary episodes do not materialize automatically from favorable structural conditions, even in the abundant presence of triggers. Rather, they develop. The onset of urban civic revolutionary contention is shaped to a greater degree than social revolutions and other forms of revolution by the features of political regimes, with corrupt, personalist, repressive governments being particularly vulnerable. But even in the presence of conducive structural conditions, and even in the presence of events that could act as triggers, the emergence of urban civic revolutionary contention has been tentative and uncertain—dependent on the actions and interactions of regimes and oppositions. Most country-years that were structurally conducive to experiencing urban civic revolution and that also experienced common triggers like financial stress or falsified elections never saw the development of urban civic revolutionary contention.

Social revolutions may function differently: they are more deeply rooted in the class structures of society than in the features of political regimes. It is possible that they more closely resemble the earthquakes to which Goldstone likened them—suddenly bursting onto the historical scene in response to an inevitable trigger. But urban civic revolutions are clearly not earthquakes waiting to happen. Though associated with specific structural conditions, their emergence has depended on the actions and interactions of regimes and oppositions in order to transform them, as it were, from tropical disturbances into perfect storms. Sometimes a regime under heightened structural risk acted to prevent urban civic contention from materializing. Occasionally, a regime that was not under significant structural risk acted in such a way as to incite revolutionary mobilization where it otherwise would have been unlikely—the cyclone bombs of revolution. Even in cases in which structure exerted its strongest influence, structural factors were significantly better at identifying *where* urban civic revolutionary challenges materialized than *when* they materialized. Ultimately, whether heightened structural risk translated into urban civic contention—even in the presence of triggers—depended on the ways in which regimes and oppositions took advantage of the structural conditions with which they were presented.

In this respect, the unpredictability of urban civic revolutions is rooted less in an unknowable structure of hidden preferences than in the dynamic character of the regime–opposition interactions that are essential to their emergence. As in the forecasting of hurricanes, any specific incident of urban civic revolution may be unpredictable, dependent as it is on these interactions. But over the long term, distinct patterns emerge—a reflection of the deeper structural factors that have shaped urban civic contention but have not determined it.

4

The Repression–Disruption Trade-off and the Shifting Odds of Success

> An insurrection when it breaks out is an idea which submits itself to trial by the people. If the people turn down their thumbs, then the idea is dead fruit, the insurrection has failed.
>
> VICTOR HUGO, LES MISÉRABLES (1862)[1]

THERE ARE TWO WAYS of judging "success" in revolution. By the minimalist criterion, a revolution can be deemed successful when, in the words of Tilly, it leads to "the displacement of one set of power holders by another."[2] I refer to this minimalist notion as "opposition success." By the maximalist criterion, a revolution can be judged successful when the revolutionary opposition displaces the incumbent regime *and* the post-revolutionary regime brings about substantive, intended, lasting change. I refer to this as "substantive success." Revolutionary outcomes need to be judged by both criteria, and indeed the maximalist criterion assumes the minimalist within it. In this chapter I examine opposition success. Given the outbreak of revolt, what factors influence whether a revolutionary opposition is able to evict an incumbent regime?

Normally incumbent regimes enjoy great advantages over revolutionary oppositions. They already occupy the high ground of government and dominate oppositions in terms of arms and resources. Occasionally, one encounters a regime so fragile that it crumbles after its first confrontations with mass

---

1. Hugo 1982 [1862], 1045.
2. Tilly 1978, 193.

unrest. In Georgia during the 2003 Rose Revolution, police defections to the opposition were aided by the fact that, on the eve of the revolution, the police had not been paid for three months. Under these circumstances the police not only gladly allowed opposition supporters to enter the legislative and state chancellery buildings; they actually cleared a path for them to storm the parliament.[3] But in the vast majority of cases incumbent regimes do not fall quite so easily. Revolutionary episodes are rare; successful revolutions still rarer. From 1900 to 2014, only 123 cases of revolutionary contention involving at least a thousand civilian participants resulted in oppositions gaining power—slightly more than a third of all episodes. Yet, as we will see, over the 1900–2014 period the odds of attaining power through revolution strikingly improved. Even as the frequency of revolutionary contention increased, the rate of opposition success more than doubled. These two trends were likely related: the increasing odds of opposition success undoubtedly incentivized growing numbers of challengers to take their chances.

As I will show, these shifting odds of opposition success were in significant part due to the movement of revolution back to cities and the proliferation of the urban civic revolutionary repertoire. As we have seen, urban revolts take place where the coercive capacity of the state is strongest, rendering revolutionary oppositions highly vulnerable to government repression. But proximity to centers of power and commerce also comes with advantages, bringing revolutionaries closer to their ultimate targets and allowing them potentially to disrupt an incumbent regime more efficiently than would be possible at greater distance. This is the repression–disruption trade-off that forms the basis for much of my understanding of the spatial dimensions of revolutionary contention.

But as people, power, and wealth concentrated in cities over the past century, the resources and opportunities available to urban revolutionaries shifted. Large cities make possible revolutionary strategies that rely on the power of numbers for countering regime repression and disrupting governments. Large cities also contain better resourced and highly networked populations, more robust means for communication, greater visibility, and greater connections to the outside world. The need to translate these advantages into opposition success led revolutionary oppositions to deploy particular mobilizational tactics: the urban civic repertoire. As opposed to armed revolts in cities or urban rioting, urban civic revolts attempt to mobilize as many people as possible in central urban spaces in a concentrated period of time, thereby paralyzing government and society with the hope of inducing regime collapse.

3. Karumidze and Wertsch 2005, 39, 47, 54.

The urban civic repertoire seeks to take advantage of the revolutionary assets and opportunities afforded by a large urban environment. The tactics, goals, and organization of such revolts are constructed in ways that leverage the revolutionary advantages of large cities, helping to explain why these revolts have achieved a relatively high rate of success.

This chapter proceeds as follows. First, using data on the outcomes of 343 revolutionary episodes around the world from 1900 to 2014, I demonstrate the increase in rates of opposition success over time, showing how this has been associated with the urbanization of revolution and the spread of the urban civic repertoire. I then examine why this might be so by unpacking the factors that have been associated with opposition success in urban and rural environments over the past century and how these relate to the urban civic repertoire. I show that the regimes most vulnerable to overthrow in the face of urban revolutionary challenges have been significantly different from those most vulnerable to overthrow from rural revolts. In urban revolutions, oppositions have been more likely to succeed when facing hybrid and personalist authoritarian regimes—a pattern that does not hold for rural revolutions. The outcomes of urban revolutions have been much more sensitive than the outcomes of rural revolutions to regime features. Thus, as authoritarian regimes grew more hybrid in the wake of the Cold War, they also grew more vulnerable to being overthrown when facing urban (and especially urban civic) revolutionary challenges.

I also show that in urban environments, the ability to mobilize large numbers in open public spaces (and the features of oppositions that facilitate this—unarmed revolt, minimalist goals, and coalitional leaderships) has been strongly associated with opposition success. These features constitute the core elements of the urban civic repertoire. The same, however, is not true in the countryside, where numbers matter less, and violence is more strongly associated with opposition victory. But even in urban revolts, there are diminishing returns to numbers, and it is only at extremely large numbers that the odds truly tip in favor of opposition victory. As urbanization concentrated large numbers in cities over the past century, the mobilization of exceptionally large numbers in revolutionary protests in cities grew more feasible, tilting the repression–disruption trade-off function in favor of the urban civic repertoire.

Revolutionary Success across a Century of Revolt

Over the past century, the odds of achieving power through revolution have markedly improved. Figure 4.1 displays the number of successful and unsuccessful revolutionary episodes from 1900 to 2014. As it shows, the number of successful revolutions peaked during World War I, the early 1960s, the late

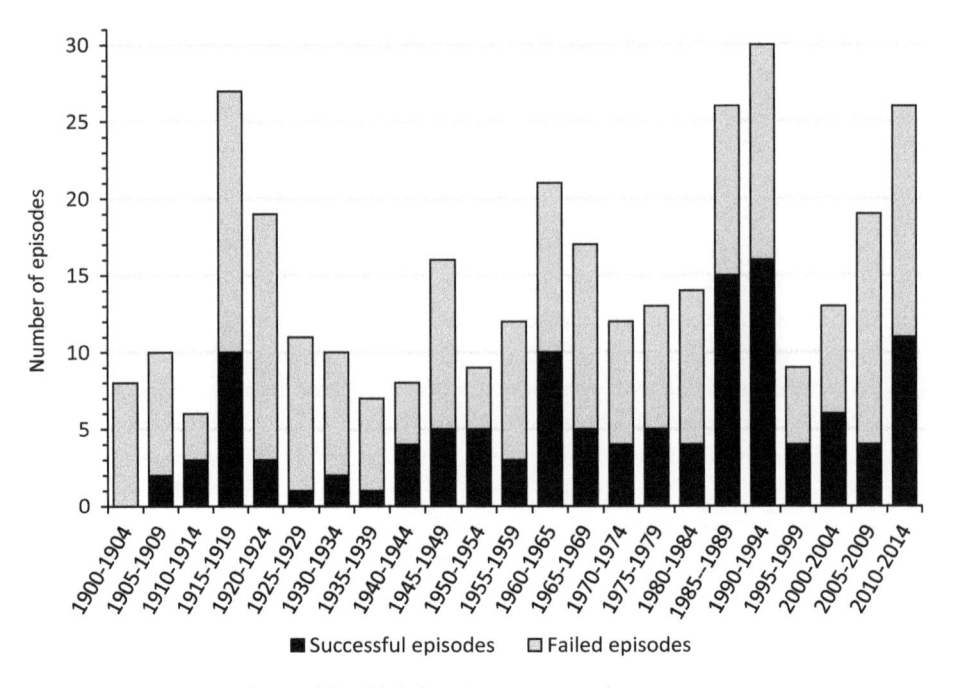

FIGURE 4.1. Successful and failed revolutionary episodes over time, 1900–2014.

1980s and early 1990s, and the 2010s. These were also moments of significant increase in the overall number of revolutionary episodes—a reflection of the impact of transnational revolutionary waves on revolutionary success. Although it is difficult to see in Figure 4.1, the number of successful revolutions has generally grown over time. This is confirmed by a simple count model, which reveals a statistically significant relationship (at the .001 level) between time and the number of successful revolutionary episodes over the 1900–2014 period.[4] By contrast, there is no statistically significant relationship between time and the number of failed revolutionary episodes. In other words, successes have been growing more frequent while failures have not. In the early twentieth century, one would have expected to find a successful revolution approximately once every two years; by the early twenty-first century, successful revolutions occurred at a rate of two every year.

The growth in revolutionary success over time is more clearly visible in Figure 4.2, which displays the proportion of successful revolutionary episodes

---

4. The findings hold even when one drops cases associated with the collapse of European communism.

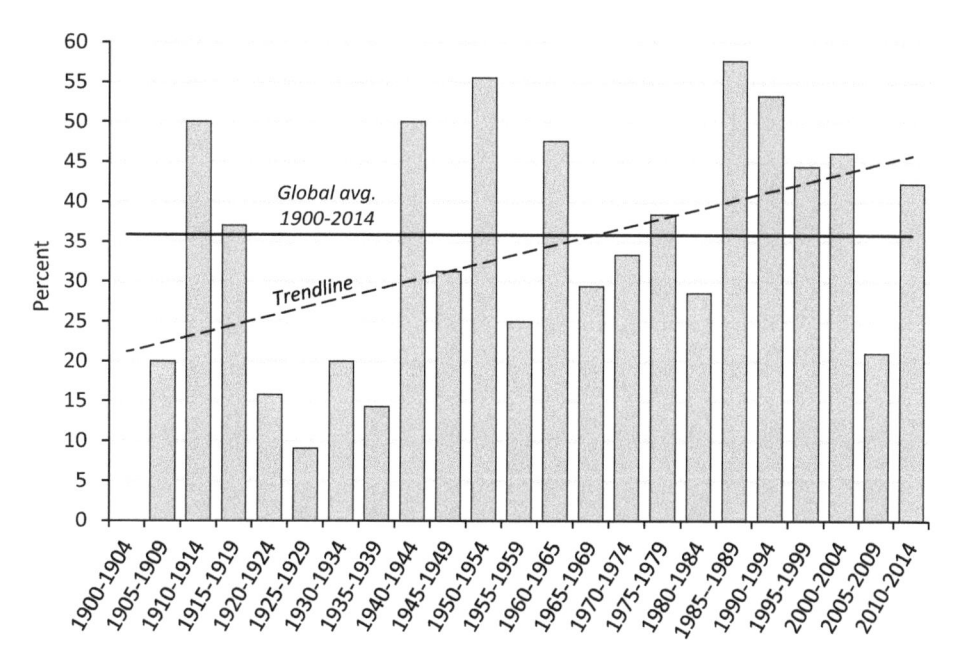

FIGURE 4.2. Percentage of successful revolutionary episodes over time, 1900–2014.

over five-year intervals from 1900 to 2014. The percentage of successful episodes has gradually risen over time. The trendline is positive, and in the post–Cold War period the proportion of episodes experiencing success was consistently above the average success rate for the 1900–2014 period as a whole (with the sole exception of the 2005–9 interval).[5] During the first half of the twentieth century, 25 percent of revolutionary episodes resulted in the opposition attaining power. During the Cold War years, the rate of success increased to 37 percent. After the Cold War, the success rate rose still further to 46 percent.[6] Despite the overall upward trend, there has still been a great deal of fluctuation in success rates over time. But the probability of success for a revolutionary

---

5. The lowered rate of success from 2005 through 2009 reflected regime learning in the wake of the spread of the color revolutions. A series of failed attempts at electoral revolution (in Azerbaijan, Belarus, Armenia, Moldova, and Iran) followed the earlier successes of the color revolutions in Serbia, Georgia, and Ukraine during the 2000–2004 period.

6. Part of this growth in opposition success was due to the collapse of European communism, which involved a large number of interconnected cases and a high rate of success (75 percent). But even excluding these cases, 41 percent of revolutionary episodes in the post–Cold War era resulted in the opposition coming to power.

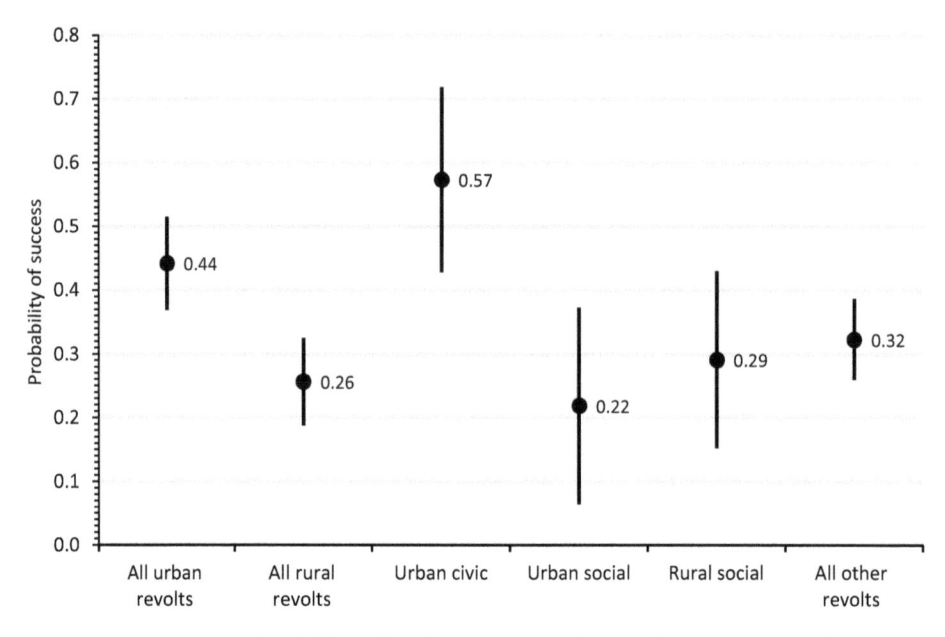

FIGURE 4.3. Marginal probability of revolutionary success by episode type, controlling for the effects of time. Logistic regression (n = 343). Point estimates, with 95 percent confidence intervals.

episode more than doubled over the 1900–2014 period, rising from .23 at the beginning of the twentieth century to .48 by 2014.[7]

This remarkable growth in opposition success has been connected in part with the shifting locations and forms of revolution. Toward the end of the twentieth century, revolutionary contention grew increasingly urban. If most revolutionary episodes in the first half of twentieth century and the Cold War occurred predominantly in the countryside and in countries whose populations were overwhelmingly rural, since the end of the Cold War revolutionary episodes have occurred primarily in cities and in societies that are increasingly urban. As Figure 4.3 shows, the urbanization of revolt has been closely associated with an increased probability of revolutionary success. Controlling for the effects of time (and thereby eliminating any period effects), urban revolts have had a probability of success (.44) that is substantially greater

---

7. Based on a logistic regression of 343 revolutionary episodes from 1900 to 2014. Statistically significant at the .01 level. See Appendix 4C for details on the logistic models used in this chapter.

than that of rural revolts (.26).[8] Location is not the only factor that mattered. Urban social revolutionary episodes, for instance, had only a .22 probability of success. They almost always involved armed rebellion in cities, where the state's coercive forces are concentrated and armed revolutionaries are at a strategic disadvantage. Their goals also typically stoked considerable resistance from propertied classes and the state. Rural social revolutionary episodes, trading disruptive capacity for safety by carrying out armed rebellion at a distance from the state's repressive apparatus, performed marginally better (a .29 probability of success). By contrast, urban civic revolutionary episodes—espousing minimalist goals of removing a corrupt and repressive regime and mobilizing large numbers in urban public spaces in proximity to command centers of power—exhibited an extraordinary record of success (a .57 probability of opposition victory).[9]

What explains the exceptional success of the urban civic model? If incumbent regimes hold the high ground in revolution and normally dominate oppositions in terms of arms and resources, revolutions are able to succeed against the odds because they effectively leverage the resources available to them in the environment within which they operate, neutralize regime advantages, raise the costs of continued support for the regime, and force disintegration of its coalition. There are numerous factors that might influence the capacity of oppositions to accomplish these tasks. In the analysis that follows, I divide them into two broad categories: first, the strengths and vulnerabilities of the regimes targeted by revolutionaries; and second, opposition goals, mobilizational capacities, and tactics. The division is artificial, since the two are often related to one another. Nevertheless, as a way of dissecting some of the patterns associated with revolutionary success over the past century, it is a useful device. As I show, the urban or rural context of rebellion has exerted a strong influence on how these factors affect revolutionary outcomes. It is not the only factor that has mattered; but it has been among the most important.

Location and Regime Strengths and Vulnerabilities

Regimes have different vulnerabilities to revolutionary challenge depending on their institutional configurations, resources, strengths, and weaknesses. As a significant literature has indicated, open regimes are better able to co-opt

---

8. Statistically significant at the .001 level.

9. The substantially higher probability of success for the urban civic model holds true even if one excludes those cases associated with the collapse of European communism, restricts the sample only to the post–Cold War period, or compares urban civic revolts only with other urban revolts.

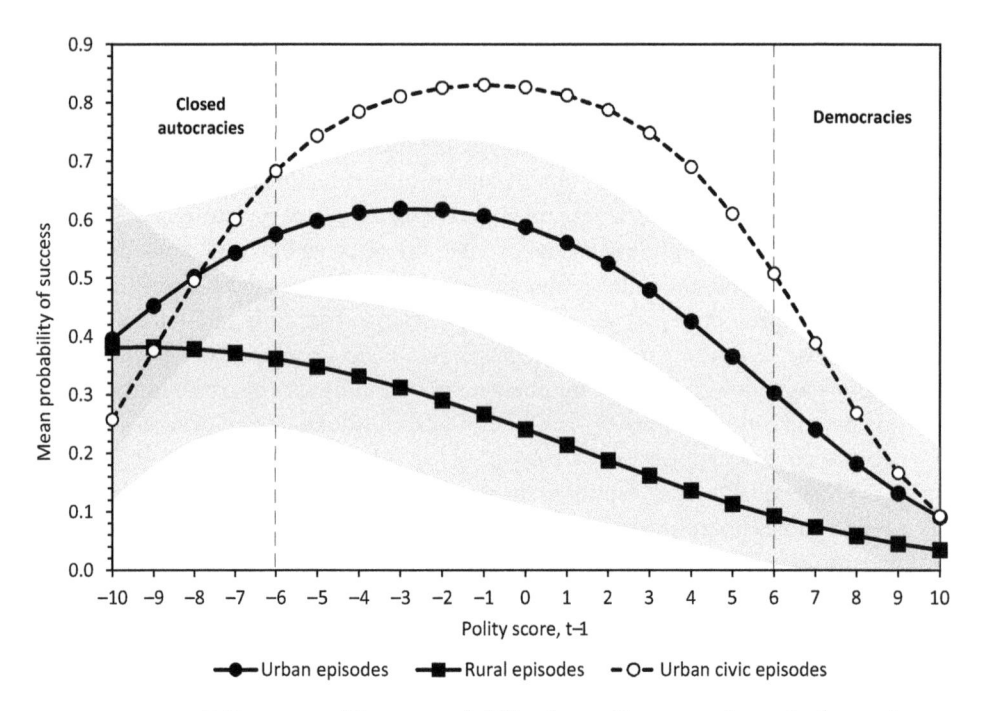

FIGURE 4.4. Polity scores and the mean probability of opposition success, by rural, urban, and urban civic episodes. Average marginal predictions of a logistic regression on twenty multiple-imputation samples (colonies excluded), with 95 percent confidence intervals. For revolutionary contention in territories that were part of another state, the Polity score for the central government was used. The quadratic form was adopted after testing for fit using the Bayesian Information Criterion (BIC).

political opponents, but are more constrained in their ability to apply force. Closed regimes are better able to marginalize revolutionary challengers by force because they are less constrained by sustaining coalitions. Nevertheless, they are less capable of co-opting opponents.[10] Figure 4.4 reports the results of tests for the effect of political openness (as measured by Polity scores) on revolutionary outcomes since 1900, given the prior materialization of a revolutionary challenge. Once a significant revolutionary challenge emerged, regimes in the more open range of the Polity scale (above zero) had less chance of being overthrown than those in the more closed range (below zero)—irrespective of the frequency with which revolutionary contention occurred.

---

10. Tullock 1971; Silver 1974; Bueno de Mesquita and Smith 2010. See also Eisinger 1973; Tilly 1978; Tarrow 1998.

To be sure, revolutionary episodes occur much less frequently in democracies.[11] Since 1900, only forty-eight episodes have occurred in countries that scored 6 or above on the Polity scale—the cut-off that is typically used to indicate regimes approaching the democratic range. Almost all of these episodes took place in lower-quality democracies. But of these forty-eight episodes, only seven (15 percent) were successful—an extremely low rate of success. As Jeff Goodwin observed, "No popular revolutionary movement ... has ever overthrown a consolidated democratic regime."[12] The reason is simple: revolutionary movements that seek to overthrow democracies confront the question of why large numbers should take the extraordinary risks associated with revolution when they could wait out the regime until it must submit itself for approval at the ballot box.[13] In this sense, among other qualities, democracies depend upon patience. Only groups that feel perpetually locked out of power (i.e., permanent minorities) would consider engaging in revolutionary mobilization against a functioning democratic regime. But such groups would be able to rely on smaller numbers and therefore would be less likely to succeed. The general effectiveness of democracies in countering revolutionary threats also points to a truism of counterrevolutionary strategy: co-optation has generally worked better than repression for neutralizing revolutionary threats.

There are, however, important differences in the vulnerabilities of regimes depending on the location and character of revolutionary challenge. As Figure 4.4 shows, urban revolts have had a far greater effectiveness against a much broader range of non-democratic regimes than rural revolts. As the proximity dilemma implies, proximity of rebellion to centers of power, commerce, and population renders most regimes more vulnerable to revolutionary overthrow than is the case when revolt is carried out at greater distance. There has been little difference between urban and rural revolutions for the most repressive and the most open regimes. But the middle ranges of the Polity scale (from −6 to 6) have been much more vulnerable to urban than rural revolution.

This has been especially true for urban civic revolutions.[14] The tactics of the urban civic repertoire—mobilizing large numbers in central urban spaces in

---

11. In a complementary log-log panel model with robust standard errors and controls for time dependence (n = 10,777 country-years from 1900 to 2014 across 164 countries), there is a negative and statistically significant relationship (at the .001 level) between the Boix, Miller, and Rosato binary measure of electoral democracy and the likelihood of experiencing a revolutionary episode.

12. Goodwin 2001, 300.

13. Obviously, in democratic regimes in which electoral fraud or manipulation occur, this dictum does not hold.

14. These findings hold even when controlling for the onset year of an episode.

a concentrated period of time—have magnified the advantages of urban location when mobilizing against non-democratic regimes in the middle ranges of the Polity scale. However, they have been less effective against the most closed regimes—even less effective than other types of urban revolts. Examples of failed urban civic revolutions that fall into this category include the 8888 Uprising and the Saffron Revolution in Burma, the 1989 Tiananmen protests in China, the 2011 Electoral Protests in Iran, and the 2005 attempt at a color revolution in Azerbaijan. The willingness of such regimes to carry out extreme measures of repression against unarmed crowds and their higher levels of cohesion in the face of revolutionary challenge rendered them harder to overthrow through the power of numbers. Less closed authoritarian regimes have had more difficulty controlling urban civic challenges, due to the greater space they afford to political opposition and their looser sustaining coalitions—all of which translated into larger opposition numbers and less ability to contain backlash when applying repression against crowds. Unlike consolidated democracies, these regimes have often lacked electoral mechanisms for co-opting opposition or engaged in extensive electoral fraud. At the end of the twentieth century, non-democratic regimes grew markedly more hybrid and competitive in response to the global advance of democracy and American hegemony.[15] As this loosening of autocracies under domestic and international pressure spread, hybrid regimes grew increasingly vulnerable to overthrow by urban civic revolt. Examples of the limited opening of highly closed autocracies that helped to facilitate successful urban civic revolt include the People Power Revolution in the Philippines in 1986, the 1987 South Korean June Uprising, the collapse of Soviet communism from 1987 to 1991, and the 2011 Egyptian Revolution. In essence, the evolution of regimes after the end of the Cold War in a more hybrid direction played to the strengths of the urban civic repertoire.

A substantial literature suggests that institutionalized forms of authoritarianism are more resilient in the face of revolutionary challenge.[16] Their sustaining coalitions are broader, and they are better able to co-opt potential opposition and monitor dissent within their institutions.[17] As we saw in Chapter 3, military and personalist autocracies have been more prone than other types of non-democratic government to experiencing revolutionary contention, while monarchies and party autocracies have been the least susceptible to facing revolutionary threats.[18]

15. Levitsky and Way 2010.
16. Gandhi and Przeworski 2006; Geddes, Wright, and Frantz 2014; Lee 2015.
17. Magaloni 2008.
18. Using the Geddes, Wright, and Frantz data on non-democratic regime-types since 1946 and based on a complementary log-log panel model with robust standard errors and controls for time dependence (n = 7,699 country-years across 148 countries), military and personalist

When faced with the outbreak of a revolutionary threat, military regimes have had a high probability (.49) of being overthrown. But so too have monarchies (a .48 probability of opposition success). One-party authoritarian regimes (.42) and competitive authoritarian regimes (.37) have been somewhat more resilient.[19] But the probability of opposition success has been significantly higher for all types of regimes if the revolutionary threat occurred predominantly in cities rather than the countryside: for monarchies—.60 versus .27; for military regimes—.58 versus .35; for one-party regimes—.48 versus .33; for competitive authoritarian regimes—.48 versus .24; and for democracies—.29 versus .05. In short, urban location has magnified the vulnerabilities of all types of regimes, but especially those with narrow coalitions.

Personalist regimes, as defined by Geddes, Wright, and Frantz,[20] have not only had a higher likelihood than other types of regimes of being challenged by revolution; they have also had a higher likelihood of being overthrown when confronting a revolutionary threat (.62)—higher than all other types of regimes. Relatedly, there has been a strong relationship between the number of years during which a regime's leader has been in power and the likelihood of a regime being toppled when confronting a revolutionary challenge. On average, a regime whose leader has been in power for only five years had only a .34 probability of being overthrown, while the equivalent probability for a regime whose leader has been in power for twenty-five years was .60.[21] Again, these vulnerabilities are magnified when the revolutionary challenge occurs in cities. Some studies suggest that older leaders—particularly in non-democracies—are more vulnerable to overthrow than younger leaders.[22] As leaders age, not only do their physical and mental abilities decline, but those surrounding them also come to anticipate their eventual exit from power. This renders a change of leadership more thinkable, and jockeying among potential successors can create splits within a regime's coalition that facilitate regime-change. There is no statistically significant relationship between the age of a leader and the emergence of revolutionary challenges, but there is a relationship between

---

autocracies were more prone to experiencing a revolutionary episode than other types of non-democracies.

19. Again, these findings hold even when controlling for onset year. Data on regime-types come from my own classification. The greater vulnerability of military regimes and monarchies to collapse in the face of revolutionary challenge is further confirmed on the smaller Geddes, Wright, and Frantz sample.

20. Geddes, Wright, and Frantz 2014.

21. Statistically significant at the .001 level using twenty multiple-imputation samples (colonies excluded).

22. Bueno de Mesquita and Smith 2010, 943.

a leader's age and the ability of that leader to survive a revolutionary challenge once a challenge has materialized.[23] Thus, a forty-year-old leader in a closed autocracy (Polity score of −6) had a .40 probability of being overthrown in the face of a serious revolutionary threat, but a seventy-five-year-old leader in the same situation had a .61 probability. Examples include Erich Honecker (aged seventy-seven at the time of the East German Revolution in 1989), Suharto (aged seventy-seven at the time of the Indonesian Revolution in 1998), Porfirio Diaz (aged eighty at the time of the Mexican Revolution in 1910), Hosni Mubarak (aged eighty-three at the time of the Egyptian Revolution of 2011), and Syngman Rhee (aged eighty-five at the time of the April Revolution in South Korea in 1960).[24]

A number of other factors affect the capacity of a regime to weather significant revolutionary challenges. Wealthier and well-resourced regimes have been better positioned than regimes that lacked resources to survive revolutionary crises because of their ability to hold their coalitions together and co-opt potential opposition supporters through side-payments or concessions.[25] Holding other variables constant at their means, a country with a GDP per capita of $1,000 had a .39 likelihood of having its regime toppled when faced with a significant revolutionary threat, while a country with a GDP per capita of $5,000 had a .25 chance of being overthrown, and a country with a GDP per capita of $10,000 only a .13 probability. And holding other variables at their means, an opposition that embarked upon revolution in a country producing no oil had a .44 chance of attaining power, whereas a revolutionary opposition in a country whose oil production was in the ninetieth percentile among countries had only a .17 probability of success. Countries experiencing urban revolutionary contention have generally tended to be wealthier than those experiencing rural revolutionary contention.[26] Thus, one of the disadvantages facing urban revolutionary oppositions—particularly in countries that have significant oil resources or are more developed—is that

---

23. Statistically significant at the .05 level using twenty multiple-imputation samples (colonies excluded), controlling for the degree of openness of the regime. The effect does not hold for aging leaders in more open regimes. Thus, in a regime with a Polity score of 6, there is only a .27 probability of overthrow through revolution for a seventy-five-year-old leader.

24. Once one controls for the number of years an incumbent leader has been in office, the relationship between leader age and revolutionary outcomes grows statistically insignificant, as the effect of age is captured by the tenure-in-office variable. For obvious reasons, the two variables are closely correlated.

25. Fearon and Laitin 2003; Collier and Hoeffler 2004; Bueno de Mesquita and Smith 2010; Knutsen 2014.

26. t = −7.039, significant at the .001 level with 286 degrees of freedom.

these regimes have greater resources for holding coalitions together and co-opting potential opposition than is the case for countries experiencing rural rebellions.

The Haitian Revolution of 1946 illustrates well how an absence of resources for maintaining a regime's coalition and co-opting political opponents facilitates opposition revolutionary success. In 1946, impoverished Haiti (GDP per capita of $1,046 and no oil resources) teetered on the brink of bankruptcy.[27] The highly repressive regime of Élie Lescot had relied on clandestine payoffs from Dominican dictator Rafael Trujillo. But in 1943 Trujillo withdrew his support, and much of the glue holding Lescot's regime dissolved. Lescot's disastrous economic policies further pushed his regime to the brink of revolt. A rubber production program sponsored by the United States confiscated land with little compensation and left the countryside completely impoverished. The Lescot regime fell apart in the course of five days in the face of a small Marxist-led urban mobilization aimed at incorporating the country's black population. Students, workers, teachers, shopkeepers, and even civil servants peeled off and joined the opposition, with a crowd of four thousand marching to the presidential palace. When soldiers shot into the small crowd, killing two demonstrators, riots broke out in the capital and strikes broadened, leading the cabinet to resign. Lescot ordered his soldiers to engage in a crackdown, but the military refused to obey, instead arresting Lescot and eventually holding elections for a new government.[28]

Contrast the ease with which the impoverished Lescot regime fell in the face of relatively small crowds with the enormous challenges facing Azerbaijan's ill-fated attempt at a color revolution in 2005. Following the example of successful revolutions in Georgia, Ukraine, and Kyrgyzstan, Azerbaijani opposition parties banded together to create the Freedom Coalition (Azadlig) in an attempt to carry out an electoral revolution. But the government of Ilham Aliyev was flush with oil cash and enjoyed unwavering American support for its potential role as a source of oil and gas for Europe in an attempt to counter Russian influence.[29] Aliyev repelled this bothersome rebellion with ease, holding his coalition together through a combination of intimidation and payoffs. Aliyev's party dominated the elections in November, receiving 62 percent of the vote. Despite opposition efforts to carry out electoral observation, vote

---

27. Holding other variables at their means, a regime with these features would have had a .50 chance of being overthrown, given the onset of revolutionary contention.

28. Smith 2004; Parkman 1990.

29. Holding other variables at their means, a regime like Azerbaijan in 2004 (with a GDP per capita of $4,597 and 15.7 million metric tons of oil produced per year) would have had only a .15 chance of being overthrown by revolution in the face of a revolutionary challenge.

fraud was rampant. Opposition protesters took to the streets, waving orange banners in imitation of Ukraine's Orange Revolution and calling for the government's removal. But the protests could only muster twenty to thirty thousand participants—hardly enough to crack Aliyev's well-funded coalition. His richly remunerated police brutally broke up the demonstrations, leaving hundreds of protesters badly injured.[30]

Since the days of Trotsky, it has been generally recognized that maintaining control over the army and police is critical for a regime's ability to weather revolutionary crises.[31] Factors known to affect military defection in revolutionary situations include the internal cohesion of the military, the degree to which it consists of conscripts, the social backgrounds of soldiers, the past record of the military's conduct toward society, and the extent to which the military is well paid and supplied. Many of these factors are difficult to quantify,[32] but one is fairly straightforward: military remuneration and supply. Zoltan Barany has argued that "[a]ll things being equal, if the regime makes a genuine effort to supply the military with the facilities and equipment that it needs, the top brass are likely to stand by their rulers."[33] By contrast, on the basis of the Arab Spring cases, Eva Bellin contended that military capacity is not the main issue for military defection in the face of revolutionary challenge, but rather military professionalism. Because it enjoys greater institutional autonomy and independence from the incumbent regime, a professionalized military sees its mission as defending the country rather than defending the regime and has less to lose from defection.[34] Resentment of its deployment as a police force was a major cause of defection of portions of the Soviet army to Boris Yeltsin during the August 1991 coup. General Aleksandr Lebed recalled that "placing police functions on the army was a great humiliation for the army. The army was

---

30. Bunce and Wolchik 2011; Valiyev 2006. For an inside look into the failure of the revolt, see the BBC documentary *How to Plan a Revolution* (O'Mahoney 2006).

31. As Trotsky wrote in his analysis of the Bolshevik Revolution, "the first task of every insurrection is to bring the troops over to its side." Trotsky 1932, vol. 3, 181. See also Skocpol 1979; Chorley 1973; Barany 2016.

32. I did test for the effect of military conscription on revolutionary outcomes using the data of Asal, Conrad, and Toronto (2017), but found no statistically significant effect on outcomes.

33. Barany 2016, 31. See also Nepstad 2013.

34. Bellin 2012. For a similar argument, see Lutterbeck 2013. Others have found, on the basis of a detailed examination, that the army in Tunisia never really defected. Anti-terrorist units within the Interior Ministry (still highly professionalized units, though not within the military) detained members of the Trabelsi and Ben Ali families as they were attempting to flee. Much of the internal security apparatus collapsed in the face of crowd-led attacks against them. See Jebnoun 2014; Pachon 2014; Grewal 2016.

Without civil war — With civil war

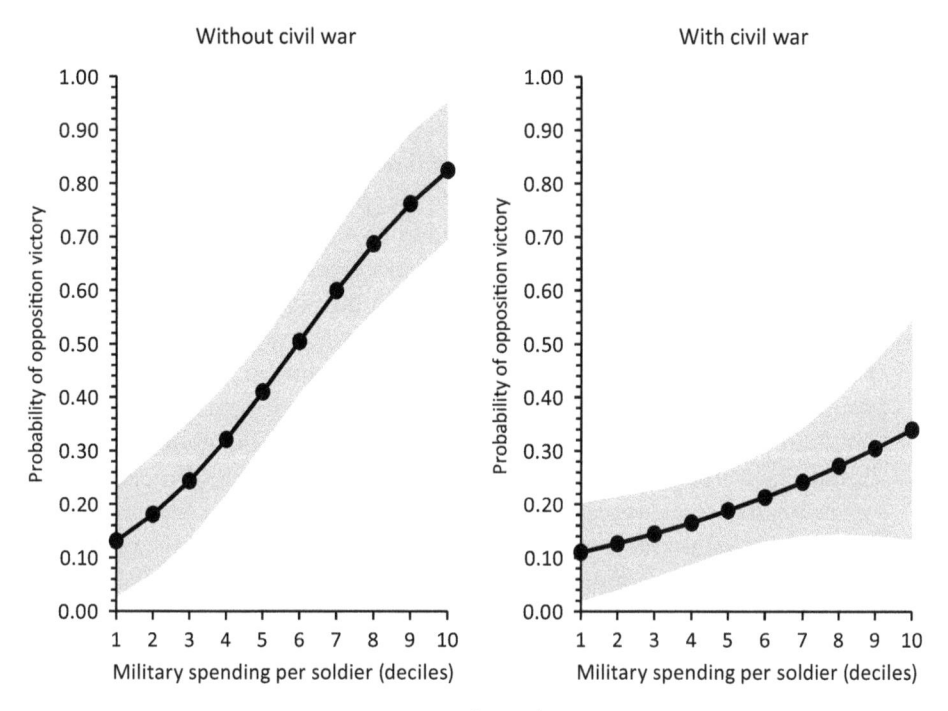

FIGURE 4.5. Military expenditure per soldier (deciles) and revolutionary outcomes, with and without civil war. Average marginal predictions of a logistic regression on twenty multiple-imputation samples (colonies excluded), holding other variables at their means. Point estimates, with 95 percent confidence intervals.

not prepared psychologically for this kind of activity, and whenever it was forced to do it, it led to one result only: enormous bitterness and the undeserved outrage of the crowd against the army."[35] By contrast, an army that is less professionalized, more patrimonial, and cemented to a regime by personal or ethnic ties is likely to be more reliable in the context of a revolutionary crisis.

I find that the relationship between military professionalism and military defection in the face of revolutionary challenge has varied according to the type of challenge involved—specifically, whether a revolution involved a civil war or not.[36] As displayed in Figure 4.5, in the context of revolutionary civil

---

35. Lebed' 1995, 249 (my translation).
36. I define a civil war as a revolutionary episode involving sustained armed combat between oppositions and an incumbent regime that lasts more than two months. See chapter 8 for details.

war, military spending per soldier (a measure of how well paid and supplied a military force is) has had a statistically insignificant (though weakly positive) relationship with opposition success. This may seem counterintuitive. One might have thought that the relationship between opposition success in revolutionary civil wars and a well-supplied and remunerated military would be strongly negative—with better paid and equipped armies leading to lower chances of opposition success. But studies have found that, while other factors—the duration of the conflict, the military capacity of rebel opposition, the administrative capacity of state institutions, the mobilizing effects of indiscriminate violence against civilians, and external intervention (particularly, pro-insurgent assistance)—are associated with outcomes in civil wars, this is not necessarily the case with regard to a regime's military capacity.[37] Indeed, revolutionary civil wars fought by conventional armies on both sides tend to be more favorable to oppositions than regimes.[38] The outcomes of revolutionary civil wars depend more on the correlation of force between regimes and rebels, the administrative capacity of the state to penetrate its territory, and the ability of rebels to sustain revolt due to popular support rather than on how well supplied and paid a regime's military may be.

However, in revolutionary contention that has not involved civil war, the opposition has had a higher probability of success when the military is better paid and better supplied. Such militaries are likely to think of themselves as professional soldiers dedicated to fighting wars, not policing populations. There are of course exceptions, as militaries are hierarchical organizations accustomed to obeying orders. But in urban environments, where revolutions rarely involve civil wars, a well-paid, professionalized military is a less useful tool for repressing revolutionary challengers than a well-paid and well-supplied police force. Police are tasked with maintaining public order; the military in many countries is not. A well-paid and well-supplied police force (like that in Aliyev's Azerbaijan) is unlikely to defect, given the large rewards it reaps for loyalty to the regime and its enhanced capabilities for carrying out its tasks. In Eduard Shevardnadze's Georgia, by contrast, the poorly paid and supplied police happily cleared a path for the opposition to take over parliament. But the situation for militaries is different. A well-paid and well-supplied military that is dispatched to put down protests can feel that it has been inappropriately diverted to the task of propping up a regime instead of focusing on its main

---

37. For an overview of the findings of the literature on civil war outcomes, see Shelton, Stojek, and Sullivan 2013. I tested for the influence of a number of other variables measuring the military capacity of a regime; none proved statistically significant.

38. Statistically significant at the .05 level.

function of defense from external attack. Moreover, when rank-and-file soldiers are deployed to put down revolts in urban environments, the possibilities multiply for revolutionary oppositions to fraternize with troops—a critical process that can induce soldiers to defect. Less professionalized militaries with extensive personal, ethnic, or family connections with ruling regimes have often been more willing to be deployed for the repression of revolutionary protests—though soldier defection can remain a challenge even in these cases.

A number of temporal conjunctures—transnational revolutionary waves, electoral campaigns, periods of reform, and external wars—are known to influence the onset of revolutionary challenges through their effects on regime cohesion, the ability of regimes to repress, and the willingness of populations to engage in risky collective action. But their influence on revolutionary outcomes has been less clear. Kurt Weyland argues that transnational waves of revolution are based on cognitive shortcuts and distorted inferences that falsely assume that success in one case can be easily transferred to another. As he put it with regard to the revolutions of 1848, successful revolution in Paris "made many people jump to the conclusion that a similar regime-change could occur in their state. This unthinking belief overwhelmed prudence, inspired enthusiasm and hope among protesters and fear among defenders of the quo." According to Weyland, this rush to revolution in the context of waves ends up producing many more failures than successes.[39] However, looking over the revolutionary record since 1900, revolutionary episodes that occurred within a transnational wave of revolution actually had a higher probability of opposition success (.51) than revolutionary episodes that occurred outside a transnational wave of revolution (.31).[40] Urban revolutions are twice as likely as

---

39. Weyland 2009, 392–93. See also Weyland 2012.

40. Statistically significant at the .001 level for twenty multiple-imputation samples. The result holds even when controlling for the effects of time, Polity scores, the number of years an incumbent regime had been in power, levels of development, military expenditures per soldier, and other forms of conjunctural influence. I coded episodes as part of a transnational revolutionary wave if, based on secondary sources, the episode was said to have drawn significant inspiration from the occurrence of a prior revolutionary episode within ten years of the episode in question. First-mover episodes that set off transnational waves were not coded as part of the wave unless they concluded after the onset of other episodes within the wave, as first-mover episodes usually set off waves because they are successful. If they concluded after the onset of other episodes in the wave, however, their success may have been influenced by the onset of other episodes. Colonies were excluded from the analysis, but as most successful anti-colonial revolutions occurred within the context of a transnational wave, had these cases been included the relationship would have undoubtedly been even stronger.

rural revolutions to occur within a transnational revolutionary wave.[41] Urban populations are better connected through mass communications and more likely to be aware of revolutionary developments in other countries. But higher rates of success for episodes within a wave hold true for both urban and rural revolutions. Thus, rural revolutions occurring within a revolutionary wave were more likely to experience opposition success (a .34 probability) than rural revolutions outside a wave (.23), and urban revolutions within a wave were more likely to be successful (.55) than urban episodes outside a revolutionary wave (.41).[42]

In short, revolutionary waves have generally been propitious times for challenging regimes from below. The reasons are several. The successful example of others injects a sense of possibility into the interactions between both regimes and oppositions. If a population can overthrow a regime in an analogous context, why not here? Example can also provide a powerful sense of momentum and direction that aids oppositions in mobilizing populations and facilitates defections from a regime's coalition. Certainly, during a transnational revolutionary wave, as Weyland argues, oppositions who would never have mobilized in the absence of a wave are inspired to act, and many have the odds heavily stacked against them. But if, historically, revolutionary oppositions have performed better when mobilizing within rather than outside waves, and opportunities for revolution materialize rarely, it is rational for revolutionaries to try to take advantage of the power of example and irrational to sit out a revolutionary wave from a guarded sense of caution. Another propitious moment may never emerge in one's lifetime. As Wendy Pearlman noted with regard to the Arab Spring, Syrian protestors

> explicitly recognized the differences among Arab countries. On the question of "whether Syria would follow in the footsteps" of its Arab neighbors, a Syria-based scholar found her interviewees to be acutely aware of the "structural differences between Syria, Tunisia, and Egypt." They consistently mentioned uniquely Syrian experiences with sectarianism and regime violence as the "important variables" governing prospects for contentious action in their country. When protestors did take to the streets, it was without illusions about the enormous obstacles that they faced. . . . They advocated revolution not out of erroneous forecasting, but out of hope.[43]

---

41. Chi-square = 23.08, statistically significant at the .001 level with 1 degree of freedom. The result includes anti-colonial revolts and excludes first-movers.

42. Statistically significant at the .05 level in twenty multiple-imputation samples.

43. Pearlman 2013, 389.

Transnational waves have grown increasingly frequent as revolution has urbanized, further reinforcing the high rates of success associated with urban revolution in the late twentieth and early twenty-first centuries.[44]

Electoral campaigns often act as lightning rods for revolutionary challenges, especially in authoritarian regimes. Not only are elections moments when regimes are forced to reach out to society for support, but electoral campaigns also have the potential to thicken opposition organization and networks. In addition, widespread fraud can function as a focal point for opposition mobilization, magnifying participation.[45] Periods of reform also multiply contention by generating discord within ruling elites, restraining repression, and encouraging oppositions to press demands—thereby potentially increasing the likelihood of opposition success.[46] And as we saw in chapter 2, external wars can weaken regimes, disrupting their repressive capacities at home and rendering them more vulnerable to revolutionary overthrow.[47] While elections, political reforms, and external war may be associated with increased onset of revolutionary contention, each had a positive but statistically insignificant relationship with revolutionary outcomes.[48]

I tested each of these regime-specific factors in both bivariate and multivariate frameworks, using both complete-case and multiple-imputation samples (Table 4.1), as well as subjecting them to a series of robustness tests. The openness/closedness of a regime (as measured by its Polity score), its degree

---

44. Revolutionary episodes that occur within waves clearly have higher success rates than those that do not. But the key challenge for identifying any independent causal effect for waves on revolutionary outcomes is the possibility that the societies that are more likely to experience successful revolutions might also be those more likely to select into revolutionary waves. Several factors associated with revolutionary outcomes are also associated with mobilizing within a transnational wave (in particular, political openness/closedness, level of development, and urban location). I used propensity score matching to identify whether there was a causal effect for mobilizing within a wave that operated independently of these factors. Using nearest-neighbor matching on the complete-case sample of 272 episodes (excluding colonies), and matching on factors associated with both revolutionary outcomes and mobilizing within a wave (urban location, level of development, and Polity score), the average treatment effect on the treated (ATET) for mobilizing within a wave was positive and substantial—a 17 percent increase in the probability of success for mobilizing within a wave (statistically significant at the .05 level, with robust standard errors). I thank Andreas Wimmer for suggesting this test.

45. Bunce and Wolchik 2011; Tucker 2007.

46. Tarrow 1998.

47. Skocpol 1979.

48. In bivariate specifications, periods of political reform were marginally significant at the .10 level, but the relationship dissolved when controlled for other factors.

TABLE 4.1. Incumbent regime characteristics and the likelihood of opposition victory in revolutionary contention[a]

	Model 1	Model 2	Model 3	Model 4	Model 5	Model 6	Model 7	Model 8	Model 9
				Multiple-imputation[b]					Complete-case[c]
Polity score, t–1	0.895 (–4.16)***		0.897 (–2.93)**	0.906 (–3.48)***	0.892 (–3.74)***	0.895 (–3.48)***	0.915 (–3.07)**	0.899 (–3.34)***	0.911 (–2.72)**
Polity score, t–1 (squared)	0.987 (–2.58)*		0.987 (–2.37)*	0.983 (–3.09)**	0.981 (–3.29)**	0.978 (–3.41)***	0.983 (–2.99)**	0.979 (–3.23)***	0.973 (–3.81)***
Monarchy		4.687 (2.82)**	1.491 (0.59)						
Military government		4.762 (3.01)**	1.228 (0.30)						
One-party authoritarian regime		3.649 (2.67)**	0.931 (–0.11)						
Competitive authoritarian regime		3.019 (2.35)*	1.129 (0.21)						
Other non-democracy		2.353 (1.44)	0.918 (–0.12)						
Years incumbent leader in power				1.045 (2.66)**	1.055 (3.12)**	1.046 (2.55)*	1.050 (2.98)**	1.043 (2.36)*	1.065 (3.13)**
Age of incumbent leader				1.014 (1.20)					
GDP per cap. ($ thousands), t–1					0.978 (–0.34)	0.850 (–2.07)*		0.830 (–2.31)*	0.842 (–2.06)*

Ln (oil production), t–1				0.895 (–3.26)**	0.887 (–3.32)***	0.893 (–3.09)**	0.864 (–3.66)***
Mil. expenditure per soldier (deciles)				1.276 (3.80)***	1.469 (4.15)***	1.471 (4.17)***	1.536 (4.46)***
Civil war					1.032 (0.04)	1.147 (0.20)	1.073 (0.09)
Civil war # Mil. expenditure per soldier					0.798 (–1.85)+	0.796 (–1.87)+	0.789 (–1.84)+
Part of transnational revolutionary wave						1.925 (2.31)*	1.583 (1.41)	
Period of political reform						1.419 (0.95)		
Electoral revolution						1.780 (1.45)		
Occurred during or in wake of foreign war						1.650 (1.51)		
n	288	288	288	288	288	288	288	233
Number of imputations	20	20	20	20	20	20	20	n.a.
F-statistic/Likelihood ratio chi-square	9.088***	2.297*	2.807**	6.804***	6.977***	6.053***	5.04***	5.60***	75.80***
Relative increase in variance (RVI)	0.03394	0.00001	0.01802	0.03336	0.05486	0.07982	0.0177	0.0708	n.a.
Fraction of missing information (FMI)	0.07178	0.00001	0.08655	0.109	0.1272	0.212	0.0896	0.2045	n.a.
AUC	0.631	0.612	0.654	0.704	0.770	0.809	0.737	0.811	0.820

(*Continued*)

TABLE 4.1. (*continued*)

	Multiple-imputation[b]								Complete-case[c]
	Model 1	Model 2	Model 3	Model 4	Model 5	Model 6	Model 7	Model 8	Model 9
Percent correctly classified (complete-case sample, n = 233)	60.9%	62.3%	63.1%	70.4%	72.1%	78.1%	71.2%	78.5%	78.1%
True positive rate (complete-case sample, n = 233)	23.9%	0.0%	28.4%	42.0%	56.8%	64.8%	46.6%	65.9%	64.8%
False positive rate for true failures (complete-case sample, n = 233)	16.6%	0.0%	15.9%	12.4%	18.6%	13.8%	13.8%	13.8%	13.8%
AIC (for complete-case sample, n = 233)	293.68	307.51	299.87	279.36	261.62	251.12	281.57	253.10	251.12
BIC (for complete-case sample, n = 233)	304.04	328.21	327.48	296.61	285.78	282.18	309.18	287.61	282.18

[a]Colonies excluded from analysis. [b]Logistic regression (odds ratios, with t-statistics in parentheses), for twenty multiple-imputation samples. [c]Logistic regression (odds ratios, with z-statistics in parentheses), based on the specification in Model 6.
+ $p < 0.10$, * $p < 0.05$, ** $p < 0.01$, *** $p < 0.001$

of personalism (based on the number of years the leader has been in power), the resources available to a regime (measured by GDP per capita and oil production), and the degree of military professionalism (measured by military spending per soldier, with its effect depending on whether the revolution involved civil war) proved robust to the influence of the other variables.[49] Taken together, these regime-specific features correctly identify the outcomes of 78 percent of revolutionary episodes over the last century, with a score of .81 for the area under the Receiver Operating Characteristic (ROC) curve accounted for by the model.[50] The area under the Receiver Operating Characteristic curve (also known as AUC) is a standard way of describing the accuracy of a classification model. A higher AUC means that the model has identified more true positives correctly while minimizing true negatives that have been falsely classified as positives. (A score of 1 represents perfect accuracy, while a score of .50 represents accuracy no better than chance.) An AUC of .81 is considered a reasonably accurate but not outstanding record of discriminating successes from failures.[51] It essentially means that there is an 81 percent chance that the model distinguished correctly between actual successes and actual failures. Nevertheless, the model does much better at correctly identifying failures (for the complete-case sample, accurate for 86 percent of actual failures) than correctly identifying successes (accurate for only 65 percent of actual successes).

As Figure 4.6 shows, the ability of these factors to classify outcomes accurately also varies substantially depending on the urban or rural location of revolutionary challenge. For urban revolutionary episodes, regime strengths and vulnerabilities categorize outcomes fairly effectively, though they are again more accurate in identifying opposition failures than opposition successes. However, for rural episodes, the features of regimes examined here have been substantially less important in determining outcomes. In the complete-case sample, they barely register much classificatory power at all, correctly identifying only a third of successful rural revolutions (though in the

---

49. The effect of transnational revolutionary waves was statistically insignificant once civil war (interacted with military spending per soldier) was included in the model. This was due to the strong relationship between civil war and the urban or rural location of revolutionary contention ($r = -.73$), as transnational waves predominantly unfold within an urban context. In the complete-case sample, a likelihood ratio test showed that the model with transnational waves was not a significant improvement over the model with waves excluded and the civil war interaction included (chi-square = 0.02).

50. The model using the complete-case sample produced an AUC of .82.

51. See Pepe 2003.

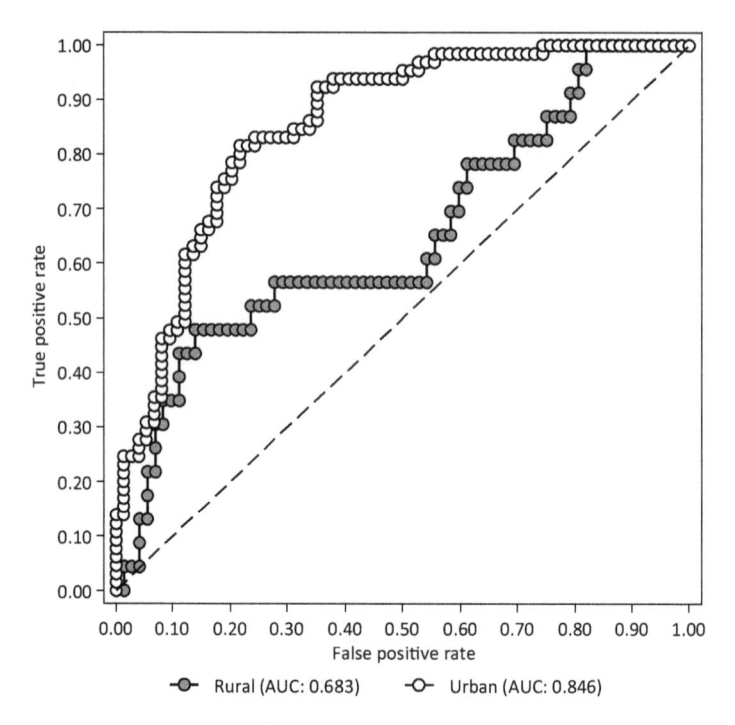

FIGURE 4.6A. ROC curve based on regime features (rural vs urban episodes), complete-case analysis. Colonies excluded, n = 233.

multiple imputation the classificatory power of regime features is greater).[52] Other factors that are not in the model (such as the capacity of states to penetrate their territory) matter more for outcomes in rural than in urban revolutions.[53] As the repression–disruption trade-off would lead us to expect, the closer a rebellion is to centers of government, the more its outcome is shaped

52. In the complete-case analysis, the difference in the areas under the ROC curve for urban and rural episodes is statistically significant at the .01 level. The complete-case estimation may be superior to multiple-imputation estimation in this instance, as there were no statistically significant relationships between whether a case contained missing data on any of the imputed independent variables and the outcome of the dependent variable. Under these circumstances the complete-case analysis can be considered free of bias due to missing observations. See Van Buuren 2018, 57–58; White and Carlin 2010.

53. Indeed, the Hanson/Sigman state capacity index is negative and marginally significant when included in the regime model, though the sample size is greatly reduced. It only has an effect on the outcomes of rural rebellions.

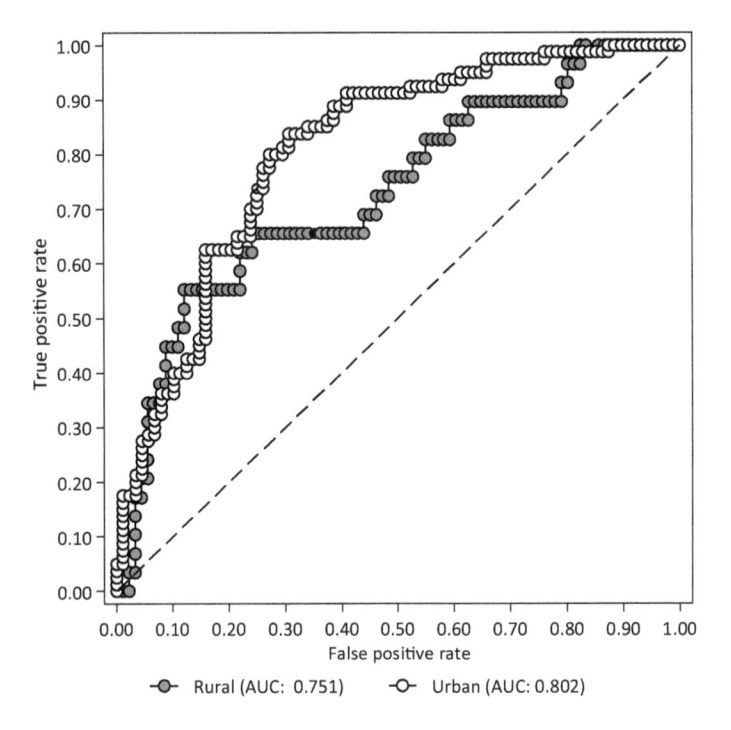

FIGURE 4.6B. ROC curve based on regime features (rural vs urban episodes), multiple-imputation analysis. Colonies excluded, n = 288. Multiple imputation was carried out using twenty samples, with 19.1 percent of cases having missing information on at least one variable.

by the features of the political regime that it opposes, while the further away a rebellion is from centers of power, the more likely it is that the outcome will be shaped by the infrastructural power of the state.

Location and Opposition Goals, Capacities, and Tactics

The factors that make regimes more fragile or durable in the face of revolutionary challenge are not the only influences on revolutionary outcomes. There have been persistent debates over the role of opposition goals, mobilizational capacities, and tactics in fostering mobilizational success. William Gamson's well-known study found that movements are more likely to succeed when their demands are less radical and less ambitious, when they deploy hierarchical rather than looser forms of organization, and when they are violent and unruly.[54] By contrast, examining a large number of episodes around the world, Erica Chenoweth and Maria Stephan argued that so-called nonviolent campaigns have been more effective than violent campaigns in achieving their ends. They contended that the ability of a movement to mobilize large numbers is the factor most closely associated with movement success. Nonviolent campaigns, they maintain, have a participation advantage over violent movements. Violence raises physical, informational, moral, and commitment-related barriers to large-scale participation, while the ability to mobilize large numbers associated with nonviolent resistance leads to "enhanced resilience, higher probabilities of tactical innovation, expanded civic disruption (thereby raising the costs to the regime of maintaining the status quo), and loyalty shifts involving the opponent's erstwhile supporters, including members of the security forces."[55]

Chenoweth and Stephan's data concern movement campaigns of all sorts rather than revolutionary contention specifically. Still, using our sample of revolutionary episodes, the ability to generate large numbers of participants stands out as one of the most important capacities of oppositions associated with revolutionary success—correctly categorizing outcomes on its own for 69 percent of revolutionary episodes over the last century (see Table 4.2).[56] Figure 4.7 illustrates the relationship and shows that, without considering the influence of any other factors, revolutionary oppositions since 1900 that were able to generate mobilizations of 180,000 or more generally had on average a 50/50 chance or better of gaining power, while those that generated less than 180,000 had a less than 50/50 chance.

The 2004 Orange Revolution in Ukraine had a hymn—"Nas Bahato" (There are many of us)—a rap song whose refrain declares, "Together we are many, no one can defeat us." Large revolutionary crowds, particularly in close proximity to government nerve centers, can create extraordinary pressure on regime coalitions and can cause enormous strain on government decision-makers—sometimes even panic. As the number of participants in revolutionary protests increases, the likelihood of network connections between crowds and a regime's institutions and elites increases. In the Orange Revolution, as the size of the crowd on Maidan soared, "the social profile of protest got broader and broader," and "the sons and daughters, even the grandparents, of

---

54. Gamson 1975. For a similar argument with respect to the effectiveness of violence, particularly for constituents without resources, see Piven and Cloward 1979. They take issue with Gamson's claim about the benefits of hierarchical organization.

55. Chenoweth and Stephan 2011, 10.

56. Revolutionary contention in colonial territories was included in the analysis of opposition-specific features.

TABLE 4.2. Opposition characteristics and the likelihood of opposition victory in revolutionary contention

	Model 1[a]	Model 2[a]	Model 3[b]	Model 4[b]	Model 5[b]	Model 6[a]	Model 7[a]
Ln (peak participation)	1.517 (5.86)***					1.307 (2.75)**	1.316 (2.85)**
Urban location		136.656 (5.16)***	3.550 (1.52)			15.920 (2.44)*	18.105 (2.55)*
Total deaths (deciles)		1.473 (3.49)***				1.282 (2.00)*	1.281 (1.99)*
Urban # Total deaths (deciles)		0.515 (−5.05)***				0.577 (−3.82)***	0.566 (−3.98)***
Demonstration tactics			6.256 (4.57)***			3.578 (2.82)**	3.685 (2.93)**
Strike tactics			1.914 (2.05)*			2.034 (2.02)*	2.027 (2.02)*
Riot tactics			0.770 (−0.83)				
Armed tactics short of civil war			1.361 (0.83)				
Civil war			7.653 (2.25)*			4.020 (2.43)*	4.111 (2.49)*
Urban # Civil war			0.119 (−2.22)*				
Goal: liberal				3.600 (3.98)***		2.428 (2.37)*	2.538 (2.55)*

(Continued)

TABLE 4.2. (*continued*)

	Model 1[a]	Model 2[a]	Model 3[b]	Model 4[b]	Model 5[b]	Model 6[a]	Model 7[a]
Goal: social				0.811 (−0.66)			
Goal: state independence				0.644 (−1.39)			
Goal: constitutional				2.880 (2.46)*		2.781 (2.04)*	2.763 (2.05)*
Goal: reversal of ethnic order				1.671 (1.51)			
Goal: Islamist				0.477 (−1.40)			
Coalitional leadership					3.000 (3.15)**	1.130 (0.33)	
Vanguard party leadership					0.565 (−1.31)		
Other party leadership					0.782 (−0.55)		
Traditional societal leadership					0.333 (−2.34)*	0.511 (−1.42)	
Paramilitary/militia leadership					0.734 (−0.84)		
Underground leadership					0.566 (−1.25)		
Liberation movement leadership					1.104 (0.27)		

n	343	343	343	343	343	343	343
Number of imputations	20	20	n.a.	n.a.	n.a.	20	20
F-statistic/Likelihood ratio chi-square	34.33***	13.08***	53.45***	47.78***	34.55***	5.93***	7.14***
Relative increase in variance (RVI)	.0168	.0059	n.a.	n.a.	n.a.	0.0057	0.0111
Fraction of missing information (FMI)	.0278	.0086	n.a.	n.a.	n.a.	0.0301	0.0258
AUC	0.717	0.723	0.724	0.713	0.694	0.804	0.800
Percent correctly classified (complete-case sample, n = 304)	68.1%	67.4%	65.8%	69.4%	67.4%	72.0%	71.1%
True positive rate (complete-case sample, n = 304)	36.0%	30.6%	30.6%	47.8%	32.4%	52.3%	49.6%
False positive rate for true failures (complete-case sample, n = 304)	13.5%	11.4%	14.0%	18.3%	12.4%	16.6%	16.6%
AIC (for complete-case sample, n = 304)	372.17	373.32	383.29	377.49	392.36	353.52	351.09
BIC (for complete-case sample, n = 304)[c]	379.60	388.19	413.02	403.51	422.10	398.13	388.26

[a]Logistic regression (odds ratios, with t-statistics in parentheses), for twenty multiple-imputation samples. [b]Logistic regression (odds rations, with z-scores in parentheses), using complete case sample. [c]Although the BIC is higher for Model 7 than for Models 1 and 2, likelihood-ratio tests indicate the superiority of Model 7 over Model 1 (chi2(8) = 37.07, significant at the .001 level) and Model 7 over Model 2 (chi2(8) = 34.23, significant at the .001 level).

+ p < 0.10, * p < 0.05, ** p < 0.01, *** p < 0.001

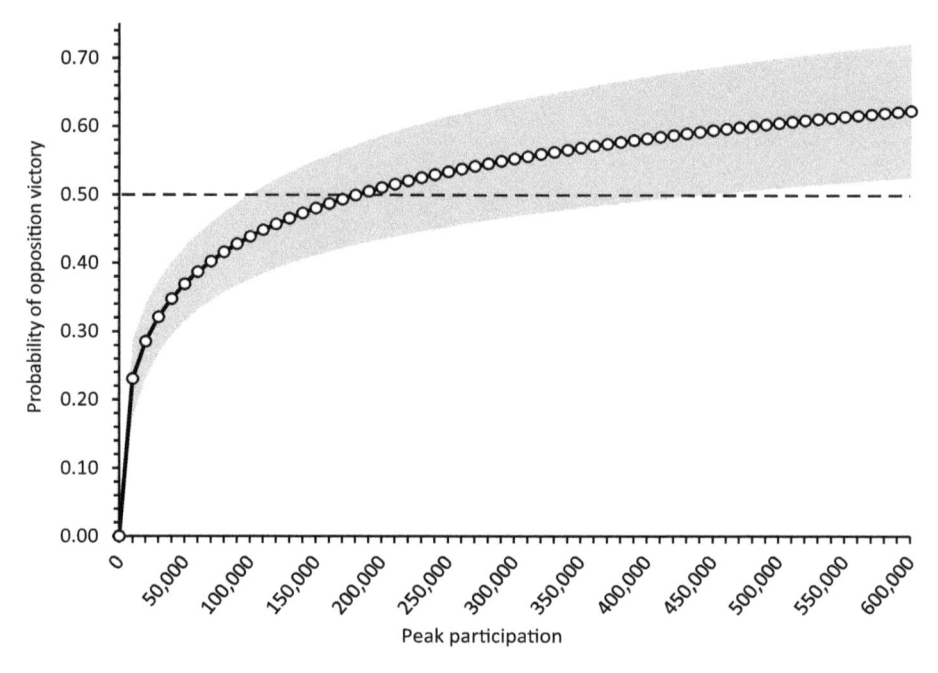

FIGURE 4.7. Peak participation and the marginal probability of opposition success. Average marginal predictions of logistic regression (point estimates, with 95 percent confidence intervals), based on twenty multiple-imputation samples (n = 343).

the militia were now on the streets," making it harder for the police to assent to the kind of crackdown that some within the regime were advocating.[57] According to some accounts, several secret police generals had wives and children demonstrating on Maidan in support of Yushchenko—a factor that likely impelled them to oppose the use of force to put down the rebellion.[58] Even the son-in-law of President Kuchma spent an evening on Maidan, reportedly saying that were he still a student, he would have camped out with the protesters.

Large-scale urbanization has been central to the proliferation of tactics relying on the power of numbers. The median urban revolt since 1900 generated peak mobilizations of about one hundred thousand participants; by contrast, the median rural revolt generated peak mobilizations of only around sixteen thousand. Over time, as the world has urbanized and larger numbers have

57. Wilson 2005, 127.
58. Chivers 2005.

concentrated in cities, the size of urban revolutionary mobilizations has increased substantially, with the median-based revolt in cities growing from 45,000 before 1985 to 150,000 thousand after 1985. As we saw in chapter 2, societies experiencing urban revolts have also been considerably more literate and have had higher levels of schooling, greater newspaper circulation and television ownership, and greater mobile phone ownership than those experiencing rural revolts—all features that further magnify the capacity to scale up in revolutionary contention. Thus, urban revolts in the late twentieth and early twenty-first centuries were well positioned to take advantage of the power of numbers in ways that rural revolts and urban revolts in earlier times simply could not.

Chenoweth and Stephan, however, seriously overstate the ability of numbers to produce success on their own. Without taking into account any other factors, the ability to generate numbers is significantly better at explaining the failure of revolutionary oppositions (correctly categorizing 90 percent of failed cases) than it is at explaining their success (correctly categorizing only 29 percent of successful cases).[59] Essentially, low numbers predict opposition failure, but high numbers on their own do not necessarily translate into opposition success. The failure to generate numbers can indeed stack the odds against a revolutionary movement; but there is clearly much more to revolutionary success than simply generating numbers.

As the size of revolutionary mobilizations rises, there are strongly diminishing returns to mobilizing more participants. As Figure 4.7 demonstrates, above a certain level, greater participation only marginally increases an opposition's chance of victory. The curve begins especially to flatten out between peak mobilizations of two hundred and three hundred thousand, and it is only after reaching the level of 450,000 participants that the 95 percent confidence interval breaks the 50/50 threshold. Put differently, only after achieving mobilizations of more than 450,000 participants could an opposition movement on average have confidence—at the 95 percent level—of better than a 50/50 chance of victory. In short, while the chances of victory greatly improve if a revolutionary opposition is able to mobilize large numbers, only extremely large mobilizations truly tip the odds in its favor.

Not all rebellions seek to maximize numbers, as maximizing participation is not always the most relevant and effective investment for the circumstances oppositions face. As Stathis Kalyvas and Matthew Kocher note, in many forms

---

59. These statistics come from the complete-case sample (n = 320). Even for urban revolutions, levels of participation are more predictive of failures than successes.

of civil war, "military success is not simply a function of manpower," as rebel movements may have few weapons or limited capacity to maintain a large army, and large numbers may be harder to generate, maintain, and control over the course of a conflict.[60] In Che Guevara's words, "the number of men that a guerrilla band can have is a matter of extremely flexible calculation adapted to the territory, to the means available of acquiring supplies, to the mass flights of oppressed people from other zones, to the arms available, to the necessities of organization."[61] Mass support is important in rural revolts, as Mao noted, but not necessarily direct mass participation in rebellion. It is not that numbers do not matter in rural revolts. But large numbers in a rural context involve difficulties of coordination and do not translate directly into military victory on the battlefield.[62] Moreover, generating large numbers in rural conflicts is further complicated by the widespread presence of violence, which multiplies the risks of revolution considerably.

In this respect, the urban/rural context of revolt makes a huge difference in terms of the effects of a particular tactic and its likelihood to contribute to revolutionary success. There is an unresolved problem in the Chenoweth and Stephan finding that nonviolence, through its ability to generate numbers, is categorically more effective than violence: can one really say that an opposition succeeded only because of a particular tactic or form of organization, irrespective of how that tactic or form of organization related to the political and social environment in which it operated and the targets against which it was oriented? In a thoughtful essay about movement outcomes, Marco Giugni referred to this as the "internal/external debate" in the study of social movement outcomes.[63] Movements choose tactics largely because their leaderships believe them to be relevant for movement goals and for the political and societal circumstances in which the movements find themselves. A tactic that might be suitable for rebellion in a sizeable urban center, where large numbers can be generated but state power is more thickly present, is unlikely to be appropriate for rebellion in a rural district, where centers of power and commerce are remote, potential participants are highly dispersed, and the strategic advantage is in eluding state power rather than confronting it directly. Indeed, over the last century, 75 percent of

---

60. Kalyvas and Kocher 2007, 212.

61. Guevara 1961, 11.

62. The US field manual guiding American counterinsurgency strategy notes that "a small number of highly motivated insurgents with simple weapons, good operations security, and even limited mobility can undermine security over a large area." Nagl et al. 2008, 13.

63. Giugni 1999.

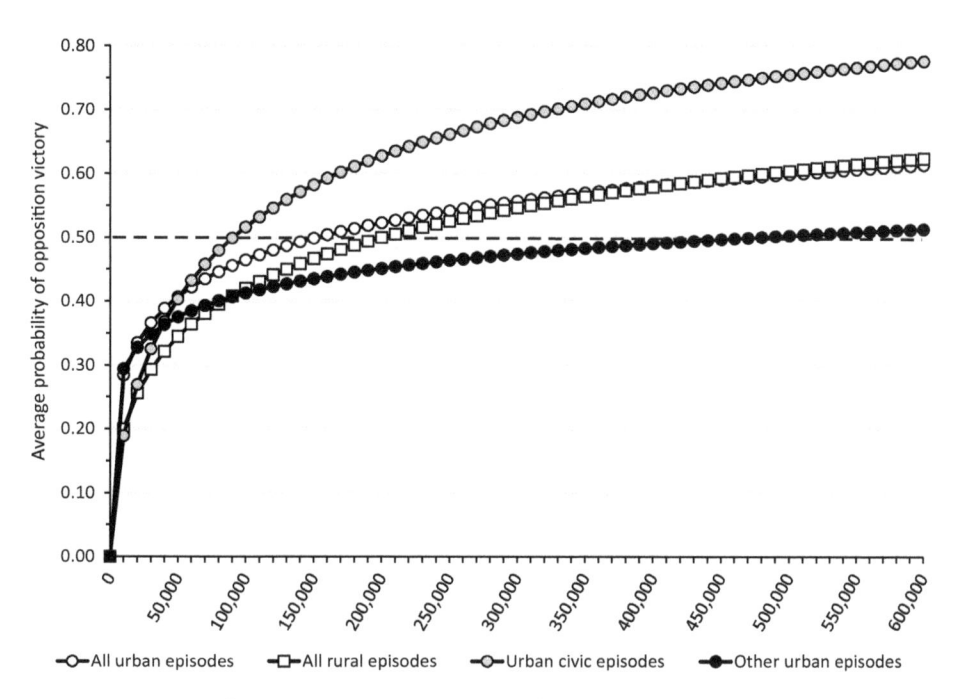

FIGURE 4.8. Peak participation and the average probability of opposition success in urban, rural, urban civic, and other urban revolutionary episodes. Average marginal predictions of a logistic regression on twenty multiple-imputation samples (n = 343). Point estimates, with confidence intervals omitted for visibility.

revolutionary episodes that occurred predominantly in the countryside began with acts of civilian armed rebellion, and 99 percent utilized arms at some point during the episode. By contrast, only 9 percent of urban episodes began with acts of armed rebellion, and only 36 percent utilized arms at any point during the episode. Instead, 69 percent of revolutionary episodes in cities began with street demonstrations or strikes. There is a logic to these tactical choices that is closely related to the spatial context within which revolt unfolds.

The contextualized nature of the relationship between numbers and revolutionary outcomes becomes evident when we compare the impact of participation on revolutionary outcomes across different locations and types of episodes (Figure 4.8). Urban revolutions have been somewhat better at translating numbers into success at participation rates below two hundred thousand. This is a reflection of their greater ability to disrupt due to proximity to centers of administration, commerce, communications, and international trade.

But above two hundred thousand, location alone exercised little impact on how numbers translated into revolutionary outcomes. Much of the difference between the success rates of urban and rural episodes boils down to the fact that only 6 percent of rural episodes ever achieved mobilizations of more than two hundred thousand, as opposed to 44 percent of urban episodes. While on average large mobilizations have affected the probability of opposition success equally in urban and rural revolts as a whole, large numbers have simply been much more difficult to generate and deploy in rural than in urban environments.

But a closer look reveals a great deal of heterogeneity among urban revolutions in their ability to transform numbers into the pressure needed to force regime-change. Even within urban episodes that displayed equally sized mobilizations, the urban civic repertoire of concentrating large numbers in central urban spaces exhibited an extraordinary efficiency in translating numbers into success. As the Figure 4.8 indicates, when they mobilized fewer than fifty thousand participants, urban civic revolutions actually had a lower rate of success on average than other types of urban revolts. Urban civic revolts succeeded at high rates not only because they were able to mobilize larger numbers, but also because they were able to do more with the numbers that they generated. Thus, on average, an urban civic revolt with a mobilization of two hundred thousand would have had a .63 probability of success. By contrast, an urban revolt that did not rely on urban civic tactics and generated a mobilization of two hundred thousand would have had only a .45 probability of success. Increasing the number of participants in an urban revolution above two hundred thousand without concentrating them in central urban spaces had little effect on outcomes. In short, if an urban opposition could mobilize more than fifty thousand, concentrating large numbers into central urban spaces was a more efficient way of translating numbers into opposition success than other ways of pressing for regime-change in cities.

Accordingly, the most effective revolutionary tactic in cities since 1900 has been the demonstration, in which large numbers mass together in public space. It is in fact the only tactic that has a statistically significant relationship (indeed, at the .001 level) with outcomes in urban revolutions, though in rural revolts demonstrations have no relationship to success. Most urban rebellions relied upon multiple tactics. But based on the revolutionary record since 1900, and controlling for the number of participants (and holding its effect at its mean), an urban revolution that relied solely on demonstrations and no other tactic would have had a .49 probability of opposition success on average. By contrast, the probability of success for an urban revolution that relied solely on armed rebellion and no other tactic would have been .20, for an urban revolution that relied solely on revolutionary riots—.14, and for an urban revolution that relied on strikes alone—.22.[64] In the countryside, however, civil war was the only tactic associated with opposition victory (statistically significant at the .05 level). Numbers certainly matter in cities. But numbers matter more when they are deployed in effective ways.

Thus, as the repression–disruption trade-off would predict, regimes are highly vulnerable to revolutionary action in cities through the unarmed occupation of public space by large numbers, while armed uprisings or revolutionary riots in cities have a reduced chance of success. Generating large numbers wards off regime repression against oppositions, and engaging in disruption of government in close proximity to a regime's nerve centers can exert considerable leverage over regimes. As a result of this confluence of tactics and environment, on average urban civic revolts exceeded a 50/50 chance of opposition success when they produced mobilizations approaching a hundred thousand[65]—far fewer participants than the 480,000 threshold necessary for other forms of urban revolt to reach the 50/50 threshold. Essentially, as urbanization concentrated large numbers in cities, it altered the character of the repression–disruption trade-off function by rendering urban civic revolutionary tactics both feasible and highly effective.

It is important to emphasize, however, that there are no optimal forms of organization, tactics, or levels of participation in the abstract, without taking into consideration the goals of revolutionary movements, the vulnerabilities of targets, and the political and ecological contexts in which movements operate. This becomes evident when one examines in more detail the relationship of violence to revolutionary outcomes since 1900. In line with Chenoweth and Stephan, it is generally true that revolutionary contention that begins with violence on the part of the opposition is less likely to be successful. However,

---

64. Combinations of tactics enhance the prospects for revolutionary success. Thus, an urban episode that deployed both demonstrations and strikes on average would have resulted in a .55 probability of success, controlling for levels of participation. But demonstrations are doing most of the heavy lifting in the relationship, not strikes.

65. In a number of urban civic revolts, anecdotal evidence points to the one hundred thousand threshold as a level where regimes begin to have difficulties managing revolt. For example, during the Orange Revolution in Ukraine, when asked to throw his support behind the revolutionary protests, the mayor of Kyiv Aleksandr Omel'chenko is said to have quipped, "If you bring out 100,000 I'm with you . . . If it'll be 99,000 I won't be" (quoted in Wilson 2005, 125). Similarly, on the eve of the January 25 protests that set off the 2011 Egyptian Revolution, Wael Ghonim, the founder of the "We Are All Khaled Said" website, posted on his site "If 100,000 take to the streets, no one can stop us." Ghonim 2012, 134.

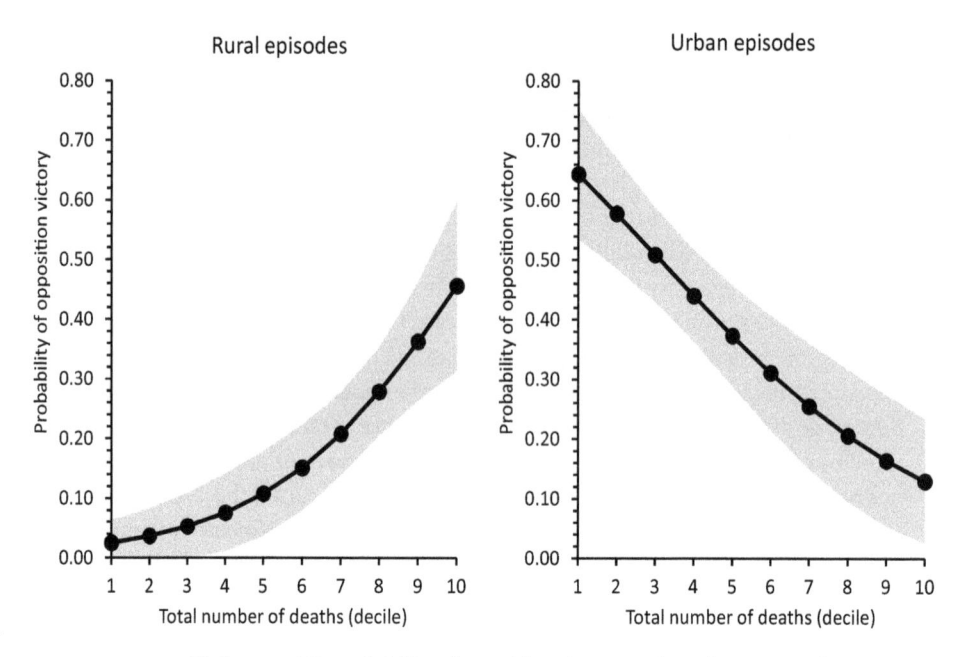

FIGURE 4.9. Violence and the probability of opposition victory, rural vs urban context. Average marginal predictions of logistic regressions (point estimates, with 95 percent confidence intervals), based on twenty multiple-imputation samples (n = 343).

what Chenoweth and Stephan miss is the contextualized nature of the disadvantage attached to violence. Less violent tactics have been effective only in urban contexts—where oppositions are at a disadvantage in pursuing armed revolt given the presence of large numbers of police and military, and where regimes are more vulnerable to disruption through numbers. But in rural revolutionary episodes, the capacity of oppositions to wield violence has actually increased their likelihood of victory. Figure 4.9 presents the relationship between revolutionary outcomes and lethal violence, as measured by the total number of deaths within a revolutionary episode, broken down into deciles.[66] As it shows, the degree of lethal violence had opposite effects on revolutionary outcomes in urban and rural environments. In rural episodes, greater lethal

---

66. Chenoweth and Stephan (2011) categorize campaigns as either violent or nonviolent, basing their finding on this binary classification. However, some of their "nonviolent" campaigns actually involved considerable numbers of deaths, and some that started off as nonviolent campaigns transformed into bloody civil wars (the Syrian Civil War, for instance). Instead of a binary classification, I use the number of people who died to measure the intensity of violence in a revolutionary episode.

violence was associated with an increased probability of opposition victory, whereas in urban episodes it was associated with a lowered probability of opposition success. Indeed, once one controls for the effect of violence, any relationship between the size of mobilizations and revolutionary success in rural revolutions disappears entirely.

More lethal violence in rural episodes generally reflects more intense and prolonged rebel resistance—conditions that can wear down an incumbent regime and its support base and increase the likelihood of opposition victory. By contrast, as Chenoweth and Stephan emphasize, higher levels of lethal violence in an urban environment exert a negative effect on participation and undermine an opposition's chances of relying on the power of numbers, which is associated with opposition success in cities. But the negative effect of lethal violence on opposition success in cities goes well beyond its adverse effect on participation and also inheres in the capacity of regimes to deploy high levels of force in cities against armed oppositions, lowering the likelihood of success. Thus, even when one controls for the effects of participation on revolutionary outcomes, violent rebellion in cities is considerably less likely to succeed[67]—irrespective of the numbers involved—largely because regimes are almost always better armed and can deploy greater force than urban revolutionary oppositions. In sum, there is no universal advantage to nonviolent tactics (or for that matter, any set of tactics) outside of the particular context in which they are pursued.

A deeper look shows that tactics, goals, organizational forms, and contextual locations in revolutionary contention are highly correlated and closely intertwined with one another. As Gamson argued, revolutionary oppositions that have less ambitious goals are more likely to succeed in gaining power. Thus, liberal revolutions and constitutional revolutions have had a significantly higher probability of success (.60 and .54 respectively) than those that sought to transform class relations (.25), attain state independence (.21), overturn a system of ethnic or racial domination (.41), or establish an Islamist political order (.17). Part of this minimalist advantage revolves around the ability to attract larger numbers when espousing limited goals that can appeal across class and cultural divisions. Only revolutionary oppositions espousing minimalist goals have had a positive and statistically significant relationship with the size of mobilizations in revolutionary contention.[68] But

---

67. See Model 3 in Table 4.2.
68. The median levels of peak participation for liberal revolutions and constitutional revolutions are one hundred thousand and ninety thousand respectively, while revolts that seek to transform class relations have a median peak participation of twenty thousand, state

revolutionary oppositions espousing minimalist goals continued to enjoy an advantage in achieving opposition success even when one controls for their capacity to attract more participants. In addition to attracting numbers, oppositions espousing minimalist goals were also more likely to be located in cities[69] and were less likely to meet violent resistance from groups in society affected by change than were movements with more ambitious and divisive goals[70]—all factors that made for higher rates of success. To complicate matters further, minimalist goals were associated with an increased likelihood of success only in cities and had no relationship with outcomes in rural revolts.

Contrary to Gamson, hierarchically organized movements had no universal advantage over looser forms of organization in revolutionary contention over the past century. In fact, quite the opposite: revolutionary oppositions that consisted of coalitions of parties, movements, and civil society groups had a significantly higher probability of success (.57) compared to oppositions led by traditional leaderships (.18), vanguard parties (.26), underground movements (.24), paramilitary organizations (.33), or liberation movements (.43).[71] But the choice of organizational forms is also deeply intertwined with the goals of a revolutionary movement, the tactics it chooses, and the locational context in which it operates. Thus, 75 percent of revolutionary episodes that employed a coalitional organizational form sought minimalist goals of containing the power of despots or monarchs, 90 percent took place primarily in cities, and 90 percent utilized demonstrations as a tactic. One of the key advantages of the city in terms of revolutionary

---

independence—of twenty thousand, reversal of ethnic or racial order—of twenty thousand, and Islamist rule—of fifteen thousand.

69. Liberal revolts and constitutional revolts have a .97 and .83 probability respectively of taking place primarily in cities, while those aimed at transformation of class relations have a .49 chance, state independence—a .29 chance, reversal of ethnic or racial order—a .25 chance, and Islamist rule—a .37 chance.

70. Thus, liberal revolts have only a .06 chance of evolving into civil war, and constitutional revolts only a .11 chance. By contrast, revolts that aim at transforming class relations have a .58 chance, state independence—a .68 chance, inversion of racial or ethnic domination—a .86 chance, and instituting an Islamist order—a .66 chance.

71. The extremely low rate of success of revolts led by traditional societal leaderships appears to be associated with the fact that most of these revolts (70 percent) occurred in the first half of the twentieth century, most (70 percent) occurred primarily in rural areas, and most aimed either at state independence (67 percent) or at instituting an Islamist political order (33 percent)—all factors associated with lowered success.

activity is the variety of groups present that can potentially be pulled into a coalition in order to maximize participation. As Byron Miller and Walter Nichols put it, "The city can be conceived of as a 'relational incubator' because it facilitates the building of networks among diverse activist groups and, in turn, the collectivization of group resources."[72] Coalitional leadership is only relevant where a variety of political forces is present, when they can agree upon a broad common aim, and where large numbers of potential participants are concentrated, since the purpose of coalitional leadership is to maximize participation by bringing the followers of disparate groups into rebellion.

Coalitional leaderships also enjoy a degree of advantage that transcends the larger numbers that they help to produce. Even controlling for the numbers that revolutionary oppositions generate, revolts with coalitional forms of leadership still had a .52 chance of success, while those that were not coalitional had only a .30 chance. By pulling a broader variety of political forces into revolt, coalitional oppositions are better equipped to induce defections from an incumbent regime due to the higher probability that the coalition contains network ties with key members of the incumbent regime. In the 2003 Rose Revolution in Georgia, for instance, a number of leaders in the opposition coalition were former government ministers or leaders who enjoyed close ties with the military and police. Opposition supporters permeated the security organs and had free access to Shevardnadze's national security advisor, who himself eventually defected to the opposition. As one revolutionary opposition leader noted, "Some of our supporters were active inside the army and police. Georgia is too small. Everybody knows everybody else."[73]

The functional equivalent of coalitional forms of leadership for rural revolts is the liberation movement—a broad-based opposition typically aimed at gaining independence by uniting different classes, cultural groups, or ideological factions under a common umbrella. Liberation movements are organized differently from coalitional forms of leadership. Whereas coalitional leaderships consist of a temporary alliance between pre-existing parties, movements, and civil society groups, liberation movements are more stable formations that typically attempt to unite broad social groups (often different ethnic groups) against a common enemy. Rarely, however, do they reflect that pluralism upward into the leadership of the movement, which

---

72. Miller and Nicholls 2013, 460. See also Nicholls 2008.
73. Karumidze and Wertsch 2005, 15, 39, 47, 54.

usually remains hierarchical.[74] Three-quarters of liberation movements since 1900 appeared in struggles aimed at achieving state independence, and 78 percent involved predominantly rural contention. Liberation movements may enjoy a marginal advantage due to their efforts to pull in a broader base of support. They displayed a higher probability of success relative to other organizational forms—with the exception of coalitional forms of leadership—though the effect is not statistically significant. In this respect, the advantage attached to coalitional forms in cities has not carried over into more loosely organized revolts in the countryside. Looser organization only provides an advantage where large numbers are concentrated and in proximity to nerve centers of government.

In short, the ways in which the spatial context of rebellion has shaped the effectiveness of numbers and the elective affinities between the goals, organizational forms, tactics, and locations of revolt render abstract arguments about the universal effectiveness of specific tactics or organizational forms problematic. To be sure, numbers have mattered greatly in achieving revolutionary success, but they have mattered mostly in urban settings. There is also the issue of how large numbers are generated. As we have seen, an opposition that seeks to maximize numbers would likely select minimalist goals, coalitional forms of leadership, and unarmed tactics. The advantages of these choices in an urban context are more than just their effects on numbers. They also aid in multiplying network connections with key members of a regime. They aid in avoiding government repression where rebels are at a disadvantage. And they reduce violent societal opposition to revolutionary goals. This bundle of choices in fact constitutes the key features of the urban civic repertoire, but would be entirely inappropriate in a rural context or in an urban setting in which large numbers could not be generated.

This is not to say that tactics drive goals rather than the other around. It is simply to note that choices of goals, tactics, and organizational forms are closely intertwined with the locations, targets, and social forces involved in revolt and cannot be easily disentangled from them. If we want to know why the urban civic repertoire has exhibited a high rate of success compared to other forms of revolution, the answer lies not simply in the affinity between tactics, goals, and organizational forms, but also in the urban environment in which it is ensconced and the targets against which it is deployed. Its ability to maximize numbers and its adoption of particular goals, tactics, and forms of organization are appropriate only in an urban context and are magnified in their effectiveness against particular types of regimes. Indeed, it is

---

74. See Gumede 2017.

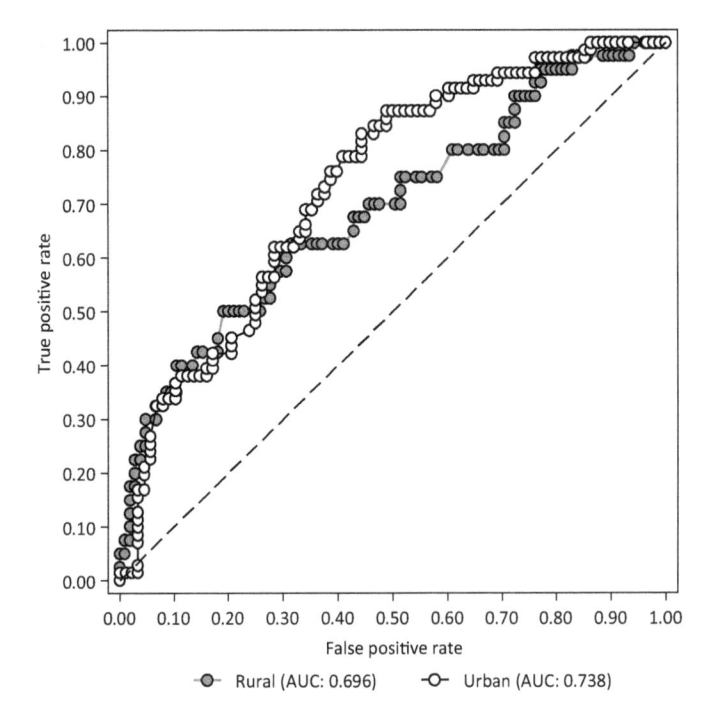

FIGURE 4.10A. ROC curves based on opposition features (rural vs urban episodes), complete-case sample (n = 304).

only within the context of large urban centers that this bundle of choices even makes sense.

Overall, the opposition goals, mobilizational capacities, and tactics identified here are able to classify the outcomes of 71 percent of revolutionary episodes correctly, with a score of .80 for the area under the ROC curve categorized by the model. This is not an overwhelmingly convincing record. But like regime strengths and vulnerabilities, opposition goals, capacities, and tactics do a much better job identifying revolutionary failure (accurate in 83 percent of actual failures) than identifying revolutionary successes (accurate in only 49 percent of actual successes). Moreover, as can be seen in Figure 4.10, opposition-specific factors had a somewhat larger impact on outcomes in urban than in rural revolts (though the difference is not statistically significant).[75]

---

75. In this instance, the multiple-imputation estimation is likely more accurate than the complete-case estimation, as there were statistically significant relationships between whether a case contained missing data on several imputed independent variables and the outcome of the dependent variable.

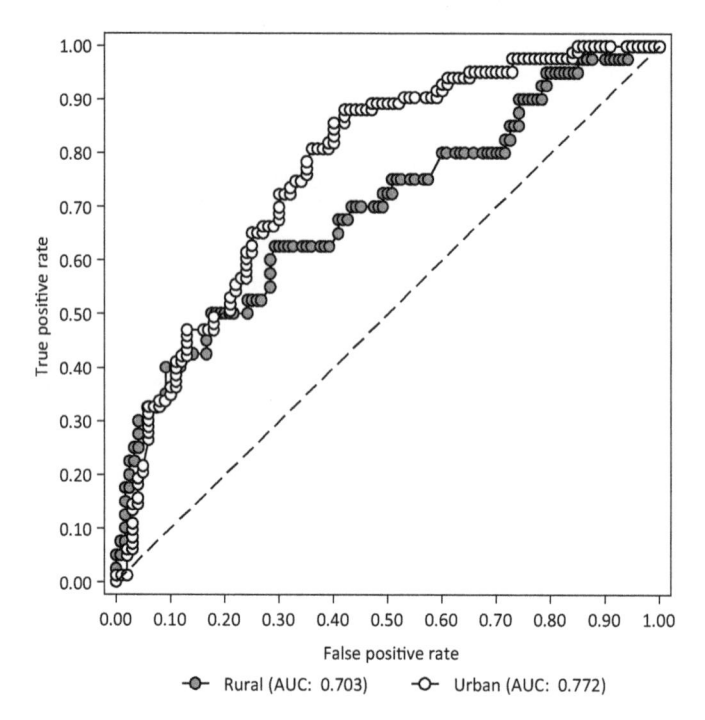

FIGURE 4.10B. ROC curves based on opposition features (rural vs urban episodes), multiple imputation (n = 343). Multiple imputation was carried out using twenty imputed samples, with 11.3 percent of observations having missing information on at least one variable.

Conclusion: The Constrained Predictability of Revolutionary Outcomes

The patterning of revolutionary outcomes over the last century has reflected the logic of the repression–disruption trade-off. The outcomes of revolutionary contention in cities were shaped more by the features of the regimes they opposed than was true of revolutionary contention in the countryside—a product of how proximity to centers of power exposed urban challengers more directly to the repressive capacities of the state. As a result of this exposure, violence in cities was generally a losing strategy, even while violence in the countryside enhanced prospects for success. Violence was detrimental to revolutionary success in cities not merely because it raised the potential costs of collective action and thereby undermined participation. Armed uprisings in cities also were far more vulnerable than rural rebellions to the coercive power of regimes. Yet, as this chapter has shown, urban revolts have been able to disrupt regimes more effectively than rural revolutions. They have had higher rates of success, and have been more effective against a broader range of regimes, than rural revolts, and they have been far better positioned to take advantage of the momentum generated by transnational revolutionary waves. Urban revolutions have also been better positioned than rural revolts to harness the power of numbers. It is only at extremely large numbers that the chances of victory truly tip in favor of oppositions—and really only in cities. Thus, the massive wave of urbanization that washed over the planet during the past century profoundly altered the repression–disruption trade-off function in revolution. It gave birth to the urban civic repertoire as a way of leveraging the strategic advantages of large cities for revolutionary challengers: proximity to centers of power and commerce; the presence of large, highly networked, and well-resourced populations; and heightened visibility and thickened connections to the outside world.

Of course, unlike the analysis in this chapter, revolutionary contention in real time is not a matter of lining up the mobilizational capacities, goals, and tactics of oppositions and the strengths and vulnerabilities of regimes. Opposition success or failure emerges out of the ability of oppositions to take advantage of the vulnerabilities of regimes and to neutralize their strengths, as well as the ability of regimes to take advantage of the weaknesses of oppositions and to neutralize their assets. This is why the tactics and organizational forms adopted by oppositions have often been related to the strengths and weaknesses of the regimes that they are challenging.[76] There is a superficiality and an artificiality to simply merging the regime and opposition models developed in this chapter into a single model. The results may reflect the larger logic of how the outcomes of episodes since 1900 were patterned, but they tell us little about how these outcomes were actually produced.

Nevertheless, for the sake of completeness, the two models combined (Table 4.3) produce an estimation that discriminates between revolutionary successes and failures with reasonable accuracy, properly classifying the outcomes of 80 percent of revolutionary episodes since 1900 (excluding revolutionary episodes in colonies) and producing a score of .89 for the area under the ROC curve. But there is overfitting in the combined model.[77]

---

76. For instance, Polity scores and the number of years in which an incumbent leader has been in power are both related to the choice of organizational forms by oppositions and the ability of oppositions to mobilize large numbers. For a more on this, see the robustness test files available from the author.

77. Overfitting is a condition in which a statistical model begins to describe the random error in the data rather than the relationships between the variables, reducing the generalizability of the model outside of the original data for which it was created and raising questions about the statistical significance and magnitude of the estimates. One cause of overfitting is multicollinearity, and

TABLE 4.3. Combined models of regime and opposition characteristics and the likelihood of opposition victory in revolutionary contention[a]

	Opposition model		Regime model		Combined model (1)		Combined model (2)	
	Complete-case[b]	Multiple imputation[c]	Complete-case[b]	Multiple imputation[c]	Complete-case[b]	Multiple imputation[c]	Complete-case[b]	Multiple imputation[c]
Ln (peak participation)	1.281 (2.30)*	1.29 (2.40)*			1.572 (2.92)**	1.603 (3.44)***	1.442 (2.59)**	1.539 (3.44)***
Urban location	15.097 (2.06)*	19.682 (2.26)*			72.675 (2.41)*	23.321 (2.09)*	24.902 (2.06)*	12.528 (1.89)+
Total deaths (deciles)	1.335 (2.01)*	1.395 (2.26)*			1.325 (1.51)	1.315 (1.65)+	1.384 (1.87)+	1.322 (1.85)+
Urban # Total deaths (deciles)	0.578 (−3.34)***	0.546 (−3.68)***			0.479 (−3.24)**	0.535 (−3.27)**	0.529 (−3.06)**	0.582 (−3.12)**
Demonstration tactics	4.189 (2.89)**	5.189 (3.42)***			10.559 (3.34)***	7.922 (3.58)***	7.482 (3.14)**	6.935 (3.56)***
Strike tactics	1.734 (1.42)	1.99 (1.85)+			0.796 (−0.43)	1.349 (0.68)		
Goal: political/civil liberties	2.043 (1.80)+	2.22 (2.09)*			0.62 (−0.86)	0.816 (−0.43)		
Goal: republican/anti-monarchical	2.586 (1.65)+	2.732 (1.87)+			0.786 (−0.30)	1.84 (0.91)		
Polity score, t−1			0.904 (−2.91)**	0.897 (−3.43)***	0.912 (−2.27)*	0.895 (−2.99)**	0.925 (−2.00)*	0.904 (−2.82)**
Polity score, t−1 (squared)			0.973 (−3.81)***	0.980 (−3.23)**	0.975 (−2.98)**	0.979 (−2.87)**	0.976 (−3.02)**	0.979 (−2.99)**
Years incumbent leader in power			1.064 (3.09)**	1.043 (2.45)*	1.069 (2.41)*	1.030 (1.33)	1.061 (2.46)*	1.036 (1.77)+

	(1)	(2)	(3)	(4)	(5)	(6)
GDP per cap. ($ thousands), t−1		0.862 (−1.81)+	0.857 (−2.02)*	0.733 (−2.98)**	0.769 (−2.89)**	0.736 (−3.07)**	0.750 (−3.27)**
Ln (oil production), t−1		0.869 (−3.56)***	0.892 (−3.23)**	0.859 (−2.96)**	0.876 (−2.87)**	0.861 (−3.16)**	0.876 (−3.12)**
Mil. expenditure per soldier (deciles)		1.496 (4.29)***	1.414 (3.99)***	1.155 (1.16)	1.213 (1.76)+	1.276 (2.90)**	1.278 (3.15)**
Civil war	2.545 (1.48)	2.451 (1.48)	1.028 (0.04)	1.196 (0.15)	0.960 (−0.04)		
Civil war # Mil. expenditure per soldier		0.808 (−1.69)+	0.873 (−1.17)	1.170 (0.95)	1.145 (0.91)		
n	255	234	288	212	288	212	288
Number of imputations	n.a.	n.a.	30	n.a.	30	n.a.	30
Likelihood ratio chi-square/F-statistic	64.51***	73.79***	6.05***	108.57***	4.16***	105.98***	6.10***
Relative increase in variance (RVI)	n.a.	n.a.	0.0751	n.a.	0.0620	n.a.	0.0601
Fraction of missing information (FMI)	n.a.	n.a.	0.1406	n.a.	0.1542	n.a.	0.1955
AUC	0.786	0.815	0.803	0.888	0.889	0.883	0.881
Percent correctly classified	71.0%	78.2%	n.a.	83.5%	n.a.	81.6%	n.a.
True positive rate	54.6%	64.8%	n.a.	75.9%	n.a.	71.1%	n.a.
False positive rate for true failures	19.0%	13.7%	n.a.	11.6%	n.a.	11.6%	n.a.
Leave-one-out cross-validated AUC	0.744	0.780	n.a.	0.833	n.a.	0.844	n.a.
AIC (common sample, n = 212)	240.28	238.03	n.a.	209.26	n.a.	201.853	n.a.
BIC (common sample, n = 212)	273.85	268.24	n.a.	266.32	n.a.	242.132	n.a.

[a]Colonies excluded. [b]Logistic regression (odds ratios, with z-scores in parentheses). Likelihood ratio chi-square for overall model provided. [c]Logistic regression (odds ratios, with t-statistics in parentheses). F-statistic for overall model provided.

+ $p < 0.10$, * $p < 0.05$, ** $p < 0.01$, *** $p < 0.00$

When statistically insignificant variables are dropped, multicollinearity is resolved, and the new model is subjected to a leave-one-out cross-validation, it accurately classifies the outcomes of 82 percent of revolutionary episodes, with a cross-validated AUC score of .84—a reasonably accurate record. However, like its component models, the combined model in Table 4.3 has a tendency to under-predict success, correctly classifying failure for 88 percent of actual failures but correctly identifying success for only 71 percent of actual successes. We saw in chapter 3 that statistical models of the onset of revolutionary contention seriously over-predict the occurrence of revolutionary contention. By contrast, statistical models of revolutionary outcomes significantly under-predict opposition success.

Why might revolutionary failure be more accurately anticipated than revolutionary success? One possibility that always lingers over any statistical model is omitted variable bias. A number of factors that make for revolutionary success are not easily quantified. This would seem to be particularly true for rural episodes, where revolutionary conflicts take the form of civil wars over extended periods of time and are less shaped by regime characteristics and levels of participation. As we saw, both regime and opposition models do better at classifying the outcomes of urban revolutionary episodes than the outcomes of rural episodes.

The strengths and weaknesses of revolutionary oppositions are also harder to identify and measure than the strengths and weaknesses of the regimes they target. Prior to revolutionary onset, the extent of opposition support is latent and unknowable. Critical aspects of opposition strengths and weaknesses are difficult to gauge. We have no systematic measures *ex ante* of the thickness of opposition network structures, the likelihood that the population will heed an opposition's call to mobilize, or even the aid and resources that an opposition receives from abroad—all factors that can make a difference in revolutionary outcomes. Some of these unmeasurables are reflected in the opposition model by *ex post* variables like peak mobilizations and levels of violence. But much about the strengths and weaknesses of revolutionary oppositions prior to mobilization is simply unknowable.

Still, to minimize possibilities for omitted variable bias, I tested the combined model against a large number of additional factors that, for theoretical reasons, might have been associated with revolutionary outcomes: population size; economic growth on the eve of revolution; youth bulges (variously

---

tests revealed a strong correlation between urban location and the presence of civil war ($r = -.70$), as well as between the presence of civil war and the number of deaths in revolutionary contention ($r = .77$). For these reasons, the civil war variable was dropped in the reduced combined model.

defined); the presence of mountainous terrain; average total years of schooling; soldiers per thousand population; the V-Dem core civil society index; V-Dem's measure of private ownership in the economy; the V-Dem index for executive corruption; the Hanson/Sigman state capacity index; and others. These variables were tested in both bivariate and multivariate specifications and for complete-case and multiple-imputation samples. I also tested whether they operated differently in urban and rural environments. Only the state capacity index exhibited a statistically significant relationship when included in the combined model. As the repression–disruption trade-off would predict, its effect functioned in opposite directions in urban and in rural settings—depressing the chances of opposition victory in the countryside, while actually enhancing it in cities.[78]

A second possible explanation for the models' greater accuracy in identifying revolutionary failure than revolutionary success is that, by its very nature, success may simply be harder to anticipate than defeat. Overthrowing an entrenched regime is difficult, whereas revolutionary failure can happen for any number of reasons. Even if a regime possesses characteristics that make it more vulnerable to overthrow by revolution, given the resources and forces that regimes have at their disposal, it is still a formidable task to evict an incumbent through revolution—one that often requires exogenous influences, serendipity, and even a dose of luck. Whereas the weaknesses of revolutionary oppositions may render defeat likely, their strengths may not translate so directly into success.

A third explanation for the weaker predictability of revolutionary success relative to revolutionary failure is that the former requires more than simply tallying the strengths and weaknesses of regimes and oppositions. These factors certainly matter for outcomes, as the models in this chapter demonstrate, but they are not the whole story. There is a dynamic, iterative, interactive character to revolutionary contention that pushes us to look beyond structure and statistical probabilities and focus instead on events—on how structural advantage and disadvantage are actually utilized in real-time in revolutionary "play." And it is to this that we turn next.

78. The strong correlation between GDP per capita and the state capacity index turned GDP per capita statistically insignificant in this specification. Results of these tests are reported in the robustness test files available from the author.

5

Revolutionary Contingency and the City

> The street is disorder. All the elements of urban life, which are fixed and redundant elsewhere, are free to fill the streets and through the streets flow to the centers, where they meet and interact, torn from their fixed abode. This disorder is alive. It informs. It surprises.
>
> HENRI LEFEBVRE, *THE URBAN REVOLUTION*[1]

STRUCTURAL CONDITIONS MATTER in conditioning the onset and outcomes of revolutionary contention. But we have also seen that there are significant limits to their explanatory power. Occasionally revolutionary contention emerges even in the absence of the structural conditions present in most other cases. Sometimes it fails to materialize even when structural conditions are conducive and potential triggers are present. The structural factors associated with opposition victory do much better at accounting for revolutionary failure than accounting for revolutionary success. As Mill observed, these deviations from the expectations of structural explanation are the result of "the extensive and constant reaction of the effects upon their causes"[2]—that is, the consequences of agency. Even when favorable structural conditions are in place, revolutions still require agency to bring them about, and with agency comes choice, and with choice, the possibility of error and the unexpected.

In this chapter, I draw upon a wide variety of revolutionary episodes to unpack the roles played by choice, contingency, and error in urban revolutionary contention. The examples presented are not meant to be a representative

---

1. Lefebvre 2003, 18–19.
2. Mill 1950, 344.

sample. They have been chosen from episodes for which we have particularly rich descriptions. Their purpose is to reveal the dynamic interactions and transformative moments that occur within urban revolutionary contention. On the basis of this material, I show how the profoundly different rhythms of urban and rural revolutions shape the ways in which revolutionary contention unfolds. The speed, intensity, and compactness of urban revolutions differ radically from the slow but punctuated tempo of rural revolts. Everything about cities is compressed: space, time, and the very parameters of daily existence. These features of urban life are further amplified in the context of revolutionary contention by what I have called the proximity dilemma. Proximity to centers of state power heightens the stakes and risks involved in revolutionary contention for both oppositions and regimes, turning urban revolutions into condensed conflicts that unfold over a matter of days and weeks rather than years. The speed and intensity of urban revolutionary contention create significant information problems for both regimes and oppositions and heighten the impact of choice, error, and chance in revolutionary processes. In turn, the consequences of these choices are acutely magnified by the proximity of urban contention to the nerve centers of the state and its concentrated coercive power.

Information problems also play an important role in rural revolutionary contention, and certainly battles between rebels and governments in the countryside are as emotion-laden, confusing, and intense as confrontations that occur in cities. But rural revolutions are more tolerant of error. As we will see, in rural contention, mistakes can be made with fewer direct consequences on outcomes due to the remoteness of the state and the impenetrability of terrain. In most instances, these factors provide a buffer for rebels and regimes to recover from missteps. This is not the case in urban revolutionary contention, where the consequences of miscalculation are direct and immediate. There is no place for oppositions to retreat to in urban revolution, and no cushion for a regime to absorb the impact of poor judgment. The margin for error is much smaller.

In a well-known study, Timur Kuran argued that revolutions almost always come as a surprise because of the problem of "hidden preferences." Kuran contends that, since true preferences for regime-change are concealed and can only be known *ex post*, revolution by its very nature is unpredictable.[3] But rural revolutions rarely surprise us. They unfold over a lengthy period, the preferences of rebel forces for regime-change are not hidden but openly revealed by the very act of taking up arms, and outcomes materialize out of a sequence of battles that stretches over years (and sometimes decades).

---

3. Kuran 1997.

Rather, it is urban revolutions that surprise. They surprise not only on account of hidden preferences, but also because of the condensed and intensified character of urban revolutionary contention and its proximity to nerve centers of government. In contrast to rural rebellions, urban revolutions typically move at a pace that outstrips the capacities of human comprehension. These intensified and condensed periods of regime–opposition interaction—what I have referred to elsewhere as "thickened history"[4]—introduce a heightened contingency into processes of contention, generating unpredictable moments out of which revolutionary outcomes materialize. Certainly, the outcome of battles in rural revolutions are often unpredictable. But battles occur sporadically in rural revolutions, and usually at a distance from centers of power. As a result, it is rare for a single battle or engagement to decide a war. But urban revolutions are condensed into a single battle, and every engagement potentially harbors within it a turning point.

Moreover, because large numbers of participants are more likely to be involved in urban revolutions, and because revolutionary organization is often coalitional and less coherent, spontaneous actions in urban revolutions can push revolutionary contention in unpredictable directions. Actions by elements of a crowd or by groups of soldiers or police in confrontation with one another can have significant consequences. In urban revolutions, sudden and unanticipated events can transform the revolutionary landscape, and rumor, miscalculation, and coincidence can directly affect the momentum and trajectory of a rebellion, with a direct impact on outcomes. Much of the fundamental unpredictability of urban revolutions derives not from falsified preferences, but from the compactness and speed of urban revolutionary processes and their adjacency to centers of government, frequently leading to unforeseen moments of transformation and shaping the ways in which urban revolutionary play unfolds.

The Revolution Game and Its Fields of Play

Revolutionary episodes have much in common with what happens on the playing field in a sporting event. Much as in political contention, sporting teams enter a competition with well-known strengths and weaknesses and a past record of accomplishment. Precisely because of general knowledge about this past and the relative assets possessed by each team, one team is usually favored over the other in any given match. Teams also enter competition with a playbook of learned and scripted ways of engaging their adversary, as well as

---

4. Beissinger 2002.

a game plan for mitigating their opponent's strengths and attacking their weaknesses. Over time, as they engage in repeated play, the strengths and weaknesses of each team manifest themselves in a pattern of outcomes. Yet, the result of any given match is hardly predetermined, and often the outcome on the field has little to do with prior expectations, game plans, or what happened in the past. Rather, what counts is what players do with the assets that they bring to the field: the decisions they make, the actions they take "in play," and the ways in which opposing players react to those actions. Indeed, outcomes often have less to do with what happens on the field than with how teams *react to* what happens on the field. Sometimes a weaker team, despite a lack of proportionate assets or a losing record, upsets a stronger one. That is, after all, why games are played out instead of the winner simply being declared ahead of time on the basis of a team's assets, past record, or reputation. Likewise, in the revolution game, incumbents are always the favored team due to their disproportionate assets and past record of domination. But while that record and those assets shape the expectations of participants and observers alike, these expectations and the best-laid plans often have little to do with what actually unfolds.

Of course, there are important differences between sports competitions and revolution. Obviously, in revolution the risks and stakes involved could hardly be higher. Moreover, the stakes are different for the contending sides. Opposition participants potentially face death, injury, imprisonment, torture, exile, harm to family or friends, or unemployment should they lose. For those who lose but survive, revolution is often an iterative affair, requiring multiple attempts before achieving success. Lenin famously described 1905 as "a dress rehearsal" without which the Bolshevik Revolution "would have been impossible."[5] For some Otpor activists, the Bulldozer Revolution in 2000 was actually their fourth attempt to overthrow Slobodan Milošević,[6] while many of the key activists in the 2013 Euromaidan Revolution had cut their revolutionary teeth during the Ukrainian student movement in 1990, the "Ukraine Without Kuchma" movement in 2000, and the Orange Revolution in 2004. It is hard to extinguish revolutionary challenges completely, as opposition networks are difficult to root out.[7] Thus, for oppositions, revolution is a potentially repeatable game, assuming that they live another day to play and retain an appetite for the risks involved. Indeed, repetition has been the mother of

5. Lenin 1977, 310.
6. See the interview with Ivan Marovic in Garfield 2004.
7. About a fifth of all revolutionary episodes over the last century bear a direct relationship to a prior unsuccessful attempt at revolution against the same target in the same country sometime over the previous twenty-five years.

revolutionary invention, as players frequently attempt to learn the lessons of prior contention.[8]

For incumbent regimes, however, the revolution game is a "win and continue to play, lose and you are out" type of contest. With occasional exceptions, incumbents evicted from power by revolution forfeit the opportunity to play a second time.[9] Should the regime lose, leaders rarely face death or imprisonment (though trials of former leaders ousted by revolution became more frequent in the 2000s under the then-prevailing liberal international order). Rare are cases like those of Gualberto Villaroel in Bolivia (who was hung from a lamp-post in front of the presidential palace), Nicolae Ceaușescu in Romania (who was captured, tried, and executed along with his wife), or Muammar Gaddafi of Libya (who was caught while hiding in a drainage pipe and beaten, tortured, and shot).[10] Only one out of every fourteen leaders evicted by revolution has been killed. Imprisonment is somewhat more common (one out of every eight). Even so, the specter of death or imprisonment haunts the imagination of every dictator.[11] In reality, exile, power-sharing agreements, or simply a return to civilian life are the modal outcomes when incumbent leaders lose revolutionary challenges—often with former leaders retaining a significant portion of their ill-gotten wealth.[12] But when incumbents lose, they lose their power, status, and whatever sources of wealth political influence provides, and the lives and fortunes of family, friends, and collaborators can suffer enormously. In the aftermath of his overthrow in South Korea in 1960, Syngman Rhee went into exile in Hawaii. But 612 of his associates lost their positions of influence (with many deprived of their civic rights). About a dozen were executed, and several committed suicide.[13]

Because of the potentially catastrophic losses involved, incumbent regimes prefer not to play the revolution game at all. They hope that their hegemonic

---

8. On the importance of learning from repeated challenges over time, see Onuch 2014a.

9. Only a handful of leaders have ever been able to return to power after being removed in a revolution—Viktor Yanukovych (ousted twice by revolution in Ukraine) being one.

10. Other leaders killed during revolutions include Samuel K. Doe of Liberia, Mohammed Daoud Khan of Afghanistan, and Juvénal Habyarimana of Rwanda. In addition, Anastasio Somoza Debayle, dictator of Nicaragua from 1967 until his overthrow in 1979, was assassinated by a Sandinista commando team in 1980 while in exile in Paraguay, and Tsar Nicholas II and family were executed by a Bolshevik firing squad in 1918.

11. For evidence that the entourage of Philippines president Ferdinand Marcos feared being lynched by mobs once the revolution was lost, see Johnson 1987, 259.

12. Out of eighty-eight successful, non-separatist revolutions from 1900 to 2014, in 51 percent the incumbent leader went into exile, in 27 percent the incumbent was allowed to retire from power and remain in the country, and in 13 percent the incumbent shared power with revolutionaries.

13. Kim 1983, 204.

position, past record of domination, and reputation for invincibility will prevent the opposition from even attempting revolutionary challenge. But in rare moments incumbents are forced to play by the moves of the opposition. In this respect, revolutionary oppositions are risk-seeking: if the revolution game is to be played at all, the opposition must seize the initiative and have significant tolerance for the dangers involved. Incumbents, by contrast, are risk-averse; they have more to lose than to gain by playing the revolution game and would prefer to avoid it altogether. In short, unlike a sporting event, the revolution game is only played when oppositions compel regimes to play it. Moreover, unlike a sporting event, there are no rules in the revolution game; each side can do whatever is necessary to prevail—constrained only by their interests, resources, wile, and occasionally moral compunction. And unlike a sporting event, the audiences in the revolution game (the population, the international community, and the regime's supporting coalition) are also potential participants. Ultimately, they decide who wins by their willingness to join in the fray or remain on the sidelines.[14]

One of the key features of the revolution game, however, is that the fields on which it unfolds vary tremendously with regard to their topography and physical location. There are radically different rhythms to the game in urban and in rural environments. In the countryside, where populations are dispersed and where distance and rough terrain potentially provide safety from the repressive actions of the regime, the revolution game stretches over years and revolves around the eventfulness of battle, which ruptures an otherwise monotonous, spartan, and frequently stressful daily routine. As Che Guevera wrote, "[T]he guerrilla fighter will live for days without approaching any inhabited place, avoiding all contact that has not been previously arranged, staying in the wildest zones, knowing hunger, at times thirst, cold, heat. . . . Within the framework of combatant life, the most interesting event, the one that carries all to a convulsion of joy and puts new vigor in everybody's steps, is the battle."[15] During Mao's Long March in 1935, communist fighters marched almost continuously for 368 days with no shelter from rain and little food across five thousand miles of forbidding Chinese territory in order to escape the armies of Chiang Kai-shek—traversing eighteen mountain ranges and grasslands in which they sometimes did not encounter another human for days. Of the hundred thousand who embarked on the journey, only eight thousand remained at the end.[16] Even so, the Chinese communist quest for power

14. Schattschneider 1960, 2.
15. Guevara 1961.
16. Snow 1973, 204–5; Schram 1966, 188.

stretched on for another thirteen years. Rural rebels constantly face the threat of discovery and ambush and are forced at times to spend chains of sleepless nights on the run. But not all rural revolution involves such extreme hardship. During the long wait between skirmishes in the Angolan War for Independence, guerrillas organized soccer leagues and typing classes, while detachments of Zimbabwean guerrillas spent much of their war for independence consuming beer in the bush.[17] Between battles in El Salvador, educated guerrillas taught their illiterate comrades to read.[18] Bulgarian partisans during World War II wintered in a hideout known as the "Submarine," replete with pots and pans, a sink, and bunk beds. As one partisan recalled, "My life went on monotonously until the snow melted: sleeping during the day, and cooking, conversing, and collecting wood logs for the stove during the night."[19] Ensconced in their mountainous sanctuaries in periods between battles, Mao's armies engaged in military drills, listened to political lectures, played table tennis and other sports, and sang songs.[20] It is sometimes feasible for rural rebels to move back and forth between revolutionary action and normal village life—as occurred, for example, during the Huk Rebellion in the Philippines.[21]

The rhythm of the urban revolutionary game is markedly different. If the key features of rural revolution are its length and its routine punctuated by intermittent battle, in cities revolutionary processes are compressed—measured in days and weeks rather than years. The 1986 People Power Revolution in the Philippines lasted for four days, the 2004 Orange Revolution in Ukraine for seventeen days, the 2011 Egyptian Revolution for eighteen days, and the 2010 Tunisian Revolution for twenty-eight days. Urban revolutions are limited in duration because they occur where the state's coercive power is strongest and its nerve centers are concentrated. It is difficult to sustain revolutionary contention in cities, because it occurs where the state is both most capable of repressing and most vulnerable to overthrow. Moreover, urban revolution directly disrupts ongoing political and economic life. It may not involve the physical hardships of cold and hunger suffered by rural rebels while attempting to evade government forces. But it can involve significant disruptions to daily life and emotionally taxing commitments for days on end for large numbers of people. Either one side prevails, or exhaustion eventually sets in. As a result, urban revolutions unfold at an extraordinarily rapid pace.

17. Harwood 1983.
18. Hammond 1998.
19. Ghodsee 2015, 73.
20. Snow 1973, 279–83.
21. Kerkvliet 1977, 70, 94, 165.

I use the term "thickened history" to describe periods in which the pace of contention quickens to the point that it becomes practically impossible to comprehend the ongoing flow of events. As Trotsky portrayed the flow of actions leading to the Bolsheviks' seizure of power in Petrograd in November 1917, "Every week brings something new to the masses. Every two months creates an epoch."[22] More than seven decades later, a Soviet journalist used eerily similar language to describe the cascading events leading to the collapse of the Soviet state that Trotsky had helped to create: "We are living in an extremely condensed historical period. Social processes which earlier required decades now develop in a matter of months."[23] The sense of time speeding up in urban revolutionary contention is echoed in numerous other accounts. As Georgian journalists wrote of the twenty-day Rose Revolution in Tbilisi in 2003, "Events were occurring with unbelievable speed in Georgia and were growing more astounding to observers by the day. Analysts tired of making predictions, many of which were outdated within hours."[24] The speed of urban revolutionary processes has accelerated still further in a world of instantaneous global communication. In 1917, it took more than a week for Lenin (then in Zurich) to learn of the outbreak of the February Revolution in Petrograd.[25] By the twenty-first century, news of urban revolutionary events is broadcast around the world over digital media in real time and "with a speed and on a scale never seen before."[26]

One of the features of thickened history is that events "begin to move so fast and old assumptions become so irrelevant that the human mind cannot process all the new information." As one seasoned observer of Soviet politics reminisced about the collapse of the Soviet Union, "[t]he flow of events was so rapid and so unexpected that no one had time to step back and reflect upon what had transpired. Observers tended to retain their interpretations of events even after they had been proved incorrect and to combine them with interpretations of later events in contradictory ways."[27] Zurab Zhvania, one of the leaders of the opposition during Georgia's 2003 Rose Revolution, used similar words to describe his inability to evaluate what was happening during the uprising: "I had no chance ... for any analysis because everything was running so fast."[28]

22. Trotsky 1932, vol. 1, 420. For the best account of the volatile and contingent character of the events that brought the Bolsheviks to power in 1917, see Rabinowitch 1991.
23. Golovanov 1989.
24. Chikhladze and Chikhladze 2005, 8.
25. Pipes 1990, 386.
26. Howard and Hussain 2011, 35.
27. Hough 1997, 3, 316.
28. Karumidze and Wertsch 2005, 41. For almost identical statements about the challenges faced by decision-makers during the collapse of the Soviet Union, see Beissinger 2002, 92.

This intensified pace of events exerts significant effects on the character of urban revolutionary play. In chess, it is well known that the probability of making blunders is increased when players are forced to play quickly due to the pressure of the clock (what is known among chess enthusiasts as *zeitnot*, or time trouble).[29] Psychological research on decision-making has similarly shown that time pressures reduce an agent's search for information, decrease openness to alternatives, increase the importance of negative information, cause defensive reactions and neglect or denial of important information, and reinforce wrong judgment and evaluation. All these effects in psychological experiments are magnified when the stakes involved are higher.[30] Indeed, as experiments show, in situations of heightened danger, time often feels more compressed than it actually is,[31] leading to rushed decision-making. In urban revolutions, the speed with which interactions between regimes and oppositions occur and the dangers associated with proximity to centers of state power increase the likelihood of errors and missteps. In moments of urban revolutionary crisis, when the risks and stakes for regimes, oppositions, and societies could not be greater, the pace of events challenges the powers of human comprehension, and the possibility that actions, decisions, rumors, miscalculations, or coincidences might affect the outcome of revolutionary contention multiplies.

Even in normal times, urban life is full of "interdependencies, unpredictability, mobility, differences, speed, and intense affects." As Julie-Anne Boudreau observes, "interdependencies characteristic of urbanity give unprecedented salience to small acts that can easily be transformed into unexpected political situations on global and local scales."[32] A key feature that distinguishes urban from rural revolutions is these heightened interdependencies and the contingencies that they introduce into revolutionary processes.

Certainly, miscalculation, chance, and uncertainty are features of rural revolts as well. Castro's Granma landing in December 1956, for instance, was a total disaster. The rebels were supposed to land at the town of Niquero, where a small group of compatriots was waiting for them with trucks, jeeps, and food. Instead, the rebels were forced to ditch their leaky boat in a swampy area fifteen miles to the south, losing most of their weapons and supplies. "The cargo was lost; there were only a few rifles left, and some sodden ammunition; the first guide was an informer; the survivors chewed sugar cane for food, scattering

---

29. Chabris and Hearst 2003; Sigman et al. 2010.
30. Edland and Svenson 1993; Zakay 1993.
31. Langer, Wapner, and Werner 1961.
32. Boudreau 2010, 55, 62.

bits all along their trail like Tom Thumb. The first attack found them cut off from each other and in a state of exhaustion; it was to take the little parties of survivors several days to regroup."[33] Most of the rebels were killed in battle or surrendered. Che Guevara then tried to guide the remaining guerrillas to the Sierra Maestra Mountains by the position of the North Star—mistakenly using the wrong star. By a stroke of luck, the rebels retreated to safety. Of the eighty-two in the original Granma landing party, only twelve made it to the mountains.[34] But in spite of this catastrophic beginning, Castro was able to recover and eventually gain control over the Cuban state two years later after fighting from his mountain sanctuaries.

The Sandinista National Liberation Front (FSLN) in Nicaragua attempted to model their revolution after the Cuban success story. After identifying what they believed was their equivalent of the Sierra Maestra mountains, a loose and ill-prepared group of sixty-three rebels (only half of whom were armed) entered Nicaragua in 1963 from neighboring Honduras. Lost, starving, wet, and cold, the guerrillas wandered the mountains for four months, occasionally encountering government forces "by accident." After a group of rebels was wiped out in a government ambush, the operation was abandoned completely.[35] Yet the FSLN bounced back, overthrowing the Somoza dictatorship sixteen years later.

Rural rebels and governments often err in choosing which targets to attack, or embark upon action without proper preparation. Much of the information on which they act is faulty, scanty, and based on unreliable informants or rumor. In rural revolutions, chance encounters between government forces and rebels are frequently the source of battles, the outcomes of which are unpredictable; and surprise attacks and decoys are mainstays of rural revolutionary warfare.[36] Many of these challenges occur because of the isolation of rural rebels, their dependence on informants, or the slowness with which information reaches them, not because of the speed of interactions. But the impact of mistakes and misinformation in rural revolution is tempered by the attributes of the playing field and the rhythm with which rural revolutionary play unfolds: the dispersed character of rural populations and rebel groups; distance from national centers of power; the availability of space into which one can retreat and the weak penetration of the state, especially in areas of rough terrain; and the punctuated and prolonged character of revolt. For regimes as

---

33. Vega 1969, 75–76.
34. Sierra n.d.
35. Zimmermann 2001, 80–82.
36. For a summary of partisan warfare principles, see Snow 1973, 275–76.

well, the remoteness of contention creates a buffer behind which they can insulate themselves or recover from mistakes. Miscalculation in rural revolution can usually be rectified because the process of contention unfolds over a protracted period, the effect of a mistake may be confined to a particular locality or impact a limited number of people, or errors occur where the state is weakest and at a distance from the seat of national power. As a result, rebels and regimes normally have opportunities to retreat and recover to fight another day. Only in rare instances do rural revolutionary battles exert a direct effect on the final outcome.

Not so in cities. Because revolutionary play in cities is compressed in time, involves simultaneous actions by large numbers of individuals, and takes place precisely where the state's coercive capacities are strongest and its nerve centers are most vulnerable, the potential for miscalculations, missteps, or mere chance to exercise a direct effect on revolutionary outcomes is considerably greater. In urban revolutions, the problem facing revolutionaries is not the scarcity of good information due to isolation, but the overwhelming speed with which events unfold, fostering decision-making based on incomplete information, outdated assumptions, and rumor. The speed of play and the irredeemable quality of mistakes, not the isolation of the players, dictate the nature of the errors. In urban civic revolutions, tendencies toward miscalculation are magnified by the structural features of those regimes most vulnerable to experiencing urban civic revolution: that is, personalist non-democratic regimes whose leaders have been in office for long periods of time. Such regimes are prone to mistakes in revolutionary play because they are arrogant, overconfident, often incompetent, and frequently lack quality information. Proximity to centers of power means that mistakes have immediate, direct, and often irreversible consequences. In short, the urban revolutionary playing field shapes how revolutionary processes unfold. It creates significant information problems and increases the likelihood that error and contingency will influence revolutionary outcomes.

Sources of Surprise in Urban Revolution

Kuran's theory about the role of hidden preferences provides critical insights into bandwagoning processes within revolutions. But it is limited as an explanation for why revolutions surprise us. For one thing, it is not at all clear what an individual's "true" preferences concerning revolution are. Among those who favor political change, reform would often be preferable to revolution were it an available option. Revolution is risky, costly, and on the whole unlikely to succeed; it may also imply a more substantial degree of change than is believed necessary. In many revolutions, a large proportion of participants do not embark upon revolutionary action with the intention of overthrowing the government. On the basis of surveys of participants in the 1989 East German Revolution, Opp found that "many citizens say that they have expected their protests to lead to reforms, . . . not to an overthrow of the system."[37] Similarly, in the 1960 April Revolution in South Korea overthrowing Syngman Rhee, "the initial motive of the students was to protest illegal actions by the government, especially with regard to the electoral process. . . . It never occurred to anyone, including those who demonstrated in Seoul and other cities, that a regime was to fall."[38] A preference for political change and a preference for revolution are not the same thing, and Kuran's theory fails to distinguish between the two.

The differences between rural and urban revolutions in this regard are conspicuous. Three-quarters of rural revolutionary episodes since 1900 began with acts of armed rebellion, and another 7 percent began with formal declarations of sovereignty. There is nothing hidden about preferences for revolution in these cases. They began with open acts of rebellion, developed over the course of years, and ended when one side gradually gained the upper hand. Moreover, in rural revolutions, rebels know ahead of time who will and who will not participate in acts of rebellion. These decisions are coordinated in advance of any engagement.

By contrast, since 1900, 33 percent of urban revolutions began with repressed demonstrations, 23 percent with unrepressed demonstrations, and 14 percent with strikes. Only 11 percent began with acts of civilian armed rebellion, and another 7 percent with military rebellions. Most urban revolutionary episodes do not start with people openly declaring their intention to overthrow the regime, but evolve toward revolution through a process of radicalization that "depends upon the reaction of the authorities and their agents to initial limited demands."[39] Sometimes this escalation of demands occurs well into the events of the episode. For example, when asked whether he thought the 2003 Rose Revolution in Georgia had been inevitable, Zurab Zhvania, one of its leaders, responded, "Absolutely not. I can tell you that even two days before President Shevardnadze's resignation he still had a chance to avoid the most dramatic scenario. People were not looking for a revolution. . . . Unfortunately, Shevardnadze and those surrounding him shut the door to dialogue and compromise with the opposition."[40]

---

37. Opp 1994, 110.

38. Kim 1983, 9–10, 104.

39. Reicher and Stott 2007, 36.

40. Karumidze and Wertsch 2005, 35–36, 46–47. Even the day before the culminating events of the revolution, the opposition was hoping to arrange a compromise solution with Shevardnadze, but he refused.

In urban revolutions, opposition activists often enter into contention with low expectations of effecting change, due to the prior record of regime dominance. For the same reasons, regimes tend to display complacency and overconfidence. As one participant in the January 25 protests that set off the 2011 Egyptian Revolution reported,

> We did not feel optimistic that the demonstrations would be very effective or even that they would be launched throughout Egypt. The source of our pessimism was our previous experience with demonstrations over the past few years. They used to be small, with only a few dozen or a few hundred people, who would end up receiving beatings with the sticks of the Central Security Forces and whose leaders would face arrest.[41]

In the words of another participant,

> Both activists and security apparatuses didn't believe that the mobilization would amount to anything on January 25. The direct consequence of that was that all players didn't plan. While activists were skeptical and most of them had no plan for an ending for what they had organized, the security apparatus never imagined that these mobilizations would differ from their previous experiences with protesters. They didn't plan an alternative strategy to their usual "beat and arrest." That is why, on the ground, most of the [Central Security Force] squads didn't know what to do. They stood confused and didn't react, at least at first. In a chain reaction, as people saw others protesting and not being repressed, more started to join.[42]

As Wael Ghonim posted on his "We Are All Khaled Said" website on the morning of the January 25 demonstration, "I have no idea what will happen today . . . I have no idea where I might end up tomorrow."[43]

The January 25 demonstration surprised both the Mubarak regime and participants themselves. As one participant notes, "No one leaving their house that morning knew that they were stepping into the largest policing failure of Mubarak's tenure. The uprising was forged in the heat of street fighting, unanticipated both by its hopeful strategists and its watchful adversaries."[44] Another participant reports, "I was shocked. Everyone was. I don't believe anyone who says they knew it would be like that."[45] Though strongly influenced by the

---

41. Rabea 2015.
42. El Chazli 2017.
43. Ghonim 2012, 174.
44. El-Ghobashy 2012, 27.
45. Khalil 2011, 121.

revolution in Tunisia, the January 25 protest did not directly demand Mubarak's resignation, but called only for disbanding parliament and holding new elections, instituting a two-term limit for the presidency, cancelling emergency rule, firing the minister of the interior, raising the minimum wage, and establishing unemployment benefits. Many of the participants had pledged to participate beforehand on Facebook. They gathered at various assembly points throughout the city, winding their way to Tahrir Square in order to avoid the police. But on numerous occasions the police blocked their path. Perhaps out of concern for a Tunisian-style scenario, the police deployed without their usual batons and riot shields—locking arms instead to thwart the progress of the crowds; but the police were severely outnumbered, and the tactic "quickly proved to be almost comically ineffective."[46] Protestors filled half of Tahrir Square before the regime unleashed tear gas and water cannon on them, with the police regaining the upper hand by the early hours of the morning. But the surprising size of the crowds, the enthusiastic encouragement of those encountered along the way, and the ineffective reactions of the police were read by the opposition as "signs of a shifting situation,"[47] encouraging them to organize another protest four days later. Still, even on the morning of the January 28 protests that led to the occupation of Tahrir Square, activists believed that "it was impossible to predict that a revolution was coming. I was still working on the assumption that we were five years away."[48]

Generally, rural revolutionaries know how many rebels they will bring with them into battle. In urban revolutions, the number of people who will show up when mass mobilization begins is fundamentally unknowable ahead of time. This is not only because of falsified preferences. Even in electoral revolutions, in which individual preferences about the regime have already been openly expressed at the ballot box and populations know with some confidence the extent to which the regime lacks societal support, levels of revolutionary participation are unknowable *ex ante*, as preferences about the regime are grossly insufficient for predicting whether an individual will act on those preferences. (This was, after all, why scholars identified the existence of a collective action problem in the first place.)[49] Even if fully revealed, preferences provide only minimal guidance as to who and how many will participate in acts of rebellion in urban revolutions.

---

46. Khalil 2011, 141.

47. El Chazli 2017. El Chazli's argument about the signals sent by the participation of ordinary people bears a similarity to that made by Lohmann (1994) concerning East Germany.

48. Quoted in Khalil 2011, 164.

49. Olson 1971.

The 2003 Rose Revolution in Georgia, for instance, occurred in the wake of parliamentary elections in which numerous public opinion polls had already openly revealed the population's true preferences about the regime, despite fraudulent official electoral results. Nino Burjanadze, one of the leaders of the revolution, described her astonishment over the turnout at the initial protests of the revolution:

> When I saw the exit polls [on the day of the parliamentary elections] . . . , it was absolutely unbelievable. . . . Of course, I had a strong emotional response. I knew I had won in Kutaisi, but it didn't matter . . . I spent three hours thinking about the situation, still hoping something might change. But when I came into my office, I told everyone there, "I am not going to tolerate this." Because I knew quite well that the elections were totally fraudulent. . . . So the next day we asked the people who were angry about the reality of what had happened to come to the State Philharmonic Hall in Tbilisi. We were expecting that 1,000 or 1,500 people would show up. . . . When we arrived at Philharmonic Hall at 5p.m. and we saw 5,000 people, it was absolutely unbelievable for us.[50]

A similar story unfolded in Ukraine in 2004 in the wake of electoral fraud. (Again, the actual preferences of the public were well-tracked by public opinion polls and widely publicized.) The opposition campaign of Viktor Yushchenko issued a call to its followers to gather on Maidan to protest the vote and force a new election. There were significant doubts as to whether the strategy would work. The Yushchenko campaign had never gathered more than seventy thousand at any previous rally, and the organizers thought they would be lucky to mobilize that many.[51] But as we have seen, even that number would have been grossly insufficient for forcing regime-change. As Dominique Arel observed, "[W]hat everybody expected was for a relatively small following to disrupt business as usual in the center, much like the small demonstrations of 'Ukraine without Kuchma' four years earlier."[52] Taras Stetskiv, one of the co-ordinators of Yushchenko's campaign, later recalled,

> When my colleagues and I came to Maidan, there were only about five hundred people. At 10a.m., there were about three or four thousand. We even had a bit of rain. We thought people would not come out to the streets. At 11 a.m. . . . people from headquarters were calling us up and asking [how many had arrived], and I said, "It's about thirty thousand people." And they

---

50. Quoted in Karumidze and Wertsch 2005, 45–46.
51. Karatnycky 2006, 42.
52. Arel 2005, 3.

said: "It's a catastrophe. With this amount, we won't be able to achieve anything."[53]

Finally, people started pouring into the square at around noon. The size of the crowd increased to eighty thousand and then swelled to two hundred thousand. To the surprise of the organizers themselves (and the Kuchma regime), Kyivans had turned out in far larger numbers than anyone had anticipated.[54]

But surprise in urban revolutions runs much deeper than simply uncertainty over who will participate. It also resides in the inherent unpredictability of regime–opposition interactions during periods of intensified confrontation. In rural revolutions, revolutionaries and regimes have the luxury of long periods between battles for plotting strategies to defeat their opponent. Urban revolutions, by contrast, are a "theatre of unpredictable action,"[55] a "constantly changing field of struggle with continuing interplay of moves and countermoves" in which "nothing is static."[56] As Ghonim observed, "The rapid pace of events drove home one of the key strategies I learned from the revolution: to achieve your vision, you need friends and communication channels more than you need plans. The world moves too fast for even the best-laid plans to hold up."[57]

The February 1917 Revolution that overthrew tsardom in Russia illustrates well how the compressed character of regime–opposition interactions in urban revolutions leads to sudden and unanticipated transformations in contentious trajectories. As Orlando Figes notes, in the February Revolution, "the speed of events took everyone by surprise."[58] Tsyuoshi Hasegawa similarly writes that "when women workers of the Vyborg District abandoned their work early on the morning of February 23, no one realized that they were witnessing the moment that would overthrow tsarism." The second day of the episode saw massive strikes, riots, and demonstrations in Petrograd over food shortages. But there were still few in the city predicting that events "would ultimately lead to a revolution," though "many felt that . . . an unusual political crisis had arrived." Even after the outbreak of a massive general strike and widespread violence on the third day (February 25), as well as radical speeches by some orators, "few believed that the crisis was truly serious enough to

---

53. Quoted in the film *Orange Revolution* (York 2007).
54. For a similar story from the People Power Revolution in the Philippines, see Johnson 1987, 81–82.
55. Bozarslan 2018, 3.
56. Sharp 2012, 34.
57. Ghonim 2012, 232.
58. Figes 1996, 333.

become a revolution,"[59] and many within the government still believed that the protests could be contained if sufficient food supplies were brought to the capital. As Figes explains, "that had been the outcome of several bread riots in the recent past and, although this one was more serious, there was no real reason yet to believe that it would end any differently."[60]

But on the evening of February 25, Tsar Nicholas II committed a major blunder that transformed a potentially manageable situation into an unmanageable one. He commanded his government to quell the disturbances forcefully and immediately, causing the authorities in Petrograd to ban all gatherings in the city, send in troops, and instruct soldiers to use their firearms against crowds to restore order in the capital. The following day, Petrograd was converted into a military camp, and confrontations between soldiers and protestors led to four significant massacres in various parts of the city, leaving scores of dead and wounded. The regime's crackdown effectively emptied the streets. Indeed, it seemed to some within the opposition that the authorities had gained the upper hand. But both the government and the opposition "underestimated the psychological impact of the shooting order on the soldiers."[61] On February 27, four regiments mutinied, leading to a total breakdown of order in the city as troops began firing on one another. Militant workers seized rifles, revolvers, and ammunition from armories, moved toward the city center, and joined the mutinous soldiers. Mob violence spread, with attacks on military barracks, police stations, and prisons. Bloody battles were waged for control of the streets. With the disintegration of its law enforcement apparatus, the regime suffered a total loss of control over the capital. In short, while in hindsight the Russian Revolution may appear the inevitable product of deeper structural conditions, this hardly explains how a bread riot transformed into a revolution. Its revolutionary character emerged tentatively, out of the ways in which the regime reacted to protests for reform.

Despite the strengths and weaknesses that both sides bring with them into revolutionary contention, the directions in which these intensified periods of interaction evolve are fundamentally unpredictable. A good example is the 1989 Tiananmen Uprising in China. It began with an accidental opportunity—the death of Hu Yao Bang, the reformist leader removed from office in 1987 by Deng Xiaoping for sympathizing with student protests. Students used the occasion of the funeral on April 22 to press demands for the abolition of censorship, freedom of speech, the prosecution of corrupt officials, and increased pay

---

59. Hasegawa 1981, 246, 258, 309, 323.
60. Figes 1996, 311.
61. Hasegawa 1981, 278.

for intellectual work. Thousands of students attempted to present a petition to the Communist Party leadership, kneeling in supplication on the steps of the Great Hall of the People. But the government refused to accept the petition. That decision backfired, as the party leadership appeared callous in the eyes of the public, inciting widespread sympathy for the students.

On April 26, a government editorial in the *People's Daily* condemned the student movement, calling it a plot to foment unrest. This angered the students and provoked them to further action. They originally planned a limited march to protest the editorial. This represented a compromise between those who wanted to proceed as far as Tiananmen Square and those who wanted to call off the march altogether. As Craig Calhoun describes it,

> They would march only a third of the way to Tiananmen, as far as the Third Ring Road. This seemed a balance between prudence and the need to act. It would be enough to show that the students rejected the April 26 editorial but would not constitute a major provocation. Still, the compromise only partly assuaged their fear, and some students wrote wills and shaved their heads in anticipation of possible death.

The students began the march "with uncertainty about what they would confront and even whom they would lead." They expected only a small turnout, in view of the government's warning. But to their surprise, eight thousand turned out from Beijing University alone. When the students moved easily through a police blockade at the Third Ring Road, they abandoned their plans for a limited march and instead pushed on to Tiananmen. This was a moment of transformation (one of many in Beijing in 1989): the weakness of the government response emboldened the protestors. While they encountered groups of unarmed police who attempted to block their way, "each time, the surging crowd easily broke through, eliciting a roar of approval and encouraging both onlookers and participants to think it possible to stand up to the army." As Calhoun writes, "A crowd-control technique more effective at building the confidence of protesters . . . is hard to imagine." The April 27 demonstration on Tiananmen Square, which attracted up to a hundred thousand participants, proved to be an enormous success and a turning point for those participating, "reshaping people's ideas about themselves and about what was possible."[62]

Unpacked and dissected at this more granular level, urban revolutions consist of compact sequences of moves and countermoves that bear enormous consequences for those involved, push events in one direction or another, and

62. Calhoun 1994, 50–52.

eventually move contention toward its ultimate outcome. They also contain tremendous emotional tension and uncertainty.[63] Bryan Johnson, a journalist for the Toronto *Globe and Mail*, provides the following description of one of the early confrontations of the 1986 People Power Revolution in the Philippines, when crowds of civilians attempted to block an armored column that could have easily wiped out the small reformist military rebellion that had ensconced itself at Camp Crame:

> The sleepy EDSA-Ortigas intersection was suddenly a chaotic "choke point," the spot on the map where People Power and the Marcos forces intersected. Just after 2:30p.m., General Tadiar had his first moment of decision as he peered through a gunner's slot at the cars, buses, and massed humanity blocking the crossroads. The Marine commander postponed the confrontation, swung his column to the right, and smashed through a concrete wall. Now it was the civilians' turn to make hard choices, though few of us actually did. The panic and horror hadn't quite settled over the crowd of the barricade before the first hotheads—or heroes—vaulted the wall and ran to the APCs. The rest of us followed like lemmings, shouting and waving and scraping our knees on the whitewashed concrete. Courage or insanity—something contagious—was certainly in the air. Tadiar and his officers were confounded by this turn of events. They stood in an angry knot beside one tank, screened off from the crowd, . . . while the entire Marine unit adopted the same frozen military glare.[64]

At the vanguard of this standoff between the tanks and the crowd were nuns, children, and housewives, who were positioned "for maximal emotional impact upon tank commanders." The confrontation with the "tense and edgy" marines stretched on for an hour, during which "a single idiot on either side could touch off a massacre."[65] The troops eventually withdrew—fearful of inducing a bloodbath.

In other cases, restraint did not prevail. In the April Revolution in South Korea against Syngman Rhee in 1960, large numbers of students assembled immediately outside the presidential residence, where the president and government ministers could hear the crowd roaring and singing outside. Police outside the building became "frantic," desperately and repeatedly appealing to their superiors for clarification as to how to respond. They were told to "use all available means to stop them," but to shoot only if the crowds attempted to

---

63. See Sewell 1996; Pearlman 2013.
64. Johnson 1987, 103–4.
65. Johnson 1987, 107, 122.

enter the residence. Only about twenty meters separated the two sides. Suddenly the police opened fire with live ammunition into the crowd (whether this was ordered by the police chief or was simply the result of a jittery trigger-finger is still unknown). The crowd scattered within thirty seconds. Left behind were 180 dead and thousands of wounded. The violence "transformed the character of the protest movement," changing what had been a mobilization for political reform into a revolution.[66] It is considered one of several key turning points in the overthrow of the Rhee regime, setting off six days of student-led protest and violence that eventually brought about the president's resignation.

Confusion is common in urban revolutionary processes, due to the dangers and stakes involved and the high degree of uncertainty surrounding intensified regime–opposition interactions.[67] During the 1986 People Power Revolution in the Philippines, crowds were literally "driven in circles by conflicting rumors" of troop movements. One of the turning points of the revolution was the defection of a group of Sikorsky attack helicopters to the rebels—equalizing the constellation of forces between the opposing sides and creating a shift of momentum. When the defecting helicopters first approached, soldiers and civilians inside Camp Crame believed that they were under attack, setting off a panic. "Thousands simply grabbed whatever they valued—including, in many cases, their children—and ran for their lives.... The problem, of course, was that no safety existed. Those who tried to flee ran smack into each other, in Keystone Kops confusion." Within minutes, panic had transformed into elation, as the protestors realized that the helicopters were defecting to the opposition. "Civilians leapt into one another's arms and fell laughing on the ground. Thousands started jumping up and down and trying to climb the walls."[68]

These kinds of emotional oscillations are typical of the urban revolutionary experience. Calhoun describes similar processes at play during the Tiananmen Uprising: "Within six weeks, these students would experience peaks of exhilaration as their movement grew beyond their short-term expectations, troughs of depression as it seemed to falter from ineffective leadership and lack of direction, and rage as soldiers following government orders killed hundreds or even thousands of protestors.... The movement was marked by wild swings of emotion, euphorias and panics, periods of calm and of intense activity, sleepless nights and midday fainting spells, all of which reshaped the consciousness of its participants."[69] During the hunger strike on the square, as

66. Kim 1983, 115–19, 136.
67. On the role of confusion in the Iranian Revolution, see Kurzman 2004.
68. Johnson 1987, 102, 166–67.
69. Calhoun 1994, 5.

bodies grew weak and tensions mounted, student tempers grew short, exacerbating conflicts among the protestors.[70] Rumors spread like wildfire, aggravated by divisions among the protestors and uncertainties over government actions. As Calhoun recalls, rumors that the army was about to attack the students "had proven false so many times that even with the army in sight I doubted them."[71] The intense and condensed character of interactions within urban revolution can be emotionally and physically exhausting. As one participant in the Tunisian Revolution reported, "I lived the Tunisian revolution moment by moment, either in the street or at home in front of my computer screen. . . . I was glued to my computer all day watching and sharing terrible videos of the police killing people, posting Facebook status updates, and expressing my anger against the oppressive regime."[72] In the 1989 Romanian Revolution, leaders of the revolutionary opposition in Timișoara did not sleep or eat for days. "Tempers were frayed, and the continuing uncertainty and possible dangers of the situation only added to the stress."[73]

Despite all this, many citizens look back at these periods of "thickened history" as some of the best memories of their lives—recalling widespread sentiments of camaraderie, unity, and national pride. Opposition loss brings with it a sense of hopelessness and depression, generating narratives of defeat that may or may not support remobilization.[74] But opposition victory invariably evokes deep emotional catharsis. As one participant in the Egyptian Revolution described the feelings associated with the moment when Mubarak resigned,

> I heard my mum scream, followed by hysterical claps and screams from my dad. I ran from the bathroom to the living room and asked, "What? What? He died? He died?!" I was hoping Mubarak was dead and that everything would be over then. My parents gleefully told me, "He stepped down. He stepped down." Endless screams were heard everywhere. I had never before seen my parents that enthusiastic, joyful, and spontaneously expressing their extreme happiness. My mother kept laughing, jumping in the air, and singing on the balcony, and my dad kept saying, "Unbelievable. Unbelievable." I went down to the street where all of Alexandria was celebrating. . . . There were fireworks and people singing and dancing. It was an unforgettable night of extremely joyous feelings, tears and smiles, and laughter and hope. . . .

70. Calhoun 1994, 102.
71. Calhoun 1994, 82–85, 92.
72. Khedhir 2015, 41–44.
73. Siani-Davies 2005, 78.
74. Beckwith 2015.

That night after watching the world celebrating with us and raising its hats honoring our revolution, a certain idea haunted me: today is the reason for my existence.[75]

Moves, Countermoves, and Missteps in Urban Revolutionary Play

Generally, regimes can respond to revolutionary challenges in one of three ways: ignore them, repress them, or make concessions. Ignoring may be possible if the numbers involved are small or the disruption to everyday life is minimal.[76] But for regimes whose dominance depends on "maintaining an air of invincibility or permanence,"[77] tolerating a revolutionary challenge can be risky business—particularly in cities, where large numbers reside and where close proximity to a regime's nerve centers renders challenges visible and immediately dangerous. It sends signals that challenge is possible precisely where the regime is most vulnerable.

Notwithstanding decades of research,[78] there is still much that remains unpredictable about the effects of repression on protest. Repression imposes costs on challengers, creates disincentives to joining rebellion, and disrupts opposition networks, rendering further mobilization more difficult. But it can also mobilize even larger numbers of challengers by becoming a widely shared grievance. While most attention has been paid to the effects of the severity of repression on mobilization, this is hardly the only factor that matters. The extent to which protest is able to persist in the wake of severe repression also depends on a long list of other factors: the size and coherence of the opposition, the thickness of its networks, and its degree of public support; regime-type and the extent to which a regime contains divisions within it; the degree of openness of the media and the communications environment; whether repression is carried out in the open or hidden from public view; the institutional capacities of the police and the military; the number of people on the streets at the time of repression and whether the opposition is already in control of public space; and exogenous events, which can shape expectations about momentum. We know quite a bit about how each of these factors works.

---

75. Hany 2015.
76. Bishara 2015.
77. Robertson 2009, 530.
78. For an overview, see Lichbach 1987; Opp and Roehl 1990; Gupta, Singh, and Sprague 1993; Opp 1994; Moore 1998; Beissinger 2002; Francisco 2004; Earl 2004; Davenport 2007; Soule and Davenport 2009.

The problem is that too many factors are simultaneously at play that affect the relationship, injecting unpredictability into outcomes.

Similarly, concessions can mobilize or demobilize. They can co-opt challengers and cause them to work within institutions. But they can also multiply challenges by making a regime appear weak and encouraging challengers to ask for more. Concessions that are not credible or are viewed as insignificant and meaningless can anger populations and spur greater mobilization, much like backlash in response to repression.[79] Regimes and oppositions tend to view concessions through markedly different lenses. Regimes treat them as transactional: in exchange for a concession, the opposition is supposed to demobilize.[80] But for some within the opposition, acquiescence to concessions may require compromising principles in unacceptable ways, or the regime's offer may be interpreted as a sign of weakness, encouraging opponents to "up the ante." Concessions often have a differentiating effect on oppositions, demobilizing moderates but mobilizing radicals. To complicate matters further, regimes often engage in a combination of punishment and reward, and the mix they choose, the groups they target, and the consistency with which they act can also be critical.[81]

As the literature indicates, regimes are more likely to resort to repression when they feel threatened and when oppositions articulate radical demands.[82] In this respect, the natural tendency for most regimes is to respond to revolutionary challenges with force, even if the use of force may be counterproductive. The sense of threat is further magnified in urban revolutions by the proximity of the challenge to nerve centers of governmental power. In the infamous "Tbilisi massacres" in the Soviet Union in April 1989, a hundred thousand demonstrators assembled outside the Georgian House of Government, only five hundred meters from the headquarters of the Georgian Communist Party. As subsequent investigations revealed, the psychological pressure on the Georgian Communist Party leadership from the close presence of the crowd and the radical nationalist speeches blaring over loudspeakers was intense. Believing their headquarters were about to be stormed, they panicked, dispatching frantic telegrams to Moscow requesting help in putting down the protests. Ironically, protest organizers had been planning to end their campaign within a few days because of fatigue and uncertain public commitment. The botched attempt by

---

79. Goldstone and Tilly 2001.

80. "You think everything is about deal-making," Wael Ghonim told the head of Egyptian state security. Ghonim, 2012, 279.

81. Lichbach 1987; Rassler 1996; Inclán 2009; Cunningham and Beaulieu 2010; Franklin 2015.

82. Davenport 2007; Sullivan 2016.

the authorities to clear the square in the early hours of April 9 left nineteen dead and 290 wounded when soldiers used poison gas and the sharpened edges of their sapper shovels to control the crowd. The Tbilisi events elicited an enormous backlash in Georgia and elsewhere in the Soviet Union, constituting a turning point in the disintegration of the Soviet regime's ability to apply force against crowds.[83]

In short, if the research on repression and concessions has demonstrated anything, it is that simplistic dicta do not hold. Regimes would like to be rational and strategic in marginalizing revolutionary challenges, and they may believe that they are acting that way. But given the large number of variables and the magnified sense of threat involved in urban revolution, the choice of actions is often dictated by emotions like hope or fear, and their impact is difficult to predict—even without considering the institutional and time constraints that regimes are under. It is easy to see how, in the heat of rapid and compact urban revolutionary contention, when the fate of a regime hangs in the balance, decision-makers might be prone to mistakes in fashioning responses to urban revolutionary challengers. As Goldstone and Tilly observe,

> the state may initially set the level of concessions or repression too low.... Protest activity will then start to mount, and the question for the state is what to do next—increase repression, or increase concessions, or both. It may swing back and forth between concessions and repression, trying to find a combination that quells protest, without success. This kind of inconsistent repression and concession is strongly associated with increasing protest actions.[84]

Due to the rapid pace of events in urban revolutionary contention, regimes may also choose concessions based on assumptions that are no longer relevant. As Valery Boldin, one of Gorbachev's advisors, observed about the Soviet regime's responses to the massive waves of mobilization that helped precipitate its collapse, "It became common to hear proposals for measures that would have been meaningful some three or five years earlier."[85] Events simply moved far faster than the capability of institutions to react to them.

But there is another dimension to decisions about repression in urban revolutionary contention: they are often made on the spot, by rank-and-file police and soldiers as they confront revolutionary challengers on the ground in real time. In urban revolutionary contention, where the opposition and the forces

---

83. Beissinger 2002, 347–354.
84. Goldstone and Tilly 2001, 188.
85. Boldin 1994, 147.

of order are in direct contact, it is not unusual for police and soldiers to act autonomously, in instinctive and unplanned ways. Spontaneous actions by elements of a crowd are also common. There is enormous space for mistakes or misinterpretations that can have fateful consequences.

This becomes clear when we examine regime and opposition decision-making across a diversity of cases. In the February 1917 Revolution in Russia, for instance, major blunders played an important role in the overthrow of the tsarist regime. Not only did the tsar, as noted earlier, senselessly order troops to fire on crowds, but much of Petrograd's central military command was in disarray and failed to act effectively in countering mutinies within its own ranks. Ironically, a substantial number of troops in Petrograd remained loyal to the regime. But the central command neglected to engage in timely action and lost communication with loyal forces. As Hasegawa observes,

> A remarkable fact of the February uprising was that it succeeded at all. What prevented the tsarist government from putting it down? When one looks into the uprising, one is struck with the extreme ineptitude of the security authorities. Not only could they not prevent the uprising from spreading through the city, but they also failed miserably to muster forces that could have rallied behind the tsarist government. The frightened, unnerved leadership made mistake after mistake, ultimately driving itself to total disintegration.... The ineptitude and confusion of the commanding authority led to the final disintegration of the loyal troops without firing a single shot.[86]

It was not only the regime that made mistakes. As Nikolai Sukhanov, one of the great observers of the revolution, remarked, opposition parties were "weak, unprepared, without initiative, and incapable of orienting themselves in the situation... [so that] in practice they did not understand, recognize, or digest the events that had turned everything upside down."[87]

The outcome of the People Power Revolution in the Philippines was the result of a long train of mistakes made by the Marcos regime due to overconfidence, misinformation, and incompetence. The revolution was set off by a snap presidential election that Marcos mistakenly called in February 1986—an idea that had been suggested to him by CIA director William Casey to help consolidate the regime, and which had originally been resisted by Marcos. Marcos was overconfident, believing that he could win the election easily. Cory Aquino waged a brilliant campaign, however, and the opposition set up

---

86. Hasegawa 1981, 294 and 310.
87. Sukhanov 1922, 127, 131.

an extensive vote-monitoring operation that identified instances of electoral fraud.[88] Marcos encountered a stroke of luck when American intelligence revealed to him the impending coup that the defense minister Juan Ponce Enrile and the deputy chief of staff Fidel Ramos were about to launch. He waited for the rebels to act before pouncing. On the first day of the revolt, the reformist rebels were "virtually defenseless" and could easily have been overrun. They were saved "only by the indecision and overconfidence of the Marcos generals." As Johnson reports, "the lopsided odds created overconfidence among the Loyalists." Despite its overwhelming military superiority, the Marcos regime agreed not to attack the rebels in exchange for a promise that the rebels not attack the presidential palace. Since the rebels had no capabilities for mounting an assault on the presidential palace, the agreement was "a gigantic blunder" that bought the rebels critical time, allowing hundreds of thousands of civilians to place themselves strategically in front of the entrance to Camp Crame, where the rebels were holed up, to block any attempted attack.[89] The soldiers eventually sent by Marcos to take Camp Crame were not equipped with crowd-control equipment, putting them in the difficult position of choosing between disobeying orders or being held responsible for a major massacre. Repeatedly, they chose retreat over massacre.[90]

Throughout the episode, the Marcos regime displayed enormous incompetence. It failed to cut off communications to Camp Crame, allowing the opposition to coordinate with its allies outside the camp. It failed to discover the radio station from which the opposition coordinated civil resistance, even though that station was located in close proximity to the presidential palace. And it guarded the Maharlika television broadcast center with an absurdly small force, allowing it to be captured easily by rebel soldiers.[91] Marcos declared a 6p.m. to 6a.m. curfew that was entirely ignored by the population; the curfew was announced at 7p.m. in the evening when a million people were on the streets, so the regime had no way of enforcing the order. Although Cory Aquino stayed at her sister's home in the suburbs of Manila, the regime never attempted to place her under arrest. Hoping to catch the rebels off-guard, on the third day of the episode the regime spread false rumors of Marcos's resignation, even while it plotted a final assault on Camp Crame. The opposition believed the rumors of Marcos's departure, causing jubilant celebrations (and even leading Enrile prematurely to declare the day as Philippine Independence

88. Johnson 1987, 90–91.
89. Johnson 1987, 14, 73–74, 85, 264.
90. Johnson 1987, 128, 132, 209–16.
91. Johnson 1987, 114, 185–87, 205.

Day). In the meantime, Marcos was sitting in his office preparing to deliver his final blow. But the scheme backfired. For one thing, it caused large numbers of government troops to defect to the opposition, since they too believed the rumors of Marcos's departure.[92] For another, Marcos sprang the trap too early. If he had waited another hour, most of the civilian crowds defending the rebel troops would have dispersed. Instead, he ordered an assault while crowds were still in place. As a result, military commanders balked, not wanting to cause large numbers of civilian casualties.[93] Another assault on Camp Crame failed when loyalist troops, masquerading as opposition supporters, attempted to sneak past crowds. They disguised themselves by tying yellow ribbons on their guns, but ineptly failed to sport other rebel markers such as armbands and a rotated Philippine flag patch. They were quickly spotted and surrounded by crowds of protestors.[94]

The more deeply one delves into the events of urban revolutions like the People Power Revolution, the more one comes to appreciate the human element in revolution and the ways in which the outcomes of revolutionary contention are often the product of faulty decisions by regimes and oppositions. The 1989 overthrow of the Ceaușescu regime in Romania displays a similar pattern of mistakes. It began on December 16, when attempts by the regime to evict a church pastor in the city of Timișoara became the occasion for anti-regime demonstrations and riots. The following day, crowds grew larger, as the authorities lost control over the city center. In response, Ceaușescu ordered a "bizarre" military parade through the city center as a show of strength against the protestors, "with flags flying and bugles blowing." But rather than demoralizing the crowds, this "left most of the onlookers thoroughly bemused and, in fact, provided a pretext for the crowd to gather and solidify."[95] The number of troops deployed to Timișoara was wholly insufficient to crush the protests. By the end of the day, the protestors had captured five army tanks and ransacked Communist Party headquarters. Having failed in his first attempt to quell the disturbances, Ceaușescu then ordered a much larger force of secret police troops and army reinforcements to crush the revolt using live ammunition, killing over sixty and wounding more than two hundred. The bodies were

---

92. In Tunisia in 2011, false rumors on the internet that the army had refused to obey orders to fire into crowds played a role in the demise of the Ben Ali government. See Grewal 2019, 259–60.

93. Johnson 1987, 188–89, 193, 198–99, 209, 213–16.

94. Johnson 1987, 120–21.

95. Siani-Davies 2005, 63–64.

loaded onto trucks and transported to Bucharest, where they were cremated—their ashes dumped into a canal.[96]

Believing the revolt to be over and the situation under control, Ceaușescu then departed on December 18 for a three-day visit to Iran—often considered one of his biggest blunders. Once security forces had driven protestors off the streets, opposition in Timișoara retreated to the factory floor. The authorities ordered official meetings at factories to explain the massacres; but these escaped official control and turned into strikes and demonstrations. On December 20, large crowds of workers marched to the center of Timișoara, picking up supporters along the way. The crowd of forty thousand took control of the city, intermingling with troops and claiming that the army had defected to their side. Eventually, the army had to be withdrawn. On Ceaușescu's instruction, the regime engaged in one more attempt to regain control over Timișoara: it mobilized twenty thousand workers from Oltenia (Ceaușescu's stronghold), arming them with clubs and dispatching them on special trains with orders to take back the city. But when they arrived in Timișoara on December 21, no one was at the train station to meet them, so the trains promptly returned to Bucharest.[97] In spite of tight censorship, word of the Timișoara events quickly spread across Romania by telephone, with disturbances breaking out in cities and towns in Banat and Transylvania.

Ceaușescu arrived back from Iran on the afternoon of December 20 and proceeded to make another fateful decision: he chose to hold a huge mass meeting on Palace Square in the heart of Bucharest as a show of popular support for his regime, to be televised live to the nation. Ceaușescu believed that he enjoyed overwhelming public support and that the demonstration would contain the further spread of revolt. Instead, it only illustrated how out of touch with reality he was. In the most famous incident of the revolution, on December 21 a hundred thousand participants were bussed to the center of the city and provided with placards expressing support for the dictator. Ceaușescu addressed the crowd from the balcony of the Central Committee building. A few minutes into the speech, a loud bang caused screams and commotion in the crowd,[98] and a number of people were injured in the pushing and shoving that ensued. Elements in the crowd began chanting "Timișoara!" Ceaușescu was visibly startled, and the live television transmission was cut off.

---

96. Siani-Davies 2005, 59–68.

97. Siani-Davies 2005, 70–77.

98. It is still unclear whether the noise was a firecracker, the short-circuiting of a loudspeaker, a gunshot, or a tear gas canister fired by the secret police at nearby protesters.

A few minutes later, Ceaușescu resumed his speech, but toward the end he was interrupted again by chants and jeers. The speech came to an abrupt end, and Ceaușescu was unceremoniously hustled off the balcony. A little later, only a few blocks away, crowds of protesters clashed with the police. Pitched battles between police and protestors stretched late into the night, leaving forty-nine dead and 463 wounded.[99]

The following morning, large crowds streamed toward the center of the capital, fraternizing with troops and overwhelming them. Shortly afterward, guards were suddenly withdrawn from Central Committee headquarters, paving the way for the downfall of the regime.[100] Ceaușescu and his wife fled from the roof of the building by helicopter only minutes before crowds would have reached them. After a series of misadventures, the couple took refuge on a military base. They were detained by soldiers, and two days after their flight were summarily tried and executed. The conflict then descended into a murky civil war on the streets of Bucharest, with soldiers and armed civilians pitted against a shadowy force of regime loyalists. Throughout the revolution opposition leaders were "overwhelmed by the sheer pace of events and were floundering in the face of the need to adapt to the dynamics of a mass popular uprising."[101] They were as stunned by the uprising as the regime itself.

The 1989 Tiananmen Uprising similarly took unexpected turns as a result of mistakes on both sides. The Chinese government attempted to undermine the student movement through a variety of means. At first, it met with student leaders on a school-by-school basis, hoping this would create rivalries among them. After that effort failed, the government staged a public dialogue with leaders of officially recognized student associations in order to feign interest in student issues, but "it convinced no one."[102] Eventually, the government invited a handful of representatives from the independent Federation of Autonomous Students to a televised dialogue, though the meeting included representatives of official student associations as well. As Calhoun notes, "It seemed . . . that the students were about to be outmaneuvered by the government's superficial hints of openness and repressive tolerance, by which they would be allowed expression but would not be taken seriously."[103] Indeed, in the following days the movement began to dwindle, as students returned to class. To revive the movement's momentum, a group of radical student activists embarked on a hunger strike on Tiananmen Square on May 13. The hunger

99. Siani-Davies 2005, 82–87.
100. Siani-Davies 2005, 88–89, 92.
101. Siani-Davies 2005, 112, 119.
102. Calhoun 1994, 55.
103. Calhoun 1994, 56.

strike was opposed by many of the independent student unions, as those with sympathies with the reformist wing of the government felt that it was too provocative. The government had actually agreed to a new dialogue with the students before the hunger strikers headed off to Tiananmen Square, though this was unknown to them at the time.[104] With the students occupying the square and Gorbachev's impending visit to China on May 15, the Communist Party leadership very much needed the protests to be resolved. Prominent reformist intellectuals stepped in, acting as mediators between the hunger strikers and the government. But the talks quickly broke down due to divisions among the hunger strikers, as radicals among them pushed for more confrontational tactics and far-reaching political demands. An historic opportunity for reform in Chinese history was thus missed, as the students' failure to compromise empowered hardliners within the party and led to the eviction of the reformist wing from the government.

Indeed, the tragedy of Tiananmen was that, through their intransigence and unwillingness to compromise, student protesters empowered the very forces that ultimately repressed them. By remaining in Tiananmen, hunger strikers forced Gorbachev to cancel his visit to the square, embarrassing the Communist Party leadership. One last attempt was made by the Party leadership to negotiate, as hardline prime minister Li Peng met with student leaders on May 18. Calhoun notes that "this meeting might have started a real dialogue had it been held in late April or the first week of May. But now the government was offering too little, too late."[105] Li Peng insisted that the students end their protest before any of their concerns could be taken up by the government. Student leaders, by contrast, lectured Li Peng about how the government needed to accept student demands before the hunger strikers would leave the square. After the meeting, reformist leader Zhao Ziyang appeared at the square with tears in his eyes, telling hunger strikers that "we have come, but too late."[106] He had been removed from office the night before, opening the path to a more forceful imposition of order.

Up to a million citizens mobilized in support of the hunger strikers on May 18, with representatives from nearly all sectors of urban society participating, including the working class. The size and diversity of the crowds led many among the hunger strikers to declare victory.[107] But the next day the regime imposed martial law, and the momentum of the movement was lost

104. Hinton 1996.
105. Calhoun 1994, 80.
106. Calhoun 1994, 81.
107. Pieke 1996, 12.

again. As the Tiananmen protests persisted, the composition of the students on the square changed, with more radical students from the provinces coming to predominate. Plagued by factions and intrigues, those left on the square denounced any effort to end the protest as "capitulationist" and called for an end to the party's dictatorship and the resignation of Li Peng.[108] As the episode stretched on, the students on the square tired, and it was increasingly evident— even to the student leadership—that they were losing.[109] Student leaders resolved to end the occupation, but it proved impossible to leave the square due to outbidding by radicals. The ensuing brutal suppression of the Tiananmen rebellion was a product of this complex dialectic between square and government office. It demonstrated how navigating urban revolutionary contention is as difficult for revolutionary oppositions as it is for incumbent regimes.

Urban Revolutionary Play and Revolutionary Endgames

As we have seen, urban revolutions have a much higher success rate than rural revolutions. Rural revolutions are harder to extinguish. The prolonged character of rural rebellion reflects the fact that rural revolutionaries are better able to evade the repressive power of the state. But proximity to centers of power and commerce provides urban revolutionaries with greater opportunities for direct disruption of a regime. In rural revolutions, life in cities can often continue without disruption in the midst of civil war. In urban revolutions, by contrast, normal daily life in cities typically comes to a halt. In Alexandria during the 2011 Egyptian Revolution, for example, "no one went to work, and as a result, the fear of food shortages haunted us. The supermarkets opened for less than three hours a day for people to buy food. People started to run out of money because withdrawing money from banks was impossible."[110] This paralysis of daily life as a result of urban revolutionary challenge can exert significant pressures on a regime politically and economically. It also takes a heavy toll on populations as revolutionary contention persists.

Opposition success in urban revolutions, in keeping with their compact character, usually materializes abruptly: through the sudden resignation or flight of a leader, or defection or seizure of power by the regime's military. The outcome itself typically takes populations by surprise. Regimes once thought to be all-powerful suddenly collapse like a house of cards. By contrast, in rural revolutions, opposition success emerges slowly, through progressive victories

---

108. On the radicalization of student demands, see Calhoun 1994, 101, 122, 184–85.
109. Calhoun 1994, 105–6; Hinton 1996.
110. Hany 2015, 67–70.

on the battlefield. It typically drags out over an extended period, often giving those associated with the old regime plenty of opportunity to flee.

Physical proximity to centers of power places urban oppositions in a propitious position to induce defections from a regime's institutions and coalition through direct contact. Network ties between the opposition and the regime played a key role in the outcome of the 2000 Bulldozer Revolution in Serbia. Prior to the election that set off the final confrontation, "opposition leaders had spent countless hours meeting with high-ranking police and military officials to get a promise that violence would not be used at peaceful rallies."[111] Former army generals within the opposition interceded with military commanders, urging them to remain neutral. In the end, military officers played a critical role in persuading Milošević to step down.[112] In the 2004 Orange Revolution in Ukraine, the opposition established ties with the secret police prior to the onset of revolutionary contention. One of these meetings (a dinner with secret police chief Ihor Smeshko) was the occasion for the infamous dioxide poisoning of Yushchenko.[113] Smeshko (a Harvard graduate who had worked as military attaché in the United States) was an outsider to the secret police. He was chosen as a compromise candidate to run the police in the wake of the scandals that had racked the Kuchma administration in the early 2000s. The Ukrainian secret police played an ambiguous role throughout the revolution. The spy agency, for instance, secretly recorded conversations by the Yanukovych campaign about election rigging and turned these tapes over to the opposition. (The tapes became key evidence used in the Supreme Court decision that annulled Yanukovych's victory and swung the outcome to the Orange side.)[114] A steady stream of revelations of pro-Yushchenko sentiment from within official institutions unfolded on Maidan. On November 23, for example, 350 Ukrainian diplomats came out in support of Yushchenko in a collective declaration. Television journalists denounced their bosses for forcing them to read the fraudulent electoral results on air. Members of the army and the security services began to make their neutrality public, with reports of troops declaring their loyalty to the Yushchenko camp.[115] The fragility of Kuchma's control over institutions, which had been weakened by persistent conflicts between factions over the distribution of property and corruption, easily fed into such defections.[116] Elite defection

---

111. United States Institute of Peace 2001, 9.
112. Cohen 2001, 417, 425; Gordy 2000, 82.
113. Kuzio 2005a.
114. Chivers 2005; Kuzio 2004; Kuzio 2005b.
115. Beissinger 2011.
116. Way 2005.

from a regime's ruling coalition is much more difficult to pull off in a rural revolution carried out by civil war.

Since normally elites will not risk defection unless revolutionary victory appears likely, the possibility of inducing defections from a regime's sustaining coalition in urban uprisings is usually dependent on a sense of momentum built up by the flow of action.[117] Opposition inaction, passivity, or hesitation provides regimes with an opening to sow doubts about the prospects for opposition victory, allowing regimes to regroup. As Trotsky wrote with reference to the February 1917 Revolution in Russia, "A revolutionary uprising that spreads over a number of days can develop victoriously only in case it ascends step by step, and scores one success after another. A pause in its growth is dangerous; a prolonged marking of time, fatal."[118] Thus, overthrowing a regime through urban revolution requires a crescendo of action that induces regime defections by signaling the inability of a regime to eliminate the threat and by demonstrating mounting popular support for regime-change. Failure to demonstrate momentum, by contrast, dooms an urban challenger to defeat by undermining opposition morale and sapping its capacity to mobilize populations or induce regime defections, opening it up to eventual repression. If prolonged, the paralysis that results from urban revolution can backfire on urban oppositions, turning populations against them, becoming a cause for opposition divisions, and legitimizing repression. Mubarak, for instance, believed that by "entrenching and stretching out the standoff, keeping the country disrupted while blaming the protestors for that disruption," he could eventually isolate and outlast them. As Ashraf Khalil notes, "It was a valid strategy. Many apolitical Egyptians were already showing signs of revolutionary fatigue at the massive interruption of daily life."[119] Because of the difficulties of sustaining revolutionary challenges in cities, a sense of momentum must be built quickly—typically within a matter of weeks and months—before exhaustion ultimately sets in. This diverges sharply from rural revolutions, where momentum might shift back and forth over years and emerge only after a succession of battles.

Unlike in rural revolutions, oppositions in urban revolutions confront military and police continuously and directly. One of the riskiest moments for regimes in urban revolutions has been when the military is commanded to engage in violence against civilians. In February 1917, Russian troops ordered to suppress crowds balked at carrying out their orders, at times refusing to

---

117. For further evidence, see Tarrow 1998; Beissinger 2002; Chenoweth and Belgioioso 2019.
118. Trotsky 1932, vol. 1, 110.
119. Khalil 2011, 216–17.

break up protests, disobeying commands to fire into crowds, deliberately shooting over the heads of demonstrators, and even occasionally defending protestors against the police.[120] After being forced to shoot directly into crowds on February 26, leaving hundreds dead, on February 27 soldiers mutinied, leading to the total breakdown of order and the eventual abdication of the tsar. In the 1986 People Power Revolution in the Philippines, even though marines loyal to Marcos had placed themselves in position to be able to wipe out the rebellion at Camp Crame with tanks and precision howitzers, the commanding officer Colonel Braulio Balbas refused to fire—even after being ordered repeatedly to do so by his superiors. As he later recalled,

> I was willing to obey all legal orders, but I did not believe I could commit an atrocity. . . . Many, many people would have been killed if I fired the heavy weapons. . . . [T]he foremost thing in my mind was not to commit atrocities against the Filipino people or my fellow soldiers. I had several things to consider. I knew that if I disobeyed and Marcos wins, then I would be arrested, court-martialed, and maybe face a firing squad. I could not defect to Camp Crame, because my family was back in Fort Bonifacio [controlled by Marcos] and maybe they would be hurt.[121]

Balbas prevaricated long enough for the situation to resolve itself, with Marcos fleeing the presidential palace.

Urban revolutionaries have greater opportunities than rural revolutionaries for face-to-face contact with the rank-and-file police or soldiers charged with suppressing them. In cities, revolution participants may even be neighbors, relatives, or friends of police or soldiers charged with repressing revolt. Given these network ties, troops drawn from other regions tend to be more reliable in repressing revolutionary threats. During urban revolutionary contention revolutionaries try to communicate directly with police or soldiers, urging them to disobey orders, to defend protestors, and to defect. Known as "fraternization," this tactic has been a mainstay of urban revolutionary contention since at least the late eighteenth century.

Neil Ketchley rightly notes that the key to fraternization as a tactic is the "physical co-presence" of revolutionaries and armed forces, with the use of ranged weapons rendering fraternization more problematic.[122] Opportunities for fraternization are relatively constricted in rural revolts due to their civil war

---

120. Figes 1996, 311–12.

121. Quoted in Johnson 1987, 147, 198–201. Johnson calls Balbas "an unsung hero of the revolution."

122. Ketchley 2017, 51, 56.

character and the need to use ranged weapons. Fraternization in rural revolts largely occurs through interaction of off-duty soldiers with civilian noncombatants whose loyalties are hidden, though it can occasionally occur through informal relationships across battle lines due to common ethnic, clan, or interpersonal ties.[123] But armies typically have strict rules against fraternization, particularly when they are deployed in combat. In rural revolts, fraternization depends on hidden personal connections between civilians and soldiers rather than on open entreaties for defection, as occurs in cities. As a result, large-scale defections in rural revolts are more likely to occur through defeat on the battlefield, issues of unit composition, or low morale due to poor supply of soldiers than through fraternization.[124]

As Ketchley observes, in the 2011 Egyptian Revolution there was little fraternization between protestors and the Central Security Forces, who were trained in crowd control and equipped with ranged weapons such as water cannon and tear gas (used for "controlling space and maintaining distance between the two sides").[125] By contrast, efforts to fraternize with the Egyptian army were extensive once it was deployed on January 28 to guard major intersections. Fraternization frequently involved acts of trespass in which civilians climbed onto military vehicles and mingled with soldiers. It is precisely to avoid the dangers of fraternization that soldiers are typically kept physically separate from civilians in barracks and camps; but this distance is dissolved when the military is deployed to police urban uprisings. In Egypt, citizens clambered on top of armored cars and tanks, took pictures with soldiers, and shared food with them, trying to convince them to protect protestors from the police and to disobey orders to repress the revolt. Fraternization in urban revolutions usually involves these kinds of ritualized interactions, in which civilians seek to exert social pressure on soldiers to disobey orders or to join revolutionaries through open entreaties or acts of kindness, such as handing flowers or food to them. Ketchley notes that there was always a tension and ambiguity to fraternization during the Egyptian Revolution, as revolutionaries never knew whether the troops that they were greeting would defend them or turn on them. (Both reactions in fact occurred.) Nevertheless, fraternization helped to foster a partial breakdown of military discipline in the area of Tahrir Square and may have stayed the hand of the regime in ordering a larger

---

123. For instances of fraternization in rural revolutions, see Wickham-Crowley 1992, 147; Daugherty 1995.
124. Kingma 1997; McLauchlin 2015.
125. Ketchley 2017, 51.

crackdown by the army. On February 3, the military even declared that it would guarantee the security of the protestors in Tahrir Square.[126]

Moments of fraternization have often constituted key turning points within urban revolutions. In the 1960 April Revolution in South Korea, the final denouement of the Syngman Rhee regime occurred when 150 elderly professors marched on the National Assembly, calling for the president's resignation. A large crowd gathered to watch. A group of tanks roared up to the Assembly building and soldiers appeared, blocking the advance of the crowd. Attracted by the sound of the tanks, more people poured into the area. Individuals in the crowd began arguing with the soldiers, attempting to convince them not to fire. After several tear gas grenades were thrown, the crowd began to sing the refrains of an army song from the Korean War. This moved the soldiers deeply. As Quee-Young Kim describes it: "Suddenly, from an Army loudspeaker opposite the Assembly came the electrifying words: 'Your demands are just. The Army recognizes that your demands are just.'"[127] Once the army had broken in one location, this set off a chain reaction of defections elsewhere, precipitating Rhee's resignation the following day.

The ability of regimes to contain fraternization is key to their survival during urban revolutionary crises. In the Tiananmen Uprising, the regime's first efforts to suppress the student revolt after the declaration of martial law on May 19 failed when citizens spontaneously created barriers at major intersections leading to the square and proceeded to fraternize with troops, attempting to persuade them not to follow orders to suppress the demonstrators. As Calhoun describes the scene at one intersection on May 21, "The troops looked very hot and a little baffled. Citizens climbed all over the open trucks the soldiers were in, occasionally offered them food, and constantly harangued them, teased them, jabbered at them."[128] Because of this exposure, the regime feared that the troops might not be reliable, so it withdrew these forces and instead brought in troops from the remote provinces for their second attempt at suppression on the night of June 3–4. The greatest bloodshed occurred when these troops fired their way through crowds manning barricades. Much of the violence against civilians was arbitrary and excessive, committed in the dark, where troops could not clearly see the faces of their victims.

---

126. Ketchley 2017, 76–77; Ketchley 2014. Women in particular were at the forefront of fraternization efforts in Egypt. For a similar observation on gender roles in fraternization during the February 1917 Revolution in Russia, see Trotsky 1932, vol. 1, 109.

127. Kim 1983, 187–88.

128. Calhoun 1994, 93.

Conclusion: The Epiphany of Urban Revolution

"It was a miracle, pure and simple," one Filipino business professor asserts about the People Power Revolution in the Philippines. "There must have been divine intervention somewhere along the line."[129] In Cory Aquino's words, "God actually came down and walked among us during those four days. There is no other explanation for what happened." The revolt, which had a deeply religious character to it, later gave rise to tales of a Blue Nun who suddenly appeared in the crowd and held back the advance of tanks.[130] Similarly, the year 1989 is known in eastern Europe as the *annus mirabilis* (miraculous year).[131] In nearly identical words, Slavoj Žižek refers to the 2011 Egyptian Revolution as "miraculous," as something "that few predicted, violating the experts' opinions, as if the uprising was not simply the result of social causes but the intervention of a mysterious agency."[132] In rural revolutions, religion and magic often fortify the courage of participants through belief in other-worldly salvation, or in the potions, oaths, totems, or spirits that villagers believe protect them from enemy bullets.[133] But the mystery of urban revolutions lies in the unexpected and transformative moments that emerge out of intensified and compressed regime–opposition interactions. These defy easy explanation and naturally give rise to narratives of conspiracy, divine intervention, and inevitability.[134]

Urban revolutions surprise. They surprise not so much because of preference falsification, though certainly this can occur, but rather because of the unanticipated outcomes that unfold from their condensed interactions, the speed with which they move, and the difficulty of fashioning rational responses under time pressure and on the basis of incomplete or faulty information—all at a close distance from nerve centers of power. Charles Kurzman has observed that revolutions are fundamentally unpredictable because "revolutionaries themselves don't know what is going to happen, and their behaviors are responses to the confusion."[135] Regimes, too, are often overwhelmed by information problems in urban revolutionary play and have little

---

129. Mamot 1986, 119.

130. Johnson 1987, 127, 274.

131. Patton 2011.

132. Žižek 2011.

133. For examples, see Iliffe 1967; Solomon 1969; Lan 1985; Salemink 1994; Behrend 1999; Askew and Helbardt 2012.

134. Polletta (2006) called these "Click!" stories—accounts that attempt to explain the inexplicable without really explaining it.

135. Kurzman 2004, 11.

conception of what the actual impact of their actions will be. Rumor, miscalculation, and coincidence play outsized roles. These are present in rural revolutions as well. But the city is unforgiving. In rural revolutions, revolutionaries and regimes can recover more easily from mistakes, thanks to the safety afforded by terrain and the buffer of distance. In urban revolutions, the consequences of mistakes are magnified a thousandfold by the proximity of contention to nerve centers of state power and the inability of oppositions to hide from government repression.

It is this which makes urban revolutions, in Teodor Shanin's words, a "moment of truth." As he put it, "The stakes are high, the lessons harsh, and there is no time for leisurely meditation.... The results are final."[136] The compactness, speed, intensity, and high stakes of urban revolution render it a particularly challenging and dangerous game for all who play.

136. Shanin 1986, 184.

6

Public Space and Urban Revolution

> As to strongholds, what is suitable to different forms of government varies; thus, an acropolis is suited to an oligarchy or a monarchy, but a plain to a democracy; neither to an aristocracy, but rather a number of strong places.
>
> ARISTOTLE, *POLITICS* 7.11.1330B[1]

AT THE BEGINNING of the twentieth century what is known today as Maidan (the Square) in Ukraine's capital Kyiv could not have served as the site for the enormous demonstrations that occurred there a century later during the Orange and Euromaidan revolutions. Not only was the city's population too small to support such mobilizations, but the physical space of Maidan was also strikingly different. At one time the site of the Lyadski Gate to the ancient city of Kyiv, and then swampland after Kyiv's destruction by the Mongols in the thirteenth century, by the 1830s the area had come to be known as Bazar Square after the shops and taverns that inhabited it. It later assumed the name Khreshchatyk Square, for the developing main commercial street of Kyiv on which it was located. In 1876, the capacious building of the Kyiv City Duma (Council) was erected at its entrance, enclosing the space, marking it as a government nerve center, and bestowing upon it a new name: Duma Square. Across the street from the City Duma, a sloping hill stretching upward along Instytutska Street (named after the "Institute for Noble Maidens" located there) was densely packed with houses and other buildings. Later, nestled at the top of the hill was one of the Russian Empire's earliest "skyscrapers"— the twelve-story Ginzburg House, built in 1912. As a result of the construction of the City Duma at the square's entrance, the open space at Duma Square was highly constricted. It consisted of the cobblestoned street of the fashionable

---

1. Aristotle 1941, 1292.

Khreshchatyk in front of the building (thirty meters wide with an electric tram running down the middle) and a small, fenced-in park behind it. The park was highly landscaped with a fountain and was mainly used for leisure strolls and as a trolley roundabout (Figure 6.1). During the Revolution of 1905, crowds of up to twenty thousand protested on the street space in front of the City Duma, though not on the small square behind. But the events of 1905 in Kyiv were scattered throughout the city rather than concentrated on any single site.[2]

Demonstrations again occurred at Duma Square in 1917. The main events of the February Revolution occurred in Petrograd, but photographs from the time show crowds of about thirty thousand gathered along Khreshchatyk in front of the City Duma building (and pushing up past the entrance to Instytutska Street) to celebrate the downfall of the tsar. In March 1917, an assembly of soldiers and civilians carried out an improvised trial and hanging of the statue of former prime minister Piotr Stolypin, which had been erected in 1913 in front of the Duma building after his assassination in Kyiv. Other locations in the city arguably functioned as more important sites for large gatherings during the revolution—among them Bessarabian Square, Volodymyrska Street, Podil, and St. Sophia Square.[3] In January 1918, the Bolsheviks staged an armed uprising at the Kyiv Arsenal, with echoes in the Podil, Shuliavka, and Demiivka neighborhoods. Duma Square played little part in these events. After the Soviets gained power, the City Duma building became the seat of Kyiv's regional government and communist party, and the square was renamed Soviet Square. In 1935, it was rechristened once again, as Kalinin Square—after Mikhail Kalinin, the powerless president of the Soviet Union, on his sixtieth birthday.

Maidan would never have become Maidan had it not been for World War II. In 1941, the Germans captured Kyiv without much physical damage to the city; but the City Duma building was blown up as a result of the notorious Khreshchatyk explosions staged by the Soviet secret police. Rather than turn the city over intact to the Nazi invader, Stalin ordered that much of Khreshchatyk be destroyed by long-distance radio-controlled explosions, sowing panic throughout the city. The Nazis used the explosions as a pretext for

---

2. Cybriwsky 2014; Antonova-Azarova 2014; Oliynyk 2015; Hamm 1993; Bilenky 2018; Zhukovsky 2008a.

3. Garboś 2018; Zhukovsky 2008b. For outstanding photographic images of the city of Kyiv during this period, see http://photohistory.kiev.ua/gal/. In April 1917, up to a hundred thousand participated in a ceremony in St. Sophia Square celebrating the downfall of the tsar. Excluding communist-organized parades, it was likely the largest demonstration in Kyiv prior to July 24, 1990, when Rukh organized a mass rally in favor of Ukrainian independence. See *Ekspress khronika*, no. 31, July 31, 1990.

FIGURE 6.1. Khreshchatyk and Duma Square in 1918, as seen from a German aerial photo. (Courtesy of VARTO Publishing House.)

massacring much of the city's Jewish population. Khreshchatyk was also left in ruins from the Second Battle of Kyiv in December 1943, when Kyiv was recaptured from the Germans after heavy fighting. After the war, the area was demolished and completely redesigned. The reconstructed square became an open space of roughly twenty thousand square meters, dominated at one end by a large fountain and stretching across Khreshchatyk up the now-vacant adjacent hill to a new Stalinist high-rise hotel where Ginzburg House once stood. Khreshchatyk was doubled in width to seventy-five meters, and a metro stop allowing for the rapid movement of people in and out of the square (with a pedestrian crossing beneath Khreshchatyk) was completed in 1976. In 1977, the square was renamed yet again, as October Revolution Square, in honor of the sixtieth anniversary of the October Revolution, and a granite monument to Lenin was erected at one end. The square was used to stage the Soviet regime's parades on May Day, Victory Day, and the anniversary of the October Revolution.

In its newly constructed configuration, Maidan's size, accessibility, role in communist rituals, and strategic location all made it a propitious space for launching an urban civic revolt. While not directly adjacent to Ukraine's centers of power, it was ten minutes' walk (less than a kilometer) from the headquarters of the Ukrainian Communist Party Central Committee (later, the presidential administration in independent Ukraine), and fifteen minutes (1.3 kilometers) from the headquarters of Ukraine's parliament. Its role as a center of communist celebration gave it a symbolic value to those seeking to challenge communist rule. Nearby European Square, marking the beginning of Khreshchatyk in one direction and leading to Mariyinsky Park and the parliament in the other, provided an adjacent space for defense of Maidan, strategic advance, and potential crowd overflow. However, Maidan's utility as a site of mass rebellion was not immediately recognized when restrictions on demonstrations loosened under glasnost in 1988 and 1989. Occasional protests were mounted there,[4] but most large-scale demonstrations during the glasnost years were held in Dynamo Stadium, St. Sofia Square, or in the vicinity of the republic's legislature near Mariyinsky Park.[5]

Maidan's potential as a revolutionary space was discovered in fall 1990—and almost by accident. Inspired by developments elsewhere in the Soviet bloc, in September 1990 a hundred Ukrainian students staged a hunger strike for new elections, a boycott of negotiations over a new union treaty for the USSR, and the resignation of pro-Moscow prime minister Vitalii Masol. Maidan was chosen as the site to pitch their tents only after the originally planned location—Mariyinsky Park near the republic's legislature—was occupied by police. The hunger strikes were soon accompanied by demonstrations of one hundred to two hundred thousand organized by the Ukrainian national movement Rukh. What came to be known as the "Revolution on the Granite" played a central role in Ukraine's progress toward independence: Masol resigned after two weeks of protest, and power shifted from the pro-Moscow faction within the Communist Party to the pro-sovereignty faction headed by Leonid Kravchuk.[6] After Ukrainian independence in 1991, the square was again renamed, as Independence Square. In 2001, a sixty-meter column was erected to commemorate Ukrainian independence, and a giant multi-level underground shopping mall

---

4. Examples include the blocked protest by the Ukrainian Culturological Club on the second anniversary of the Chernobyl accident in 1988 and the demonstration by the Ukrainian Helsinki Union and Gromada Club during Gorbachev's visit to Kyiv on February 19, 1989.

5. In February 1990, the square was used by the Ukrainian national movement Rukh to hold an electoral rally, though Rukh held similar rallies in other locations in the city as well. The large April 25 rally in 1990 over Chernobyl was held in St. Sophia Square.

6. Beissinger 2002; Torba 2016; Kowal and Wapiński 2014. I code the episode as "quasi-revolutionary."

FIGURE 6.2. Khreshchatyk and Independence Square in 2017. (© Viacheslav Tykhanskyi | Dreamstime.com.)

was installed under the square (see Figure 6.2).[7] Since then, Maidan has served as a space for successive urban civic revolts: the failed "Ukraine without Kuchma" campaign in 2001, the Orange Revolution in 2004, and the Euromaidan Revolution in 2013. The use of the square for one revolt multiplied its symbolic value as a site for future revolts.

The example of Maidan illustrates how public space plays an important role within urban revolutionary contention. Revolutionary contention in close proximity to centers of power heightens the dangers to both regimes and oppositions, simultaneously increasing opposition exposure to repression and regime vulnerability to opposition disruption. As we have seen, this proximity dilemma shapes the tempo and character of urban revolution. It also affects the ways in which spatial factors play into urban revolt. The design of a medieval fortress and its relationship to the natural environment shaped the ability of armies to defend or to storm it. The configuration and disposition of urban public space affects whether certain tactics of mass siege are available to oppositions and regimes and the extent to which these tactics are likely to prove effective.

This is true all the more insofar as urban civic revolts rely on a strategy of rapidly concentrating large numbers in central urban locations and taking advantage of the spaces between buildings rather than using the city's built environment as cover for armed attack. Some types of space are more appropriate

---

7. During the Orange and Euromaidan revolutions, protestors could literally shop or dine at the food court between revolutionary demonstrations.

than others for mobilizing large numbers and paralyzing government. As we will see, the shape, location, visibility, and symbolic value of public space are critical in explaining the efficacy of urban civic revolutionary tactics. Capacious public space (particularly space that is highly visible and bears strong symbolic significance) aids the concentration of large numbers, and public space located in proximity to governmental centers facilitates visibility, increases the threat to incumbent regimes, and magnifies opposition leverage. Regimes seek, by contrast, to keep revolutionary contention at safe distance and to design and regulate access to public space in such a way as to minimize these threats.

All cities are hubs of governmental power. Capital cities are distinguished from other cities by the presence of the seat of government and core state institutions, and as a result exhibit "special demands and ambitions."[8] As states have multiplied and consolidated and as urbanization has proceeded, large open spaces in proximity to governmental centers of power have proliferated throughout the world, especially in capital cities. Beginning in the seventeenth and eighteenth centuries, a conscious concern for urban planning and the creation of large, monumental spaces arose in European capitals. As James Leith has noted, "Medieval cities grew up in a haphazard fashion in which open spaces were often accidental rather than the result of conscious planning. Even the great cathedrals that dominated the horizons of such cities usually had very little space around them to set them off and to allow the public to get an overall view of them, especially to encompass their rich facades. In many cases the space in front and around them is the result of later planning, usually involving the destruction of ancient buildings that had cluttered their surroundings."[9] As cities grew in size, smaller historical squares once bustling with markets were emptied of their commerce and were expanded into grand monumental spaces celebrating state power. The outer fortifications of cities were torn down and replaced with wide boulevards to ease passage or for recreational outings. Public parks emerged out of royal gardens or hunting grounds and from common grazing areas, becoming a fundamental element of urban design by the nineteenth century.[10] Traffic junctions and circles were added to burgeoning cities to facilitate movement. All of these elements of modern urban design spread transnationally with the rise of colonialism, urbanization, and the globalization of the modern state.

Particularly in capital cities, many of these spaces had their roots in attempts by regimes to validate their authority and display their dominance

8. Hall 1997, 328.
9. Leith 1991, 6. See also Pollak 1991.
10. Hall 1997, 57, 300, 314–15. The French word *boulevard* originally meant a military rampart or wall of a fortification.

through the physical redesign of the city, creating areas for displays of loyalty, inculcating a sense of shared identity, and impressing upon citizens the power, grandeur, and majesty of the state. Tiananmen Square, for instance, was once a narrow, T-shaped approach to the Forbidden City, occupied by a series of gates, government ministries, trolley tracks, and market stalls. It was transformed in the 1950s into a vast open space intended for mass displays of loyalty to the communist regime.[11]

As Wolfgang Braunfels observed, "Each city lets us know who governs it and how it is governed. We can read in a skyline or in any ground plan the standing of the controlling powers."[12] Aristotle had this idea in mind in his observations about regime-type and urban design: certain spatial arrangements are more suitable to particular configurations of political power. Lawrence Vale perhaps put it more bluntly: "urban design, like war, can be seen as an extension of politics by other means."[13] But urban public spaces not only project an idealized image of power. They also represent a potential threat to power, for what can be used to display the authority of the state to citizens can also be used by citizens to challenge the authority of the state. When states created monumental spaces to celebrate their power, transformed fortifications into boulevards, converted royal gardens into public parks, and fashioned traffic circles to facilitate movement, they unwittingly produced the public spaces in which urban civic revolutions have unfolded. As I show in this chapter, much of the politics of urban civic revolutionary contention revolves around a struggle for control over this public space—a contest as to whether regimes maintain it as a site of order, or oppositions subvert it for purposes of rebellion.

Public Space and Urban Civic Revolt

Simply defined, public space is space that in principle is accessible to anyone. Public space is distinct from private space, where the owner retains the right to restrict access (e.g., private dwellings, land holdings, and commercial establishments), and state space, where the state exercises its right to ban or severely limit public access (e.g., government residences, government offices, military bases, and prisons).[14] Public space is the product of customary or formal legal property regulations governing who has the right to use which

---

11. Hung 1991.
12. Braunfels 1988, 2.
13. Vale 2014, 35. See also Tonkiss 2005.
14. For a discussion of these distinctions, see Rose 1986. On the relationships between public, private, and state property in the Russian Empire, see Pravilova 2014.

physical spaces in the built and natural environment. In rural areas, these public physical spaces have largely involved rights of way, fishing or hunting rights, access to water, communal lands for cultivation, conservation areas, and common land for grazing. In cities, by contrast, public space manifests itself in streets, squares, markets, mass transit, and parks. As cities are centers of dense population settlement and concentrations of political and commercial power, in urban areas there has tended to be a formal and well-defined delineation between public space and other types of space, demarcating where individuals can or cannot go freely. The boundaries between these spaces are often differentiated by fences, signs, gates, or built structures, and their use is regulated and enforced by law.[15] In rural areas, customary rights are more often observed.

I differentiate between public space and the public sphere, in that the public sphere is a domain for discursive exchange that does not necessarily exist in a specific physical space. The public sphere (particularly mass media and the internet, but also physical spaces such as salons, clubs, banquets, mosques, and cafes) provides domains for coordination and dialogue that are central to revolutionary processes. But while revolutions may be talked about in salons, they are not carried out there. Discourse alone lacks the forceful qualities that armed rebellion and the physical occupation of squares and streets involve and that allow a revolutionary opposition to impose regime-change upon an intractable government. In the 1998 Indonesian Revolution, "the major contribution of the internet . . . was that it provided spaces where people could mingle without the overt control of the state." However, for the revolution to force the issue of regime-change, it ultimately required action within physical space.[16] As John Parkinson has put it, "while revolutions most certainly are televised, what television, YouTube, Twitter, and others disseminate are pictures and narratives of physical events, . . . contests over physical space, performed by flesh-and-blood people."[17]

Urban public space serves multiple purposes. Simply due to the density of urban settlement, the daily movement of people and goods (as well as opportunities for engaging in work and commerce) would be impossible without it. It can also be a source of enjoyment and amusement for city inhabitants. But as the debate over public space and the "right to the city" affirms,[18] urban public space and the very division of urban space into public and private are physical manifestations of power relations in society. They signal class

15. Madanipour 1999.
16. Lim 2002, 393.
17. Parkinson 2012, 1–2.
18. Lefebvre 1991; Lefebvre 2003; Harvey 2010; Harvey 2013; Sennett 1978; Castells 1983.

relations, and who is or is not favored by political power. States also require the existence of public space to be able to penetrate and surveil society, for bureaucrats to execute the state's directives, and for the military and police to deploy. In Amman, Jordan in the 2000s, for example, roads were widened in key areas of the city to allow the movement of armored vehicles in the event of unrest.[19] Just as there is a tension between public and private space, there is also a tension between public and state space. The extent to which state spaces are open to the public varies across and within societies, and states often regulate the use of public spaces in ways that can transform them de facto into state spaces. Public space also serves broader political and symbolic functions for states. States frequently use public space in cities to project and represent political power and to inculcate a sense of allegiance. This is what Lefebvre referred to as "monumental space"[20]—that is, the symbolic use of public space in ways that are intended to instruct individuals about their membership and place in society.[21]

The ultimate goal of all revolutions is to capture state space—specifically, that state space where the command centers of government reside. But in cities contention for control over public space often plays a critical role in this process. This is due in part to the proximity of certain public spaces to government centers of power, and in part to the multifunctional character of public space. Urban public space can serve multiple purposes depending on who controls it. Normally, it is a site of political order due to the concentration of state capacity in cities. As Jeroen Gunning and Ilan Zvi Baron note, public space in Egyptian cities under Mubarak was "predominantly the space where the regime and its agents ruled."[22] But public space has always contained a subversive potential as well and is subject to what Kristin Ross calls *détournement* (hijacking)—that is, "using the elements or terrain of the dominant social order to one's own ends, for a transformed purpose."[23] At times, for instance, public space has been associated with crime and informality. It can also be made to serve purposes of rebellion.

This reappropriation of public space in urban revolutionary contention stands in marked contrast to the spatial politics of rural revolutions. Rural rebels typically declare zones of alternative sovereignty in areas beyond governmental control. They often attempt to establish systems of governance in

19. Schwedler 2018, 199.

20. Lefebvre 1991, 220.

21. In Levinson's (1998, 10) words, "those with political power within a given society organize public space to convey (and thus teach the public) desired political lessons."

22. Gunning and Baron 2014, 251.

23. Ross 1988, 42. James Scott (1990) refers to such moments of inversion as ruptures in the public transcript of power and notes how they are imbued with catharsis and emotion.

populated areas within these zones, setting up courts, police, and schools, providing public goods, and engaging in taxation. But unlike urban public space, which is relatively fixed and demarcated by the built environment of the city, rebel territory in rural revolutions is amorphous and ambiguous, lacks any clear sense of boundedness, and frequently changes hands over the course of a conflict.[24] Land occupations are also common in peasant uprisings. In most land occupations, peasants seek to increase access to land, forest, and water that they claim has been illegitimately alienated from them by landed elites, the church, or the state but which they covet or require for subsistence. During the Russian Revolution of 1917, for instance, peasant communities organized themselves into assemblies (*skhody*) and took control of land, though much of the process was disorderly, involving dispersed acts of squatting, looting, and vandalism. Fallow land owned by the gentry particularly was targeted, but so also was land owned by the state, the church, and independent peasants. Peasants harvested wood and cleared land for farming and grazing in government and privately owned forests, and local mills were seized.[25] Eric Hobsbawm noted with respect to revolutionary land occupations in Latin America that "the most usual case is one in which such land is simultaneously claimed by peasants and landlords, neither of whom may, or indeed in most cases will, have a valid property right under official law."[26] In the Mexican Revolution, land seizures were not meant to be visible acts of defiance performed for a national audience, but were rather village affairs aimed at addressing local inequities. They involved acts of squatting and surreptitious colonization, the burning of estate buildings, theft of livestock or other property, and attacks on manor houses and estate employees.[27] Thus, in contrast to the seizure of public space in urban revolutions, land occupations in peasant revolutions targeted private or state lands—not rural public spaces such as commons, markets, thoroughfares, or natural preserves. Contention revolved around local issues such as land use and land ownership, not around national issues such as who should control the state. And land occupation in rural revolutions was not a conscious strategy for paralyzing a regime or precipitating its downfall, but was rather a means for redistribution. When used as a tactic by revolutionary movements, land seizures could magnify peasant participation in rebellion,[28] create chaos, and

24. Kasfir 2015.
25. Gill 1979, 40; Channon 1992; Badcock 2007, 181–210; Retish 2008; Figes 2014, 79.
26. Hobsbawm 1974, 121.
27. Coatsworth 1988, 25. See also Knight 1986.
28. Controlling for time and the number of deaths involved in revolutionary contention, land seizures in rural revolutions are positively associated with levels of participation at the .05 level. On average, revolutions involving land seizures were associated with a hundred thousand

undercut a regime's bases of support in the countryside. But they were usually insufficient on their own to topple a government.

Public space played a more important role in the armed revolts and urban rioting that dominated urban revolutions in the nineteenth and early twentieth centuries. But use of public space in these revolts was largely subordinated to military tactics. Urban revolts in the nineteenth and twentieth centuries generally assumed a number of action forms: armed crowds, barricaded insurrections, military mutinies, mob actions (or what George Rudé called "political riots"),[29] funeral processions, marches, and parades. The militarization of crowd action was a central feature. In the French Revolution, for instance, the storming of the Bastille was "not a case of crowds versus troops so much as an instance of troops leading the crowds."[30] Those participating in peaceful marches and processions often carried sabers, knives, pikes, and firearms with the "intent of making a show of strength and to defend against very real threat of government repression."[31] Rebellious crowds in nineteenth-century Europe did not always have the intention of carrying out violence, but they nevertheless needed to be prepared in the event that the authorities resorted to attacks against them. In the February Revolution in Russia in 1917, demonstrating workers brought knives, hammers, wrenches, and iron bars to marches—both for fighting the regime's soldiers and for looting food shops.[32] Armories were frequent targets of collective action in order to obtain firearms. As if at war, rebels besieged any location used by the regime to command and coordinate force—barracks, police headquarters, prisons, railway stations, and communications hubs.

The spatial features advantageous for urban armed revolts differed substantially from those conducive to contemporary urban civic revolutions. Narrow, twisting streets and fortified houses facilitated barricade warfare by making construction and defense easier. Much barricade warfare was carried out from houses, with combatants shooting at troops or dropping objects on them. Thus, private space provided critical cover for mounting armed attacks in public space. The cobblestoned streets that formed much of public space in a world of horse-drawn transport proved conducive to barricade building and violent rioting. As Mark Traugott shows, barricades in Paris tended to be constructed

---

more participants than those not involving land seizures, holding the effect of other factors constant at their means.

29. Rudé 1995, 93.

30. House 2014, 25.

31. Alpaugh 2014, 2–3; House 2014, 19. Tilly (2008, 79–84) argues that the peaceful protest demonstration did not become a regular part of the protest repertoire of French citizens until the late nineteenth century.

32. Figes 2014, 69.

in identical locations in 1830 and 1848[33]—a tactical response to the built environment and network structures of the city. Large, open urban public spaces provided locations where those involved in urban armed revolts and revolutionary riots could mill, join up with like-minded individuals, and be recruited to action.[34] They also functioned as staging grounds for assaults or as sites for looting private shops. But they offered no cover from the firepower of the regime's forces, and they were certainly not strategic targets for occupation.

It was really only in the late twentieth and early twenty-first centuries, with the proliferation of the urban civic repertoire, that the occupation of squares, intersections, traffic circles, and parks became a common revolutionary tactic in cities. In the 1980s, armed revolt in cities began to decline sharply: prior to 1985, 70 percent of urban revolutionary episodes involved armed rebellion (and before 1950, 76 percent); but from 1985 onward, that proportion dropped to 27 percent.[35] Some revolutionary tactics in cities do not require physical occupation of public space. Strikes, for instance, can be highly disruptive to regimes simply through the act of staying home, without ever occupying public space. Strikes can increase the chances of revolutionary success when participation is broad and when they occur in strategic branches of the economy. But staying at home lacks the confrontational, symbolic, and spectacle-like qualities that the physical occupation of public space entails. As we saw in chapter 4, an urban revolutionary episode that engages in strikes but no other tactic has a fairly low probability of opposition success.[36] Beginning in the 1990s, the use of strikes in urban revolutions declined sharply, as neoliberal economics weakened the power of labor unions and the middle class came to assume a larger role in urban revolutionary contention.[37] By contrast, the use

---

33. Traugott 2010, 8–9.

34. One of the earliest urban public spaces to be used for revolutionary purposes was the Palais-Royal, a large complex that had once been the childhood home of Louis XIV. It had come to be owned by the duke of Orleans and was gradually transformed in the years leading up to the French Revolution into a public space of gardens, squares, galleries, clubs, and cafes. The Palais-Royal served as a staging ground for the French Revolution and a place where "crowds numbering as many as ten thousand gathered." One such crowd set off to storm the Bastille. "The 'fruits' of this endeavor—severed heads—were returned on pikes amidst general approbation to the place from which their bearers had departed, the garden of the Palais-Royal." McMahon 1996, 1–2.

35. There is a negative and statistically significant relationship (at the .001 level) between the year of onset of an urban revolutionary episode and the probability that it was armed.

36. Controlling for time and the use of other tactics, an urban revolution that utilized strikes but no other tactic had a .22 probability of success.

37. There is a negative and statistically significant relationship (at the .001 level) between the year of onset of an urban revolutionary episode and the probability that it involved strikes, with

of demonstrations in urban revolutions has increased dramatically over the past century. From 1900 to 1985, 63 percent of urban revolutionary episodes involved demonstrations (and before 1950, 55 percent). Since the Cold War that proportion has risen to 93 percent.[38]

As cities grew in size, they also became increasingly vulnerable to disruption through the occupation of public space by large numbers. By reappropriating and occupying urban public space, urban revolutionary oppositions put on display not only the illegitimacy and impotence of a regime, but also the existence of its alternative. These tactics proved exceedingly effective. Thus, as we saw earlier, urban revolutionary episodes that have engaged in rallies, protests, or processions in public space have had a significantly higher rate of success than those that engage in other tactics but do not use demonstrations—irrespective of the level of mass participation involved. The power of numbers is critically important to revolutionary success in cities, but so too is the visibility and theatrical quality of the demonstration and the public space in which it occurs.

The types of public space used for urban civic revolts have varied. Some unfold in the mundane spaces of traffic circles, boulevards, or public parks. The People Power Revolution in the Philippines in February 1986, for instance, began with mass rallies of up to a million people in Rezal Park in central Manila. But its key events unfolded along a section of the Epifanio de los Santos Avenue, the main traffic route that circumnavigates Manila (commonly referred to by its acronym "EDSA"). This particular stretch of the EDSA highway constituted the main access route to two military camps, Camp Crame and Camp Aguinaldo. The site was chosen by Cardinal Jaime Sin for defensive reasons: in particular, to protect soldiers revolting against the Marcos regime who had taken refuge in Camp Crame. Up to a million people mobilized to block the highway, providing a human barrier that shielded rebel soldiers from the regime's attacks.[39] In the Indonesian Revolution in 1998, the towering Monas monument (colloquially known as "Sukarno's last erection") and the busy Hotel Indonesia traffic circle in Jakarta "suddenly blossomed as insurgent civic spaces,"[40] becoming sites for massive protests that ultimately helped to topple the Suharto regime. Revolutionary protestors in Bahrain in 2011 chose the Pearl Roundabout, "previously considered an

---

the proportion of urban revolutions involving strike action dropping from 57 percent in the first half of the twentieth century to 28 percent in the post–Cold War period.

38. There is a positive and statistically significant relationship (at the .001 level) between the onset year of an urban revolutionary episode and whether it involved a demonstration.

39. Abinales and Amoroso 2005.

40. Douglass 2008, 10.

inaccessible traffic island with a grandiose monument,"[41] to mount their rebellion by taking ownership over this hitherto forbidden territory. The roundabout "offered not only enough space for a large demonstration, but also a strategic location at the center of the capital. By protesting here, the uprising was highly visible to others in the country and beyond."[42] Istanbul's Gezi Park is a site that "normally is governed by the rhythm of work and consumption" adjacent to the transportation center and nationalist monument of Taksim Square.[43] The occupation of Gezi Park in 2013, which challenged the authority and growing repressiveness of the Erdogan regime through its overbearing plans for redeveloping the city, involved the reappropriation of the park as a space of resistance.

Other spaces for urban civic revolt are chosen in part for their symbolic importance. More than two-thirds of urban civic revolts unfold in spaces that bear significant national or religious symbolism. An important aspect of public space is its ability to take on meaning—what geographers and social theorists refer to as "place."[44] As Clifford Deaton notes, when urban public space bears concentrated symbolic national or religious meaning, it can "connect with salient political memories that inspire and help scale-up mobilization."[45] For example, Cathedral Square, the main square of the Old Town in Vilnius, is one of the most widely known symbols of Lithuania, with its distinctive thirteenth-century bell tower and monument to Gediminas, the founder of the Grand Duchy of Lithuania. The cathedral contains the crypts of Lithuanian kings, though under Soviet occupation it was converted into a warehouse and stripped of its treasures. The fate of the cathedral in deeply Catholic Lithuania was itself a grievance and a symbol of Soviet occupation. In June 1988, Cathedral Square became the site of the first mass meetings of Sajudis, the Lithuanian independence movement, when fifty thousand people gathered to meet with Lithuania's delegates to the Nineteenth Party Conference in Moscow.[46] Though it had been transformed in shape and dimensions under communist rule, Tiananmen Square had a history as a center of Chinese political life when Beijing's student activists decided to use it to stage a hunger strike in April 1989. It had been the site of protests during the May Fourth Movement in 1919, the place where Mao proclaimed the People's Republic of China into existence in 1949, and the location of most major government parades, funerals, and celebrations. Surrounded

41. Khalaf 2013, 270.
42. Ollamh and Lanthier 2016, 150.
43. Yaka and Karakayali, 2017, 58.
44. Agnew 1987; Agnew and Duncan 2014; Massey 1994.
45. Deaton 2015, 210.
46. Misiunas and Taagepera 1993, 316.

by government buildings and Mao's mausoleum, it constituted a highly symbolic place where student activists could insert their dissent into the rich history of twentieth-century Chinese student activism—further symbolized by their choice of the Monument to the People's Heroes in the center of the square as the locus of their hunger strike.[47]

The use of nationalism or religion substantially multiplies participation in revolutionary contention, and space constitutes one element of this symbolic politics. Strongly symbolic places can function as focal points for mobilization, lessening the need for formal organization. Urban civic episodes that unfold in spaces bearing strong national or religious symbolism mobilize on average two to three times more participants than those that do not.[48] Urban civic revolts rely on numbers for protection from repression and to exert leverage over a regime. Mobilizing in symbolic spaces provides a strategic advantage for urban civic revolutionary contention, for it aids movements in scaling up. In rural settings, by contrast, the symbolic meanings attached to place tend to be highly localized and dispersed, and therefore less capable of magnifying participation.

The meaning of a place is of course not static. As we saw in the case of Kyiv's Maidan, revolutionary contention itself contains the power to attach new meanings to place. In the Philippines in 1993, the government erected a monument commemorating the 1986 People Power Revolution on the EDSA site. In 2001, that monument became the locus for two more Filipino urban revolts—each of which sought to mobilize competing constituencies using the same symbolic space of the EDSA shrine.[49] The use of a particular space for revolutionary purposes transforms that space into a potential focal point for future challenges by imbuing it with symbolic meaning. The focal point for Thai student protests in 1973 was the Democracy Monument—located in a traffic circle in the middle of Bangkok. The monument was commissioned in 1939 by Thailand's military government to commemorate the 1932 military coup that established constitutional monarchy but that also launched military dictatorship in the country. The story represented in the monument—and even its name—was a gross misrepresentation of what occurred in 1932. But in 1973, the symbolism of the monument lent itself to reappropriation by those seeking to democratize Thailand's military dictatorship.[50]

47. Hershkovitz 1993; Zhao 2004; Calhoun 1994; (Nelson K.) Lee 2009.

48. Statistically significant at the .05 level in a two-sided t-test (t = −2.025, with 52 degrees of freedom). For an argument that the absence of adequate symbolic space in central Minsk hampered Belarusian protests against Lukashenko, see Hansen 2017.

49. Abinales and Amoroso 2005.

50. Herzfeld 2016, 78–79.

As cases like the Democracy Monument in Bangkok or Maidan in Kyiv illustrate, revolutionary spaces do not exist in the abstract. They must be discovered and made, and that invention proceeds dynamically and dialectically. Symbolism is important. But meanings can also be created. When a space desired for mounting challenges is inaccessible due to restrictions imposed by the authorities, other spaces can be sought out. Some of these will prove unsuitable; others will turn out to be strategically advantageous; still others will go on to be swallowed by the development of the city. Through a process of trial and error, move and countermove, revolution and evolution, urban revolutionary space is made and remade over time.

Urban Revolution and the Configuration of Public Space

The size, shape, and location of the public space are an inherent part of the urban revolutionary process. In Saskia Sassen's words, the arrangement of public space in the city can be crucial in "giving the powerless rhetorical and operational openings," allowing them to become "present, visible, to each other," and making "visible the limits of superior military power."[51] Alternatively, public space can be a factor undermining revolutionary potential and rendering exhaustion or repression easier. Since the days of Haussmann, numerous regimes have dreamed of revolution-proofing their cities by engineering the built environment in ways that make revolution more difficult. In Haussmann's time, whole neighborhoods were razed to modernize Paris and eliminate the narrow streets that the working class had found so useful for mounting urban armed revolts. Boulevards were built to the width of an extended cavalry squadron, corner buildings were set back from intersections to make streets more difficult to barricade, macadamized surfaces prevented insurgents from digging up cobblestones, and circles were spaced to allow for interlocking fields of cannon fire.[52]

Haussmann's Paris became the paradigm for modernity in urban design in the late nineteenth and early twentieth centuries. Tahrir Square in Cairo, for example, was modeled on Haussmann's Paris. It was originally named Ismailia Square, after the then-ruler Pasha Ismail, who had been educated in Paris and was enamored with Haussmann's remaking of the city. Yet, these same reconstructions of the city into open squares and broad boulevards created possibilities for novel repertoires of revolt. Once it assumed its current shape at the beginning of the twentieth century, Ismailia Square became a frequent site for protests against British colonial rule, in significant part because British

---

51. Sassen 2011, 573–74.
52. Traugott 1995, 158; Gould 1995, 65–95; Simpson 2013; Harvey 2003.

military barracks were located there. Major protests occurred in Ismailia Square against the British during the 1919 Egyptian Revolution—hence its renaming, after the British were evicted, as Tahrir (Liberation) Square. Under Nasser, Tahrir Square gained new strategic importance when a number of government buildings were erected there—including the headquarters of the ruling party. The square remained a focal point for Egyptian protest, functioning in 1977 as a staging ground for demonstrations of workers and students after the Sadat government cut subsidies for food staples, prompting large numbers of Egyptians to take the streets in two days of violent protest.[53] Despite attempts by the Mubarak regime to fence off, dismantle, and depopulate Tahrir Square by transforming it into a glorified traffic circle, it remained a magnet for revolutionary challenge because of its history, central location, and proximity to centers of power.[54]

Urban designs involving large public squares are often thought to facilitate revolutionary mobilization. Acts of mass defiance in large public squares can help to crystallize the realization that one is part of a movement of like-minded people, rendering the square a potent symbol of resistance. In Asef Bayat's words, "The power of the square lies in its visible and persistent defiance of authorities, for the square puts on display to both the people and politicians the power of the opposition and the feebleness of the regime."[55] Parkinson similarly emphasizes the visibility of revolts that occur in squares, noting that "the number of people we can get into a square has an impact on the degree to which organizers can show the scale of popular displeasure with a government."[56] Visibility is particularly important to urban civic revolutionary tactics, which rely heavily on numbers rather than arms to ward off repression.

Certainly, there are ways in which the occupation of a square differs from linear forms of protest such as marches or street processions. In the occupation of a square there is no destination, route, or end-point—"just a beginning without a visible end."[57] This spatial fixedness but temporal uncertainty can signal resolve and commitment—part of what Tilly identified as central to

---

53. Illugadóttir 2013; Paraskevas 2011; El-Hamalawy 2001; Attia 2011.

54. Elshahed 2011.

55. Bayat 2017, 126.

56. Parkinson 2012, 149. As Martin and Miller (2003, 155) note, "One hundred people occupy space very differently than 1,000 or 100,000. The difference is meaningful in terms of demonstrating support for a cause and in terms of the types of reactions—such as police behavior—it may instigate."

57. Nikos (a participant in the Syntagma Square anti-austerity protests in Greece in 2011), as quoted in Kavada and Dimitriou 2017, 77.

successful protest performances.[58] Occupations of squares involve "an art of duration and endurance" that presumes that revolution is "a lengthy process" rather than "an event that is over and done with, reducible to a date on the calendar." Such seizures of public space communicate "an insistence on being heard and seen," consciously provoking a response from the authorities.[59] Moreover, as opposed to filling a street or boulevard with people, massing large numbers in a square symbolically establishes a kind of liberated territory and provides a physical expression of the dual sovereignty that lies at the heart of revolutionary claims—as Bayat puts it, "a microcosm of the alternative order the revolutionaries seem to desire."[60] David Patel argues that the presence of a well-known, centrally located square also functions as a focal point that helps to overcome collective action problems and maximize numbers with minimal formal coordination, since people know where to go to challenge a regime. He claims that the absence of a well-known, centrally located square in some Arab countries rendered revolutionary protests more difficult during the Arab Spring.[61] Matt Ford similarly argues that the public square constitutes the "epicenter of democratic expression and protest, and the lack of one—or the deliberate manipulation of such a space—as a way for autocrats to squash dissent through urban design."[62]

However, the flip side of visibility is vulnerability. Mobilizing in large public squares without producing sufficient numbers to protect against regime attacks leaves oppositions highly vulnerable to repression. The shape and size of public space are never sufficient on their own to explain revolutionary outcomes. Moreover, large-scale revolutionary mobilizations are hardly precluded in the absence of a capacious public square. As Parkinson notes, "Activists work with the places they have; they do not just give up and go away when unable to find a plaza in front of the presidential palace or a marching route conducive to high visibility."[63] Nevertheless, the shape and availability of public space does influence the kinds of tactics and targets available to revolutionary oppositions, as well as the character of the interactions between regimes and oppositions. In Egypt's second city, Alexandria, for instance, because of the city's narrow and elongated layout along forty kilometers of coastline, and because government headquarters were over two hundred kilometers away in

58. Tilly 2008, 121.
59. Mitchell 2013, 102–6.
60. Bayat 2017, 115.
61. Patel 2013.
62. Ford 2014.
63. Parkinson 2012, 160.

the capital Cairo, revolutionary mobilizations followed "a rather different morphology than its Cairene counterparts":

> Whereas marches in Cairo were usually planned to start from a multitude of points around Tahrir Square and then converge and end on the square with a sit-in..., there was a preference in Alexandria for marches without end points that would instead fill and circle around the main arteries of the city. When Alexandrians tried to replicate the Cairene model by initiating a sit-in at different spots in the city..., they quickly realized that it wouldn't work because of these geographical peculiarities: no square was as big, central, and equidistant from all the protest sites as Tahrir Square was in Cairo.[64]

In Alexandria, the narrow streets in neighborhoods off major thoroughfares provided protection against police attack.[65] But revolutionary mobilization in Alexandria was forced to assume the form of linear marches rather than the territorial occupations of squares, due simply to the physical layout and design of the city.

When revolutionary protests broke out in Yemen's capital Sana'a in the wake of Mubarak's resignation in Egypt, pro-regime loyalists occupied Tahrir Square in Sana'a (symbolically named and located in the central business district of the city) in an attempt to preclude its seizure by revolutionary protesters. In response, revolutionary protesters set up a protest camp outside the gates of Sana'a University. The area came to be dubbed "Change Square," becoming the focal point for the 2011 Yemeni Revolution. Change Square did not possess the strategic quality of Sana'a's Tahrir Square; it was not located in proximity to the presidential palace and was unsuited to paralyzing daily life in the city. But as it was adjacent to the university's gates, it had ready access to restaurants, photocopy machines, internet cafes, photography studios, and vendors "selling everything from cucumber snacks, sunglasses, and anti-government posters."[66] As a result, protests in Change Square assumed a festive quality—replete with art exhibits, music, dance, and theater—that contrasted sharply with the violence of the Yemeni Revolution elsewhere.[67] In Aden, three hundred kilometers to the south, revolutionary protestors occupied seven different squares, reflecting the disagreements among them. With their divisions reinforced by this spatial divide, it proved impossible to find a way of uniting the opposition.[68]

64. El Chazli 2016.
65. On the vulnerability of protestors in Syntagma Square during the quasi-revolutionary anti-austerity protests in Greece in 2011, see Kavada and Dimitriou 2017, 85.
66. Alwazir 2011.
67. BBC 2011.
68. Shaiban 2012, 170.

In short, space constrains the tactics available to revolutionary oppositions, defines the character of interactions between regimes and oppositions, and shapes social relationships within oppositions. The relationship between participants and non-participants also differs according to whether an opposition embraces a territorial or a linear strategy of revolt. In linear marches and processions, participation is "a deliberate and open act of support," with the movement of participants creating "a boundary between the static onlookers and the marching participants."[69] No such boundary exists in the occupation of a square, which transforms onlookers into participants simply by their presence. Prior to the spread of mass communications, marches had an advantage over stationary strategies of rebellion in terms of spreading revolutionary messages to a larger number of people and recruiting new participants, as onlookers could potentially be recruited along the route.[70] This may be one reason why the occupation of squares was a less common tactic prior to the second half of the twentieth century. With the rise of television and social media, the recruitment advantage of marches was greatly diminished.

But linear strategies of revolt do increase the likelihood of violent confrontations.[71] As marches and processions move through streets, revolution participants typically pass through neighborhoods where onlookers jeer or oppose them, come upon buildings or establishments associated with the regime, encounter members of disliked groups, or confront roadblocks from the police or other opposing forces. Indeed, revolutionaries often route processions precisely in order to engage in such confrontations. In the absence of a focal point, and with the seat of government two hundred kilometers away, Egyptian revolutionaries in Alexandria were left with the dilemma of where to direct their protest. In this case, much of the energy of protesters was focused against police stations, which were attacked and burned.[72] Certainly, significant violence can develop in revolts that occupy squares—as the Egyptian and Euromaidan revolutions demonstrate. But the violence involved in the occupation of squares often occurs in the process of getting to the square (as in Cairo in 2011), when police assault the occupants of a square to dislodge them (Cairo in 2011 and Kyiv in 2013–14), or when protestors venture away from squares in order to assault government centers (Kyiv in 2013–14). By contrast, revolts that assume the form of marches and processions frequently unleash revolutionary violence against stores, police stations, government offices, or ethnic minorities encountered along the route—targeting any object or group associated with the ruling regime.

69. Reiss 2007, 3.
70. Rucht 2007, 55.
71. On the tension involved in marches, see Rucht 2007, 55.
72. El Chazli 2016.

Some linear processions assume a militaristic character. Much of the European labor movement prior to World War I adopted a military style of marching as a way of communicating power and discipline to its audiences—a style emulated by Mussolini during his ascent to power. Mussolini's fascist marches were aggressive, meant to convey a sense of "strength, discipline, inexorability, and intransigence."[73] They often transgressed into the territory of adversaries, provoking fear and discomfort among opponents. Other linear marches can be carnivalesque. In the quasi-revolutionary anti-Milošević protests in Belgrade in 1996–97, for instance, participants banged pots and pans and blew whistles while "smiling, conversing, and laughing," maneuvering giant satirical puppets of Milošević and his wife along the protest's path—all while being accompanied by ten brass bands.[74] The route took participants past the City Council, Milošević's office, and the buildings of the state television channel and the main state-owned newspapers, providing opportunities for protestors to jeer, chant slogans, and throw eggs (and occasionally stones). Still other linear revolutionary protests have involved funeral processions for victims of regime repression—as occurred, for example, during the October Revolution in Sudan in 1964. When police broke into Khartoum University to disperse a symposium called to discuss the ongoing conflict in southern Sudan, violent clashes with students occurred, leading police to open fire with live ammunition and killing Ahmad al-Qurayshi, a twenty-one-year-old student from a village outside Khartoum. Al-Qurayshi's death served as "a catalytic event, rapidly leading others in Khartoum to begin mobilizing in protest." At the student's funeral, thirty thousand people marched silently and solemnly behind his bier in a massive religious ceremony that drew in anti-regime protestors across political boundaries. As W. J. Berridge describes it, "once the religious ceremony was complete and just as al-Qurayshi's body was being dispatched in a lorry to his home village, the scene was set for the crowds to rail against the government. Chanting 'the soldiers will fall,' they started to attack police vehicles."[75]

Judging by revolutionary outcomes, the strategic advantage of squares has been greatly exaggerated, as the rate of success is practically identical for urban civic episodes that coordinate around squares and those that do not.[76] Moreover, many urban revolutions combine elements of linear and territorial strategies. The belief that squares make a difference in revolutionary outcomes is in

---

73. Reiss 2007, 160; Reichardt 2007, 183.
74. Dimitrov 2007, 241.
75. Berridge 2015, 22; Kushkush 2012.
76. Chi-square = 0.2884, statistically insignificant (with 1 degree of freedom).

fact less a function of their size and shape than their strategic location, visibility, and proximity to centers of power. Ford, for example, points to how Tahrir Square's location within Cairo rendered it "the perfect place to launch a revolution." As he puts it, "Centrally located in Egypt's largest city, Tahrir sits near the Egyptian parliament, Mubarak's political party headquarters, the presidential palace, numerous foreign embassies, and hotels filled with international journalists to broadcast footage of the protests for audiences around the world."[77] Examining the spatial politics of protests in Teheran in 2009, Reza Nejad argues that the structural influence of urban design on revolutionary outcomes is due less to the width of streets or the size of squares than to "the way that a street or square is positioned and related to the other parts of a city." For Nejad, "the topology of a city is primarily not about the geometrical properties of parts of the city but about the way that the parts are constituted as a whole," which affects not only the materialization of crowds, but also their effectiveness.[78]

Certainly, the location and shape of public space influences the character of revolutionary action. But the most important spatial factor that affects outcomes in urban civic revolutionary episodes is proximity to centers of power. Generally, the closer crowds are to centers of power, the more visible they are to the nation and the world, and the more they are able to paralyze government and generate pressure on a regime's institutions and supporting coalition. In a significant number of urban civic episodes, the public spaces chosen for revolutionary mobilization were located immediately in front of presidential palaces or governmental headquarters, exerting psychological pressure on political elites. In March 1920, when the Danish king set off a political crisis by dismissing the government and claiming that he was the highest authority in the land, tens of thousands of Danes filled Amelienborg Palace Square. Raucous crowds chanting slogans for republican rule and an end to the monarchy directly outside palace windows ultimately swayed the monarch to relent.[79] As detailed in chapter 5, similar dynamics occurred in Tbilisi in 1989, when crowds adjacent to governmental centers of power caused local leaders to panic, ordering the clearing of the square and leading to a massacre of civilians.

A little over a quarter of all urban civic episodes occur within five hundred meters of the palace or headquarters of the chief executive, 49 percent within two kilometers, and 75 percent within four kilometers.[80] As Figure 6.3 shows,

77. Ford 2014.
78. Nejad 2013, 162.
79. Lidegaard 2009, 89–93.
80. Distance calculations are based on geo-coded references for the coordinating locations closest to the executive center of power where revolutionary oppositions organized major protests (n = 54 urban civic revolts for which information was available).

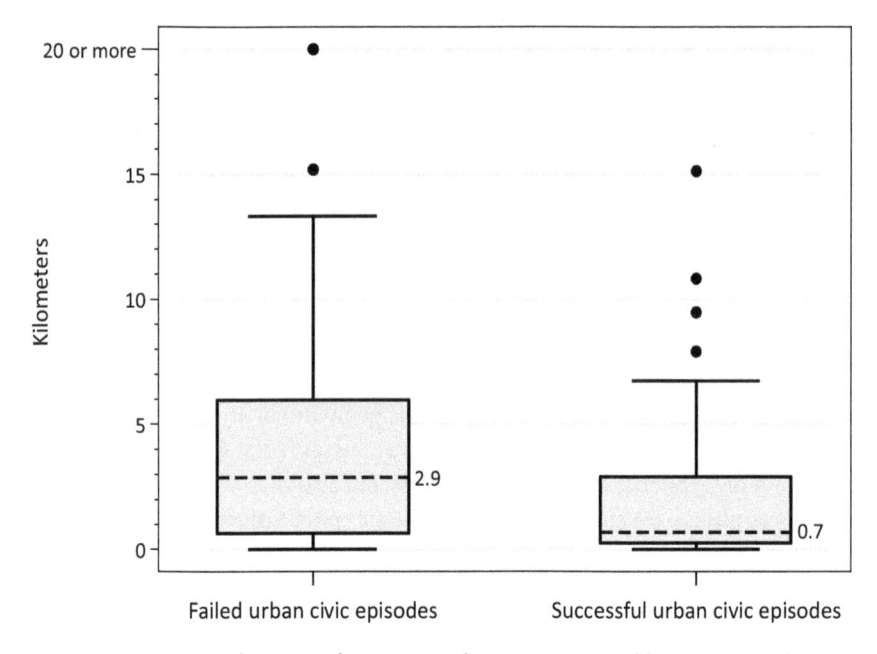

FIGURE 6.3. Distance from seat of government, by outcome. Dotted lines represent the median; the box, the 25th and 75th percentiles; and the whiskers, the lower and upper adjacent values.

urban civic episodes whose mobilizations occurred in close proximity to the executive seat of government have been more likely to attain power than those located farther away. A majority of successful urban civic revolts occurred within seven hundred meters of the seat of power. By contrast, a majority of failed urban civic episodes occurred at least 2.9 kilometers from the seat of power.[81] There is a statistically significant relationship at the .05 level between proximity to centers of power (whether the main coordinating point for an urban civic revolt was located within three-quarters of a kilometer of the seat of power) and revolutionary outcomes—even when one controls for levels of participation and for other variables associated with revolutionary outcomes.[82] In short, distance from command centers of government matters in urban civic revolutionary contention for leveraging oppositional success.

81. In a one-tailed difference of means test, statistically significant at the .05 level (t = 1.7231, with 56 degrees of freedom). The extreme outlier of Naypyitaw was reduced to the maximum of twenty kilometers distance.
82. The relationship holds even when further controls for Polity score, level of economic development, oil production, military spending per soldier, and number of years in which the incumbent regime has been in power are introduced.

In this respect, because they are where the seat of national government is located, capital cities play an important role in urban civic revolutionary contention. Certainly, a significant number of urban civic episodes begin in provincial towns and cities.[83] The April 1960 revolution against Syngman Rhee in South Korea began with protests against electoral fraud in the southeastern town of Masan; violent repression of the protests sparked student demonstrations in Seoul that eventually overthrew the regime. The East German Revolution in 1989 began with the Monday demonstrations in Leipzig, eventually spreading throughout East Germany and making their way to the Berlin. The 2010 Tunisian Revolution began in small towns and cities of the south and, aided by the circuits of the internet, progressed to the capital. Indeed, an urban civic episode that is also able to generate significant mobilization outside the capital generally has a higher probability of success than one that does not.[84] Protest outside the capital signals widespread opposition to a regime that protest occurring within the capital only does not.

But while they may not always begin in capital cities, almost all successful urban civic revolts end in the capital, for it is in the capital that the nerve centers of the central government—the ultimate target of revolution—reside. Over the last century, capital cities have come to represent a growing proportion of the populations of their respective countries, rendering the mobilization of large numbers in proximity to centers of power increasingly feasible. Figure 6.4 shows the growing concentration of population around capital cities since 1900, with the average proportion living in the capital almost tripling from 6.8 percent in 1900 to 17.2 percent in 2014. Capital cities also tend to be places where there is a greater variety of political forces, media attention is higher, foreign connections are thicker, and there is a concentration of education and wealth. They are also places in which there is an abundance of monumental public space. All this renders capital cities highly conducive sites for mounting urban civic revolts.

Spatial Strategies for Countering Urban Civic Revolt

If the shape, location, and symbolic value of public space affect the tactics, levels of participation, and outcomes of urban civic revolutionary contention, then they also matter for regimes in countering urban revolutionary threats. Public order policing in cities is spatial by its very nature. As Steve Herbert writes with regard to maintaining public order in Los Angeles, "the police are expected, when they are summoned, to exercise their coercive power to secure control over space. In fact, control over space is a fundament of overall

---

83. For an argument for the importance of secondary cities in the Arab Spring, see Ersoy 2015.
84. Chi-square = 16.4395, significant at the .001 level (with 1 degree of freedom).

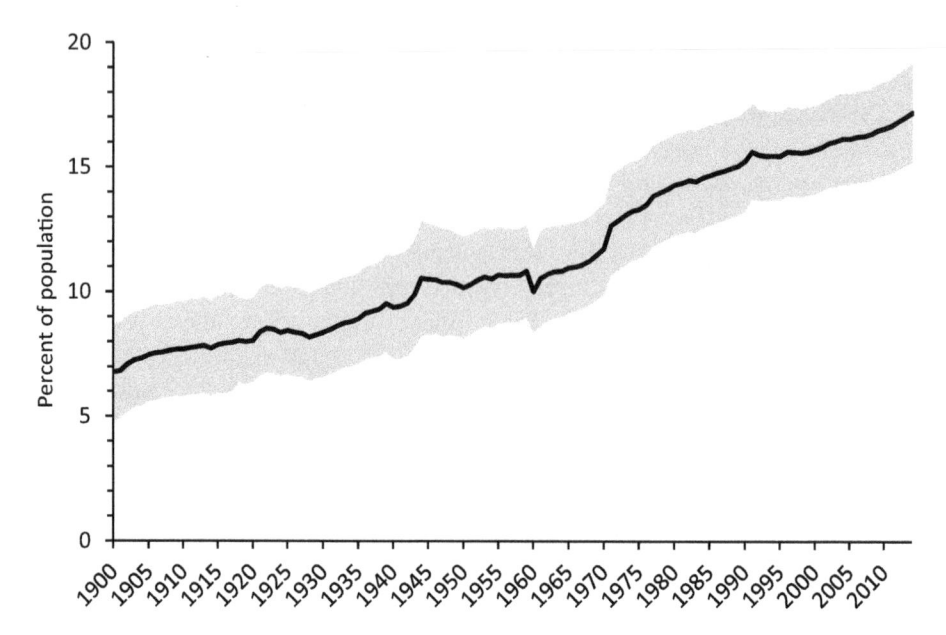

FIGURE 6.4. Mean concentration of populations in capital cities, 1900–2014. Means, with 95 percent confidence intervals.

police efforts at social control."[85] This is particularly true with regard to countering urban civic revolutions in view of the role that mobilization in public space plays within them. Countering urban civic revolutionary challenges is largely a matter of maintaining control over public space (particularly, public space in close proximity to the nerve centers of power).

This contention over strategically located public space contrasts sharply with the ways in which regimes counter rural revolutions and urban armed rebellions. Rural rebels thrive by gaining popular support in diffuse clusters of population located in safe zones beyond the reach of the regime. Fully policing such zones is impossible, given their size and inaccessibility. Thus, rural counterinsurgency "is fundamentally a struggle over people, not territory."[86] Modern counterinsurgency strategies in rural environments emphasize not control over space, but the need to gain the allegiance of noncombatants through co-optation, provision of public goods, side-payments, playing on divisions, and eliminating individual rebel fighters. In urban armed revolts, the spaces over which regimes and oppositions contend are dispersed throughout a city. As Jonathan House describes the

---

85. Herbert 1997, 10. See also Yarwood and Paasche 2015; Mitchell and Staeheli 2005; Wahlström 2010.

86. Berman, Shapiro, and Felter 2011, 773.

challenges facing authorities in Paris in 1848, crowds "tended to gather ... at points that were difficult to predict." Even after crowds were dispersed, they often reassembled in other locations. Thousands of barricades could suddenly appear throughout the city, and barricades that were cleared would sometimes reappear only a short distance away, behind the troops who had just cleared them. Sniper fire was a constant threat, and high numbers of casualties occurred on both sides. Troops needed to be concentrated in large detachments, for otherwise they were vulnerable to attack or to being overrun by mobs or armed insurgents. Cavalry was useful for clearing mobs from boulevards, and artillery was an important tool for disposing of barricades. But counterinsurgency operations in urban armed revolts ultimately involved house-to-house sweeps similar to contemporary urban warfare, with soldiers taking up positions in doorways in order to engage insurgents on the opposite side of the street who were shooting at them from upper-story windows. Other forces would take control of buildings around barricades and shoot down on insurgents from the second floor (sometimes even tunneling into buildings adjacent to barricades). As House notes, "Instead of frontal assaults, the problem required moving through, over, and around houses to outflank the enemy, followed by artillery fire and rapid pursuit to scatter or seize the rebels."[87] In this kind of urban warfare, the distinction between public and private space is obliterated.

But where revolutionary contention relies on the concentration of numbers in highly visible central urban spaces, the struggle for control over public space is pivotal in determining outcomes. In repressing the 2009 electoral protests in Iran, the regime gradually pushed protests away from public spaces in the center of Teheran to the city's periphery, and eventually to the rooftops of private residences:

> As civil unrest proceeded and the response of the authorities became harsher, protests were further limited to peripheral/residential areas.... Protests continued, but because they were fragmented in segregated parts of the city, their effect on the city was minimized. [Eventually], after months of suppression, the protest was pushed out of public spaces altogether and delimited to rooftops of residential buildings where people were chanting 'God is great' after dark. Collective action no longer appeared as a mass occurrence in a public space; rather, it was the voice of people that created the space of protest. People could not see each other; instead, the sense of being together was perceived as they heard each other.[88]

---

87. House 2014, 6, 48, 54, 184, 194, 196, 200–212.
88. Nejad 2013, 173–74.

Similarly, in 2011 in Bahrain, the brutal suppression of revolutionary protests in Manama's Pearl Roundabout deliberately pushed them into neighborhoods and villages of high Shiite concentration on the capital's periphery, where they remained largely out of sight and distant from centers of power. The government's response to protests in these peripheral areas was considerably more restrained and aimed at "limiting protesters to the confines of their villages." As a result, "those protests that do occur are easier to suppress and generally less visible. The overarching goal here is to minimize the potential impact of these activities. Significantly, however, the government has not acted to eliminate these protests altogether—instead, it has sought to monitor and regulate activities."[89] In short, effective defense against urban civic challenges requires the insulation and clearing of public spaces in proximity to government nerve centers, thereby isolating and marginalizing opposition.

Aside from the occupation and policing of public space, one strategy that regimes have occasionally used to insulate themselves from challenge is to move the capital to a new location in the hinterland—away from more contentious and populated urban centers. By moving the capital to a remote location, regimes shield members of their coalition from the influence of opposition movements and render it more difficult for urban revolutionary challengers to disrupt the activities of the government. The classic example is the decision of the Burmese junta in 2005 to relocate their capital from Yangon to Naypyitaw (a remote, uninhabited site 350 kilometers to the north)—an instance of what some have referred to as "dictatorship by cartography."[90] During the 8888 Uprising in 1988, some civil servants and soldiers participated in anti-government street demonstrations. The regime believed this occurred because civil servants and military officers lived intermixed with the rest of the Yangon population rather than in separate encampments. Many civil servants during the uprising felt a direct personal danger to themselves and their families due to their residence in proximity to revolutionary upheaval. By moving the capital, the regime could keep key administrative personnel and the military isolated from rebellious population centers and "create a better space for managing state affairs in any contingency."[91] Indeed, the move may have helped the regime survive the challenge of the Saffron Revolution in August 2007 by allowing the military to open fire directly into crowds and arrest thousands of monks without experiencing significant harassment from friends, relatives, or neighbors.[92]

89. Ollamh and Lanthier 2016, 158.
90. Quoted in Kennard and Provost 2015.
91. Myoe 2008, 9. See also Seekins 2009.
92. Selth 2008; Thawnghmung and Myoe 2008.

The new capital Naypyitaw was designed on Haussmann-like scale, with twenty-lane highways to allow for aircraft landings, massive roundabouts, public gardens, golf courses, and ample monumental space. The city is divided into zones, "making it very hard to work out where the center ... actually lies,"[93] and the parliamentary complex is surrounded by a moat intended to keep public intrusions at bay. There are Orwellian touches as well: the roofs of housing are color-coded according to the rank of the inhabitants, while high-ranking military officers and officials are segregated in a separate complex isolated from regular government employees. All this was estimated to have cost in the range of $5 billion in a country whose per capita income was only $280 per year. Ironically, the enormous expense of building a new capital caused a severe budget deficit and cuts to fuel subsidies—providing the initial spark for the 2007 Saffron Revolution. Naypyitaw contained a much smaller population than Yangon and was disproportionately filled with government employees, making it difficult for revolutionary challengers, should they appear in Naypyitaw, to mobilize a critical mass. But within a decade of its founding, Naypyitaw had already blossomed into a city of over a million, raising questions about whether moving the capital ever really solves the problem of urban civic rebellion or merely buys a regime time. Like a magnet, power draws populations to it, as politicians, bureaucrats, and soldiers must be fed, serviced, lobbied, and entertained. Indeed, when the Burmese military seized power in a coup in 2021, Naypyitaw, like the rest of the country, experienced sizeable protests—perhaps on a scale smaller than elsewhere, but significant nonetheless.

Another spatial strategy of control that regimes have sometimes used to prevent revolts is to expunge sites of revolutionary protests completely. After months of massive anti-regime protests at the Pearl Monument in Manama, the ruling Khalifa dynasty declared martial law in Bahrain and, with the support of Gulf Cooperation Council forces, suppressed the rebellion. Days after the invasion, the government sealed off access to the monument and razed it to the ground in an attempt to obliterate the symbolic center of resistance. The regime then turned the area into a seven-street intersection, surrounded the site with barbed wire and concrete barricades, and posted guards on a round-the-clock basis in order to prevent the site from ever being used again as a place of challenge. It also attempted to wipe out all memory of the monument by removing coins, postcards, and photographs with its image from circulation. Predictably, representations of the monument—painted as graffiti on walls or circulated on the internet—became a symbol of continuing resistance to the regime.[94]

---

93. Kennard and Provost 2015.
94. Khalaf 2013; Ollamh and Lanthier 2016, 151.

Alternatively, incumbent regimes can render revolutionary public space unsuitable for rebellion by allowing the city to swallow it—transforming it into commercial space, privatizing it, or overrunning it with traffic.[95] Manezh Square in Moscow, for example, is an enormous area that lies between the entrance to Red Square and Tverskaya, Moscow's main boulevard, and at the confluence of three metro stations. In the nineteenth century, the area had been filled with commercial booths, shops, and religious shrines and was flanked on one side by the old buildings of Moscow University (built in 1793), on the other side by the Kremlin, and at the far end by the Manezh, the tsars' enormous horse stables (built in 1817), from which the square gained its name. But in the 1930s, the commercial and religious structures were razed, and the square was completely redesigned into an enormous parade ground to glorify Stalin, bounded at one end by the Manezh and at the other by the newly built Hotel Moscow, located at the entrance to Red Square.[96] Because of its strategic location, in the communist period citizens were forbidden even from walking on the square, which remained a vast empty expanse except during official Soviet holidays, when it transformed into the gathering point for official parades in front of the Kremlin leadership atop the Lenin mausoleum.[97] During the glasnost period, however, Manezh Square was reclaimed by opposition movements and functioned as a site for large-scale protests against the communist regime. It was the site of the largest protest in Russian history, on March 10, 1991, when up to a half a million citizens gathered to express their support for Boris Yeltsin, the resignation of Mikhail Gorbachev, and an end to the Soviet regime.[98]

After a communist-led revolt against his young government in 1993, Yeltsin grew concerned that Manezh Square might be used as a staging ground for revolt against his own regime—much as he had used it against Gorbachev. He convinced the mayor of Moscow Yuri Luzhkov to build an underground shopping center on the spot—fencing off the area from the public once again during construction.[99] The resulting shopping center not only placed huge profits in the hands of Luzhkov and his associates, but also transformed the physiognomy of the square, planting the mall's enormous glass-domed roof and skylights in its middle, locating fountains and other installations at its far end, and imparting a Disney-like atmosphere to it by erecting fairy-tale statues on its edge. Since the square now contained a major shopping mall, an additional

95. For a critique of such practices in democracies, see Sennett 1978.
96. Solov'ev n.d.
97. Khazanov 1998, 291–92.
98. Beissinger 2002, 419.
99. Hoffman 2002.

reason for banning protests could be concocted: that they interfered with private commercial activity. As one Russian urban designer has observed, as a result of these changes Manezh Square "is no longer associated with the past spirit of protests and manifestations, [and] the rare events that did happen there are not widely known among people. It is no longer the place that draws attention to people's rights and desires. In this sense, the goal of eliminating such a chance was achieved."[100] Another source notes that "Manezh Square can serve as a perfect example of an attempt to transform space in such a way ... that it is not possible to use it in order to mobilize citizens."[101]

Aside from moving the capital, obliterating squares, or filling them with commercial centers, the most common way that regimes control revolutionary threats in urban public space is through physical control and regulation. Police formations have been trained to form lines, wedges, echelons, and diamonds for preventing crowds from entering sensitive areas. Barricades, fencing, steel cordons, barbed wire, and other physical barriers are ubiquitous tools of crowd policing. Their purpose is to insulate vulnerable areas of the city from the presence of the crowd, though these physical barriers themselves often set up a confrontation between police and the crowd at points of territorial demarcation. More feasible when crowds are smaller are kettling tactics: surrounding and herding crowds into confined spaces (a controversial tactic in liberal democracies that became common in the 2000s as a spatial strategy of control).[102] All of these techniques have spread globally through the publication of policing manuals and instructional materials.

Legal regulation of access to and use of public space is also used pervasively to counter urban revolutionary threats. Beginning with the American Bill of Rights, the right to peaceful assembly came to be defined as an individual right and an integral part of democratic freedoms, eventually finding its way into the Universal Declaration of Human Rights and the constitutions of democracies and non-democracies alike. But the right to assembly has always been subject to restriction, even in democratic countries, and governments routinely utilize regulations covering the use of public space to minimize disruption from acts of protest.[103] Such restrictions have been especially prevalent in authoritarian regimes as a way of defending against rebellion. Given that the effectiveness of revolutionary protest depends heavily on its location, regimes have sought to undermine revolutionary challenges by dislocating them,

100. Nedosekina 2011.
101. Topolyan 2017.
102. Neal, Opitz, and Zebrowski 2019.
103. McCarthy and McPhail 1998; Parkinson 2012, 3–4.

transforming visible public spaces in proximity to government centers into state "safe spaces" for the exclusive use of government. They have created protest-free zones, limited the manner in which protest can be carried out, and closed off access routes.[104] Some regimes have set aside special zones for protest, far removed from government centers, in an attempt to insulate themselves from revolutionary threats. By distancing protest from centers of power, regimes deprive oppositions of visibility to a broader audience and the ability to gain leverage over government through proximity to its nerve centers.

These techniques of spatial control have been replicated and perfected by regimes throughout the world and are part of a repertoire widely used for suffocating challenging dissent. Until 1987, the Soviet Union had no procedure for authorizing demonstrations, since all demonstrations were illegal. In April 1981, when four Jewish refuseniks applied to the local government in Novosibirsk to hold a demonstration in the city center, it "provoked panic among city officials." In response, the police cordoned off whole neighborhoods and immediately granted two of the would-be organizers permission to emigrate.[105] But in 1987, after the introduction of glasnost had sparked a series of troublesome demonstrations in central Moscow, new legislation was introduced to provide local authorities with the ability to regulate protests and to decide which demonstrations they wanted to allow. Potential protestors were supposed to register and obtain a permit at least seven days in advance of a demonstration, and protests were barred from Red Square and other areas adjacent to the Kremlin. However, the actual details of the regulations were never published, and the new rules were wielded in such a way as to provide authorities with a legal tool for eliminating protests not to their liking. Subsequent rules further refined these legal regulations, extending the time needed to obtain a permit to ten days and introducing penalties of up to two months in prison for violations. Ultimately, the rules were never implemented, as the authorities were overwhelmed by an explosion of acts of defiance occurring entirely outside this new legal framework. Since authority to confer permits was left to local governments, enormous disparities existed in how applications were handled. Some localities followed the rules; others ignored them altogether, permitting no demonstrations. In most cases, groups who were denied permits protested anyway; out of 724 "mass events" in Ukraine during the first nine months of 1989, 47 percent took place without a permit. In short, the attempt to introduce a regulatory framework for protests by the Soviet regime failed miserably.[106]

104. Moeckli 2016.
105. Alexeyeva 1985, 195.
106. Beissinger 2002, 334–342.

In the 1990s, the Yeltsin government was relatively lax in enforcing regulations about protest. But in the wake of the color revolutions, the Putin regime developed a new spatial strategy for undermining the potential for urban civic revolution by enforcing tighter regulations over permits. In April 2007, when human rights activists sought to organize a "Dissenters' March" against Putin in Pushkin Square in Moscow, they were denied permission by the authorities supposedly on the grounds that a permit for a demonstration in the same location for the same time had already been granted to a pro-Kremlin youth group. The authorities proposed that the human rights rally instead be held in a more peripheral location. The pro-Kremlin rally never took place, but the square was blocked by the police, nonetheless. When opposition activists attempted to hold their rally on the empty square, they were surrounded by riot police, beaten, and arrested.[107]

Large-scale opposition burst out once again in the wake of widespread electoral fraud in 2011 and Putin's decision to run for president for a third time after the interim term of his loyal lieutenant Dmitry Medvedev. This time, the Kremlin allowed protests but carefully licensed them, ensuring that they occurred in spaces that kept demonstrations contained and distant from more central and symbolic parts of Moscow such as Tverskaya Street, Revolution Square, or Manezh Square.[108] After long negotiations, one of the places permitted by the authorities was Bolotnaya (Swamp) Square, located on an island in the middle of the Moskva River in plain sight of the Kremlin. Not only did its location in the middle of the river make it easy for police to surveil, but the limited space of the park constrained the size of crowds that could fit there, so that participants were forced to spill over bridges and embankments to the opposite side of the river. Eduard Limonov, one of the opposition's leaders, refused to direct his followers to the Bolotnaya rallies, believing that the square was "the most worthless piece of territory where protests could be held"—in his words, "an island isolated from everything" and potentially "a trap" due to the overcrowding that would ensue.[109] Indeed, at the May 6, 2012 rally against Putin's inauguration, police efforts to constrict the number of protestors on the island provoked clashes, leading to brutal beatings at the hands of the police, four hundred arrests, and imprisonment of several opposition activists.

Ultimately, the Putin regime became caught in a spiral of increasingly draconian penalties in order uphold its spatial hegemony over the streets. Fines of

---

107. Kozenko 2007.

108. On the Kremlin's "spatial segregation policy" with regard to protests, see Gabowitsch 2017, 213–20.

109. Quoted in Abramova 2015.

up to a year's average salary were introduced for those who organized protests without government permission or who failed to comply with the specified conditions of the permit (such as the number of participants allowed or the location of the event). In 2014, in the wake of Euromaidan, these penalties were expanded further to include fines of up to two years' salary and prison sentences of up to five years for those who engaged in three violations of the law.[110] The government also set aside special zones for protests—so-called speakers' corners in Gorky Park and Sokolniki Park—far from any bystanders or protest targets. The strategy was eventually replicated in other cities throughout Russia. Because these spaces lacked visibility, were located in remote corners of the city, and were unsuitable for protest, they generally went unused.[111]

Regimes use numerous other tricks to prevent oppositions from utilizing public space to stage challenging protests. In December 2011, health officials in Moscow issued a warning to the public that people could catch respiratory infections if they participated in anti-Putin protests, and on the day before the protests, the Moscow Department of Education suddenly required all high school students to report for a mandatory examination at the very time that protests were scheduled to take place.[112] In 2005, the Ethiopian government detained all young men living in neighborhoods near the prime minister's palace—irrespective of their political orientations or whether they had participated in any acts of protest—in order to keep protests away from regime nerve centers in the wake of fraudulent elections.[113] In other instances, regimes have used sound to disrupt and contain revolutionary protest. During the revolt against the Maduro regime in Venezuela in 2014, the National Guard blasted Venezuelan folk music over loudspeakers mounted on trucks in order to prevent opposition protesters marching through Caracas from being heard.[114]

Some regimes attempt to ban protest altogether. In the wake of a wave of "clapping protests" in which anti-regime protesters simply occupied public space and clapped, the Lukashenko regime in Belarus introduced a set of extraordinary measures outlawing "the joint mass presence of citizens in a public space . . . for the purpose of a form of action or inaction that has been planned beforehand and is a form of public expression of public or political sentiments

---

110. Demirjian 2014.
111. The authorities eventually closed the Gorky Park facility as part of their increasing restrictions over protest in the capital.
112. Schwirtz 2011.
113. Arriola 2014.
114. Ellsworth 2014.

of protest."[115] These Kafkaesque regulations did not prevent citizens from eventually mounting a major revolutionary challenge to Lukashenko in 2020. Indeed, broad bans against protest can backfire. In the midst of the Euromaidan Revolution, the government of Viktor Yanukovych introduced strict laws against protests. The new law criminalized "extremist activity," handing out three years in prison for repeat offenders, up to five years in prison for anyone blocking a government building, up to two years for drivers of motorcade protests, and amnesty from prosecution for police committing violence against protesters. The laws themselves energized and multiplied revolutionary mobilization; within two weeks the government was compelled to revoke most of their provisions, and Yanukovych was eventually forced from office.[116] Similarly, on January 28, 2011, Hosni Mubarak ordered troops and tanks onto the streets and declared a general curfew for Cairo, Alexandria, and Suez, restricting all civilians from going onto the streets after 6p.m. But protestors openly defied the curfew, and given their overwhelming numbers, there was no way that the regime could possibly enforce it.[117]

Conclusion: Urban Civic Revolt and the Struggle for Control over Public Space

Tilly observed that "the geography of policing, safe spaces, spatial claims making, and political struggle over control of spaces emerge as specific problems of western cities over the last few centuries" whose "coincidence depends on the presence of dense settlements containing well defined public spaces, with governments exercising more or less continuous jurisdiction and surveillance inside their territories." He notes, by contrast, that "[i]n thinly settled rural areas, nomadic pastoral economies, lineage-dominated settlements, or zones of civil war, . . . we can reasonably expect to find somewhat different spatial dynamics."[118]

As we have seen, spatial politics differ dramatically between urban and rural revolutionary contention. In rural revolutions, contention revolves not around control over space, but control over scattered clusters of population. In urban revolutions, spatial politics are defined by proximity to the nerve centers of government, large concentrations of population, and the density of the built

---

115. Mouzykantskii 2011.
116. Wilson 2014, 80–83.
117. Kirkpatrick 2011a.
118. Tilly 2000, 152.

environment. As the repression–disruption trade-off in revolution suggests, proximity of revolutionary challenges to centers of power breeds danger for revolutionaries by exposing them to the full repressive capacity of the state, even while it increases their potential for disrupting and overthrowing regimes, amplifying the dangers to regimes as well. Over time, as cities have grown in size and states have become increasingly powerful, revolutionary oppositions have come to rely more on the power of numbers than the power of arms to exert leverage over regimes and protect themselves from regime repression. This in turn has meant using the built environment of the city differently from the past—less as cover for armed attacks, and more as spaces in which large numbers can be concentrated.

As a result, public space has become increasingly central to urban revolutionary contention, and the outcomes of urban revolution have come to hinge on a struggle for control over it. Numbers, visibility, and proximity to centers of power are all important elements of the urban civic revolutionary repertoire. Each in turn is influenced by the space within which collective action unfolds. Public space that is highly visible to domestic and international audiences, is located on public transportation routes, and bears strong symbolic significance aids urban revolutionaries in scaling up. Public space that is located in proximity to governmental centers increases the threat posed by revolutionary oppositions and magnifies opposition leverage.

Conversely, regimes seek to protect themselves by keeping revolutionary challenges at safe distance from government nerve centers, by policing and regulating access to public space, and by designing cities in such a way as to minimize threats. Since the invention of modern revolution, regimes have attempted to revolution-proof their cities. They have razed neighborhoods, moved capitals, paved roads, laid down boulevards, obliterated protest sites, and smothered them in traffic or commerce. They have limited the use of public space through laws and regulations, created "safe zones" in proximity to government centers, and established special zones for protest in outlying areas. Yet, none of these efforts have ultimately succeeded in completely eliminating revolutionary challenges. On the contrary, over time revolutionary contention in cities has multiplied, subverting urban public space with increasing frequency and transforming it into a site of political challenge.

7

The Individual and Collective Action in Urban Civic Revolution

> What is a rebel? A man who says no[.]
> ALBERT CAMUS, THE REBEL (1951)[1]

WHY INDIVIDUALS participate in revolutionary collective action has long been a central concern of scholarship. Three issues have dominated the conversation: who participates in revolutionary mobilizations; what motivates them; and how individuals who participate are connected to one another and to the societies from which they are drawn.

The answers to these questions vary according to the location and character of revolutionary action. In small-population settings, revolutionary movements are typically organized as vanguard parties, militias, or conventional armies. Thanks to low population densities, they are often able to monitor individuals locally, providing opportunities for rebels to wield selective incentives to stimulate participation, control who does and does not participate, and establish organizational and ideological coherence.[2] A significant proportion of rural revolts have also taken advantage of the authority of traditional societal leadership, further allowing for monitoring and control of populations through village hierarchies or religious institutions. Rural revolutions sometimes consist of multiple rival movements vying for control over a state. But each of these movements usually possesses a degree of internal cohesion, reinforced through hierarchical command, localized patterns of recruitment, personal ties, and the heat of combat. Frequently, as a result of efforts to inculcate

---

1. Camus 1991 [1956], 13.
2. Popkin 1979; Weinstein 2007.

organizational norms and ideologies, rural rebel movements are able to obtain obedience even "in risky and dangerous environments where central leaders cannot easily monitor or punish local units."[3] Protracted struggle stretching over years and shielded by distance or terrain also greatly facilitates socialization efforts.

For the urban revolutions that have become more common around the world, however, the factors that motivate and bind participants together are less clear. As we have seen, as a result of the repression–disruption trade-off and the enormous risks that such revolts pose for oppositions and governments, urban revolutions tend to be extremely compact in time, lasting for weeks and months rather than years and decades. The urban armed revolts that predominated in the nineteenth and early twentieth centuries necessarily organized themselves clandestinely due to the dangers posed by the repressive capacity of regimes in cities. In nineteenth-century France, for instance, urban revolution was carried out by dozens of small secret societies that counted on the broader population rising up after these armed bands took to the barricades or seized key points in the city. House describes the dilemma faced by such groups:

> [T]he success of such a plot depended upon secrecy from the police, yet final victory required widespread popular support. . . . Even in those rare instances where the police failed to predict and preempt such a conspiracy, the limited numbers of rebels involved and the violence of their methods normally meant that police and troops did not hesitate to repress the conspirators forcefully.[4]

Safety from arrest for rebels depended upon secrecy from the very populations on which they depended for victory.

As states grew more powerful and cities expanded in size, urban civic tactics of mobilizing large numbers in central urban spaces proliferated. Where the goal of revolutionary oppositions is to mobilize large numbers in a concentrated window of time, revolutionary movements face difficult challenges in deploying selective incentives. They cannot normally monitor individuals within large anonymous population centers, clearly differentiate or control who participates and who does not, or provide more than the weakest of selective incentives to stimulate participation.[5] Nor would they

---

3. Staniland 2014, 6.
4. House 2014, 19.
5. Among participants in the Orange Revolution, only 5 percent said that people participated in revolutionary protests in order to experience solidarity with others or be with friends,

want to filter participants, as they seek to maximize numbers in order to protect themselves against repression and exert leverage on regimes. Anyone who participates, irrespective of purpose, contributes to these goals. In rapidly assembled rebellions like urban civic revolutions, there is little opportunity or capability to socialize participants into movement norms. Leadership plays the role of a convener of crowds rather than a dispenser of incentives or inculcator of norms or ideologies. Selective incentives wielded by regimes do often *prevent* individuals from participating in urban civic revolutions.[6] Indeed, they are generally of greater significance in urban revolutions, where the reach of the state is greater, than in rural rebellions. Rosenfeld found, for instance, that because middle-class employees in the public sector in postcommunist countries are significantly dependent on their regimes, they are less likely than their private sector counterparts to participate in anti-regime protests.[7] But while regime selective incentives often explain why some individuals do not participate in urban revolutionary action, they provide little guidance as to why other individuals do or to how those who participate are connected to one another.

In the face of large numbers assembled on the streets, and in the absence of much information about those participating, there has been a tendency among observers to homogenize the crowd and attribute its motivations to the master-narratives that opposition leaderships articulate to justify revolt. In cases as diverse as the collapse of communism, the color revolutions, and the Arab Spring, observers claimed that individual participation in these revolts was a manifestation of emerging democratic values in these societies, brought about by secular processes of education, modernization, or globalization.[8] Societal values tend to change relatively slowly (usually as the result of generational replacement), and the values that one adheres to in early adulthood generally persist throughout one's lifetime.[9] One would therefore expect changes in values to be relatively enduring in their effects. Yet, commitment to

---

because they were compelled to participate by their superiors, or because they were paid money to participate.

6. Olsson-Yaouzis 2010.

7. Rosenfeld 2021. This tends to be less true where public employees are poorly paid or suffer a significant decline in their standard of living. As we will see, government employees mobilized in revolutionary protests disproportionately to their numbers in society in both the Tunisian and Egyptian revolutions. They have also played important roles in revolutionary protests throughout sub-Saharan Africa.

8. See, for example, Lewin 1991; Karatnycky 2005; Diuk 2006; Alexander 2011; Dalacoura 2012.

9. Abramson and Inglehart 2009.

democratic values in the wake of many urban civic revolutions has been fleeting. As one study of student participants in the April 1960 revolution in South Korea that brought down Syngman Rhee concluded, "The slogans [that the students] shouted favored democracy and free elections. . . . However, commitment to democracy could not have been the real reason for the revolt, since polls show that the students actually favored autocratic leadership and thought democracy 'unsuitable' for Korea."[10]

To be sure, most participants in urban civic revolutions are motivated by a keen sense of injustice and a deep sense of anger. But to maximize participation in urban civic revolts, cooperation must be obtained across markedly divergent groups within a large population in a matter of days or weeks, necessarily drawing on a wide variety of values and grievances. Given that revolutionary organization in such situations cannot provide ideological coherence, filter participants, or socialize them, these revolts by their very nature lack ideological consensus.

Generally, there has been a dearth of systematic information about the individuals who compose urban revolutionary crowds. There are of course numerous eyewitness and memoir accounts of specific revolutions that provide a sense of the animus underpinning revolt. There are also occasional ethnographies that delve more deeply into individual motivations.[11] While enormously valuable, such studies are based on small and non-random samples. This is especially problematic when participants number in the hundreds of thousands and when revolutionary mobilizations materialize and dissipate in a matter of days or weeks. Archival research on revolutionary participation has typically been based on lists of those arrested or killed.[12] Such studies may or may not be representative of the crowds from which these individuals were drawn, but they usually tell us little about revolution participants other than when they were born, when they died, their occupations, and the localities from which they hailed.

In this chapter, I address questions about participation in urban civic revolutions through an unusual series of nationally representative surveys conducted in the aftermath of four successful revolutions: the 2004 Orange Revolution, the 2010 Tunisian Revolution, the 2011 Egyptian Revolution, and the 2013 Euromaidan Revolution. These surveys provide an unprecedented look at the values, backgrounds, lifestyles, modes of communication, and network connections of those who participated in four of the most significant urban

---

10. Douglas 1963, 584. Surveys of Korean students at the time showed that over 80 percent felt that Western democracy was not suitable for South Korea and that their two most frequently mentioned worries were "livelihood" and "political and economic instability."

11. For urban revolutions, see Feldman 1991; Kubik 1994; Fournier 2006; Wedeen 2019.

12. See Tilly 1964; Gould 1991; Tezcür 2016.

civic revolutions of the early twenty-first century. Moreover, they allow us to compare these individuals to other individuals in society. In this respect, they offer a unique window into urban civic revolutionary collective action.

They show, for instance, that even in revolutions known for their enormous protests, participants constituted a small minority of society. In all four cases, a majority or plurality supported revolution. But significant segments of society often opposed it, and many remained apathetic. In this respect, revolutionary mobilizations are not simple reflections of societal preferences with regard to regime-change, but are refracted through the ability of oppositions and regimes to mobilize their respective supporters and demobilize the supporters of their opponents. The surveys also show that outsized revolutionary crowds in cities can be assembled in a variety of ways—on the basis of different configurations of societal cleavage (gender, age, class, and cultural difference). In this respect, the model of urban civic revolution is highly portable to a broad range of contexts.

Despite this variety, in all four revolutions better resourced and better educated citizens participated disproportionately. The extent of this middle-class bias varied: some urban civic revolts approximated broad cross-class alliances among urban inhabitants, while others were more narrowly constructed (though still with some degree of participation from other urban groups). Nevertheless, class was not the dominant category around which revolutionary mobilizations formed in all four revolts. Disaffection from abusive government constituted the major glue holding revolutionary coalitions together—cemented further through shared symbols of civic nationalism. As we will see, participants in these urban civic revolts had little in common in terms of views on public policy other than their fierce rejection of the incumbent regime. Within each society, revolution participants represented a greater variety of political tendencies than either revolution supporters who did not participate or those who supported the incumbent regime. They constituted a hastily assembled negative coalition, united at the moment of revolt by their common disaffection from the government.

Despite the fact that urban civic revolutions are often framed as "democratic," economic matters, corruption, and cultural and national issues tended to be more widespread concerns among participants in all four revolutions than civil and political freedoms. Certainly, some participants were motivated by democratic aims. But as we will see, they were a minority within the revolutionary crowds, and commitment to democratic values among most participants was weak. In this respect, these revolutions are better understood as revolutions against repressive and abusive government than for democracy. They were more about what people were struggling *against* than what they were struggling *for*.

Finally, the ways in which these urban civic revolutions were coordinated varied across cases. Civil society associations (parties, trade unions, youth groups, religious organizations) sometimes played important roles. But urban civic revolts have increasingly come to be digitally coordinated, as there is a strong affinity between the urban civic model and the ability of digital forms of communication to scale up crowds quickly. Digital coordination constitutes an effective tool for multiplying participation, but it has come at a price: it has reinforced and exaggerated tendencies already inherent in the urban civic model toward fragmented political organization, diminished strategic coordination, and diluted collective identities.

Identifying Revolutionary Participation

Much about revolutionary participation can only be studied retrospectively. This is especially true for urban revolutions, where it is impossible to know ahead of time who will participate and who will not, and the temporally compressed character of revolutionary collective action renders measurement in the context of rebellion difficult. Moreover, individual participation in revolutionary protests can vary significantly over time, so that measurement at any one point would not accurately reflect individual patterns of participation throughout an episode.[13]

But retrospective studies have their own issues. First, there are concerns about memory recall. The further in time a study is from the actual events of the revolution, the more severe these issues are likely to be. Even more significant are the challenges posed by preference falsification, particularly if those on the losing side fear prosecution, or those who wavered in conviction feel pressure to declare loyalty to the winning side. Failed revolutions, violent revolutions, or revolutions that bring highly repressive governments to power are especially likely to suffer from such problems.[14] But they are present even in a pluralist post-revolutionary environment.

In this chapter, I use retrospective nationally representative surveys to examine participation in four successful urban civic revolutions.[15] The Orange Revolution from November 21, 2004 through January 10, 2005 was one of the

---

13. Tarrow 1991.

14. Survey questions on participation in civil wars, for example, have extremely low response rates: Wood 2009, 122. See also Beath, Fotini, and Enikolopov 2011; Lyall, Blair, and Imai 2013; Matanock and García-Sánchez 2017.

15. For other studies that have utilized retrospective surveys to probe revolutionary participation, see Lohmann 1994; Opp, Voss, and Gern 1995; Humphreys and Weinstein 2008; Mueller 2013; Brym et al. 2014; Doherty and Schraeder 2014; Onuch and Sasse 2016.

most spectacular displays of urban revolutionary protest on the European continent since the end of the Cold War. Up to a million citizens turned out on Maidan, the main square of Kyiv, in temperatures as cold as −12 degrees centigrade to call for the annulment of falsified elections and an end to the corrupt regime of Leonid Kuchma, despite threats of a police crackdown. The Tunisian Revolution began with protests following the self-immolation of street vendor Mohamed Bouazizi in the provincial town of Sidi Bouzid on December 17, 2010 and lasted until the flight of President Zine El Abidine Ben Ali on January 14, 2011. Large numbers participated in the hundreds of revolutionary protests that spread from towns and small cities of the south to the capital Tunis, with 338 dying and over two thousand injured in the course of the revolt. The Egyptian Revolution began with protests on January 25, 2011 and ended with the resignation of President Hosni Mubarak on February 11, 2011, with at least 846 dying in protests and clashes during the revolt and another six thousand injured. Millions protested in Cairo's Tahrir Square or in one of the thousands of protests against the Mubarak regime in various cities around the country. The Euromaidan Uprising in Ukraine began on November 21, 2013 after the government of President Viktor Yanukovych suspended preparations for signing an association agreement with the European Union and ended, after a prolonged series of protests and violent clashes, with the flight of Yanukovych to Russia on February 23, 2014. At least 121 died and 1,800 were injured in the violence that accompanied the overthrow of the Yanukovych regime.[16] Protests occurred throughout Ukraine during the revolt, and crowds in Kyiv reached eight hundred thousand.

Nationally representative surveys could be used to study revolutionary participation in these cases only because all four revolutions were successful and participation in them was large enough to be able to identify a significant sample of participants. Participants would be unlikely to identify themselves after a failed revolution, and nationally representative surveys would not be an appropriate research strategy for revolutions involving smaller numbers. Each survey was structured differently. The 2005 and 2014 Ukrainian Monitoring surveys were conducted by the Institute of Sociology of the Ukrainian Academy of Sciences. Monitoring surveys have been organized by the Institute every year since 1994 as a means for analyzing trends within Ukrainian society. The surveys consist of a representative sample of 1,800 adults (eighteen years or older) in all provinces of Ukraine[17] and are composed of two parts: a battery

---

16. Many more, of course, died in the separatist war in the Donbas that followed the revolution.

17. Crimea could not be included in the June 2014 sample, as it was under Russian occupation.

of questions repeated annually or biennially, and a series of one-time questions designed to probe topical issues.[18] In both the March 2005 and June 2014 surveys, a battery of one-time questions was added that dealt with the events of the Orange and Euromaidan revolutions respectively.

Most studies assume that individuals face a binary choice during revolutions: participate or remain on the sidelines. But as Petersen noted,[19] the choices within revolutions are more complex. Most individuals do not participate in revolutionary collective action. But some non-participants support revolution and some oppose it. Others remain indifferent. Among those who support the revolution but do not participate, some choose to provide aid to revolutionaries. And some opponents of revolution choose to mobilize against revolution in support of the incumbent regime. Each of these positions encompasses various degrees of ambiguity and commitment.[20]

The Monitoring surveys in Ukraine allow us to identify many of these differences in behavior. In the March 2005 survey, respondents were asked, among other questions, to identify the candidate for whom they voted in each of the three rounds of the 2004 presidential election that precipitated the Orange Revolution, and whether they had participated in any protest actions during the revolt. Assuming that those who voted for the regime's candidate Viktor Yanukovych did not demonstrate for the opposition's candidate Viktor Yushchenko (and vice versa), in essence these questions allow us to identify seven distinct categories of individuals according their behaviors: 1) revolutionaries (those who voted for Yushchenko in the third round of voting on December 26, 2004[21] and who also participated in revolutionary protests); 2) revolution helpers (those who voted for Yushchenko and provided food, money, or clothing to protesters, but did not participate themselves in protests);[22] 3) revolution supporters (those who voted for Yushchenko in

---

18. For sampling procedures, see Panina 2005, 17–18. For studies that utilized the aggregated results of the 2005 Monitoring survey, see Stepanenko 2005; Lane 2008; White and McAllister 2009. For a study comparing individual participation in the Orange and Euromaidan revolutions based on the Monitoring data, see Reznik 2016. I thank Viktor Stepanenko for providing me with access to the surveys.

19. Petersen 2001.

20. See, for instance, Wedeen 2019.

21. I use the third round of voting as the clearest expression of whether an individual supported Yushchenko. The first round included numerous other candidates, and the second round occurred prior to the onset of revolutionary events.

22. About 11 percent of those who participated in revolutionary protests (thirty respondents) also indicated that they provided food, clothing, or money to protesters. They were counted as revolution participants rather than revolution helpers.

the third round but did not participate in demonstrations or aid protestors); 4) revolution opponents (those who voted for pro-incumbent candidate Viktor Yanukovych or voted against all candidates in the third round and did not participate in protests); 5) counterrevolutionaries (those who participated in protest demonstrations but voted for Yanukovych, voted against all candidates, or willingly chose not vote);[23] 6) the inactive or apathetic (those who neither voted nor participated in any protests); and 7) the uncommunicative (those who refused to answer any one of these questions).[24]

Survey respondents were asked similar questions about the Euromaidan Revolution in the June 2014 Monitoring survey. But as an election that might capture political preferences did not accompany the revolution, respondents were instead asked directly whether they supported the demands of the Euromaidan protests or the demands of the anti-Maidan protests (i.e., the counterrevolutionary mobilizations that accompanied the revolution).[25] These questions again allow one to identify the same seven behavioral categories: revolutionaries, revolution helpers, revolution supporters, revolution opponents, counterrevolutionaries, the inactive or apathetic,[26] and the uncommunicative.[27]

These behavioral categories for both revolutions are compared in Figure 7.1. Since Crimea (an area of opposition to Euromaidan) was not included in the 2014 survey (as it was under Russian occupation at the time), I also provide the results for the Orange Revolution excluding Crimea for the sake of comparison.[28] As the surveys show, participation was significantly greater in the Orange

23. During the Orange Revolution there were pro-incumbent demonstrations organized by the Yanukovych campaign. The largest involved about seventy thousand participants.

24. Two respondents indicated that they had participated in protests during the Orange Revolution but were disqualified from voting. I classified them into revolutionary and counterrevolutionary categories respectively, based on other characteristics (prior voting behavior and political attitudes on key issues). Due to the small number indicating that they were counterrevolutionaries, unless otherwise stated I lumped them together with revolution opponents and dropped the uncommunicative from the analysis.

25. On the anti-Maidan protests, see Portnov and Portnova 2015, 62–63. The largest anti-Maidan protest is alleged to have gathered sixty to a hundred thousand participants.

26. This group consisted of those who did not participate in protests or aid protestors and who also indicated that it was "hard to say" whether they supported the demands of Euromaidan protests and "hard to say" whether they supported the demands of anti-Maidan protests.

27. Again, due to the small number indicating that they were counterrevolutionaries, unless otherwise indicated I lumped them together with revolution opponents and dropped the uncommunicative in subsequent analyses.

28. These results differ only marginally, increasing the proportion of revolutionaries and revolution supporters and decreasing the proportion of revolution opponents in the Orange Revolution.

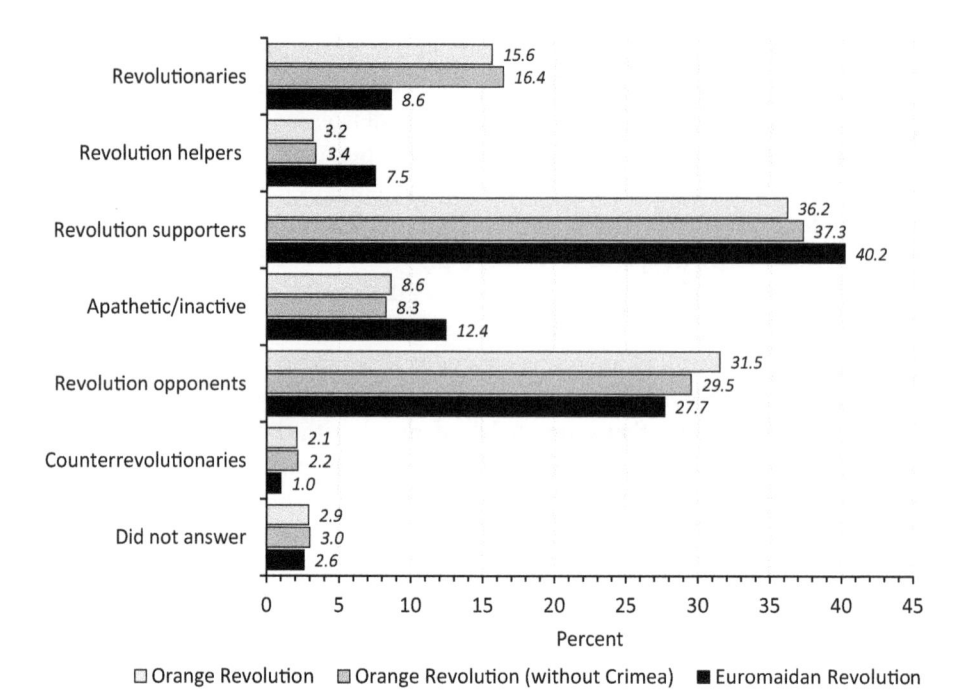

	Orange Revolution	Orange Revolution (without Crimea)	Euromaidan Revolution
Revolutionaries	15.6	16.4	8.6
Revolution helpers	3.2	3.4	7.5
Revolution supporters	36.2	37.3	40.2
Apathetic/inactive	8.6	8.3	12.4
Revolution opponents	31.5	29.5	27.7
Counterrevolutionaries	2.1	2.2	1.0
Did not answer	2.9	3.0	2.6

FIGURE 7.1. Behavioral categories in the Orange and Euromaidan revolutions (2005 and 2014 Monitoring surveys). Euromaidan survey excludes Crimea.

Revolution than in Euromaidan (15.6 versus 8.6 percent), but more people aided protestors in Euromaidan than in the Orange Revolution (7.5 versus 3.2 percent). When one combines the two groups, overall levels of activism in the two revolutions were roughly similar, with society somewhat more involved in the Orange Revolution than in Euromaidan. The proportions of revolution supporters who did not participate and of the apathetic were slightly larger in Euromaidan than in the Orange Revolution, while the proportion of revolution opponents was marginally smaller. Not surprisingly, in both revolutions, those who admitted to being counterrevolutionaries was small.

The second round of the Arab Barometer survey provides another rare opportunity to study revolutionary participation systematically and in a broader context.[29] It was fielded in Egypt in June 2011 and in Tunisia in

29. The Arab Barometer consists of a set of nationally representative surveys on political life, governance, and political, social, and cultural values regularly administered in eleven Arab countries. The principal investigators of the Arab Barometer surveys are Amaney Jamal, Bassma Kodmani, Khalil Shikaki, and Mark Tessler. The Egyptian survey was administered by the

October 2011—shortly after the revolutionary waves that swept both countries. Like the Monitoring surveys, the Arab Barometer was not designed to study revolutionary participation, but an additional battery of questions was added to probe participation in and attitudes toward these revolutions. In Egypt, 1,220 people were surveyed, while in Tunisia the sample size was 1,196. Respondents were asked whether, during the events of these revolutions, their positions were closer to supporters of the regime, the opposition, or neither side. They were also asked whether they had participated in the protests of these revolutions (and whether they had offered assistance such as food, money, or transportation to participants). Again, putting these questions together, in Egypt one can identify seven behavioral categories: 1) revolutionaries (those who participated in the protests and supported the opposition to Mubarak); 2) revolution helpers (those who supported the opposition to Mubarak and provided food, money, or transportation to protesters, but did not participate in protests); 3) revolution supporters (those who did not participate in protests or aid protestors, but indicated that their position was closer to the opposition than the regime); 4) revolution opponents (those who did not participate in protests but whose position was closer to the regime); 5) counterrevolutionaries (those who said that they participated in protests but that their position was closer to the regime or who supported neither side);[30] 6) the apathetic/inactive (those who did not participate in protests and who supported neither side); and 7) the uncommunicative (those who refused to answer). The question on aiding revolutionaries was not asked in the Tunisian survey, but using the same criteria one can identify six behavioral categories in the Tunisian Revolution: revolutionaries, revolution supporters, revolution opponents, counterrevolutionaries, the apathetic/inactive, and the uncommunicative.[31]

Al-Ahram Center for Political and Strategic Studies, led by Gamal Abdel Gawad. The survey in Tunisia was administered by the Sigma Group, led by Youssef Meddeb. Both surveys relied on area probability sampling. I especially thank Amaney Jamal for including my suggestions in the design of the survey.

30. On pro-Mubarak demonstrations during the Egyptian Revolution, see Ketchley 2016. Pro-Mubarak protests began on January 28 (the "Friday of Anger") and frequently coincided with anti-regime demonstrations as a way of harassing and repressing revolution participants.

31. Again, due to the small number of those indicating that they were counterrevolutionaries in Tunisia and Egypt, I treated them as revolution opponents and dropped the uncommunicative from subsequent analyses. The wording of the question in the Arab Barometer may also have contributed to under-reporting of counterrevolutionary action. In Egypt, the question asked, "Did you participate in the protests against former president Hosni Mubarak between January 25 and February 11, 2011?" In Tunisia, the question was, "Did you participate in the

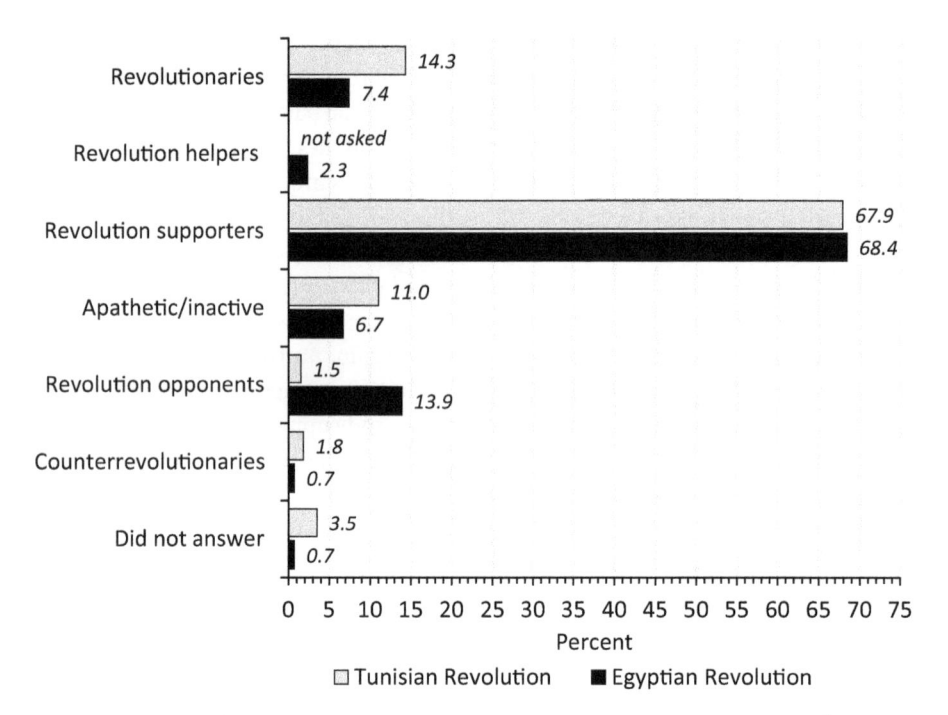

FIGURE 7.2. Behavioral categories in the Tunisian and Egyptian revolutions (Arab Barometer surveys).

These behavioral categories for the Tunisian and Egyptians revolutions are shown in Figure 7.2. As a proportion of the population, participation rates in the Tunisian Revolution were significantly greater than in the Egyptian Revolution—even though, as noted in the media at the time, the size of protests in Egypt far exceeded those in Tunisia. Differences in population size between the two countries largely explain this (Tunisia had a population of 10.7 million at the time of the revolution, whereas Egypt's population was 82.5 million). According to the surveys, the proportion of revolution supporters was roughly similar in both societies, whereas Egypt had more respondents who admitted to being revolution opponents.[32]

Preference falsification is an issue in all four surveys, leading to an understatement of opposition to these revolutions and of counterrevolutionary activity more generally. The fact that all four revolutions were successful

---

protests against former president Zain Al-Abdeen Ben Ali between December 17th, 2010 and January 14th, 2011?"

32. The survey was conducted two years before the Egyptian Counterrevolution of 2013.

mitigated the risks associated with identifying oneself as a participant. But it created incentives to conceal opposition to these revolts and to overstate the degree to which one supported them. A nationally representative survey taken in the midst of the Orange Revolution gives some sense of the magnitude of the problem in Ukraine. Conducted by the Kyiv International Institute of Sociology (KIIS) over December 10–14, 2004,[33] the survey was a "bare-bones" instrument focused almost entirely on voting and protest behavior, asking respondents whether they had participated in revolutionary demonstrations and their electoral preferences in the upcoming third round of the presidential election. As the survey was carried out prior to the third round of voting and the final outcome of the revolution, it may be a more accurate reflection of who participated in revolutionary protests but a less accurate reflection of individual regime preferences (12.2 percent of the sample said that they were likely to vote but did not know yet for whom or indicated no electoral preference). The KIIS survey found a lower proportion of revolutionaries (13.6 percent) than the Monitoring survey (15.6 percent)—but within the margin of error of both surveys.[34] But it also reported a significantly lower proportion of revolution supporters (26.9 percent in the KIIS survey versus 36.2 percent in the Monitoring survey)[35] and somewhat higher proportions of revolution opponents (35.6 percent versus 31.5 percent)[36] and counterrevolutionaries (4.0 percent versus 2.1 percent).[37] Some of these differences could have been due to different sampling strategies in the two surveys. However, the patterns also fit what one would expect to find under conditions of preference falsification.

The likelihood is that both surveys involve an element of preference falsification. In the retrospective Monitoring survey, the effect is to inflate the number of revolution supporters and to deflate the number of revolution opponents and counterrevolutionaries. In the Monitoring survey, 62 percent of those who claimed to have voted in the third round of the 2004 presidential election indicated that they voted for Yushchenko, even though the official results of the election showed that Yushchenko received only 52 percent of the vote. In the KIIS survey, however, only 43 percent of those who indicated that they would

33. The sample consisted of 2,044 adults (eighteen years or older). I thank Valery Khmel'ko, Dmytro Khutkyy, and Tatiana Petrenko of the Kyiv International Institute of Sociology (KIIS) for providing me with access to the data.

34. The difference from the Monitoring sample is not statistically significant.

35. Statistically significant at the .001 level (chi-square = 38.1937, with 1 degree of freedom).

36. Statistically significant at the .01 level (chi-square = 7.4308, with 1 degree of freedom).

37. The difference for counterrevolutionaries is smaller than the margin of error for the sample as a whole (3 percent).

likely participate in the third round of voting said that they would vote for Yushchenko (far below the official results). Since vote fraud was not a major issue in the election's third round, one can presume that in the midst of revolutionary crisis, when the outcome was still uncertain, some individuals were reluctant to identify their allegiance to the opposition openly and instead declared themselves "undecided" (captured in the KIIS survey by the large number who had not yet declared their electoral preference). It could also be that this portion of the population was genuinely undecided and subsequently tipped to the opposition because of the outcome of revolutionary protests. The bottom line is that we will never know the "true" distribution of preferences with regard to regime-change in the Orange Revolution (if such a thing even exists).

Given the higher level of violence involved in Euromaidan and its aftermath, one would expect that preference falsification would be a more severe issue in the 2014 Monitoring sample. The violence following the revolution also created sampling problems. Crimea, which constituted 5 percent of the 2005 Monitoring sample, could not be included in the 2014 survey, as it was under Russian occupation. Moreover, fighting had just begun in the Donbas, creating potential issues with the Donbas portion of the sample (though survey responses in the Donbas fit the pattern one would expect from the region). Tellingly, 36 percent of Donbas residents responded that it was "hard to say" or refused to answer whether they had supported the anti-Maidan movement, and the odds that a respondent from Donbas would refuse to answer this question were twice as great as for a respondent from central Ukraine. The 2014 Monitoring survey underestimates the proportion of counterrevolutionaries and revolution opponents, misplacing some of them in the inactive/apathetic category and failing to survey others.

Preference falsification is also present in the Arab Barometer surveys. The Tunisian survey contains an extremely low proportion of revolution opponents (1.5 percent) and a higher percentage of respondents who refused to answer than the Egyptian survey. At the same time, the proportion of revolution supporters in both the Tunisian and Egyptian surveys is high (68 percent in both cases), leading to suspicions that some respondents might have misrepresented their support out of fear or concern for their reputation. For these revolutions, we do not have surveys that measure revolutionary participation in the midst of these revolts. But other surveys of participation carried out after these revolutions reflect patterns similar to those found in the Arab Barometer.[38] Preference

---

38. An analogous participation rate (18.5 percent) was reported in a survey of the six Tunisian provinces where revolutionary mobilization was concentrated (Doherty and Schraeder 2014). This is almost identical to the Arab Barometer's participation rate in these same six governorates

falsification is a problem in all social scientific research—including ethnographic and eye-witness accounts. Survey research is no different.

Despite the issues noted, the surveys represent the best available systematic record of participation in these four revolutions. Each survey provides an approximation of the differences between revolutionary participants and other behavioral groupings in society. All of them show that participants in these revolutions (as well as those who aided participants) were small minorities within their respective societies. Revolutionaries appear to have enjoyed majority or plurality support in all four revolutions; but incumbent regimes also frequently possessed significant pockets of support—especially in Ukraine. The Monitoring surveys show that in both revolutions, Ukrainian society was narrowly divided over regime-change. The degree of incumbent-regime support in Tunisia and Egypt is likely masked by preference falsification. Even in Egypt, however, 15 percent of society had no qualms about identifying itself as opposed to the revolution only months after it occurred. In all four revolutions, there were many more opposition supporters who mobilized against these regimes than regime supporters who mobilized in support of them. This is particularly striking in the Ukrainian cases, where society was roughly evenly divided over revolution according to mass preferences, but where counterrevolutionary mobilization was small. Thus, on the basis of the KIIS survey conducted in the midst of the Orange Revolution (which probably reflected the degree of opposition to the revolution more accurately but underestimated the degree of support for it), one in every three opposition supporters mobilized against the regime, while only one in every ten regime supporters mobilized in its defense.[39] According to the 2005 Monitoring survey (which overestimated support for the revolution and underestimated support for the regime), one

---

(18.4 percent). Moreover, a similar participation rate was reported in two Gallup polls conducted in Egypt in March–April 2011 and September 2011 using a representative sample over the age of fourteen (Brym et al. 2014). The March–April sample found that 11 percent reported both participating in the protests of the Egyptian Revolution and supporting protests in favor of the removal of Mubarak, while in the September sample 8.4 percent did so. As in the Arab Barometer results, 70 percent reported in the March–April sample (and 67 percent in the September sample) that they supported the protests for removal of Mubarak but had not participated in them. Of course, preference falsification is likely an issue in these surveys as well. Whenever relevant, I use the Doherty/Schraeder and Gallup data as further checks on the findings. I thank the Gallup Organization for allowing me access to their surveys.

39. Corroborating these patterns, the KIIS survey also found that 51 percent of Yushchenko voters who did not participate in protests themselves knew someone (a friend, relative, or acquaintance) who participated. By contrast, only 18 percent of Yanukovych voters who did not participate themselves knew someone who participated.

in every four opposition supporters mobilized against the regime, while one in twenty regime supporters mobilized in its defense.

In this respect, patterns of mobilization were not a simple reflection of societal preferences regarding regime-change. Rather, those preferences were refracted through the capacity of oppositions and regimes to mobilize supporters and demobilize opponents. Thus, in the KIIS survey conducted in the midst of the Orange Revolution, when respondents were asked whether it was necessary to engage in protest actions in order to defend one's choice for president, 75 percent of those who indicated that they were intending to vote for opposition candidate Yushchenko answered affirmatively, while only 23 percent of those who indicated that they would vote for regime candidate Yanukovych did so. In short, support for the regime was "soft," as regime supporters were less committed to defending the regime than opposition supporters were to overthrowing it. This "soft" support for the regime is a feature of many authoritarian regimes where regime supporters tolerate widespread regime abuses in exchange for policy or material advantage.

What is particularly exciting about these surveys as instruments for studying revolutionary participation is the degree of detail that they provide about the values, beliefs, behaviors, and lifestyles of respondents. In the two Monitoring surveys, over 350 questions were asked of each respondent, covering a wide variety of topics. In addition to questions about the respondent's age, gender, marital and family status, level of education, place of residence, religion, nationality, language use, and economic and material situation, the surveys asked respondents about their attitudes toward privatization, Ukraine's geo-political orientation, citizenship and language policy, and political institutions. They asked about respondents' political self-identification, participation in civil society associations, trust in other people and in institutions, evaluations of political leaders, interactions with the state over the previous twelve months, attitudes toward various nationalities, respondents' biggest fears and desires in their lives, their health and drinking habits, height and weight, the size of their living space and how well it was heated, how they spent their free time and what consumer goods they owned, access to the internet and cellphone ownership, and numerous other questions. Never before has such an extensive record of the personal habits, behaviors, beliefs, and backgrounds of participants in a revolution been available (though this was not the overt purpose of these surveys).

To illustrate what one can learn from this kind of information, controlling for the effects of age and gender, Orange revolution participants had more living space than other members of Ukrainian society (on average, 60.5 versus 43.0 square meters) and were more likely to heat their apartments at a normal temperature in the winter (a .71 probability versus .60). They were more likely to have attended church in the past week than others (a .27 probability versus .14), somewhat less likely to smoke (.68 versus .75), more likely to say that they had true friends (.64 versus .54) and that they never experienced loneliness (.43 versus .33), more likely be satisfied with their lives as a whole (.41 versus .26), and more likely to remain politically active after the revolution (.08 versus .03).[40] Scholars have long argued that "biographical availability" (the "absence of personal constraints that may increase the costs and risks of movement participation, such as full-time employment, marriage, and family responsibilities")[41] functions as a filter for high-risk collective action. While the Monitoring surveys show no statistically significant relationship between marriage and revolutionary participation, they do show that, controlling for age and gender, a person who participated in the Orange or Euromaidan revolutions was much less likely to have children below the age of six than were those who supported these revolutions but did not participate. Similarly, controlling for gender and age, those who participated in the Orange or Euromaidan revolutions were in significantly better health than those who supported these revolutions but did not participate.[42]

In this chapter, I focus primarily on the choice to participate in revolutionary protests. However, the surveys have a great deal to tell about other choices individuals made in revolutionary situations. For instance, the 2005 Monitoring survey reveals that, controlling for gender and age, there was a .42 probability that a person who participated in counterrevolutionary protests against the Orange Revolution had exercised in the last seven days (compared to only .22 for other revolution opponents and .17 for the rest of Ukrainian society). There was a .16 probability that counterrevolutionaries had visited a lawyer sometime in the last twelve months (.05 for other revolution opponents and .05 for the rest of society), and a .80 probability that they were dissatisfied with the amenities and sanitary conditions of their home (.64 for other revolution opponents and .39 for the rest of society).[43] They also drank alcohol more regularly than other revolution opponents and the rest of Ukrainian society[44] and were more likely to come from Yanukovych's stronghold and fiefdom in the Donbas (a .47 probability) than other revolution opponents (.38).[45] Those who aided

---

40. Based on a logistic model of participants versus other members of society, controlling for age and gender. See Appendix 4C for estimation details. All differences were statistically significant at the .001 level.

41. McAdam 1986, 70.

42. Based on a multinomial logistic model (see Appendix 4D for model details). All relationships were statistically significant at the .05 level or better.

43. For instance, counterrevolutionaries were less likely to own a refrigerator or washing machine than other revolution opponents (statistically significant at the .001 level).

44. Statistically significant at the .05 level or better.

45. The KIIS survey found an even higher concentration of counterrevolutionaries in the Donbas. Controlling for age and gender, there was a .72 probability that a counterrevolutionary came from the Donbas but only a .33 probability for other Yanukovych voters.

participants in the Orange Revolution were similar in political views and background to those who participated. But they tended to be older (on average, forty-seven years old, as opposed to forty for participants), and, controlling for age and gender, were more likely to own a car (a .25 probability, compared to .13) than revolution participants.[46] And those who were apathetic during the Orange Revolution were younger, poorer, more likely to be female, and more likely to speak Russian at home compared to the rest of Ukrainian society.[47]

In short, the richness of the Monitoring surveys and their ability to identify different behavioral categories within the population with respect to revolution make them unique in the study of revolutionary politics.[48] While the Arab Barometer surveys do not contain the same level of detail, they nevertheless provide their own insights. They show, for instance, that women, the less educated, the more secular, Christians, and farmers disproportionately opposed the Egyptian Revolution relative to their proportions within society,[49] while 82 percent of Egyptians who aided revolution participants had friends or acquaintances in the crowds (compared to only 24 percent of revolution supporters more generally). A number of questions in the Arab Barometer surveys about the frequency of revolutionary participation, media use during revolutionary contention, and the revolutionary activity of friends and family also add dimensions that are absent in the Monitoring surveys.

Variable Assembly: Social Structure and Urban Civic Revolts

The surveys show that each revolt had roots in a somewhat different set of societal cleavages. In this respect, urban civic revolutions can be assembled in a variety of ways, rendering the repertoire portable to a wide range of contexts.

---

46. Statistically significant at the .01 level or better.
47. Statistically significant at the .05 level or better.
48. Recent efforts to survey crowds in urban civic revolts (Tufekci and Wilson 2012; Onuch and Sasse 2016) involve thin survey instruments out of necessity and do not allow comparisons with non-participants. For an effort to use case-control methods to compare participants with the broader population from which they are drawn, see Rosenfeld 2017.
49. All relationships statistically significant at the .05 level or better. Disproportionate opposition to the revolution is confirmed in the Gallup data for women, Christians, rural populations, and the less educated.

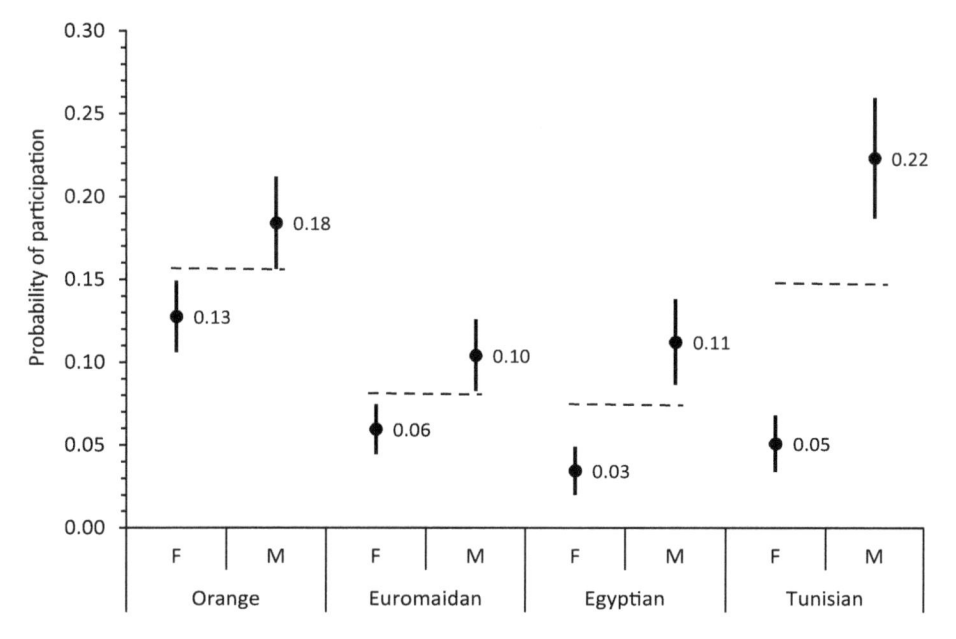

FIGURE 7.3. The probability of participating in revolutionary protests, by gender. Multinomial logistic regression, controlling for the effects of age. Point estimates, with 95 percent confidence intervals. Dashed lines represent the average probability of participation for all non-missing observations in the sample.

All four revolutions were highly gendered, though to varying degrees (Figure 7.3). Gender differences in participation were particularly strong in the Arab Spring revolts: in Tunisia the probability of a male citizen participating in revolutionary protests was almost four times the probability of a female participating (.23 versus .06), and in Egypt almost three times greater (.11 versus .04).[50] Males were also overrepresented in the Ukrainian revolutions, though by smaller margins: the probability of male participation was twice as great as that of female participation (.11 versus .06) in Euromaidan and 58 percent higher (.19 versus .13) in the Orange Revolution. Clearly, the cultural milieus in which these revolutions unfolded shaped gender roles within them. But cultural norms were not the only factors that mattered; higher levels of violence also pushed women into auxiliary roles—as the results in Ukraine

---

50. These patterns are confirmed in the Doherty/Schraeder and Gallup data. Despite disproportionate male participation in Egypt, there was significant participation by Egyptian housewives, who constituted 13 percent of Egyptian Revolution participants. See Ketchley 2014, 160–61; Hafez 2012.

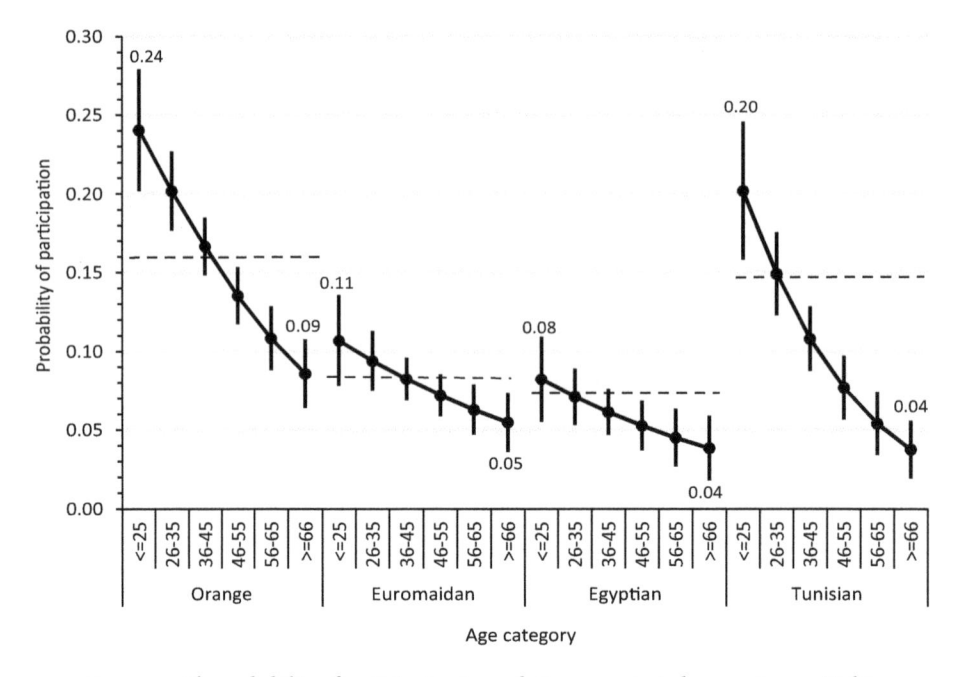

FIGURE 7.4. The probability of participating in revolutionary protests, by age category. Multinomial logistic regression, controlling for the effects of gender. Point estimates, with 95 percent confidence intervals. Dashed lines represent the average probability of participation for all non-missing observations in the sample.

in two revolutions separated by a decade demonstrate. In the more violent Euromaidan, women were more likely to aid participants than to participate themselves; this was not the case in the less violent Orange Revolution.[51]

Age also structured participation differentially in all four revolts (Figure 7.4). Egypt, Tunisia, and Ukraine have radically different age structures. At the time of these revolutions, Egypt had a fast growing population, with 19 percent of society aged between fifteen and twenty-four, while Ukraine had an aging population, with only 10 percent of society in that age range. Tunisia lay somewhere in-between, with 15 percent of society aged between fifteen and twenty-four. Despite the popularity of youth bulge explanations of revolution,[52]

---

51. This is similar to the findings of Parkinson 2013. In both Orange and Euromaidan revolutions, women were overrepresented among the apathetic, but gender played little role in structuring support or opposition to the revolution more generally. By contrast, in Egypt women were overrepresented among those opposing the revolution—a finding replicated in the Gallup survey.

52. Hart, Atkins, and Youniss 2005; Goldstone 2002; Urdal 2006.

there was a statistically significant relationship between age and participation in all four revolutions, irrespective of the proportion of youth in the population. Revolutions are often thought to involve disproportionate participation by the young because the young are the most physically capable within a population, tend to be more risk-taking and less burdened by social responsibilities, and are often more idealistic.[53] But age mattered a great deal more in structuring participation in the Orange and Tunisian revolutions than in the Egyptian and Euromaidan revolts. Youth activism was greatest in the Orange Revolution, due to the key role played by revolutionary youth movements that consciously sought to appeal to youth through music, logos, and brand marketing.[54] By contrast, Euromaidan was the "oldest" of the four revolutions, with half of participants aged forty-two or older. This pattern might seem puzzling given the outsized role played by Ukrainian youth only a decade earlier. But repeated revolutions in Ukraine created a cohort effect: the cohort that participated in the Orange Revolution was, by 2013, nine years older, and studies showed that 63 percent of Euromaidan participants had also participated in the Orange Revolution.[55]

The Tunisian Revolution was also disproportionately led by youth, spearheaded by young cyber-activists in urban centers and by unemployed youth (many of them university graduates) in cities and towns of the southern hinterland.[56] A quarter of participants in the Tunisian Revolution were aged twenty-two or younger, and half were younger than thirty. By contrast, half of participants in the Egyptian Revolution were thirty-five or older.[57] The April 6 Youth Movement played a critical role in organizing the early protests of the Egyptian Revolution. But its connections with Egyptian youth were limited to large cities, whereas Egyptian youth (those between eighteen and twenty-five years of age) were predominantly rural (69 percent), reflecting Egypt's high rural population growth. Conversely, Tunisian youth were predominantly urban (73 percent) and highly networked through the internet. At the time of the revolution, 69 percent of Tunisians twenty-five years old or younger accessed the internet at least once a month; the corresponding figure for Egyptians was 29 percent. Despite a youth bulge in Egypt, age played a smaller role in structuring participation in the Egyptian Revolution because the revolution

---

53. However, in the Orange Revolution (though not the other three revolutions), youth was not only associated with greater participation, but also with a higher likelihood of being apathetic.

54. Garfield 2004; Nikolayenko 2017.

55. Onuch and Sasse 2016, 569.

56. Honwana 2013. This is confirmed as well in the Doherty/Schraeder data.

57. The Gallup poll finds a slightly more youthful core of participants in the Egyptian Revolution, but still half were thirty-three or older.

was urban, while Egyptian youth was predominantly rural.[58] Thus, patterns of mobilization across these revolutions illustrate the shortcomings of youth bulge theories as applied to urban civic revolutions. Mobilizational structures aimed at youth, the rural or urban location of youth, and their structural position within the economy were more important than the sheer size or proportion of youth in society. Cohort effects were significant at times as well.

Successful revolutions have long been thought to require cross-class alliances.[59] But these four revolutions were assembled out of societies with radically different class structures. Ukraine is an aging post-communist economy with a large number of pensioners, a high rate of female participation in the workforce, a large industrial working class, a significant technical intelligentsia, a substantial number of professionals and office workers, and a growing element of small business. The agricultural sector constitutes only 6 percent of the workforce. Registered unemployment ranged between 8 and 10 percent, with a quarter of the population living below the poverty line. By contrast, Egypt is a developing country with low rates of female participation in the workforce, a large public sector (27 percent of the Egyptian labor force), a significant tourism industry, a growing professional class, and large numbers of shopkeepers and craftsmen. The agricultural sector in Egypt made up 32 percent of the workforce on the eve of revolt. Official unemployment in Egypt was 9 percent—similar to Ukraine. But much of the Egyptian economy flowed through its informal sector, and youth unemployment at the time stood at around 26 percent, with a quarter of the population living below the poverty line. In Tunisia, the agricultural sector constituted 15 percent of the workforce on the eve of revolution. But the Tunisian economy in the years prior to revolt also featured a substantial working class and a growing middle class. The official unemployment rate of 15 percent was twice that level among youth—and even higher (44 percent) among educated youth. Not surprisingly, unemployed educated youth played an important role in the revolution. And with a Gini index of 41, income inequality was higher in Tunisia than in Egypt or Ukraine (the result of years of neoliberal economic reforms). Inequality was especially felt between the more prosperous north and the rest of the country. In all three countries, the state, which once dominated these economies, experienced significant contraction in the years preceding revolution due to privatization, economic reform, and externally induced structural adjustment resulting from neoliberal development. This fueled substantial economic grievances not only among the poor, but also within the middle class.

---

58. In Egypt, rural youth were more likely than other age categories to oppose the revolution. As Basheer Saqr, founder of Egypt's Farmers Solidarity Committee, said, "The revolution was largely a revolution of the cities.... The countryside didn't really take part in it." Quoted in El-Kouny 2012. For a contrary view, see Abu-Lughod 2012.

59. Dix 1984; Goldstone 1994; Goodwin 2001; Goldstone 2011.

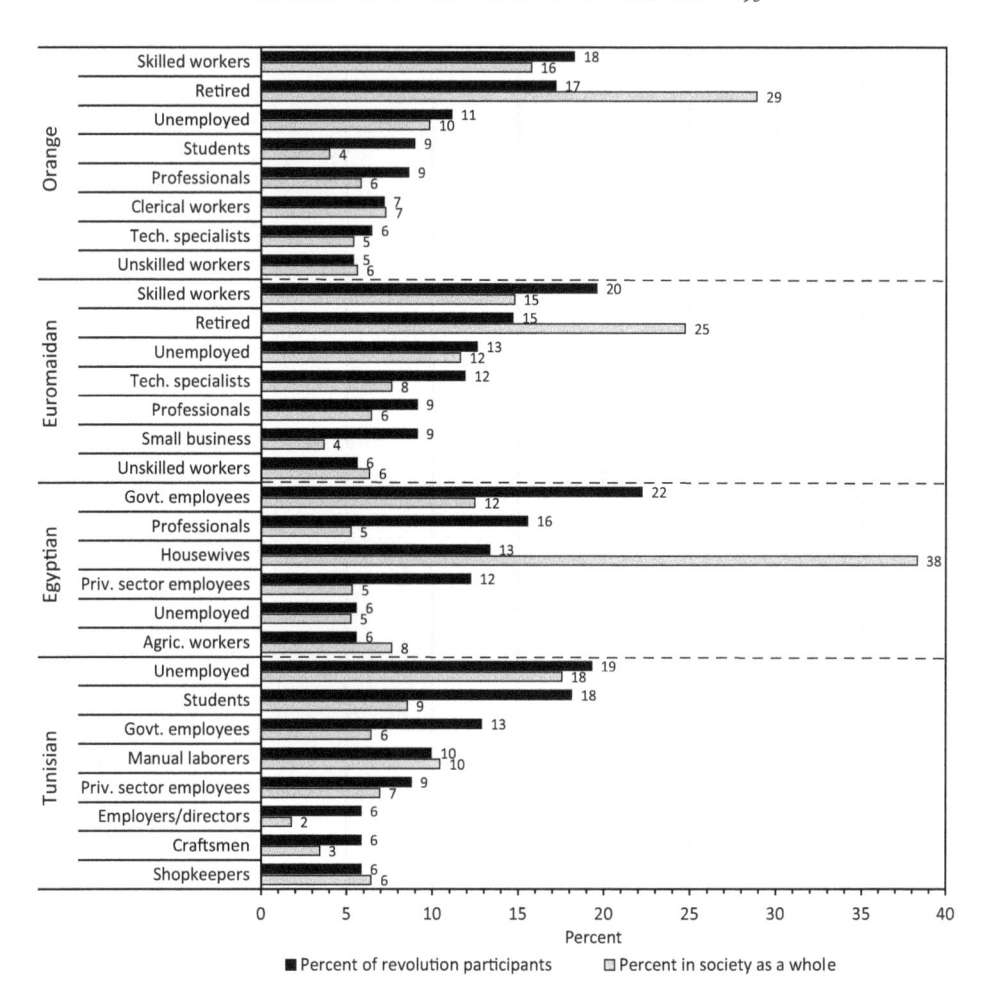

FIGURE 7.5. Occupations of participants in revolutionary protests (percentage of participants), relative to percentage of occupation in society as a whole. Occupational groups were included only if they represented at least 5 percent of revolution participants. The percentage of the occupation in society as a whole was based on the average for the entire sample.

These broader societal patterns were reflected in the occupational backgrounds of participants (Figure 7.5). In the Orange Revolution, participants consisted predominantly of skilled workers, retirees, the unemployed, students, the professional and technical intelligentsia, and clerical workers. Of these, students and professionals participated disproportionately relative to their weight within society.[60] Most of these same occupational groups (with the exception

60. Statistically significant at the .05 level or better.

of students and clerical workers and the addition of small business) were well represented in the crowds that protested in Euromaidan a decade later—this time with skilled workers and small business overrepresented relative to their proportion within society.[61] Tunisian Revolution participants consisted of a different permutation of occupational groups: the unemployed, students, manual laborers, and employees from public and private sectors (as well as smaller contingents of employers, craftsmen, and shopkeepers). While participants represented a broad cross-class coalition of groups centered around cities and towns, students, government employees, employers, and craftsmen were overrepresented in the crowds relative to their share in society.[62] The unemployed, though a substantial percentage of revolutionary crowds in Tunisia, were actually no more likely to participate than in proportion to their presence in society as a whole. By contrast, crowds in the Egyptian Revolution consisted of a somewhat narrower coalition of government employees, professionals, housewives, and private sector employees (with smaller contingents of the unemployed and agricultural workers).[63] Government employees and professionals were particularly likely to participate relative to their share within society.[64]

In short, there is no single constellation of groups composing the crowds within urban civic revolutions. Sometimes the unemployed play a significant role, sometimes they do not; sometimes skilled workers participate disproportionately, and in other revolutions they do not; sometimes government employees are important, but in other cases they are not; sometimes students are important, and in other cases they are conspicuously absent. These different patterns reflected not only the different occupational structures of these societies, but also the different constellations of grievances and the different mobilizational structures that manifested themselves within these revolutions. In this respect, the urban civic model is transposable to a variety of situations and social structures, with varying assembly.

Nevertheless, in all four revolutions educated and middle-class individuals participated disproportionately relative to their weight within society. This becomes clearer when we look at patterns of income, consumption, and

61. Statistically significant at the .05 level or better.
62. All these differences statistically significant at the .05 level or better. The relatively small group of employers and directors in Tunisia inexplicably participated with high probability, according to the survey. One cannot rule out that these results are a product of preference falsification or simply sample size.
63. For an explanation of these different class patterns of mobilization in Tunisia and Egypt, see Beissinger, Jamal, and Mazur 2015.
64. Statistically significant at the .01 level or better.

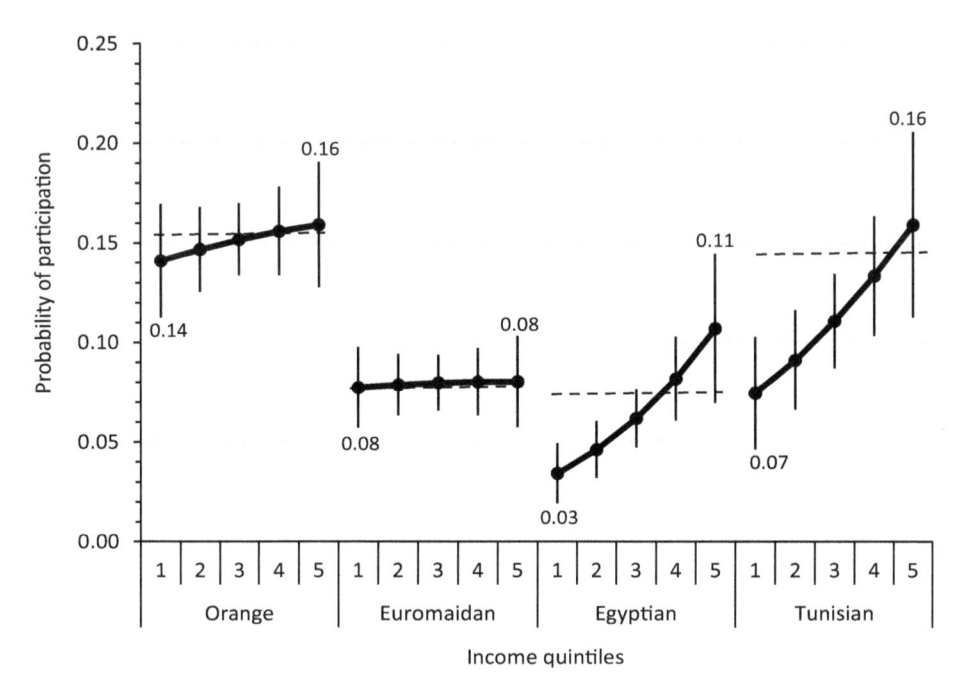

FIGURE 7.6. The probability of participating in revolutionary protests, by income quintiles. Multinomial logistic regression, controlling for the effects of gender and age. Point estimates, with 95 percent confidence intervals. Dashed lines represent the average probability of participation for all non-missing observations in the sample.

education among participants. As Figure 7.6 shows, controlling for the effects of gender and age, reported income was strongly related to participation in the Egyptian and Tunisian revolutions, with the poor participating at much lower rates than the better-off.[65] In both revolutions, only about a quarter of participants belonged to the bottom two income quintiles. In the two Ukrainian revolutions, there was no clear relationship between reported income and participation—most likely because of widespread under-reporting of income (a common phenomenon in surveys in Ukraine). But class differences made themselves evident in Ukraine's revolutions in other ways—particularly through differences in consumption. Controlling for the effects of gender and age, the number of durable consumer goods owned by a Ukrainian citizen (out

---

65. The results were replicated in Egypt in the Gallup sample and in Tunisia in the Doherty/Schraeder sample.

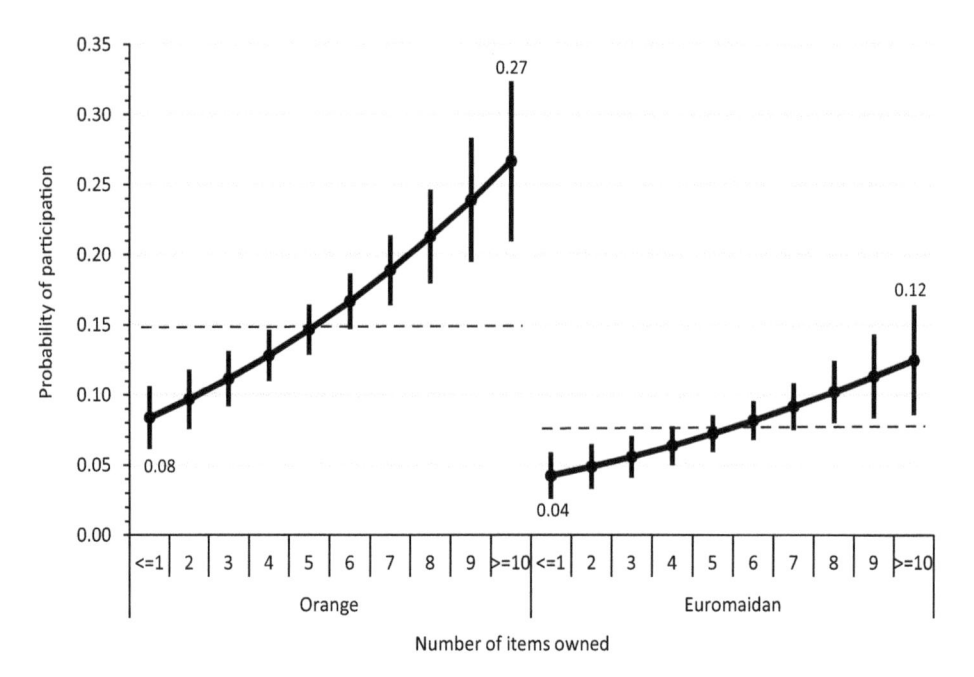

FIGURE 7.7. The probability of participating in revolutionary protests, by consumer goods ownership. Multinomial logistic regression, controlling for the effects of gender and age. Point estimates, with 95 percent confidence intervals. Data represent the number of items owned from a list of sixteen. Dashed lines represent the average probability of participation for all non-missing observations in the sample.

of a list of sixteen)[66] was strongly related to participation in both revolutions (Figure 7.7). Consumption more strongly tracked participation in the Orange Revolution than in Euromaidan, as the violence of Euromaidan pushed many of the better-off into aiding revolutionaries rather than participating directly. But in all four revolutions, better resourced and better educated citizens were more likely to participate than the poor or disadvantaged.

Participation in all four revolutions was also strongly related to education (Figure 7.8). Controlling for gender and age, in both Ukrainian revolutions those with higher education were twice as likely to participate as those with only a primary education, while in the Arab Spring revolts the relationship

66. Respondents were asked whether they owned any of the following items: a dacha, a garden plot, a car, a color television, nice furniture, a library of more than a hundred books, stereo and video equipment, a tape recorder or radio receiver, sports or tourist equipment, a refrigerator, a washing machine, a sewing machine, fashionable clothing, a computer, fishing equipment, or a motorboat.

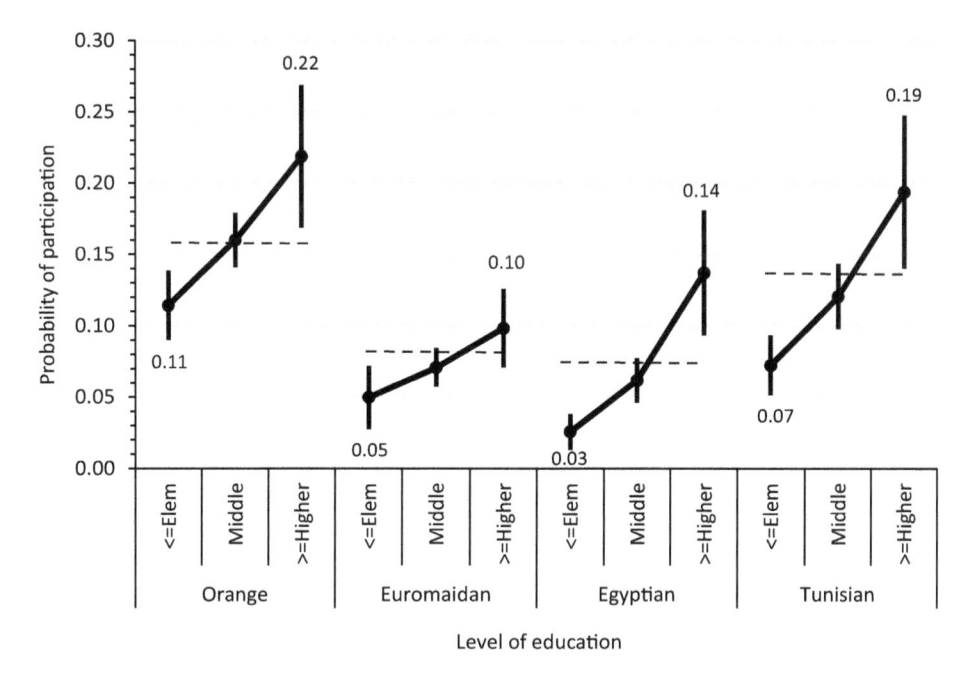

FIGURE 7.8. The probability of participating in revolutionary protests, by level of education. Multinomial logistic regression, controlling for the effects of gender and age. Point estimates, with 95 percent confidence intervals. Dashed lines represent the average probability of participation for all non-missing observations in the sample.

between higher education and participation was even stronger, especially in Egypt.[67] The exceedingly high level of unemployment among those with a higher education doubtless played a role in instigating revolutionary participation in Egypt and Tunisia; but in neither country did the highly educated unemployed participate at greater rates than the highly educated employed, though the highly educated unemployed participated at much higher rates than the less educated unemployed.[68] Education was more weakly associated

---

67. These findings were replicated in the Gallup poll, where those who had completed higher education had a .15 probability of participating in the Egyptian Revolution, while those with eight years or less of education had only a .05 probability of participating. They were also replicated in the Doherty/Schraeder poll, where those with a higher education had a .23 probability of participation in the Tunisian Revolution, while those with basic education or less had only a .09 probability of participation.

68. Thus, in Tunisia those with higher education who were unemployed participated with a .24 probability—much greater than the probability of participation for the unemployed without higher education (.14). But those with higher education who were employed participated

with participation in Euromaidan, as violence pushed many of the better educated into aiding participants rather than participating themselves.

While the bulk of attention in the study of revolution and regime-change has fallen on social class,[69] nationalism and cultural difference have always been important elements in revolutionary mobilization.[70] Social class was clearly important in all four revolutions discussed here. But it was not the dominant cleavage around which revolutionary mobilizations formed. Rather, these revolutions predominantly pitted a variously imagined civic "nation" against the political class.

The roles of nationalism and cultural difference were particularly evident in Ukraine, where region, language use, religion, and national identity played outsized roles in structuring individual behavior during revolution. Behavior in both Ukrainian revolutions was strongly shaped by region of residence, with participation concentrated in the west and center of Ukraine and opposition primarily concentrated in the east and south. Overall, 49 percent of Orange revolutionaries and 56 percent of Euromaidan revolutionaries were residents of western Ukraine, the historical center of Ukrainian nationalism, even though the region accounted for only 18 percent of the country's population.

Region in the Ukrainian context, however, is in part a container for deeper cultural differences based in language use, religion, and attitudes toward the Ukrainian national project. Thus, controlling for age, gender, education, and class (measured as consumer goods ownership), if a person primarily spoke Ukrainian at home, he or she was almost six times more likely to participate in the Orange Revolution and almost five times more likely to participate in the Euromaidan Revolution than if he or she did not (Figure 7.9). Moreover, a person who did not speak Ukrainian at home was almost six times more likely to oppose the Orange Revolution and almost four times more likely to oppose the Euromaidan Revolution than a person who did. Language use in Ukraine is complex, with many individuals switching between Ukrainian and Russian depending on context.[71] But quite literally, revolutionaries and revolutionary opponents tended to speak different languages in

---

with a .28 probability. Similarly, in Egypt those with higher education who were unemployed participated with a .18 probability, significantly greater than the participation rate of the unemployed without higher education (.07). At the same time, those with higher education who were employed participated with a .20 probability.

69. For a critique of the excessive focus on class in the literature on democratic transitions, see Haggard and Kaufman 2012.

70. Nationalism and religion played critical roles in many of the large-scale urban civic revolts of East Asia, Southeast Asia, and communist Europe. See Kubik 1994; Slater 2009; Lieven 1993; Beissinger 2002; Fink 2009.

71. Arel 2002; Bilaniuk 2005; Kulyk 2011.

THE INDIVIDUAL AND COLLECTIVE ACTION 299

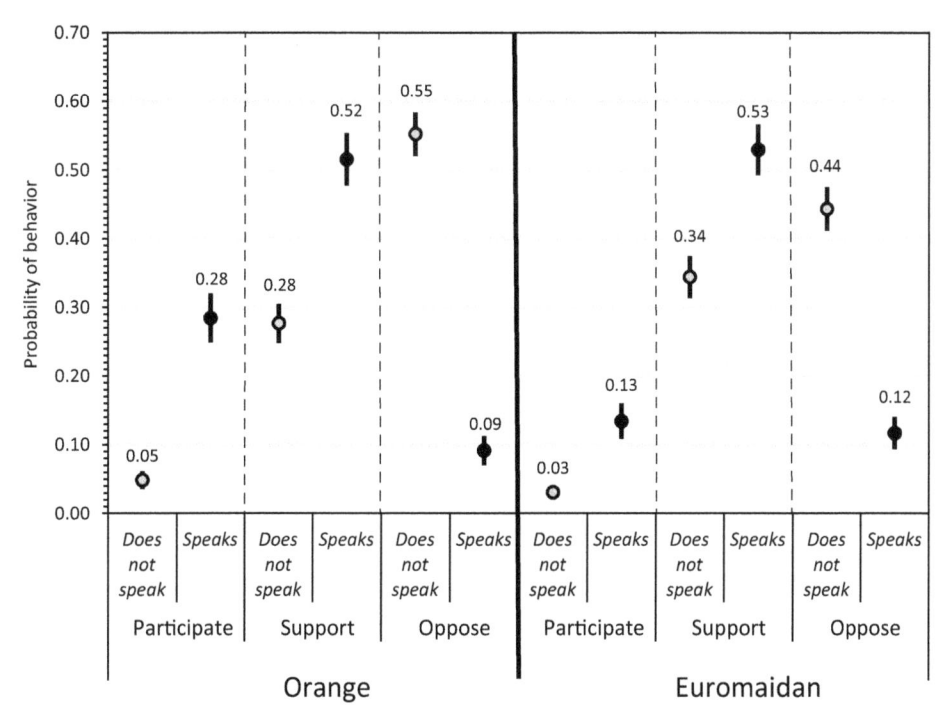

FIGURE 7.9. Probability of participation in, support of, or opposition to revolution, by whether respondent speaks Ukrainian at home (Orange and Euromaidan revolutions). Multinomial logistic regression, controlling for the effects of gender, age, education, and consumer goods ownership. Point estimates, with 95 percent confidence intervals. Euromaidan sample excludes Crimea.

their everyday lives: almost three-quarters of participants in both the Orange and Euromaidan revolutions spoke primarily Ukrainian at home, as opposed to only two-fifths of the country as a whole. Religious difference also formed an important cleavage in both revolutions. Though they make up only 7 percent of Ukrainian society, Uniates comprised 22 percent of participants in the Orange Revolution and 31 percent of participants in the Euromaidan Revolution.

These cultural differences translated into very different attitudes toward the Ukrainian state. Thus, 75 percent of Orange Revolution participants and 83 percent of Euromaidan participants indicated that they primarily identified as citizens of Ukraine, and 78 percent of Orange Revolution participants and 90 percent of Euromaidan participants indicated that they were proud to be citizens of Ukraine. By contrast, only 46 percent of Orange Revolution opponents and 44 percent of Euromaidan opponents primarily thought of themselves as citizens of Ukraine (with significant numbers identifying as inhabitants of their village, region, or the former Soviet Union). Only 34 percent of Orange Revolution opponents and 30 percent of Euromaidan opponents indicated that they were proud to be citizens of Ukraine. Civic nationalism was one of the main tropes of both revolutions (with tones of ethnic nationalism surfacing more visibly in Euromaidan). Participants in these revolts were precisely those with whom such appeals resonated.[72] The urban civic revolutionary crowd functions as a simulated nation—a site where claims about ownership over the state are put forth and nationhood becomes seemingly tangible.

Civic nationalism similarly helped to cement a diverse coalition in the Egyptian and Tunisian revolutions. Wael Ghonim has written of how "the sense of solidarity transcended differences of age, class, culture, education, and religion" during the Egyptian Revolution.[73] One of the chief slogans of the Egyptian Revolution and other Arab Spring revolts—"The people want to bring down the regime!"—exemplifies the collective reclaiming of an alienated state that urban civic revolutions represent.[74] The mobilizations of the Arab Spring were not revivals of the old anti-colonial Arab nationalisms of previous revolutions in Egypt and Tunisia. Rather, they represented a new nationalism revolving around the shared fate of living for decades under corrupt and repressive regimes that were viewed as having stolen and usurped that which rightfully belonged to the nation. Expressions of national pride pervaded the Egyptian Revolution, and national flags were ubiquitous.[75] Asmaa Mahfouz, one of the founders of the April 6 Youth Movement, declared after the January 25 protest, "This is the Egyptian people we have always dreamed of. I can now say I am proud to be an Egyptian."[76] And as a thirty-eight-year-old Egyptian mother of three proclaimed in the midst of the uprising, "For the first time I am proud to be an Egyptian."[77] In short, urban civic revolutions are associated with an upsurge in civic nationalism, which aids oppositions in holding together a diverse coalition.

While the square transcended divisions,[78] cultural difference still played a role in structuring participation in Arab Spring revolutions. Religion was a

---

72. Kuzio 2010; Kuzio 2015; Arel 2007; Marples and Mills 2014. Certainly, reverse causation accounted for part of these patterns, in that revolutionary participation undoubtedly magnified identity with and pride in country, while those who lost in these revolutionary struggles might be expected to demonstrate less pride in country.

73. Ghonim 2012, 265.

74. Abulof 2015.

75. Filiu 2011, 27.

76. Quoted in Khalil 2011, 159.

77. Sherwood 2011.

78. This indeed is the central theme of the widely acclaimed Egyptian/American documentary "The Square" depicting the Egyptian Revolution and its aftermath.

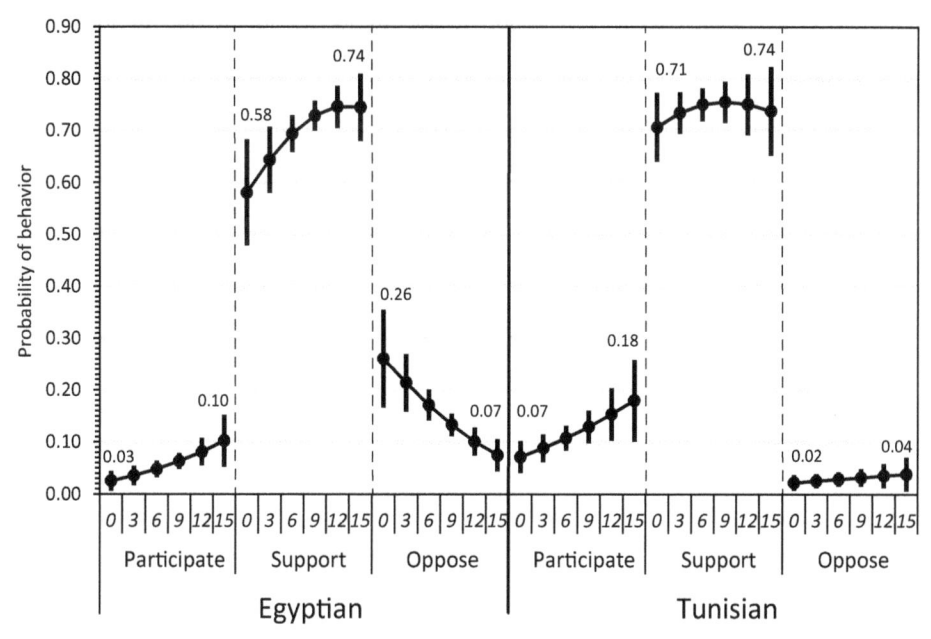

FIGURE 7.10. Probability of participation, support, or opposition to revolution, by level of religiosity among Muslims (Egyptian and Tunisian revolutions). Multinomial logistic regression, controlling for gender, age, and income quintile (and in Egypt, for whether a respondent was Christian). Point estimates, with 95 percent confidence intervals. Religiosity was measured as a 0–15 scale based on five religious behaviors.

particularly important mobilizing vector. Both the secular and the religious were represented within revolutionary crowds in Egypt and Tunisia. But religion was a significant mobilizing force in both revolutions. Although Egyptians were considerably more pious than Tunisians,[79] controlling for gender, age, and class (measured by income quintile), Islamic religious practice was related to participation in both revolutions,[80] with the more pious participating at higher rates than the less pious (Figure 7.10). This was partially the result of mobilization by followers of Islamist movements. In Tunisia, slightly over a fifth of revolution participants were Ennahda supporters, while in Egypt

---

79. Respondents were asked to identify whether they "always, most of the time, sometimes, or rarely" prayed daily, watched or listened to religious broadcasts on radio or TV, attended religious lessons in mosques, read the Quran, and read religious books. These scores were added and placed on a 16-point scale, from 0 to 15 (See Beissinger, Jamal, and Mazur 2015). On this 0–15 scale, Egyptian Muslims averaged 8.5, while Tunisian Muslims averaged 6.0.

80. The Egyptian results were controlled for whether a respondent was Muslim or Christian.

about a quarter of participants supported the Muslim Brotherhood.[81] In Egypt (though less so in Tunisia), support for and opposition to revolution were strongly structured by religious piety. Thus, controlling for gender, age, and class, the religious in Egypt were considerably more likely to support the revolution and less likely to oppose it. Christians in Egypt were twice as likely to be apathetic or to oppose the revolution as Muslims—largely out of fear of how the revolution might affect their position as a religious minority.

Political Beliefs and Negative Coalitions

Urban civic revolutions are typically led by coalitional leaderships, which help to maximize participation through bloc recruitment and increase the likelihood of network connections to the elite. In the Orange Revolution, for instance, 46 percent of revolution participants indicated that their electoral support for Yushchenko was conditional upon the endorsements of other politicians–in particular, Yulia Timoshenko (36 percent), Oleksandr Moroz (18 percent), and Anatoliy Kinakh (13 percent). Thus, coalitional leadership practically doubled the number of participants.

The factional groupings that composed the Orange coalition at the elite level reflected themselves downward in the composition of crowds, which represented a multiplicity of political orientations and lacked consensus over basic values and goals. The dissensus that results from coalitional leadership in urban civic revolts is further exacerbated by the rapidity with which revolutionary participants are assembled and the absence of any filtering or socialization of participants by revolutionary organization. As a result, participants have little in common in terms of public policy preferences other than their strong rejection of the incumbent regime. The reasons for this rejection vary enormously—both across revolutions and across participants within revolutions.

The Monitoring surveys provide an unprecedented look into the political orientations and beliefs of participants. As they show, in terms of political orientations, participants in both the Orange and Euromaidan revolutions represented a more diverse set of political groupings than those who supported these revolutions but did not participate and those who opposed them (Figure 7.11). The Herfindahl index,[82] displayed on the far side of the Figure, shows that, in both revolutions, two participants chosen at random were more

---

81. In the Gallup survey, 28 percent of participants indicated that they supported the Muslim Brotherhood.

82. A Herfindahl index measures the probability that any two individuals drawn at random represent the same type. It is calculated by the formula $H = \sum_{i=1}^{N} s_i^2$ where N is the number of types within a population, and s is the share of each type within the population.

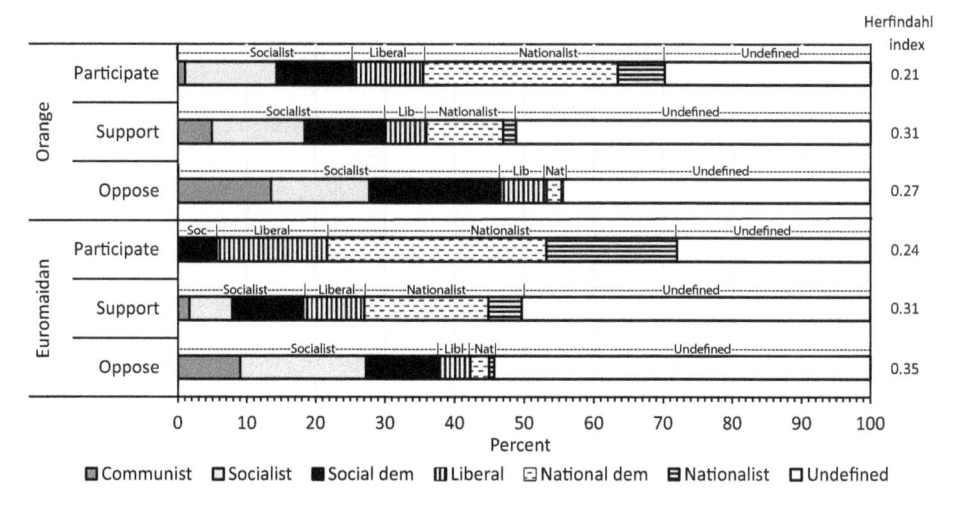

FIGURE 7.11. Political self-identification among participants, supporters, and opponents of revolution (Orange and Euromaidan revolutions). Herfindahl indices represent the probability that two individuals chosen at random from the population represent the same type.

likely to be of different political persuasions than two revolution supporters chosen at random or two revolution opponents chosen at random. (A lower Herfindahl score index indicates a higher degree of diversity.)[83]

The Arab Barometer surveys do not offer as clear a picture of the political orientations of participants. But they do reveal the variety of motivations brought together through revolution. Respondents were asked to identify the most important and second most important reasons why citizens participated in these revolutions.[84] Among revolution participants, improving the economic situation was the most frequently cited motivation—identified

---

83. Participants in the Orange Revolution were somewhat more diverse than participants in Euromaidan. The collapse of the Socialist Party in 2007 significantly reduced the socialist contingent of participants in Euromaidan.

84. The question asked, "A number of citizens participated in the protests between January 25 and February 11, 2011 [for Tunisia, December 17, 2010 and January 14, 2011] for various reasons. In your opinion, what were the most important and the second most important reasons for the protests?" Possible replies included the economic situation, civil and political liberties, corruption, replacing the current regime with an Islamic regime, protesting pro-Western state policy, protesting pro-Israel state policy (Egypt only), protesting passing leadership to Gamal Mubarak (Egypt only), or some other reason specified by the respondent that was not among those listed. The question did not ask participants directly why they as individuals participated in the revolution. But given that the respondents examined here were all

as the primary reason for participation by 38 percent of Egyptian and 58 percent of Tunisian participants. An additional 30 percent of Egyptian and 19 percent of Tunisian revolution participants cited the economy as a secondary reason for rebellion. In both revolutions, combating corruption was the reason for rebellion cited second most frequently by participants—noted as a primary or secondary reason by 56 percent of Egyptian and 60 percent of Tunisian revolutionaries.[85] Despite the fact that they were frequently framed as "democratic,"[86] in both revolutions civil and political freedoms were less frequently cited by participants as motivations—named by only 29 percent of Egyptian and 50 percent of Tunisian participants as *either* a primary *or* a secondary reason (and cited as the primary reason for revolt by only 18 percent of Egyptian participants and 20 percent of Tunisian participants). In short, while demands for civil and political freedoms were salient for a minority of participants, most participants in both Arab Spring revolutions saw issues of the economy and corruption as more important motivators of revolt. Judging from the motivations mentioned by participants themselves, these were revolutions not for democracy, but against corrupt and abusive rule.

Further evidence shows a high degree of dissensus over major policy issues among participants in the Orange and Euromaidan revolutions. Using a series of questions from the Monitoring surveys that captured opinions on a variety of issues related to democracy, a market economy, cultural issues, and foreign and political orientations,[87] I performed a latent class cluster analysis to identify how opinions on various issues clustered together among revolution participants.[88] For both samples, statistical tests indicated that a three-cluster model

---

revolution participants, one would expect their answers to be informed by their own concerns and experiences.

85. Relatedly, in Egypt, another 36 percent of revolution participants identified the succession of Mubarak's son Gamal as a primary or secondary reason for participation.

86. Howard and Walters 2015.

87. The questions concerned attitudes toward a multi-party system, toward privatization of large enterprises, privatization of land, the right to buy and sell land, the general role of the state in the economy, Ukraine's possible NATO membership and its foreign policy orientation, whether Russian language should be accorded official status, and how revolutionaries identified themselves on the political spectrum.

88. Latent class cluster analysis is a finite mixture approach used to identify groupings of individuals who share similar interests, values, characteristics, or behaviors. Individuals are classified into clusters based on the probabilities of their membership, which (unlike traditional k-means cluster analysis) are estimated directly from the model. Unlike traditional k-means clustering, latent class cluster variables can be continuous, nominal, or ordinal (Vermunt and Magidson 2002). Latent Gold 4.5.0 was used to perform the analyses. The analyses were

was appropriate.[89] Figure 7.12 displays the cluster profile plots for the three clusters in each revolt. Based on the patterns of responses, I labeled them pro-market nationalists, anti-market nationalists, and socialists. In both revolutions, pro-market nationalists supported a multi-party system, privatization of large enterprises and land, the purchase or sale of land, a Western foreign policy orientation, and NATO membership for Ukraine, but opposed official status for the Russian language. When asked to identify themselves on a political spectrum, they predominantly chose "nationalist" or "national-democratic." In both revolutions they constituted about a third of all participants. Like their pro-market counterparts, anti-market nationalists also identified themselves predominantly as "nationalist" or "national-democratic," preferred a Western orientation for Ukraine, were favorably disposed to NATO membership, and opposed official status for the Russian language. But unlike pro-market nationalists, they were strongly against privatization of large enterprises, privatization of land, and the purchase or sale of land. At the time of the Orange Revolution, they were also sharply divided over the desirability of a multi-party system in Ukraine, though by the Euromaidan Revolution their support for multi-party democracy had increased. They had also drifted away from central planning, even though they continued to oppose privatization and other market-oriented measures. Anti-market nationalists constituted slightly less than half of the participants in both revolutions. Socialists opposed privatization of large enterprises, privatization of land, and the purchase or sale of land and were most likely to favor a centrally planned economy for Ukraine. At the time of the Orange Revolution, this cluster opposed a Western orientation in Ukraine's foreign policy and supported making Russian an official language. They also did not support a multi-party system for Ukraine. By the time of the Euromaidan Revolution, they had grown divided over foreign policy orientation and had come to oppose official status for Russian,[90] even though they

---

performed on both revolution participants and revolution helpers, since the violence of Euromaidan tended to drive some revolutionaries into auxiliary roles.

89. Simulations suggest that the Bayesian Information Criterion (BIC) and the Akaike Information Criterion with a per-parameter penalty of 3 (AIC3) are the most accurate measures for adjudicating the number of clusters in a latent class cluster analysis (Fonseca 2008). For the Orange Revolution model, the lowest BIC suggested a three-cluster model, while the lowest AIC3 suggested a four-cluster model. However, only a small number of cases were classified into the fourth cluster (4 percent of the sample), pointing to the wisdom of a three-cluster model. For Euromaidan participants, BIC suggested a two-cluster model and AIC3 a three-cluster model. In this case, the third cluster was large and made substantive sense, so a three-cluster model was adopted for the Euromaidan sample as well.

90. These shifts were most likely due to the Russian invasion of Crimea in the aftermath of the revolution and the onset of the rebellion in Donbas.

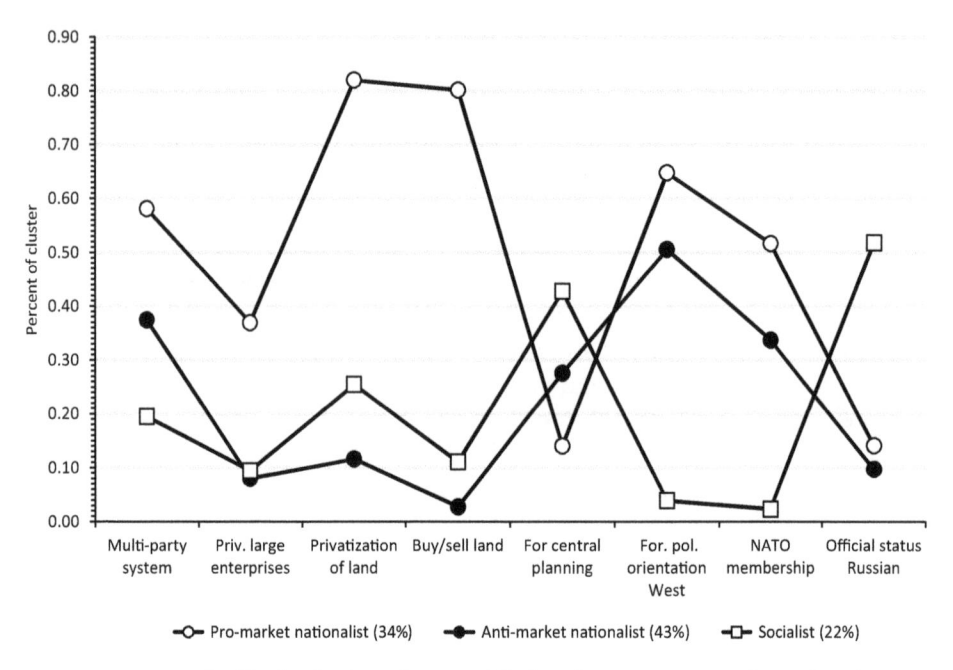

FIGURE 7.12A. Profile plots for three-cluster model of revolution participants: Orange Revolution. Latent cluster analysis.

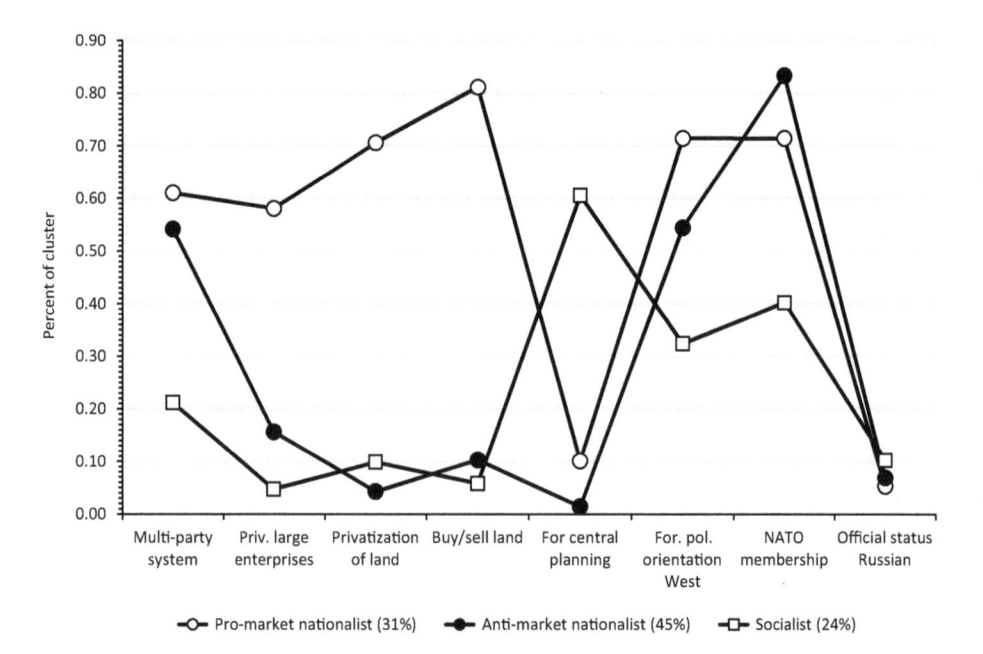

FIGURE 7.12B. Profile plots for three-cluster model of revolution participants: Euromaidan Revolution. Latent cluster analysis.

continued to be tepid about multi-party democracy. This cluster most frequently identified as socialist, social-democratic, or moderate left at the time of the Orange Revolution, but by Euromaidan they did not identify with any political tendency due to the disintegration of the Socialist Party in 2007. They constituted a little less than a quarter of participants in both revolutions.

Again, despite the frequent framing of these revolutions as "democratic," the Monitoring surveys reveal that commitment to democratic values and norms was weak among most Orange and Euromaidan revolutionaries. For instance, 66 percent of Orange Revolution participants and 62 percent of Euromaidan participants agreed with the statement "Several strong leaders can do more for our country than laws and discussions," while only 33 percent of Orange Revolution participants and 52 percent of Euromaidan participants believed that Ukraine needed a multi-party system. Only 27 percent of Orange Revolution participants and 42 percent of Euromaidan participants believed that Gypsies should be allowed to be inhabitants of Ukraine, while 45 percent of Orange Revolution participants and 70 percent of Euromaidan participants believed that Jews should be allowed to be inhabitants of Ukraine.[91]

Certainly, the Ukrainian revolutions and the Arab Spring revolts were broadly "civic" in the sense that citizens mobilized against government misrule and corruption. But the democratic master-narratives that accompanied these revolts functioned as holders for a variety of grievances and purposes, assembled through common rejection of these regimes and through shared symbols of nationhood rather than shared democratic values. In revolts that depend heavily on the rapidly assembled power of numbers, individual motivations to engage in revolutionary action are often weakly related to revolutionary master-narratives.[92]

Civil Society, Personal Networks, and Information

The collective action and resource mobilization paradigms placed great emphasis on the role of formal organization (political parties, social movement organization, labor unions, professional associations, churches, youth groups, etc.) for solving collective action problems.[93] But it is well known that parties and civil society associations are weak in Ukraine, Egypt, and Tunisia. In Ukraine, somewhere between 13 and 16 percent of citizens report belonging

---

91. Actually, participants in the Orange and Euromaidan revolutions were as prejudiced toward Gypsies and Jews as the rest of the population of Ukraine.
92. Klandermans 2010.
93. McCarthy and Zald 1977.

to *any* civil society association,[94] while the corresponding figures are 15 percent for Egypt and 7 percent for Tunisia.[95] To put this in perspective, the 2010 Life in Transitional Societies II (LITS II) survey found that 40 percent of French, 32 percent of Germans, 40 percent of Great Britons, and 57 percent of Swedes reported active membership in at least one civil society association, and another 32 percent of French, 50 percent of Germans, 34 percent of Great Britons, and 78 percent of Swedes reported passive membership.[96]

Given this weakness of civil society associations, it is hardly surprising that ties to parties, movements, or civil society associations were noticeably absent among the vast majority of participants in these urban civic revolutions. To be sure, urban civic revolutions are often led by coalitions of parties, movements, or civil society associations, and participation is considerably greater for those belonging to a political party or civil society association than for those who do not. But in all four revolutions, members of parties or civil society associations were a minority of revolution participants (22 percent in the Orange Revolution, 29 percent in Euromaidan, 21 percent in the Tunisian Revolution, and 43 percent in the Egyptian Revolution). In the Egyptian Revolution, these were mainly members of the Muslim Brotherhood, informal trade unions, and liberal civil society associations.[97]

How, then, do urban civic revolutions scale up to include hundreds of thousands—even millions—of citizens? As we have seen, one of the great advantages of large urban environments for revolutionary collective action is the density of weak ties, mass media, and mass communications networks. Digital technologies have further magnified mobilizational possibilities in urban centers. Beginning in the 1990s, and particularly in the first decade of the 2000s, a transformation in communications technologies unfolded around the world, as the internet and mobile phones gained widespread use. In 2000, only 7 percent of the world's population used the internet and 8 percent used a cellphone. By 2014, internet usage had reached 40 percent of the world's population

---

94. This was defined as a political party, socio-political movement, environmental movement, public organization, independent trade union, artistic union, sports club or association, professional association, student society or youth organization, religious organization or church community, farmer association, or some other organization, society, or movement.

95. In the Arab Barometer surveys, this was defined as a political party, charitable society, professional association, trade union, youth association, cultural association, sports club, family or tribal association, local development association, cooperative association, or some other type of association.

96. The data are available at http://www.ebrd.com/pages/research/economics/data/lits.shtml.

97. See Clarke 2014; Beissinger, Jamal, and Mazur 2015.

and cellphone ownership—63 percent.[98] The impact of digital communications has been particularly evident in cities. Thus, in 2019, 72 percent of households living in urban areas around the world had access to the internet at home. The corresponding figure for rural households was 38 percent. While virtually all of the urban population around the world was covered by mobile broadband networks in 2019, this was true of only 17 percent of the rural population in less developed countries.[99] This transformation in communications technologies has had a profound impact on the ways in which revolutionary opposition is coordinated—facilitating greatly the kind of rapid scaling up characteristic of the urban civic repertoire. As digital technologies and television came to dominate communications processes, visuality, simultaneity, and self-coordination have grown increasingly central to revolutionary processes.

The four revolutions examined in this chapter represent different moments in the digitalization of revolution. In fall 2004, when the Orange Revolution broke out, digital communications technologies had only begun to make inroads into Ukraine. YouTube, Twitter, and Instagram did not exist, and Facebook was just beginning to emerge. In all, 10 percent of Ukrainian society were internet users and 26 percent were mobile phone users (with 29 percent having access to either technology). The mobilizations of the Orange Revolution were primarily organized by conventional civil society organizations. But digital communications (email, SMS messaging, and the internet) played a role in providing alternative sites for news, coordinating the Orange electoral campaign and the youth movement Pora, and spreading information about protest events.[100] Orange Revolution participants were considerably more likely to be internet (20 percent) or mobile phone (36 percent) users than other members of Ukrainian society, with 41 percent of revolution participants having access to either technology. But civil society membership and digitally enabled participation were largely separate phenomena: among participants, 77 percent of digital communications users were not members of any civil society association, while 56 percent of participants who were members of a civil society association were not digital communications users. Most significantly, almost half of all participants neither belonged to a civil society association nor had access to digital communications. Television (in particular, the independent

---

98. These figures come from the World Bank (https://data.worldbank.org/indicator/IT.NET.USER.ZS) and the 2014 Ericson Mobility Report (https://www.ericsson.com/assets/local/mobility-report/documents/2014/ericsson-mobility-report-november-2014.pdf).

99. International Telecommunication Union, "Measuring Digital Development: Facts and Figures 2020," at https://www.itu.int/en/ITU-D/Statistics/Pages/facts/default.aspx.

100. Lysenko and Desouza 2010.

station Channel 5) played a critical role in informing these participants about events.[101]

Nearly a decade later, at the time of Euromaidan, digital communication had sunk deep roots into Ukrainian society, with 41 percent using the internet and 89 percent using cellphones. Among participants in Euromaidan, 70 percent were internet users and 92 percent used either a cellphone or the internet. Civil society associations played a role in mobilizing participants in Euromaidan. Church congregations were particularly important mobilizing structures among Uniates, who constituted almost a third of all participants in the revolution.[102] However, Euromaidan was overwhelmingly a digitally coordinated revolution. Facebook, Twitter, SMS messaging, internet-based television, and other social technologies were key in coordinating the uprising, with 49 percent of participants reporting that they had learned about the protests through Facebook alone.[103] Social media became a vehicle for providing real-time information about protests, and in the wake of police brutality activists shared photos and video recordings to identify perpetrators and bring them to justice. Digital media were also widely used to coordinate aid to participants and to connect the uprising to supporters abroad.[104] Two-thirds of digitally connected participants in Euromaidan belonged to no civil society associations; but the vast majority of those revolution participants who did belong to a civil society association (86 percent) were digitally connected. Significantly, social media were also used by anti-Maidan groups, by the regime, and by its Russian allies to disrupt revolutionary mobilization and to organize counterrevolution.[105]

The Arab Spring revolutions broke out at a time of rapid change in the information sphere within the Arab world, with the rise of Al Jazeera, satellite television, and the spread of digital technologies into the region.[106] In 2010, 37 percent of Tunisians and 22 percent of Egyptians used the internet, while 90 percent of Tunisians and two-thirds of Egyptians used mobile phones.[107] The

---

101. Dyczok 2014.

102. Controlling for age and gender, a Uniate who attended church regularly had a .38 probability of participating in Euromaidan, while a Uniate who did not attend church regularly had only a .20 probability. By contrast, a non-Uniate who attended church had only a .11 probability of participating, and a non-Uniate who did not attend church—only a .06 probability.

103. "Ukrainian Protest Project," as reported in Onuch 2014b.

104. Bohdanova 2014.

105. Gruzd and Tsyganova 2015.

106. Lynch 2006; Lynch 2011; Lynch 2012.

107. Data come from the World Bank, at https://data.worldbank.org/indicator/IT.NET.USER.ZS; Jorba and Bimber 2012, 17.

introduction of an Arabic version of Facebook in 2009 greatly accelerated the impact of social media and played an important role in both revolutions. Despite the regime's efforts to censor it, a vibrant internet culture, fed by blogger communities and connected to a large Tunisian diaspora abroad, emerged in Tunisia prior to the revolution. The initial protests in Sidi Bouzid were recorded by cellphone camera, posted on Facebook, picked up by the Tunisian diaspora, and disseminated back into the country.[108] Shortly thereafter, footage of the carnage from government repression of protestors in Kasserine went viral, fed by very high levels of Facebook usage among Tunisian youth. (In the Arab Barometer survey, 63 percent of Tunisians under the age of twenty-five reported having a Facebook page, as opposed to 18 percent of the rest of society.) One can debate whether the Tunisian Revolution would have been possible without Facebook, given the regime's heavy censorship of official media. Certainly, satellite television also played an important role in spreading information about the revolt, and no revolt ever succeeds simply because of communications technologies. But on whatever side of the debate one falls, it is difficult to deny that Facebook played an important role in the processes that unfolded during the revolution, or that the use of Facebook greatly facilitated the overthrow of the Ben Ali regime.[109]

In the years leading up to the Egyptian Revolution, high levels of television censorship drove many Egyptians to seek out news from satellite television and independent blogs. The brutal beating and murder of Egyptian blogger Khaled Said at the hands of the police in June 2010 inspired a Facebook page in his name that became a hive of opposition information and activity. It played an important role in communicating information about the initial protests of the revolution. The April 6 Movement, the key organizer of the January 25 protests, primarily coordinated the protest through Facebook and other social media. Video and photos from protests quickly found their way online and were shared globally. The Mubarak regime attempted to contain the power of digital communications by cutting off internet and cellular phone communication across Egypt for five days, though activists nonetheless found ways around the interruptions.[110]

Civil society associations were more important for coordinating revolutionary participation in Egypt, while digital coordination was more important for coordinating revolutionary protests in Tunisia. As we saw, 43 percent of Egyptian Revolution participants belonged to at least one civil society

---

108. Breuer, Landman, and Farquhar 2014.
109. See Ryan 2011.
110. Eltantawy and Wiest 2011. For evidence that the strategy backfired, see Hassanpour 2014.

association, as opposed to only 21 percent of Tunisian Revolution participants. While the Arab Barometer surveys contain no information on mobile phone use, they show that 64 percent of Tunisian Revolution participants and 51 percent of Egyptian Revolution participants were internet users.[111] There was also more hybridization of civil society membership and internet use among revolution participants in Egypt than in Tunisia. Accordingly, in the Egyptian Revolution, 59 percent of participants who were internet users were also members of a civil society association, while in Tunisia the corresponding figure was only 28 percent. The Arab Barometer surveys asked respondents about the sources of information that they relied on to follow the events of these revolutions. Whereas 33 percent of Tunisian Revolution participants replied that they relied primarily on internet-based sources (mostly Facebook), only 14 percent of Egyptian Revolution participants did so. The internet played an important role in coordinating early mobilizations in the Egyptian Revolution.[112] But as events unfolded and larger numbers of citizens became involved, television became the most important source of information for the vast majority of participants. Overall, 81 percent of participants in the Egyptian Revolution indicated that they relied primarily on television (largely Al Jazeera) for information about revolutionary protests; in Tunisia that proportion was 61 percent (a mix of Al Jazeera and French television).

Thus, conventional modes of communication and civil society organization coexist and hybridize with digital coordination in urban civic revolution, and urban civic revolutions have varied in the extent to which they are digitally or organizationally coordinated. The Orange Revolution (and to a lesser extent, the Egyptian Revolution) approximated more closely what Lance Bennett and Alexandra Segerberg label "organizationally-enabled connective action," whereby digital communication supplements civil society associations, which use the internet as a tool of coordination and mobilization, "relaxing their need to recruit and manage formal members and exclusively brand or frame their own campaigns." By contrast, Euromaidan and the Tunisian Revolution approximated more closely what Bennett and Segerberg call "crowd-enabled connective action." They were more digitally coordinated and coordinated less through civil society associations, with "few central organizations, few formal leaders, little in the way of brokered coalitions, and action frames that are

111. Mobile phone ownership was likely near-universal among participants in both revolutions. According to the Gallup poll, 91 percent of Egyptian revolution participants owned mobile phones. Mobile phones played an important role in documenting the revolution, spreading information to news organization, and for voice-to-voice communication. See Tufekci and Wilson 2012.

112. Clarke and Kocak 2020.

inclusive and individualized."[113] During the Tunisian Revolution, union activists played a role in spreading protests beyond Sidi Bouzid and in bringing them to Tunis. But they did so independently of their national unions, which had come under strict state control in the years leading up to revolt.[114]

Some have questioned whether digital coordination undermines commitment to high-risk collective action, which has generally been thought to require the presence of "strong" network ties (kinship relationships, friendships, and face-to-face personal relationships).[115] Studies have shown, however, that on average 80 percent of regular interpersonal digital communications across media platforms are with the same four or five individuals, with most communications revolving around the status of loved ones, family, and friends.[116] As one study of the effect of digital communications observed,

> The traditional human orientation to neighborhood- and village-based groups is moving towards communities that are oriented around geographically dispersed social networks. People communicate and maneuver in these networks rather than being bound up in one solidary community. Yet people's networks continue to have substantial numbers of relatives and neighbors—the traditional bases of community—as well as friends and workmates. The internet and email play an important role in maintaining these dispersed social networks.

As the study concluded, "The connectedness that the internet and other media foster within social networks has real payoffs: People use the internet to seek out others in their networks of contacts when they need help."[117]

Revolutionary crises are one such circumstance when people typically seek help from those in their extended networks. Contrary to the popular image of the internet as a community of strangers, revolutionary participation coordinated through the internet is actually more likely to occur along the lines of strong ties (that is, among groups of family and friends) than revolutionary participation that is not coordinated through the internet. Overall, 87 percent

---

113. Bennett and Segerberg 2013, 11–13. The quasi-revolutionary electoral protests in Russia in 2011–12 also represent an example of predominantly digital coordination. Overall, 70 percent of participants in the protests reported that they relied primarily on the internet as their main source of information about the protests; by contrast, 81 percent of the Russian population as a whole relied upon television as its main source of information about them. See Volkov 2012, 21.

114. Mabrouk 2011, 631; Beissinger, Jamal, and Mazur 2015.

115. Gladwell 2010.

116. Chambers 2013, 9.

117. Boase et al. 2006, i.

of participants in Egyptian Revolution protests had friends or family who also participated—compared to only 24 percent of those who did not participate. (In Tunisia the corresponding figures were 88 percent and 33 percent.) But 97 percent of revolutionary participants who primarily used the internet as their main source of information during the revolution indicated that their friends and family also participated—true for only 82 percent of other revolutionary participants; the figures for Tunisia were 96 percent and 81 percent respectively.[118] As Figure 7.13 shows, internet use during revolution magnified considerably the effects of strong ties. In Egypt, those who used the internet as their primary source of information during the revolution but did not have friends or family who participated had only a .06 probability of participating in the revolution's protests, while those who had friends or family who participated but did not use the internet as their main source of information had a .21 probability of doing so. But those who both used the internet and had family or friends who participated had a .46 probability of participating. Analogous patterns occurred in Tunisia.[119]

Some have argued that the fluidity of social media, with their easy entry and exit, imbues digital activism with a lack of commitment.[120] But internet-based participants in revolution participate more (not less) regularly than those who participate without relying on the internet. In the Egyptian Revolution, revolutionary participants who utilized the internet as their primary source of information participated in substantially more revolutionary demonstrations than revolutionary participants who did not.[121] Similar patterns occurred in the quasi-revolutionary electoral protests in Russia in 2011–12, where there was a strong, statistically significant relationship between whether a person used the internet as their primary source of information about the protests and the number of protests in which they participated.[122] In short, the digitalization of revolutionary mobilization does not necessarily translate into reduced commitment on the part of participants.

There are, however, a number of tendencies inherent in the urban civic model that digital coordination accentuates and exaggerates: fragmented political organization, diminished strategic coordination, diluted collective identities, and the condensed and compressed character of revolutionary collective

---

118. For Egypt, chi-square = 3.894, significant at the .05 level (with 1 degree of freedom). For Tunisia, chi-square = 9.518, significant at the .01 level (with 1 degree of freedom).

119. For both Egypt and Tunisia, statistically significant at the .001 level or better.

120. Van Laer 2010.

121. Participants using the internet participated on average in 1.18 more demonstrations during the revolution than participants who did not (statistically significant at the .001 level).

122. Beissinger 2017, 365.

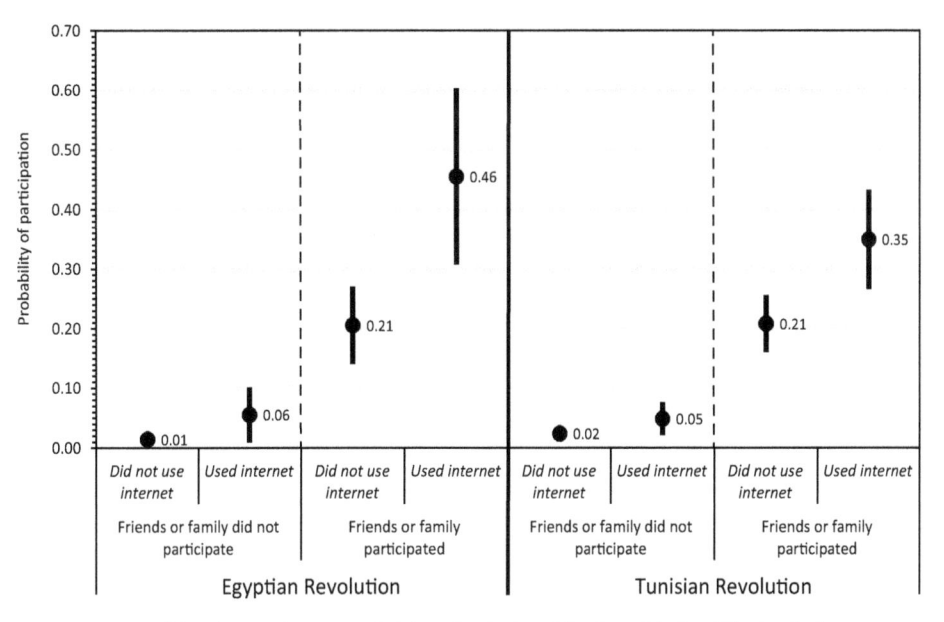

FIGURE 7.13. Probability of participation in revolutionary protests, by participation of friends or family and the use of internet as the primary source of information about the revolution (Egyptian and Tunisian revolutions). Multinomial logistic regression, controlling for gender and age. (For Egypt, a quadratic specification for age was used.) Point estimates, with 95 percent confidence intervals.

action. Bennett and Segerberg argue that digitally mediated networks allow large numbers of people to coordinate without a heavy organizational presence and without sharing common identities. Personal expression and self-motivation play larger roles than externally derived incentives in motivating action.[123] In the Euromaidan Revolution, for example, radical groups like Pravyi Sektor (Right Sector) came together relatively quickly through the internet in the midst of revolutionary mobilization, without much associational life prior to the onset of the revolutionary crisis. As a result of their weak connections with those on the square, conventional opposition politicians were distrusted by crowds on Maidan and had great difficulty controlling their actions. On a number of occasions, key events were driven by the radicalism of the crowds rather than by the leaders of opposition parties. Similarly, in the 2009 Iranian electoral uprising, angry Tehranis, coordinated largely by Twitter and other

123. Bennett and Segerberg 2013.

social media, began protesting and chanting "Death to the Dictator!" against the wishes of reformist leaders. The leaders had been denied a permit to hold a protest demonstration by the authorities, feared the possibility of violence, and attended these digitally coordinated protests in order to dissuade rather than encourage protestors. However, they lacked any ability to contain the internet-generated crowds, who clashed violently with riot police and the Basij paramilitary.[124] Thus, digital coordination injects an additional element of unpredictability into regime–opposition interactions during urban civic revolutions. As the Ukrainian and Iranian cases suggest, the inability of opposition groups to direct and restrain crowds increases the likelihood of crowd violence.

By diluting leadership, digital coordination also undermines strategic coordination. The most authoritative leaders of the quasi-revolutionary and largely digitally coordinated electoral protests in 2011–12 in Russia were not politicians, but a loose collection of bloggers and media personalities. A public opinion poll asked participants what they thought the movement's weakest points were. Topping the list (named by 49 percent of participants) was "the absence of a clear program of action," with 25 percent also naming "the disunity of the movement and conflicts among leaders" and another 23 percent naming "the absence of authoritative and influential figures."[125] Strategic vision for the movement was almost completely lacking. In Egypt and Tunisia as well, those coordinated exclusively through social media lacked the political organization necessary for mounting effective electoral campaigns in the wake of revolution, instead ceding the electoral field to more established Islamist parties organized along conventional civil society lines. Thus, digital coordination of revolutionary mobilization may reinforce the urban civic model by facilitating the mobilization of large numbers, but it does not provide a foundation for strategic coordination or for building stable political organization after revolution.

Finally, the identities nurtured by digitally coordinated revolutions are ad hoc, inclusive, and oppositional—amplifying tendencies toward fragmentation already inherent within the urban civic model. Indeed, in both the Orange and Euromaidan revolutions, participants who used the internet represented a somewhat more fragmented set of political groupings (as measured by Herfindahl indices) than participants who did not.[126] As Bennett and Segerberg

---

124. Kadivar 2018b.

125. See http://www.levada.ru/17-09-2012/opros-na-marshe-millionov-v-moskve-15-sentyabrya.

126. Thus, in the Orange Revolution, the Herfindahl index for revolution participants who did not use the internet was .221, while for those who used the internet it was .200. A higher Herfindahl index reflects less fragmentation. Similarly, for Euromaidan, the Herfindahl index

note, in digitally coordinated mobilization "the identity reference is more derived through inclusive and diverse largescale personal expression rather than through common group or ideological identification." Its central feature is its symbolic inclusiveness, in that "personal action frames are inclusive of different personal reasons for contesting a situation that needs to be changed" and focus attention not on "who are we" but "who are you"—that is, they orient diverse individuals toward the lowest common denominator of what they oppose rather than what they stand for.[127]

Conclusion: The Individual in the Urban Civic Revolutionary Crowd

Much about individual participation in revolutions is shaped by the proximity dilemma. As states have grown more powerful and cities have expanded in size, tactics that rely on the power of numbers in cities have come to predominate over tactics that rely on the power of arms. Unlike rural revolutions, which unfold over a protracted period of time among scattered populations and are carried out by hierarchical organizations, revolutions that depend on the power of numbers cannot monitor individuals, control who does or does not participate, provide significant selective incentives, or socialize participants into movement norms. This creates significant challenges for mobilizing populations and forces urban civic oppositions to rely instead on hastily assembled and highly diverse coalitions, an inclusive civic nationalism, and broadly "civic" minimalist demands of reclaiming the state from corrupt and abusive regimes—least common denominators that attract as many participants as possible.

This has significant consequences in terms of who participates in urban civic revolutions, what motivates participants, and how individuals who participate are connected to one another. To be sure, urban civic revolutionary crowds consist disproportionately of better resourced and better educated individuals and are built out of myriad nodes of family and friends—even when mobilization is digitally coordinated. But because these revolutions involve hastily constructed negative coalitions that pull in all who favor the

---

for revolution participants who did not use the internet was .251, while for those who used the internet it was .241. If one includes all digital media users (internet and cellphone) for Euromaidan, the differences in Herfindahl indices are still starker: .302 for those who were not digital media users, and .239 for those who were. In short, digitally coordinated participants were somewhat more politically fragmented than participants who were not digitally coordinated.

127. Bennett and Segerberg 2013, 40, 57–59.

removal of the incumbent regime irrespective of purpose, disaffection with government constitutes the glue holding revolutionary participants together—cemented further by shared symbols of civic nationhood. Though a democratic master-narrative predominated in all four of the revolutions examined in this chapter, participants were more frequently motivated by economic grievances and opposition to corruption than by a desire for political and civil liberties. They shared neither basic values nor common beliefs regarding the desired directions of public policy.

Thus, urban civic revolutions are better understood not as revolutions for democracy, but as revolutions against a corrupt and predatory political class. As we will see, the fragmentation inherent in urban civic crowds comes back to haunt these revolutions once they come to power. The new governments they bring to power find it difficult to build stable political organization, forge societal consensus, and sustain governing coalitions, rendering their durability and capacity to effect substantive change problematic.

8

The Pacification of Revolution

[V]iolence was the beginning and ... no beginning could be made without using violence, without violating.

HANNAH ARENDT, *ON REVOLUTION* (1965)[1]

UNTIL THE LAST DECADES of the twentieth century, large-scale violence was considered an inherent attribute of revolution—even an integral part of the definition of revolution itself.[2] Yet, the relationship between violence and revolution has never been straightforward. To be sure, social revolutions at times produced outsized numbers of deaths. An estimated one million people died during the Mexican Revolution from 1910 to 1917, three million during the Russian Revolution from 1917 to 1920, 2.1 million during the final phase of the Chinese Revolution from 1946 to 1949, and 790,000 during the Algerian Revolution from 1954 to 1962. Additionally, a number of the most horrific genocides of the twentieth century—the Armenian Genocide (1915–16), the Cambodian Genocide (1975–79), and the Rwandan Genocide (1994)—were closely associated with revolution.[3]

But even in social revolutions, deadly violence has varied considerably. Six cases (Russia, China, Mexico, Algeria, Vietnam, and Cambodia) account for 85 percent of deaths that occurred in social revolutionary contention over the last century. A quarter of all social revolutions in which the opposition succeeded in coming to power involved fewer than 2,100 deaths, and half involved fewer than twenty-five thousand deaths. While social revolutionary contention has produced more deaths than other forms of revolution, mass

---

1. Arendt 1965, 10.
2. Calvert 1967; Huntington 1968, 264; Dunn 1972, 12; Skocpol 1979; Johnson 1982.
3. Melson 1992; Straus 2006; Straus 2015; Kiernan 1996; Mayer 2000.

killing is also frequently due to actions taken by authorities to suppress social revolutionary challenges or by post-revolutionary regimes after they gained power as part of their efforts to transform their societies. Of the forty-four instances of mass killing ("politicide" and genocide) identified by the Political Instability Task Force from 1955 to 2017, more than two-thirds (68 percent) involved government efforts to counter revolutionary threats, 18 percent involved the use of terror by post-revolutionary governments after they gained power, and 7 percent involved the use of terror by revolutionary groups as a tactic for gaining power.[4] As Goldstone observed, "far more violence is committed by new revolutionary regimes after seizing power—in order to consolidate their control of society, or in civil wars between revolutionaries and counterrevolutionaries—than is committed by revolutionary actors against authorities before the latter are overthrown." Thus, violence in revolution should be seen as "complex and contingent, with old regimes, revolutionary oppositions, and new revolutionary regimes all capable of violence or nonviolence to varying degrees at different times."[5]

Once one moves beyond the social revolutionary world to the broader revolutionary universe, the association between revolution and deadly violence breaks down further. Thirty percent of successful revolutions since 1900 involved ten thousand deaths or more. By contrast, 42 percent involved fewer than one hundred. Only a tiny proportion of revolutionary episodes (5 percent) involve no fatalities whatsoever, though in these cases lesser degrees of violence invariably were present. Even in so-called nonviolent revolutions, street battles between police and crowds remain a frequent affair. Thus, the key questions that need to be addressed about the relationship of violence to revolution are not *whether* revolutions are violent, but rather *how much* violence they involve and what explains that variation.

As I show in this chapter, in general the number of people dying in revolutionary contention declined dramatically in the late twentieth and early twenty-first centuries. This decline in revolutionary mortality occurred despite increasing numbers of revolutionary episodes over the same period. Most of this decrease in lethal violence has been due to changes in the character and incidence of revolutionary civil war. But deaths in revolutionary contention not involving civil war have also declined substantially, suggesting broader

---

4. Genocide and politicide are defined by the Task Force as "the promotion, execution, and/or implied consent of sustained policies by governing elites or their agents—or in the case of civil war, either of the contending authorities—that result in the deaths of a substantial portion of a communal group or politicized non-communal group." The definition and list of cases are available at http://www.systemicpeace.org/inscrdata.html. See also Goldstone et al. 2010.

5. Goldstone 2003, 53–54.

structural forces at work. Enormous variation in the number of deaths in revolutionary contention remains. But looked at as a whole, revolutionary contention has grown remarkably less lethal.

I attempt to estimate some of the factors associated with this decline in revolutionary mortality. As we will see, a large part of the decline appears to be rooted in geopolitics: the end of the bipolar competition associated with the Cold War. But urbanization and the return of revolution to cities have also played important roles. As we have seen, the greater state capacity, economic development, global exposure, and increased visibility associated with urban location renders armed rebellion in cities problematic. The proliferation of the urban civic repertoire and its reliance on numbers rather than arms is a reflection of this. But so also is the sea-change that has taken place in the ways in which governments confront unarmed crowds in cities. Over time, civil wars have been fought with increasingly sophisticated weapons aimed at killing rebels more efficiently. By contrast, urban rebellion has moved in precisely the opposite direction. Fearful of the effects of lethal violence on populations in close proximity to centers of power, governments have progressively embraced less lethal technologies for controlling urban crowds. As a result, the risks involved in urban revolution have declined dramatically. By the late twentieth century, global norms had emerged concerning the use of deadly force against unarmed protesters, though their impact on revolutionary violence remains ambiguous. Nevertheless, as revolution has urbanized and as cities have grown in size, wealth, and power, mortality in revolution has diminished, and revolution has become seemingly more "civilized"—if by civilized we mean more pacified, more contained, and less tolerant of deadly violence on all sides.[6]

Revolutionary Mortality, 1900–2014

Table 8.1 provides statistics on mortality across the 325 revolutionary episodes from 1900 to 2014 for which information on deaths was available.[7] An estimated twenty-six million people died in revolutionary contention from 1900 to 2014; 48 percent of these deaths occurred in episodes that began during the first half of the twentieth century, and another 41 percent in episodes that

---

6. Elias 1994; Pinker 2011. For a study that places emphasis on the liberal international order as a source of the pacification of revolution, see Ritter 2015.

7. Information on the number of deaths for each revolutionary episode was drawn from a wide variety of sources. Estimates include both civilian and government deaths and were aggregated for the entire period of the episode. Divergent estimates were averaged. Data on deaths could not be found for eighteen cases; these cases were dropped from the analysis.

TABLE 8.1. Number of deaths in revolutionary episodes, by period of onset

Deaths category	1900–1949	1950–1984	1985–2014	Total
<=10 deaths	6.3%	7.7%	25.2%	13.9%
>10 and <=100 deaths	14.4%	9.9%	16.3%	13.9%
>100 and <=1,000 deaths	16.2%	12.1%	15.5%	14.8%
>1,000 and <= 10,000 deaths	28.8%	20.9%	22.0%	24.0%
>10,000 and <=50,000 deaths	14.4%	22.0%	8.9%	14.5%
>50,000 deaths	19.8%	27.5%	12.2%	19.1%
Total deaths in time period	12,067,089	10,725,404	2,833,791	25,626,284
Average deaths per episode	109,009	115,385	22,122	77,911
Median deaths per episode	2,700	9,567	149	2,100
n	111	91	123	325

began during the Cold War; only 11 percent died in revolutionary episodes that began during the post–Cold War period.[8] But as the table indicates, revolutionary episodes tended to be most violent during the Cold War, with 48 percent involving more than ten thousand deaths—compared to 34 percent during the first half of the twentieth century and only 21 percent in the post–Cold War period. By contrast, 42 percent of revolutionary episodes in the post–Cold War period involved a hundred or fewer deaths, as opposed to only 17 percent during the Cold War and 21 percent during the first half of the twentieth century. In all, deaths from revolutionary contention declined by almost 7.9 million during the post–Cold War period compared to the Cold War.

How does one explain this extraordinary falloff in lethal revolutionary violence? By and large, the explanation revolves around the changing character and incidence of revolutionary civil wars, which account for the overwhelming number of people who died in revolutionary contention. But as we will see, deaths in revolutions that have not involved civil wars (what I call in this chapter "contained revolutionary contention") have also been declining.

---

8. Ongoing episodes (nineteen cases, as of the end of 2014) were included in the analysis. All ongoing episodes have involved civil wars and produced significant numbers of deaths. Thus, the number of dead for the post–Cold War period is underestimated. But even if all of these cases eventually produced the average level of civil war deaths for other episodes during the post–Cold War period, total deaths from revolutionary episodes starting in that period would still only amount to a total of 3,854,972 fatalities (about a third of the deaths in either the first half of the twentieth century or the Cold War).

There is a large literature on the incidence and lethality of civil wars.[9] Much of that literature studies civil wars in isolation from the phenomenon of revolution. Not all civil wars are revolutionary by the definition used in this book; some are drug wars, while others are irredentist in character or involve struggles against recent foreign invaders rather than established governments. Moreover, many revolutionary episodes do not entail civil wars. In this respect, thinking about the role of civil war violence within revolutionary contention is a different exercise, with different purposes, from thinking about civil war violence in general.

Most of the literature on civil wars already defines a civil war by the number of deaths occurring in a conflict.[10] Obviously, if one is interested in explaining variability in deaths across revolutions, defining a civil war by the number of deaths involved would be circular. Accordingly, I define a civil war not by the number of people who died, but by the contentious process that it represents: as sustained armed combat between an opposition and an incumbent regime. The notion of war implies sustained armed conflict between two parties, with repeated battles and campaigns waged on multiple fronts—not a single battle or short-lived armed uprising. Some definitions of civil war emphasize the prolonged and widespread character of civil war conflict that distinguishes it from other forms of armed violence.[11] With this in mind, I operationalized the notion of sustained armed combat as armed combat that lasted for more than two months. Those episodes in which armed conflict lasted for more than two months were said to involve civil wars. Those that never involved armed conflict or that involved armed conflict that lasted for less than two months I classified as "contained" episodes. They were contained in the sense that their development into civil war remained blocked, prevented, or never contemplated.

There is obviously a degree of arbitrariness in the selection of the two-month threshold, just as there is an element of arbitrariness in the selection of the twenty-five or one thousand annual battle-deaths threshold for defining civil war that dominates much of the civil wars literature.[12] I chose the

---

9. For studies of the onset of civil wars, see Collier and Hoeffler 2004; Barbieri and Reuveny 2005; Fearon and Laitin 2003; Ross 2006; Gleditsch 2007; Cederman, Wimmer, and Min 2010. For studies examining deaths in civil wars, see Lacina 2006; Kalyvas 2006; Weinstein 2006; Heger and Salehyan 2007; Balcells and Kalyvas 2014.

10. The Correlates of War (COW) definition requires one thousand cumulative battle deaths, while the Armed Conflict Dataset (ACD) definition requires a minimum of twenty-five battle deaths per year. See Singer and Small 1994; Gleditsch et al. 2002.

11. See Gersovitz and Kriger 2013; Florea 2012.

12. See Sambanis 2004.

two-month threshold after a careful examination of revolutionary episodes and as a way of distinguishing civil wars from single-event armed rebellions that end quickly in victory or defeat but do not evolve into sustained armed combat. In cases like the 1919 Spartacist Uprising in Germany (three thousand dead over ten days of rebellion), the 1920 Ruhr Uprising in Germany (1,500 dead over thirty-one days), the 1928 Kampang Buluh Uprising in British-controlled Malaysia (a thousand dead over eleven days), the 1932 APRA Rebellion in Peru (2,500 dead over five days), the 1952 MNR Revolution in Bolivia (six hundred dead over eight days), the 1956 revolution in Hungary (3,200 dead over twenty days), the 1989 Romanian Revolution (1,100 dead over thirteen days), or Black January in 1990 in Azerbaijan (282 dead over thirteen days), armed uprisings were intense but brief, as rebels either quickly succeeded in overturning the incumbent regime or were swiftly repressed. The contained character of violence in these cases better qualifies them as armed uprisings than as civil wars. Civil war involves sustained combat precisely because neither side has the ability to defeat the other completely through the immediate application of force. In contained revolutionary conflict, by contrast, one side—the government or the opposition—is swiftly defeated, usually in a matter of days. On average revolutionary episodes with civil wars lasted a little over nine years (with a median of 4.5 years). Some revolutionary civil wars lasted as long as thirty-five to forty years.[13] By contrast, most armed uprisings that do not develop into civil war by my definition last less than twenty-three days. They might have developed into civil wars had neither side been able to defeat the other. But for a variety of reasons (urban location being one of them) this did not occur.[14]

There are clearly limits to the number of people who can be killed in armed revolutionary combat in sixty days. Not surprisingly, the presence of civil war by this definition (i.e., sustained armed combat) is the single most powerful factor associated with mortality in revolution.[15] Overall, 63 percent of revolutionary episodes that involved civil wars resulted in more than ten thousand

---

13. Examples of particularly long-lasting civil wars include the Guatemalan Civil War, the Colombian Civil War, the Moro Rebellion, the Manipur Insurgency, and the Shan State Rebellion.

14. Thus, 76 percent of armed uprisings that did not develop into civil wars occurred primarily in cities.

15. In contrast to much of the civil wars literature, I include all deaths associated with revolutionary contention—not only battlefield deaths, but also civilian deaths. Moreover, in accordance with my definition of revolution, the sampling frame for revolutionary civil wars used here excludes the drug wars, irredentist conflicts, and resistance to foreign invasion that are typically included in datasets of civil wars.

deaths (with 38 percent resulting in more than fifty thousand deaths). By contrast, 55 percent of contained episodes produced fewer than a hundred deaths. In this respect, selection into civil war is critical for explaining patterns of revolutionary lethality.

In the analysis that follows, I unpack some of the factors associated with the decline in lethal violence in revolutions since 1900 and estimate the degree to which each of these factors is responsible for the overall decline in revolutionary mortality. I divide my analysis into three parts: first, variation in levels of mortality within civil wars; second, variation in the likelihood that a revolutionary episode selected into civil war; and third, variation in patterns of mortality in contained episodes that did not involve civil wars.

There is obviously a great deal of endogeneity built into these processes. The process of selecting into civil war is related to the processes producing deaths within each of these modes of contention. Failure to account for these selection effects would produce biased estimates of the factors associated with each.[16] Thus, for this analysis, I employed an endogenous switching model.[17] This is one of a number of selection models appropriate for situations in which the relationship between an outcome of interest and a set of explanatory factors varies across two discrete regimes. In the well-known Heckman selection model, only one of two regimes is observed, and the model corrects for this selection bias. By contrast, in the endogenous switching model, two regimes are observed (in this case, deaths in revolutionary episodes with and without civil wars), and the analysis models the outcomes within each regime, taking into account the effects of the sorting process between them. Like all selection models, an assumption of the endogenous switching model is the joint normality of the error terms, though this assumption is often violated.[18] Statisticians have found ways to correct for these violations by using copulas (coupling functions that transform a joint probability distribution into uniform marginal values).[19] The copula-based endogenous switching model that I use in this chapter estimates the effects on revolutionary mortality due to factors associated with selection into civil war, as well as the effects of factors associated with mortality within revolutionary civil wars and in episodes not involving civil war—correcting for violations of joint normality that otherwise would yield inconsistent estimates.[20]

---

16. Maddala and Nelson 1975.
17. For more details on the endogenous switching model, see Appendix 4E.
18. Moffitt 1999, 1390–93; Bushway, Johnson, and Slocum 2007.
19. See Lee 1983; Smith 2003; Bhat and Eluru 2009; Hasebe 2013.
20. Manning and Mullahy 2001. As deaths in revolutionary contention vary tremendously across episodes (ranging from zero to three million), the natural log of deaths was used as the

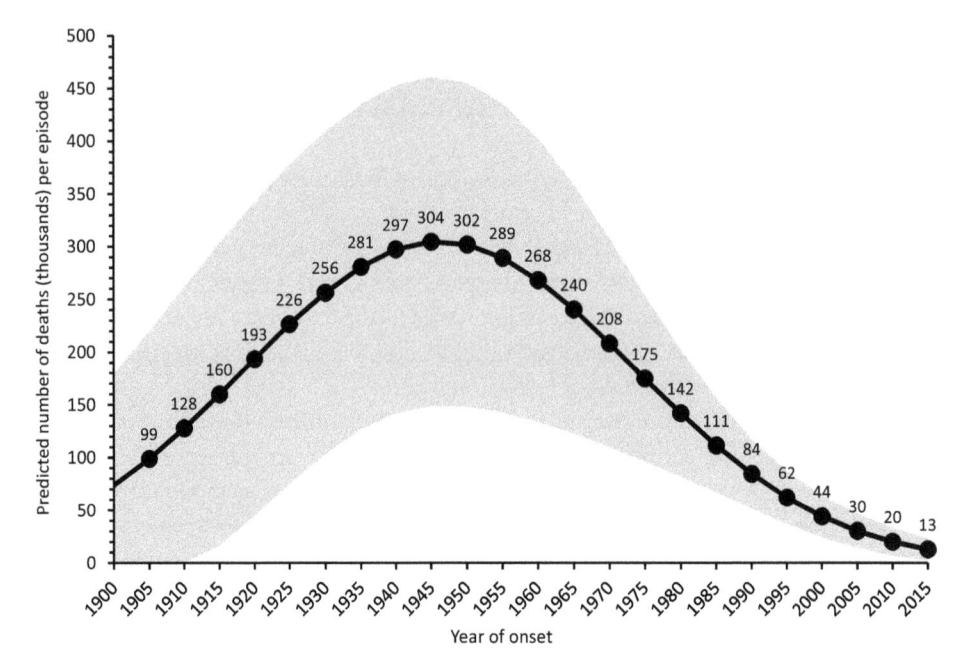

FIGURE 8.1. Average predicted deaths (thousands) per revolutionary episode involving civil war, by year of episode onset. Average marginal predictions (GLM estimation, using log link and gamma variance function), with 95 percent confidence intervals and robust standard errors (n = 162 episodes).

Of course, the model should be understood as merely a rough estimation. Much of what it tells us depends on the types of measures available to capture key processes, and these are quite limited. Nevertheless, the model does provide an opportunity to gain some leverage on the types of factors shaping the decline in revolutionary mortality over the long term, and geopolitics, urbanization, and the return of revolution to cities play important roles in this story.

Changing Mortality within Revolutionary Civil Wars

Changes in the nature of civil warfare and the conditions under which revolutionary civil wars were fought account for a large portion of the decline in mortality in revolutions during the post–Cold War years. As Figure 8.1 shows, heightened mortality in revolutionary civil wars was a particular phenomenon of the mid-twentieth

---

dependent variable, back-transforming the results into numbers of deaths. For purposes of comparison, I also report alternative estimates produced by a GLM model that uses the raw number of deaths rather than its logged form. It does not take into account selection effects.

century. Civil wars during the post–Cold War years were significantly less deadly on average than at any time during the prior century. The number of deaths in revolutionary episodes involving civil wars rose sharply in the wake of World War I, peaking in the 1940s and 1950s, declining gradually over the rest of the Cold War, and then falling off to significantly lower levels in the post–Cold War period.[21] The narrowing confidence intervals for the post–Cold War period in Figure 8.1 indicate declining variation in the lethality of civil war combat.

A dramatic leap in mortality in revolutionary civil wars began during the first half of the twentieth century with the Mexican Revolution (over one million deaths) and accelerated during the Bolshevik Revolution and Civil War (over three million deaths). The Mexican Revolution and the Russian Civil War were some of the first conflicts to apply the infinitely more lethal weaponry of industrial warfare characteristic of World War I to the practice of civil war (machine guns, modern artillery, aerial bombardment, armored trains, etc.).[22] In many ways the Russian Revolution and Civil War has been rightly considered an extension of the total warfare of the First World War. The Bolshevik Revolution also utilized new political technologies of mass mobilization, engaging a large portion of the population in revolutionary conflict. In both conflicts, the carnage was further magnified by the extreme division and complexity of the contending sides. Both conflicts were also highly internationalized, with European and American powers intervening and reinforcing the warring parties. All of these factors rendered these revolutions unusually deadly. A series of social revolutions in the middle of the twentieth century—the Chinese Revolution and Civil War (two million dead from 1927 to 1936, and another 2.1 million dead from 1946 to 1949), the Vietnamese Revolution (645,000 dead from 1945 to 1954), and the Algerian National Revolution (790,000 dead from 1954 to 1962)—also accounted for massive numbers of casualties, marking the high point of revolutionary civil war mortality in the bloody twentieth century. But with the end of the Cold War, revolutionary civil wars grew markedly less lethal. On average, during the first half of the twentieth century revolutionary civil wars produced 223,000 deaths, and during the Cold War 175,000. By contrast, revolutionary civil wars in the post–Cold War period averaged fifty-eight thousand deaths.[23]

21. For similar findings in the civil wars literature, see Lacina 2006; Lacina, Gleditsch, and Russell 2006; Buhaug et al. 2008; Melander, Öberg, and Hall 2009; Einsidel 2014.

22. On Russia, see Holquist 2002. On Mexico, see Jowett and Quesada 2013. For evidence that conventional civil wars are particularly lethal on the battlefield, see Kalyvas and Balcells 2010; Balcells and Kalyvas 2014.

23. The Rwandan Civil War and Genocide (eight hundred thousand dead from 1990 to 1994) was the only conflict during the post–Cold War period to rival the bloodshed of the most intense mid-twentieth century revolutions.

What explains this sharp decline in the lethality of revolutionary civil wars from the Cold War to the post–Cold War era? I used the endogenous switching model to identify factors associated with deaths in revolutionary civil wars, controlling for selection effects. I then employed the model to engage in a counterfactual analysis aimed at estimating deaths in revolutionary civil wars in the post–Cold War period had the conditions associated with mortality in civil wars been the same as prevailed during the Cold War period. I then compared that to deaths associated with the actual conditions of the post–Cold War period to estimate how the changes in the factor concerned may have affected revolutionary mortality. Details on the how these estimates were produced can be found in Appendix 4E.

Table 8.2 presents the results of the civil war portion of the endogenous switching model and the estimated counterfactual differences. It shows that the changing duration of revolutionary civil wars was powerfully associated with the decline in revolutionary mortality in civil wars during the post–Cold War period. The Cold War period witnessed high levels of fatality in revolutionary civil wars due in significant part to the ways in which superpower competition prolonged conflict by fortifying the opposing sides with weapons and support. The duration of revolutionary civil wars increased dramatically during the Cold War thanks to the availability of significant amounts of foreign weaponry and aid, allowing both sides in a conflict to persist. Revolutionary civil wars during the first half of the twentieth century lasted on average four years and seven months. By contrast, those that began during the Cold War lasted on average fifteen years and one month—that is, more than three times longer. The end of the Cold War caused a marked decline in the duration of revolutionary civil wars, with the average duration dropping to six years and three months. Other studies have also shown that the duration of conflict is strongly associated with the number of deaths produced in a civil war.[24] Controlling for the effects of other factors associated with mortality in civil war and for selection into civil war, the switching model estimates that the shorter length of civil wars was associated with approximately 2.9 million fewer deaths in the post–Cold War years (or 38 percent of the total decline in deaths from revolution that occurred after the end of the Cold War).[25]

---

24. Lacina 2006. Kalyvas and Balcells provide evidence that the shifting durations associated with the end of the Cold War were also closely connected with changes in technologies of warfare. See Kalyvas and Balcells 2010; Balcells and Kalyvas 2014.

25. The GLM model finds a significantly lower but still quite substantial decline in deaths due to changing civil war duration: 2.1 million.

TABLE 8.2. Estimated impact of changing conditions of contention on deaths in revolutionary civil wars, Cold War vs post–Cold War periods

	Endogenous switching model ("civil war" portion of model only)[a]							Estimated effect on deaths, 1985–2014 vs 1950–1984 (Model 3)	Percentage of total change in deaths, 1985–2014 vs 1950–1984
Variable	Model 1	Model 2	Model 3[b]	Model 4[b]	Model 5[b]	Model 6	Model 7		
Duration of civil war (in months)	1.457 (2.72)**	1.802 (3.85)***	1.784 (3.97)***	1.747 (3.87)***	1.736 (3.85)***	1.781 (3.93)***	1.902 (4.08)***	−2,978,943	−37.7%
Level of urbanization, t−1		0.971 (−2.34)*	0.971 (−2.44)*	0.972 (−2.39)*	0.972 (−2.45)*	0.971 (−2.37)*	0.970 (−2.53)*	−1,454,948	−18.4%
Opposition victory			3.244 (3.12)**	2.922 (2.85)**	3.379 (3.29)**	3.261 (3.10)**	3.108 (3.00)**	−867,369	−11.0%
Polity score, t−1				0.951 (−1.71)+					
Population size (in population, t−1)					1.280 (1.91)+				
Aimed at altering ethnic/racial order						0.964 (−0.09)			
Social revolutionary episode							0.646 (−1.05)		
n	308 (150)	230 (93)	230 (93)	230 (93)	230 (93)	230 (93)	230 (93)		

(Continued)

TABLE 8.2. (*continued*)

Endogenous switching model ("civil war" portion of model only)[a]

Variable	Model 1	Model 2	Model 3[b]	Model 4[b]	Model 5[b]	Model 6	Model 7	Estimated effect on deaths, 1985–2014 vs 1950–1984 (Model 3)	Percentage of total change in deaths, 1985–2014 vs 1950–1984
Akaike Information Criterion (AIC)[c]	1186.571	1183.191	1175.817	1174.940	1174.257	1177.808	1176.726		
Bayesian Information Criterion (BIC)[c]	1241.581	1241.638	1237.702	1240.263	1239.580	1243.132	1242.049		
sigma(1)	2.056	1.908	1.827	1.799	1.792	1.826	1.818		
theta(1)	−0.315	1.000	1.000	1.000	1.000	1.000	1.000		
Kendall's tau(1)	0.070	−0.222	−0.222	−0.222	−0.222	−0.222	−0.222		
LR test (independence of errors)	4.292+	5.846*	8.298**	7.972*	8.362**	7.801*	8.578**		
Estimated total impact of factors on deaths in civil wars								−5,301,260	−67.2%
Actual decline in deaths, post–Cold War period vs Cold War period								−7,891,613	−100%

[a]Coefficients with z-scores in parentheses. Copulas used were Clayton and FGM (Farlie-Gumbel-Morgenstern), with a normal marginal distribution of the error terms. All parameters were calculated using the switchcopula command written by Hasebe 2013.

[b]Likelihood ratio tests indicate that one cannot conclude with confidence that Model 4 is a better fit than Model 3, chi2(1) = 2.88, p = 0.0899 or that Model 5 is a better fit than Model 3, chi2(1) = 3.56, p = 0.0592.

[c]Performed on a common sample of n = 230 (93).

+ $p < 0.10$, * $p < 0.05$, ** $p < 0.01$, *** $p < 0.001$

Urbanization and development also exercised significant effects on revolutionary mortality in civil wars. Several studies suggest that urbanization reduces the risk of occurrence of civil war.[26] But the concentration of people, power, and wealth in cities also constrains mortality within a civil war once it has broken out. For one thing, state capacity is greater in societies that are more urbanized,[27] constraining the ability of oppositions to contest power through civil war and reducing the intensity of civil war conflict when it does occur. Urbanization is also closely associated with economic development.[28] The more urban and developed a society is, the more disruptive civil war is to economic life, creating strong incentives for political elites to contain the destruction. And as the literature on civil wars has suggested, the more developed a society, the less incentive populations might have to join rebel groups.[29]

But there are other reasons why urbanization might lead to a decline in deaths during civil wars. As Sassen notes, "killing civilians in a city is a different type of horror from killing people—far more people—in the jungle and in villages."[30] The visibility of violence in urban contexts acts as a deterrent. Kalyvas notes that much violence in rural areas is invisible, with deaths remaining largely hidden from the media and from international observers.[31] Rural rebellions are dominated by less literate populations who have difficulty making atrocities in the countryside known to a wider audience. The inaccessibility of these revolts also limits the presence of outside observers. By contrast, the presence of media and foreign observers in cities renders violence within them more visible to the country as a whole and to the international community, making massacres in urban environments harder to carry out and more politically consequential. These effects have been greatly magnified by digital communications, which have transformed the ability of oppositions to document and share images of urban revolutionary violence across the globe.

Thus, controlling for other factors associated with mortality in revolution and selection into civil war, the endogenous switching model indicates a substantive and statistically significant negative relationship between urbanization on the eve of revolutionary contention and the number of deaths occurring in a revolutionary civil war. On average, societies experiencing revolutionary

---

26. Urdal 2008; Collier and Hoeffler 2004; Auvinen 1997.

27. The Hanson/Sigman state capacity index is correlated with urbanization ($r=.54$).

28. Across more than twelve thousand country-year observations for 164 countries for which information is available, urbanization and GDP per capita have a .68 correlation.

29. Fearon and Laitin 2003; Collier and Hoeffler 2004; Hegre and Sambanis 2006; Blattman and Miguel 2010, 33.

30. Sassen 2011, 577.

31. Kalyvas 2004, 165.

civil wars during the Cold War were 16 percent urban. By contrast, those experiencing revolutionary civil wars in the post–Cold War period were 27 percent urban. The effect of this, according to the model, would have been to reduce the number of deaths in revolutions after the Cold War by approximately 1.5 million (or 18 percent of the actual total decline in revolutionary mortality in the post–Cold War period).[32]

Other factors are also associated with mortality in revolutionary civil wars. Civil wars in which the opposition prevails, for instance, tend to be more deadly than those in which the opposition loses.[33] In civil wars in which the opposition wins, combat penetrates more deeply into populated urban zones controlled by the incumbent regime, heightening casualties. There were fewer revolutionary civil wars in the post–Cold War period that the opposition won than during the Cold War (sixteen and twenty-one, respectively). The estimated effect would have been to reduce revolutionary mortality by another 867,000 (or 11 percent of the total decline after the Cold War).[34]

I tested for the effects of a series of other factors often thought to be associated with mortality in civil wars but found no consistent relationships. Other studies have found that the degree of openness/closedness of a regime is related to the number of people who die in civil wars,[35] as more closed governments are more willing to use indiscriminate violence against oppositions and civilians. I found only a marginally significant effect.[36] Larger populations experiencing revolutionary civil wars might have been expected to produce larger numbers of fatalities; but as other studies have found, population size was only marginally related to civil war deaths in the endogenous switching model.[37] Social revolutions and ethnic civil wars are both thought to involve higher levels of mortality than other types of conflicts. But controlling for selection effects and the influence of other factors, I found no relationship. It is

---

32. The GLM model finds an even stronger impact for urbanization on civil war deaths—a decline of 1.9 million deaths after the Cold War.

33. In a one-sided t-test, t = −3.3269, significant at the .001 level.

34. In the GLM model, opposition victory was associated with 852,000 fewer deaths.

35. Lacina 2006; Heger and Salehyan 2007. On the general relationship between collective violence and regime-type, see Tilly 2003.

36. A likelihood-ratio test showed that the inclusion of Polity scores did not substantially improve the model. In the GLM model, Polity score was not statistically significant.

37. Again, a likelihood-ratio test showed that the inclusion of population size did not improve the model. For a similar finding, see Lacina 2006. Population size was statistically significant in the GLM model and associated with an increase of 643,000 deaths in the post–Cold War period due to the larger populations subjected to civil war violence.

true that, on average, more people have died in social revolutions than in any other type of revolution. But much of the reason for this has been that social revolutionary civil wars have been longer than other civil wars[38]—particularly after social revolutions migrated to the countryside. Controlling for duration, neither social revolution nor ethnic civil wars produced more deaths than would otherwise have been expected.[39] As we will see, however, both do influence revolutionary mortality through their impact on selection processes.

In all, the model projected that 5.3 million fewer deaths in the post–Cold War period (or 67 percent of the estimated actual decline in revolutionary mortality after the Cold War) can be accounted for by three factors: a decline in the duration of civil war conflicts; increased levels of urbanization in the societies experiencing civil wars; and changing patterns of opposition success. Most of the decline was due to the changing duration of civil wars due to the end of Cold War competition. But urbanization and development played substantial roles as well.

Selection Effects and Deaths in Revolutionary Civil Wars

Part of the decline in mortality in revolutionary contention after the Cold War was due to changing selection into civil war—in particular, a sharp drop in the probability that revolutionary contention involved civil war. Clearly, the decision to embark upon civil war rests in part on choices made by revolutionaries and incumbent leaders. For instance, after revolutionary crowds stormed his presidential palace in the 1986 People Power Revolution in the Philippines, Ferdinand Marcos seriously contemplated embarking on an armed struggle from his home province of Ilocos Norte in order to regain power, as his wife Imelda and some of his close associates were urging him to do. Many believed that Marcos had the capability to wage and even win such a war, bloody as it would have been. But the aging dictator was more interested in preserving his wealth and image than in engaging in a protracted fight for power. He demanded only that the revolutionary opposition issue a statement praising him for all he had done for the country—after which he promptly packed up and fled, taking much of his fortune with him.[40] Critical junctures like this abound in the politics of revolution. But other factors also determine whether armed

---

38. In a two-tailed t-test, $t = -4.358$, significant at the .001 level.

39. Some ethnic civil wars did not qualify as revolutionary by the definition used in this book, as they were focused on irredentist goals. But for those that were revolutionary, they lasted about as long as other civil wars on average.

40. Johnson 1987, 268–69.

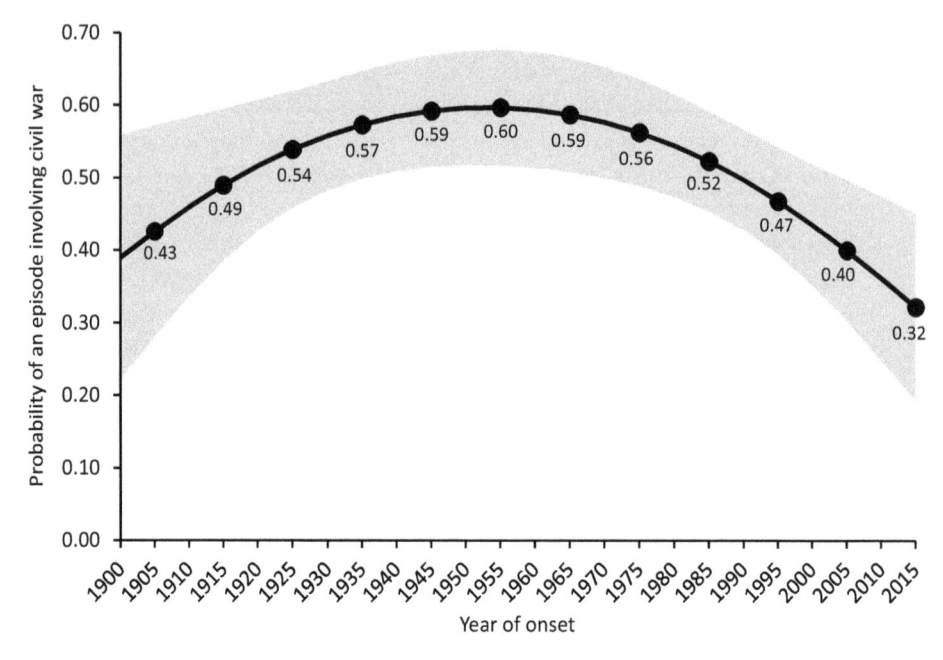

FIGURE 8.2. The probability of a revolutionary episode involving civil war, by year of episode onset. Average marginal predictions (logistic regression) with 95 percent confidence intervals (n = 343 episodes).

combat, once embarked upon, will become sustained. Clearly, an imbalance of force between regimes and insurgents should make a large difference, as this would likely lead to the rapid victory of one side. The ability of insurgents to hide from superior government forces, on the other hand, should make rapid victory harder and be more likely lead into civil war.

As Figure 8.2 shows, the probability that a revolutionary episode developed into a civil war rose sharply over the first half of the twentieth century, reaching a peak during the Cold War years, and then dropping precipitously thereafter. At the height of the Cold War, three-fifths of revolutionary episodes involved civil wars. By the early 2000s, that proportion had dropped to about a third.

I again used the endogenous switching model to explore further the effect of selection into civil war on changing mortality in revolutions. I identified factors associated with whether revolution did or did not assume civil war form and then employed the model to estimate what the effect on mortality would be had Cold War conditions prevailed in the post–Cold War period, calculating the difference between this and the effects of these factors at actual post–Cold War levels (again, details can be found in Appendix 4E). The results (presented in Table 8.3) show that the location of contention and the character of revolutionary goals constituted the most important factors shaping selection into civil war—specifically, the rural or urban location of revolutionary contention, whether an opposition articulated goals of class transformation, and whether the opposition articulated goals of altering an ethnic or racial order.[41] In all, the effect of these three factors on selection into civil war accounted for about a quarter of the total estimated decline in deaths from revolutionary contention during the post–Cold War years.

As we have seen, armed revolt in cities is particularly dangerous for rebels, because it occurs where the coercive capacity of the state is strongest. By the middle of the twentieth century, most armed revolutionary challengers chose instead to utilize the rough terrain of the countryside for protection against government retaliation. A large proportion of armed rebellions occurring in cities (43 percent) have lasted only two months or less (as opposed to only 8 percent of rural armed rebellions). As a result, civil wars unfolding primarily in cities are much rarer than civil wars taking place primarily in the countryside. Only 19 percent of urban revolutionary episodes have involved civil wars, compared to 87 percent of rural episodes.[42] Thus, the difference between deaths in civil wars and deaths outside of civil wars closely corresponds to the urban/rural divide in revolution. Over time, the proportion of urban revolutions involving civil wars has declined, roughly halving from 22 percent between 1900 and 1984 to 11 percent since 1985. As cities grew in size and states became more powerful, civil war came to occupy a reduced role within urban revolutionary practice due to the disruption and destruction involved, the stacked odds against armed rebellion in cities, and the growing possibilities for unarmed rebellion relying on the power of numbers. Controlling for other factors, the estimated overall effect on revolutionary mortality of the return of revolution to the city in the post–Cold War period would have been a drop of approximately 664,000 deaths compared to the Cold War period (or 8 percent of the total decline in revolutionary deaths after the Cold War).

Declining selection into civil war was also very much a product of a broader shift in the goals of revolutionary contention after the Cold War. Social revolutionary episodes were particularly prone to selection into civil war because attempts to transform the class structure of society encountered violent resistance from propertied classes and governments, necessitating armed rebellion

---

41. In a separate probit estimation on all 343 revolutionary episodes, these three factors alone correctly identified whether civil war occurred in 85 percent of episodes and accounted for 89 percent of the area under the curve—a relatively accurate record of prediction.

42. For exceptions, see Staniland 2010.

TABLE 8.3. Estimated impact of selection processes into or away from civil war on deaths in revolutions in the Cold War and post–Cold War periods

Endogenous switching model (selection portion of model only)[a]

Variable	Model 1	Model 2	Model 3	Model 4	Model 5	Model 6	Estimated change in number of deaths, 1985–2014 vs 1950–1984 (Model 3)	Percentage of total change in deaths, 1985–2014 vs 1950–1984
Rural/urban location of episode	0.106 (−10.04)***	0.102 (−9.52)***	0.110 (−9.12)***	0.111 (−9.07)***	0.118 (−8.51)***	0.117 (−8.67)***	−664,218	−8.4%
Episode aimed at altering ethnic/racial order		3.792 (5.24)***	4.477 (5.57)***	4.496 (5.62)***	4.356 (5.36)***	4.53 (5.50)***	+560,234	+7.1%
Social revolutionary episode			1.743 (2.44)*	1.723 (2.39)*	1.73 (2.36)*	1.705 (2.31)*	−1,708,210	−21.6%
Polity score, t−1				1.014 (0.82)				
GDP per cap. ($ thousands), t−1					0.950 (−1.13)			
Ln (oil production), t−1						0.972 (−1.16)		
Dummy for major diamond producer						1.628 (1.26)		

n	230 (93)	230 (93)	230 (93)	230 (93)	230 (93)	228 (92)
Akaike Information Criterion (AIC)[b]	1196.037	1172.261	1168.497	1169.752	1169.174	1169.932
Bayesian Information Criterion (BIC)[b]	1250.907	1230.559	1230.225	1234.910	1234.332	1238.519
LR test (independence of errors)	1.575	7.831*	8.298**	8.748**	6.97*	9.588**
Estimated total impact						−1,812,193
Actual decline in deaths						−7,891,613

	−23.0%
	−100%

[a]Coefficients with z-scores in parentheses. Copulas used were Clayton and FGM (Farlie-Gumbel-Morgenstern), with a normal marginal distribution of the error terms. All parameters were calculated using the switchcopula command written by Hasebe 2013.

[b]Computed on common sample of 228 observations for purposes of comparison.

+ p<0.10, * p<0.05, ** p<0.01, *** p<0.001

on the part of revolutionary oppositions. Social revolutions had a .63 probability of developing into civil war, compared to only .47 for all other episodes. As we saw in chapter 2, as social revolutionary contention declined, urban civic revolutionary contention proliferated. These episodes had an extremely low probability (.09) of selecting into civil war, largely because they relied on the power of numbers rather than the power of arms (though repression has at times pushed urban civic oppositions into armed rebellion). Controlling for the effects of other factors on civil war deaths, the shift of revolutionary practice away from social revolution toward urban civic contention after the Cold War exerted a powerful effect on revolutionary mortality through selection into civil war, lowering deaths by approximately 1.7 million (or 22 percent of the total decline in revolutionary mortality).

As many have pointed out, the rise of ethnic civil wars after the Cold War cut in the opposite direction, increasing the number of deaths in revolution. Revolutionary contention aimed at altering an ethnic or racial order has had a strong tendency (a .78 probability) to select into civil war due to the ways in which these conflicts challenge the dominance of privileged ethnic groups.[43] Rebellions against central governments dominated by minority ethnic groups have been particularly likely to involve civil war, as minority-dominated governments are reluctant to incorporate majority demands for power-sharing.[44] Through its influence on selection into civil war, the multiplication of revolutionary contention challenging ethnic or racial domination after the Cold War was associated with an additional 560,000 revolutionary deaths (a 7 percent increase in revolutionary mortality).

Mortality in Revolutionary Episodes without Civil Wars ("Contained" Episodes)

Taken together, factors associated with the incidence and severity of civil war in the endogenous switching model accounted for about 90 percent of the total actual decline in revolutionary deaths after the Cold War. Two factors in particular stand out: geopolitical change and urbanization. The end of the Cold War affected the conduct of civil war by leading to markedly shorter wars. It also contributed to the marginalization of social revolution, thereby reducing selection into civil war. Simply in these two ways, geopolitical change may have led to as many as 4.7 million fewer deaths from revolution in the post–Cold War period (59 percent of the total estimated decline in

---

43. For a similar finding, see Eck 2009.
44. Cederman, Wimmer, and Min 2010; Collier 2003, 57–63.

revolutionary mortality). But the growing concentration of people, power, and wealth in cities also appears to have exercised a major effect on revolutionary mortality. It enhanced state capacity, increased demand for containing the economic fallout from civil war, altered revolutionary repertoires, reduced incentives to join rebel groups, and created constraints on government use of violence by rendering it more visible to citizens and the outside world. As a result of the shifting proportion of revolutionary episodes located in cities, revolutionary contention was much less likely to assume civil war form due to the overwhelming presence of the state's coercive apparatus. These factors were associated with as many as 2.1 million fewer deaths from revolution (or 27 percent of the total decline in revolutionary mortality after the Cold War).

Although they account for far fewer deaths, revolutionary episodes that did not involve civil wars ("contained" revolutionary contention) have also experienced a decline in mortality over time (Figure 8.3). In contrast to deaths in civil wars, this decrease was gradual, beginning in the 1930s and continuing over the post–Cold War period. Thus, in the first half of the twentieth century, 36 percent of these contained episodes experienced a thousand or more deaths. During the Cold War, that proportion fell to 23 percent, and in the post–Cold War era to 13 percent.[45] Contained episodes that involved more than a hundred deaths similarly dropped from 62 percent in the 1900–49 period, to 47 percent from 1950 to 1984, to 32 percent from 1985 to 2014. At the same time, the proportion of contained episodes that involved ten deaths or fewer rose from 12 percent in the first half of the twentieth century, to 23 percent during the Cold War era, to 41 percent in the post–Cold War period. As the confidence intervals in Figure 8.3 indicate, there was also much greater variability in deaths in contained episodes in the first half of the twentieth century than in the late twentieth and early twenty-first centuries.

Applying the same method, I used the endogenous switching model to identify factors associated with mortality in contained revolutionary contention (controlling for selection effects) and estimated the impact of these factors on revolutionary mortality (Table 8.4). In this case, given the gradual

---

45. In the first half of the twentieth century, six episodes that did not involve civil wars (by the definition used in this study) resulted in ten thousand deaths or more: the 1905 Revolution in Russia, the 1911 Xinhai Revolution in China, the August 1924 Uprising in Soviet Georgia, La Matanza in 1932 in El Salvador, the 1945 Setif Uprising in French-controlled Algeria, and the 228 Uprising in 1947 in Taiwan. Since 1947, only one episode without civil war involved more than ten thousand deaths: the 1991 Uprising in Iraq, in which Iraqi Arabs and Kurds revolted against Saddam Hussein in the aftermath of the Gulf War. This uprising is not classified as a civil war since it lasted only thirty-six days before it was crushed.

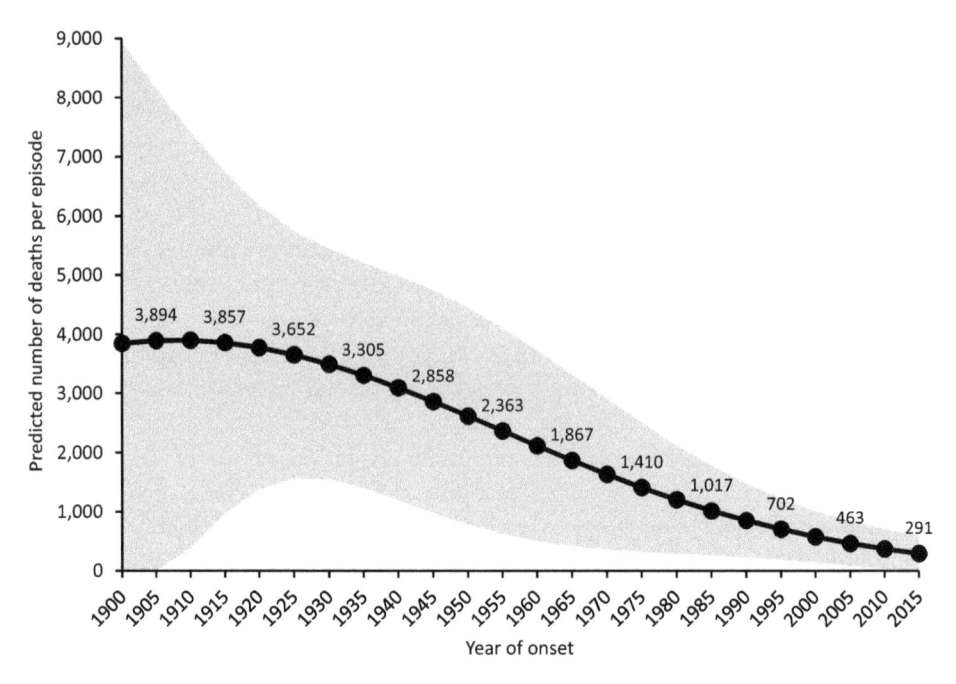

FIGURE 8.3. Average predicted deaths per revolutionary episode without civil wars, by year of episode onset. Average marginal predictions (GLM estimation, using log link and gamma variance function), with 95 percent confidence intervals and robust standard errors (n = 163 episodes).

decline of deaths in episodes without civil wars over the past century, I compared patterns after the Cold War with those during the first half the twentieth century, as this provided a better baseline for understanding how mortality in these episodes evolved.

As the results show, the relocation of revolution to cities also played a significant role in the diminution of revolutionary mortality in revolutionary contention short of civil war. The stronger presence of a regime's coercive capacities and increased visibility of repression in cities constrained lethal violence in these episodes. Among episodes without civil wars, there is a strong negative relationship between whether the episode occurred in an urban or rural environment and the number of people who died in it. More people died in episodes short of civil war in rural contexts—away from the visibility of the city and where the state's coercive capacities were weaker—than in urban ones. In first half of the twentieth century, 74 percent of episodes that did not develop into civil wars occurred primarily in cities; by the post–Cold War period that proportion had risen to 97 percent. This shift

TABLE 8.4. Estimated impact of changing conditions of contention on deaths in episodes without civil wars, first half of twentieth century vs post–Cold War period

Endogenous switching model ("no civil war" portion of model only)[a]

Variable	Model 1	Model 2	Model 3	Model 4[c]	Model 5[c]	Model 6	Model 7	Estimated effect on deaths, 1985–2014 vs 1900–1949 (Model 5)	Percentage change in deaths in episodes without civil wars, 1985–2014 vs 1900–1949
Rural/urban location	0.001 (−3.97)***	0.005 (−3.31)***	0.008 (−3.52)***	0.010 (−4.58)***	0.009 (−5.33)***	0.010 (−5.64)***	0.007 (−5.24)***	−94,630	−48.6%
Urban civic episode		0.134 (−4.39)***	0.153 (−4.15)***	0.131 (−4.69)***	0.186 (−3.91)***	0.226 (−3.31)***	0.162 (−3.74)***	−73,912	−37.9%
Opposition victory			0.364 (−2.29)*	0.225 (−3.41)***	0.193 (−3.88)***	0.216 (−3.56)***	0.203 (−3.81)***	−14,697	−7.5%
Polity score, t−1				0.886 (−3.39)***	0.904 (−2.93)**	0.902 (−3.01)**	0.902 (−2.73)**	+32,394	+16.6%
GDP per cap. ($ thousands), t−1					0.798 (−3.63)***	0.801 (−3.60)***	0.794 (−3.19)**	−44,044	−22.6%
Social revolutionary episode						2.352 (1.51)			
Human rights treaty ratifications (0–4)							0.816 (−0.97)		
Year of onset							1.012 (1.28)		

(Continued)

TABLE 8.4. (*continued*)

	Endogenous switching model ("no civil war" portion of model only)[a]							Estimated effect on deaths, 1985–2014 vs 1900–1949 (Model 5)	Percentage change in deaths in episodes without civil wars, 1985–2014 vs 1900–1949
Variable	Model 1	Model 2	Model 3	Model 4[c]	Model 5[c]	Model 6	Model 7		
n	241 (101)	241 (101)	241 (101)	233 (96)	230 (93)	230 (93)	227 (93)		
Akaike Informatin Criterion (AIC)[b]	1190.782	1176.603	1173.38	1163.427	1155.94	1155.004	1158.224		
Bayesian Information Criterion (BIC)[b]	1235.306	1227.977	1228.179	1221.651	1217.589	1220.078	1226.723		
sigma(0)	2.722	2.549	2.504	2.369	2.293	2.296	2.245		
theta(0)	0.773	0.666	0.662	0.843	1.038	1.204	0.941		
Kendall's tau(0)	−0.279	−0.250	−0.249	−0.297	−0.342	−0.376	−0.320		
LR test (independence of errors)	2.529	3.481	4.223+	4.627+	8.298**	9.780**	8.446**		
Estimated total impact								−194,889	−125.2%
Actual decline in deaths in episodes without civil wars, 1985–2014 vs 1900–1949								−155,696	−100.0%

[a] Coefficients with z-scores in parentheses. Copulas used were Clayton and FGM (Farlie-Gumbel-Morgenstern), with a normal marginal distribution of the error terms. All parameters were calculated using the switchcopula command written by Hasebe 2013.
[b] Computed on common sample of 227 observations for purposes of comparison.
[c] A likelihood ratio test indicates that one cannot conclude with confidence that Model 6 is a better fit than Model 5, chi2(1) = 2.42, p = 0.1195
+ p < 0.10, * p < 0.05, ** p < 0.01, *** p < 0.001

would have been associated with ninety-five thousand fewer deaths during the post–Cold War years compared to the first half of the twentieth century—or 49 percent of the total decline in revolutionary deaths in contained episodes.[46]

The proliferation of the urban civic repertoire also pushed down mortality in contained episodes. Their minimalist goals, unarmed character, and imperative of maximizing numbers reduced lethal violence within revolutionary contention, even relative to other contained episodes. Thus, urban civic contention involved 1,500 fewer deaths on average than other urban uprisings that did not involve civil war.[47] Controlling for other factors, the growth of the urban civic repertoire after the Cold War would have thus been associated with an additional reduction of seventy-four thousand deaths (or 38 percent of the total decline estimated by model).[48]

Economic development was also associated with a substantial reduction in mortality in contained episodes. Again, the wealthier the country, the more incentive there is for both sides to avoid the destruction and disruption involved in armed revolutionary violence. The average GDP per capita of countries experiencing contained revolutionary contention increased from $1,556 in the first half of the twentieth century to $4,715 by the end of the twentieth and early twenty-first century. According to the model, this would have been associated with a reduction of forty-four thousand deaths in the post–Cold War period compared to the first half of the twentieth century (or 23 percent of the total decline in deaths in contained revolutionary episodes).[49]

Other factors appear to have exercised smaller effects. While opposition victory in civil wars was associated with higher levels of mortality due to the resistance generated as civil war moved into more populated regime-controlled areas, in contained episodes opposition victory was associated with lower levels of mortality. Defeating a revolutionary opposition in these cases involved higher levels of repression on the part of regimes than when regimes were

---

46. The endogenous switching model overestimated the number of deaths ascribed to contained revolutions by about 25 percent (or thirty-nine thousand deaths). The GLM model finds a smaller decline (sixty-four thousand fewer deaths) due to the changing locations of rebellion.

47. In a two-tailed t-test, statistically significant at the .05 level (t = 2.099, with 143 degrees of freedom).

48. The GLM model finds a smaller decline in deaths in the post–Cold War period (twenty-six thousand) associated with the proliferation of the urban civic repertoire.

49. The GLM model identifies thirty-three thousand fewer deaths in the post–Cold War period that were due to changing levels of economic development.

toppled, multiplying the number of deaths. The probability of opposition victory in episodes without civil wars increased over the past century from .32 in the first half of the twentieth century to .53 by the post–Cold War period. The overall effect would have been to reduce deaths by about fifteen thousand (or 8 percent of the decline estimated by the model).[50] The degree of openness of a regime on the eve of contention was also negatively associated with mortality in contained episodes. During the post–Cold War years, regimes that experienced revolutionary contention short of civil war were actually slightly more repressive on average (Polity score of −2.3) than those that experienced contained revolutionary contention in the first half of the twentieth century (Polity score of −1.7).[51] The effect would have been to add an additional thirty-two thousand deaths in the post–Cold War period relative to the early twentieth century (or 17 percent of the total change estimated by the model).[52]

Lethality and Changing Technologies of Counter-Rebellion

Obviously, not all factors affecting revolutionary mortality can be adequately captured in a statistical model. In particular, one of the major drivers of revolutionary mortality has been changes in technologies of rebellion and counter-rebellion. Much of the higher mortality in civil wars during the Cold War, for instance, was pushed by the supply of heavy conventional weapons to both sides of these conflicts.[53] Generally, over the course of the twentieth century, civil wars have been characterized by the application of increasingly sophisticated and deadly weaponry, evolving from infantry and cavalry to more mechanized instruments of war such as tanks, aerial bombing, and artillery. Modern weaponry is vastly more destructive than the bolo knives used by Moro insurgents in the early twentieth century against American forces, the shotguns and Mauser bolt rifles used by Irish rebels during the Easter Uprising, or the Lee-Enfield carbines employed by the British in putting down colonial uprisings.

---

50. The GLM model finds a decline of ten thousand deaths as a result of changing patterns of opposition success in the post–Cold War period.

51. They were, however, less repressive than those that experienced contained revolutionary contention during the Cold War (Polity score of −3.3).

52. The GLM model identifies an additional eleven thousand deaths in the post–Cold War period that were due to more repressive regimes experiencing contained revolutionary contention.

53. Kalyvas and Balcells 2010; Balcells and Kalyvas 2014.

That does not mean that earlier conflicts were fought with less brutality.[54] Indeed, massacres of noncombatant civilians have occurred in response to armed rebellion throughout much of modern history.[55] But the purpose of weaponry in countering armed rebellion is not to disperse rebels but to kill them (though the consequence may often be simply to maim or disable them). Given their ability to evade government forces, dispersing armed rebels only invites them to regroup and return.

The number of deaths in civil wars has declined due to shifting durations of conflict, urbanization, economic development, and other factors. Nevertheless, over the long term, the lethality of the weapons used in civil wars has grown. By the late twentieth and early twenty-first centuries rebels in revolutionary civil wars were commonly equipped with automatic weapons, mortars, improvised explosive devices, land mines, rocket-propelled grenades, and shoulder-fired missiles—weapons that armed rebels in the early twentieth century could barely imagine. In some cases, they have even had access to tanks, artillery, helicopters, and aircraft. Governments are often fitted out with even more destructive weapons: cruise missiles, cluster bombs, "bunker busters," and (on occasion) even chemical weapons. Remotely controlled smart weapons, drones, and precision-guided munitions have aimed to minimize exposure of government forces to rebel fire while mitigating the blowback from the "collateral damage" of noncombatant deaths.[56] Nevertheless, they are meant to kill insurgents more efficiently. Generally, over time, the weaponry involved in civil wars has grown increasingly sophisticated and deadly, and the international market for such weapons remains brisk.

By contrast, urban revolutionary contention has pushed in the opposite direction: away from lethality toward less lethal means of rebellion and counter-rebellion. From the eighteenth through the early twentieth century, urban revolutions were extremely violent affairs. They generally assumed two forms: armed uprisings, which usually involved shooting battles for control over city streets; and what Rudé called "political riots,"[57] in which lightly armed crowds attacked the symbols and agents of the regime. Urban armed uprisings were intense but brief, producing large numbers of deaths in a concentrated period and leading to severe punishment for those who lost. Four thousand people were killed in the five-day June Uprising in Paris in 1848, including over eight hundred soldiers and members of the Mobile Guard.

---

54. Lyall and Wilson 2009; Boot 2002.
55. Valentino, Huth, and Balch-Lindsay 2004.
56. See Koplow 2010; Scharre 2018.
57. Rudé 1995, 93.

Approximately fifteen thousand more were arrested, with further thousands transported across the Mediterranean to Algeria.[58] During the so-called "bloody week" of the Paris Commune in May 1871, twenty-five thousand rebels were killed or executed on the spot. Of the forty thousand Communards captured, twenty-five thousand were executed and twelve thousand deported to penal colonies or imprisoned for periods of up to twenty years.[59] In the Revolution of 1905 in Russia, Nicholas II regained control over his realm by killing nineteen thousand rebels (including the execution of two thousand) and imprisoning seventy thousand. Two thousand rebels were massacred in one event alone—the quashing of demonstrations in support of the *Potemkin* naval mutiny.

Urban armed insurrection thus bred savage methods of suppression. A significant part of the explanation for high levels of mortality in urban rebellions in the nineteenth and early twentieth centuries can be attributed to extremely violent repertoires of rebellion and repression. For most of the nineteenth century, the policing of urban unrest in Europe was entrusted to the military and governed by a doctrine of "necessity." As Alex Bellamy put it, "Necessity served as both an enabler and a constraint on mass atrocities in that it permitted their use whilst limited the circumstances in which they might be legitimately employed and the scale of permissible killing."[60] What exactly "necessity" involved was unclear (indeed, purposefully so). Usually, it was a euphemism for expediency or whatever unfolded in practice on the ground. At other times, it meant whatever a regime thought was needed to ensure its own survival, though regimes usually erred on the side of greater savagery, just to be certain and to deter future challengers. But for all that it was arbitrary and bloody, the doctrine of necessity assumed that lethal force against crowds required a justification—even a cynical one. That fact alone indicated a sense of moral unease with shooting directly into crowds that has driven in part the evolution of urban counterrevolutionary tactics over time.

There were also strategic reasons why rulers tended to believe that lethal violence against crowds should be used as a last resort. Shooting into crowds inflamed targeted populations and often had a severe negative effect on soldiers' morale, constituting a leading cause of mutiny and military defection. In nineteenth-century barricade fighting, which resembled a battlefield in its direct exchange of fire between soldiers and revolutionaries, fraternization (and the presence of women and children) posed a significant challenge for

---

58. Lees and Tilly 1972, 31–32; Traugott 2002, 201–2.
59. Gould 1991, 718; Merriman 2014.
60. Bellamy 2012, 42–43.

troop loyalty.[61] In the revolutions of 1830 and 1848, for instance, the French army demonstrated little inclination to defend the government, preferring in many instances to lay down its arms rather than fight.[62]

One ever present alternative to shooting into crowds was to shoot over their heads as a warning. Even when ordered to fire directly into crowds, soldiers frequently chose to fire over their heads anyway—or not to fire at all.[63] However, shooting over their heads often had the unintended effect of inciting crowds rather than dispersing them. For example, after ordering a gathering in Dublin in December 1789 to disperse, a local sheriff commanded his soldiers to shoot a warning volley over the heads of the protestors. Instead of dispersing them, the volley provoked them to attack soldiers with bricks and stones, eventually instigating troops to fire directly into the assemblage.[64] As late as the early twentieth century, the British Colonial Office advised its forces overseas that if firearms had to be used, they should "make early, accurate use of lethal force to disperse a crowd," as "delaying the order to fire or shooting ineffectually either over protesters' heads or at their legs ... antagonized demonstrators without terrorizing them."[65]

Thus, the search for less lethal approaches to crowd control was rooted in the moral unease associated with shooting into unarmed crowds as a means of dispersing them and the fear of how shooting at or over crowds often undermined military discipline and incited anger within civilian populations. This backlash from lethal responses to unarmed rebellion was especially dangerous to regimes in cities, where government institutions and commercial enterprises were vulnerable. One alternative was simply to parade a large military force before crowds in an effort to intimidate without inflicting casualties, with the hope that a mere show of outsized force would be sufficient to disperse rebels. Indeed, in England and Ireland in the eighteenth and nineteenth centuries crowds were "frequently overawed simply by the arrival or the parading of troops; sometimes the rumor of soldiers coming was sufficient to scatter a crowd."[66] But this often did not have the intended effect.

The British were the pioneers of less lethal approaches to crowd control in the eighteenth and nineteenth centuries. The English Riot Act of 1714 established a ritualized procedure of crowd management that relied heavily on the threat but not the use of force. It allowed local magistrates to summon troops

61. Traugott 2010, 206–12.
62. Palmer 1988, 13–14.
63. Palmer 1988, 68.
64. Black 1988, 252.
65. Thomas 2012, 75–76.
66. Palmer 1988, 67.

in the event of disorders and to prohibit assemblies of twelve or more persons, subjecting violators to threats of arrest, conviction, and execution as felons. Magistrates were required to read a proclamation of warning to the crowd and to wait for one hour prior to taking any action, allowing time for the crowd to depart. But the reading of the proclamation in many cases had no effect on rioting crowds (in most cases it could not be heard above the din of disorder).[67] Moreover, troop reliability remained a constant problem throughout the eighteenth and early nineteenth centuries. Part-time militias—usually locally recruited—were reluctant to enforce the Riot Act,[68] given the outsized punishment they were being asked to mete out to their neighbors.

British policy was guided by a philosophy of minimum force that gradually whittled away at the doctrine of necessity. Firearms were not supposed to be used against rioters unless they were armed or were inflicting grievous injury on others. Higher levels of force were authorized against armed insurrection—an argument that Brigadier-General Reginald Dyer falsely used to justify his order to fire directly into an unarmed crowd of twenty thousand in Amritsar in April 1919 (without even issuing a warning), massacring 379 Indians and wounding over a thousand.[69] Dyer's actions were a violation of British military policy at the time, and the reaction to the Amritsar massacre in Britain reflected the moral unease that surrounded the use of killing as a tool of crowd control. Nevertheless, the official investigation into the massacre blamed Dyer more for continuing to fire into the crowd for as long as he did than for the decision to shoot into it in the first place. Dyer's actions demonstrated the considerable degree of discretion that military commanders on the ground retained in making decisions about the use of force, even under guidelines of "minimum force." This was particularly so in colonial settings, where the difference between protest and insurrection was often difficult for the colonizer to parse. As Martin Thomas noted, colonial governments were unsure of how to act when confronted with mass unrest: "Some reacted too slowly, others too quickly; some with insufficient shows of strength, others with excessive brutality."[70]

One alternative to infantry firepower was to employ cavalry charges. At the Peterloo Massacre in 1819 in Manchester, for instance, a gathering of sixty thousand was cleared in ten minutes by Hussar light cavalry, who charged into the crowd swinging their sabers. Most of the casualties were caused by people

---

67. Vogler 1991, 2–3.
68. Palmer 1988, 57–61.
69. Lloyd 2010.
70. Thomas 2012, 71, 75.

crushed or smothered by the fleeing crowd.[71] In an effort to reduce casualties, French cavalry were instructed to use the flat sides of their sabers to beat protestors rather than slash them. Even so, deaths from laceration were common.[72] Cavalry were also the method of choice for dispersing crowds in the Russian Empire in the early twentieth century. Horsemen would line up across the full width of a street and charge at full speed into a gathering, with Cossacks swinging their *nagaiki* (whips) at the crowd or swiping at them with sabers. To prepare for battle against such assaults, protestors donned heavy sheepskin coats or placed pads of cotton on their shoulders and backs. Others scattered sharp nails on the streets to counter mounted troops or brought broken bottles and knives that could be used to stab horses. One of the turning points in the February Revolution in 1917 was when Cossack cavalry refused to ride full speed into crowds and instead stopped short, signaling their refusal to carry out the orders of their commanders.[73]

Thus, throughout the nineteenth and early twentieth centuries, high levels of mortality were an inherent part of the urban revolutionary experience, as armed rebellion, the doctrine of necessity, and the militarization of crowd control complemented and amplified one another. But the use of military force to contain urban revolt harbored numerous dangers for regimes. Not only did it lead to outsized numbers of deaths and injuries that risked regime division, backlash mobilizations, and erosion of regime support. It also was a heavy strain on military forces and soldiers' morale. As European militaries professionalized, generals resented deployment to put down domestic revolt, preferring instead to focus their attention on external threats and the art of inter-state warfare. As Anja Johansen put it, "fighting street battles against crowds of men, women, and children was not [considered] a worthy activity for the glorious French army," while in Prussia "military commanders actively sought to avoid getting involved in the policing of civilians" and "increasingly saw disengagement from involvement in protest policing as being in the best interest of the army."[74] Military force nevertheless remained central to countering revolutionary threats in cities well into the twentieth century throughout much of Europe. Not until 1921 was the French army relieved of its duties of policing strikes and demonstrations. But particularly in Germany, Austro-Hungary, and Great Britain, the role of the military in containing urban revolt

71. Read 1958, 139.

72. Johansen 2005. 132. For similar use of cavalry to disperse crowds in Germany in the first half of the nineteenth century, see Husung 1982, 40–41.

73. Hasegawa 1981, 225, 248.

74. Johansen 2005, 90, 282.

had shrunk by the early twentieth century, as professional police forces developed to assume these functions.[75]

Over the course of the nineteenth century, police units were organized across the European continent for assisting the military in containing urban disorders. Based largely on the French model of the "King's police," these militarized units were armed, under the strict control of central governments, and lived in barracks. In most of Europe, they played the role of a force supplementary to the military in containing crowds. They were grossly understaffed and generally overwhelmed by the waves of industrial unrest that swept through Europe in the nineteenth century.

In this respect, the British model of "citizens' police" was an outlier. It aimed at demilitarizing crowd control by arming police not with guns, but with truncheons.[76] In 1830, the "baton charge" was invented when London's newly established Metropolitan Police assailed an unruly protest multiple times *en masse*, beating participants with truncheons until the dazed crowd dispersed. As a result, "for the first time in English history," urban disorders were suppressed "without any resort to soldiers and by a large civil force armed only with pieces of wood."[77] Obviously, cracking heads with batons produced severe injuries, including many deaths. Baton charges were little less than police-initiated brawls designed to disperse crowds, inflict injury, and instill fear among insurgents. Still, as a substitute for shooting directly into crowds or the cavalry charge, the baton charge was considered at the time to be a "more humane" alternative. The practice of beating rather than shooting crowds spread globally with the emergence of professional police forces over the nineteenth century. The composition of the truncheons has changed over the years—from wood to metal or metal-tipped, to plastics, and to rubberized plastic. But the truncheon and the baton charge remain as a mainstay of policing urban revolutionary contention to this day.

The search for ways to reduce mortality in urban crowd control accelerated in the late nineteenth and early twentieth centuries—spurred in particular by the need to mitigate the propaganda value of police violence for social-democratic oppositions. In Paris, where police had gained a reputation for "mindless brutality" in attacking crowds, police prefect Louis Lépine introduced a series of strategic measures in the 1890s that were aimed at reducing fatalities from police violence. These included a massive increase in the size of the police force, issuing warnings to crowds prior to dispersal, limiting military

---

75. Johansen 2005, 4.
76. Della Porta and Reiter 1998, 4–5.
77. Palmer 1988, 310.

involvement in crowd control, and creating separate spaces for peaceful protest.[78]

As Figure 8.3 shows, however, it was really only in the 1930s that deaths in urban revolutionary contention began to drop substantially. This decline was aided by the development of a series of less lethal technologies of crowd control that continue to be widely used today. Tear gas was first developed for police use in 1912 by French scientists as a way of forcing urban rebels to abandon barricades.[79] It quickly found application in the gas warfare of World War I. After the war, tear gas began to be produced commercially in the United States and marketed globally. By the 1930s, it was applied broadly in North and South America against urban protestors (as well as in British, American, French, Spanish, and Italian colonies to subdue anti-colonial unrest).[80] As Anna Feigenbaum describes, marketing for tear gas at the time emphasized how "it could demoralize and disperse a crowd without live ammunition. Through sensory torture, tear gas could force people to retreat. These features gave tear gas novelty value in a market where only the billy club and bullets were currently available. Officers could disperse a crowd with 'a minimum amount of undesirable publicity.'"[81]

Tear gas and its later cousin, pepper spray, are classified as chemical weapons by the 1993 Chemical Weapons Convention and are prohibited from use in conventional warfare. There is, however, no restriction on their use for civilian crowd control. Deaths occur from the use of gas weapons against crowds—either from the impact of dispersal canisters or from secondary effects. The April 1960 Revolution in South Korea that overthrew Syngman Rhee, for instance, was touched off when the use of tear gas at close range lodged a tear gas canister in the eye of a seventeen-year-old boy during protests in the city of Masan. The backlash eventually provoked protests around the country.[82] But the use of gas weapons vastly reduced mortality in urban revolutionary contention, altered the tactics of both police and oppositions, and lowered the risks involved in urban revolution. Police no longer needed to engage directly with crowds by smashing heads: they could disperse crowds at a safe distance and with fewer fatalities, bolstering morale and lowering police casualties. Urban revolutionaries no longer prepared for cavalry charges with cotton, sheepskin, knives, nails, and broken bottles but instead donned swim goggles,

---

78. Johansen 2005, 99–100.
79. (John) Lee 2009, 4.
80. Feigenbaum 2017a; Feigenbaum 2017b; Shoul 2008; Thomas 2012, 80–81.
81. Feigenbaum 2017b, 28.
82. Kim 1983, 115–19, 136.

bandanas, and gas masks, toting spray bottles of vinegar to counteract the effects of gas.[83]

A second major innovation involved the use of pressurized water to disperse urban crowds. The first known use of fire-fighting equipment to attack crowds was in the middle of the nineteenth century,[84] but the practice accelerated in the late nineteenth century when the invention of steam-driven fire pumps and rubber-lined fire hoses facilitated the direction of high-pressure jets of water against contentious gatherings. The combustion engine greatly enhanced the ability to deliver streams of pressurized water. The first truck-mounted water cannons were deployed in Germany in 1931.[85] By 1934, French gendarmes were authorized to mix tear gas into high-pressure water jets sprayed from fire equipment to break up demonstrations in France and North Africa, offering, in Thomas's words, "a modern, humanitarian alternative to policemen's bullets."[86] But it was not until the early 1950s that the water cannon came to be used as a regular part of urban crowd control. Dyes, tear gas, and other noxious substances were typically added to the water stream to identify or further disable protest participants. During the 1957 revolution in Colombia against the regime of Gustavo Rojas Pinilla, for example, police used red-dyed water sprayed from a water cannon to mark demonstrators for later identification.[87]

Much of the contemporary arsenal of crowd control was developed only in the second half of the twentieth century, when a further decline in urban revolutionary mortality occurred. The rise of the urban civic repertoire coincided with the emergence of new and more sophisticated crowd-control technologies. Numerous types of riot-control vehicles—most of them armored, capable of demolishing barricades, and equipped with powerful water cannons and other less lethal weaponry—came to be produced during the Cold War on both sides of the Iron Curtain.[88] After the Cold War, global competition among the dozen or so private corporations marketing these vehicles grew "intense."[89] Several additions completed the modern arsenal of less lethal weaponry for countering urban rebellion. In the late 1950s, British police in Hong Kong began experimenting with ricocheting wooden bullets off the

---

83. Khalil 2011, 157–58.

84. See, for instance, the image of firefighters using hoses to break up a workhouse protest by women in 1849, at https://www.gettyimages.ie/detail/news-photo/cartoon-depicting-a-woman-leading-a-workhouse-rebellion-news-photo/959260452?adppopup=true.

85. McNab 2015, 11.

86. Thomas 2012, 80.

87. Associated Press 1957. See also Leibenluft 2008.

88. McNab 2015.

89. Future Market Insights 2019.

ground with the aim of wounding protestors in the legs. This approach was later adapted by British forces policing the Troubles in Northern Ireland, with rubber bullets substituting for wood. Later, plastic bullets replaced rubber, due to significant injuries caused by the tendency of rubber to ricochet uncontrollably. Rubber and plastic bullets (and other so-called kinetic impact projectiles such as bean bag rounds and shot pellets) rapidly became part of the global arsenal of urban crowd control. These kinetic impact projectiles are meant to cause pain but not significant injury, though they have in fact led to thousands of severe injuries, ranging from lacerations to blindness, and have caused scores of deaths.[90] Still, there is little doubt that they have enormously reduced fatalities in urban revolutionary contention. Riot shields first appeared among British soldiers during the Cyprus Emergency in the 1950s, and later among French police during the May 1968 uprising.[91] They became standard issue to British police after 1977 as part of a trend toward para-militarization of crowd control.[92] By the 2000s, these weapons (along with pepper gas, concussion grenades, Tasers, body armor, and Long-Range Acoustic Devices) had become the instruments of choice for suppressing urban civic revolts.[93]

Indeed, a key reason why the confidence intervals in Figure 8.3 narrow so sharply for the late twentieth and early twenty-first centuries is the global diffusion of these less lethal technologies for crowd control, which have come to be deployed for combating urban crowds in nearly every corner of the world. Some within the less-lethal weapons industry have peddled a utopian vision of a world in which the killing of urban protestors will be eliminated completely, reducing the policing of urban crowds to a matter of sophisticated technologies.[94] Such a fantasy contrasts sharply with the marketing of increasingly lethal weapons to both sides in predominantly rural civil wars.[95]

The Doctrine of Necessity, Human Rights, and Unarmed Urban Rebellion

Despite the wide availability of less lethal forms of crowd control, there are still many instances in which regimes shoot directly into unarmed urban crowds when threatened by revolt—as cases as diverse as Myanmar in 1988, China and

---

90. Haar et al. 2017.
91. French 2015, 120; Samuelson 1968.
92. Waddington 1987.
93. For an overview, see Davison 2009; Wood 2014.
94. Smith 2019.
95. Moore 2012.

Romania in 1989, Lithuania, Mali, and Madagascar in 1991, Thailand in 1992, Russia in 1993, Bahrain in 1994, Venezuela in 2002, Myanmar in 2007, Kyrgyzstan in 2010, Tunisia, Egypt, Bahrain, Yemen, Syria, and Libya in 2011, Ukraine in 2014, and many other cases testify. Shooting into crowds may be less frequent than in the early twentieth century, but it still occurs often enough. There are also numerous instances in which troops refuse orders to fire into crowds. But given the widespread presence of technological alternatives, by the late twentieth century the long-standing doctrine of necessity could no longer be so easily deployed to justify lethal force against unarmed revolutionary challengers.

Indeed, over the past century, the reputational costs associated with the application of lethal force against unarmed crowds have reversed. In the nineteenth century, regimes that failed to deal with rebellion with sufficient severity feared reputational costs deriving from their seeming weakness and lack of resolve. In a world dominated by monarchs and landed elites, rulers sought to cultivate reputations as strongmen who were defending civilization against the madness of revolution and the savagery of the crowd. From the point of view of Tsar Nicholas II, less severe force toward his revolutionary opponents in 1905 was not an option. It would have been seen as undermining his reputation as an imperial autocrat at home and abroad and as opening the door to the barbarism that the revolutionary masses supposedly represented.[96] It was also thought to encourage future challengers. As Arno Mayer noted, outsized repressions were meant not simply to restore order, but "to serve as a warning to would-be rebels in years to come"[97] from leaders who gained little by showing mercy toward their opponents.

In the latter part of the twentieth century, these reputational incentives were inverted. Excessive severity against oppositions had become a badge not of state strength and civilizational prowess but of state weakness and moral turpitude—of "caddish, disreputable, and unsavory" behavior and a signal that a government was "rogue" and did not "belong to the family of nations."[98] This sea-change in reputational costs attached to lethal repression was rooted in the human rights revolution and the emergence of international norms concerning how states should treat noncombatant citizens.

There is, of course, no right to rebellion in international law.[99] But neither is rebellion prohibited; indeed, a significant proportion of the world's regimes

---

96. Ascher 1988/1994; Figes 2014, 30.
97. Mayer 2000, 109
98. Rotberg 2008, 8.
99. The closest international law comes to a right of rebellion is the right to self-determination, which in practice has been heavily weighted in favor of the territorial integrity of states and restricted in interpretation to formal colonial situations, foreign military occupations, or subordinated racial groups. See Cassese 1995.

trace their origins to revolution.[100] States have the right to criminalize revolution, and most do. However, whereas the doctrine of necessity once reigned supreme, today governments are not considered to have a right to massacre unarmed citizens engaged in efforts to overthrow them.

At least, this is the case in the eyes of international law. Protection of noncombatant civilians in the Geneva conventions was originally restricted to cases of inter-state warfare. But in 1977 additional protocols extended these protections to noncombatant civilians more generally. Human rights law as it developed after World War II prohibited the intentional killing of civilians across a wide variety of contexts, eventually establishing a responsibility on the part of the international community to protect civilian populations when states egregiously failed to live up to these obligations.[101] As the practice of revolution evolved with the proliferation of the urban civic repertoire in the late twentieth century, revolutionaries were increasingly no longer armed combatants, but rather unarmed civilians peacefully protesting the abuses of their governments. Thus, the shift in urban revolutionary tactics from armed revolt to unarmed revolt relying on the power of numbers altered the relationship of revolution to the prescriptions of international law.

Though regimes widely violate these norms in practice, a variety of international covenants (including the 1948 Universal Declaration of Human Rights and the 1976 International Covenant on Civil and Political Rights) established a right to peaceful, unarmed assembly.[102] International normative guidelines developed over the use of lethal violence in dealing with unarmed protests.[103] For instance, the "Code of Conduct for Law Enforcement Officials," adopted by the UN General Assembly in 1979, stipulates that "firearms should not be used except when a suspected offender offers armed resistance or otherwise jeopardizes the lives of others and less extreme measures are not sufficient to restrain or apprehend the suspected offender."[104] In its "Basic Principles on the Use of Force and Firearms by Law Enforcement Officials" (adopted in 1990), UN bodies further established that "in the dispersal of assemblies that are unlawful but non-violent, law enforcement officials shall avoid the use of force or, where

100. Bellal and Doswald-Beck 2011, 11–13.
101. Bellamy 2012, 20–22.
102. Bellal and Doswald-Beck 2011, 8–10.
103. Armed rebellion is also not completely devoid of international legal regulation. Once a revolutionary opposition utilizes weapons and organizes itself into an armed force, international humanitarian law applies.
104. "Code of Conduct for Law Enforcement Officials," adopted by General Assembly resolution 34/169 of 17 December 1979 (at https://www.ohchr.org/EN/ProfessionalInterest/Pages/LawEnforcementOfficials.aspx).

that is not practicable, shall restrict such force to the minimum extent necessary." The document then added that "exceptional circumstances such as internal political instability or any other public emergency may not be invoked to justify any departure from these basic principles."[105] These guidelines have been further backed by multiple decisions in international courts.[106] None of these prescriptions actually outlaws the application of lethal force against unarmed crowds, and "the minimum extent necessary" still leaves considerable leeway in judgment. But insofar as these normative prescriptions, encoded in international laws and regulations, whittle away at the circumstances under which regimes can plausibly claim that shooting into unarmed crowds is legitimate to save a regime, they further circumscribe the doctrine of necessity. Paradoxically, they may also inadvertently provide incentives for regimes to falsely claim that unarmed crowds were actually armed, to plant weapons on opposition movements, or instigate violence on the part of revolutionaries or their supporters, thereby legitimating harsher government repression.[107] All of these practices have become part of the repertoire of authoritarian regimes when facing unarmed revolutionary threats.

These norms have also influenced the tactics of oppositions, further incentivizing them toward unarmed rebellion in the hope of generating external pressure on their regimes.[108] But their effects in constraining regimes has obviously depended on the costs that regimes suffer from violating them. At best, they function as a weak constraint. As Beth Simmons observed, "governments have typically been reluctant to impose costs of any description on all but the most egregious rights abusers."[109] The Chinese government, for instance, suffered little as a result of its brutal suppression of the 1989 Tiananmen protests. To be sure, governments around the globe (with the exception of countries ruled by hardline communist regimes) condemned the Chinese government: France temporarily froze its relations with China and cut back on cultural exchanges; Australia reduced aid and loans; and a few countries temporarily banned exports of military equipment to China. But by and large it was "business as usual" after the Tiananmen massacres.[110]

---

105. "Basic Principles on the Use of Force and Firearms by Law Enforcement Officials," adopted by the Eighth United Nations Congress on the Prevention of Crime and the Treatment of Offenders, Havana, Cuba, August 27 to September 7, 1990 (at https://www.ohchr.org/en/professionalinterest/pages/useofforceandfirearms.aspx).

106. Bellal and Doswald-Beck 2011, 16–18.

107. See Lupu and Wallace 2019.

108. Ritter 2015.

109. Simmons 2009, 154.

110. Seymour 1990.

However, there have been cases in which the international response to outsized repressions of revolutionary protests has been substantial and consequential. After Muammar el-Qaddafi attacked unarmed protestors with live ammunition, tanks, artillery fire, and helicopter gunships in February 2011, the United States froze billions of dollars of Libyan assets, the International Criminal Court issued a warrant for Qaddafi's arrest for crimes against humanity, and NATO engaged in a major air campaign aimed at supporting Qaddafi's overthrow. Still, international reactions such as this have been extremely rare.

There are other reputational costs that can at times attach themselves to governments that deploy lethal force against unarmed challengers. Studies have found that human rights violations that gain widespread notoriety can reduce foreign direct investment, as multinational corporations that invest in the countries in which they occur can themselves be tainted by involvement with these regimes.[111] After the repressions of the Myanmar 8888 Uprising, for instance, a number of branded multinationals, in response to activist campaigns in advanced industrial countries, rapidly disinvested from Myanmar due to the negative publicity they encountered and the harm that accrued to their brands.[112]

It is possible that some regimes opt to utilize less lethal technologies of crowd control for fear of the international consequences of using more substantial force, and it may be that some rulers eschew shooting into crowds because they have internalized norms about the use of force against unarmed civilians. But there is little evidence of any systematic effect for human rights norms on revolutionary mortality—measured either by the number of human rights treaties ratified by a state, or alternatively (given the linear growth of human rights law) by the simple linear effect of time (Model 7 in Table 8.4). While shooting directly into crowds may involve significant reputational costs, fear of domestic backlash remains a more powerful deterrent to shooting into crowds than ill repute.

Conclusion: Urbanization and the "Civilizing" of Revolution

Mortality in revolutionary contention peaked in the mid-twentieth century and then experienced a marked decline, resulting in approximately 7.9 million fewer deaths in revolution in the post–Cold War period compared to the Cold War. A large portion of this decrease can be ascribed to geopolitical

---

111. Barry, Clay, and Flynn 2013; Garriga 2016
112. David and Holliday 2012, 129.

change—in particular, the shortening of revolutionary civil wars and a decline in social revolutionary contention. But urbanization and related factors (economic development, the shifting location of revolution to cities, and the proliferation of the urban civic repertoire) also played significant roles.

By shifting revolutionary contention to areas of greater state capacity, by increasing the visibility of violence, by reducing incentives to engage in violent disruption and embark upon civil war, and by altering the tactics of states and revolutionary oppositions, the concentration of people, power, and wealth in cities has functioned to reduce revolutionary mortality on a massive scale. The development of less lethal technologies of crowd control facilitated these trends, providing opportunities for regimes to counter revolutionary crowds without having to shoot directly into them. By the late twentieth and early twenty-first centuries, international norms reinforced these developments—though their effect in reducing mortality has been inconsistent and at best ambiguous. All this has greatly reduced the risks involved in urban revolution.

So, has revolution—once virtually defined by its extreme violence—grown "civilized," if by "civilized" we mean "tamer," less violent, more peaceful? It would seem so. But one should be cautious about unidirectional thinking when it comes to revolutionary mortality. For one thing, there has always been a great deal of variance in deaths in revolution across episodes. While that variance (and the scale of outlier events) has declined over time (in episodes both with and without civil war), singular outbreaks of large-scale violence have repeatedly occurred over the last century. Moreover, trends in revolutionary deaths since 1900 have not been unilinear. Deaths peaked in the mid-twentieth century and subsequently declined. This pattern was driven in part by geopolitics and the end of bipolar competition. With the decline of American power by the 2010s and the emergence of a multipolar world in which states like Russia, Saudi Arabia, and Iran have displayed an increased willingness to involve themselves in civil wars in places like Yemen, Libya, and Syria, a reversal of the trend is fully possible.

The return of revolution to cities and the rise of repertoires relying on the power of numbers rather than the force of arms have acted as constraints on revolutionary mortality, though they in no way preclude the deployment of lethal violence. Still, much of the pacification of revolution has been driven by structural and strategic factors. To the extent that it has occurred, the "civilizing of revolution" is rooted as much in the shifting locations and conditions of revolt as in the moral unease associated with revolutionary killing and "the better angels of our nature."[113]

---

113. Pinker 2011.

9
The Evolving Impact of Revolution

[T]here is nothing more difficult to carry out, nor more doubtful of success, nor more dangerous to handle than to initiate a new order of things.

NICCOLÒ MACHIAVELLI, *THE PRINCE*[1]

DO REVOLUTIONS MATTER? Certainly, those attempting to bring them about believe that they will. They would hardly engage in the kind of high-risk collective action that revolution involves if they thought that nothing would come of it. For the most part, people do not embark upon revolution lightly. As Jeff Goodwin observed, they do so because they believe that there is "no other way out"[2]—that the status quo has become intolerable and that there are no alternative remedies for addressing their miseries.

But no one should enter into revolution with the illusion that it will resolve the fundamental conflicts and trade-offs inherent in the human condition. Revolutions are well known to be accompanied by an explosion of hopes and expectations. Yet they are equally associated with disappointment and disillusionment. We should not be surprised that the record of revolutionary movements that have managed to gain power in achieving substantive change has been mixed. Some have introduced sweeping, lasting change. Others have effected only minor modifications or change that proved short-lived. Some regimes brought to power by revolution have endured for decades. Others barely lasted for months. Sometimes post-revolutionary change has come at a high price, costing more lives than were lost in revolutionary contention itself; even those instrumental in bringing the new regime to power can be among the individuals suffering the most. As is true of politics more generally, advancement in one area

1. Machiavelli 1952, 49.
2. Goodwin 2001.

often comes at the cost of deterioration in another. Moreover, most revolutions bring with them consequences completely unanticipated by revolutionary participants, opponents, and observers. The path of substantive change in the wake of revolution has never been straight. It has always been arduous, circuitous, and contested—with detours, roundabouts, and dead ends.

Take, for instance, the case of the Hungarian Revolution of 1919. After two months of major strikes, riots, and street protests, a coalition of communists and social democrats led by Béla Kun forced the resignation of the democratic government of Mihály Károlyi and proclaimed a Hungarian Soviet Republic in March 1919. The new government enacted a dizzying array of changes: it nationalized land, industry, housing, and commercial enterprises; abolished aristocratic titles and privileges; and declared healthcare and education free. But the inflation and food shortages that ensued quickly led to the collapse of the revolutionary coalition. Kun resorted to terror to prop up his regime, and Czechoslovak and Romanian troops invaded, forcing Kun to flee after only 134 days in office.[3] Cases like the 1919 Hungarian Revolution often lie forgotten in the annals of revolution. Their main contribution lay in how they precipitated what followed—in the Hungarian case, the repressive and semi-fascist regime of Admiral Horthy that dominated Hungarian politics for more than two decades.

In the history of revolution, stories like Béla Kun's are more common than one might think. The 1960 April Revolution in South Korea ushered in a democratic republic that lasted only eight months, displaced by a military coup launched by General Park Chung-hee, who ruled the country for the next eighteen years. The Morsi government brought to power by the 2011 Egyptian Revolution lasted twelve months, giving way to the dictatorship of General Abdel Fattah el-Sisi. Within two years of the Orange Revolution in Ukraine, the crippled regime of Viktor Yushchenko had so unraveled that Viktor Yanukovych, whom Yushchenko had defeated in the revolution, won his way back to power through the ballot box. The main legacy of the Orange Revolution was to set the stage for Yanukovych's corrupt regime and for the societal disappointment that helped precipitate a second revolution in 2013–14. But even that revolution struggled mightily to achieve substantive change in its wake.

The literature on revolution is vast, but so much more has been written about the causes and processes of revolutions than about their consequences, as the questions of how and why revolutions matter have taken back-stage relative to the question of why they occur in the first place.[4] All revolutions come

---

3. Tőkés 1967.
4. See Goldstone 2001, 167.

with two goals: to gain power and to enact substantive change after gaining power. Difficult as overthrowing an incumbent regime through revolution may be, achieving substantive change in the wake of revolution is harder still. As Arthur Stinchcombe observed, after revolution,

> all aspects of government tend to be unsettled and difficult to manage: which ethnicity will dominate a nation, where state and subnationality boundaries will be drawn, which classes will be mobilized into politics or collective bargaining under the regime, who will pay taxes to which political budgets, which property will be secure, how economic going concerns will be created and governed, who will recruit and sustain armies to fight whom, who will arrest juvenile delinquents or organize them into gangs, who will back the promises of commercial contracts with force, and who will select legislative bodies or authorities to make policy on all these matters.[5]

Governing after revolution is probably the most challenging context that any government can possibly face. Not only are all of the problems of the old regime that led to revolution still there, but hopes have been raised to a maximum, populations have been activated, followers of the old regime persist, and all fundamental issues of politics are potentially on the table. Add to this the destruction that revolutionary contention can inflict on societies and economies and it is easy to see why revolutions usually disappoint the colossal hopes of those who brought them about.

Indeed, the frame most commonly used to discuss the consequences of revolutions is profoundly pessimistic—the metaphor of Thermidor, named after the month in the French revolutionary calendar when the radical faction of the revolutionary government was evicted from power. For Crane Brinton, all revolutions end in Thermidor, which he viewed as convalescence from the fever of the extreme passions and asceticism unleashed by revolution. During Thermidor, society returns to its pre-revolutionary habits and pleasures, and politics takes a decided turn toward the conservative. Nevertheless, Brinton believed that revolutions still exercised a deep impact on state and society over the long term—increasing the efficiency of the state, centralizing power, transferring property, and sweeping away many of the abuses of the old regime and restrictions on societal development.[6] Robert Fishman argues that the revolutionary path to democracy followed in Portugal developed a set of institutional and cultural practices that were significantly more inclusionary than those of the pacted transition in neighboring

---

5. Stinchcombe 1999, 52.
6. Brinton 1965, 205–41.

Spain. As a result of the 1974 Carnation Revolution, Portuguese institutions remained more open to societal influence than Spanish institutions decades after the events in question.[7]

Why do some revolutions leave behind persisting consequences, while others exert little lasting impact? And what would the likely path of development have been had revolution not occurred in the first place or had the revolutionary opposition failed? After all, revolutions need to be judged not merely by what post-revolutionary governments achieve or do not achieve in their wake, but also by the counterfactuals that they naturally suggest and by the conditions of society that revolutionaries inherit.

In this chapter, I examine the critical period following revolutions, evaluating the record of post-revolutionary governments according to a set of common standards on a series of issues faced by all governments: their ability to establish order, generate economic growth, mitigate inequality, institute political freedoms, and create institutions accountable to society. These are the key values that we, as citizens, care about. Obviously, they are not achievable simultaneously, and all regimes are forced to make choices between them. I explore the impact of revolution on order, growth, equality, freedom, and accountability through multiple comparisons and counterfactual analyses. As I show, the ways in which revolutionary governments come to power exert a substantial impact on post-revolutionary outcomes, though sometimes in unanticipated ways. Post-revolutionary governance also plays a critical role. As Rod Aya observed, most changes brought about by revolutions "were rammed through, not in the cross fires of a revolutionary situation when power was up for grabs, but afterwards as the settled policy of government officials."[8] Nevertheless, the goals and organizational forms of revolutionaries and the manner by which they come to power exercise a powerful effect on the extent to which order, growth, equality, freedom, and accountability have been achieved after revolution.

In line with the thrust of this book, I am particularly interested in comparing the impact of the social revolutions that have dominated social science theorizing about revolution with the urban civic revolutions that have become increasingly prevalent since the end of the Cold War. The regimes that came to power through social revolution generally excelled at providing order and mitigating inequality, but had strongly negative effects on freedom, economic growth, and accountability. These results were closely related to the egalitarian ideologies, modes of organization, and tactics of contention that accompanied

---

7. Fishman 2011.
8. Aya 1979, 48.

social revolutions. Urban civic revolutions also lead to substantial improvements in some areas and significant damage in others. Their main achievement has been a marked improvement in political freedoms. But this progress generally falls short of what one would expect from an electoral democracy (minimally defined), and in many cases deteriorates over time. Moreover, urban civic post-revolutionary regimes are more fragile than those brought to power by successful social revolutions, a condition that frequently places their achievements in jeopardy. This fragility is in part the product of the hastily convened coalitional character of urban civic revolts, as well as of the significant social and economic problems that urban civic post-revolutionary regimes experience. Reflecting their minimalist goals and revolutionary tactics, the immediate impact of successful urban civic revolutions on economic growth, though negative, is small. But over time these regimes tend to experience a crisis of stagnating economic growth. The fact that they largely inherit the state of the old regime intact—with its embedded relationships of corruption—places severe limits on their ability to address issues of economic development, enact political change, or respond to the widespread social demands that accompany these revolutions. Class inequalities and ethnic tensions tend to worsen after urban civic revolutions, though some forms of inequality (access to education and healthcare, and women's civil liberties) marginally improve. In sum, as revolution has evolved away from social revolution and toward urban civic forms, the impact of revolution on society has not only changed; it has also grown more precarious and uncertain.

Parameters of Post-Revolutionary Analysis

Identifying the impact of a revolution is a challenging task. Some outcomes could be the product of pre-revolutionary patterns, while others may be the result of revolutionary contention or of post-revolutionary governance. In this regard, it is useful to distinguish between revolutionary *aftermaths*—referring to political, social, and economic developments in the immediate wake of a revolutionary seizure of power—and revolutionary *legacies*—referring to longer-lasting patterns of political and social behavior that result from revolution. Legacies are relationships that are produced and reproduced across time, whereas the persistence of aftermaths is unknowable: they may endure and become legacies, they may feed into the production of some new pattern of behavior through the circumstances that they create, or they may simply be temporary conditions that are swept aside by subsequent developments. Legacies only become fully apparent decades after the events in question, though their outlines are likely visible even during the years immediately following a revolution.[9] The further one moves in time from the end of revolutionary contention, the more likely it is that other factors besides the experience of revolution (post-revolutionary governance or other domestic and international developments) will shape post-revolutionary outcomes, and aftermaths will either dissipate or transform into legacies.

To explore these patterns, I engaged in three types of systematic comparison. First, I explored whether trajectories of development after the end of revolutionary contention were similar to or different from trajectories before revolutionary contention began. Here, I examined the extent to which order, growth, equality, freedom, and accountability were affected by the experience of revolutionary contention or by post-revolutionary developments relative to the pre-revolutionary situation that revolutionary governments inherited. I was particularly interested in comparing these patterns across different types of revolutions, juxtaposing patterns of development in social revolutions with those of urban civic revolutions. Second, I compared patterns of order, growth, inequality, freedom, and accountability in countries that experienced successful revolutions with those that experienced failed revolutions. As we have seen, once a revolutionary episode materializes, whether a revolutionary opposition is able to gain power is partially a structured outcome and partially the product of unpredictable regime–opposition interactions. The implicit counterfactual probed in these comparisons was how patterns of order, growth, equality, freedom, and accountability after revolution might have been different had the revolutionary opposition lost and the old regime continued in office. Hardly anything has been written about the consequences of failed revolutions,[10] despite the fact that revolutionary failure is more common than revolutionary success. Yet, as we will see, societies that experience failed revolutions often display distinctive patterns of development. Finally, I compared patterns of order, growth, inequality, freedom, and accountability in countries that experienced successful revolutions with those in countries that were roughly similar in critical respects at the time revolution broke out but did not experience a revolutionary episode during this period. As in Fishman's comparison of Portugal and Spain in the wake of their transitions to democracy, the implicit counterfactual pursued in these comparisons is how things might have turned out had a significant revolutionary challenge never materialized in the first place.

I use a difference-in-differences research design to explore these questions. Difference-in-differences is a quasi-experimental setup that utilizes longitudinal

---

9. Beissinger and Kotkin 2014. Zimmermann (1990, 36) maintained that one generation is the minimal amount of time needed to judge the long-term impact of revolutions.

10. For an exception, see Slater and Smith 2016.

data from treatment and control groups to think counterfactually about the effects of a particular intervention or treatment, such as the passage of a law or the enactment of a particular policy.[11] Known in econometrics as part of the Rubin causal model,[12] it posits that every unit has different potential outcomes depending on its "assignment" to a particular condition. In this case, the "assignment" or "treatment" is experiencing a revolutionary episode, a successful revolution, or a particular type of revolution, depending on the nature of the comparison being made. The difference-in-differences model can be used to estimate a treatment effect that is the difference between the observed value of the dependent variable and the value that the dependent variable would have taken under the assumption of parallel trends (i.e., had there not been any treatment at all). The parallel trends assumption presumes that, in the absence of treatment, the difference between the compared groups would have remained constant over time.

I use the difference-in-differences setup to compare patterns of political and societal development on the eve of a revolutionary episode with those at the end of the episode. As the length of episodes varies across cases, I exclude the "treatment" years of revolutionary contention with the exception of the final year of the episode, comparing outcomes in the year prior to the onset of the episode directly with outcomes at the episode's conclusion, regardless of episode length. This allows identification of the direct effect of the period of revolutionary contention on outcomes. It is important to note, however, that this should not be interpreted as a "treatment effect" for revolution, as we do not know that revolutionary contention was entirely responsible for the difference. Exogenous events (such as external wars or global financial crises) that accompany or pre-date revolutionary contention could also exert a significant influence. (This was certainly the case for patterns of economic growth in the wake of a number of well-known revolutions, such as the Russian Revolution of 1917 and the Indonesian Revolution of 1998.) For longer revolutionary episodes, it is also highly likely that other factors occurring during the period of revolutionary contention could affect outcomes. Nevertheless, comparing the situation on the eve of revolutionary contention with the situation at the end of contention provides a rough and intuitive way of thinking about the impact of the *period* of revolutionary contention on outcomes of interest.

To improve the quality of the comparison, I included an additional two years before the onset of a revolutionary episode in the difference-in-differences estimation (for a total of three years prior to the onset of revolution). Including several years prior to the onset of the episode allows for better assessment of

11. Card and Krueger 1994.
12. Rubin 1973a; Rubin 1973b; Rubin 1974.

pre-revolutionary trajectories and the parallel trends assumption. I also analyzed the seven years following the end of a revolutionary episode to assess the impact of the period of revolutionary contention on subsequent development, as well as to identify other potential violations of the parallel trends assumption.[13]

There are several reasons why the difference-in-differences setup cannot be used for causal inference with regard to the impact of revolutions on subsequent societal development. I provide a more extended discussion of this in Appendix 4G, which gives an overview of the difference-in-differences model. Chief among these reasons are violations of the parallel trends assumption. In causal inference, the parallel trends assumption is considered the most critical supposition of the differences-in-differences model for isolating treatment effects, though it is often an assumption that is difficult to meet in practice—especially when the number of time periods is large. It requires that the difference between treatment and control groups would have remained constant over time in absence of treatment. Violations of the assumption can be understood as a form of omitted variable bias—that is, something was not accounted for before or after treatment that affected the outcome of interest. For instance, societies that experienced successful revolutions could have had higher levels of economic contraction before the onset of revolution than societies that experienced failed revolutions, so that a contracting economy in the wake of successful revolution could simply be a continuation of pre-revolutionary trends. Alternatively, the pattern of outcomes may have emerged only after the end of revolutionary contention, as a result of post-revolutionary governance or other post-revolutionary developments. It is possible that the effect of revolutionary contention on outcomes, if any, was fleeting (simply a temporary phenomenon of revolutionary aftermaths). It also could prove more long-lasting (reproduced over time, as one would expect from a legacy in formation). Each of these potential relationships is pictured in Figure 9.1.[14]

Violations of the parallel trends assumption are frequent in the analyses that follow—whenever pre-revolutionary or post-revolutionary developments affect outcomes. Accordingly, I do not use the difference-in-differences setup for identifying causal relationships, but rather use it for purposes of controlled comparison. It allows us to examine patterns of development before and after successful

---

13. Multiple imputation was used to fill in missing values within the dependent variables. Results were always compared with those from the complete-case sample.

14. Given that data for many of the dependent variables of order, growth, inequality, freedom, and accountability were not available for colonies or for territories seeking independent statehood, these cases were dropped from the analysis. This left 217 "treated" observations in which a revolutionary episode occurred.

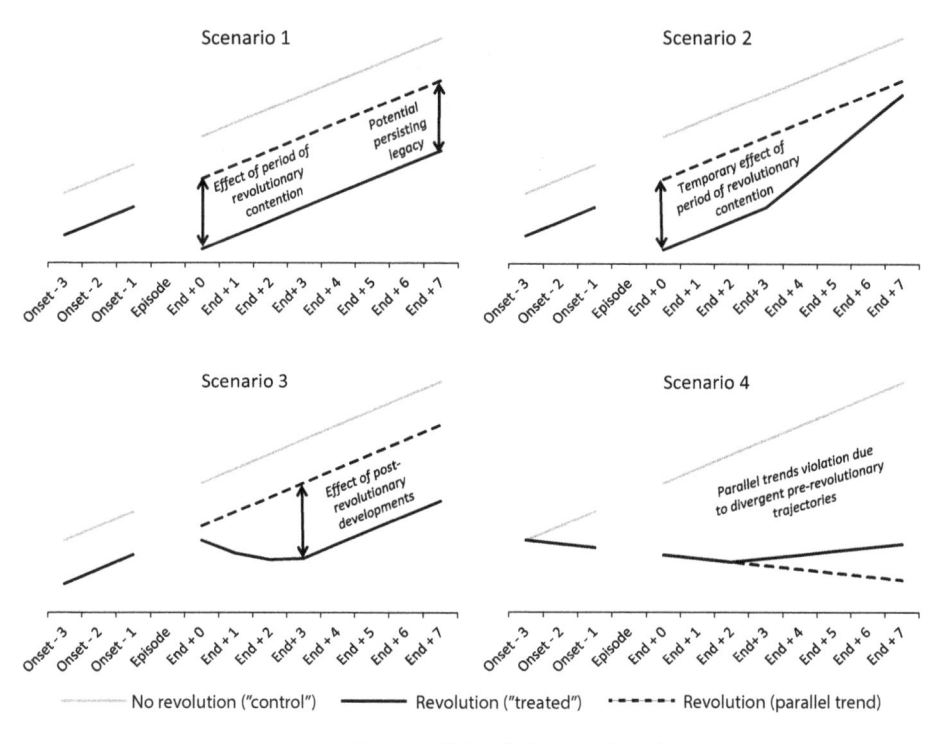

FIGURE 9.1. Conceptualizing the impact of revolution.

revolution, to compare them to other societies that did not experience revolution over the same time period or that experienced failed revolutions, and to ascertain the presence of particular violations of the parallel trends assumption.

To explore the counterfactual of what might have happened had revolutionary contention never occurred in the first place, I engaged in matching, integrating this into the difference-in-differences design. Revolutionary episodes are rare events, so the list of potential comparison cases that did not experience revolution is quite extensive. Many of these cases do not share initial starting conditions with or were on a substantially different trajectory from those cases that experienced revolution. To address this problem, matching was used to identify the most reasonable comparison cases for each revolutionary episode. I identified those cases that did not experience a revolutionary episode but were similar in key regards in the year prior to when the revolution occurred in "treated" cases (particularly on variables found earlier to be associated with revolutionary onset or success).[15] Since a chief concern of the

---

15. Details of matching procedures can be found in Appendix 4H.

difference-in-differences setup is that treatment and control groups should not differ in ways (other than assignment) that could affect their trends over time, matching on case characteristics in the year prior to revolutionary onset enhanced the validity of the analysis by eliminating potential confounders and imposing a similar distribution of key covariates onto treatment and control groups to the extent possible.[16] Of course, matching occurs on measured variables only, and, especially when comparing countries, there are many confounding influences that could also be at play in shaping levels of order, growth, inequality, freedom, and accountability—before, during, or after revolution. I used country fixed-effects to control for some of these differences. The fixed-effect essentially absorbed country-specific differences as they existed on the eve of revolutionary contention.[17] Moreover, I confined matches to the same world-region or to contiguous neighbors in order to mitigate the effects of additional unmeasured confounders. Given that the logic of matching is similar to the logic of a "most similar" research design in qualitative research,[18] I assumed that, holding all measurables equal, countries in the same world region were more likely to display similar unmeasurables that could confound the results (such as historical and cultural background, diffusion effects, or spillover effects from contiguous wars or natural disasters) than countries in different corners of the world.[19]

Due to matching restrictions, the unmatched sample contained a larger number of revolutionary episodes (176 successful and unsuccessful revolutionary episodes) than the matched sample (123 successful and unsuccessful revolutionary episodes, with 304 matched "control" cases). The matched sample was important for probing the counterfactual of what might have occurred had no revolutionary episode materialized. The unmatched sample included a larger number of revolutionary episodes and was more appropriate for exploring patterns in different types of revolutions and under different outcomes of revolutionary contention. I present analyses from both, depending on the question explored.[20]

---

16. Heckman, Ichimura, and Todd 1997; Abadie 2005.

17. A fixed-effects framework (combined with using the year prior to revolutionary onset as the base year) constrained starting points across cases to be equal in the year prior to the onset of mobilization, thus allowing one to see trends relative to the situation on the eve of revolution more clearly.

18. Nielsen 2016.

19. On the importance of region as a container for unmeasured causal effects, see Bunce 1995; Beissinger and Young 2002; Mainwaring and Pérez-Liñán 2007.

20. Full regression results can be found in the Stata output files available from the author.

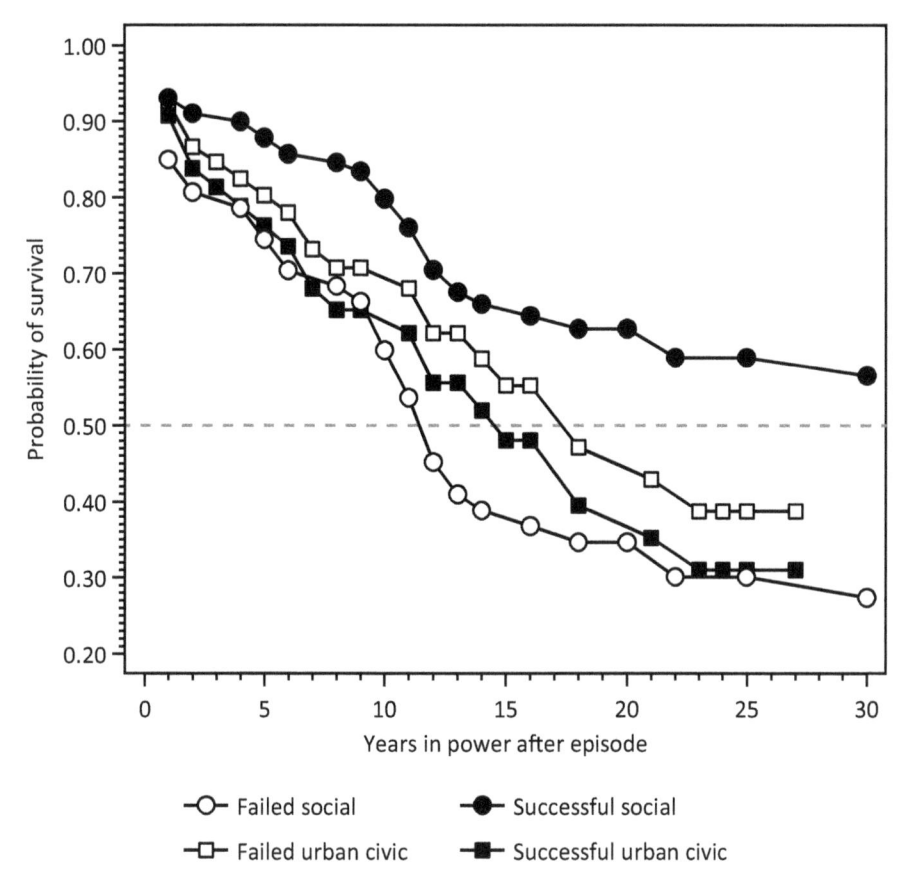

FIGURE 9.2. Survival functions for regimes after social and urban civic revolutionary episodes. Cox proportional hazards model.

Revolutions and Post-Revolutionary Political Order

One of the fundamental differences between post-revolutionary politics after successful social and urban civic revolutions is regime longevity. Figure 9.2 reports the survival curves from a Cox proportional hazards model of regime duration for social and urban civic revolutions.[21] Post-revolutionary regimes resulting from successful social revolutions have been significantly more durable than post-revolutionary regimes resulting from successful urban civic revolutions. In all, 25 percent of successful urban civic revolutions lasted only three years or less in power, as opposed to only 9 percent

21. For more on the model, see Appendix 4F.

of successful social revolutions; and 39 percent of successful urban civic revolutions lasted only eight years or less in power, as opposed to 23 percent of successful social revolutions. On average, new regimes created out of successful urban civic revolutions lasted for 11.9 years. By contrast, social revolutions produced extraordinarily long-lasting regimes, persisting in power on average for 28.9 years.[22]

Thus, regimes produced by social revolution have clearly been exceptional in their longevity. But why? The conventional answer invokes political repression after social revolutions, and there is some truth in this. The V-Dem measure for repression of civil society (averaged across the first five years after the end of revolutionary contention) has a U-shaped relationship with the durability of post-revolutionary regimes: durability is increased at low levels and high levels of repression, but regimes in the middle had lowered chances of survival.[23] Successful social revolutions produced regimes that were considerably more repressive toward civil society than other regimes produced out of revolution[24]—with most situated in the top quarter of post-revolutionary regimes in terms of repressiveness. But this cannot explain the difference in survival rates, as urban civic post-revolutionary regimes tended to be more open toward civil society than other regimes produced by revolutions.[25] Moreover, while the openness or repressiveness of post-revolutionary regimes mattered for survival, the effect is significantly weaker than that of other factors that shape post-revolutionary regime durability.

Communist regimes and vanguard parties have also been thought to produce more long-lasting post-revolutionary governments. But when compared to other post-revolutionary regimes, no statistically significant relationship exists between regime durability and whether a post-revolutionary regime came to power by means of a vanguard party. Communist regimes generally were longer lasting than other post-revolutionary regimes; but the question of why this should be the case remains, and the effect grows statistically insignificant once one controls for other factors. Indeed, a number of regimes that came to power through social revolution (for instance, the Mexican PRI and the Islamist regime in Iran) have been long-lasting in the absence of vanguard parties or communist rule.

Here is where the experience of revolutionary contention matters greatly. Levitsky and Way have argued that "the identities, norms, and organizational

22. See also Levitsky and Way 2012; Lachapelle et al. 2020; Levitsky and Way 2022.
23. Statistically significant at the .01 level.
24. In a two-tailed t-test, t = −3.5875 (significant at the .001 level).
25. In a two-tailed t-test, t = 4.9695 (significant at the .001 level).

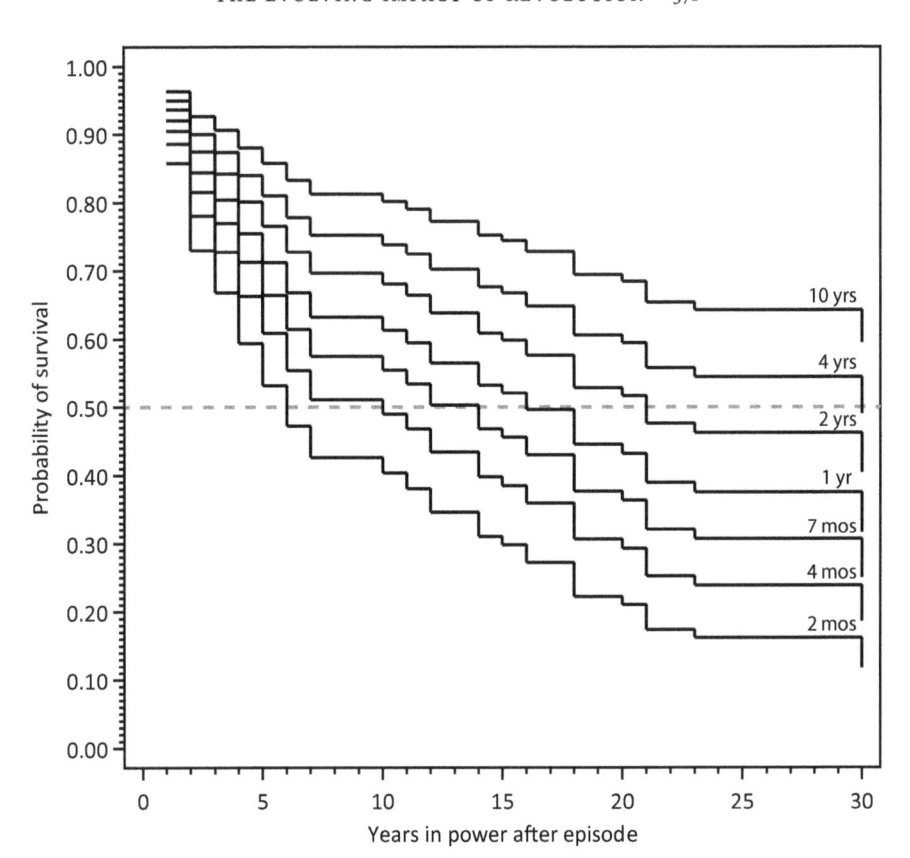

FIGURE 9.3. Survival functions for post-revolutionary regimes, by length of revolutionary episode (n = 119 successful revolutions). Cox proportional hazards model.

structures forged during periods of sustained, violent, and ideologically-driven conflict are a critical source of cohesion" for post-revolutionary regimes. Prolonged revolutionary contention aids revolutionary state-building, eliminates counterrevolutionary threats, fosters more coherent post-revolutionary regimes, and creates a strong security apparatus closely tied to the new regime.[26] There is good evidence to support the claim that sustained revolutionary struggle produces more durable post-revolutionary regimes. As pictured in Figure 9.3, there is a strong, statistically significant, and robust relationship between the duration of a revolutionary episode and the duration of the

---

26. Levitsky and Way 2012, 869. See also Huntington 1968, 418; Lachapelle et al. 2020; Levitsky and Way 2022; Clarke 2018; Clarke 2020; Slater and Smith 2016, 1478.

government produced from revolution.[27] There are, of course, numerous other factors that affect the longevity of regimes over the course of their lifetimes, such as their ability to deliver benefits to their populations, the coherence of their elites, their capacity to marginalize challengers, and the degree of division within society. But for post-revolutionary regimes, the length of revolutionary contention is one of the most important features that influences longevity—irrespective of ideology, regime repressiveness toward civil society after revolution, the experience of having survived a civil war, models of revolutionary organization, or the number of people who died in revolution.[28] As Levitsky and Way note, among successful revolutionary movements, prolonged revolutionary contention fosters elite cohesion, a sense of identity, a hardened discipline, and an organizational capability that carry over into the post-revolutionary era. These features of prolonged revolutionary contention "raise the cost of defection and provide leaders with additional (non-material) resources that can be critical to maintaining unity and discipline, even when a crisis threatens the party's hold on power."[29]

The effect of prolonged revolutionary contention on the longevity of post-revolutionary governments transcends social revolutions. Indeed, the length of revolutionary contention is a good predictor of the duration of post-revolutionary regimes, irrespective of whether the revolution was a social revolution or a different type of revolution.[30] Thus, even among successful liberal revolutions, the duration of revolutionary contention is strongly related to the longevity of post-revolutionary regimes.[31] Successful social revolutions were particularly drawn out—generally more protracted than other types of successful revolutions.[32] The average duration of successful social revolutionary episodes was eight years and eight months, and half experienced five or more years of revolutionary struggle. Simply based on the bivariate relationship between the length of revolutionary contention and post-revolutionary regime survival, regimes produced out of successful social revolutions on average would have had more than a 50 percent chance of surviving thirty years or more. By contrast, 79 percent of successful urban civic revolutions

27. Statistically significant at the .001 level. See Stata output files for results.
28. All of these other factors (with the exception of repressiveness toward civil society) proved statistically insignificant in the Cox proportional hazards model.
29. Levitsky and Way 2012, 870.
30. For both, the relationship is statistically significant at the .01 level
31. Statistically significant at the .05 level. See also Kadivar 2018a.
32. Thus, among revolutions that involved civil wars, successful social revolutions lasted on average more than twice as long as other successful revolutions (in a two-tailed t-test $t = -3.14$, significant at the .01 level with 46 degrees of freedom).

experienced four months or less of revolutionary contention, and 58 percent experienced two months or less. As a result, almost three out of every five governments brought to power by urban civic revolutions would have had less than a 50 percent chance of surviving more than six years, while four out of five would have had less than a 50 percent chance of surviving more than ten years.

As we have seen, because they occur where the coercive capacity of the state is strongest, and because sustaining disruption and high levels of participation over long periods of time within an urban environment is difficult, urban civic revolts tend to be highly concentrated in time, unfolding over a matter of days and weeks rather than years. It is impossible to forge a common sense of loyalty and identity in such a compact period of time. Moreover, to maximize participation, urban civic revolts tend to resort to loose coalitional forms of leadership and espouse minimalist goals, constructing rapidly assembled negative coalitions that pull in all who favor removal of the incumbent regime, irrespective of purpose. They have neither the desire nor the ability to filter or socialize participants, as occurs in revolutions that extend over longer periods of time. Urban civic tactics have a much higher rate of opposition success than social revolutions—in large part because of the greater efficiency of the power of numbers when located in close proximity to government nerve centers. But the consequences of this success come back to haunt them once power is attained. The regimes that come to power through urban civic revolutions are notoriously fractious, and in many cases fall apart months after the incumbent regime is driven from power. They lack the loyalty and cohesion characteristic of social revolutions.[33] These facts constrain the ability of urban civic revolutions to deliver substantive change in their wake.

Social revolutions forcefully push aside the old regime and its ruling elites. But successful urban civic revolts often leave many of the elites associated with the old regime in place, potentially providing them with the opportunity to reorganize and regain power.[34] One of the vexing issues for oppositions in many urban civic revolutions has been when to leave the square and under what circumstances mobilization should be ended. Urban civic revolutions sometimes end when the military seizes power or when the incumbent leader resigns. But in some circumstances, this can leave power in the hands of those who were part of or closely associated with the old regime—raising questions

---

33. Foran and Goodwin (1993) note that social revolutions also experience elite fragmentation in the wake of revolution that can threaten the achievement of goals. However, the prolonged contention associated with social revolutions tends to produce more disciplined and coherent regimes relative to other forms of revolution.

34. See Clarke 2018; Clarke 2020.

about what exactly revolutionaries actually accomplished. Ambiguous outcomes manifested themselves in Egypt in 2011 and Algeria in 2019. In such instances, the resignation of the incumbent leader divided the opposition, and exhausted participants found it difficult to sustain mobilization. The dilemma facing urban civic oppositions in such circumstances is whether to prolong contention (usually with smaller crowds and diminished enthusiasm) in order to challenge the ambiguous outcome, or to demobilize and threaten remobilization if change does not materialize. But remobilization after revolution is often quite difficult, given the desire of many within the population to return to normality. Even when urban civic oppositions do gain more direct control, elites closely associated with the old regime usually remain in positions of authority, becoming an opposition capable of recapturing power once the post-revolutionary regime's legitimacy begins to slip. In short, there can be downsides to relying on the power of numbers rather than the power of arms that manifest themselves once revolutionary contention ends.

Dan Slater and Nicholas Rush Smith have argued that counterrevolutions (by which they mean "collective and reactive efforts to defend the status quo and its varied range of dominant elites against a credible threat to overturn them from below")[35] produce distinctly durable political orders, as the threat of revolution unifies these regimes, inducing cooperation among a wide array of elites. Their argument may apply to the specific regimes that they analyzed. But it does not hold when looked at more systematically across cases. As Figure 9.2 shows, old regimes that survive social revolutionary threats are substantially less durable than new regimes that emerge out of social revolutions, and less durable than old regimes that survived urban civic revolutions. Moreover, new regimes produced from urban civic revolutions have approximately the same staying power as old regimes that survive urban civic revolutionary threats. The exception in the politics of durability are successful social revolutions—due to their ability to eliminate opponents and to produce cohesive and coherent post-revolutionary governments.

Durability is not the only dimension by which to judge a regime's ability to provide order. State capacity—the ability of the state to penetrate society, extract resources, and implement its goals—is severely challenged by the experience of revolution. The disorder produced by revolution disrupts the ongoing functioning of state institutions, can lead to significant challenges to territorial integrity, and undermines revenue collection. Successful social revolutions have been widely thought to lead over the long term to a state capacity greater than that of their pre-revolutionary antecedents. They remove class impediments to

---

35. Slater and Smith 2016, 1475.

state bureaucratization and mass incorporation, and are thought to forge more rationalized, centralized, and powerful states.[36] External war—with its considerable state-building implications[37]—was once closely associated with social revolution, and civil war has almost always been a component of social revolution. While civil war challenges the state capacity of incumbent regimes, the protracted contention of social revolution provides significant state-building opportunities for revolutionaries to create a disciplined military force for defeating the incumbent regime, to organize alternative governments in liberated zones, and to provide public goods and services to civilian populations. All this translates into governments after social revolutions that are more capable and more penetrative. While there is a great deal of case-specific evidence for these propositions, they have rarely been tested in a systematic way. We also know little about what happens to state capacity as a result of urban civic revolutionary contention. Urban civic revolutions tend to occur in countries that already have higher levels of state capacity than the societies that undergo social revolutions. But does the experience of revolution alter this?

Cross-national measures of state capacity are notoriously problematic. But the few measures that are available lend credence to the standard story. They also show that urban civic revolutions provide little state-building advantage—even weakening the state in some areas. The absence of civil war and large-scale violent contention in urban civic revolutions provides no impetus for building military capacity. Moreover, the compact nature of urban civic revolutions essentially means that state-building has largely been extracted from the revolutionary process, with post-revolutionary governments inheriting the state of the old regime intact rather than, in Leninist terms, smashing it and building a new one. As we will see, the implications of this for the persistence of a host of social and political relationships are profound.

V-Dem provides, for instance, an estimate of the proportion of a country's territory under the control of the central government. As those data show, the ability of a government to control its territory is tested to a far greater degree in social revolutionary than in urban civic contention. On average, the proportion of territory controlled by the new central government in successful social revolutions is 4.2 percent lower during the last year of revolutionary contention compared to the situation on the eve of revolution. In successful urban civic revolutions, it is 2 percent lower. After both social and urban civic revolutions, territorial control tends to be restored to pre-revolutionary levels relatively quickly. But in successful social revolutions, the proportion of territory

36. Brinton 1965; Skocpol 1979.
37. Tilly 1990.

controlled by the new central government seven years after the end of revolutionary contention is actually higher (by 2.9 percent, on average) than the proportion controlled by the old central government prior to the onset of revolution. By contrast, for successful urban civic revolutions, the proportion of territory controlled by the new central government seven years after the end of revolution is lower (by 1.3 percent, on average) compared to the proportion controlled by the old central government before the onset of revolution.[38]

The association of social revolutions with war and civil war translates into significantly more militarized societies after social revolutions than after urban civic revolutions. In the seven years following successful social revolutions, government military spending tended to increase substantially, growing at almost twice the rate of military spending following successful urban civic revolutions.[39] There are, of course, exceptions. Russia's annexation of Crimea and war against Ukraine over the Donbas precipitated the militarization of Ukraine in the wake of the Euromaidan Revolution. But by and large, social revolutions were associated with a more far-reaching militarization of society than has been true of urban civic revolutions.

The Hanson/Sigman measure of state capacity—one of the few cross-national measures that seeks to capture state capacity in an integral manner, incorporating extractive, coercive, and administrative dimensions—covers only a portion of the time period analyzed by the data on revolutionary contention, severely limiting sample size (particularly for social revolutions). But for the cases for which information is available, state capacity declined much more sharply during social revolutionary contention than during urban civic revolutionary contention. However, state capacity also recovered much more rapidly in the wake of successful social revolutions than after successful urban civic revolutions. In general, state capacity in regimes brought to power by social revolutions attained or exceeded the level of matched counterparts five to seven years after the end of revolutionary

---

38. Based on the average marginal predictions of a fixed-effects difference-in-differences regression (with cluster-robust standard errors) of thirteen successful social revolutions and twenty-nine successful urban civic revolutions for which data were available, using ten multiple-imputation samples. Data imputed for 3.4 percent of observations. Findings confirmed in the complete-case sample.

39. See Appendix 3 for the sources of data. Results based on the average marginal predictions of a fixed-effects difference-in-differences regression (with cluster-robust standard errors) of thirteen successful social revolutions and twenty-eight successful urban civic revolutions for which data were available, using twenty multiple-imputation samples. Data imputed for 11.1 percent of observations. In the complete-case sample, growth in military expenditure is more than three times greater after successful social revolutions than after successful urban civic revolutions.

contention. By contrast, state capacity after successful urban civic revolutions lagged significantly behind matched counterparts.[40]

Social revolutions and urban civic revolutions also display contrasting capabilities in providing law and order. Successful revolutions, irrespective of type, are almost invariably followed by an explosion in crime and criminality—in large part because they typically cause a weakening of the police and legal institutions, which tend to be closely associated with old regimes. In some cases, revolutions have also been accompanied by a breakdown of the prison system and the mass release of ordinary criminals into society, further complicating efforts to re-establish legality.[41] The collapse of the tsarist regime in February 1917, for instance, led to a huge burst of crime and mob justice in Russian society that aided the rise to power of the Bolsheviks by further delegitimizing the Provisional Government. Crime initially grew worse under the Bolsheviks, as they encouraged efforts to "smash" existing police and law enforcement bureaucracies.[42] Similarly, in the decade after the revolutions that overthrew communism, property crimes increased in central and eastern Europe by 72 percent, vehicle theft by 236 percent, robbery by 100 percent, and murder by 30 percent.[43] After its 2011 revolution, Egypt experienced a crime wave "unlike anything the country has experienced in its recent history," with crime tripling from 2011 to 2013.[44] All this can quickly undercut the legitimacy of a post-revolutionary government. In Egypt during the 2012 presidential election (the first competitive election after the 2011 revolution), districts where crime increased most significantly were also districts most likely to vote for Ahmed Shafiq, the candidate most closely associated with the Mubarak regime.[45]

Post-revolutionary regimes have differed radically in their ability to contain this upsurge in criminality. The Bolsheviks opted to crush it by entrusting the problem to the Cheka, the secret police. It turned ordinary crime into counter-revolutionary offenses and was granted the power to "arrest, try, imprison,

---

40. Based on the average marginal predictions of fixed-effects difference-in-differences regressions (with cluster-robust standard errors) on four successful social revolutions and fifteen matched cases and twenty-one successful urban civic revolutions and forty-seven matched cases for which data were available, using twenty multiple-imputation samples. Data imputed for 11.4 percent of observations. Patterns confirmed in the complete-case sample, which included six successful social revolutions and twenty-one matched cases and twenty-four successful urban civic revolutions and fifty-four matched cases.

41. This occurred, for instance, in China in 1949. See Dikötter 1997, 148.

42. Hasegawa 2017.

43. Caparini and Marenin 2005.

44. Daragahi 2013. See also Kirkpatrick 2011b.

45. Abadeer et al. 2019.

execute, and deport criminals to forced labor camps."[46] This—not political dissent—was in fact the origin of the GULAG. A similar approach was used in China after the communist victory in 1949.[47] Governments that come to power through urban civic revolutions typically lack the authoritarian impulse and institutional coherence to see through such a draconian strategy. In cases in which urban civic post-revolutionary governments have confronted the problem with heavy-handed tactics, the approach has tended to backfire. To deal with rampant crime after the Rose Revolution in Georgia in 2003, for instance, the Saakashvili government pushed aside existing law enforcement institutions, created new centralized police organizations, and engaged in a major campaign against criminality and organized crime. But over-enforcement led to crowding in prisons and to prison riots that eventually shook the regime and helped lead to its electoral defeat in 2013.[48] In other instances, persisting crime and criminality played significant roles in undermining public support for urban civic post-revolutionary regimes and helped to fuel continued political instability.

In sum, the regimes resulting from successful social revolutions excelled at producing political order in multiple ways. They had significantly greater longevity, were more militarized, fostered greater state capacity, and were better able to contain the illegality released by revolution than regimes produced out of successful urban civic revolutions—despite (or more accurately, because of) the challenges emerging from prolonged violent contention. By contrast, post-revolutionary urban civic regimes largely inherited the state, with all its baggage, from the old order, struggled to maintain political stability, and had difficulty containing post-revolutionary criminality. Unlike social revolutions, urban civic revolutions generally left no long-term legacies of state-building; on the contrary, they were associated with a weakening of the state. Thus, as revolution has shifted from social to urban civic forms, post-revolutionary regimes have become less stable and less capable of producing coherent and orderly states.

The Impact of Revolution on Economic Growth

There is a large literature in economics and political science that argues that revolutions have sharply negative consequences for economic growth.[49] Much about this relationship, however, remains unpacked.[50] For one thing, most

---

46. Hasegawa 2017, 265.

47. Dikötter 1997, 148.

48. Kukhianidze 2009; Slade 2012.

49. See, for instance, Huntington 1968; Barro and Lee 1993; Alesina et al. 1996; Ades and Chua 1997.

50. As one economist notes, "precisely what is being measured, what it means, how it operates, and what its relationship is to economic growth are shrouded in mystery" (Hart 1993, 301).

empirical studies lump revolutions together with other forms of political instability (such as military coups and assassinations) and assume that their effects on economic growth are identical and additive.[51] Most studies also fail to differentiate between the effects of failed and successful revolutions,[52] though logically one would expect that economic policies emerging after successful revolutions would differ from those in regimes that survive revolutionary challenges. Few studies probe whether different types of revolutions variously influence economic development, though revolutionary episodes differ dramatically from one another. Some involve cataclysmic civil wars that decimate human and physical capital.[53] Others involve minimal lethal violence and leave behind little physical destruction. Some last for years, even decades. Others are compact, occurring within weeks and days. These differences should have enormous effects on patterns of economic development after revolution.

Moreover, some post-revolutionary governments prioritize redistribution over economic growth and aim to remake societal relationships totally, leading to major economic dislocation. By contrast, early modern revolutions were thought to have facilitated economic growth by pushing aside landed elites, establishing secure property rights, and permitting a greater influence of commercial classes over government.[54] Olson argued that, so long as they do not become chronic, revolutions and other destabilizing events disrupt economic activities in the short term, but set the stage for more rapid growth over the long term by upending distributional coalitions that had blocked needed change in pre-revolutionary regimes.[55]

The literature is right to stress the negative economic effects of revolution. As can be seen in Figure 9.4, countries that experienced revolutionary contention (whether failed or successful) had lower levels of GDP per capita at the end of contention (point End+0) compared to the eve of contention (point Onset-1). To compare economies at different starting levels, I standardized

51. For evidence of the problematic character of this assumption, see Jong-A-Pin 2009.

52. Much of economics literature, for instance, has studied the impact of revolutions and political instability on economic growth based on political instability variables taken from the Cross-National Time-Series Data Archive, which is derived from a reading of *The New York Times*. Many of these studies lump attempted revolutions, coups, and assassinations together into an additive score based on the yearly frequency of their occurrence and do not differentiate between the economic impact of successful and failed revolutions. For examples, see Barro and Lee 1993; Alesina et al. 1996.

53. Collier 1999; Kang and Meernik 2005; Murdoch and Sandler 2002.

54. See Acemoglu, Johnson, and Robinson 2005. For a study showing the positive impact of democratic transition on economic growth, see Rodrik and Wacziarg 2005.

55. Olson 1982. See also Moore 1966; Acemoglu and Robinson 2005.

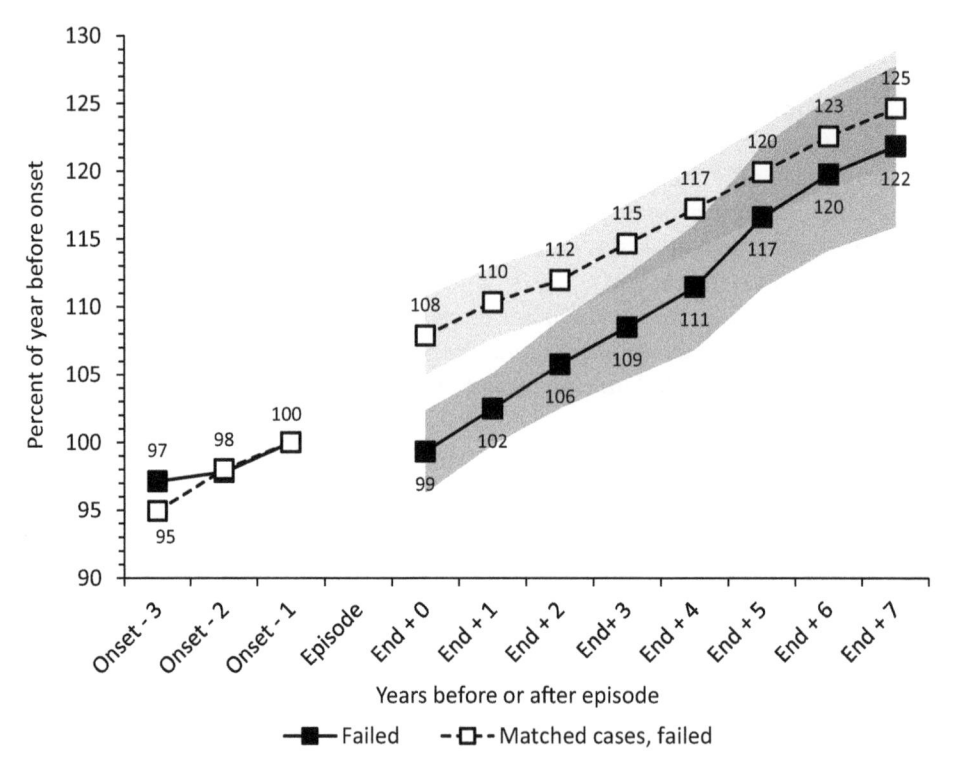

FIGURE 9.4A. Growth in GDP per capita for failed revolutions, relative to matched cases (100 = GDP per capita in the year prior to revolutionary onset). Average marginal predictions from fixed-effects difference-in-differences regressions (with 95 percent confidence intervals and cluster-robust standard errors) on 64 failed revolutions and 158 matched cases, using ten multiple-imputation samples. Data were imputed for 5.8 percent of observations.

GDP per capita at 100 for the year prior to revolutionary onset, comparing economic development before and after a revolutionary episode to this initial value. The differences between the matched samples and both failed and successful revolutions are striking. Thus, by the end of revolutionary contention the economies of countries that experienced failed revolutions (9.4a) had contracted on average by one percent compared to their level at the onset of revolution. Yet, over the same period the matched sample experienced an 8 percent increase in GDP per capita. The economic cost of failed revolution is partially rooted in the disruption caused by revolutionary contention. But it is compounded by the opportunity costs of missed growth during the period of revolutionary contention. Nevertheless, the negative effects of failed revolution are temporary. They fade away during the following years, so that what

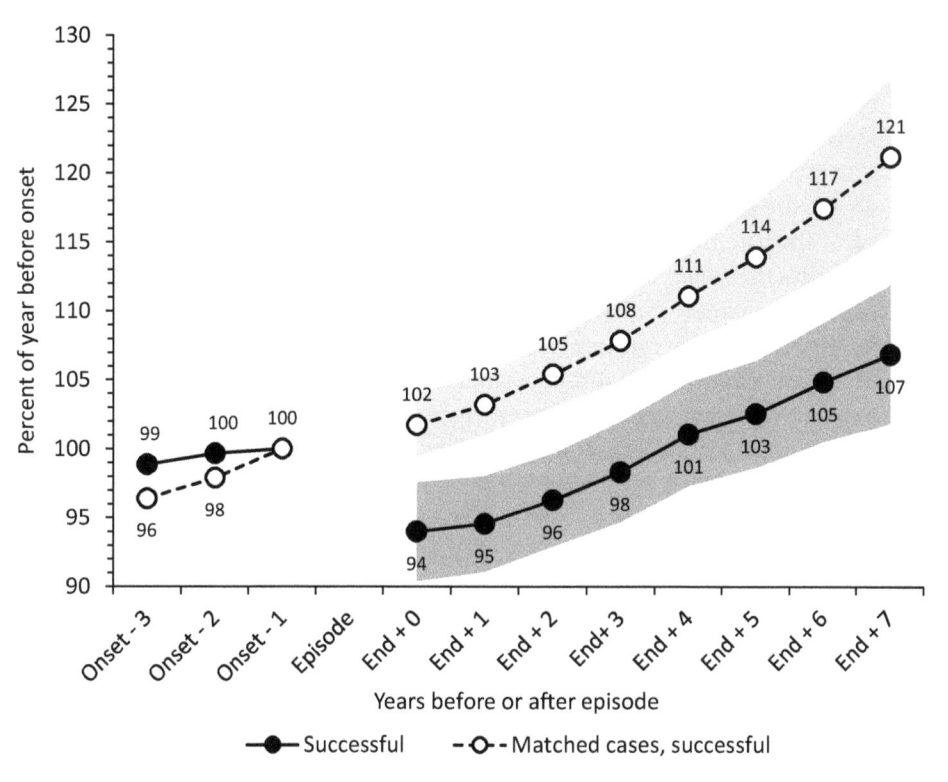

FIGURE 9.4B. Growth in GDP per capita for successful revolutions, relative to matched cases (100 = GDP per capita in the year prior to revolutionary onset). Average marginal predictions from fixed-effects difference-in-differences regressions (with 95 percent confidence intervals and cluster-robust standard errors) on 59 successful revolutions and 146 matched cases, using ten multiple-imputation samples. Data were imputed for 5.8 percent of observations.

was once a 9 percent gap with the matched sample at the end of revolution was only a 3 percent gap five to seven years later.

The situation is markedly different for countries that experienced successful revolutions (9.4b). These countries on average underwent a 6 percent contraction in their economies during the period of revolutionary contention—even while their matched counterparts grew on average by 2 percent during the same period.[56] But what is striking is that this gap increased over time. Thus,

---

56. Using the larger unmatched sample of 176 episodes (ninety-one failed and eighty-five successful revolutions) as a robustness check, the effect of successful revolutions on GDP per capita is similar (a 6.6 percent drop as a result of revolutionary contention). But the model also indicates no negative effect of revolutionary contention for failed revolutions. This raises

what had been an 8 percent gap at the end of revolutionary contention had grown on average to a 14 percent gap seven years later. The economic costs of successful revolution were compounded over time and exacerbated by post-revolutionary governance and developments. One other feature merits attention in Figure 9.4b: the apparent violation of the parallel trends assumption during the pre-revolutionary period. In contrast to their matched counterparts, the pattern of economic growth prior to revolutionary contention for countries that experienced successful revolutions was flat. This suggests that some of the poor record of post-revolutionary economic performance might be attributable to factors that transcend the revolutionary divide (position in the global economy, persistent corruption, lower human capital, etc.). The more upward trend in growth that emerged three or four years after successful revolutions remained at a slower pace than that of matched counterparts. In short, countries that experienced successful revolutions suffered a significant economic penalty due to the effects of revolutionary contention, and in the wake of revolution they generally failed to overcome pre-revolutionary patterns of sluggish growth—at least during the period examined here.

But the picture grows more nuanced as we examine different types of revolutions. There are sharp differences in the economic impacts of social versus urban civic revolutions (Figures 9.5 and 9.6). Successful social revolutions (9.5a) generally precipitated a steep drop in GDP per capita, with revolutionary contention alone contracting these economies by 8 percent on average compared to pre-revolutionary levels of development (14 percent lower than their matched counterparts that did not experience revolution over the same time period).[57] In some cases, the contraction was catastrophic. At the end of the Russian Revolution in 1920, for instance, the economy of Russia was less than half of what it had been in 1916, while the Nicaraguan economy in 1979 was two-thirds of its level on the eve of revolution in 1977. On average, the economies of countries experiencing successful social revolutions only recovered to pre-revolutionary levels of GDP per capita four years after the end of revolutionary contention,[58] though the gap between them and their matched counterparts actually widened to 20 percent during the first two years after the revolution as a result of post-revolutionary governance and developments.

---

profound questions about the assumption that both failed and successful revolutions exert similar negative economic effects.

57. Confidence intervals in Figure 9.5a overlap largely because of the small number of successful social revolutions (nine) in the sample, as standard errors are clustered on the revolutionary episode.

58. In the Soviet case, for instance, industrial production recovered to pre-World War I levels by 1926 (Davies 1990, 6).

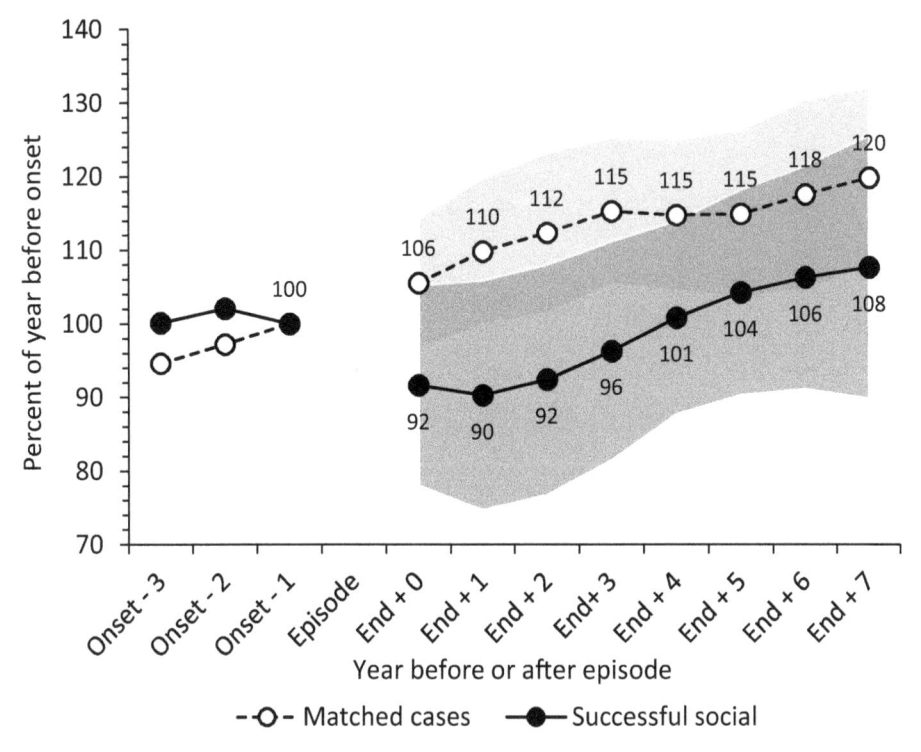

FIGURE 9.5A. Growth in GDP per capita for successful social revolutions, relative to matched cases (100 = GDP per capita in the year prior to revolutionary onset). Average marginal predictions from fixed-effects difference-in-differences regressions (with 95 percent confidence intervals and cluster-robust standard errors) on 9 successful social revolutions and 25 matched cases, using ten multiple-imputation samples. Data were imputed for 5.8 percent of observations.

The governments brought to power through social revolution promoted goals of social equality over economic growth, often used violence as a tool for transforming societies, and were known to implement utopian anti-market schemes. (During War Communism, for instance, the Bolsheviks attempted to destroy capitalist trade by demeaning the value of money, printing it in such large quantities as to purposely make it worthless.) Redistributive policies and violence against formerly dominant classes incited large-scale emigration and led to a loss of human capital (especially skilled human capital) that lowered productivity.[59] All this had a strongly negative impact on economic development, causing post-revolutionary regimes to lag far behind their matched

59. Gyimah-Brempong and Camacho 1998.

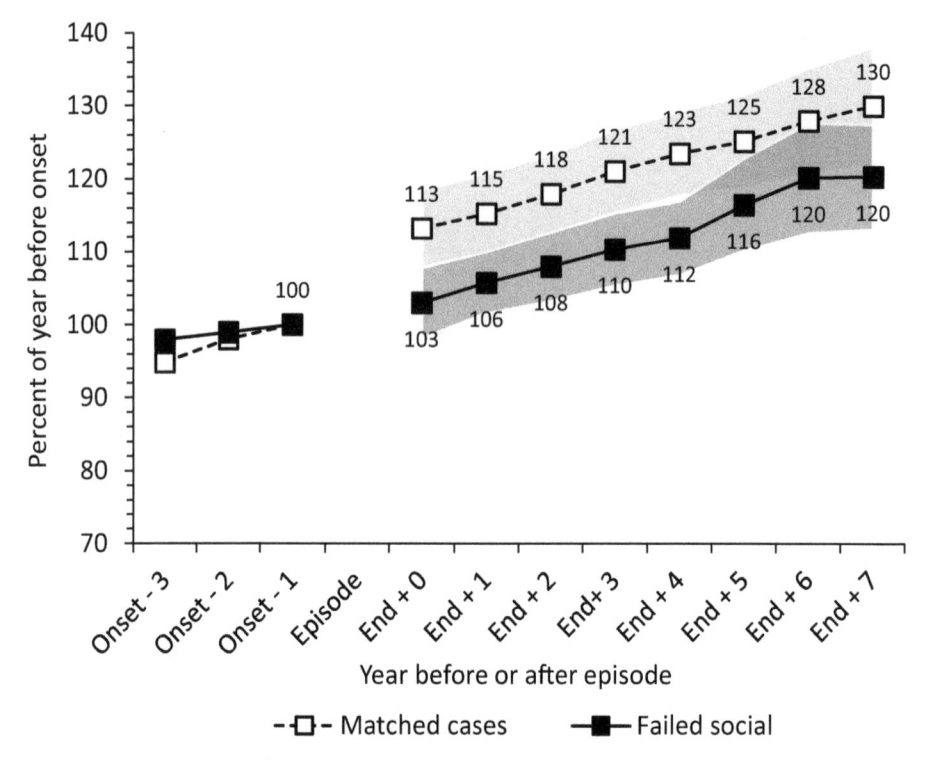

FIGURE 9.5B. Growth in GDP per capita for failed social revolutions, relative to matched cases (100 = GDP per capita in the year prior to revolutionary onset). Average marginal predictions from fixed-effects difference-in-differences regressions (with 95 percent confidence intervals and cluster-robust standard errors) on 23 failed social revolutions and 53 matched cases, using ten multiple-imputation samples. Data were imputed for 5.8 percent of observations.

counterparts. Four years after the end of revolution, as the economies of these societies began to recover, the gap with matched counterparts began to narrow (also due in part to stagnating growth among matched counterparts). Still, for successful social revolutions, the economic impact of revolution and post-revolutionary governance persisted over time, with these societies continuing to display a 12 percent gap on average relative to matched counterparts seven years after the end of revolutionary contention. Societies that experienced failed social revolutions (9.5b) also displayed a 10-point gap relative to their matched counterparts—a gap that remained largely stable over the post-revolutionary period and was due to the destruction and lingering effects of revolutionary contention. Thus, both failed and successful social revolutions left significant negative economic legacies in their wake.

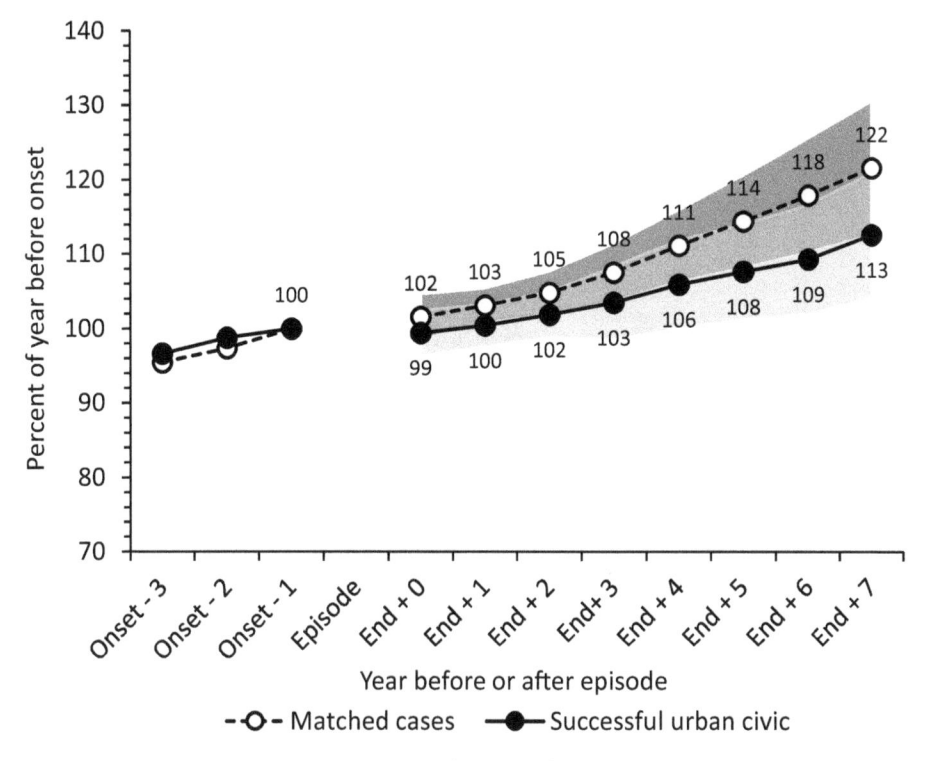

FIGURE 9.6A. Growth in GDP per capita for successful urban civic revolutions, relative to matched cases (100 = GDP per capita in the year prior to revolutionary onset). Average marginal predictions from fixed-effects difference-in-differences regressions (with 95 percent confidence intervals and cluster-robust standard errors) on 26 successful urban civic revolutions and 60 matched cases, using ten multiple-imputation samples. Data were imputed for 5.8 percent of observations.

There were also some violations of the parallel trends assumption, as hints of divergent trajectories had already appeared prior to the onset of social revolutionary contention. In successful social revolutions growth turned sharply downward in the year prior to the onset of revolution—foreshadowing and compounding the economic crises that would plague these societies after revolution. Similarly, societies that experienced failed social revolutions displayed somewhat less robust patterns of growth before the onset of revolutionary contention compared to matched counterparts. But aside from the harmful economic effects of revolutionary contention, for failed social revolutions trajectories were largely parallel with matched counterparts in the aftermath of revolution, as these societies' patterns of economic growth came to resemble those of their matched counterparts more closely after revolutionary contention than before.

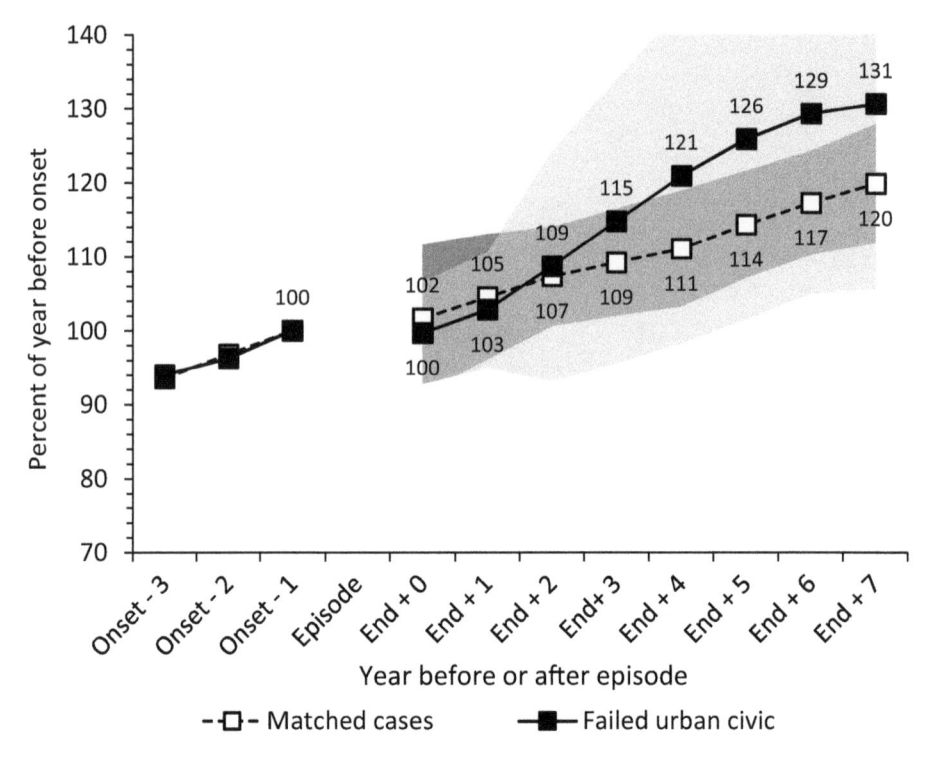

FIGURE 9.6B. Growth in GDP per capita for failed urban civic revolutions, relative to matched cases (100 = GDP per capita in the year prior to revolutionary onset). Average marginal predictions from fixed-effects difference-in-differences regressions (with 95 percent confidence intervals and cluster-robust standard errors) on 10 failed urban civic revolutions and 28 matched cases, using ten multiple-imputation samples. Data were imputed for 5.8 percent of observations.

By contrast, for societies that experienced successful urban civic revolutions (9.6a) there was relatively little immediate effect of the period of revolutionary contention on GDP per capita. Rather, the difference between these societies and their matched counterparts emerged slowly over the years following revolutionary contention, developing gradually into a 9-point gap, on average, six to seven years after the new revolutionary regime came to power. The immediate damage of urban civic revolutionary contention on economic development was minimal. But sluggish growth after urban civic revolutions was cumulative and substantial—and starkly visible years later. The threat posed by sluggish growth to post-revolutionary urban civic regimes is well illustrated by the 2010 Tunisian Revolution. In the immediate wake of the revolution, Tunisia's economy contracted by 1.4 percent. But over the following years the country's economic development was hobbled, growing a total of 6 percent over the subsequent five years. Tunisia's tourism industry suffered significant blows as a result of occasional outbursts of terrorism and continuing unrest. Even as unemployment rose well above pre-revolutionary levels, Tunisia's parties were plagued by infighting that paralyzed efforts to deal with the problem.[60] Particularly hard hit were areas of Tunisia that had been at the forefront of the 2010 revolution. In January 2016, a young man from the town of Kasserine committed suicide by electrocuting himself in desperation over his economic plight. Over the ensuing days, protests in solidarity spread to neighboring towns, including Sidi Bouzid, where the 2010 Tunisian Revolution began. The January 2016 demonstrations eventually spread to sixteen governorates and the capital Tunis, where the government was forced to impose a curfew.[61]

But the economic impact of failed urban civic revolutions (9.6b) is especially surprising. While there is a great deal of variation across these cases, societies that underwent failed urban civic revolutions on average experienced higher levels of economic growth than their matched counterparts— particularly in the two- to five-year window following revolutionary contention. For example, economic growth in Azerbaijan in the wake of its failed color revolution in 2005 was 67 percent greater in the following seven years than in its matched case of Kazakhstan over the same period. (Both were oil states in the midst of major economic expansions and affected by the same conditions of the international oil market.) Growth in China in the wake of the Tiananmen protests was 3.5 percent higher in the seven years following the episode than its matched case of Vietnam over the same period. (Both countries underwent major economic reforms during this period that integrated them into the world economy.) On average, societies that experienced failed urban civic revolutions had opened up a 9 percent gap over matched counterparts seven years after the end of revolutionary contention. The confidence intervals are particularly wide, however, and the finding here may simply be the result of the outsized influence of a few exceptional cases like China or Azerbaijan. Not all old regimes that survived urban civic challenges fared so well; but a number that did received major injections of foreign investment after crushing revolutionary challengers. In these cases, successful repression of revolution appears to have assured foreign investors eager to buy into profitable opportunities. In contrast to social revolutions, there are no clear violations of the parallel trends assumption in the pre-revolutionary period for urban civic revolutions. The divergent patterns of

---

60. Berman 2018.
61. Stephen 2016.

development manifest themselves entirely after the end of revolutionary contention (even if they may be rooted in the features of revolutionary contention characteristic of these cases).

What accounts for the slowly emerging gap with matched counterparts for societies experiencing successful urban civic revolutions, as opposed to the suddenly imposed and persistent gap associated with social revolution? Certainly, a significant part of the explanation lies in variations in the degree of destruction and disruption that occurred during revolutionary contention. Differences in the duration and violence of revolutionary contention explain why social revolutions brought on sudden large declines in GDP per capita while urban civic revolutions did not. The number of deaths that occurred within a revolutionary episode is strongly correlated with the degree of economic contraction during the period of revolutionary contention.[62] Without controlling for the effect of any other factor, a revolution that involved ten thousand deaths would be associated with an immediate drop of approximately $49 in GDP per capita by the end of revolutionary contention (or 3 percent of GDP per capita for the average country experiencing revolution); a revolution that involved fifty thousand deaths, an $85 contraction (on average, 6 percent of GDP per capita); and a revolution that involved 250,000 deaths, a $128 contraction (on average, a 9 percent contraction of GDP per capita). By contrast, countries undergoing revolutions involving fewer than a thousand deaths suffered no direct negative impact on economic development.[63] More than four-fifths of successful social revolutions involved more than a thousand deaths, while 94 percent of successful urban civic revolutions involved fewer than a thousand. The median successful social revolution generated twenty-six thousand deaths and would have been expected to produce an immediate contraction of $105 in GDP per capita (or 7.2 percent)—simply as result of the death and destruction caused by revolutionary contention.

Conversely, for countries undergoing urban civic revolutions, the nemesis of economic development is not the violence and destruction of revolutionary contention, nor redistributive and coercive post-revolutionary government, but weak and corrupt institutions. As we have seen, urban civic revolutions weaken

---

62. Using the unmatched sample of 163 revolutionary episodes, there is a statistically significant negative relationship (at the .01 level, using robust standard errors) between the logged number of deaths in a revolutionary episode and the degree of change that occurred in GDP per capita between the onset and the end of revolutionary contention.

63. Of course, these estimations do not include the ways in which the destruction occurring during revolutionary contention further reflected on economic growth in the years following a revolutionary episode.

states, and the loose and rapidly assembled coalitions that underpin urban civic revolutions result in fractious post-revolutionary governments that are fragile and less stable than those produced after social revolutions. This lack of coherence hinders urban civic post-revolutionary governments from dealing with the economic challenges that they face in the wake of revolutionary contention, particularly in comparison with their matched counterparts. By Witold Henisz's measure of political constraints (which captures the number of veto points in government and the distances of political preferences among them),[64] political executives in post-revolutionary urban civic governments were on average three to four times more constrained in terms of producing policy change than their pre-revolutionary predecessors on the eve of revolution, and twice as constrained as their matched counterparts over the same period of time.[65] Over the course of the seven years following revolution, they were subject to significantly higher constraints than political executives in governments emerging either from successful social revolutions or from failed urban civic revolutions.[66] By contrast, there are no statistically significant differences between constraints on political executives in governments produced by social revolutions and those of either their pre-revolutionary predecessors or their matched counterparts. For urban civic post-revolutionary regimes, constraints on policy change generally peak two to five years after revolutionary contention—precisely when these regimes begin to experience stagnating growth and should be introducing reforms to ensure an environment conducive to development. In short, urban civic post-revolutionary governments are more divided, more constrained, and much less capable of producing policy change than their pre-revolutionary predecessors and their logical comparison sets.

Particularly troubling for economic development after urban civic revolutions are persisting high levels of corruption. Corruption (as measured by the

---

64. Henisz 2002.

65. Based on the average marginal predictions of fixed-effects difference-in-differences regressions (with cluster-robust standard errors) for nine successful social revolutions and twenty-five matched cases and twenty-four successful urban civic revolutions and fifty-five matched cases, using ten multiple-imputation samples. Data imputed for 6.8 percent of observations. Findings hold in the complete-case sample.

66. Based on the average marginal predictions of fixed-effects difference-in-differences regressions (with cluster-robust standard errors) for thirteen successful and thirty-nine failed social revolutions and twenty-seven successful and twenty-one failed urban civic revolutions, using ten multiple-imputation samples. Data imputed for 4.8 percent of observations. Findings hold in the complete-case sample.

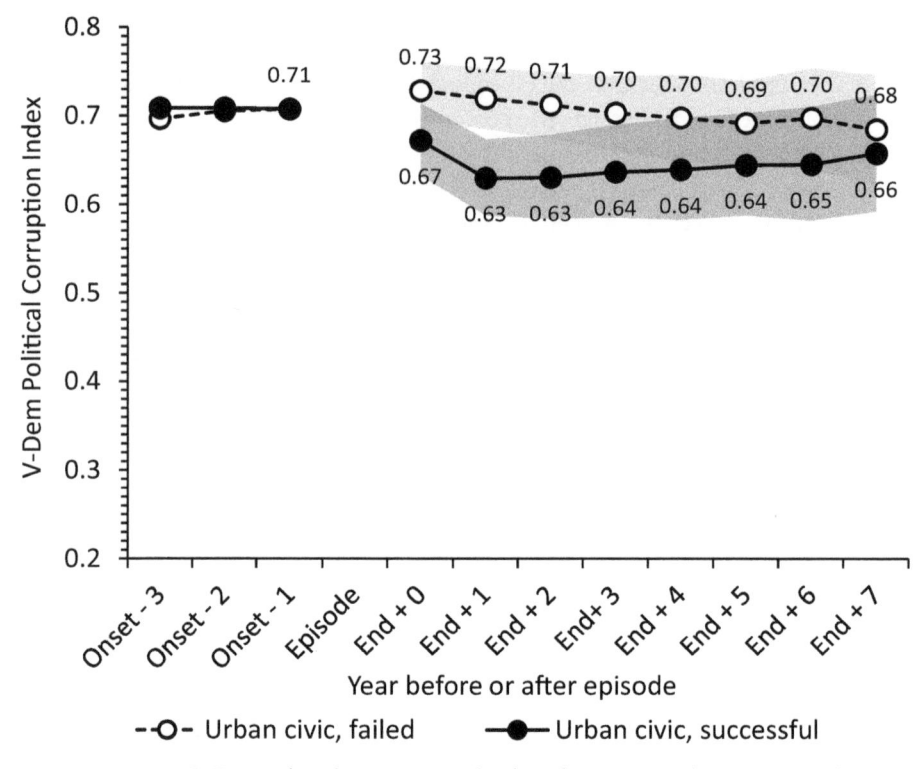

FIGURE 9.7A. V-Dem political corruption index for urban civic revolutionary episodes, failed vs successful episodes. Average marginal predictions from fixed-effects difference-in-differences regressions (with 95 percent confidence intervals and cluster-robust standard errors) on 20 failed and 29 successful urban civic revolutions, using ten multiple-imputation samples. Data were imputed for 2.9 percent of observations.

V-Dem corruption index)[67] is substantially higher in countries that experience urban civic revolutions than in those that experience social revolutions (Figure 9.7). In the wake of successful urban civic revolutions (9.7a), corruption initially declined slightly; but it remained at elevated levels in subsequent years, with small and statistically insignificant differences from pre-revolutionary regimes, regimes experiencing failed urban civic revolutions, and matched counterparts. The initial modest and relatively insubstantial decline in corruption eroded over time. The compact character of urban civic revolutionary processes has meant that urban civic post-revolutionary regimes largely inherit the state of the old regime—including its pervasive corruption

67. Coppedge et al. 2016.

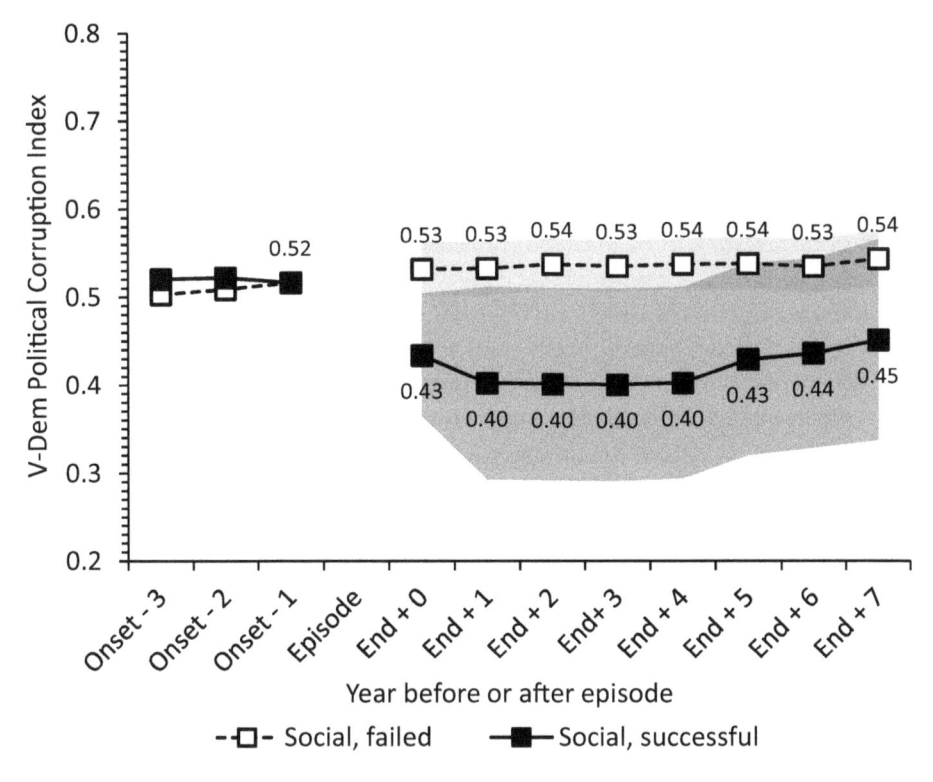

FIGURE 9.7B. V-Dem political corruption index for social revolutionary episodes, failed vs successful episodes. Average marginal predictions from fixed-effects difference-in-differences regressions (with 95 percent confidence intervals and cluster-robust standard errors) on 40 failed and 14 successful social revolutions, using ten multiple-imputation samples. Data were imputed for 2.9 percent of observations.

(a feature strongly associated with the onset of urban civic revolutionary contention in the first place). By contrast, there was a much more sizeable decline in corruption after successful social revolutions relative to its levels in pre-revolutionary regimes and regimes experiencing failed social revolutions (9.7b)—though even here some retrenchment over time is evident.[68] Corruption is well known to exercise a negative effect on economic growth.[69] Thus, despite the lower level of violence associated with urban civic revolutionary contention, a series of features of urban civic post-revolutionary governance—heightened constraints on political power, high levels of political uncertainty,

68. Findings hold in the matched sample as well.
69. Mauro 1995, Mo 2001.

and persisting corruption—exert a negative effect on economic growth that accumulates over time, producing a gap between these societies and their matched counterparts.

There are numerous other ways in which revolutionary contention and post-revolutionary governance can harm economic growth. Revolutions are generally thought to undermine societal incentives for investment (including foreign investment) by generating insecurity and eroding property rights.[70] In successful social revolutions, total investment relative to GDP dropped on average by 9 percent merely as a result of revolutionary contention.[71] This gap was exacerbated in subsequent years as property rights deteriorated, with investment never recovering to pre-revolutionary levels during the seven years following revolutionary contention and lagging far behind matched counterparts.[72] Successful urban civic revolutions displayed a markedly different pattern. The brief period of revolutionary contention was associated with an immediate drop of 2 percent in total investment as a percentage of GDP. Yet property rights actually strengthened in the wake of successful urban civic revolutions,[73] and investment recovered, on average, to pre-revolutionary levels within three years, with no statistically significant difference from matched counterparts. In short, economic growth after successful social revolutions was deeply affected by a sharp decline in investment, but this was not the chief cause of economic stagnation after successful urban civic revolutions.

Both urban civic and social revolutions also generated significant price inflation. For social revolutions, high levels of inflation were often a feature of

70. Barro and Lee 1993, 287; Alesina et al. 1996; Büthe and Milner 2008.

71. Based on the average marginal predictions from a fixed-effects difference-in-differences regression (with cluster-robust standard errors) on eight successful social revolutions and twenty-five successful urban civic revolutions for which data were available, using ten multiple-imputation samples. Data imputed for 7.7 percent of observations.

72. Based on the average marginal predictions of fixed-effects difference-in-differences regressions (with cluster-robust standard errors) on five successful social revolutions and sixteen matched cases for which data were available and twenty-two successful urban civic revolutions and forty-seven matched cases, using ten multiple-imputation samples. Data imputed for 8.2 percent of observations. Patterns replicated in the complete-case sample.

73. According to the V-Dem property rights index, property rights in societies experiencing successful urban civic revolutions not only increased in the wake of revolution relative to pre-revolutionary levels but were significantly stronger than in their matched counterparts. Based on the average marginal predictions of a fixed-effects difference-in-differences regression (with cluster-robust standard errors) on twenty-six successful urban civic revolutions and sixty matched cases for which data were available, using ten multiple-imputation samples. Data imputed for 4.1 percent of observations, and the results confirmed in the complete-case sample.

pre-revolutionary situations[74] and carried over into the revolutionary and post-revolutionary periods. But revolutions also disrupt commerce and supply chains and often lead to shortages of goods and hoarding behavior. The Bolshevik and the Chinese revolutions produced some of the most egregious instances of hyperinflation in history. Social revolutions have frequently been accompanied by rampant shortages of basic consumer items—shortages that have often been aggravated by post-revolutionary economic policies. In societies that experience successful social revolutions, the average annual rate of inflation in the final year of revolutionary contention was 77 percent, with heightened inflation often continuing in the 20–60 percent range over the ensuing seven years.[75] High rates of inflation were not necessarily a feature of urban civic pre-revolutionary situations. But inflation nonetheless spiked as a result of urban civic revolutionary contention and accelerated during the first years of post-revolutionary governance, peaking at an average annual rate of 37 percent and then subsiding to the 10–25 percent range. It remained significantly higher than in matched counterparts,[76] often becoming a source of societal dissatisfaction.

Successful revolutions—irrespective of type—also produce an explosion of governmental debt in their wake.[77] There are many reasons for this: a decline in extractive capacity associated with the disruptions of revolutionary contention and weakening of state capacity;[78] economic contraction and capital

74. On the connection between inflation and the onset of early modern revolutions, see Goldstone 1991.

75. On the association between political instability and inflation, see Cukierman, Edwards, and Tabellini 1992; Aisen and Veiga 2006; Aisen and Veiga 2008. Results based on the average marginal predictions of a random-effects difference-in-differences regression on eleven successful social revolutions and twenty-eight successful urban civic revolutions for which data were available, using ten multiple-imputation samples. Data imputed for 5.2 percent of observations.

76. Based on the average marginal predictions of a fixed-effects difference-in-differences regression (with cluster-robust standard errors) on twenty-five successful urban civic revolutions and fifty-three matched cases for which data were available, using ten multiple-imputation samples. Data imputed for 6.9 percent of observations.

77. Results based on the average marginal predictions of a fixed-effects difference-in-differences regression (with cluster-robust standard errors) on forty-nine successful revolutions and fifty-eight failed revolutions for which data were available, using twenty multiple-imputation samples. Data imputed for 10.4 percent of observations. Even controlling for the contraction in GDP per capita that accompanied revolution, government debt as a proportion of GDP increased significantly in the wake of successful revolutions. By contrast, failed revolutions exerted only a small impact on government debt.

78. Besley and Persson 2008.

flight;[79] the costs of revolutionary or post-revolutionary wars and increased security as public order erodes; spending to repair the destruction caused by revolutionary contention; and increased societal demands on government as a result of the political opening caused by regime-change. For successful social revolutions, government debt rose on average from 51 to 70 percent of GDP simply over the course of revolutionary contention. But reflecting these revolutions' social agenda and their understanding of the proper role of the state in the economy, over the seven years following revolution government debt as a proportion of GDP climbed rapidly, to 88 percent on average.[80]

For successful urban civic revolts, government debt also jumped: from 51 to 59 percent of GDP in the immediate wake of revolutionary contention. As we have seen, economic demands have usually been central to the outbreak of urban civic contention, and the contraction in public goods, subsidies, and employment opportunities for urban groups under the pressure of neoliberal economics has often fueled the grievances underpinning these revolts. In the immediate wake of successful urban civic revolutions, post-revolutionary governments have been under conflicting pressures. On the one hand, the mobilized public has demanded redress and has sought increased public spending for jobs, subsidies, and provision of public goods. On the other hand, their indebted states have continued to be at the mercy of international financial institutions, which have insisted on containment of government spending as a condition of new loans. International financial institutions have generally won this battle. After three years of heightened public spending by urban civic post-revolutionary regimes, government debt has tended to decline sharply— dropping to pre-revolutionary levels as fiscal pressures (often externally generated) kicked in.

In sum, revolutions can be damaging to economic development in almost every way imaginable: they can destroy physical and human capital; undermine investment; and spur inflation and government debt. However, the degree to which they have been harmful, the length of the pain, and the manner in which this has occurred has varied. While countries undergoing both failed and successful revolutions experienced contractions in the wake of revolutionary contention, the effects tended to be temporary after failed revolutions,

---

79. Alesina et al. 1996.

80. Results based on the average marginal predictions of a fixed-effects difference-in-differences regression (with cluster-robust standard errors) on four successful social revolutions and twenty-two successful urban civic revolutions for which data were available, using ten multiple-imputation samples. Data imputed for 10 percent of observations. Patterns further confirmed in the complete-case sample.

whereas the economic costs of successful revolution have generally been significant and more enduring.

But sharp distinctions can be observed between the ways in which different types of revolutions influence the economy. Successful social revolutions produced sudden economic declines in their wake that persisted over subsequent years, exacerbated by redistributive and coercive post-revolutionary government, lagging investment, high inflation, and burgeoning government debt. By contrast, urban civic revolutions exerted less immediate impact on economic growth. The fact that they occurred within a concentrated period of time minimized direct disruption of the economy compared with the effects of the protracted civil wars associated with social revolutions. Moreover, the hastily convened negative coalitions on which urban civic revolutions rested were not capable of engaging in the kinds of disruptive post-revolutionary transformations that social revolutions were able to carry through. In all these respects, urban civic revolutions minimized the short-term costs of revolution. But as we have seen, instability, governance problems, and continuing corruption plagued these regimes, creating a significant problem of sluggish growth over the longer term.

Thus, there is still an economic price to be paid for urban civic revolution, though the true costs emerge only gradually. While urban civic revolutions exert a more contained impact than social revolutions on investment, inflation, and debt, they still experience windows of significant economic disruption in the wake of revolution that can fuel considerable societal discontent. Their fractious and less coherent post-revolutionary governments often struggle to contain the fallout. The 2011 Egyptian Revolution illustrates well the political perils that reduced investment, increased inflation, and rocketing government debt can entail for a fledgling urban civic revolution. In the two years following the revolution, the tourist industry collapsed, investment dropped from 17 to 14 percent of GDP, inflation and unemployment shot up, and government debt soared from $30 billion to $40 billion, as the Morsi government struggled to cover popular food and fuel subsidies. All this fed into the mass discontent that helped to precipitate the 2013 protests and coup that ended Morsi's rule.[81] The political make-up of urban civic post-revolutionary regimes leaves them more exposed to the fallout that inevitably accompanies economic decline

---

81. Clarke 2018; Clarke 2020; Dorell 2013; Butter 2013. Some element of these economic disruptions in Egypt may have been purposefully instigated by elites from the old regime, though as we have seen, they are common to successful urban civic revolutions more generally.

after revolution than is the case for the cohesive and more durable regimes brought to power by social revolutions.

Revolution and Inequality

By definition, social revolutions aim to transform class relations, and regimes emerging from social revolutions prioritize equality over economic growth—at least in the immediate aftermath of revolution.[82] Thus, it comes as no surprise that regimes brought to power through social revolutions reduced a wide variety of inequalities. Following social revolutions, large private land holdings were broken up, redistributed to poorer peasants, and/or nationalized; state ownership over the economy increased substantially; income was redistributed downward; and education and healthcare were nationalized and made more accessible.[83] Indeed, analysis of the V-Dem Equal Distribution of Resources Index (a synthetic measure that attempts to gauge how equally resources are distributed in society based on access to public goods, access to welfare provisions, educational equality, health equality, and equality of political representation) shows that societies that underwent successful social revolutions experienced a substantial leap in equality compared to matched counterparts (Figure 9.8a).

Compared to what we know about social revolutions, we know relatively little about inequality after urban civic revolutions. They have occurred in societies already at a much higher level of equality than those experiencing social revolutions. But as Figure 9.8b shows, even these societies experienced a small but statistically significant increase in overall levels of equality after revolution compared to matched counterparts—at least as measured by the V-Dem index. The results suggest that revolutions, irrespective of type, lessen inequalities. When those who are traditionally excluded from the political sphere are suddenly included, there are clear egalitarian effects.[84]

But these findings conceal a great deal. Inequality comes in a wide variety of forms, and there has been significant variation across forms of inequality after different types of revolutions and in the nature of the redistribution taking place. In general, relative to matched counterparts, access to education and

---

82. Because they occurred in less developed societies, social revolutions tended to become modernizing revolutions as well, and over time goals of economic growth gained increased priority over equality. See Johnson 1970.

83. Eckstein 1982. Research has suggested that the equality introduced by social revolutions tends to fade over time. See Kelley and Klein 1977; Weede and Muller 1997.

84. Boix 2003.

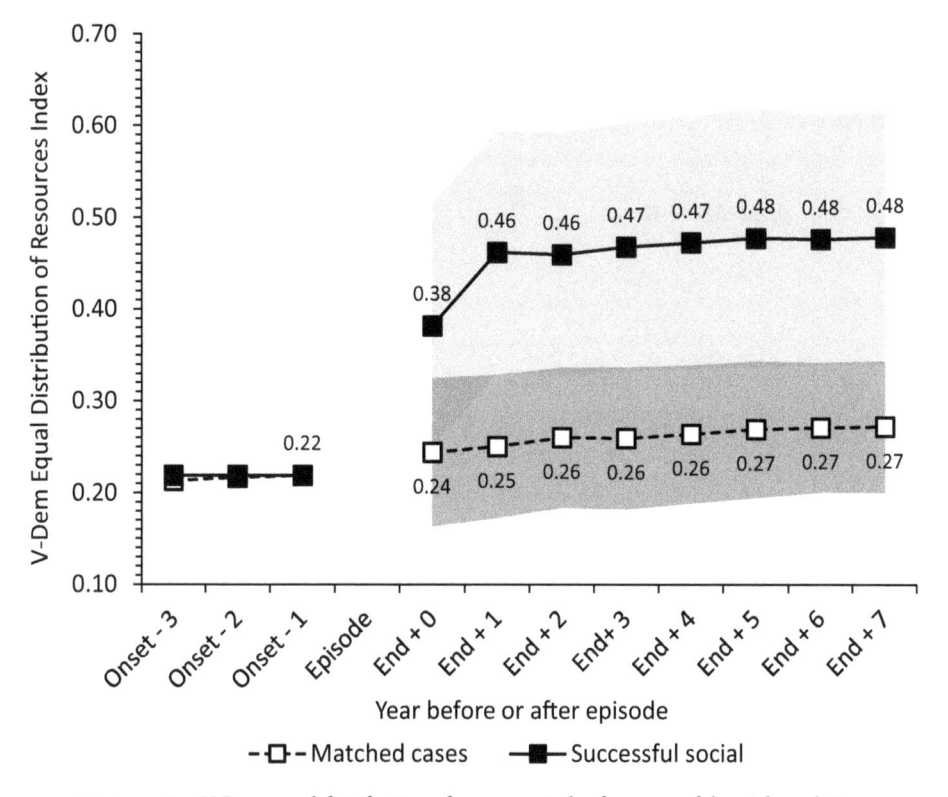

FIGURE 9.8A. V-Dem equal distribution of resources index for successful social revolutions, relative to matched cases. Average marginal predictions from fixed-effects difference-in-differences regressions (with 95 percent confidence intervals and cluster-robust standard errors) on 9 successful social revolutions and 25 matched cases, using ten multiple-imputation samples. Data were imputed for 4.1 percent of observations.

healthcare improved in the wake of both social and urban civic revolutions. Not surprisingly, the impact of social revolutions on educational and health access was large and persisting, while the effect of urban civic revolutions has been relatively small, peaking in the first years after revolution and then decaying.[85] Infant mortality and under-five child mortality reduced at faster rates after both successful social and successful urban civic revolutions compared

85. Based on the average marginal predictions of fixed-effects difference-in-differences regressions (with cluster-robust standard errors) for nine successful social revolutions and twenty-five matched cases and twenty-six successful urban civic revolutions and sixty matched cases for which the V-Dem variables for health equality and educational equality were available, using ten multiple-imputation samples. Data imputed for 4.1 percent of observations.

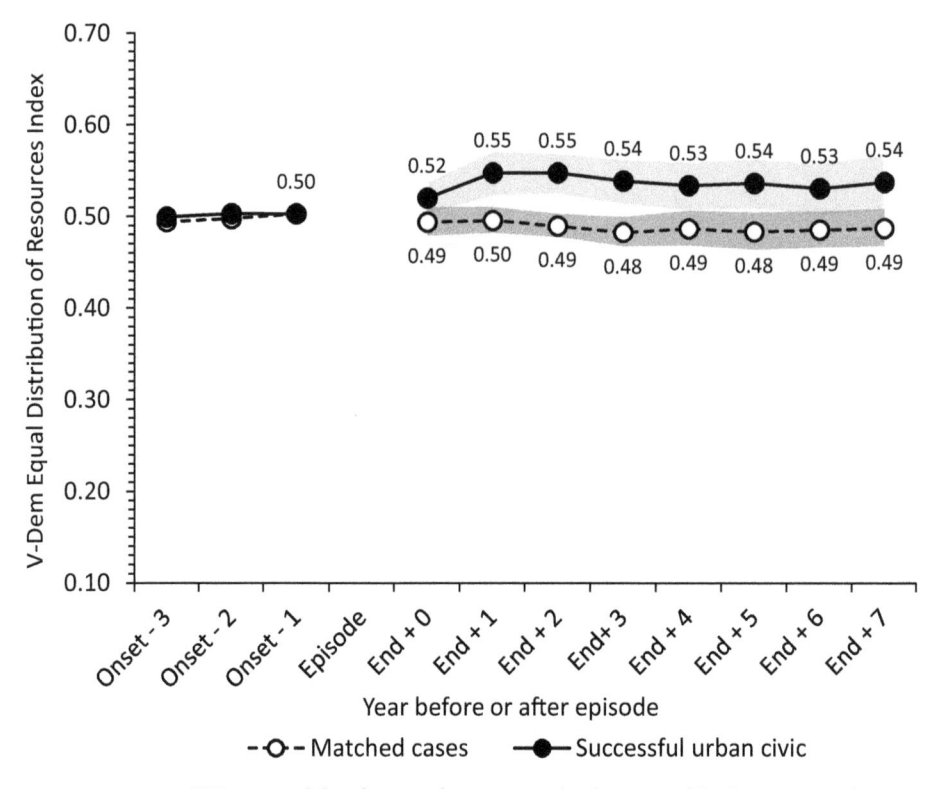

FIGURE 9.8B. V-Dem equal distribution of resources index for successful urban civic revolutions, relative to matched cases. Average marginal predictions from fixed-effects difference-in-differences regressions (with 95 percent confidence intervals and cluster-robust standard errors) on 26 successful urban civic revolutions and 60 matched cases, using ten multiple-imputation samples. Data were imputed for 4.1 percent of observations.

to matched counterparts. Again, the effect was much stronger after social than after urban civic revolutions.[86] Certainly, part of the more substantial increases in welfare access and greater reductions in poverty after social revolutions can

86. For infant mortality, results based on the average marginal predictions of a fixed-effects difference-in-differences regression (with cluster-robust standard errors) on six successful social revolutions and nineteen matched cases and twenty-five successful urban civic revolutions and fifty-five matched cases, using ten multiple-imputation samples. Data imputed for 4.3 percent of observations. For under-five child mortality, based on the average marginal predictions of a fixed-effects difference-in-differences regression (with cluster-robust standard errors) on nine successful social revolutions and twenty-five matched cases and twenty-four successful urban civic revolutions and fifty-four matched cases, using ten multiple-imputation samples. Data imputed for 3.2 percent of observations.

be ascribed to the different periods and types of societies in which social and urban civic revolutions occurred: lack of access to health and education, infant mortality, and under-five child mortality were considerably greater in the early and mid-twentieth century, when social revolutions occurred, than in the late twentieth and early twenty-first centuries, when urban civic contention has been prevalent. The types of societies that experienced social revolutionary episodes were much poorer than those vulnerable to urban civic revolution. But this still does not fully explain why social revolutions performed better than urban civic revolutions in addressing these inequalities relative to matched counterparts over the same time period. The egalitarian ideologies and commitments of those coming to power after social revolution clearly played the critical role. Moreover, many urban civic revolutionary regimes came under strong international pressure to curb public spending, limiting their ability to respond to the social needs of their populations, even if they wanted to do so.

Once we move to other forms of inequality, the effects of social and urban civic revolutions diverge more sharply. Income equality, as measured by Gini indices, has moved in opposite directions after successful social and urban civic revolutions (Figure 9.9).[87] Income distributions tend to change slowly, so trends should be considered more important than confidence intervals. Moreover, the number of successful social revolutions for which data on income inequality were available was small. But generally, successful social revolutions brought about a substantial downward trend in income inequality (9.9a), while successful urban civic revolutions tended to usher in increased income inequality (9.9b). Certainly, one would have expected this for those urban civic revolutions involving the transition from state socialism. But the pattern holds even when transitions from state socialism are dropped from the analysis. As we saw in chapter 7, participants in urban civic revolutions are generally better off economically than the rest of society. Their interests are usually better represented in the wake of successful urban civic revolutions than the interests of the poor, who are better represented after social revolutions than well-off citizens. And unlike social revolutions, successful urban civic revolutions were associated with a transfer of state property into private hands,[88] further exacerbating class differences. Sluggish economic growth, high levels of government debt that constrain public spending, persistent corruption, and ineffective governance all render it harder for urban civic postrevolutionary regimes to devise coherent social policy responses that might

---

87. Patterns further confirmed in the complete-case sample.

88. This holds true even when those cases associated with the collapse of communism are excluded from the sample.

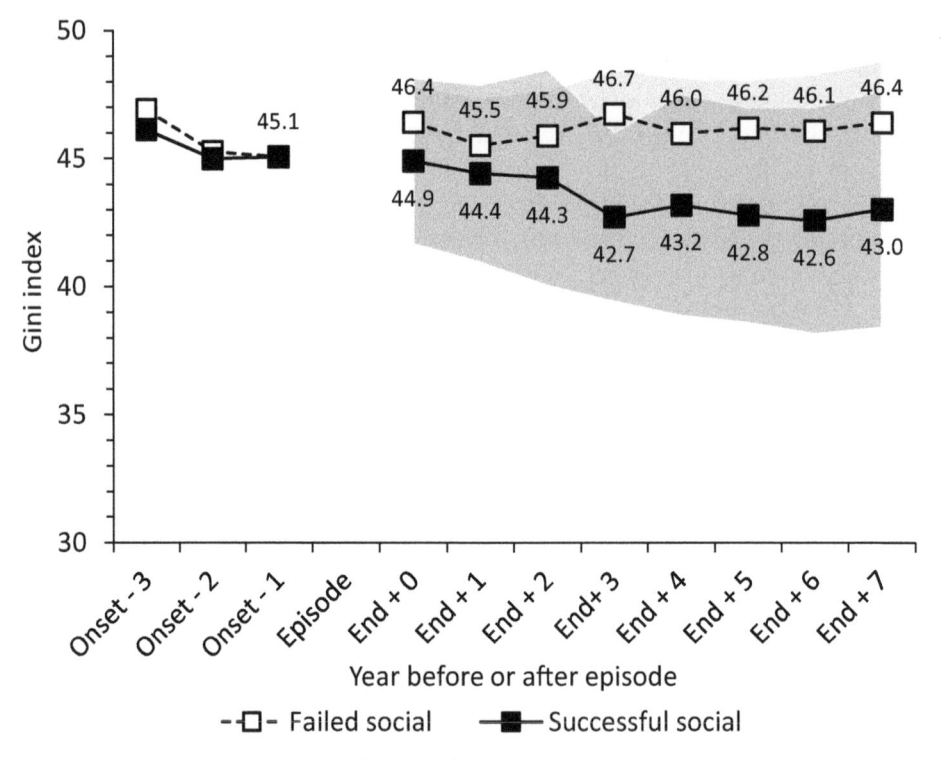

FIGURE 9.9A. Income inequality (Gini index) for social revolutions (successful vs failed revolutions). Average marginal predictions from fixed-effects difference-in-differences regressions, with 95 percent confidence intervals (cluster-robust standard errors) for 6 successful and 17 failed social revolutions, using ten multiple-imputation samples. Data were imputed for 4.5 percent of observations.

address growing class inequalities, even if they have the desire to do so. Ironically, regimes that survived failed urban civic revolutions experienced a slight decline in income inequality—in some cases the result of efforts to co-opt and buy off opposition.[89]

But class inequalities are only one of the forms of inequality with which post-revolutionary governments must grapple. Ethnic stratification may or may not intersect with class, and cultural divisions can play a significant role in revolution. Social revolutions have frequently exacerbated separatist conflict, as efforts at class and social transformation can incite minority cultural groups to seek exit. The Bolshevik accession to power in October 1917, for instance, accelerated the breakup of the Russian Empire, as nationalist elites

89. Berman 2019.

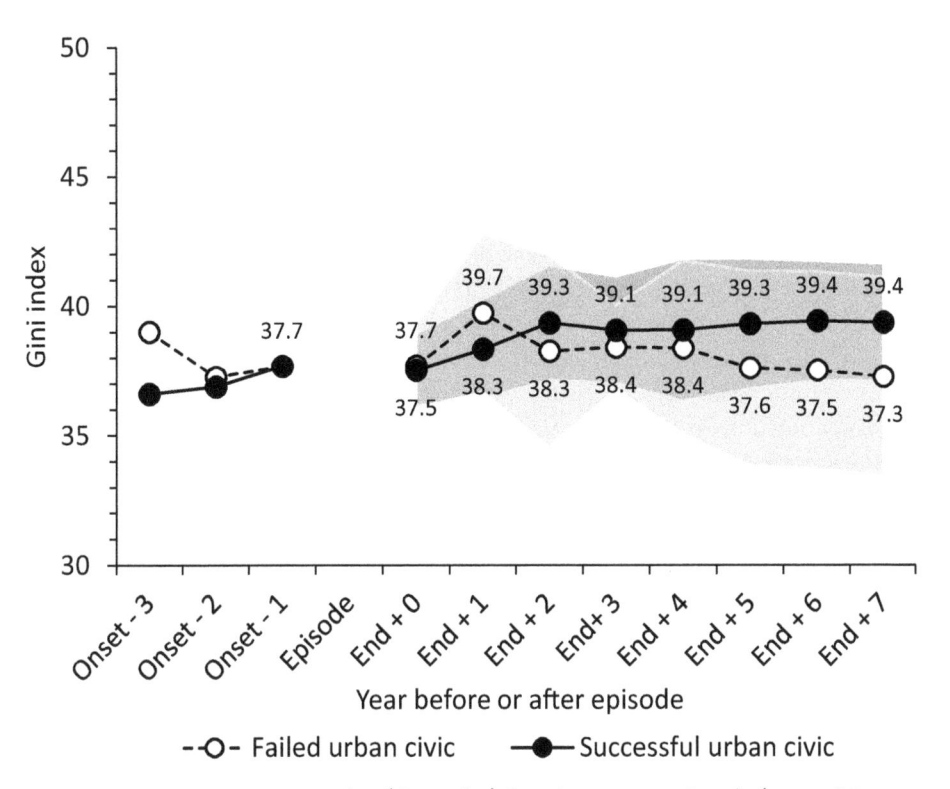

FIGURE 9.9B. Income inequality (Gini index) for urban civic revolutions (successful vs failed revolutions). Average marginal predictions from fixed-effects difference-in-differences regressions, with 95 percent confidence intervals (cluster-robust standard errors) for 26 successful and 18 failed urban civic revolutions, using ten multiple-imputation samples. Data were imputed for 4.5 percent of observations.

in non-Russian areas feared the radical and egalitarian agenda that the Bolsheviks espoused, preferring independence to Bolshevik radicalism. Nevertheless, successful social revolutions have generally been associated with a marked reduction in ethnic inequalities in their wake—largely the result of efforts by post-revolutionary regimes to incorporate marginalized ethnic groups and weaken separatist sentiments. After successful social revolutions, there was a sharp decline in the share of population belonging to ethnic groups excluded from central executive power (as defined in the Ethnic Power Relations dataset).[90] In the wake of the Bolshevik Revolution, for instance, the Soviet

---

90. Based on the average marginal predictions of fixed-effects difference-in-differences regressions (with cluster-robust standard errors) on nine successful and twenty-three failed social revolutions and twenty-eight successful and sixteen failed urban civic revolutions for

government sought to incorporate national minorities by creating what Terry Martin called an "Affirmative Action Empire." The regime attacked "Great Russian chauvinism" and attempted to disarm non-Russian nationalisms by granting diminished forms of nationhood through the establishment of national territories, cultural autonomy, and indigenous leaderships (a policy that, in the context of its time, was widely viewed as progressive).[91] Ethnic Power Relations measures indicate no such reduction in the politically marginalized status of ethnic groups after successful urban civic revolutions. Indeed, in many cases, by empowering majorities, successful urban civic revolutions have exacerbated cultural conflict, inciting outbreaks of ethnic violence, provoking interethnic tensions, and raising fears among minority groups of increased discrimination. In cases as diverse as the "Singing Revolutions" in the Baltic, the Kyrgyz Revolution in 2010, the Egyptian Revolution in 2011, and the Euromaidan Revolution in 2014, minorities previously protected by the old regime feared a reversal of their situation, experienced hostile popular backlash, or engaged in separatist actions.[92] Lack of coherent political organization, extensive corruption, and economic stress have further complicated government efforts to incorporate cultural minorities after urban civic revolutions.

As we have seen, women often play important roles in revolutionary contention, though the manner of their participation has varied depending on cultural norms and levels of violence. This participation has generally translated into greater female empowerment in the wake of successful revolutions—at least compared to the situation before revolution and to matched cases.[93] The effect has been particularly strong in successful social revolutions, where postrevolutionary regimes frequently prescribed formal quotas for female representation and continued to mobilize women at high rates as part of their efforts to transform society.[94] After the October Revolution, for instance, the Bolsheviks created a women's department (*zhenotdel*) that mobilized women

---

which data were available, using twenty multiple-imputation samples. Data imputed for 12.6 percent of observations. On the measure of ethnic exclusion used in the Ethnic Power Relations dataset, see Wimmer, Cederman, and Min 2009.

91. Martin 2001; Himka 1992.

92. Beissinger 2002; Kutmanaliev 2015; Tadros 2011; Kuzio 2015.

93. Results based on fixed-effects difference-in-differences regressions of the V-Dem indices for women's political empowerment, women's civil liberties, women's political participation, and women's participation in civil society for nine successful social revolutions and twenty-five matched cases and twenty-six successful urban civic revolutions and fifty-eight matched cases for which information was available, using ten multiple-imputation samples. Data imputed for 4.2 percent of observations.

94. Massell 1974; Lapidus 1978; Mason 1992; Luciak 2001; Johnson 2009.

in a wide variety of areas: "child and orphan care, school service and inspection, food distribution, housing supervision, preventive medicine and public health, anti-prostitution campaigns, war work, education, legislation, placement, family service, and mass propaganda for every campaign that the Party decided to undertake."[95] Social revolutions were usually accompanied by efforts to supply women with greater familial and social rights—including rights to divorce, freedom from forced marriage, and access to abortion, work, and education. Still, male-dominated political and economic hierarchies survived even the most thorough social revolutions.

By contrast, women's descriptive representation increased only marginally under urban civic post-revolutionary regimes, though their opportunities to express themselves and to participate in civil society associations rose sharply. In this regard, the mobilization of women into politics after urban civic revolutions was inconsistent. Civil liberties for women (defined by V-Dem as the ability of women to make meaningful decisions in key areas of their lives—such as freedom of movement, freedom from forced labor, property rights, and access to justice) increased more substantially after urban civic than after social revolutions, and more substantially than in matched counterparts. But urban civic post-revolutionary regimes have at times backtracked on women's familial and social rights—though the record is mixed.[96]

Thus, in line with their goals, successful social revolutions performed well in addressing all forms of social inequality—whether rooted in class, cultural difference, or gender. Successful urban civic revolutions, by contrast, usually exercised smaller effects on access to health and education and outperformed matched counterparts in reducing infant and under-five child mortality. Nevertheless, they have tended to lead to increased class and ethnic inequalities relative to pre-revolutionary patterns and matched counterparts, while exercising mixed effects in the realm of gender.

Revolution, Political Freedoms, and Government Accountability

"A revolution," Engels wrote in 1872, "is certainly the most authoritarian thing there is."[97] Engels's assertion is unquestionably true of social revolutions. A number of the most egregious instances of government-sponsored mass violence and terror during the twentieth century—Soviet collectivization (1928–31),

---

95. Stites 1976, 188.
96. See, for instance, Hrycak 2007; Khalil 2014; Eltahawy 2018.
97. Engels, in Tucker 1972, 665.

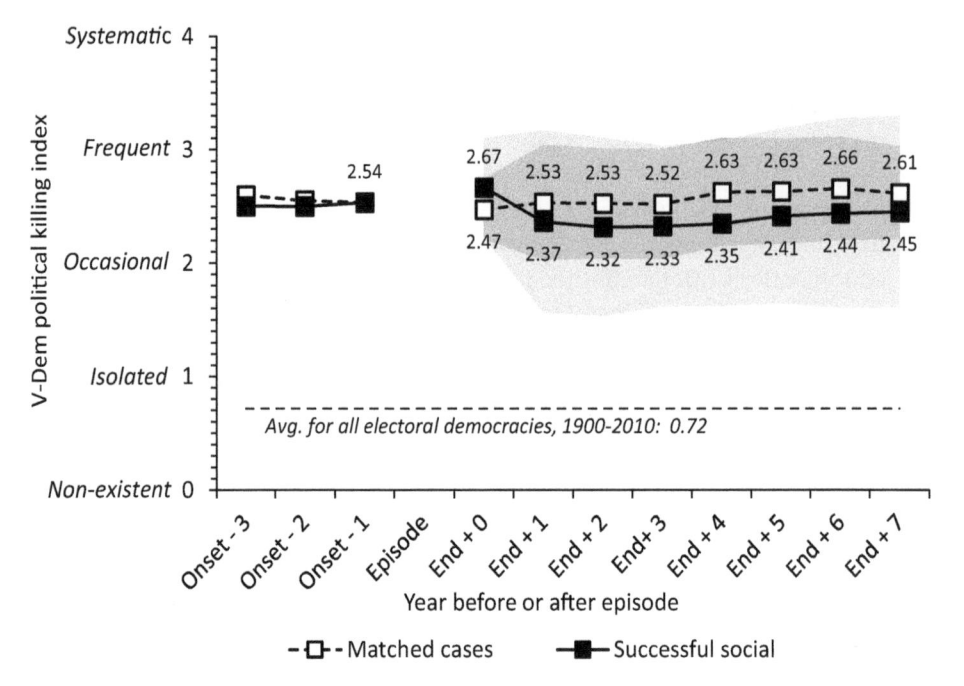

FIGURE 9.10A. V-Dem political killing index for successful social revolutions, relative to matched cases. Average marginal predictions from fixed-effects difference-in-differences regressions, with 95 percent confidence intervals (cluster-robust standard errors) for 9 successful social revolutions and 25 matched cases, using ten multiple-imputation samples. Data were imputed for 4.1 percent of observations.

the Great Purge (1936–38), collectivization in China (1955–56), the Chinese Cultural Revolution (1966–1976), and the Cambodian Genocide (1975–79)— were carried out by governments brought to power by social revolutions. Most of this political killing (for example, forced collectivization and the Great Purge in the Soviet Union, and the Cultural Revolution in China) occurred well after revolutionary contention ended, with post-revolutionary politics, regime efforts at societal transformation, and the resistance that this encountered playing central roles in instigating them.

While systematic information on the number of people killed after revolutions is not available, the V-Dem freedom from political killings index uses expert ratings to estimate the extent to which a society is free from political killing by the state or its agents for the purpose of eliminating political opponents, coding political killings as either systematic, frequent, occasional, isolated, or non-existent.[98] As Figure 9.10 shows, the average level of political

98. I reversed the V-Dem measure so that it ran from 0 (non-existent) to 4 (systematic).

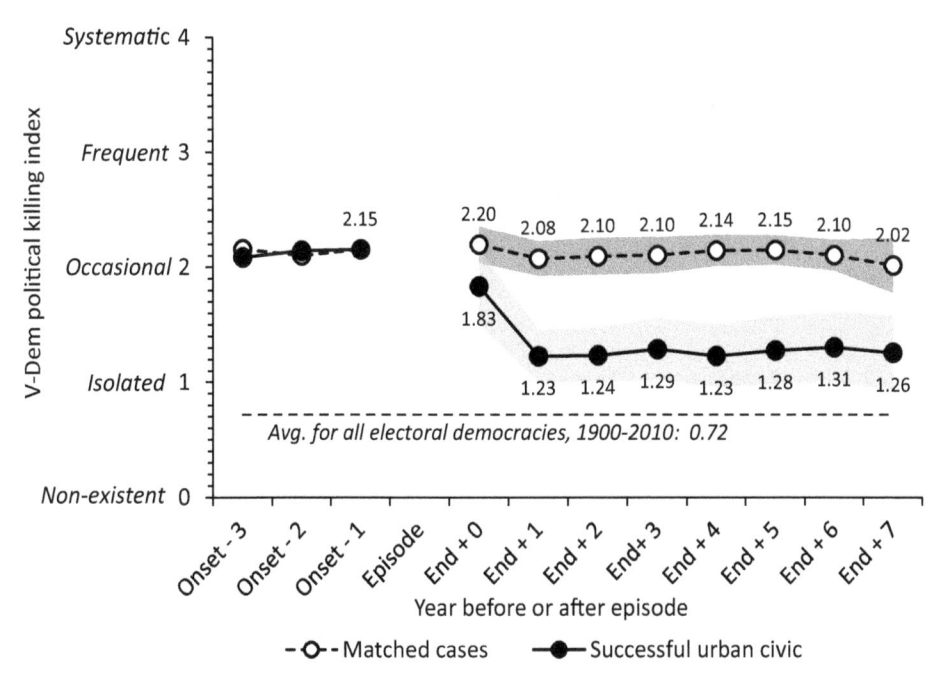

FIGURE 9.10B. V-Dem political killing index for successful urban civic revolutions, relative to matched cases. Average marginal predictions from fixed-effects difference-in-differences regressions, with 95 percent confidence intervals (cluster-robust standard errors) for 26 successful urban civic revolutions and 60 matched cases, using ten multiple-imputation samples. Data were imputed for 4.1 percent of observations.

killing for successful social revolutions during the seven years following revolutionary contention (9.10a) was in the "occasional" to "frequent" range (a poor record), and several of the better known social revolutions (the Bolshevik Revolution, the Chinese Revolution, and the Mexican Revolution) fell into the "frequent" to "systematic" range. But the average level of violence against civilians by governments coming to power through social revolution was approximately the same as the average for their matched counterparts (in the "occasional" to "frequent" range).[99] By contrast, successful urban civic revolutions (9.10b) led to a sharp decline in political killings, with killing moving on average from "occasional" to "isolated." This stands out relative to matched counterparts, which displayed no change over the same period. In short, while crime generally increased after urban civic revolutions, state-initiated violence declined. But political killings after urban civic revolutions still remained

99. Indeed, there was no statistically significant difference between the two groups.

higher on average than for electoral democracies as a whole (as classified using Boix, Miller, and Rosato's minimalist definition of free and fair elections and universal suffrage) over the twentieth and twenty-first centuries.[100]

As opposed to electoral democracy, liberal democracy is a composite concept that includes not only the periodic accountability of the governing to the governed through free and fair elections and universal suffrage, but also the rule of law and observance of political and personal freedoms.[101] Historically, political rights and modern democracy had their origins in revolution,[102] and urban civic revolutions have frequently been dubbed "democratic" revolutions. However, as we have seen, participants in these revolutions are usually motivated by a variety of concerns, and for most, political and civil and freedoms rank low among them. Moreover, the majority of participants in urban civic revolutions have often demonstrated a weak commitment to democratic values. Urban civic revolutions usually usher in significant progress along a number of democratic dimensions. But in many areas, the record of these post-revolutionary governments has fallen well short of what one would expect on average to find in an electoral democracy (minimally understood).

Figure 9.11 shows the level of expressive political liberties (such as freedom of speech and association) after revolution, as measured by the V-Dem political civil liberties index.[103] In societies experiencing successful social revolutions (9.11a), the level of expressive political freedoms—already low prior to revolutionary contention—eroded further after revolution (though there is no statistically significant difference from matched counterparts). By contrast, following successful urban civic revolutions (9.11b) freedoms of speech and association on average underwent a sudden and fundamental shift (on a 0–1 scale, from .41 to .79), with a strong and abiding difference from matched counterparts. The average scores for these cases were still below the average for electoral democracies (though the 95 percent confidence interval approached

---

100. Boix, Miller, and Rosato (2013) define electoral democracies as countries whose "political leaders [are] chosen through free and fair elections and satisfy a threshold value of suffrage." By their definition, 118 out of 172 countries (67 percent) have been electoral democracies at some point over the 1900–2010 period. Many of these regimes would not qualify as liberal democracies.

101. Dahl 1971.

102. Arendt 1965, 22.

103. The index is formed by combining separate indicators on government censorship, harassment of journalists, media self-censorship, freedom of discussion for men and women, freedom of academic and cultural expression, whether there are bans on or barriers to political parties, opposition party autonomy, civil society association entry and exit, and civil society repression.

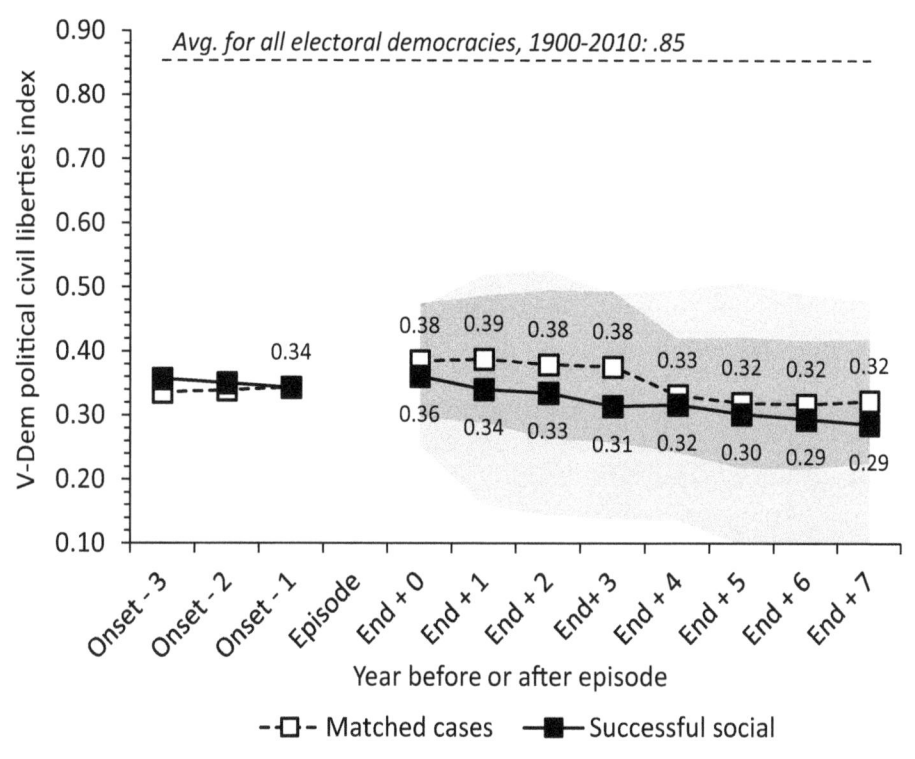

FIGURE 9.11A. V-Dem political civil liberties index for successful social revolutions, relative to matched cases. Average marginal predictions from fixed-effects difference-in-differences regressions, with 95 percent confidence intervals (cluster-robust standard errors) for 9 successful social revolutions and 25 matched cases, using ten multiple-imputation samples. Data were imputed for 4.1 percent of observations.

the electoral democracy average), and a slight erosion of these liberties occurred over ensuing years. Nevertheless, an abrupt and substantial increase in expressive political liberties constitutes the single most palpable achievement of urban civic revolutions.[104]

Similar patterns emerge for private civil liberties. The V-Dem private civil liberties index measures the degree to which governments respect private civil liberties such as freedom of movement, freedom of religion, freedom from forced labor, and property rights.[105] As can be seen in Figure 9.12 using the matched samples, successful social revolutions (9.12a) generally led to a

---

104. No such increase occurs in cases of failed urban civic revolutions relative to matched counterparts. Findings replicated in the complete-case sample.

105. Coppedge et al. 2018.

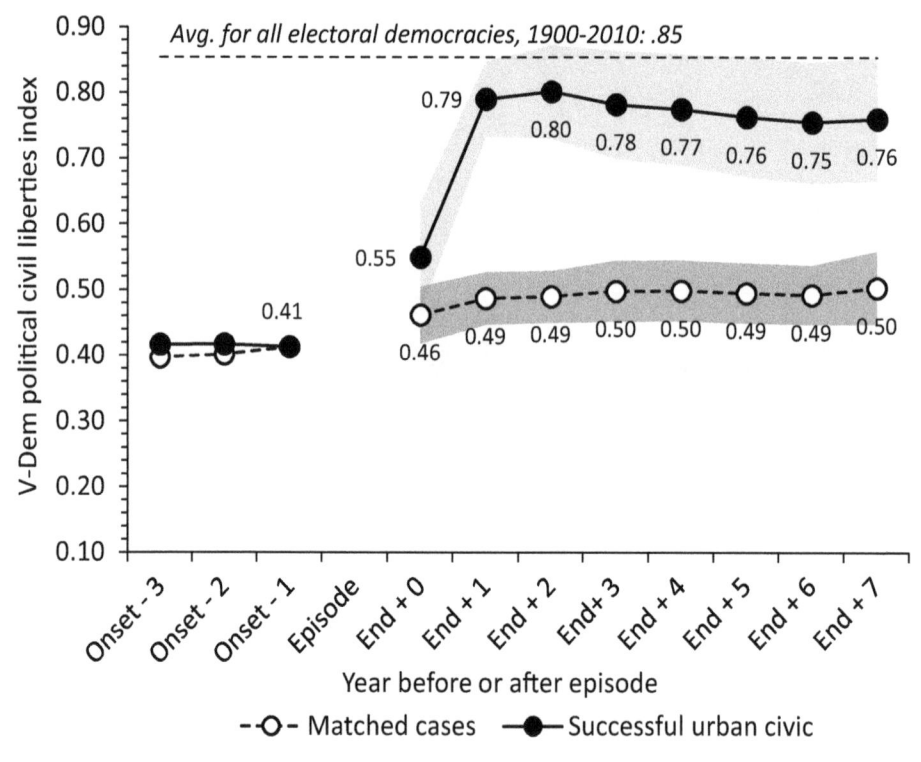

FIGURE 9.11B. V-Dem political civil liberties index for successful urban civic revolutions, relative to matched cases. Average marginal predictions from fixed-effects difference-in-differences regressions, with 95 percent confidence intervals (cluster-robust standard errors) for 26 successful urban civic revolutions and 60 matched cases, using ten multiple-imputation samples. Data were imputed for 4.1 percent of observations.

deterioration in private civil liberties in their aftermath, as new regimes sought to transform class inequalities, restrict movement of populations, and attack established social institutions such as organized religion and existing patterns of property ownership. By contrast, successful urban civic revolutions (9.12b) brought a substantial and statistically significant increase in private civil liberties in their wake compared to matched counterparts, though again, the record remained below what one would expect from the average electoral democracy.[106]

---

106. Again, no such improvement occurred after failed urban civic revolutions relative to matched counterparts. Findings are replicated in the complete-case sample.

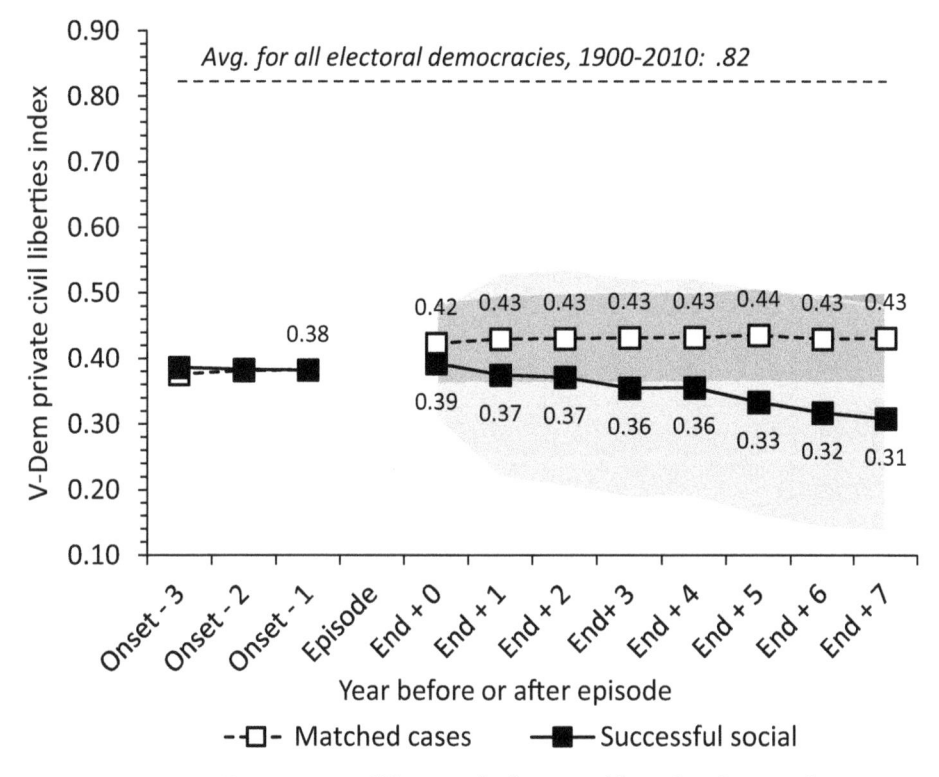

[Graph showing V-Dem private civil liberties index from Onset-3 to End+7, with Matched cases (open squares) remaining around 0.42-0.44 and Successful social (filled squares) declining from 0.38 to 0.31. Dashed line at top shows "Avg. for all electoral democracies, 1900-2010: .82"]

FIGURE 9.12A. V-Dem private civil liberties index for successful social revolutions, relative to matched cases. Average marginal predictions from fixed-effects difference-in-differences regressions, with 95 percent confidence intervals (cluster-robust standard errors) for 9 successful social revolutions and 25 matched cases, using ten multiple-imputation samples. Data were imputed for 4.1 percent of observations.

Urban civic revolutions were also accompanied by an improvement in the rule of law. The V-Dem rule of law index measures the extent to which laws are enforced in a transparent, predictable, impartial, and equal manner and government officials actually comply with laws. Using the V-Dem scale (Figure 9.13), successful social revolutions exhibited no difference in the degree to which the rule of law prevailed compared to pre-revolutionary levels or matched counterparts (9.13a). By contrast, successful urban civic revolutions were followed by a statistically significant increase in the rule of law in the years following revolutionary contention, relative to pre-revolutionary levels and matched cases (9.13b).[107] However, the rule of law in these societies

---

107. Similarly, no improvement occurred after failed urban civic revolutions relative to their matched counterparts, and the findings are replicated in the complete-case sample.

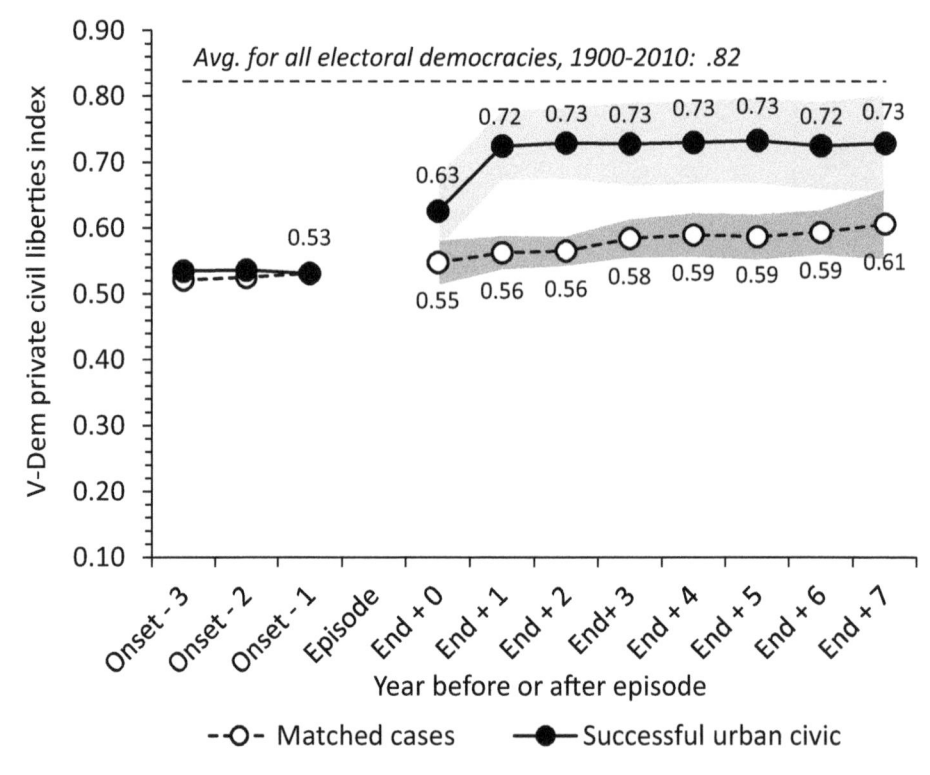

FIGURE 9.12B. V-Dem private civil liberties index for successful urban civic revolutions, relative to matched cases. Average marginal predictions from fixed-effects difference-in-differences regressions, with 95 percent confidence intervals (cluster-robust standard errors) for 26 successful urban civic revolutions and 60 matched cases, using ten multiple-imputation samples. Data were imputed for 4.1 percent of observations.

remained far below the average levels exhibited by all electoral democracies since 1900.

Finally, successful urban civic revolutions led to a substantial increase in the degree of accountability of government to citizens (Figure 9.14). The V-Dem government accountability index measures the constraints on the government's use of political power as a result of a population's ability to hold government accountable through elections, checks and balances between institutions, and oversight by civil society associations and the media.[108] After successful social revolutions, government accountability noticeably declined, though the differences from matched counterparts are not statistically

---

108. Lührmann, Mechkova, and Marquardt 2017; Coppedge et al. 2018.

0.90 —
0.80 — Avg. for all electoral democracies, 1900-2010: .79

0.70 —
0.60 —
0.50 —
0.40 — 0.34 0.36 0.36 0.36 0.36 0.34 0.33 0.33
       0.32
0.30 —
0.20

Year before or after episode: Onset-3, Onset-2, Onset-1, Episode, End+0, End+1, End+2, End+3, End+4, End+5, End+6, End+7

-□- Matched cases   —■— Successful social

V-Dem rule of law index

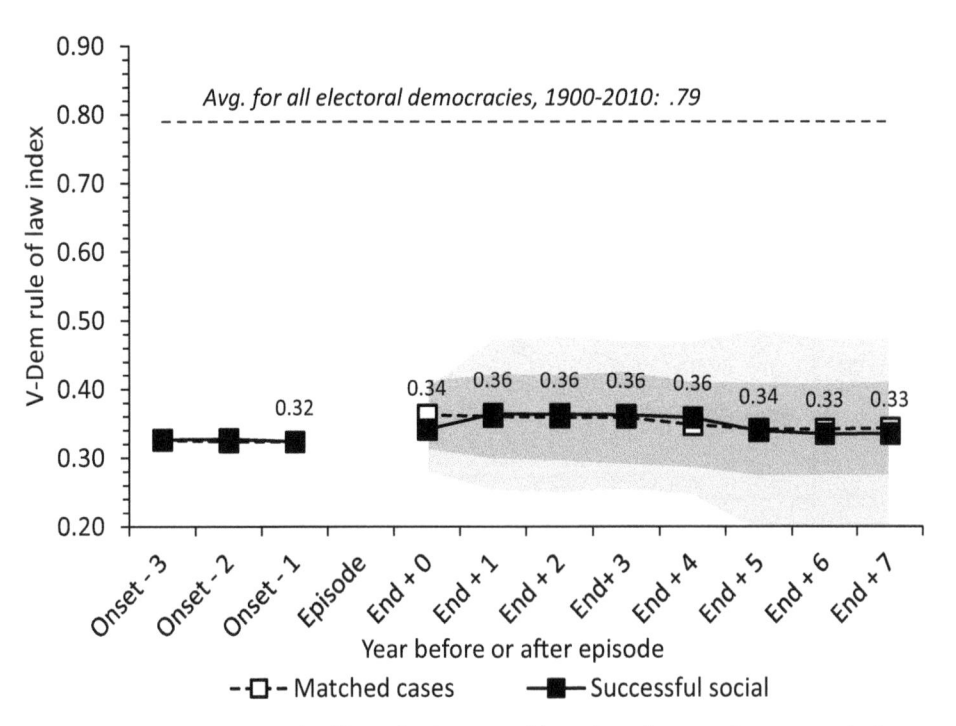

FIGURE 9.13A. V-Dem rule of law index for successful social revolutions, relative to matched cases. Average marginal predictions from fixed-effects difference-in-differences regressions, with 95 percent confidence intervals (cluster-robust standard errors) for 9 successful social revolutions and 25 matched cases, using ten multiple-imputation samples. Data were imputed for 4.1 percent of observations.

significant. But after successful urban civic revolutions, government accountability substantially increased, with the differences from matched cases statistically significant at the .01 level or better. Once again, however, the achievements of urban civic revolutions fell significantly short of the average level one would expect from an electoral democracy since 1900.

Thus, while urban civic revolutions ushered in substantial improvements in most dimensions of democratic practice, on average these regimes consistently fell short of most electoral democracies since 1900—and on some dimensions the gap has been considerable. There has also been a troubling tendency in a significant number of urban civic post-revolutionary regimes toward erosion of a number of these achievements over time. Indeed, in half or more of successful urban civic revolutions for which data are available, the V-Dem scores for political liberties, rule of law, and government accountability seven years after the end of revolutionary contention were lower than their scores one year after revolution. Democratic backsliding in these cases

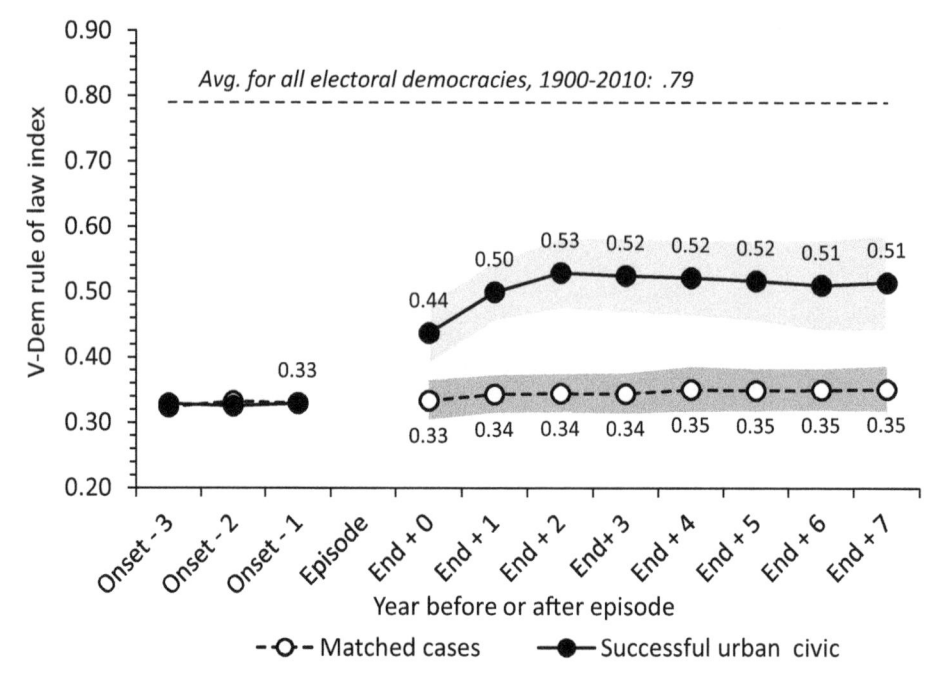

FIGURE 9.13B. V-Dem rule of law index for successful urban civic revolutions, relative to matched cases. Average marginal predictions from fixed-effects difference-in-differences regressions, with 95 percent confidence intervals (cluster-robust standard errors) for 26 successful urban civic revolutions and 60 matched cases, using ten multiple-imputation samples. Data were imputed for 4.1 percent of observations.

has been fueled by the persistent corruption, continued presence of elements of the old regime, sluggish economic growth, and instability characteristic of urban civic post-revolutionary regimes. In a number of cases (the April 1960 Revolution in South Korea, the October 1964 Revolution in Sudan, the 1973 Thai Democracy Movement, and the 2011 Egyptian Revolution), these conditions helped to precipitate military coups that completely reversed the progress on political rights and accountability achieved by the original revolutions. But backsliding has sometimes manifested itself in more subtle ways.[109] After both the Orange Revolution in Ukraine and Bulldozer Revolution in Serbia, representatives or supporters of the evicted incumbent regime eventually won their way back to power through the ballot box. In still other cases, leaders brought to power by urban civic revolutions themselves subverted government accountability and political freedoms. After the 2003 Rose

109. Bermeo 2016.

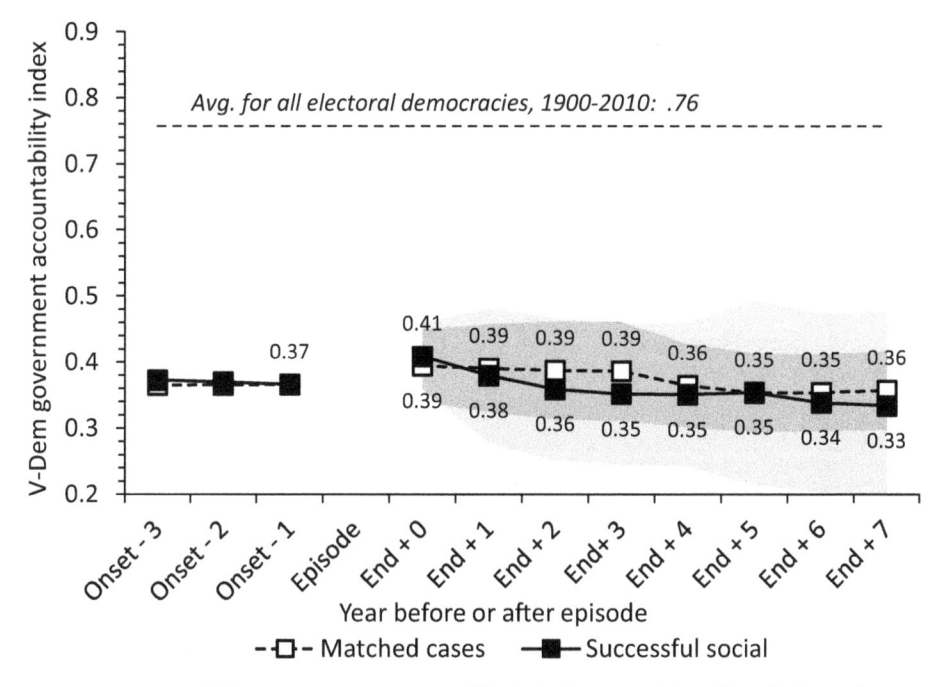

FIGURE 9.14A. V-Dem government accountability index for successful social revolutions, relative to matched cases. Average marginal predictions from fixed-effects difference-in-differences regressions, with 95 percent confidence intervals (cluster-robust standard errors) for 9 successful social revolutions and 25 matched cases, using ten multiple-imputation samples. Data were imputed for 5 percent of observations.

Revolution in Georgia, the Saakashvili regime harassed political opponents and pressured the media, closing down television stations critical of the government and compromising the rule of law.[110] After the 2002 electoral revolution in Madagascar, the Ravalomanana regime turned in an increasingly authoritarian direction, closing opposition media and precipitating a new uprising in 2009.[111]

The point here is not that the outcomes of urban civic revolution do not matter. In fact, the evidence demonstrates quite the opposite: urban civic revolutions bring about substantial gains in most areas of democratic practice. Rather, the point is to recognize that even these gains generally fall significantly short of what one would expect on average from a democracy (even

110. De Waal 2013.
111. Hinthorne 2011.

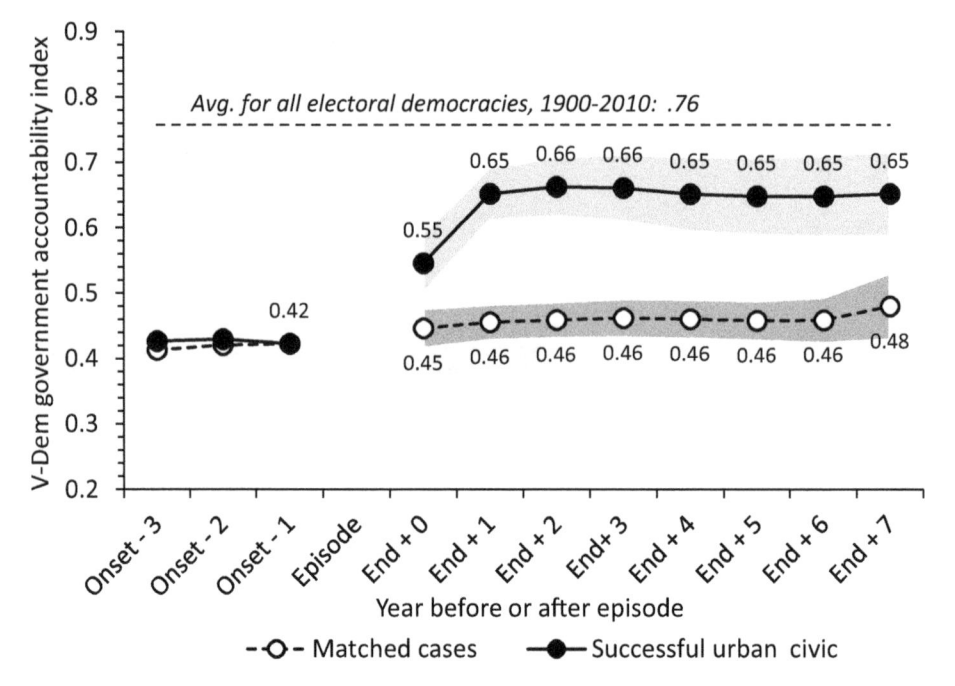

FIGURE 9.14B. V-Dem government accountability index for successful urban civic revolutions, relative to matched cases. Average marginal predictions from fixed-effects difference-in-differences regressions, with 95 percent confidence intervals (cluster-robust standard errors) for 25 successful urban civic revolutions and 58 matched cases, using ten multiple-imputation samples. Data were imputed for 5 percent of observations.

when defined in a minimalist fashion) and to note the significant challenges that these societies face in making further progress along a democratic path.

Conclusion: The Post-Revolutionary Balance Sheet

Jack Goldstone observed that "revolutionaries frequently claim that they will reduce inequality, establish democracy, and provide economic prosperity. In fact, the record of actual revolutions is rather poor in regard to all of these claims."[112] Yet as we have seen, compared to pre-revolutionary patterns of development and patterns in similar societies that did not experience revolution, revolutions have generally brought some substantial positive changes in their wake. Regimes that have come to power by social revolutions have brought about major improvements with regard to almost all forms of societal

---

112. Goldstone 2001, 167.

inequality and have excelled at providing stability and order. Urban civic post-revolutionary regimes have delivered progress in terms of political and civil freedoms, the rule of law, and government accountability, as well as marginal improvements in some areas of societal inequality (gender relations and access to health and education).

Nevertheless, these changes often came at a steep price, and progress in some areas was frequently accompanied by regression in others. Invariably, revolutions have been deleterious for economic growth and almost always generated explosions in criminality. For successful social revolutions, the economic damage that accompanied revolution was significant, rooted in the violent character of revolutionary contention, and exacerbated by ideologically driven post-revolutionary governance. Successful social revolutions were accompanied by a substantial deterioration in political freedoms and government accountability, and political killing remained at a high level—in the "occasional" to "frequent" range (by V-Dem categories), with some cases escalating into the "systematic." For successful urban civic revolutions, the immediate economic damage caused by revolutionary contention was small; but countries experiencing urban civic revolutions nonetheless suffered declines in investment, increased inflation and debt, and a slowly developing crisis of economic growth in their wake—at times helping to undermine fragile post-revolutionary governments. International financial pressures often kept new regimes from dealing with the economic and social demands that had helped to fuel revolt in the first place. Moreover, serious issues of governance and corruption persisted. Urban civic revolutions also contributed to increased income inequality, class differentiation, and, at times, greater ethnic tensions.

As social revolutions have become marginalized and urban civic revolutions have proliferated, the overall impact of revolutions has grown less conspicuous and more uncertain. Urban civic revolutions may achieve power more frequently than other types of revolutions due to their urban location and ability to harness the power of numbers in proximity to government nerve centers. But many of the same advantages that aid urban civic revolutions in capturing power hinder the prospects for substantive change in their wake. As a result of their rapidly convened coalitional character, urban civic revolutions produce new regimes that are more fragile and last for significantly less time than those produced by social revolutions. Their minimalist goals limit their ambition, and the fact that they largely inherit the state intact from the old regime (including its pervasive relationships of corruption) dampens economic growth and renders further political reform problematic. Because of their unarmed character, urban civic revolutions tend to leave those associated with the old regime at large, providing opportunities for them to regain power as post-revolutionary regimes unravel. A number of the achievements of urban civic revolutions (increased freedoms, rule of law, and government accountability) not only fall short of the average level for an electoral democracy, but in many instances have deteriorated over time.

For all these reasons, urban civic revolutions do not only exert an impact markedly different from that of social revolutions. They are also far less dramatic and clear-cut in their effects. As we have seen, revolutions continue to matter in important ways. But their impact is much more ambiguous and far less durable than was the case in the past.

10

The City and the Future of Revolution

> —[O]ur revolution was the last revolution, and there can be no more. Everyone knows that [...].
> —And why do you think there is a "last" revolution? There is no such thing as the "last" revolution; the number of revolutions is infinite.
>
> YEVGENII ZAMIATIN, MY [WE][1]

THERE HAS NEVER BEEN A DEARTH of predictions about the demise of revolution. As exemplified by the parroted propaganda lines of his protagonist D-503 in Zamiatin's 1924 dystopian novel *We*, revolutionaries usually imagine theirs to be the last revolution. The hopes unleashed by revolutions, as well as the guileful pronouncements of post-revolutionary rulers, often encourage such rationalizations. But as Zamiatin's character I-330 understood, there is no such thing as the last revolution. Revolution had limitless possibilities—including the revolution that she herself was hoping to bring about.

The example that Zamiatin had in mind, of course, was Russia's October Revolution, which the Bolsheviks touted as the revolution to end all revolutions.[2] Yet, seven decades later, the Soviet regime it brought to power was itself overthrown by revolution. Ironically, the revolutions that overthrew communism were heralded in similar language—as revolutions to end all revolutions,

---

1. Zamiatin 1967.
2. Malia 2006, 253.

as revolutions against the very idea of revolution.[3] But since the collapse of communism many of these same post-communist countries have also experienced revolutions—in some cases, multiple times. In 1840, de Tocqueville predicted that the global growth of the middle class would render revolutions increasingly rare.[4] Yet the twentieth century saw an explosion of revolutionary activity. Others have variously argued that revolutions would vanish due to the dominance of technocracy, the transformations associated with modernization, the multiplication of democracy, the hegemony of neoliberal capitalism, and the exhaustion of revolutionary ideologies.[5] As one commentator put it, "Historically outmoded, exhausted as an ambition, ruptured as political ontology, discredited by contemporary political epistemology—revolution is unquestionably finished."[6]

None of these predictions have proven true, at least with regard to political revolutions. Despite forecasts of its demise, revolution as a mode of regime-change—in Trotsky words, "the forcible entry of the masses in the realm of rulership over their own destiny"[7]—is hardly extinct, nor has it even grown rarer. On the contrary, over the long term revolutionary contention has occurred with increasing frequency around the world, transpiring at a greater pace today than during either the first half of the twentieth century or the Cold War. It is impossible to kill an idea like revolution. It lives as long as injustice without redress persists. It adjusts to the needs and constraints of its times, the social forces it services, and the variety of wrongs we endure. Revolution has not died. It has evolved.

This book has focused attention on this evolution, and in particular on how the concentration of people, power, and wealth in cities has affected the forms, frequency, outcomes, and consequences of revolution. As Skocpol noted, a generalizable causal theory of revolutions that would cover all of its various manifestations is not possible, due to the diversity of purposes and social forces involved and the changing character of revolutions across historical

---

3. Fukuyama 1992; Sakwa 2001. As Kumar (2008, 227) notes, "in the commentaries on the 1989 revolutions there were numerous statements to the effect that these were the 'last' revolutions, that perhaps they were not even revolutions, and that in any case they pointed to the exhaustion of the revolutionary tradition, at least in the West."

4. Tocqueville 1969, 634–45.

5. Malecki 1973; Fukuyama 1992; Snyder 1999; Nodia 2000; Goodwin 2003. For excellent critiques, see Parsa 2003; Kapustin 2019.

6. Brown 2005, 112. Brown goes on to mourn the demise of revolution, as "this death seems to carry with it our dreams for a better world."

7. Trotsky 1932, vol. 1, xvii.

time.[8] But theories of particular types of revolutions and of how and why revolutions have evolved (and with what consequences) are achievable, and that is what I have attempted to accomplish in this book. In so doing, I have paid particular attention to the spatial and historical contexts in which revolution has unfolded and the ways in which these have shaped revolutionary tactics and interactions, the social forces and actors involved, and the processes and outcomes of revolutionary contention.

Much of the evolution of revolutionary contention since 1900 has been influenced by a certain spatial logic of rebellion—what I have called the proximity dilemma. Cities are spatial locations in which state power is highly concentrated. This fact establishes a trade-off for revolutionaries between exposure to repression and disruptive potential: revolutionaries in cities are more directly exposed to the repressive capacities of the state, but cities are also where the state is most vulnerable to overthrow and disruption due to the concentrated presence of nerve centers of power and commerce. Revolutionaries can protect themselves by moving further from the city, but only at the expense of their ability to disrupt government. They can increase their ability to disrupt regimes by operating in proximity to government nerve centers, but only at the expense of greater exposure to a regime's repressive capacities. As in evolutionary biology, the most efficient locations for nourishment and reproduction are also those that are the most dangerous for falling to predators.

This repression–disruption trade-off has been variously managed across the history of modern revolution. Throughout the nineteenth and early twentieth centuries, revolution was predominantly an urban affair, as cities were where regime nerve centers were located and where the social forces seeking regime-change (the bourgeoisie and working class) were concentrated. Industrialization and proletarianization reinforced this urban focus, as it created a volatile mixture within cities in close proximity to state centers of power. Urban rebellions in the nineteenth and early twentieth centuries relied primarily on the power of arms and on the revolutionary riot. Cities were generally too small, communications technologies too limited, and regimes too willing to use deadly force against unarmed crowds to rely on the power of numbers. But because these revolutions unfolded where the coercive capacity of the state was strongest, regimes were in a far better position than revolutionaries in terms of arms, number of combatants, and quality of fighters, and over time, as states grew stronger and modern weaponry grew more powerful, the odds increasingly came to be stacked against armed urban revolutionaries.

---

8. Skocpol 1979, 288.

As a result of the dangers of rebellion in cities, social revolutionaries eventually migrated to the countryside, where rebels used distance and rough terrain for protection against government retaliation. The repression–disruption trade-off was managed through spatial relocation—by trading disruptive capability for safety from repression. In the process of doing this, rebels discovered the revolutionary potential of the peasant. Prior to the twentieth century, social revolution had predominantly been an urban affair, though peasant disruptions often played an important role within them. But social revolutions occurred in overwhelmingly rural societies. They were, as Skocpol observed, a phenomenon of "agrarian-bureaucratic society," in which control over and extraction of resources from peasants relied on a coordination and division of labor between a semi-bureaucratic state and a landed upper class.[9] By the mid-twentieth century, social revolution had come to be waged primarily from the countryside, with peasants becoming the main social force underpinning it. While peasant revolutions were able to hide more effectively from government repression, rural location reduced the ability of revolutionaries to disrupt regimes directly. As a result, rural revolutions unfolded over protracted periods of time, exhibiting a punctuated rhythm determined by the timing of battles. Urban revolution, of course, never disappeared. But it ceded the main stage to rural rebellion. This was the basic pattern of revolution up until the late twentieth century. Reflecting these patterns, most theories of revolution placed the character of rural society at the center of their explanations.

The age of social revolutions is now over. Social revolutions died in part as a result of the collapse of European communism, the decline of inter-state warfare, and the slow growth and territorial consolidation of state power. But they also disappeared in no small part due to the demise of agrarian-bureaucratic society. Under the impact of democratization, communism, and state-led development, the political power of landed elites was undermined. Massive urbanization, development, and land reform eroded the revolutionary potential of peasants. But many of the same conditions that undermined the prospects for social revolution in the late twentieth century—massive movements of rural inhabitants to cities, the consolidation and proliferation of states, the shift of political power and patronage from landed to urban elites, economic development, the rise of unipolar American power, neoliberal economics, and globalization—created conditions for the multiplication of new forms of urban revolution in the late twentieth and early twenty-first centuries.

As population, power, and wealth shifted to cities, so too did the phenomenon of revolution. Revolution returned to the city. The new urban

---

9. Skocpol 1979.

revolutions of the late twentieth and early twenty-first centuries occurred in a social, political, and global context fundamentally different from that of the urban revolutions of the nineteenth and early twentieth centuries. Most importantly, the world had come to be dominated by large cities that were many times the size of cities in the early twentieth century. In 1900, only thirty-six cities in the world had more than five hundred thousand inhabitants, and only sixteen had more than a million. Contrast this with 2018, when 1,146 cities had more than five hundred thousand inhabitants, and 548 had more than a million. In 1900, only nine countries in the world had cities of over a million inhabitants. By 2018, 125 countries contained cities of over a million, and fifty-six countries contained more than one city with over a million.[10] By the late twentieth century, globalization and digital communications had transformed the scope, intensity, and speed of interactions across these global political and population centers. Neoliberal economic growth not only facilitated the expansion of cities, but also led to the growth of a new global middle class in developing and emerging economies and periodically fostered the economic distress that at times played into revolt. In the unipolar international order that followed the collapse of communism, American democracy promoted challenges to autocratic regimes, and the spread of democracy encouraged the proliferation of hybrid forms of authoritarianism. As regimes grew more hybrid and less outwardly autocratic, more dependent on fostering economic growth for their legitimation, and more integrated into global economic, normative, and information orders, they grew increasingly vulnerable to disruption through urban revolution.

The new urban revolutions of the late twentieth and early twenty-first centuries were associated with a set of structural conditions starkly different from that which underpinned the social revolutions of the early and mid-twentieth century. Rather than being correlated with poverty, external war, land inequality, and weak state infrastructural power, the new urban revolutions tended to occur in lower-middle and middle income non-democracies with repressive, highly corrupt regimes whose leaders had been in power for a long time and lacked the rents provided by oil resources. They were not products of the infrastructural weakness of the state. On the contrary, they occurred precisely where the infrastructural capacity of the state was strong—in cities. They were more closely related to regime-type and political opportunities than were the social revolutions of the past. Not peasants and workers, but the urban middle class participated disproportionately in them, with a variable array of other urban groups: workers, clerical staff, craftsmen, small business

---

10. Data come from United Nations 2019 and 1905 *World Almanac*.

owners, students, pensioners, housewives, and the unemployed. These revolutions were diverse in the social groups they encompassed and the grievances they articulated. But what united them were their revolutionary tactics of concentrating large numbers in central urban spaces and their broadly "civic" goals of reclaiming power from corrupt and abusive rulers.

Large-scale urbanization had brought increasing numbers of people into regular contact with the state, including the state's unrivaled predatory and repressive capabilities. The urban civic revolutions that proliferated in the late twentieth and early twenty-first centuries involved extraordinary explosions of mass mobilization aimed at reclaiming the state from the control of lawless, corrupt, and oppressive governments in the name of those to whom these states theoretically belonged—their citizens.

Urban civic revolutions involved a new revolutionary repertoire that relied on the power of numbers rather than the power of arms. Urbanization had concentrated vast numbers in close proximity to the state's nerve centers, rendering these regimes increasingly vulnerable to challenge by large, unarmed crowds. They sought to harness the structural advantages of large cities—numbers, diverse networks, available resources, robust communications, heightened visibility, and proximity to centers of power and wealth—to mobilize as many people as possible in central urban spaces, using the power of numbers to protect against government repression, disrupt the normal operations of commerce and administration, and incite defections from an incumbent regime. These revolutions displayed a remarkably high rate of success relative to other forms of revolution and accounted for the global increase in revolutionary contention that occurred during the late twentieth and early twenty-first centuries. Alterations in the repression–disruption trade-off function due to large-scale structural change (the concentration of people into cities, greater global connectedness, the rise of digital communications, and greater vulnerability of governments to urban disruption) combined with tactical innovation on the part of oppositions to create more favorable conditions for urban revolutionary oppositions.

The spatial politics of urban revolution in the late twentieth and early twenty-first centuries differed markedly from the past. Urban armed revolts of the nineteenth and early twentieth centuries employed the cityscape as rough terrain—as cover from which to contest state power—obliterating the distinction between public and private property. By contrast, urban civic revolts unfolded in the spaces between buildings—in the modern city's spacious public squares and broad boulevards—which provided a propitious setting for concentrating large numbers. They sought visibility, not cover, with the hope of exploiting the power of moral shocks, network ties, and social pressure to induce regime defections. Therefore, an inherent part of the politics of urban civic revolution was contention over public space, through its appropriation, regulation, and policing. Like all urban revolutions, the speed, intensity, and compactness of contention injected an unpredictable element into urban civic revolutionary processes. The proximity dilemma renders urban revolutions a high-risk/high-stakes endeavor for both regimes and oppositions. As a result, these revolutions have tended to be extremely compact in time, exhibiting a rhythm radically different from the slow but punctuated tempo of rural revolutions. This speed and compactness of interaction creates significant information problems—the consequences of which are greatly magnified by proximity to centers of state power and the absence of any buffer zone into which oppositions or regimes can retreat.

As revolution grew more urban, and as urban revolutions came to rely more on numbers rather than arms, the revolutionary process became increasingly "civilized" (in the sense of becoming less violent and less disruptive of everyday life). In particular, the moral unease associated with shooting into unarmed crowds, along with regime fears of the unpredictable effects of backlash or defections in close proximity to nerve centers of government, led to a search for less lethal methods of repression—even while the weaponry involved in countering rural rebellions grew markedly *more* lethal. The widespread killing that had once been considered a defining hallmark of urban revolution came to be eschewed by both regimes and oppositions. In the process, the risks that oppositions took in embarking on urban revolution were lowered considerably.

Revolutionary processes that concentrate hundreds of thousands into central urban spaces in a matter of days or weeks—as urban civic revolutions do—necessarily draw on a wide variety of grievances and political forces. As we have seen, participants in urban civic revolutions exhibited a lack of consensus over ends. Revolutionary organization in such situations could not provide ideological coherence, filter participants, or socialize them into movement norms, and maximizing participation involved attaining cooperation across widely divergent groups. To maximize numbers, these revolutions typically constructed a broad negative coalition rapidly assembled in a makeshift manner, pulling in all who favored the removal of the incumbent regime, irrespective of purpose. They relied on coalitional leaderships (and sometimes, no leadership), advancing broadly "civic" minimalist demands for reclaiming power from unscrupulous and overbearing rulers—a least common denominator across the broadest possible number of people.

Consequently, having attained power, urban civic oppositions produced post-revolutionary governments that were fractious and less durable than governments brought to power by social revolutions. These revolutions did lead to substantial gains in political freedoms and government accountability relative to pre-revolutionary regimes. But their achievements generally fell short of what one would expect from an electoral democracy (defined in a minimalist way) and even displayed a tendency to deteriorate over time. Urban civic revolutions did not push aside the state, but rather inherited the pre-revolutionary state largely intact, with all its deformities and defects. These embedded relationships of corruption, the greater constraints these regimes were under, and their greater fragility limited the responses of urban civic regimes in addressing the social and economic grievances that often had played a role in inciting revolution in the first place. The immediate economic disruptions these revolutions caused were minimal; but over time, the societies in which they had occurred experienced crises of sluggish growth that dragged at the legitimacy of new revolutionary regimes. These regimes also faced difficulties in grappling with the waves of crime unleashed by revolution, generally brought greater income inequality in their wake, and frequently exacerbated ethnic tensions.

In short, the achievements of urban civic revolutions are constrained by their mode of organization, the contexts in which they occur, and the societies they inherit. But this should not be construed as an argument against revolution. John Dunn once observed that "[a]ll post-revolutionary governments do considerable damage."[11] There is some truth to this, though Dunn's assessment begs to be placed in context: the incumbent regimes overthrown by revolutions also generate enormous harm. Revolutions often improve some aspects of the human condition at the expense of others, and the costs of revolution can sometimes be considerable. But generally, people do not embark upon revolution lightly. They do so because of the significant injuries inflicted upon them by pre-revolutionary governments and the absence of alternative means for redress.[12] This is where the larger tragedy of revolutions lies: that in the societies that experience them, the harms done are considerable both in revolution's presence and in its absence. But those who embark upon revolution need to do so with eyes wide open and to understand just how difficult achieving real progress is. It is not achieved by episodic acts like revolutions, but through difficult, protracted, iterated struggle—with or without revolution. No one should enter upon revolution believing that it is a panacea for the ills we confront, or that post-revolutionary life will not involve considerable adversity, difficult trade-offs, and failures.

Yet, as revolution has evolved toward urban civic forms, its impact on politics and society has grown more ambiguous and tentative. The damage done, the

---

11. Dunn 1972, 17.
12. Goodwin 2001.

risks involved, and the advantages gained have all narrowed considerably. Revolution is not dying. In fact, quite the opposite: it is proliferating and becoming more common. But it is also becoming less disruptive and more uncertain in its effects, even as it becomes a more normalized part of the political landscape.

What of the future? Will future revolutions continue to resemble those of today? Will they continue to be less disruptive and more ambiguous in their effects than revolutions of the past? Will they continue their trend toward lowered mortality? Can the urban civic repertoire continue to produce high rates of success? Will we look back at the late twentieth and early twenty-first centuries as an unusual age of revolution, much as Seton-Watson, in the mid-twentieth century, looked back at his century's first fifty years? And will new forms of revolution emerge alongside the urban civic repertoire and possibly displace it?

If anything should be clear from this book, it is that when it comes to revolution, the future is never the past. Certainly, the spatial logic that underpins many of the arguments advanced in this book—the inherent trade-off between repression and disruption associated with proximity to or distance from state centers of power—is unlikely to change. It seems as embedded in the nature of revolutionary contention as the growth versus predation-risk trade-off is within evolutionary biology. But as in evolutionary biology, learning behavior and environmental change alter patterns of behavior over time. We should expect that to be true in the future with regard to revolutions as well.

Given the continuing concentration of people, power, and wealth in cities, the future of revolution will undoubtedly remain predominantly urban. The United Nations projects that, by 2050, almost seven out of every ten inhabitants of the planet will live in cities—including half of the population in low-income countries and three-fifths in lower-middle income countries.[13] While centers of the world economy will likely shift eastward and southward, wealth, power, and human capital will continue to concentrate in massive urban centers, bringing increasing numbers of people into close proximity with the state. If the arguments of this book hold, these urban centers, with their vast concentrations of people, power, and wealth, should remain highly susceptible to disruption from urban civic revolutionary contention—particularly where governments remain predatory and repressive. The global retreat of democracy in the second half of the 2010s virtually ensures that there will be no shortage of such regimes in the future.

Current trends suggest that revolutionary contention will continue to occur at a rapid pace. The data used in this book were right-censored after

---

13. United Nations 2019.

2014—an arbitrary cut-off due to the historical accident of when I embarked upon analysis and writing. But since 2014, revolutionary contention has continued to unfold with great frequency. During the 2015–19 period, new mass revolts seeking regime-change broke out in Central America (Guatemala, Honduras, and Nicaragua), the Balkans (Moldova, Macedonia, Romania, Serbia, Montenegro, and Albania), the Middle East (Algeria, Lebanon, Iran, and Iraq), and South America (Venezuela and Bolivia). New bouts of civil war (in most cases, based on long-standing conflicts) occurred in Burundi, Turkish Kurdistan, Yemen, and Cameroon. In 2017, a coupvolution ousted Robert Mugabe in Zimbabwe, and in 2018, revolutions overthrew corrupt and repressive regimes in Armenia and Sudan. Spectacular outbursts of separatist revolt occurred in Hong Kong and Catalonia, while failed citizen uprisings took place in Haiti and Togo. The year 2019 was one of global protest and revolt not unlike 2011 or 1989. In all, 5.4 new revolutionary episodes occurred annually from 2015 to 2019 (averaged over the 2010–19 decade, 5.3 episodes per year).[14] That compares with a pace of 2.44 new episodes per year during the first half of the twentieth century, 2.80 during the Cold War, and 4.10 during the post–Cold War period. Of the new revolutionary episodes that occurred from 2015 to 2019, 89 percent took place primarily in cities (a proportion greater than at any five-year period since 1900), and 63 percent were urban civic in character—unarmed, relying on the power of numbers, and broadly civic in their demands.

In short, urban revolutionary contention has continued to grow more frequent and to assume urban civic form. Yet one thing has changed substantially: the rate of opposition success.[15] In the second half of the 2010s, there was a palpable decline in successful revolutions, with the probability of success for urban revolts dipping to .25 (and for urban civic revolts, to .24). This compares with a success rate of .54 for urban revolts and .59 for urban civic revolts during the 1985–2014 period. Averaged over the entire decade of the 2010s, the probability of opposition success in urban revolutionary episodes was .36—lower than for any decade since the 1930s. Several trends appear to be conspiring to attenuate the success of the urban civic repertoire and its ability to capitalize on the revolutionary advantages of cities.

Certainly, regime learning in a world in which revolution has grown increasingly prevalent is a large part of these changes. Regimes are now thoroughly familiar with the urban civic repertoire and have developed a number

---

14. This does not count quasi-revolutionary episodes that occurred during the 2015–19 period in Ethiopia in 2016, Iraq in 2016, South Korea in 2016, and Chile, Ecuador, and Colombia in 2019.

15. For a similar observation, see Chenoweth 2017.

of tactics to counteract it. They have grown craftier in their approaches to repressing urban civic oppositions, targeting key activists outside of periods of mobilization—away from the crowd and the eye of the cellphone camera. They have become more skillful at co-opting elements of diverse oppositional coalitions prior to the onset of mobilization. And they have been more adamant in holding onto power in the face of contention and in prolonging episodes in order to exhaust revolutionary fervor. Governments have grown shrewder in exercising control over public space and in keeping oppositional challenges to locations outside city centers, where the disruption they inflict is less pronounced.

It is also true that in recent years, urban revolutionary contention has been growing more violent in ways that may erode or alter the urban civic repertoire. In places as far-flung as Myanmar, Hong Kong, and Belarus, regimes have shown an increased willingness to use violence against unarmed crowds, including in some cases shooting directly into them. The violence of the 2014 Euromaidan Revolution in Ukraine stood in stark contrast to the peaceful protests of the Orange Revolution only a decade earlier. Euromaidan began as an urban civic revolt, with protests of hundreds of thousands in Maidan in a fashion similar to the Orange Revolution. But the regime was much more violent in its approach to revolutionary protests than in 2004, and numbers proved insufficient to dislodge Yanukovych from power a second time. This empowered more radical and violent elements within the crowd.[16] Alongside massive protests of up to a million, groups of Euromaidan protesters utilized "the old-fashioned methods of throwing Molotov cocktails and bits of their own city" at Berkut riot police, while the police responded with increasingly savage tactics. Injured protesters "were snatched from their hospital beds," and "activists were seized at night, beaten, and dumped in local forests."[17] Riotous violence was further compounded by the inability of conventional party and civil society leaders to control leaderless, digitally mobilized crowds. In their keenness to counter the urban civic repertoire, regimes have embraced more violent tactics toward unarmed crowds; crowds in turn have reverted to the enduring tactic of the revolutionary riot. This new, more volatile synthesis may in fact represent the future of revolution in cities.[18]

As in the past, large-scale structural change is at work altering the repression–disruption trade-off function and changing the character of revolutionary contention. As we have seen, since 1900, revolution has evolved as a

---

16. Kudelia 2018.
17. Wilson 2014, 86, 97.
18. See Kudelia 2018; Kadivar and Ketchley 2018.

result of the concentration of people into cities, changing patterns of political and economic power, altered social structures, new technologies of rebellion and counterinsurgency, and shifting currents of geopolitics. Like the impact of climate change on processes of natural selection, these forces continue to mold revolutionary practice—periodically tilting the advantage toward either oppositions or regimes.

We may in fact be entering a new period of "climate change" in the practice of revolution. Especially significant in this regard has been the incorporation of advanced digital technologies into repertoires of repression. Digital media have grown increasingly important to the coordination of urban revolt, and they initially proved a disruptive force, empowering oppositions vis-à-vis regimes. But over time, regimes developed new ways of disrupting and censoring digital communication and using the internet to identify, harass, and confuse oppositions.[19] Oppositions in turn have found ways to counter these efforts, and technological innovation has not been a one-way street. The encrypted Telegram communications platform, for example, became an important means for evading government efforts to quash digitally based opposition and for coordinating uprisings in such varied places as Iran, Hong Kong, and Belarus.[20] Telegram was developed by Nikolai and Pavel Durov, founders of the most popular Russian social media platform Vkontakte. The Durov brothers were ousted from their company by Putin for failing to share user information with the Russian secret police. Telegram was their answer to Putin. Governments have rushed to ban Telegram, but efforts to penetrate or outlaw the platform have had mixed results.[21] For example, despite repeated government efforts to block it, 60 percent of Iran's population was using Telegram as of 2019.[22] The cat-and-mouse game over digital communications will continue to be played out, though it is doubtful that there will ever be an outright winner. At different times the advantage will shift to one side or the other.

Still more ominous are the ways in which regimes have been experimenting with digital systems of citizen surveillance. One of the big advantages of mobilizing in large crowds is the ability of individual participants to conceal their identities in order to avoid government retaliation. In the past, repressive

---

19. Gunitsky 2015; King, Pan, and Roberts 2013; Roberts 2018.

20. Maréchal 2018.

21. Doffman 2019; Litvinova 2020. The Starlink global satellite network is another potential development that could bypass government censorship when accessing the internet, allowing internet use from virtually any location on the planet. See, for instance, the appeals of the Belarusian opposition to Elon Musk to deploy the Starlink network during the attempted revolution in Belarus in 2020 after Lukashenko cut off the Belarusian internet (Hamacher 2020).

22. Akbari and Gabdulhakov 2019.

regimes sometimes resorted to spraying protest participants with dyed water, in the hope that the stains would allow police to round up those who had participated after protests ended.[23] But this was not a particularly efficient way of identifying participants. Technology has come to play a growing role in this effort—especially with the development of facial recognition software. In China, for instance, the Sharp Eyes program has aspired to connect security cameras on all squares, roads, shopping malls, transportation hubs, and buildings into a single nationwide surveillance network based on facial recognition—even rating individuals captured by these cameras on the basis of their behavior and using the information to reward and punish them.[24] In Moscow, thousands of security cameras have been fitted with facial recognition software and linked into a police database.[25] The Chinese government has promoted the export of these systems—with authoritarian regimes in Zimbabwe, Venezuela, and Belarus lining up as early customers.[26] Facial recognition surveillance in places like China and Russia no doubt exerts a chilling effect on potential participants in urban protests, and could undermine the urban civic repertoire by weakening the protection that large numbers provide against government repression. This is turn could constrain the size of crowds, diluting a key dimension of the urban civic repertoire and tilting the repression-disruption trade-off function in favor of governments.

All this is part of the global trend toward "smart cities"—that is, the use of sensors and integrated data collection to manage daily urban life. Smart cities have already come into existence in China and in the much of the advanced industrial world; they are rapidly being promoted in parts of the developing world as well. They harbor great promise for improving the daily lives of urban dwellers with regard to congestion, delivery of services, business development, sustainability, recreation, and civic involvement. But they also contain enormous implications for the policing and surveillance of public space, as the Chinese example has shown. Many worry that it is not a far leap from smart cities to surveillance cities, and if this does transpire, the global implications for the ability of populations to contain out-of-control political elites could be profound.

The broader geopolitical context has also shifted in ways sharply detrimental to urban civic oppositions. By the 2010s, questions were emerging as to whether American power had begun to recede under the impact of costly wars,

---

23. Leibenluft 2008.
24. Denyer 2018.
25. McGoogan 2017.
26. Cave et al. 2019; Greitens 2019; Xu 2020.

financial crisis, and domestic political gridlock. These trends accelerated greatly under the Trump presidency, as American hegemony and the liberal international order rapidly retreated, and the United States turned inward to face its own problems of polarization and economic distress. Along with this, the American emphasis on human rights and promotion of democracy greatly thinned. At the same time, Russia and China came to play larger roles in supporting autocratic allies in the Middle East, Africa, and Latin America—providing investment, resources, and weapons and training for their armed forces and police. Having been spooked by waves of rebellion in the post-communist region and the Middle East, Russia and China came to define themselves as counterrevolutionary powers—even to the extent that the Putin regime ignored the hundredth anniversary of Russia's October Revolution lest its celebration somehow inspire those questioning the status quo. The Biden administration promised to revive American power and renew commitment to promoting democracy and human rights abroad. But the decline of American power and the growth of globalized autocratic powers like Russia and China are not so easily reversed. They have altered the geopolitics of regime-change, raising doubts that the international environment will be as conducive to the success of urban civic revolution in the future as it was in the post–Cold War past.

Superficially, urban civic revolutions share elements with twenty-first century right-wing populism. Both attack corrupt political establishments, both tap into the animus emanating from the deteriorating economic position of portions of the middle class, and both champion a reclaiming of the state and popular sovereignty. But a closer inspection reveals important differences. If urban civic revolutions are directed against corrupt and abusive authoritarian regimes in lower-middle and middle-income countries, populist movements are instead a disease of democracies, including those in upper-middle income and advanced industrial countries. Right-wing populism resembles the fascist movements of the 1920s and 1930s more than the urban civic oppositions of the post–Cold war era. Such movements in the past occasionally inspired revolutionary mobilizations, such as Mussolini's 1922 March on Rome or Hitler's 1923 Beer Hall Putsch, and they could very well do so in the future.[27]

Twenty-first century populist movements have sought to undermine the constraints on power that epitomize democratic government (the rule of law, checks and balances, and accountable government) and to establish the

---

27. The January 6, 2020 Capitol Riot in the United States lacked the sustained commitment of a revolutionary mobilization to force through regime-change and was aimed at keeping Donald Trump in office by pre-empting electoral processes. Nevertheless, it revealed new possibilities for right-wing rebellion.

dominance of executive power, riding roughshod over civil society, the press, and individual freedoms. They have utilized racism, xenophobia, and nationalism to divide citizens and create a sense of cultural warfare and perpetual crisis, introducing a deepened personalism and corruption into government in place of the impartiality that typifies democratic procedure. By contrast, urban civic revolutions have sought to unite citizens across existing divides and to impose constraints on government, curb unchecked power, and liberate society from government predation and corruption. In populism, strong charismatic leaders have sought to gain power in established democracies through the ballot box, targeting an alienated electorate. They have taken advantage of free and fair elections and the rule of law to subvert democracy through democratic means. Urban civic revolutions, conversely, have generally lacked coherent leaderships, sought to constrain autocratic leaders, and gained power through an extra-institutional siege of government—largely because genuine electoral institutions and the rule of law were absent. If urban civic revolutions drew support disproportionately from the educated urban middle classes, the support base for right-wing populism has tilted toward the less educated, the blue-collar, and the rural, tapping into grievances over being left behind by globalization, immigration, and the privileges of the professional classes. The religious/secular divide also forms a significant cleavage on which populist movements have thrived. And in newer democracies, right-wing populist movements have flourished in the wake of the failure of urban civic revolutions to deliver on their promises.

Where right-wing populist movements have attained power, democratic quality has rapidly deteriorated. Once in power, these regimes finagle electoral rules and manipulate the contours of the electorate to sustain themselves in office, blurring the line between democracy and electoral authoritarianism. These diluted democracies in many respects resemble the types of regimes that in the past have proven vulnerable to urban civic revolt. But out of power, right-wing populist movements have also represented a threat to democracy, especially where they encourage the growth of armed extremism. They have made the return of armed revolt in cities imaginable once again. Democracies have long been thought to be immune to revolution, largely because free and fair electoral mechanisms deflect opposition from revolutionary challenge. Democratic backsliding and extreme polarization have been undermining that immunity—even within long-established democracies. Polarization and information bubbles have eroded commitment to the democratic process and belief in the integrity of democratic procedures. This crisis of democracy may well lead to new forms of revolutionary challenge in the future.

Yet another challenge to the urban civic repertoire emerges from growing inequalities. Despite what might be deduced from the decline in social revolutions aimed at addressing class inequalities, the neoliberal era brought a deepening of economic inequality and a widening gulf between rich and poor. Within-country income inequalities increased for a large portion of the world's population in the late twentieth and early twenty-first centuries.[28] Social issues were never completely off the agenda of urban civic revolution, as the surveys of participants from multiple urban civic revolutions analyzed in this book revealed; indeed, economic issues were prominent among the grievances that fueled these mobilizations. But redistribution was not the main focus of these revolutions, and income inequalities tended to increase in their wake. Particularly in the global south, urbanization has concentrated large numbers of poor people in cities and will continue to do so at a rapid pace. While the urban poor have traditionally played a less conspicuous role in revolutionary mobilizations, that could change in the future as the pace of urbanization in the developing world accelerates.

In 2020 and 2021, issues of class inequality became intertwined with the devastation of a global pandemic. The pandemic led to the largest global economic contraction since the Great Depression, impoverishing hundreds of millions across the planet. Deprivation on such a scale will undoubtedly reverberate for many years. One consequence could be a deepening of the social agenda of revolution to address broader issues of inequality, redistribution, and poverty.[29] Without significant redistributive reform, economic inequality is likely to push itself back onto the revolutionary agenda. The resulting conflicts would not be driven by the poverty of peasants located far from urban centers of power, but by the precariousness of urban subsistence in close proximity to the state, juxtaposed with the extravagance of the richest one percent. How this might manifest itself in revolutionary repertoires is unclear, though in the past, efforts at addressing class inequalities through revolution provoked high numbers of deaths and were incapable of generating the kind of broad civic coalitions that would allow revolutionaries to rely on the power of numbers rather than the power of arms.

The pandemic brought a sudden but temporary halt to the massive waves of anti-regime protests that swept the world in 2019 and early 2020. As *The New York Times* reported, "The daily burden of acquiring face masks or food overshadows debates about corruption and abuse of power."[30] It is hard to imagine a more powerful neutralizer of crowds than the atomizing consequences of an epidemic. Yet, even a pandemic could not shut down the impulse to rebellion

28. United Nations 2020.
29. Sly 2020.
30. Wang, Abi-Habab, and Yee 2020.

in many parts of the world, as large numbers of revolutionary protestors continued to brave the streets in places like Thailand, Belarus, Armenia, Mali, and Myanmar.

Revolutions have transformed the physiognomy of our world, and most states have experienced a revolution at some point in their modern histories. Despite repeated predictions of its demise, revolution as a mass political project of regime-change from below has displayed phoenix-like resilience. It has altered tremendously over time in location, substance, and form—moving from the city to the countryside and then returning to the city over the course of a century, relying on different social forces and displaying different tactics with each transition. Revolutions of the future will look different from those of today, as revolutionary contention continues to be buffeted by the forces that have shaped it over the past three hundred years. As contemporary trends suggest, revolutionary contention in the future may be less successful and perhaps more violent and riotous than in late twentieth and early twenty-first centuries, as urban civic tactics come under duress. It may gain a deeper social agenda or become a tool of right-wing politicians, and it may spread to democracies in ways that have not traditionally been the case. But it is likely to remain both urban and frequent. For as Zamiatin well understood, there is no such thing as the last revolution. The number of revolutions is infinite.

APPENDIX 1

Construction of Cross-National Data on Revolutionary Episodes

A CENTRAL EMPIRICAL strategy of this study was the creation of a cross-national dataset on revolutionary episodes for understanding global patterns of revolutionary contention since 1900 and the structural forces that have shaped these trends. I defined a revolutionary episode as a mass siege of an established government by its own population with the aim of displacing the incumbent regime and substantially altering the political or social order—irrespective of whether the opposition successfully gained power.

To identify possible episodes that fit this definition, a team of research assistants and I scoured a large variety of sources. In all, eight published encyclopedias,[1] nine existing global datasets on wars, civil wars, ethnic conflict, and instances of nonviolent resistance,[2] nine online encyclopedias and databases of conflict events,[3] and all files of Keesing's *World News Archive* from

---

1. These included Minahan 2002; Ness 2009; Phillips and Axelrod 2005; Creveld 1996; Colby 1908; Kohn 1999; Goldstone 1998b; and various editions of the *Encyclopedia Britannica* (including the classic 1910–11 edition).

2. These were: Correlates of War Dataset (Sarkees and Wayman 2010); Cross-National Time-Series Data Archive (Banks and Wilson 2015); Ethnic Power Relations Dataset (Wimmer, Cederman, and Min 2009); the "Ethnicity, Insurgency, and Civil War" dataset (Fearon and Laitin 2003); Minorities at Risk Dataset (Minorities at Risk Project 2009); Political Instability Task Force Dataset (Goldstone et al. 2010); Nonviolent and Violent Conflict Outcomes Dataset (Chenoweth and Shay 2020); Uppsala Conflict Dataset (Pettersson and Wallensteen 2015); and the "From Empire to Nation-State" Dataset (Wimmer and Min 2006).

3. These included: Armed Conflict Events Database (https://www.onwar.com/#gsc.tab=0); Dynamic Analysis of Dispute Management (DADM) Project (https://uca.edu/politicalscience/dadm-project/); Global Nonviolent Action Database (https://nvdatabase.swarthmore.edu/); GlobalSecurity.org (https://www.globalsecurity.org/); International Center on Nonviolent

1931 to the present were examined in their entirety. Moreover, 135 other occasional sources (newspapers, websites, and online encyclopedias) and over eight hundred scholarly books and articles were consulted on specific episodes in order to identify whether an episode qualified for inclusion. The sources consulted for each episode are documented in the full dataset available from the author. (Unless directly cited in the book, they are not represented in this book's references.)

Short narratives were composed on each potential case, and at weekly meetings of the research team, each episode was discussed to determine whether it met the criteria of the definition and should be included in the dataset. In all we identified 345 episodes. (For a full listing of the episodes, see Appendix 2.) Episodes that fell close to but short of the definition for one reason or another (as detailed below) were tracked (131 cases in all). A list of these cases and the reasons why each was rejected are included in the full dataset.

To ensure the mass character of revolutionary episodes and to distinguish them from terrorist actions, coups d'état, and small armed mutinies, I required that each revolutionary episode have, at a minimum, a peak mobilization of at least a thousand civilian participants. The threshold measures the highest number of participants directly engaged in revolutionary action during any event of the episode (or in the case of civil wars, the highest total size of rebel forces).[4] This threshold was chosen after extensive examination of episodes above and below this cut-off point. Many of the episodes examined in this study were able to mobilize very large numbers of participants, with 10 percent mobilizing over five hundred thousand, 25 percent over a hundred thousand, 45 percent over fifty thousand, 64 percent over twenty thousand, and 81 percent over ten thousand. But there are obviously many episodes that do not meet the thousand-person cut-off. According to Cunningham, Gleditsch, and Salehyan (2013), the median level of mobilization in civil wars from 1945 to 2011 was four thousand armed participants, with 25 percent of civil wars involving fewer than a thousand participants.[5] However, only three out of the

---

Conflict (https://www.nonviolent-conflict.org/resource-library/); the Modern Conflicts Database (https://www.peri.umass.edu/modern-conflicts); Online Encyclopedia of Mass Violence (https://www.sciencespo.fr/ceri/en/ouvrage/oemv); and Wikipedia.

4. As noted in chapter 7, revolutions involve participation by civilians in various ways. But direct participation is central to the disruption that revolutionary action seeks to generate, and so I use it for identifying the mass character of mobilization.

5. Of civil wars with less than a thousand participants, 42 percent were classified as ethnic, secessionist, or autonomy conflicts, 11 percent as coups, and 9 percent as terrorist actions.

ninety-one civil wars identified by Cunningham, Gleditsch, and Salehyan with fewer than a thousand participants ended in victory for the opposition, and two of these three cases were classified by them as coups d'état. Moreover, a number of these cases were not aimed at regime-change. By contrast, seven out of the 110 civil wars they identified that involved between one thousand and four thousand participants ended in opposition victory, and none of these cases were classified by them as a coup d'état. I collected information on episodes that met my definition but had fewer than a thousand participants and placed them on my alternative list. In all, thirty-one episodes fit this description, including such cases as the 1904 Liberal Revolt in Paraguay, the 1915 Chilembe Revolt in British Nyasaland, the Tallin Uprising in 1924, the 1935 Fier Uprising in Albania, the 1948 Costa Rican Civil War, the 1959 Mosul Uprising in Iraq, the 1964 Zanzibar Revolution, the 1979 Granadan Revolution, the 1996 Popular Revolutionary Army Uprising in Mexico, and the 2004 Central African Bush War. All of these episodes were small armed uprisings, and only three involved the opposition gaining power. Their inclusion would not have affected this study's substantive arguments.

I included anti-colonial and separatist mobilizations aimed at independence in the dataset, as these sought regime-change within a portion of a country's territory. Indeed, many of the major revolutions of history have been anti-colonial or separatist revolts, including the Vietnamese Revolution (1945–54), the Algerian Revolution (1954–62), and the Estonian Singing Revolution (1987–91).[6] But I excluded irredentist conflicts that sought to detach a particular territory from one state and place it within the boundaries of another state (such as the Northern Ireland Civil War of 1969–98, the Nagorno-Karabakh Conflict of 1988–94, and the Bosnian Civil War of 1992–95) on the grounds that these conflicts were better understood as instances of switching allegiances from one state to another rather than regime-change per se.[7] Irredentist conflicts also frequently involve significant participation and intervention by an external national homeland, to the point that it is often difficult to identify the strength and degree of autonomy of local actors.

---

6. Many scholars have noted the fundamental similarities between revolution and secession. For a discussion, see Buchanan 1991. In all, 18 percent of the sample consisted of revolutionary episodes that solely articulated demands for independence without articulating other revolutionary goals, while another 17 percent of the sample consisted of episodes in which demands for independence were made alongside other revolutionary goals.

7. On the distinctiveness of irredentist conflicts and how the politics of irredentism differs in fundamental ways from other separatist conflicts, see Chazan 1991.

I also excluded resistance to foreign invasions or foreign-imposed regime-change (such as the Moroccan Wars against Spain and France in 1908–12, the large number of partisan wars and resistance movements against Nazi occupation across Europe during World War II, and the so-called Forest Brotherhoods in the immediate aftermath of Soviet occupation of the Baltic following World War II). These mobilizations were not oriented toward the overthrow of an established government, but rather were a direct consequence of invasion. They sought to evict an occupying army in wartime or a domestic regime directly imposed by a foreign power. Similarly, I excluded instances of resistance to the imposition of colonial rule (what Terence Ranger called "primary resistance" to colonialism[8]) and included only those cases of resistance to established colonial governments.

Finally, if an opposition came to power through the ballot box or through elite negotiations without engaging in a mass siege of government (even if it perpetrated extensive violence against opponents, as the Nazis did in Germany in 1932–33), these cases also were excluded. By contrast, Mussolini's March on Rome in October 1922 and Hitler's 1923 Beer Hall Putsch were included in the dataset, as they constituted mass sieges of government with the intent of imposing regime-change.

For each of the 345 episodes that qualified by these criteria, a narrative was composed that described the causes and major events of the episode, how it unfolded, and how it ended using a variety of secondary sources. The episode narratives and the sources on which they were based were used throughout this study as case material to illustrate patterns and trends and to examine in more depth the processes that occurred within specific episodes.

Information on each episode was coded for a wide variety of fields: the timing of the episode's beginning and end; its outcome; features of the incumbent regime prior to onset of the episode; the goals and grievances articulated by revolutionary oppositions; the peak size of civilian mobilization involved; the class and ethnic characteristics of participants; tactics of revolutionary resistance and forms of revolutionary organization; how the episode began and how it ended; how long the government in place at the end of the episode lasted in power; the number of deaths that occurred during the episode; features of government, society, and economy during the decade following the episode; whether the episode was part of a revolutionary wave and which prior revolutionary episodes were related to the episode and in what way; and the sources consulted for each case. All this information was tied together in a relational database available from the author in spreadsheet form.

8. Ranger 1968.

Of course, it is difficult to assess how comprehensive the data are, since there are no other datasets on revolutionary episodes that are completely comparable. There are, however, two datasets that are somewhat analogous: Djuve, Knutsen, and Wig's "Historical Regimes Data" on instances of regime-change from 1789 to 2016;[9] and the NAVCO 1.3 data on so-called maximalist campaigns from 1900 to 2019.[10] Unlike the data on revolutionary episodes in this book, the Historical Regimes Data do not include cases of failed revolutions. For the 1900–2014 period covered by my revolutionary episodes data, they do, however, include 126 civil wars or popular uprisings that led to regime-change—the equivalent of successful revolutionary episodes within my data. The sample used in this book found 123 successful revolutionary episodes over the same time span. The NAVCO 1.3 data cover what Chenoweth and Shay call "maximalist campaigns" (campaigns over regime-change, secession, self-determination, and major social change) that involved at least a thousand participants. For the 1900–2014 period, their data include 550 campaigns, compared to the 343 episodes that I identified as revolutionary over the same time span. However, a closer examination reveals that a large proportion of the "maximalist" campaigns in the NAVCO data involved instances of resistance to foreign invasions or foreign occupations, were irredentist in character, or were quasi-revolutionary episodes, reformist campaigns, or non-revolutionary sieges of government as outlined by my definitions in chapter 1. There are also 106 cases in the revolutionary episodes dataset used this book (31 percent of all episodes) that do not appear in NAVCO dataset.

Because I was interested in identifying changing patterns of revolution over time, I was acutely aware of the potential biases that could be introduced by relying only on more contemporary sources, which would likely have thinner coverage of earlier episodes and over-represent more recent ones. I took particular care to ensure coverage of revolutionary episodes during the first half of the twentieth century. This was reflected in the substantial variety of sources that were consulted. The result is a far more representative sample of revolutionary episodes than appears in comparable sources. Thus, sixty-five revolutionary episodes in the dataset that occurred from 1900 through 1950 (53 percent of all episodes in the dataset during these years) are not represented in the NAVCO 1.3 dataset of maximalist campaigns.

No dataset provides complete coverage, and readers will undoubtedly identify particular episodes that they believe qualify as revolutionary by the definition

---

9. Djuve, Knutsen, and Wig 2020.
10. Chenoweth and Shay 2020.

used in this book and that should have been included. They may disagree with my definition of revolution, with my interpretation of particular cases, or the inclusion of a particular case in the analysis. Such differences of opinion are inherent to an enterprise of this kind. But for the goals of this study, the revolutionary episodes included in the dataset provide a reasonable representation of how revolutionary contention evolved around the world since 1900—the main purpose for which the data were created.

APPENDIX 2

Revolutionary Episodes, 1900–2014

TABLE A2.1. Revolutionary episodes, 1900–2014

Start year	End year	Name of episode	Location of episode	Location	Goals	Tactics	Outcome
1899	1902	Philippine–American War	American-occupied Philippines	R	Ind (AC)	A (CW)	Failed
1899	1920	Dervish Rebellion	British-controlled Somalia	R	Ind (AC), Isl	A (CW)	Failed
1900	1900	War of the Golden Stool	British-controlled Ghana	R	Ind (AC)	A (CW)	Failed
1900	1900	Huizhou Uprising	China	R	Const	A	Failed
1901	1903	Liberating Revolution	Venezuela	R	Oth	A (CW)	Failed
1901	1913	Moro Wars	American-occupied Philippines	R	Ind (AC), Isl	A (CW)	Failed
1903	1903	Ilinden Revolt	Ottoman Empire-controlled Macedonia	RU	Soc, Ind	A (CW)	Failed
1904	1907	Herero Rebellion	German-controlled Southwest Africa	R	Ind (AC)	A (CW)	Failed
1904	1904	Sasun Uprising	Ottoman-controlled Armenia	R	Ind	A (CW)	Failed
1904	1904	Vaccine Revolt	Brazil	U	Oth	R, A	Failed
1905	1906	1905 Revolution in Russia	Russian Empire	UR	Soc, Const	R, S, D, L, A	Failed
1905	1905	Argentinian Revolution of 1905	Argentina	U	Lib	A	Failed
1905	1907	Maji-Maji Rebellion	German colony of Tanganyika	R	Ind (AC)	A (CW)	Failed
1905	1906	Persian Constitutional Revolution	Persia	U	Const	S	Successful
1906	1906	Cuban Liberal Revolution of 1906	Cuba	UR	Lib, Oth	A (CW)	Failed
1906	1907	Ping-liu-li Uprising of 1906	China	R	Const	A	Failed
1908	1909	Hanoi Poison Plot and Related Revolts	French-controlled Vietnam	R	Ind (AC)	R, A, D	Failed

1908	1908	Young Turk Revolution	Ottoman Empire	U	Const	A, CV, S, D	Successful
1909	1910	Hauran Druze Rebellion	Ottoman-controlled Syria	R	Ind	A (CW)	Failed
1909	1909	Tragic Week in Catalonia	Spain	U	Soc	R, S, D	Failed
1910	1912	Albanian Uprisings 1910–1912	Ottoman-controlled Albania	R	Ind	A (CW)	Failed
1910	1910	1910 Portuguese Revolution	Portugal	U	Const	A, S	Successful
1910	1919	Mexican Revolution and Civil War	Mexico	RU	Soc, Const, Oth	A (CW), L, S, D	Successful
1911	1912	Xinhai Revolution	China	RU	Const	A (CW), CV	Successful
1914	1914	Red Week	Italy	U	Soc	R, S, D	Failed
1914	1915	Maritz Rebellion	South Africa	R	Ind, Oth	CV, A	Failed
1915	1921	Jangal Rebellion	Iran	R	Soc, Ind, Const	A (CW), L	Failed
1915	1917	Volta–Bani War	French-controlled Burkina-Faso	R	Ind (AC)	A (CW)	Failed
1916	1916	Easter Uprising	British-controlled Ireland	U	Ind	A	Failed
1916	1918	Arab Revolt of 1916–1918	Ottoman-controlled Arab lands	R	Ind (AC)	A (CW)	Successful
1916	1916	Borgawa Revolt in Dahomey	French-controlled Dahomey	R	Ind (AC)	A (CW)	Failed
1916	1920	Kaocen Rebellion	French-controlled Niger	R	Ind (AC), Isl	A (CW)	Failed
1917	1917	Chambelona Revolt	Cuba	R	Lib, Oth	A (CW), CV	Failed
1917	1917	February Revolution in Russia	Russian Empire	U	Const	R, S, D, A	Successful
1917	1918	Barue Rebellion	Portuguese-controlled Mozambique	R	Ind (AC)	A (CW)	Failed
1917	1920	October Revolution and Civil War	Russian Empire	UR	Soc	A (CW), S, D, L	Successful
1917	1926	Basmachi Revolt	Russian-controlled Central Asia	R	Ind (AC), Isl	A (CW)	Failed
1918	1918	Finnish Civil War	Finland	U	Soc	A (CW)	Failed

(*Continued*)

TABLE A2.1. (*continued*)

Start year	End year	Name of episode	Location of episode	Location	Goals	Tactics	Outcome
1918	1918	Egba Revolt in Nigeria	British-controlled Nigeria	R	Ind (AC)	A	Failed
1918	1918	Austrian Revolution of 1918	Austria	U	Const	R, S, D, A	Successful
1918	1918	Aster Revolution	Hungary	U	Const	R, D, A	Successful
1918	1918	German Revolution	Germany	U	Const	S, D, A	Successful
1918	1921	War of the Insane	French Indochina	R	Ind (AC)	A (CW)	Failed
1918	1920	Haitian Revolt of 1918	American-occupied Haiti	R	Ind	A (CW)	Failed
1918	1919	Sparticist Uprising/related revolts	Germany	U	Soc	A, S, D	Failed
1918	1921	Greater Polish Uprising/related revolts	German-controlled Poland	RU	Ind	A (CW)	Successful
1919	1919	Hungarian Revolution of 1919	Hungary	UR	Soc	A, S, D, L	Successful
1919	1922	Christmas Uprising	Yugoslav-controlled Montenegro	R	Ind, Oth	A (CW)	Failed
1919	1922	Irish War of Independence	British-controlled Ireland	UR	Ind	A (CW), S	Successful
1919	1926	Rif Rebellion	French- and Spanish-controlled Morocco	R	Ind (AC), Isl	A (CW)	Failed
1919	1920	Samil Independence Movement	Japanese-controlled Korea	U	Ind (AC)	D, CR	Failed
1919	1922	Egyptian Revolution of 1919	British-controlled Egypt	UR	Ind (AC), Const	R, S, D, A, CR	Successful
1919	1924	Mahmud Barzanji Revolt	British-controlled Iraqi Kurdistan	R	Ind (AC)	A (CW)	Failed
1920	1920	1920 Guatemalan Revolution	Guatemala	U	Lib, Oth	A, D	Successful
1920	1920	Ruhr Uprising	Germany	U	Soc, Oth	A, S	Failed

1920	Easter Crisis	Denmark	U	Const	D (UC)	Failed
1920	Arab Insurrection in Iraq	British-controlled Iraq	UR	Ind (AC)	A (CW), S, D	Failed
1920	Indian Non-Cooperation Movement	British-controlled India	U	Ind (AC)	S, D, R, CR	Failed
1920	Tambov Rebellion	Soviet Russia	R	Oth	A (CW), L	Failed
1920	Kocgiri Rebellion	Turkish-controlled Kurdistan	R	Ind	A (CW)	Failed
1921	Kronstadt Rebellion	Soviet Russia	U	Lib, Oth	A, S, D	Failed
1921	March Action	Germany	U	Soc	A, S	Failed
1921	Rand Revolt	South Africa	U	Soc, Oth	R, S, A	Failed
1922	Bajram Currie Revolt	Albania	R	Eth, Oth	A	Failed
1922	Senussi Rebellion	Italian-controlled Libya	R	Ind (AC)	A (CW)	Failed
1932	Irish Civil War	Ireland	RU	Oth	A (CW)	Failed
1923	March on Rome	Italy	U	Oth	A, R, D	Successful
1922	September Uprising	Bulgaria	R	Soc	A	Failed
1923	Beer Hall Putsch	Germany	U	Oth	A	Failed
1923	De la Huerta Rebellion	Mexico	RU	Oth	A (CW), CV	Failed
1924	Albanian Uprising of 1924	Albania	RU	Lib, Eth	A, D, CV	Successful
1924	August 1924 Uprising in Georgia	Soviet-controlled Georgia	R	Ind	A	Failed
1925	Sheikh Said Rebellion	Turkish-controlled Kurdistan	R	Ind	A (CW)	Failed
1925	Druse Rebellion	French-controlled Syria and Lebanon	UR	Ind (AC)	A (CW)	Failed
1927	Nicaraguan Civil War of 1926	Nicaragua	R	Oth	A (CW)	Failed
1927	1926 Indonesian Communist Revolt	Dutch-controlled Indonesia	UR	Soc, Ind (AC)	A	Failed

(*Continued*)

TABLE A2.1. (*continued*)

Start year	End year	Name of episode	Location of episode	Location	Goals	Tactics	Outcome
1927	1929	Cristero Rebellion	Mexico	R	Oth	A (CW)	Failed
1927	1936	Chinese Civil War Part 1	China	RU	Soc	A (CW), L	Failed
1927	1934	Sandino Rebellion	Nicaragua	R	Soc, Eth, Oth	A (CW)	Failed
1927	1930	Agri Rebellion	Turkish-controlled Kurdistan	R	Ind	A (CW)	Failed
1928	1928	1928 Kampang Buluh Uprising	British-controlled Malaysia	R	Ind (AC), Isl	A	Failed
1928	1931	Kongo-Wara Rebellion	French-controlled Cameroun/Equitorial Africa	R	Ind (AC)	A (CW)	Failed
1928	1929	Afghan Civil War of 1928–1929	Afghanistan	R	Isl, Oth	A (CW)	Successful
1930	1931	Salt March and related campaigns	British-controlled India	U	Ind (AC)	D, CR	Failed
1930	1931	Vietnamese Uprisings (Yen Bai)	French-controlled Vietnam	R	Soc, Ind (AC)	A (CW), L	Failed
1930	1932	Saya San Rebellion	British-controlled Burma	R	Ind (AC)	A (CW)	Failed
1931	1934	Kumul Rebellion/related revolts	Chinese-controlled Xinjiang	R	Ind, Isl	A (CW)	Failed
1931	1931	1931 Chilean Revolution	Chile	U	Lib	A, S, D, R	Successful
1932	1932	La Matanza	El Salvador	R	Soc	A, L	Failed
1932	1932	First APRA Rebellion	Peru	U	Soc	A	Failed
1932	1932	Constitutionalist Revolution (Brazil)	Brazil	U	Const, Oth	A (CW), CV	Failed
1933	1933	Cuban Revolution of 1933	Cuba	U	Lib, Oth	S, D, R, CV	Successful
1934	1934	Asturias Uprising and Catalan Revolt	Spain	U	Soc, Lib	A, S	Failed

1935	1935	Cuban General Strike of 1935	Cuba	U	Lib	A, S	Failed
1935	1935	Sakdal Uprising	American-occupied Philippines	R	Ind (AC)	A	Failed
1935	1935	Goharshad Mosque Rebellion	Iran	U	Isl	D, R	Failed
1935	1935	1935 Communist Rebellion in Brazil	Brazil	U	Soc	A, CV	Failed
1936	1936	1936 Syrian General Strike	French-controlled Syria	U	Ind (AC)	S, D, R	Failed
1936	1936	Arab Revolt in Palestine	British Controlled Palestine	UR	Ind (AC)	S, A	Failed
1936	1939	Spanish Civil War	Spain	RU	Oth	A (CW), CV	Successful
1940	1944	1940–1944 Insurgency in Chechnya	Soviet-controlled Chechnya	R	Ind	A (CW)	Failed
1942	1944	Quit India Uprising	British-controlled India	U	Ind (AC)	S, D, R, CR	Failed
1943	1943	Woyane Rebellion of 1943 (Ethiopia)	Ethiopia	R	Eth, Oth	A (CW)	Failed
1944	1947	Jewish Insurgency in Palestine	British-controlled Palestine	U	Ind (AC), Oth	A (CW), D, S, R	Successful
1944	1944	El Salvador Revolution of 1944	El Salvador	U	Lib	S, D, A, CV	Successful
1944	1944	Glorious May Revolution 1944	Ecuador	U	Lib	D, A, CV	Successful
1944	1944	Guatemalan Revolution	Guatemala	U	Lib	S, D, A, CV	Successful
1944	1949	Greek Civil War	Greece	RU	Soc	S, D, A (CW)	Failed
1945	1945	Setif Uprising	French-controlled Algeria	UR	Ind (AC)	D, R, A	Failed
1945	1949	Indonesian War of Independence	Dutch-controlled Indonesia	R	Ind (AC)	A (CW)	Successful
1945	1954	Vietnamese Revolution	French-controlled Vietnam	RU	Soc, Ind (AC)	A (CW), L	Successful
1946	1946	Haitian Revolution of 1946	Haiti	U	Lib	S, D, R, CV	Successful
1946	1949	Chinese Civil War Part 2	China	R	Soc	A (CW), L	Successful

(Continued)

TABLE A2.1. (*continued*)

Start year	End year	Name of episode	Location of episode	Location	Goals	Tactics	Outcome
1946	1946	Bolivian Revolt of 1946	Bolivia	U	Lib	S, D, R, A	Successful
1946	1954	Huk Rebellion	Philippines	R	Soc	A (CW)	Failed
1947	1947	228 Uprising	Taiwan	U	Lib, Eth	R	Failed
1947	1948	Madagascar Rebellion	French-controlled Madagascar	R	Ind (AC)	A (CW)	Failed
1948	1948	Al-Wathbah	Iraq	U	Soc, Const	S, D, R	Failed
1948	1979	Communist Insurgency in Burma	Myanmar	R	Soc	A (CW)	Failed
1948	1958	La Violencia	Colombia	UR	Soc, Oth	R, A (CW)	Failed
1948	1960	Malayan Emergency	British-controlled Malaysia	R	Soc, Ind (AC)	A (CW)	Failed
1948	1948	Callao Revolt	Peru	U	Soc	A, CV	Failed
1949	1976	Karen Revolt	Myanmar-controlled Karen-ni	R	Ind	A (CW)	Failed
1949	1962	Darul Islam Guerrilla War	Indonesia	R	Ind, Isl	A (CW)	Failed
1950	1950	Moluccan Independence Movement	Indonesian-controlled Molucca Islands	RU	Ind	A (CW)	Failed
1951	1975	First Naga Rebellion	Indian-controlled Nagaland	R	Ind	A (CW)	Failed
1952	1956	Tunisian Independence Movement	French-controlled Tunisia	R	Ind (AC)	A (CW)	Successful
1952	1952	Egyptian Revolution of 1952	Egypt	U	Const	S, D, R, A, CV	Successful
1952	1952	Bolivian MNR Revolution	Bolivia	U	Soc, Oth	A, D	Successful
1952	1952	Rosewater Revolution	Lebanon	U	Eth, Oth	S, D	Successful

1952	Mau-Mau Revolt	British-controlled Kenya	R	Ind (AC)	A (CW)	Failed
1953	East German Uprising	East Germany	U	Lib, Oth	S, D, R	Failed
1954	Algerian National Revolution	French-controlled Algeria	R	Soc, Ind (AC)	A (CW)	Successful
1955	Cameroon War of Independence	French-controlled Cameroon	R	Ind (AC)	A (CW)	Failed
1955	First Sudanese Civil War	Sudanese-controlled South Sudan	R	Ind, Eth	A (CW), CV	Failed
1956	Tibetan Uprising	Chinese-controlled Tibet	UR	Ind, Oth	A (CW), R	Failed
1956	Peronist Revolt	Argentina	U	Oth	S, D, R, A	Failed
1956	Hungarian Revolution of 1956	Hungary	U	Lib, Oth	D, A	Failed
1956	Cuban Revolution	Cuba	RU	Soc	D, A (CW)	Successful
1957	Colombian 1957 Revolution	Colombia	U	Lib	S, D (UC), CV	Successful
1958	1958 Venezuelan Uprising	Venezuela	U	Lib	S, D, A, CV	Successful
1958	Paraguayan Uprisings	Paraguay	R	Lib	A (CW)	Failed
1958	First Lebanese Civil War	Lebanon	U	Eth	R, A (CW)	Failed
1958	Shan State Rebellion	Myanmar-controlled Shan State	R	Ind	A (CW)	Failed
1958	Mon Uprising	Myanmar-controlled Mon State	R	Ind	A (CW)	Failed
1960	April Revolution	South Korea	U	Lib	D (UC)	Successful
1960	Anti-Apartheid Movement	South Africa	UR	Soc, Lib, Eth	S, D, R, A (CW), CR	Successful
1960	Congo Crisis	Zaire	R	Soc, Ind, Oth	A (CW)	Failed
1960	Guatemalan Civil War	Guatemala	R	Soc	A (CW)	Failed
1961	Angolan War of Independence	Portuguese-controlled Angola	R	Soc, Ind (AC)	A (CW)	Successful
1961	Eritrean War of Independence	Ethiopian-controlled Eritrea	R	Soc, Ind, Eth	A (CW)	Successful

(*Continued*)

TABLE A2.1. (*continued*)

Start year	End year	Name of episode	Location of episode	Location	Goals	Tactics	Outcome
1962	1964	First Tuareg Rebellion in Mali	Tuareg-inhabited regions of Mali	R	Ind, Isl	A (CW)	Failed
1962	1994	First Kachin Rebellion	Myanmar-controlled Kachin	R	Ind, Oth	A (CW)	Failed
1962	1969	Venezuelan Insurgency	Venezuela	RU	Soc	A (CW), CV	Failed
1962	1976	Dhofar Rebellion	British-controlled Oman	R	Soc, Const, Eth	A (CW)	Failed
1962	1962	Brunei Rebellion	British protectorate of Brunei	UR	Ind (AC), Const, Oth	A	Failed
1963	1974	Guinea-Bissau Revolution	Portuguese-controlled Guinea/Cape Verde Islands	R	Soc, Ind (AC)	A (CW)	Successful
1963	1963	15 Khordad Uprising	Iran	U	Isl	D, R	Failed
1963	1963	Ar-Rashid Revolt	Iraq	U	Soc	A, CV	Failed
1963	1963	Trois Glourieuses	Congo-Brazzaville	U	Soc, Oth	A, S, D, R, CV	Successful
1963	1967	Aden Emergency	British-controlled Aden	RU	Soc, Ind (AC)	A (CW)	Successful
1964		Manipur Insurgency	Indian-controlled Manipur	R	Soc, Ind	A (CW)	Failed
1964	1964	Simba Rebellion	Zaire	R	Soc, Eth	A (CW)	Failed
1964	1979	Rhodesian Bush War	Rhodesia	R	Soc, Eth	A (CW)	Successful
1964	1975	Mozambique War of Independence	Portuguese-controlled Mozambique	R	Soc, Ind (AC)	A (CW)	Successful
1964	1964	October Revolution in Sudan	Sudan	U	Lib	S, D (UC), R	Successful
1965	1965	March Intifada	British-controlled Bahrain	U	Soc, Ind (AC), Const	S, D, R	Failed
1965	1965	Dominican Civil War	Dominican Republic	U	Soc, Lib	A (CW), CV	Failed

1965	1982	Thai Communist Insurgency	Thailand	R	Soc	A (CW)	Failed
1965	1979	First Chadian Civil War	Chad	R	Eth, Oth	A (CW)	Successful
1966	1986	Mizo Uprising	Indian-controlled Mizoram	R	Ind	A (CW)	Failed
1966	1966	1966 Ecuador Unrest	Ecuador	U	Lib	S, D, R, CV	Successful
1966	1990	Namibian War of Independence	South African-controlled Namibia	RU	Soc, Ind (AC)	A (CW), S, CR	Successful
1967	1975	Cambodian Civil War	Cambodia	RU	Soc, Oth	A (CW), D	Successful
1967	1972	First Naxalite Uprising	India	R	Soc	A (CW), L	Failed
1967	1970	Nigerian Civil War	Nigerian-controlled Iboland	RU	Ind	A (CW)	Failed
1967	1975	Tupamaros	Uruguay	U	Soc	A	Failed
1968	1971	Bangladesh Secession	Pakistan-controlled East Pakistan	UR	Ind	S, D, A (CW)	Successful
1968	1968	May 1968 in France	France	U	Soc	S, D, R	Failed
1968	2011	Basque Separatist Movement	Spanish-controlled Basque Lands	U	Soc, Ind	A	Failed
1968	1989	Second Malayan Emergency	Malaysia	R	Soc, Eth	A (CW)	Failed
1969		NPA Communist Revolution	Philippines	R	Soc	A (CW)	Failed
1969	1977	ERP/Montoneros Rebellion	Argentina	U	Soc	A (CW)	Failed
1970	1970	Black Power Revolution in Trinidad	Trinidad and Tobago	U	Soc, Eth	S, D, CV	Failed
1970	1971	Black September in Jordan	Jordan	UR	Eth, Const	A (CW)	Failed
1971	1971	Monima Revolt	Madagascar	R	Soc	A, R	Failed
1971	1971	1971 JVP Insurrection	Sri Lanka	R	Soc	A	Failed
1972	1972	1972 Rotaka Revolution	Madagascar	U	Oth	S, D, R, CV	Successful
1972	1972	First Burundi Civil War	Burundi	R	Eth	A (CW)	Failed

(*Continued*)

TABLE A2.1. (*continued*)

Start year	End year	Name of episode	Location of episode	Location	Goals	Tactics	Outcome
1972	2012	Moro Rebellion	Philippines-controlled Mindinao	R	Ind, Isl	A (CW)	Failed
1973	1978	Baloch Insurgency	Pakistan-controlled Baluchistan	R	Ind	A (CW)	Failed
1973	1973	1973 Thai Democracy Movement	Thailand	U	Lib	D (UC)	Successful
1973	1973	Greek Polytechnic Uprising	Greece	U	Lib	D (UC)	Failed
1974	1975	Carnation Revolution	Portugal	U	Soc, Lib	A, S, D, CV	Successful
1974	1991	Ethiopian Civil War	Ethiopia	R	Eth	A (CW)	Successful
1975	1990	Second Lebanese Civil War	Lebanon	U	Eth	A (CW), CV	Failed
1975	2002	Angolan Civil War	Angola	R	Eth, Oth	A (CW)	Failed
1975	1990	Laotian Guerilla War	Laos	R	Oth	A (CW)	Failed
1976		Colombian Civil War	Colombia	RU	Soc, Oth	A (CW)	Failed
1976	2005	Aceh Insurgency	Indonesian-controlled Aceh	R	Ind, Isl	A (CW)	Failed
1977	1992	Mozambican Civil War	Mozambique	R	Oth	A (CW)	Failed
1978	1979	Iranian Revolution	Iran	U	Soc, Const, Isl	S, D, R, A	Successful
1978	1979	Sandinista Revolution	Nicaragua	RU	Soc	S, R, A (CW)	Successful
1978	1978	Saur (April) Revolution	Afghanistan	U	Soc, Oth	D, A, CV	Successful
1978	1979	Ugandan Civil War	Uganda	R	Eth, Oth	A (CW)	Successful
1979	1992	Afghan Civil War	Afghanistan	R	Isl, Oth	A (CW)	Successful
1979	1992	El Salvador Civil War	El Salvador	RU	Soc	D, A (CW)	Failed
1979	1982	Islamist Uprising in Syria	Syria	U	Isl	S, D, A (CW)	Failed
1980		Second Naga Insurgency	Indian-controlled Nagaland	R	Soc, Ind	A (CW)	Failed

1980	1983	Second Chadian Civil War	Chad	R	Oth	A (CW)	Successful
1980	1999	Sendero Luminoso	Peru	R	Soc, Eth	A (CW)	Failed
1980	1980	Kwangju Uprising	South Korea	U	Lib	D, A	Failed
1980	1983	Solidarity Uprising	Poland	U	Lib	S, D	Failed
1981	1986	Uganda Bush War	Uganda	R	Lib, Eth, Oth	A (CW)	Successful
1981	2003	Mujahideen Rebellion	Iran	UR	Soc	D, A (CW)	Failed
1981	1995	Sikh Separatist Insurgency	Indian-controlled Punjab	U	Ind	A (CW)	Failed
1982	1990	Contra Wars	Nicaragua	R	Oth	A (CW)	Failed
1982	1982	Bolivian Anti-Military Protests	Bolivia	U	Lib	D (UC)	Successful
1983	2005	Second Sudanese Civil War	Sudanese-controlled South Sudan	R	Ind, Eth	A (CW)	Successful
1983	2009	Sri Lankan Civil War	Tamil-inhabited northern and eastern Sri Lanka	R	Soc, Ind	A (CW)	Failed
1984	1999	PKK Kurdish Rebellion in Turkey	Turkish-controlled Kurdistan	RU	Soc, Ind	D, R, A (CW)	Failed
1984	1988	New Caledonian Uprising	French-controlled New Caledonia	R	Ind (AC)	D, R	Failed
1985	1985	Sudanese 1985 Revolution	Sudan	U	Lib	S, D, R, CV	Successful
1985	1986	Haitian Uprising	Haiti	U	Lib	S, D, R, CV	Successful
1986	1986	People Power Revolution	Philippines	U	Lib	D (UC)	Successful
1986	1991	Somali Revolution	Somalia	RU	Eth, Oth	D, R, A (CW)	Successful
1986	1987	Ugandan Holy Spirit Movement	Uganda	R	Eth, Oth	A (CW)	Failed
1987	1987	South Korean June Uprising	South Korea	U	Lib	D (UC)	Successful
1987	1987	Panamanian Civic Crusade	Panama	U	Lib	S, D (UC)	Failed
1987	1989	1987 JVP Insurrection	Sri Lanka	U	Soc, Oth	S, A	Failed

(*Continued*)

TABLE A2.1. (*continued*)

Start year	End year	Name of episode	Location of episode	Location	Goals	Tactics	Outcome
1987	1989	1987 Tibetan Uprising	Chinese-controlled Tibet	U	Ind	D, R	Failed
1987	1993	First Intifada	Israeli-occupied West Bank and Gaza	U	Ind	R, S, CR	Failed
1988	2003	Bodo Insurgency	Indian-controlled Bodoland	R	Ind	A (CW)	Failed
1988	1988	8888 Uprising	Myanmar	U	Lib	S, D (UC)	Failed
1988		Lord's Resistance Army Insurgency	Uganda	R	Eth	A (CW)	Failed
1988	1991	Estonian Singing Revolution	Soviet-controlled Estonia	U	Lib, Ind	D (UC)	Successful
1988	1991	Lithuanian National Revolution	Soviet-controlled Lithuania	U	Lib, Ind	D (UC)	Successful
1988	1991	Latvian Singing Revolution	Soviet-controlled Latvia	U	Lib, Ind	D (UC)	Successful
1988	2001	Papua New Guinean Civil War	Papua New Guinea-controlled Bougainville	R	Ind	D, A (CW)	Failed
1988	1991	Georgian National Revolution	Soviet-controlled Georgia	U	Ind	D, R	Successful
1989	1989	Tiananmen Protests	China	U	Lib	D (UC)	Failed
1989	1989	East German Revolution	East Germany	U	Lib, Oth	D (UC)	Successful
1989	1990	Bulgarian Revolution of 1989	Bulgaria	U	Lib	S, D (UC)	Successful
1989	1989	Velvet Revolution	Czechoslovakia	U	Lib	S, D (UC)	Successful
1989	1990	Beninese Revolution	Benin	U	Lib	S, D (UC)	Successful
1989	1990	1990 Mongolian Revolution	Mongolia	U	Lib	D (UC)	Failed
1989	1989	Romanian Revolution	Romania	U	Lib	S, D, A	Successful
1989	1996	First Liberian Civil War	Liberia	R	Eth	A (CW)	Successful

1990	Second Naxalite Rebellion	India	R	Soc	A (CW), L	Failed
1990	Black January in Baku	Soviet-controlled Azerbaijan	U	Ind	D, R, A	Failed
1990	Nepalese People's Movement	Nepal	U	Const	R, D (UC)	Successful
1990	Baren Uprising	Chinese-controlled Xinjiang	R	Ind, Isl	D, A	Failed
1996	Second Tuareg Rebellion in Mali	Tuareg-inhabited regions of Mali	R	Ind	A (CW)	Failed
1990	Assam Rebellion	Indian-controlled Assam	R	Soc, Ind	A (CW)	Failed
1995	Nigerien Civil War	Tuareg-inhabited reigons of Niger	R	Ind	A (CW)	Failed
1990	Kosovo War for Independence	Serbian-controlled Kosovo	UR	Ind	A (CW), CR	Successful
1994	Rwandan Civil War	Rwanda	R	Eth	A (CW)	Successful
1990	1990 Revolution in Bangladesh	Bangladesh	U	Lib	S, D (UC)	Successful
1996	Third Chadian Civil War	Chad	R	Eth	A (CW)	Successful
1991	Togo 1991 Revolution	Togo	U	Lib, Eth	S, R, A	Failed
1991	1991 Uprisings in Iraq	Iraq	UR	Eth	D, A (CW)	Failed
1991	March 1991 Revolution in Mali	Mali	U	Lib	S, D (UC), CV	Successful
2002	Sierra Leonean Civil War	Sierra Leone	R	Oth	A (CW)	Failed
1991	Albanian Anti-Communist Protests	Albania	U	Lib	S, D (UC)	Successful
1991	1991 Madagascar Revolution	Madagascar	U	Lib	S, D (UC)	Successful
1991	Russian Revolution of 1991	Soviet Union	U	Lib, Ind	D (UC)	Successful
1991	Chechen Revolution	Russian-controlled Chechnya	U	Ind	D, A	Successful
1993	Georgian Civil War of 1991–1993	Georgia	U	Lib, Oth	D, A (CW)	Successful
2002	Algerian Civil War	Algeria	RU	Isl	A (CW)	Failed

(*Continued*)

TABLE A2.1. (*continued*)

Start year	End year	Name of episode	Location of episode	Location	Goals	Tactics	Outcome
1992		Oromo Rebellion	Ethiopia	R	Ind, Oth	A (CW)	Failed
1992	1997	Tajikistan Civil War	Tajikistan	UR	Eth, Isl, Oth	D, A (CW)	Failed
1992	1992	Black May in Thailand	Thailand	U	Lib	D (UC), R	Successful
1993	1993	Russian Constitutional Crisis of 1993	Russian Federation	U	Oth	D, A	Failed
1993	2005	Second Burundi Civil War	Burundi	R	Eth	A (CW)	Successful
1994	1996	Taliban Revolution	Afghanistan	R	Isl	A (CW)	Successful
1994	1994	Chiapas Rebellion	Mexico	RU	Soc	D, A	Failed
1994	2000	1994 Bahrain Uprising	Bahrain	UR	Eth, Const	R, D, A	Successful
1994	1996	First Chechen War	Russian-controlled Chechnya	R	Ind	A (CW)	Successful
1995	1995	1995 Yining/Ghulja Disturbances	Chinese-controlled Xinjiang	U	Ind	S, D, A	Failed
1996	2006	Nepalese Civil War	Nepal	R	Soc, Const	A (CW), L	Failed
1996	1997	Congo Civil War	Zaire	R	Eth, Oth	A (CW)	Successful
1997	1997	Albanian Pyramid Scheme Revolt	Albania	U	Eth, Oth	R, D, A (CW)	Failed
1997	1999	Republic of Congo Civil War	Republic of Congo	R	Eth, Oth	A (CW)	Successful
1998	1998	Indonesian Revolution	Indonesia	U	Lib	R, D (UC)	Successful
1999	1999	1999 Shia Uprising in Iraq	Iraq	U	Eth, Isl	R, A	Failed
1999	2003	Second Liberian Civil War	Liberia	R	Eth, Oth	A (CW)	Successful
1999	2009	Second Chechen War	Russian-controlled Chechnya	R	Ind, Isl	A (CW)	Failed
2000	2000	Bulldozer Revolution	Serbia	U	Lib	S, D (UC)	Successful
2000	2005	Second Intifada	Israeli-occupied West Bank and Gaza	U	Ind	R, S	Failed

2001	EDSA 2 Revolution	Philippines	U	Oth	D (UC)	Successful
2001	EDSA 3	Philippines	U	Oth	D, R	Failed
2001	December 2001 Uprising in Argentina	Argentina	U	Oth	D, R	Successful
2002	Madagascar Electoral Revolution	Madagascar	U	Lib, Eth, Oth	S, D (UC)	Successful
2002	2002 Anti-Chavez Revolt	Venezuela	U	Oth	S, D (UC), CV	Failed
2002	First Ivoirian Civil War	Ivory Coast	R	Eth, Oth	A (CW), CV	Failed
2003	Rose Revolution	Georgia	U	Lib	D (UC)	Successful
2004	Patani Revolt	Thailand-controlled Patani	R	Ind, Isl	A (CW)	Failed
2004	Second PKK Kurdish-Turkish Rebellion	Turkish-controlled Kurdistan	R	Ind	A (CW)	Failed
2004	Black Friday in Maldives	Maldives	U	Lib	D (UC)	Failed
2004	Orange Revolution	Ukraine	U	Lib	D (UC)	Successful
2005	Tulip Revolution	Kyrgyzstan	U	Lib, Eth, Oth	R, D (UC)	Successful
2005	Azerbaijan Color Revolution Attempt	Azerbaijan	U	Lib	D (UC)	Failed
2005	Fourth Chadian Civil War	Chad	R	Eth	A (CW)	Failed
2006	Belarus Jeans Revolution	Belarus	U	Lib	D (UC)	Failed
2006	April Revolution in Nepal	Nepal	U	Lib, Eth, Const	S, D (UC)	Successful
2006	2006 Hungarian Protests	Hungary	U	Oth	D, R	Failed
2007	2007 Guinean General Strike	Guinea	U	Lib	S, D, R	Failed
2007	2007 Tuareg Rebellion in Niger	Tuareg-inhabited regions of Niger	R	Eth	A (CW)	Failed
2007	Civil War in Ingushetia	Russian-controlled Ingushetia	RU	Ind, Isl	D, A (CW)	Failed

(*Continued*)

TABLE A2.1. (*continued*)

Start year	End year	Name of episode	Location of episode	Location	Goals	Tactics	Outcome
2007	2007	Saffron Revolution	Myanmar	U	Lib	D (UC)	Failed
2008	2008	Armenian Color Revolution Attempt	Armenia	U	Lib, Oth	D (UC)	Failed
2008	2008	2008 Tibetan Unrest	Chinese-controlled Tibet	U	Ind	D, R	Failed
2008	2008	PAD Revolution	Thailand	U	Oth	D, R, A	Successful
2009	2009	2009 Malagasy Political Crisis	Madagascar	U	Lib, Oth	D, R, CV	Successful
2009	2009	Pro-Thaksin Revolution	Thailand	U	Oth	D, R, A	Failed
2009	2009	Moldovan Twitter Revolution	Moldova	U	Lib	R, D (UC)	Failed
2009	2009	Niger Constitutional Crisis	Niger	U	Lib, Oth	S, D (UC)	Failed
2009	2009	Iranian Election Protests	Iran	U	Lib	D (UC), CR	Failed
2009	2009	Boko Haram Rebellion	Nigeria	R	Isl	A (CW)	Failed
2010	2010	Red Shirts Protests 2010	Thailand	U	Oth	D, R, A	Failed
2010	2010	Kyrgyz 2010 Revolution	Kyrgyzstan	U	Lib, Eth, Oth	D, R, A	Successful
2010	2011	Tunisian Revolution	Tunisia	U	Lib	D (UC), R	Successful
2011	2011	Egyptian Revolution 2011	Egypt	U	Lib	D (UC), R, CV	Successful
2011	2012	Yemeni Uprising 2011	Yemen	UR	Lib, Eth, Oth	D (UC), A (CW)	Successful
2011	2011	Djiboutian Uprising 2011	Djibouti	U	Lib, Eth	D (UC), R	Failed
2011	2011	2011 Green Movement Protests in Iran	Iran	U	Lib	D (UC)	Failed
2011	2012	Pearl Revolution	Bahrain	U	Lib, Eth, Const	D (UC)	Failed

2011	2011	Libyan Revolution 2011	Libya	U	Lib, Eth, Oth	D, R, A (CW)	Successful
2011		Syrian Civil War	Syria	UR	Lib, Eth, Isl	D, R, A (CW)	Failed
2011		Second Kachin Rebellion	Myanmar-controlled Kachin	R	Ind	A (CW)	Failed
2011		Sunni Insurgency in Iraq (ISIL)	Iraq	RU	Eth, Isl	A (CW)	Failed
2011	2012	2011–2012 Protests in Maldives	Maldives	U	Oth	D, A, CV	Successful
2012		2012 Tuareg Rebellion	Tuareg-inhabited regions of Mali	R	Ind, Isl	A (CW)	Failed
2012		M23 Rebellion	Democratic Republic of Congo	R	Eth, Oth	A (CW)	Failed
2012	2013	Central African Conflict	Central African Republic	R	Eth, Oth	A (CW)	Successful
2013		Anti-Balaka Revolt	Central African Republic	R	Eth	A (CW)	Failed
2013		Gezi Park Protests	Turkey	U	Lib	D (UC)	Failed
2013		2013 Egyptian Counter-Revolution	Egypt	U	Oth	D, CV	Successful
2013	2014	Euromaidan Uprising	Ukraine	U	Lib	D (UC), R	Successful
2013		South Sudanese Civil War	South Sudan	R	Eth, Oth	A (CW)	Failed
2014		2014 Bosnian Spring	Bosnia-Hercegovina	U	Lib	D, R	Failed
2014		2014 Venezuelan Protests	Venezuela	U	Lib	D (UC), R	Failed
2014		Libyan Civil War	Libya	R	Isl, Oth	A (CW)	Failed
2014	2015	September 21 Revolution in Yemen	Yemen	RU	Eth, Isl	D, A (CW)	Successful
2014	2014	2014 Burkinabe Uprising	Burkina Faso	U	Lib	D (UC), R, CV	Successful

Note: If the episode was ongoing as of December 31, 2014, the end year is left blank.

Key—Location: *U* (predominantly urban), *R* (predominantly rural), *UR* (predominantly urban with a secondary rural component), *RU* (predominantly rural with a secondary urban component); **Goals:** *Ind* (independence), *AC* (anti-colonial), *Soc* (social), *Const* (constitutional/anti-monarchical), *Lib* (liberal), *Isl* (Islamist), *Eth* (ethnic stratification), *Oth* (other); **Tactics:** *A* (armed uprising), *CW* (civil war), *L* (land seizures), *CV* (coupvolution), *R* (rioting/crowd violence), *S* (strikes), *D* (demonstrations), *UC* (urban civic), *CR* (civil resistance tactics)

APPENDIX 3

Data Sources Used in Statistical Analyses

ALL DATA FILES (along with Stata do-files, output files, and robustness test files) used in statistical analyses are available from the author. In addition to the original data on revolutionary episodes collected by the author and described in Appendix 1, the following sources were used:

1   *Social and demographic data*

Education: average total years schooling: Barro and Lee 2013. For population aged fifteen or over.

Ethnic and religious fractionalization: Fearon 2003 and Wimmer and Min 2006. Data for Belize, Brunei, Equatorial Guinea, Iceland, Qatar, and Suriname come from Alesina et al. 2003.

Internet usage by country: World Bank (at http://data.worldbank.org/indicator/IT.NET.USER.P2).

Literacy: percent literate: Vanhanen 2000; Banks and Wilson 2015; CIA (at https://www.cia.gov/library/publications/the-world-factbook/fields/print_2103.html); UNESCO (at http://data.uis.unesco.org/index.aspx?queryid=166).

Media: newspaper circulation, televisions, and radios per hundred thousand population: Banks and Wilson 2015.

Mobile phone usage by country: International Telecommunications Union (at http://www.itu.int/en/ITU-D/Statistics/Pages/stat/default.aspx).

Mortality: infant mortality: Gapminder (https://www.gapminder.org/documentation/documentation/gapdoc002.pdf) and Clio-Infra (https://clio-infra.eu/Indicators/InfantMortality.html).

Mortality: under-five child mortality: Gapminder (at http://www.gapminder.org/data/documentation/gd005/). Under-five child mortality is defined as the probability (expressed as a rate per thousand live births) that a child born in a specific year will die before reaching the age of five if subject to current age-specific mortality rates.

Population: Wimmer and Min 2006, supplemented by the Population Statistics website (http://www.populstat.info/) and Gapminder (https://www.gapminder.org/). Some data points were interpolated to fill in missing values, with clear outlier estimations dropped.

Population: proportion below age fifteen: EarthTrends (http://earthtrends.wri.org).

Population: proportion between ages fifteen and twenty-four: United Nations Population Division (https://esa.un.org/unpd/wpp/dataquery/).

Population: proportion between ages twenty and thirty-nine: United Nations Population Division, accessed at Gapminder (https://www.gapminder.org/).

Religion: percent Muslim: Kettani 2010a; 2010b; 2010c; 2010d; 2010e. Interpolated for the 1950–2014 years, with 1950 values used for years prior to 1950.

Territory: proportion covered by rough terrain: Fearon and Laitin 2003.

Territory: size of territory: World Bank (http://data.worldbank.org/).

Urbanization: World Bank World Development Indicators (http://databank.worldbank.org/data/reports.aspx?source=world-development-indicators) for the years 1960–2014, supplemented by United Nations 2006; Vanhanen 2000; Banks and Wilson 2015; and EUGene (Bennett and Stam 2000).

2   Political data

Battle deaths: from external war: Correlates of War (COW) (Sarkees and Wayman 2010) through 2007, supplemented by Wikipedia and PRIO (Lacina and Gleditsch 2005). External war is defined as including wars classified by COW as inter-state wars, as well as those classified by COW as extra-state wars (for states engaged in warfare beyond their borders). Battle deaths were averaged and evenly distributed over the course of the years of a war. For a state to be considered a war participant, it had either to commit at least one thousand troops or to suffer at least one hundred battle-related deaths.

Battle deaths: global: Data for 1900–1988 come from Lacina, Gleditsch, and Russett 2006. For 1989–2014, UCDP Battle Deaths Dataset v.5–2015, 1989–2014 (Pettersson and Wallensteen 2015).

Boix-Miller-Rosato dichotomous measure of democracy: Boix, Miller, and Rosato 2013.
Civil society index (V-Dem): Coppedge et al. 2016.
Conscription practice: Asal, Conrad, and Toronto 2017.
Electoral democracy index (V-Dem): Coppedge et al. 2016.
Executive bribery and corruption (V-Dem): Coppedge et al. 2016.
Executive corruption index (V-Dem): Coppedge et al. 2016.
Free and fair elections (V-Dem): Coppedge et al. 2016
Government accountability index (V-Dem): Coppedge et al. 2016.
Human rights treaty ratifications: Nielsen and Simmons 2015; United Nations Treaty Collection (at https://treaties.un.org/Pages/ViewDetails.aspx?src=TREATY&mtdsg_no=IV-9&chapter=4&lang=en). Measured as the number of ratifications of four key human rights treaties by state (ranging from 0 to 4). The four treaties were the International Covenant on Civil and Political Rights (ICCPR), the Optional Protocol of the ICCPR, the Convention Against Torture, and Article 22 on the authority of the International Covenant on Civil and Political Rights of the Committee Against Torture.
Incumbent leaders: number of years in power and ages: Calculated from "Archigos: A Data Base on Leaders 1875–2014" (Goemans, Gleditsch, and Chiozza 2009), supplemented by information from Rulers (https://www.rulers.org/). In years of revolutionary episodes or coups, the data refer to the leader in power prior to the onset of the episode.
Liberal democracy index (V-Dem): Coppedge et al. 2016.
Media censorship (V-Dem): Coppedge et al. 2016.
Military coups: For 1950–2014 (Powell and Thyne 2011); for 1946–49 (Marshall and Marshall 2015 and other sources).
Military personnel (number): EUGene (Bennett and Stam 2000) and World Bank (http://data.worldbank.org/indicator/MS.MIL.TOTL.P1).
Military spending: EUGene (Bennett and Stam 2000) and Stockholm International Peace Research Institute (SIPRI), at https://www.sipri.org/databases/milex.
Non-democratic regimes: types: Geddes, Wright, and Frantz 2014.
Political civil liberties index (V-Dem): Coppedge et al. 2016.
Political constraints: Henisz 2002. The measure is based on the number of independent branches of government with veto power over policy change, adjusted to take into account the extent of alignment across branches of government using data on the party composition of the executive and legislative branches.

Political killing index (V-Dem): Pemstein et al. 2018; Coppedge et al. 2018. I reversed the measure so that it ran from 0 (non-existent) to 4 (systematic).

Polity scores: Polity IV Project, Political Regime Characteristics and Transitions, 1800–2014, available at http://www.systemicpeace.org/inscrdata.html. Polity scores were revised in line with the advice contained in Plümper and Neumayer 2010. Interregnum scores were coded as missing and then interpolated relative to the endpoints of known scores.

Private civil liberties index (V-Dem): Coppedge et al. 2016.

Rule of law index (V-Dem): Coppedge et al. 2016.

State capacity index: Hanson and Sigman 2013 (obtained from authors on request).

Territory under state authority (percent) (V-Dem): Coppedge et al. 2016.

3 Economic data

Diamond production: Levinson, Gurney, and Kirkley 1992, supplemented by the *USGS Minerals Yearbook* (http://minerals.usgs.gov/minerals/pubs/commodity/diamond/index.html#myb). The data were transformed into a dummy variable differentiating major diamond producers from those that were not.

Dollar exchange rates: Clio infra (https://clio-infra.eu/Indicators/ExchangeRatestoUSDollar.html).

Electric power consumption (kWh per capita: World Bank (http://data.worldbank.org/indicator/EG.USE.ELEC.KH.PC).

Financial crises: Reinhart and Rogoff 2009 (http://www.carmenreinhart.com/data/browse-by-topic/topics/7/).

GDP per capita (in 1990 international dollars): Angus Maddison, "Historical Statistics of the World Economy: 1–2008 AD" (available at http://www.ggdc.net/maddison/oriindex.htm) through 2008, revised and supplemented by the Maddison Project (Bolt and van Zanden 2014); Barro and Ursúa 2008; the Penn World Tables 6.3 (Heston, Summers, and Aten 2009); Wimmer and Min 2006 for some early data points; and estimations using indexed growth rates from the World Bank (http://data.worldbank.org/indicator/NY.GDP.PCAP.KD) for data after 2010. Data points for Cyprus and Iceland were calculated in part from data on GDP in 1990 international dollars from the Knoema search engine (http://knoema.com/).

Global economic growth: Calculated from annual global population data from the US Census Bureau (https://www.census.gov/population /international/data/idb/informationGateway.php) and world GDP PPP (Gapminder, at http://www.gapminder.org/data/documentation/gd001 /). GDP PPP is measured in billions of 2005 international dollars.

Government debt: ratio to GDP: Clio infra (https://www.clio-infra.eu /Indicators/TotalGrossCentralGovernmentDebtasaPercentageof GDP.html#) and IMF, at http://www.imf.org/external/datamapper /DEBT1@DEBT/OEMDC/ADVEC/WEOWORLD.

Inflation rates: Clio Infra (at https://www.clio-infra.eu/Indicators /Inflation.html); the World Bank (http://data.worldbank.org/ indicator/FP.CPI.TOTL.ZG); and Mitchell 2007a; 2007b; 2007c. Annual rates were winsorized at the top 2 and bottom 2 percent (i.e., plus 300 and minus 11 respectively) in order to avoid the undue effect of hyperinflation and hyper-deflation on the estimations.

Investment relative to GDP: Penn World Tables (Feenstra, Inklaar, and Timmer 2015). Data available since 1946.

Nominal trade as percentage of nominal GDP: CEPII's TRADHIST dataset, located at http://www.cepii.fr/CEPII/en/bdd_modele /presentation.asp?id=32 and referenced in Fouquin and Hugot 2016.

Oil production: Wimmer and Min 2006; the World Bank (http://data .worldbank.org/); Ross and Mahdavi 2015; and "Historical Energy Production Statistics" produced by The Shift Project (at http://www .tsp-data-portal.org/Energy-Production-Statistics#tspQvChart). All production statistics were converted into metric tons per year. East German data were interpolated from the National Petroleum Council 1964, 11 and UN statistics (at https://knoema.com/UNSDESD2016 /un-statistics-division-energy-statistics-database-1990-2013?tsId =1224700).

Property rights index (V-Dem): Coppedge et al. 2016.

State ownership of the economy (V-Dem): Coppedge et al. 2016.

4   *Data on inequality*

Educational equality index (V-Dem): Sigman and Lindberg 2015; Coppedge et al. 2018

Equal distribution of resources index (V-Dem): Coppedge et al. 2016; Sigman and Lindberg 2015.

Ethnic groups: (percentage of population consisting of) Discriminated ethnic groups; Ethnic groups excluded from central power;

Ethnic groups with local power only; Powerless ethnic groups (Ethnic Power Relations Dataset): Wimmer, Cederman, and Min 2009.

Family farms: Vanhanen 2003.

Gini index (income): UNU-WIDER 2017; Coppedge et al. 2018 (missing data interpolated to 2012).

Health equality index (V-Dem): Sigman and Lindberg 2015; Coppedge et al. 2018

Land Ginis: Compiled from FAO 1955; FAO 1971; FAO 1981; FAOSTAT (data at http://www.fao.org/economic/the-statistics-division-ess/world-census-of-agriculture/additional-international-comparison-tables-including-gini-coefficients/table-2-number-and-area-of-holdings-and-ginis-index-of-concentration-1990-1980-and-1870-rounds-of-agricultural-censuses1/en/ and at http://www.fao.org/economic/the-statistics-division-ess/world-census-of-agriculture/additional-international-comparison-tables-including-gini-coefficients/table-1-number-and-area-of-holdings-and-ginis-index-of-concentration-1990-round-of-agricultural-censuses/en/); Frankema 2010; Deininger and Olinto 1999, 24; Lipton 2009, 286–87; Moyo 2014; Tai 1974, 310; Nafziger and Lindert 2013, 16; Pryor 1992; Russett 1964; Tillack and Schulze 2012, 466; Lambini et al 2014; Deininger, Nizalov, and Singh 2013; IFAD 2001; Lowder, Skoet, and Singh 2014. Land Ginis for more recent years were calculated using data from Eurostat (http://ec.europa.eu/eurostat/statistics-explained/images/3/3a/Utilised_agriculture_area,_by_size_of_the_holding_(UAA)_(hectares)_AgriPB13.png) and country-specific statistical websites using the POVCAL tool for computing Gini indices from grouped data, available from the World Bank. For socialist countries, the data exclude periods of predominantly collectivized agriculture. Data were interpolated between measurement points.

Land reform: Albertus 2015 (http://www.michaelalbertus.com/research.html).

Women's civil liberties index (V-Dem): Sundström et al. 2015; Coppedge et al. 2018.

Women's civil society participation index (V-Dem): Sundström et al. 2015; Coppedge et al. 2018.

Women's political empowerment index (V-Dem): Sundström et al. 2015; Coppedge et al. 2018.

Women's political participation index (V-Dem): Sundström et al. 2015; Coppedge et al. 2018.

TABLE A3.1. Cross-sectional data, means and distributions

Variable description	N	Mean	SD	Min	Max
Ln (population), t−1	299	9.14	1.6	4.49	13.91
GDP per cap. ($ thousands), t−1	267	2.65	2.55	0.28	12.53
Polity score, t−1	272	−1.49	5.89	−10.00	10.00
Democracy (Boix et al.), t−1	209	0.16	0.37	0	1
Major diamond producer (0-1), t−1	345	0.08	0.27	0.00	1.00
Percent under age 15, t−1	157	38.60	9.73	14.85	57.51
Percent population aged 20–39	175	29.13	3.39	22.56	42.68
Years incumbent leader in power, t−1	341	7.14	8.67	0.00	42.00
Incumbent age, t	339	55.94	11.56	5.00	85.00
Ln (oil production + 1), t−1	289	3.19	4.24	0.00	12.88
Percent urban, t−1	246	23.35	20.59	0.00	97.57
Under-5 child mortality rate, t−1	285	201.20	143.02	6.60	503.06
Ethno-linguistic fractionalization	143	0.45	0.30	0.00	0.90
Number military personnel, t−1	272	515.85	1,215.82	0.00	9,050.00
Military expenditure per soldier, t−1	182	6,447.51	9,750.39	10.10	53,719.01
Use of military conscription (0–1)	158	0.63	0.49	0.00	1.00
Proportion territory covered by mountains	303	18.93	20.05	0.00	81.00
Percent family farms	175	32.08	21.34	0.00	84.00
Average total years of schooling, t−1	129	4.19	2.87	0.35	11.71
Percent literate, t−1	210	54.52	31.80	1.00	100.00
Geddes regime class: personal autocracy	139	0.28	0.45	0.00	1.00
Geddes regime class: party autocracy	139	0.25	0.44	0.00	1.00
Geddes regime class: military autocracy	139	0.14	0.35	0.00	1.00
Geddes regime class: monarchical autocracy	139	0.07	0.26	0.00	1.00
Electoral democracy index (V-Dem), t−1	249	0.26	0.19	0.01	0.89
Liberal democracy index (V-Dem), t−1	249	0.17	0.14	0.01	0.83
Core civil society index (V-Dem), t−1	252	0.40	0.25	0.02	0.94
V-Dem executive corruption index	261	0.60	0.27	0.02	0.97
V-dem executive bribery (0–4), t−1	254	2.57	1.17	0.00	4.00
Private ownership of economy (0–4) (V-Dem), t−1	252	2.34	0.87	0.04	3.77
Equal distribution of resources index (V-Dem), t−1	252	0.34	0.25	0.02	0.96
Property rights (V-Dem), t−1	252	0.48	0.26	0.01	0.91
V-Dem media censorship, t−1	250	1.12	1.23	0	4
State capacity index	121	−0.52	0.81	−2.74	1.44

(Continued)

TABLE A3.1. (*continued*)

Variable description	N	Mean	SD	Min	Max
Electricity consumption per capita, t–1	114	1,545.03	2,886.98	11.52	21,665.44
Trade as percentage of GDP, t–1	155	24.36	102.97	0.15	1,081.99
Percent ethnically discriminated population (EPR), t–1	143	0.08	0.18	0.00	0.85
Percent ethnically powerless population (EPR), t–1	143	0.09	0.17	0.00	0.85
Percent ethnically excluded population (EPR), t–1	143	0.20	0.22	0.00	0.90
Size of largest excluded group (EPR), t–1	143	0.14	0.17	0.00	0.85
Newspaper circulation per 10,000 population, t–1	109	680.96	1,063.61	1.00	5,930.00
Radios per 10,000 population, t–1	111	2,160.21	6,539.22	0.00	68,406.00
Televisions per 100,000 population, t–1	112	7,142.82	12,579.08	0.00	75,603.00
Mobile phones per 100,000 population, t–1	54	13,820.35	25,502.90	0.00	104,000.00
Internet users (percent), t–1	59	13.80	17.38	0.00	77.00

APPENDIX 4

Choices of Statistical Models

THIS APPENDIX PROVIDES short justifications for the modeling choices made and how to interpret results. Each statistical model is dealt with roughly in the order in which it appears in the book. Further details on the statistical tests performed throughout the book can be obtained from the Stata do-files and datasets available from the author. Separate files that detail robustness checks are also available from the author. All analyses were performed using the 14.2 version of Stata.

4A. Count Models of the Annual Number of Revolutionary Episodes

A number of event count models were used throughout the book. Event count models are appropriate when the dependent variable cannot be negative but varies within a defined range greater than or equal to zero; in these circumstances the assumptions of a normal distribution are violated, since event counts are non-negative, are always integers, and are often small (at times, zero). Poisson regression models are used to estimate the probability of a given number of events occurring in a fixed interval of time. They assume that the event count y is Poisson distributed and is a function of the event rate vector (λ). The rate λ is determined by a set of k predictors $\mathbf{X} = (X_1, \ldots, X_k)$ and the expression relating these quantities is

$$\lambda = \exp\{\mathbf{X}\beta\}$$

The Poisson regression model for observation i is

$$P(Y_i = y_i \mid \mathbf{X_i}, \beta) = \frac{e^{-\exp(\mathbf{X}_i\beta)} * \exp\{\mathbf{X_i}\beta\}^{y_i}}{y_i!}$$

The model is estimated by maximum likelihood.[1]

---

1. Long 1997, 217–50.

Negative binomial regression is an alternative to the Poisson model that is appropriate when there is overdispersion in the distribution of events. All event count models used in the book were tested for Poisson distribution assumptions using deviance and Pearson goodness-of-fit statistics provided by post-estimation commands in Stata.[2] I report the exponentiated values of the regression coefficients, which constitute incidence rate ratios representing the incidence rate corresponding to a one unit increase in the independent variable. As recommended, robust standard errors were used to control for mild cases of overdispersion.[3] In chapter 2, I also utilized a time-series Poisson model (as implemented by the ARPOIS package) that allowed for correction of autocorrelation and overdispersion.[4]

4B. Panel Analyses of the Onset of Revolutionary Episodes

For the analyses reported in chapters 2 and 3 examining the factors associated with the onset of a revolutionary episode, onset was measured as a binary outcome that began (or did not begin) in one of 165 fixed territories during a particular year. The territories largely correspond to the boundaries of the state system in 2001.[5] Because I was interested in placing revolutionary contention in historical perspective, the panels were long and wide, involving 115 years across a large number of countries, with the sample left-censored (before 1900) and right-censored (after 2014).

The length and breadth of the panels (a total of 18,389 possible observations) was obviously a challenge for obtaining data on independent variables. As a result, the panels were unbalanced, with information missing for a significant number of country-years. Dependent variables were observed for all country-years in the panel (with the exception of military coup attempts, which were available only from 1946 onward). But data for some key independent variables were not completely Missing at Random (MAR). For instance, data on Polity scores and the number of years an incumbent leader was in power were almost completely absent for colonies, territories of another state,

---

2. See Cameron and Trivedi 2005, 266.
3. Cameron and Trivedi 2009, 560–61.
4. See Schwartz et al. 1996. ARPOIS was written by Aurelio Tobias and Michael J. Campbell.
5. The territories (countries) were derived from the Waves of War dataset compiled by Andreas Wimmer and Brian Min (2006). Four states that became independent since 2001 were treated as parts of their former states: Timor-Leste, South Sudan, Montenegro, and Kosovo. The West Bank and Gaza were treated as a separate unit from 1950 onward. Yemen was treated as a single unit, rather than as separated into North and South Yemen. Yugoslavia was measured as Serbia, Montenegro, and Kosovo.

or countries under foreign occupation. If a territory was not an independent state, there was a .96 probability that its Polity score was missing over the period examined by the data and a .99 probability that the number of years the incumbent leader was in office was missing. By contrast, if the territory was an independent state, there was only a .04 chance that its Polity score was missing and a .05 chance that the number of years the incumbent leader was in office was missing. I tried modeling these data with multiple imputation, but the results did not make intuitive sense. The issue was deeper than simply the imputation model. There are no Polity scores for colonies because the meaning of the component variables that make up Polity scores (in particular, the regulation, competitiveness, and openness of executive recruitment, executive constraints, and the competitiveness of participation) are not identifiable or comparable to these same measures within independent states. It is not even clear who should be considered the incumbent leader in a colony—should it be the local colonial governor, or the leader of the occupying state?[6] The situation is somewhat different in territories of independent states, where one could use the Polity score of the central government to represent conditions in the country as a whole. But because of these issues, I chose to limit the sample to independent states only. That, of course, eliminated some revolutionary episodes from the analysis.[7] A Little test showed that, with only independent states included in the sample, the data were Missing at Random.[8]

The resulting dataset of 11,742 cases of all independent states during the 1900–2014 period contained missing data on one or more variables for 1,226 country-years (10.4 percent of the total). In chapters 2 and 3, I sometimes used complete-case analyses to compare forms of revolutionary contention at a rudimentary, bivariate level. In chapter 3, I supplemented this with multiple imputation to ensure that relationships were robust and that estimations were unbiased. Multiple imputation allows us to estimate effects given the presence of missing values by creating different plausible sets of imputed data and

---

6. V-Dem's political democracy variables do cover many colonies. But from the description of how these measures are composed, it appears that colonies and independent states were coded according to different criteria.

7. The consequences were likely more important for social revolutionary than for urban civic revolutionary contention. In all, fourteen social revolutionary episodes (18 percent of the total) occurred in colonies, state territories, or states under occupation (These included the Vietnamese Revolution, the Algerian Revolution, revolutions in the Portuguese colonies, and the Eritrean Revolution). Only three urban civic revolutionary episodes (5 percent of the total) occurred in colonies, state territories, or states under occupation (These were the Baltic revolutions from 1987 to 1991).

8. Chi-square = 2961.4810, significant at the .001 level.

TABLE A4.1. Multiple imputation for panel data, summary statistics

Variable	Complete-case sample							Multiple-imputation samples[a]				
	mean	s.d.	min	max	N	% missing	mean	s.d.	min	max	N	m
Ln (population), t−1	8.932	1.560	4.679	14.117	11742	0.00%						
Ln (population density), t−1	3.497	1.378	0.379	7.137	11742	0.00%						
Post–Cold War period, dummy	0.398	0.490	0	1	11742	0.00%						
GDP per cap. (1990 $ thousands), t−1	4.659	5.382	0.207	42.916	11042	5.96%	4.504	5.286	0.207	42.916	11742	20
Annual growth rate, GDP per cap, t−1	1.869	6.395	−62.214	104.658	10980	6.49%	1.878	6.397	−62.214	104.658	11742	20
Polity score, t−1	0.334	7.342	−10	10	11328	3.53%	0.346	7.345	−10	10	11742	20
Years incumbent leader in power	6.227	8.081	0	67	11661	0.69%	6.224	8.077	0	67	11742	20
V-Dem measure of executive corruption, t−1	0.480	0.309	0.009	0.978	11580	1.38%	0.481	0.309	0.009	0.978	11742	20
Ln (annual oil prod., thousands metric tons), t−1	3.470	4.340	0	13.320	11560	1.55%	3.447	4.332	0	13.320	11742	20
Percent urban, t−1	43.334	23.864	1.533	99.061	11318	3.61%	42.756	23.828	1.533	99.061	11742	10
Average number of years of schooling	5.101	3.273	0	13.424	7132	39.26%	4.548	3.136	0	13.424	11742	10
Child mortality under the age of 5, t−1	146.030	129.093	2.100	577.900	11537	1.75%	146.468	129.141	2.100	577.900	11742	10
Military personnel per 1,000 pop, t−1	8.073	12.676	0	556.777	11038	6.00%	8.078	12.723	0	556.777	11742	10
Percent adult pop. aged 15–24, t−1	28.961	6.974	11.223	42.064	8527	27.38%	29.313	6.749	11.223	42.064	11742	10
Trade as percent of GDP, t−1	19.871	32.738	0.004	447.719	7235	38.38%	20.387	33.123	0.004	447.719	11742	10
Ln (dollar exchange rate), t−1	2.540	2.245	0	28.918	8826	24.83%	2.472	2.231	0	28.918	11742	10
Age of incumbent leader	56.058	11.534	11	92	11651	0.77%	56.034	11.540	11	92	11742	10
Mil. expenditure ($ thousands) per soldier, t−1	17.455	54.616	0	2416.67	9925	15.47%	15.943	51.623	0	2416.667	11742	10

[a] Estimated by predictive mean matching (k=10).

combining the results from each, taking into account the uncertainties surrounding the estimates. It thereby takes advantage of existing information and decreases the bias of estimations that would occur by dropping cases with missing information in the complete-case sample. For the multiple imputation of core variables in Table 3.1, I used predictive mean matching to create twenty imputed samples. For additional variables used in robustness tests in chapter 3, I used ten imputed samples. Predictive mean matching calculates the predicted value of the target variable according to the imputation model and then randomly draws a missing entry from a specified number (k) of donors whose predicted values are closest to the predicted value for the missing entry. The observed value of the donor replaces the missing value.[9] In this case, as recommended for large samples, I set k to 10.[10] One of the great advantages of predictive mean matching is that it yields plausible imputations and preserves the original data structure and distributions. Means, standard deviations, and distributions are presented in Table A4.1.

Revolutionary episodes are rare events and require special methods of analysis. In instances in which one of the outcomes of a binary dependent variable overwhelmingly dominates (as was the case for the panel data on revolutionary onset, as the absence of revolutionary contention was overwhelmingly preponderant), the maximum likelihood estimates of logistic regression contain substantial biases that can inflate the size of coefficients and confidence intervals.[11] Two rare-event estimation frameworks have been developed precisely for such situations: penalized logistic regression and rare events logit. Penalized logistic regression penalizes the log-likelihood of logistic regression by one-half of the logarithm of the determinant of the information matrix I (also known as the Jeffreys prior) to minimize the bias resulting from maximum likelihood estimation.[12] Thus, if logistic regression is estimated by using the formula

$$\Pr(Y=1) = \pi = [1 + \exp(-\mathbf{X}\beta)]^{-1}$$

where $\mathbf{X}$ is a set of predictors, and the maximum likelihood estimation has a log-likelihood $L_{ML}(\beta)$ that is biased as the proportion of events within the sample grows smaller, then the penalized log-likelihood $L_{PML}(\beta)$ proposed by Firth[13] to correct for this bias is

---

9. Little and Rubin 2002; Van Buuren 2018.
10. Morris, White, and Royston 2014; Allison 2015.
11. Nemes et al. 2009.
12. Heinze and Schemper 2002.
13. Firth 1993.

$$L_{PML}(\beta) = L_{ML}(\beta) + \frac{1}{2}\log \det(I(\beta))$$

This correction has been shown to work well for rare event situations. Rare events logit,[14] by contrast, utilizes a case control method of selection on the dependent variable to reduce bias by sampling among the cases in which no outcome occurred; it can sometimes overcorrect for bias, leading to some preference for the penalized approach.[15]

Both methods, however, pool across panels, and this could lead potentially to bias if there were important unobserved panel-specific features not captured in the independent variables.[16] Normally, country fixed-effects could be used to correct for unobserved heterogeneity in a panel regression. But country fixed-effects are not appropriate for rare events, as they remove panels completely from the analysis where the dependent variable does not change (i.e., countries in which revolution never occurred during the period analyzed). This situation applied to a quarter of the countries in the sample. These cases contained information that was important to our understanding of when and where revolutionary episodes materialize, so their removal would have been problematic.[17]

Event history methods provide a different framework for thinking about these issues.[18] Complementary log-log models are often used in discrete-time event history analyses when the probability of an outcome is either very small or very large. The log-likelihood function for the complementary log-log model is

$$\ln L = \sum_{j \in S} \ln F(x_j \beta_j) + \sum_{j \notin S} \ln(1 - F(x_j \beta_j))$$

where S is the set of all observations j such that $y_j \neq 0$ and $F(z) = 1 - \exp(-\exp(z))$. The complementary log-log model shares similar properties with Poisson models and is consistent with the Cox proportional hazards model, as the exponentiated coefficients can be interpreted in terms of hazard ratios.[19] A random-effects complementary log-log panel model is available as a Stata command (xtcloglog) that can be combined with robust standard errors clustered on panel subjects (in this case, territories/countries). In all models, I

---

14. King and Zeng 2001a; King and Zeng 2001b.
15. Allison 2012; Leitgöb 2013.
16. Green, Kim, and Yoon 2001.
17. See Beck and Katz 2001; Nel and Righarts 2008; Wright 2009.
18. Allison 2014.
19. Allison 1982; Jenkins 1995; Beck, Katz, and Tucker 1998; Carter and Signorino 2010.

included controls for time dependence.[20] An additional advantage of the random-effects complementary log-log panel model is that it can determine whether unobserved heterogeneity ("frailty") is a problem that affects the estimation. Stata computes the proportion of the total variance contributed by the panel-level variance component rho (ρ) that tests the extent to which the estimates are affected by unobserved heterogeneity. When ρ is zero, the panel-level variance component is not important, and the panel estimator is no different from what a pooled estimator would produce. A likelihood-ratio test of this condition is included with the Stata output and is reported in the regression tables for the panel models. In the models used to analyze the onset of urban civic revolutionary contention in Table 3.1, this test turned out to be statistically insignificant, as ρ approached zero. This indicated that a pooled estimation would produce similar results. Consequently, I moved to a pooled estimation framework. The pooled models (both complementary log-log and penalized logit estimations) produced nearly identical results and patterns of statistical significance. The penalized pooled model[21] proved superior to its alternatives in correctly identifying above-average risk for urban civic contention (This was true in both the complete-case and multiple-imputation samples). I used it with multiple-imputation samples for producing the predictions of the annual risk of urban civic contention for specific countries.

A key challenge for any rare-event analysis is overfitting, when too many regression parameters chase a limited number of data points. When a model is overfit, it can begin to describe the random error in the data rather than the relationships between variables. The result can be biased coefficients and inflated standard errors. The issue in rare-event analyses is not necessarily the overall size of the sample (which in this case is quite large), but rather the skewed distribution of the outcome variable: the number of events to be explained (i.e., onsets of urban civic revolutionary contention) is small relative to the number of explanatory parameters. A minimum of ten events per variable has traditionally been taken as a rough guide. But simulation studies of survival and logistic models suggest a lower limit of five events per variable is permissible in rare event studies.[22] In the analyses presented in Tables 3.1 and

20. See Carter and Signorino 2010.
21. Estimated using Coveney 2008.
22. Peduzzi et al. 1996; Vittinghoff and McCulloch 2007; Courvoisier et al. 2011; Allison 2012; Van Smeden et al. 2016. A variance inflation test showed that multicollinearity was not a significant problem other than when the squared term for GDP per capita was included in the specification. Since the relationship between GDP per capita and urban civic contention was quadratic, the variable needed to be included. To err on the side of caution and ensure that multicollinearity did not exercise an effect on the estimation, I created an alternative GDP per

3.2, the number of events per variable ranged between a low of five and a high of twenty-eight.

I subjected the models in Table 3.1 to a large number of robustness tests. I used the pooled complementary log-log model in Table 3.1 to bootstrap 157 country-clusters (taking one thousand samples of the data) to see if the inclusion or omission of any single country significantly affected the results. All variables in the specification remained statistically significant, and no major changes in the size or direction of relationships occurred. I also estimated a variety of population-averaged panel models with different correlation structures[23] and a pooled rare-event logistic regression model.[24] All produced similar results. I tested the robustness of the model to the inclusion or omission of each variable and to different combinations of variables in the specification in an attempt to minimize overfitting while retaining those factors that demonstrated consistent relationships. The variables in the model generally proved exceedingly resilient to different combinations of component variables, remaining statistically significant in all specifications with the sole exceptions of oil production and (occasionally) executive corruption.[25] I tested for the impact of regional fixed-effects, since the Middle East, the post-communist region, South and Southeast Asia, and East Asia experienced higher rates of urban civic contention than Africa, Latin America, Western Europe, or North America.[26] None of the regional dummies was statistically significant or changed any of the model's relationships.

---

capita variable centered on its mean and used visual inspection and a Hausman test to see whether this had any influence. I found no effects on other variables from inclusion of the original GDP per capita squared term.

23. The population-averaged model used Generalized Estimating Equations (GEE) to estimate the probability of an average state experiencing a revolutionary episode. I tested for a variety of correlational structures using the Quasi-Likelihood Information Criterion (QIC) on an identical sample; an exchangeable (equal correlation) structure proved the most efficient. See Hu et al. 1998; Neuhaus, Kalbfleisch, and Hauck 1991; Pan 2001.

24. See King and Zeng 2001b.

25. This was done using the checkrob procedure for Stata written by Mikkel Barslund. Executive corruption was statistically insignificant only when no control for level of development was included, while oil production was insignificant when either level of development or the degree of political openness/repressiveness was excluded. Oil production was the only variable that did not to have a statistically significant bivariate relationship with urban civic revolution. Nevertheless, there were sound theoretical reasons for its inclusion, and a likelihood ratio test confirmed the superiority of the model with the oil production variable included ($chi2(1) = 12.19$, significant at the .001 level).

26. See Neumayer and Plümper 2017, 138–39. Given concerns over the number of events per variable, I also rotated each regional dummy into the regression.

One of the major concerns of any statistical model is omitted variable bias. I tested separately for the influence of eleven additional variables that logically and theoretically could have been related to the onset of urban civic contention: military spending per soldier; military personnel per thousand population; average years of schooling; levels of urbanization; population density; youth as a proportion of the larger population; nominal trade as percentage of nominal GDP; the logged dollar exchange rate; the presence of financial crisis on the eve of revolution; child mortality under the age of five; and the age of the incumbent leader.[27] Each was individually tested for both a bivariate relationship with the onset of urban civic contention (controlling for time dependence) and for whether it was statistically significant or changed the signs or statistical significance of other variables when inserted into the multivariate specification in Model 4 in Table 3.1. I also tested each of these variables using ten imputed samples generated through multiple imputation that filled in missing data. Only three variables (military spending per soldier, population density, and the age of the incumbent leader) enjoyed a statistically significant bivariate relationship with urban civic contention. Each, however, was statistically insignificant when included in the multivariate model that controlled for the influence of other factors.[28] Two variables proved to be marginally significant when added to the multivariate model (youth as proportion of the larger population and under-five child mortality), though neither enjoyed a bivariate relationship with the onset of urban civic revolutionary contention. Both, however, were negatively related to urban civic revolutionary contention. Lower child mortality and smaller youth populations were associated with the onset of urban civic contention, essentially reflecting the correlation of urban civic revolution with development. Indeed, the degree of urbanization, the proportion of youth, and child mortality could each substitute in the model for GDP per capita at a statistically significant level without affecting the signs or levels of statistical significance of any of the other variables in the specification—though these models had poorer fits than the model using GDP per capita.

Of course, the relatively consistent association of the variables included in the model with the outbreak of urban civic contention does not preclude the possibility that there are other variables that might affect its onset. Some of these may have been present in particular cases but not in others, depending on case-specific circumstances. Moreover, measurability constrains the authority of all statistical inference. It is entirely possible (even likely) that there are unmeasured factors that are not captured in the statistical model, but are

27. All variables were lagged by a year.
28. The results were repeated in the multiple-imputation sample.

nevertheless associated with the onset of urban civic revolution. This is of course one of the limitations of all statistical models.

4C. Cross-Sectional Analyses of Episode Outcomes

While data on the outcomes of revolutionary episodes were complete for the entire sample (n = 343), information on a number of independent variables was incomplete. In chapter 4, I analyzed both complete-case and multiple-imputation samples, presenting the results of both estimations. As studies show, the number of imputations (M) should be equal to or greater than the percentage of cases with some incomplete data. For the regime and opposition models in chapter 4, twenty multiple-imputation samples satisfied this requirement; for the combined model, thirty multiple-imputation samples were needed.[29] Sample means, standard deviations, and distributions for the regime and opposition models are presented in Table A4.2.

Logistic regression was used for analyzing revolutionary outcomes in chapters 4 and 6. In theory, a selection model (for example, probit with sample selection) might have been used to analyze revolutionary outcomes, given that societies first selected into revolution prior to any determination of outcomes. But there are several challenges with doing so. For one thing, as noted in Appendix 4B, the rare-event character of revolutionary contention renders the standard errors from estimations based on probit or logit inaccurate. More importantly, as chapter 3 laid bare, there is no single selection process into revolution, since different types of revolutions occur for different reasons, mobilize different social forces, and are associated with distinct causal factors.

Logistic regression calculates the log-odds as

$$\ln\frac{P(Y_i=1)}{1-P(Y_i=1)} = \ln(Odds)_i = a + \sum_{k=1}^{K} \beta_k X_{ik}$$

and the predicted probabilities of an outcome are calculated as

$$\pi_i = \frac{\exp(\beta x_i)}{1+\exp(\beta x_i)}$$

$$= \frac{1}{1+\exp(-\beta x_i)}$$

---

29. White, Royston, and Wood 2011. Other numbers of imputed samples (M) were necessary for the additional variables tested in robustness checks. See the robustness test files available from the author.

TABLE A4.2. Multiple imputation for cross-sectional data, summary statistics

Variable	Complete-case sample						Multiple-imputation samples[a]					
	mean	s.d.	min	max	N	% missing	mean	s.d.	min	max	N	m
Regime model[b]												
Polity score, t−1	−1.446	5.987	−10	10	276	4.17%	−1.397	5.9735	−10	10	288	20
Polity score, t−1 (squared)	37.801	28.707	0	100	276	4.17%	37.9	28.763	0	100	288	20
Incumbent government, military	0.142	0.350	0	1	288	0.00%	0.142	0.350	0	1	288	0
Incumbent government, monarchy	0.108	0.310	0	1	288	0.00%	0.108	0.310	0	1	288	0
Incumbent government, one-party	0.222	0.416	0	1	288	0.00%	0.222	0.416	0	1	288	0
Incumbent government, competitive authoritarian	0.295	0.457	0	1	288	0.00%	0.295	0.457	0	1	288	0
Incumbent government, democracy	0.146	0.354	0	1	288	0.00%	0.146	0.354	0	1	288	0
Incumbent government, other	0.087	0.282	0	1	288	0.00%	0.087	0.282	0	1	288	0
Years incumbent leader in power	7.566	8.771	0	42	286	0.69%	7.555	8.755	0.000	42.000	288	20
Age of incumbent leader	55.493	11.823	5	85	284	1.39%	55.486	11.829	5.000	85.000	288	20
GDP per cap. (1990 $ thousands), t−1	2.738	2.598	0.279	12.530	283	1.74%	2.719	2.590	0.144	12.530	288	20
Ln (annual oil prod, thousands metric tons), t−1	3.859	4.544	0.000	13.095	285	1.04%	3.842	4.541	0.000	13.095	288	20
Military expenditure per soldier, t−1 (deciles)	5.733	2.915	1	10	240	16.67%	5.532	2.911	0.168	10.000	288	20
Civil war	0.479	0.500	0	1	288	0.00%	0.479	0.500	0	1	288	0
Civil war x Military expenditure (deciles)	2.467	3.221	0	10	240	16.67%	2.524	3.228	0.000	10.000	288	20

(*Continued*)

TABLE A4.2. (*continued*)

Variable	Complete-case sample					Multiple-imputation samples[a]				
	mean	s.d.	min	max	N	% missing	mean	s.d.	min	max	N	m
Opposition model												
Ln (peak participation)	10.518	1.857	6.908	16.118	320	6.71%	10.563	1.864	6.908	16.118	343	20
Urban location of contention	0.534	0.500	0	1	343	0.00%	0.534	0.500	0	1	343	0
Total number of deaths (deciles)	5.462	2.864	1	10	325	5.25%	5.527	2.825	0.905	10.000	343	20
Urban x Deaths (deciles)	2.166	2.718	0	10	325	5.25%	2.128	2.735	0.000	10.000	343	20
Goal: political/civil liberties	0.257	0.437	0	1	343	0.00%	0.257	0.437	0	1	343	0
Goal: class transformation	0.230	0.422	0	1	343	0.00%	0.230	0.422	0	1	343	0
Goal: state independence	0.347	0.477	0	1	343	0.00%	0.347	0.477	0	1	343	0
Goal: republican/anti-monarchical	0.082	0.274	0	1	343	0.00%	0.082	0.274	0	1	343	0
Goal: reversal of ethnic order	0.157	0.365	0	1	343	0.00%	0.157	0.365	0	1	343	0
Goal: Islamist	0.085	0.279	0	1	343	0.00%	0.085	0.279	0	1	343	0
Coalitional leadership	0.201	0.401	0	1	343	0.00%	0.201	0.401	0	1	343	0
Vanguard party leadership	0.122	0.328	0	1	343	0.00%	0.122	0.328	0	1	343	0
Other party leadership	0.096	0.295	0	1	343	0.00%	0.096	0.295	0	1	343	0
Traditional societal leadership	0.122	0.328	0	1	343	0.00%	0.122	0.328	0	1	343	0
Paramilitary/militia leadership	0.155	0.362	0	1	343	0.00%	0.155	0.362	0	1	343	0
Underground leadership	0.099	0.299	0	1	343	0.00%	0.099	0.299	0	1	343	0
Liberation movement leadership	0.157	0.365	0	1	343	0.00%	0.157	0.365	0	1	343	0

[a]Estimated by chained equations. Predictive mean matching (with k = 3) was used for Polity scores, oil production, years the incumbent leader was in power, the age of the incumbent leader, peak participation, and all interaction variables, while truncated regression was used for GDP per capita, military expenditures per soldier, and deaths. [b]Colonies excluded from analysis.

In regression tables I reported the exponentiated value of the regression coefficient, otherwise known as the odds ratio (the odds that the outcome occurred given a one-unit exposure to the independent variable, compared to the odds of the outcome occurring in the absence of that one-unit exposure). For easier interpretation, I discuss the results as average predicted probabilities at particular values of the independent variable, holding other variables constant at their means. The full sample of 343 revolutionary episodes over the 1900–2014 period has sufficient power to be able to handle maximum likelihood estimation without concerns. In Table 4.3, the complete-case logistic regression with the fewest cases per variable (the estimation combining regime and opposition models) was carried out on a sample of 212 episodes using fourteen variables (15.1 observations per variable). The analysis exhibited signs of overfitting. When statistically insignificant variables were dropped, the reduced combined model (consisting of ten covariates, or 21.2 observations per covariate) produced a more efficient and robust classification of episode outcomes. These results are reported in the tables.

In chapter 6, I also used a logistic regression on a subsample of fifty-four urban civic revolutions to examine the probability of opposition success associated with physical proximity to centers of power. The regression included only two covariates (distance from the seat of government and levels of participation), but the small sample size potentially posed a problem for maximum likelihood estimation. In this case, in robustness tests I replicated the analysis using both Ordinary Least Squares (OLS) and penalized maximum likelihood estimation (as elucidated in Appendix 4B)—the latter often considered preferable for small samples.[30] I also bootstrapped the estimation using one thousand samples of the data. The results remained the same.

4D. Analyzing Individual Behavior in Urban Civic Revolutions from Survey Data

In several discussions in chapter 7, I examined those who participated in revolution relative to the rest of the population. In these cases, a simple logistic regression model (as described in Appendix 4C) was adequate. However, one of the great advantages of the Monitoring and Arab Barometer survey data analyzed in chapter 7 is that they allow us to view the behavior of populations during revolutionary episodes as not simply a binary outcome (participate or do not participate), but through the lens of a much richer array of choices:

---

30. Rainey and McCaskey 2015.

support the revolution and participate in protests; support the revolution but fail to participate directly, and instead aid participants with food, clothing, or money; support the revolution but fail to participate directly or aid participants; oppose the revolution; oppose the revolution and participate in counterrevolutionary protests; or remain completely apathetic and inactive. Thinking of individual behavior during revolution in this way moves away from the binary of participate/do not participate, providing a more realistic analysis of the behavior of populations during revolutionary crises.

One could argue that the choices made by citizens during revolutions are ordered by their degree of opposition to or support for the regime and that an ordered logistic model would be an appropriate modeling choice. But ordered logistic regression relies on an assumption of proportional odds—that is, that the predictors consistently have the same effect on the odds of an outcome as one moves from lower-ordered outcomes to higher-ordered outcomes. In fact, in all four of the surveys, Brant tests showed that the proportional odds assumption was violated even in the simple base models that included only age and gender.[31]

Multinomial logistic regression is the appropriate modeling choice in this situation. It is used to analyze a categorical dependent variable with more than two outcomes that have no natural ordering, and unlike ordinal logistic regression it does not assume parallel slopes. The multinomial logistic model estimates $M-1$ models, where M is the number of levels of the dependent variable, and the omitted level constitutes the reference group against which the other outcomes are judged.[32] Assuming the first category is the reference category, then for $m = 2, \ldots, M$, the log odds of choosing category m over the first (reference) category is estimated by

$$\ln \frac{P(Y_i = m)}{P(Y_i = 1)} = a_m + \sum_{k=1}^{K} \beta_{mk} X_{ik}$$

For most analyses in chapter 7, I used the group of respondents who supported the revolution but did not themselves participate in it as the reference category, comparing participants to this group. The exponentiated coefficients of the multinomial logistic model produce a relative risk ratio, which measures the risk of a particular outcome (participation, aiding the revolution, opposing

---

31. Brant 1990; Long and Freese 2014. The Brant test compares the slope coefficients of the binary logistic regressions implied by the ordered regression model. Results of the tests can be found in the robustness test files available from the author.

32. Long 1997, 148–86; Greene 2012, 763–66.

the revolution, or remaining apathetic) compared to the risk of falling into the reference group (support the revolution but do not participate in it or aid it) that is associated with a one-unit change in the independent variable. However, for simplicity of interpretation, I generally reported average predicted probabilities at particular values of the independent variable, holding other variables constant at their means.

One of the assumptions of the multinomial logistic model is the Independence of Irrelevant Alternatives (IIA): the odds of choosing one alternative over another should not depend on the presence of other alternatives (i.e., deleting outcomes should not affect the odds among the remaining outcomes). Several statistical tests have been developed to assess the IIA assumption, though they are inconsistent and often provide conflicting results. More important from a theoretical point of view is that the alternatives be logically distinct, weighted independently by decision-makers, and not constitute close substitutes for one another.[33] These conditions generally apply to the choices of individuals during a revolutionary crisis that are analyzed in the survey data (the one exception is the choice between participating in or aiding revolution). I did test the IIA assumption using both Hausman-McFadden and Small-Hsiao tests.[34] In both instances, there was no statistical evidence that the IIA assumption was violated.[35]

4E. Revolutionary Mortality and the Endogenous Switching Model

To provide an estimate of how and why mortality in revolutionary contention has changed since 1900, in chapter 8 I analyzed the factors associated with deaths in revolutionary episodes that did and did not involve civil wars. I defined a civil war as armed combat lasting for more than two months. Civil wars by this definition accounted for the vast majority of deaths in revolutionary contention, though only half of all revolutionary episodes involved civil wars. Therefore, any attempt to estimate the factors associated with mortality in revolutions needed to account for selection into civil war, as well as for factors affecting deaths in episodes not involving civil war.

For this analysis, I used an endogenous switching model. The model is part of a family of selection models appropriate for situations in which the relationship between an outcome of interest (in this case, deaths in revolutionary

---

33. Long and Freese 2014, 407–11.
34. Hausman and McFadden 1984; Small and Hsiao 1985.
35. Results can be found in the robustness test files available from the author.

contention) and a set of explanatory factors varies across two discrete regimes. The best known of these selection models is the Heckman selection model, in which only one of two regimes is observed, and the model (consisting of a selection model and an outcome model) is used to correct for the omitted variable bias due to selection into the observed state.[36] In the endogenous switching model, both regimes are observed (in this case, deaths in revolutionary episodes with civil wars, and deaths in episodes without civil wars), and the analysis models the outcomes within each regime, taking into account the effects of the sorting process between them. The process of selecting into "civil war" and "no civil war" regimes is likely related to the processes producing deaths within each regime,[37] and failure to account for this endogenous selection would produce biased estimates. Thus, the endogenous switching model consists of three equations: a selection model

$$S_i = \begin{cases} 0 \text{ if } S_i^* = z_i'\gamma + \varepsilon_{si} \leq 0 \\ 1 \text{ if } S_i^* = z_i'\gamma + \varepsilon_{si} > 0 \end{cases}$$

where S_i is an indicator of selection and z_i is a vector of covariates, and two outcome equations

$$y_{1_i} = x_{1_i}'\beta_1 + \varepsilon_{1_i} \text{ if } S_i = 1$$
$$y_{0_i} = x_{0_i}'\beta_0 + \varepsilon_{0_i} \text{ if } S_i = 0$$

where x_{0_i} and x_{1_i} are vectors of covariates, and for observation i and observable outcome y_i is either y_{0_i} or y_{1_i}. The error terms, ε_{0_i} and ε_{1_i} are assumed to be dependent on ε_{si}. The model is estimated using maximum likelihood. Also known as the Roy model, the approach has been used frequently in economics to study wage differences across economic sectors.[38]

Like all selection models, one of the assumptions of the endogenous switching model is the joint normality of error terms. This assumption is often violated in reality.[39] But when the joint normality assumption is violated, maximum-likelihood estimates are inconsistent and can provide misleading inferences, especially for small samples. Statisticians have found ways to correct for these violations by using copulas (coupling functions that transform a joint probability distribution into uniform marginal values).[40] The

---

36. Heckman 1979.
37. Maddala and Nelson 1975.
38. See Lee 1978; Adamchik and Bedi 2000.
39. Moffitt 1999, 1390–93; Bushway, Johnson, and Slocum 2007.
40. See Lee 1983, Smith 2003.

copula-based endogenous switching model employs maximum-likelihood to estimate the factors associated with selection into regimes as well as those associated with the outcome of interest within each regime—correcting for violations of joint normality that would otherwise yield inconsistent estimates. The error terms of each of the two outcome models are assumed to be dependent on the error terms of the selection model, and different copulas assume different dependence patterns.

Various copula functions are available. The best combination of copulas is chosen by comparing log-likelihoods from all possible permutations. In this case, the combination of Clayton and FGM (Farlie-Gumbel-Morgenstern) copulas (with normal distribution of the marginal terms) proved to have the highest log-likelihood. The superiority of this combination over the joint normal assumption was demonstrated through a comparison of AIC and BIC scores, as well as by a Vuong test.[41] The model generates a dependence parameter θ that can be transformed into Kendall's τ (ranging from −1 to 1); it is often reported as a measure of the degree of dependence between the errors of the selection and outcome models. The model also generates a scale parameter (σ), which is related to the standard deviation of the error of the outcome equation. All calculations were performed in Stata using the switchcopula module developed by Takuya Hasebe.[42]

The copula-based endogenous switching model uses probit for the selection portion of the estimation. For the two outcome portions of model, the copula-based endogenous switching model uses ordinary least squares (OLS). Standard criteria (AIC and BIC, and in the event of disagreement between them, a likelihood ratio test of the nested models) were used to identify the most accurate specification. As deaths in revolutionary contention vary tremendously across episodes (ranging from zero to three million), the natural log of deaths was used as the dependent variable to control for heteroskedasticity, back-transforming the results into numbers of deaths for interpreting effects.[43]

The counterfactual analysis carried out in chapter 8 proceeded in several stages. For the civil wars portion of the model, I first identified a series of variables associated with deaths in revolutionary civil wars, using the endogenous switching model and standard criteria to select the most accurate specification. Then, for each independent variable (x_j), I calculated the mean for the Cold War [$\bar{x}_j$**Cold**] and the mean for post–Cold War [$\bar{x}_j$**Post**] periods, as

41. As recommended by Hasebe 2013.
42. See Hasebe 2013.
43. Manning and Mullahy 2001. To avoid taking the log of zero, one death was added to the dependent variable.

well as the marginal effects on civil war deaths at each of these mean values, holding other factors constant at their means [i.e., $\frac{\partial y}{\partial x_j}|x_j = \bar{x}_j, Cold$ and $\frac{\partial y}{\partial x_j}|x_j = \bar{x}_j, Post$]. Finally, I produced an estimate of the increase or decrease in the number of deaths in civil wars between the Cold War and post–Cold War periods due to change in independent variable x_j by multiplying the difference between these two marginal effects by the number of civil wars in the post–Cold War period. This same procedure was followed for calculating estimates for the impact of factors associated with the decline of deaths in episodes without civil wars ("contained" episodes) using the non–civil war portion of the model.

For the selection portion of the model, I used the endogenous switching model to identify factors affecting the probability that a revolutionary episode would or would not involve civil war. These were then checked in a separate probit model. For each binary factor x_j identified as systematically associated with selection into civil war,[44] I computed: 1) the marginal probabilities that an episode would involve civil war [$P(war|x_j)$] and would not involve civil war [$P(not\ war|x_j)$] associated with the factor, holding other variables constant at their means; 2) the difference between the number of episodes (n) with the factor present during the Cold War and the number of episodes with the factor present in the post–Cold War period [i.e., $(\Delta n|x_j = 1) = (n|x_j = 1, Post = 1) - (n|x_j = 1, Cold = 1)$]; 3) for the entire 1950–2014 period, the difference between the average number of deaths ($\bar{D}$) in episodes with the factor present that experienced civil war and the average number of deaths in episodes that did not have the factor present but that experienced civil war [i.e., $\Delta \bar{D}_{war} = (\bar{D}_{war}|x_j = 1) - (\bar{D}_{war}|x_j = 0)$]; and 4) for the entire 1950–2014 period, the difference between the average number of deaths in episodes not experiencing civil war in which the factor was present and deaths in episodes not experiencing civil war in which the factor was not present [i.e., $\Delta \bar{D}_{not\ war} = (\bar{D}_{not\ war}|x_j = 1) - (\bar{D}_{not\ war}|x_j = 0)$]. I used these estimates to calculate: 1) the overall increase or decrease in deaths in the post–Cold War period (relative to the Cold War) resulting from the influence of the factor on selection into civil war ($\Delta d_{war}|x_j$)) [i.e., $(\Delta d_{war}|x_j) = P(war|x_j) * (\Delta n|x_j = 1) * \Delta \bar{D}_{war}$], and 2) the overall increase or decrease in deaths in the post–Cold War period (relative to the Cold War) resulting from the influence of the factor on the decision not to select into civil war ($\Delta d_{not\ war}|x_j$) [i.e., $(\Delta d_{not\ war}|x_j) = P(not\ war|x_j) * (\Delta n|x_j = 1) * \Delta \bar{D}_{not\ war}$].

---

44. Although I tested for the effects of a number of continuous variables (GDP per capita, Polity scores, and oil production), all of the variables that proved statistically significant were binary dummy variables representing particular features of revolutionary contention.

The sum of these values ($\Delta d_{war} \mid x_j + \Delta d_{not\,war} \mid x_j$) provided a rough estimate of how the presence or absence of the factor altered revolutionary mortality from the Cold War to the post–Cold War period due to selection processes.

For purposes of comparison, I also report alternative estimates using a different estimation method that did not take into account selection effects and employed a Generalized Linear Model (GLM) with a log link (and gamma distribution family). The GLM estimation also produces different results because it fits the model $y = e^{X\beta} + \epsilon$, whereas regression with a logged dependent variable fits the model $\ln(y) = X\beta + \epsilon$.

4F. Survival of Regimes after Revolutionary Contention

In chapter 9, I fit a Cox proportional hazards model of the survival of post-revolutionary regimes. The Cox model estimates the influence of competing risk factors on the hazard rate—that is, the risk of failure, given that a subject has survived up to a particular point in time. In this model the hazard function is estimated as

$$h(t) = h_0(t) \exp(X\beta)$$

where t represents the survival time, $h_0(t)$ is the baseline hazard function, X represents the set of covariates, and β is the set of estimated regression coefficients. The estimated coefficients represent the change that is expected in the log of the hazard ratio relative to a one-unit change in the risk factor, holding other predictors constant. The hazard ratio (the ratio of the hazards associated with a one-unit change in the covariate) is produced by exponentiating the regression coefficients from the Cox model.[45]

Compared to other types of survival models, the Cox model is semi-parametric in that it makes no assumptions about the shape of the baseline hazard function, but rather estimates the effects of competing risk factors on survival time. It does, however, assume that the survival times between subjects are independent of one another, that there is a multiplicative relationship between the risk factors and the hazard, and that the relative risk of failure is constant over time—that is, the proportional hazards assumption that the hazard for individual m is proportional to the hazard for individual n.[46] Risk factors generally should be time-independent (at a minimum, time-dependent covariates need to be used with caution).

---

45. Kalbfleisch and Prentice 2002, 95–147.
46. Stata provides a post-estimation test of the proportional hazards function (estat phtest). For these tests, see the Stata output and robustness test files available from the author.

For each regime that experienced revolutionary contention, I considered the time of origin to be the year that revolutionary contention ended. Regime failure was measured by overthrow of the regime, regime-change through other irregular means, or by a fundamental change in the character of the regime through reform. Data on the duration of regimes after revolutionary contention was collected from Rulers (https://www.rulers.org/), with follow-up research on individual cases.

4G. Difference-in-Differences for Comparing Revolutionary Aftermaths

Difference-in-differences (DID) is a quasi-experimental research design that uses observational panel data from treatment and control groups to obtain an estimate of the causal effect (the average treatment effect) of a particular intervention or treatment through counterfactual reasoning. It posits that every unit has different potential outcomes depending on its assignment to a specific condition. The difference-in-differences model estimates the difference between the observed value of the dependent variable and the value that the dependent variable would have taken under the assumption of parallel trends (i.e., had there not been any treatment at all). The parallel trends assumption presumes that, in the absence of treatment, the differences between treatment and control groups would have remained constant over time.[47]

In chapter 9, I use the difference-in-differences setup to analyze developments after revolutions. In these analyses the "treatment" is experiencing a period of revolutionary contention—irrespective of its length. Exogenous events such as wars or financial crises can accompany revolution, and the effect of these exogenous events cannot be separated from the effect of revolutionary contention. Moreover, revolutionary contention can last for different lengths of time. Thus, "treatment" should not be understood as revolutionary contention per se, but rather as the *period* of revolutionary contention—including whatever other events occurred during this interlude. To identify the relationship of experiencing a period of revolutionary contention to patterns of subsequent development, the DID setup compared "treated" countries prior to the onset of and after the conclusion of revolutionary contention, relating these patterns of development to different countries that had not been "treated." Three different types of "treatment" were examined: 1) whether a

---

47. For explanations of the DID model, see Card and Krueger 1994; Imbens and Woolridge 2009, 67–72.

country experienced a revolutionary episode, compared to those that did not (based on a matched sample);[48] 2) whether, given the outbreak of revolutionary contention, a country experienced a successful or a failed revolution; and 3) whether a country experienced a successful or failed social revolution, or experienced a successful or failed urban civic revolution. I examined patterns of post-revolutionary development along a wide variety of measures of political order, economic growth, inequality, freedoms, and political accountability. Comparisons were made between "treated" and "control" cases for these outcome variables for the three years prior to revolutionary contention, the final year of revolutionary contention, and seven years following the end of revolutionary contention. For the matched cases that did not experience revolutionary contention, outcomes were compared over the same years as their matched counterparts that experienced revolutionary contention.

DID is typically used for causal identification and estimation of a treatment effect for a particular intervention. A series of strong assumptions is necessary for DID to be used for these purposes. Many of these assumptions do not fully hold for the study of revolutions. The exchangeability assumption, for instance, requires that outcomes in the control group would have been the same as in the treated group had the control group been subjected to treatment. This of course is a counterfactual that can never be tested, since assignment to revolution cannot be randomized. A positivity assumption requires that there be at least some probability that all subjects could have been assigned to the treated group. Given that a large proportion of countries have experienced revolutionary contention at some point in their histories, one could make a case that this assumption holds. But during the 1900–2014 period, a quarter of all countries experienced no revolutionary contention, and whether all of these cases ever faced a serious threat of a revolutionary challenge during this period is questionable. In view of the stochastic element at play in whether revolutionary oppositions succeed, one could argue that there was some positive probability that all countries that experienced revolutionary contention could have been "assigned" to successful or failed revolution groups. However, as we saw, particular features were associated with opposition success, and in some cases the odds were heavily stacked against opposition victory. Thus, "assignment" was never truly random. Moreover, the DID model assumes that assignment to treatment or control groups should not be determined by the baseline outcome. But "assignment" to revolutionary contention was often related to the outcomes of interest. (Economic growth, levels of inequality,

---

48. On matching procedures, see Appendix 4H.

political liberties, or government accountability—outcomes of interest—were related to the onset of revolutionary contention.)

The Stable Unit Treatment Value Assumption (SUTVA) is also problematic. SUTVA is an exclusion restriction that requires that for causal inference to hold, the application of the treatment to one subject cannot affect the outcomes for another subject, and there can be only one version of treatment during the period under observation. But revolutionary contention often diffuses, and revolution in one country can alter the probability of revolution in another. Moreover, one can imagine circumstances in which revolution in a country could affect government policies in a neighboring or related country (for instance, increased government repression to prevent the cross-national spread of revolution). A country experiencing one revolution could also experience another during the period under observation. I excluded anti-colonial and separatist revolts from the analysis, due to the frequent absence of data on variables of interest prior to the onset of revolutionary contention. Out of 175 non-separatist revolutionary episodes in ninety-seven countries with sufficient information to be included in the full difference-in-differences sample, there were seven instances in which a revolution occurred within seven years of the end of a prior revolution. Part of the analysis focused on a reduced sample of urban civic and social revolutionary episodes, comparing successful urban civic revolutions with failed urban civic revolutions and successful social revolutions with failed social revolutions. For these cases, there was no overlap of "treatments" during the periods under observation. But separatist revolts, even though they were excluded, could still have affected outcomes if they occurred during the same period as the episodes in the sample.

A final assumption of a difference-in-differences model is the parallel trends assumption, which requires that the differences between the treatment and control groups remain constant over time in order to assign causal effects to a treatment. This is often considered the most critical assumption for causal inference in a DID model—and frequently the hardest to fulfill. The greater the number of data points before and after treatment, the more rigorous the test of the parallel trends assumption, and the more likely it is that the parallel trends assumption will be violated. In the analysis in chapter 9, I examined each variable of interest for three years prior to revolutionary contention and for seven years afterward (in addition to the final year of contention). As detailed in the chapter, violations of the parallel trends assumption both before and after revolution were rampant.

Thus, the difference-in-differences model could not be used to estimate average treatment effects for revolution, or to identify causation with any confidence. Rather, I used it for purposes of controlled comparison: to examine trends before and after revolution and to compare them with cases that did not experience revolution, that experienced failed revolution, or that experienced different types of revolution. By calculating average marginal effects, I was able to provide an estimate of the immediate impact of the period of revolutionary contention on the outcome of interest, relative to the situation on the eve of revolution (subject to the caveats noted above). But I also used the difference-in-differences setup to identify the timing of violations of the parallel trends assumption: whether post-revolutionary trajectories differed from pre-revolutionary trajectories or reflected pre-revolutionary trends, and how long any change that accompanied the period of revolutionary contention lasted during the seven years following revolution. These trajectories provided evidence for whether the developments after revolution reflected pre-revolutionary legacies, were temporary aftermaths of revolution, or potentially became longer-lasting legacies in the making.

Ordinary Least Squares (OLS) were used to estimate the difference-in-differences models. I used country fixed-effects to control for unmeasured confounding influences. Thus, the difference-in-differences model was estimated by

$$Y_{it} = \beta_1 Treat_i + \beta_2 Year_t + \beta_3 Treat_i * Year_t + \gamma_2 Cntry_2 + \cdots + \gamma_n Cntry_n + \varepsilon_{it}$$

where Y_{it} is the outcome of interest for country i in year t (with years standardized to the number of years before or after the onset or end of an episode), $Treat_i$ is the indicator of treatment status of country i (a dummy variable for whether a country experienced a successful revolutionary episode—with the comparison set varying depending on the analysis undertaken), $Year_t$ is the year indicator before or after revolutionary contention, and $Cntry_n$ is a dummy variable for country i, with γ representing the country fixed-effect for each country (omitting one). For each model, average marginal effects were estimated for the interaction $Treat_i * Year_t$. This allowed identification of the difference on the outcome of interest between the year before revolution and the last year of revolutionary contention, as well as trends prior to and following revolutionary contention. The use of country fixed-effects, together with using the year prior to revolutionary onset as the base year for the regression, constrained the coefficients to be equal in the year prior to the onset of contention, thus placing the analytical emphasis on temporal change relative to the year prior to onset. As the literature notes, there can be issues with the standard errors produced from difference-in-differences estimations due to autocorrelation.[49] To correct for this, I used cluster-robust standard errors (clustered by country) in all estimations.

---

49. Bertrand, Duflo, and Mullainathan 2004.

I employed multiple imputation to fill in missing values on the time-series outcome variables. Analysts have debated whether multiple imputation should be used for estimating outcome variables. Some believe that the use of predictor variables to estimate outcomes biases estimates. Others contend that outcome variables can be imputed under certain circumstances.[50] Complete-case analysis was always conducted as a robustness check. In all analyses in chapter 9, the independent variables were fully complete, while the eleven time points of the dependent variables had various degrees of missingness (with missingness in the dependent variable ranging from 2.8 percent to 12.5 percent of observations). For cross-sectional studies, complete-case analysis is often used when observations are missing on a dependent variable only, as multiple imputation is thought to add little in these circumstances.[51] But for a dependent variable that is observed multiple times, complete-case analysis drops any observations in a series characterized by missingness, thereby including different sets of cases at each time point (as well as uneven numbers of cases) and potentially biasing estimates. In this circumstance, multiple imputation provides a much better basis for estimation. There is a high degree of serial correlation in these time series, allowing other values to be used for estimating missing values using regression imputation. However, when there was no information available on all of the pre-treatment values, imputation of pre-treatment outcomes violated the spirit of the difference-in-differences setup, as post-treatment outcomes would be used to predict pre-treatment values. Thus, I excluded revolutionary episodes from the analysis if they contained missing information for all pre-treatment years. On several occasions this reduced sample size (particularly when analyzing successful social revolutions). But results were always checked against the complete-case record.

4H. Matching for Difference-in-Differences Analysis of Revolutionary Aftermaths

When comparing countries that experienced revolutionary contention with those that did not in chapter 9, matching was used to identify the most relevant comparisons for each revolutionary episode and to control for the effect of unmeasured confounders. I matched countries on their characteristics in the year before revolutionary contention broke out, identifying a reasonable comparison set based on those features associated with revolutionary onset and a series of other factors that might confound comparison.

50. Van Ginkel et al. 2020.
51. Little 1992, 1227.

The most common approach to matching is propensity score matching,[52] which identifies matched cases based on the probability of belonging to the treatment group (in this case, the probability of experiencing a revolutionary episode in a given year) and weights them by the inverse of the propensity score. Revolutions, however, are rare events, so that the probability of treatment is quite low for all cases (even for the most structurally propitious ones). Moreover, as we saw, there is not a great deal of confidence in predicting the onset of revolutionary episodes (particularly, when they will break out), and the structural factors that influence the onset of revolutionary episodes differ across types of episodes (e.g., social revolutionary versus urban civic).

For these reasons, I used a combination of methods (propensity scores with calipers, Mahalanobis scores with calipers, coarsened exact matching, and nearest-neighbor matching) to identify potential matches for each revolutionary episode. The goal was to identify matches that exhibited relatively similar starting positions, much like the logic of comparison in small-n studies. In a first stage, I created propensity scores based on population size, level of development, economic growth, political openness, levels of corruption, and military capacity—factors shown in earlier chapters to be associated with revolutionary onset or success. In a second stage, I used Mahalanobis distance matching based on a country-year's propensity score, level of development, and general population size, as well as exact matching based on whether a country was a democracy or non-democracy, whether it was ruled by a communist regime, and whether it was a significant oil producer. At this stage, I confined potential matches to the same world-region or to contiguous neighbors in order to mitigate further the effects of unmeasured confounders, assuming that countries in the same world region were more likely to display similar unmeasurables that could confound results than countries in different corners of the world.[53] I also used calipers to eliminate observations that were beyond a reasonable distance from the "treated" observation. Finally, I used nearest neighbor matching (by propensity scores and Mahalanobis distances) to identify up to four potential matched control cases per revolutionary episode that lay within a reasonable caliper distance of each "treated" observation.[54]

---

52. Rosenbaum and Rubin 1983.

53. I recognized that region can be an artificial construct. For countries that spanned multiple regions (for instance, Russia, Turkey, Iran, and China), I included potential matches from multiple regions in the matching algorithm.

54. For propensity scores, I kept observations that were within one-quarter of the square root of a standard deviation (i.e., one-quarter of the variance) of the propensity scores for the

TABLE A4.3. Covariate balances before and after matching

Before Matching

Variable	Treated Mean	Treated Variance	Treated Skewness	Control Mean	Control Variance	Control Skewness	Balance Standardized difference	Balance Variance ratio
Ln (population), t–1	9.6314	1.9280	0.4585	9.2496	1.9617	0.4418	0.2738	0.9828
GDP per cap. (1990 $ thousands), t–1	3.0216	7.2603	1.3820	4.8405	29.8226	2.0501	-0.4224	0.2434
Annual growth rate, GDP per cap., t–1	1.0130	39.2672	-0.4590	1.9536	35.4174	0.5093	-0.1539	1.1087
Polity score, t–1	-2.0237	33.6542	0.4602	0.9587	54.7354	-0.0590	-0.4486	0.6149
Democracy, t–1 (0–1)	0.1420	0.1226	2.0511	0.4018	0.2404	0.4007	-0.6098	0.5099
Communist, t–1 (0–1)	0.0769	0.0714	3.1754	0.0759	0.0701	3.2040	0.0040	1.0189
Ln (oil production), t–1	4.2929	21.1520	0.3678	3.8159	19.4456	0.5520	0.1059	1.0878
Mil. expenditure ($ thousands) per soldier, t–1	5.9983	81.0333	2.9758	16.5095	1758.7370	6.0109	-0.3466	0.0461
V-Dem measure of exec. bribery, t–1 (0–4)	2.6746	1.3756	-0.4350	1.9948	1.7237	0.0458	0.5461	0.7981

After Matching

Variable	Treated Mean	Treated Variance	Treated Skewness	Control Mean	Control Variance	Control Skewness	Balance Standardized difference	Balance Variance ratio
Ln (population), t–1	9.5721	1.7573	0.4745	9.4883	1.9953	0.0050	0.0612	0.8807
GDP per cap. (1990 $ thousands), t–1	2.8347	6.0773	1.5526	3.0532	6.7097	1.5626	-0.0864	0.9058
Annual growth rate, GDP per cap., t–1	1.2766	34.5483	0.0386	1.9002	31.9510	-0.9091	-0.1082	1.0813
Polity score, t–1	-2.2992	33.4494	0.5626	-2.6390	36.4446	0.8184	0.0575	0.9178
Democracy, t–1 (0–1)	0.1417	0.1226	2.0544	0.1424	0.1225	2.0465	-0.0019	1.0007
Communist, t–1 (0–1)	0.0551	0.0525	3.8989	0.0554	0.0525	3.8866	-0.0013	0.9997
Ln (oil production), t–1	4.2526	20.0793	0.3410	4.7607	21.4678	0.1981	-0.1115	0.9353
Mil. expenditure ($ thousands) per soldier, t–1	5.4070	69.6059	3.3574	7.8199	227.2096	4.7665	-0.1981	0.3064
V-Dem measure of exec. bribery, t–1 (0–4)	2.7087	1.3510	-0.4520	2.4112	1.3423	-0.0778	0.2563	1.0064

As noted, one of the assumptions of the difference-in-differences model is that the composition of "treatment" and "control" groups is stable. In identifying potential matches the panel character of the data needed to be taken into account. Multiple revolutionary episodes do occur in the same society, and a society that did not experience a revolutionary episode in one year might experience one in the next. If the occurrence of the episode were in close proximity to a preceding episode, this would contaminate the separation of treatment and control groups—a key assumption of the model. I also expected that the effects of experiencing a revolution would gradually fade over time, as other factors (including post-revolutionary governance and exogenous events) came to influence patterns of development. Following the advice of Imai, Kim, and Wang,[55] I matched each revolutionary episode with control observations from other countries exclusively according to the features of countries during the year prior to the onset of revolutionary contention in the "treated" country, and only among countries that did not experience a revolutionary episode during the previous five years, during the period of revolutionary contention in the "treated" country, and during the five years following the end of the episode. This exclusionary time window kept "treated" and "control" cases reasonably separate, while also allowing for cases that experienced revolutionary episodes eventually to rejoin the pool of cases for potential reassignment. I also dropped any revolutionary episode from the matched sample that occurred within five years of the end of another revolutionary episode in the same society, in order to avoid the confounding influence of the subsequent revolution.[56]

Four matches were identified by these criteria for 34 percent of revolutionary episodes, three matches for 7 percent of cases, two matches for 30 percent, and one match for 28 percent. Having multiple matches allowed me to leverage as much relevant information as possible from multiple control cases through variable ratio matching (weighting by the inverse of the number of control cases identified as matches).[57] Table A4.3 presents the covariate balances for treatment and control groups on the variables used for matching—before and

---

sample as a whole. For Mahalanobis distances, the caliper was based on the critical value for a .95 probability, according to the chi-square distribution (with 6 degrees of freedom).

55. Imai, Kim, and Wang 2018.

56. As a result of these rules, the number of "treated" cases in the matched difference-in-differences sample that were to be matched with "control" cases was reduced to 123. In only three cases did more than one revolutionary episode occur in the same country in the same year: 1917 in Russia, 1918 in Germany, and 2001 in the Philippines. In these cases, the latter episode was used in place of the earlier episode, except if the latter episode was unsuccessful and the earlier episode was successful.

57. See Ming and Rosenbaum 2001; Stuart 2010; King, Lucas, and Nielsen 2017.

after matching. Scholars have proposed various standards for judging whether balance between treatment and control groups has been achieved. Rubin suggested a standardized difference in means greater than 0.25 as an indicator of imbalance and also recommended the use of the ratio of treated and control variances (where balance is defined by values close to 1.0 and variables are considered out of balance if the ratio is greater than 2.0 or less than 0.5).[58] As Table A4.3 indicates, by these standards the matching procedure largely achieved its goals, though there was still some imbalance on the military spending and executive corruption variables.

58. Rubin 2001.

REFERENCES

Abadeer, Caroline, Alexandra Domike Blackman, Lisa Blaydes, and Scott Williamson. 2019. "Did Egypt's Post-Uprising Crime Wave Increase Support for Authoritarian Rule?" Unpublished paper (available at https://blaydes.people.stanford.edu/sites/g/files/sbiybj1961/f/crime.pdf).

Abadie, Alberto. 2005. "Semiparametric Difference-in-Differences Estimators." *The Review of Economic Studies* 72, 1: 1–19.

Abdyrazakov, Sydyk. 2005. "Boiling Over." *Transitions Online*, March 21.

Abinales, Patricio N. and Donna J. Amoroso. 2005. *State and Society in the Philippines*. Lanham, MD: Rowman & Littlefield.

Abramova, Evgenia. 2015. "The Bolotnaya Square: Urban Design in Moscow between Social Activities and Political Protests." *Widok: Teorie i praktyki kultury wizualnej* 3, 9, at http://pismowidok.org/index.php/one/article/view/272/554.

Abramson, Paul R. and Ronald F. Inglehart. 2009. *Value Change in Global Perspective*. Ann Arbor, MI: University of Michigan Press.

Abulof, Uriel. 2015. "'The People Want(s) to Bring Down the Regime': (Positive) Nationalism as the Arab Spring's Revolution." *Nations and Nationalism* 21, 4: 658–80.

Abu-Lughod, Lila. 2012. "Living the 'Revolution' in an Egyptian Village: Moral Action in a National Space." *American Ethnologist* 39, 1: 21–25.

Acemoglu, Daron, Simon Johnson, and James Robinson. 2005. "The Rise of Europe: Atlantic Trade, Institutional Change, and Economic Growth." *American Economic Review* 95, 3: 546–79.

Acemoglu, Daron and James A. Robinson. 2005. *Economic Origins of Dictatorship and Democracy*. Cambridge: Cambridge University Press.

Acemoglu, Daron and James A. Robinson. 2006. "Economic Backwardness in Political Perspective." *American Political Science Review* 100, 1: 115–31.

Adamchik, V. and V. Bedi. 2000. "Wage Differentials between the Public and the Private Sectors: Evidence from an Economy in Transition." *Labour Economics* 7: 203–24.

Ades, Alberto and Hak B. Chua. 1997. "Thy Neighbor's Curse: Regional Instability and Economic Growth." *Journal of Economic Growth* 2, 3: 279–304.

Agnew, John A. 1987. *Place and Politics: The Geographical Mediation of State and Society*. Boston, MA: Allen & Unwin.

Agnew, John A. and James S. Duncan, eds. 2014. *The Power of Place: Bringing Together Geographical and Sociological Imaginations*. London: Routledge.

Aisen, A. and F. J. Veiga. 2006. "Does Political Instability Lead to Higher Inflation? A Panel Data Analysis." *Journal of Money, Credit, and Banking* 38: 1379–89.

Aisen, A. and F. J. Veiga. 2008. "The Political Economy of Seigniorage." *Journal of Development Economics* 87: 29–50.

Akbari, Azadeh and Rashid Gabdulhakov. 2019. "Platform Surveillance and Resistance in Iran and Russia: The Case of Telegram." *Surveillance & Society* 17, 1/2: 223–31.

Albertus, Michael. 2015. *Autocracy and Redistribution: The Politics of Land Reform*. Cambridge: Cambridge University Press.

Albertus, Michael, Thomas Brambor, and Ricardo Ceneviva. 2018. "Land Inequality and Rural Unrest: Theory and Evidence from Brazil." *Journal of Conflict Resolution* 62, 3: 557–96

Alesina, Alberto, Sule Özler, Nouriel Roubini, and Phillip Swagel. 1996. "Political Instability and Economic Growth." *Journal of Economic Growth* 1, 2: 189–211.

Alesina, Alberto, Arnaud Devleeschauwer, William Easterly, Sergio Kurlat, and Romain Wacziarg. 2003. "Fractionalization." *Journal of Economic Growth* 8, 2: 155–94.

Alexander, Jeffrey C. 2011. *Performative Revolution in Egypt: An Essay in Cultural Power*. London: Bloomsbury Academic.

Alexanian, Janet A. 2011. "Eyewitness Accounts and Political Claims: Transnational Responses to the 2009 Postelection Protests in Iran." *Comparative Studies of South Asia, Africa and the Middle East* 31, 2: 425–42.

Alexeyeva, Ludmilla. 1985. *Soviet Dissent*. Middleton, CT: Wesleyan University Press.

Allinson, Jamie. 2019 "A Fifth Generation of Revolution Theory?" *Journal of Historical Sociology* 19, 1: 142–51.

Allison, Paul D. 1982. "Discrete-Time Methods for the Analysis of Event Histories." *Sociological Methodology* 13, 1: 61–98.

Allison, Paul 2012. "Logistic Regression for Rare Events." *Statistical Horizons*, February 13, at https://statisticalhorizons.com/logistic-regression-for-rare-events.

Allison, Paul. 2015. "Imputation by Predictive Mean Matching: Promise & Peril." *Statistical Horizons*, March 5, at https://statisticalhorizons.com/predictive-mean-matching.

Allison, Paul D. 2014. *Event History and Survival Analysis: Regression for Longitudinal Event Data*. Thousand Oaks, CA: SAGE Publications.

Alpaugh, Micah. 2014. *Non-Violence and the French Revolution: Political Demonstrations in Paris, 1787–1795*. Cambridge: Cambridge University Press.

Alwazir, Atiaf Zaid. 2011. "The Square of Change in Sana'a: An Incubator for Reform." *Arab Reform Brief* 48 (April), at http://storage.arab-reform.net.s3.amazonaws.com/ari/2019/10/16150441/Arab_Reform_Initiative_2011-04_Policy_alternatives_en_The_Square_of_Change_in_Sanaa_an_Incubator_for_Reform.pdf.

Amann, Peter. 1962. "Revolution: A Redefinition." *Political Science Quarterly*, 77, 1: 36–53.

Antonova-Azarova, Anna. 2014. "Kiev: Symphony of Three Squares and Two Streets." *Interdisciplinary Studies of Complex Systems* 4: 58–73.

Appadurai, Arjun. 1996. *Modernity at Large: Cultural Dimensions of Globalization*. Minneapolis: University of Minnesota Press.

Arel, Dominique. 2002. "Interpreting 'Nationality' and 'Language' in the 2001 Ukrainian Census." *Post-Soviet Affairs* 18, 3: 213–49.

Arel, Dominique. 2005. "The 'Orange Revolution': Analysis and Implications of the 2004 Presidential Election in Ukraine." Paper presented at the Third Annual Stasiuk-Cambridge Lecture on Contemporary Ukraine, University of Cambridge (available at http://www.ukrainianstudies.uottawa.ca/ukraine_list/ukl346_13.html).

Arel, Dominique. 2007. "Why and How It Happened: Orange Ukraine Chooses the West, but without the East." In Ingmar Bredies, Andreas Umland, and Valentin Yakushik, eds, *Aspects of the Orange Revolution III: The Context and Dynamics of the 2004 Ukrainian Presidential Election*. Stuttgart: Ibidem-Verlag, 35–53.

Arendt, Hannah. 1965. *On Revolution*. New York: The Viking Press.

Aristotle. 1941. *The Basic Works of Aristotle*, ed. Richard McKeon. New York: Random House.

Arriola, Leonardo R. 2014. "Suppressing Protests during Electoral Crises: The Geographic Logic of Mass Arrests in Ethiopia," at https://www.princeton.edu/politics/about/file-repository/public/Arriola_Protests.pdf.

Asal, Victor, Justin Conrad, and Nathan Toronto. 2017. "I Want You! The Determinants of Military Conscription." *Journal of Conflict Resolution* 61, 7: 1456–81.

Ascher, Abraham 1988/1994. *The Revolution of 1905*, 2 vols. Stanford, CA: Stanford University Press.

Ascher, Abraham. 2004. *The Revolution of 1905: A Short History*. Stanford, CA: Stanford University Press.

Ashworth, G. J. 1991. *War and the City*. London: Routledge.

Askew, Marc and Sascha Helbardt. 2012. "Becoming Patani Warriors: Individuals and the Insurgent Collective in Southern Thailand." *Studies in Conflict & Terrorism* 35, 11: 779–809.

Aspinall, Edward. 2005. *Opposing Suharto: Compromise, Resistance, and Regime Change in Indonesia*. Stanford, CA: Stanford University Press.

Associated Press. 1957. "Bogota Police Disrupt Mass in Attacking Demonstrators." *The Baltimore Sun*, 6 May: 4 (from ProQuest Historical Newspapers).

Attia, Sahar. 2011. "Rethinking Public Space in Cairo: The Appropriated Tahrir Square." *Trialog* 109, 1: 10–15.

Auvinen, J., 1997. "Political Conflict in Less Developed Countries 1981–89." *Journal of Peace Research* 34: 177–95.

Aya, Rod. 1979. "Theories of Revolution Reconsidered: Contrasting Models of Collective Violence." *Theory and Society* 8, 1: 39–99.

Aytaç, S. Erdem and Susan C. Stokes. 2018. *Why Bother? Rethinking Participation in Elections and Protests*. Cambridge: Cambridge University Press.

Badcock, Sarah. 2007. *Politics and the People in Revolutionary Russia: A Provincial History*. Cambridge: Cambridge University Press.

Baland, Jean-Marie and James A. Robinson. 2008. "Land and Power: Theory and Evidence from Chile." *American Economic Review* 98, 5: 1737–65.

Balcells, Laia and Stathis N. Kalyvas. 2014. "Does Warfare Matter? Severity, Duration, and Outcomes of Civil Wars." *Journal of Conflict Resolution* 58, 8: 1390–418.

Banks, Arthur S. and Kenneth A. Wilson. 2015. "Cross-National Time-Series Data Archive." Databanks International. Jerusalem.

Barany, Zoltan. 2016. *How Armies Respond to Revolutions and Why*. Princeton, NJ: Princeton University Press.

Barbieri, Katherine and Rafael Reuveny. 2005. "Economic Globalization and Civil War." *The Journal of Politics* 67, 4: 1228–47.

Barro, Robert J. and Jong-Wha Lee. 1993. "Losers and Winners in Economic Growth." *The World Bank Economic Review* 7, Supplement 1: 267–98.

Barro, Robert J. and Jong-Wha Lee. 2013. "A New Data Set of Educational Attainment in the World, 1950–2010." *Journal of Development Economics* 104: 184–98, at http://www.barrolee.com/data/yrsch.htm.

Barro, Robert J. and José F. Ursúa. 2008. "Macroeconomic Crises since 1870." *Brookings Papers on Economic Activity* (Spring): 255–335, at https://scholar.harvard.edu/barro/publications/barro-ursua-macroeconomic-data.

Barry, Colin M., K. Chad Clay, and Michael E. Flynn. 2013. "Avoiding the Spotlight: Human Rights Shaming and Foreign Direct Investment." *International Studies Quarterly* 57, 3: 532–44.

Bates, Robert. 1981. *Markets and States in Tropical Africa*. Berkeley, CA: University of California Press.

Baudais, Virginie and Grégory Chauzal. 2011. "The 2010 Coup d'État in Niger: A Praetorian Regulation of Politics?" *African Affairs* 110, 439: 295–304.

Bayat, Asef. 2000. "From 'Dangerous Classes' to 'Quiet Rebels': Politics of the Urban Subaltern in the Global South." *International Sociology* 15, 3: 533–57.

Bayat, Asef. 2017. *Revolution without Revolutionaries: Making Sense of the Arab Spring*. Stanford, CA: Stanford University Press.

BBC. 2011. "Change Square: The Heart of Yemen's Creative Revolution." *BBC News*, June 19, at https://www.bbc.com/news/world-middle-east-13747858.

Beath, Andrew, Fotini Christia, and Ruben Enikolopov. 2011. "Winning Hearts and Minds? Evidence from a Field Experiment in Afghanistan." MIT Political Science Working Paper No. 2011–14.

Beck, Colin J. 2011. "The World-Cultural Origins of Revolutionary Waves: Five Centuries of European Contention." *Social Science History* 35, 2: 167–207.

Beck, Colin J. 2014. "Reflections on the Revolutionary Wave in 2011." *Theory and Society* 43, 2: 197–223.

Beck, Colin J. 2018. "The Structure of Comparison in the Study of Revolution." *Sociological Theory* 36, 2: 134–61.

Beck, Nathaniel and Jonathan N. Katz. 2001. "Throwing Out the Baby with the Bath Water: A Comment on Green, Kim, and Yoon." *International Organization* 55, 2: 487–95.

Beck, Nathaniel, Jonathan N. Katz, and Richard Tucker. 1998. "Taking Time Seriously: Time-Series-Cross-Section Analysis with a Binary Dependent Variable." *American Journal of Political Science* 42: 1260–88.

Beckwith, Karen. 2015. "Narratives of Defeat: Explaining the Effects of Loss in Social Movements." *The Journal of Politics* 77, 1: 2–13.

Behrend, Heike. 1999. *Alice Lakwena and the Holy Spirits: War in Northern Uganda, 1986–97*. Athens, OH: Ohio University Press.

Beissinger, Mark R. 2002. *Nationalist Mobilization and the Collapse of the Soviet State*. Cambridge: Cambridge University Press.

Beissinger, Mark R. 2007. "Structure and Example in Modular Political Phenomena: The Diffusion of Bulldozer/Rose/Orange/Tulip Revolutions." *Perspectives on Politics* 5, 2: 259–76.

Beissinger, Mark R. 2011. "Mechanisms of Maidan: The Structure of Contingency in the Making of the Orange Revolution." *Mobilization: An International Quarterly* 16, 1: 25–43.

Beissinger, Mark R. 2013. "The Semblance of Democratic Revolution: Coalitions in Ukraine's Orange Revolution." *American Political Science Review* 107, 3: 574–92.

Beissinger, Mark R. 2017. "'Conventional' and 'Virtual' Civil Societies in Autocratic Regimes." *Comparative Politics* 49, 3: 351–71.

Beissinger, Mark R., Amaney A. Jamal, and Kevin Mazur. 2015. "Explaining Divergent Revolutionary Coalitions: Regime Strategies and the Structuring of Participation in the Tunisian and Egyptian Revolutions." *Comparative Politics* 48, 1: 1–24.

Beissinger, Mark and Stephen Kotkin, eds. 2014. *Historical Legacies of Communism in Russia and Eastern Europe*. Cambridge: Cambridge University Press.

Beissinger, Mark and M. Crawford Young, eds. 2002. *Beyond State Crisis? Post-Colonial Africa and Post-Soviet Eurasia in Comparative Perspective*. Baltimore: Johns Hopkins University.

Bellal, Annyssa, and Louise Doswald-Beck. 2011. "Evaluating the Use of Force during the Arab Spring." *Yearbook of International Humanitarian Law* 14: 3–35.

Bellamy, Alex J. 2012. *Massacres and Morality: Mass Atrocities in an Age of Civilian Immunity*. Oxford: Oxford University Press.

Bellin, Eva. 2012. "Reconsidering the Robustness of Authoritarianism in the Middle East: Lessons from the Arab Spring." *Comparative Politics* 44, 2: 127–49.

Bennett, D. Scott, and Allan Stam. 2000. "EUGene: A Conceptual Manual." *International Interactions* 26: 179–204 (available at http://eugenesoftware.org).

Bennett, W. Lance and Alexandra Segerberg. 2013. *The Logic of Connective Action: Digital Media and the Personalization of Contentious Politics*. Cambridge, UK: Cambridge University Press.

Berman, Chantal. 2018. "Why Do Tunisians Keep Protesting." *The Washington Post*, January 19, at https://www.washingtonpost.com/news/monkey-cage/wp/2018/01/19/why-do-tunisians-keep-protesting/?noredirect=on&utm_term=.0881cdfa3f8c.

Berman, Chantal. 2019. "Protest, Social Policy, and Political Regimes in the Middle East." PhD dissertation, Princeton University.

Berman, Eli, Jacob N. Shapiro, and Joseph H. Felter. 2011. "Can Hearts and Minds Be Bought? The Economics of Counterinsurgency in Iraq." *Journal of Political Economy* 119, 4: 766–819.

Bermeo, Nancy. 2016. "On Democratic Backsliding." *Journal of Democracy* 27, 1: 5–19.

Berridge, W. J. 2015. *Civil Uprisings in Modern Sudan: The "Khartoum Springs" of 1964 and 1965*. London: Bloomsbury.

Bertrand, Marianne, Esther Duflo, and Sendhil Mullainathan. 2004. "How Much Should We Trust Differences-in-Differences Estimates?" *The Quarterly Journal of Economics* 119, 1: 249–75.

Besley, Timothy and Torsten Persson. 2008. "Wars and State Capacity." *Journal of the European Economic Association* 6, 2/3: 522–30.

Bhat, Chandra R. and Naveen Eluru. 2009. "A Copula-Based Approach to Accommodate Residential Self-Selection Effects in Travel Behavior Modeling." *Transportation Research. Part B: Methodological* 43, 7: 749–65.

Bilaniuk, Laada. 2005. *Contested Tongues: Language Politics and Cultural Correction in Ukraine*. Ithaca, NY: Cornell University Press.

Bilenky, Serhiy. 2018. *Imperial Urbanism in the Borderlands: Kyiv, 1800–1905*. Toronto: University of Toronto Press.

Billington, James H. 1980. *Fire in the Minds of Men: Origins of the Revolutionary Faith*. Princeton, NJ: Princeton University Press.

Binswanger, Hans P., Klaus Deininger, and Gershon Feder. 1995. "Power, Distortions, Revolt and Reform in Agricultural Land Relations." *Handbook of Development Economics* 3: 2659–772.

Bishara, Dina. 2015. "The Politics of Ignoring: Protest Dynamics in Late Mubarak Egypt." *Perspectives on Politics* 13, 4: 958–75.

Black, Jeremy. 1988. "The 'Bloody 64th': The Army and Crowd Control in Ireland in 1789." *Journal of the Society for Army Historical Research* 66, 268: 252.

Blattman, Christopher and Edward Miguel. 2010. "Civil War." *Journal of Economic Literature* 48, 1: 3–57.

Boase, Jeffrey, John B. Horrigan, Barry Wellman, and Lee Rainie. 2006. *The Strength of Internet Ties*. Washington, DC: The Pew Internet and American Life Project.

Bohdanova, Tetyana. 2014. "Unexpected Revolution: The Role of Social Media in Ukraine's Euromaidan Uprising." *European View* 13, 1: 133–42.

Boix, Carles. 2003. *Democracy and Redistribution*. Cambridge: Cambridge University Press.

Boix, Carles, Michael K. Miller, and Sebastian Rosato. 2013. "A Complete Data Set of Political Regimes, 1800–2007." *Comparative Political Studies* 46, 12: 1523–54.

Boix, Carles and Milan W. Svolik. 2013. "The Foundations of Limited Authoritarian Government: Institutions, Commitment, and Power-Sharing in Dictatorships." *The Journal of Politics* 75, 2: 300–316.

Boldin, Valery. 1994. *Ten Years That Shook the World*. New York: Basic Books.

Bolt, J. and J. L. van Zanden. 2014. "The Maddison Project: Collaborative Research on Historical National Accounts." *The Economic History Review* 67, 3: 627–51.

Boone, Catherine. 2014. *Property and Political Order: Land Rights and the Structure of Politics in Africa*. Cambridge: Cambridge University Press.

Boot, Max. 2002. *Savage Wars of Peace: Small Wars and the Rise of American Power*. New York: Basic Books.

Bosi, Lorenzo. 2013. "State Territories and Violent Political Organisations." *Nationalism and Ethnic Politics* 19, 1: 80–101.

Boswell, Terry and William J. Dixon. 1993. "Marx's Theory of Rebellion: A Cross-National Analysis of Class Exploitation, Economic Development, and Violent Revolt." *American Sociological Review* 58, 5: 681–702.

Boudreau, Julie-Anne. 2010. "Reflections on Urbanity as an Object of Study and a Critical Epistemology." In Jonathan S. Davies and David L. Imbroscio, eds, *Critical Urban Studies: New Directions*. Albany, NY: SUNY Press, 55–72.

Boudreau, Vincent. 2004. *Resisting Dictatorship: Repression and Protest in Southeast Asia*. Cambridge: Cambridge University Press.

Box, George E. P. and Norman R. Draper. 1987. *Empirical Model-Building and Response Surfaces*. New York: Wiley.

Bozarslan, Hamit. 2018. "Introduction." In Hamit Bozarslan, Gilles Bataillon, and Christophe Jaffrelot, eds, *Revolutionary Passions: Latin America, Middle East, and India*. London: Routledge, 1–6.

Brant, Rollin. 1990. "Assessing Proportionality in the Proportional Odds Model for Ordinal Logistic Regression." *Biometrics* 46: 1171–78.

Braunfels, Wolfgang. 1988. *Urban Design in Western Europe: Regime and Architecture, 900–1900* (translated by Kenneth J. Northcott). Chicago: University of Chicago Press.

Breuer, Anita, Todd Landman, and Dorothea Farquhar. 2014. "Social Media and Protest Mobilization: Evidence from the Tunisian Revolution." *Democratization* 22, 4: 764–92.

Brinton, Crane. 1965. *The Anatomy of Revolution* (revised and expanded edition). New York: Vintage.

Brown, Joel S. 1988. "Patch Use as an Indicator of Habitat Preference, Predation Risk, and Competition." *Behavioral Ecology and Sociobiology* 22, 1: 37–47.

Brown, Wendy. 2005. *Edgework: Critical Essays on Knowledge and Politics*. Princeton, NJ: Princeton University Press.

Brush, Stephen G. 1996. "Dynamics of Theory Change in the Social Sciences: Relative Deprivation and Collective Violence." *Journal of Conflict Resolution* 40, 4: 523–45.

Brym, Robert, Melissa Godbout, Andreas Hoffbauer, Gabe Menard, and Tony Huiquan Zhang. 2014. "Social Media in the 2011 Egyptian Uprising." *The British Journal of Sociology* 65, 2: 266–92.

Buchanan, Allen E. 1991. *Secession: The Morality of Political Divorce from Fort Sumter to Lithuania and Quebec*. Boulder, CO: Westview Press.

Bueno de Mesquita, Bruce and Alastair Smith. 2010. "Leader Survival, Revolutions, and the Nature of Government Finance." *American Journal of Political Science* 54, 4: 936–50.

Bueno de Mesquita, Ethan. 2010. "Regime Change and Revolutionary Entrepreneurs." *American Political Science Review* 104, 3: 446–66.

Buhaug, Halvard, Scott Gates, Havard Hegre, and Havard Strand. 2008. "Global Trends in Armed Conflict." Oslo: Center for the Study of Civil War, PRIO.

Bunce, Valerie. 1995. "Should Transitologists Be Grounded?" *Slavic Review* 54, 1: 111–27.

Bunce, Valerie J. and Sharon L. Wolchik. 2011. *Defeating Authoritarian Leaders in Postcommunist Countries*. Cambridge: Cambridge University Press.

Bushway, Shawn, Brian D. Johnson, and Lee Ann Slocum. 2007. "Is the Magic Still There? The Use of the Heckman Two-Step Correction for Selection Bias in Criminology." *Journal of Quantitative Criminology* 23, 2: 151–78.

Büthe, Tim, and Helen V. Milner. 2008. "The Politics of Foreign Direct Investment into Developing Countries: Increasing FDI through International Trade Agreements?" *American Journal of Political Science* 52, 4: 741–62.

Butter, David. 2013. "Egypt in Search of Economic Direction." Chatham House Briefing Paper, MENAP BP 2013/01 (available at https://www.chathamhouse.org/sites/default/files/public/Research/Middle%20East/bp_butter1113.pdf).

Calhoun, Craig J. 1994. *Neither Gods nor Emperors: Students and the Struggle for Democracy in China*. Berkeley, CA: University of California Press.

Calvert, Peter A. R. 1967. "Revolution: The Politics of Violence." *Political Studies* 15, 1: 1–11.

Calvino, Italo. 1972. *Invisible Cities* (translated by William Weaver). New York: Harcourt Brace Jovanovich.

Cameron, A. Colin and Pravin K. Trivedi. 2005. *Microeconometrics: Methods and Applications*. New York: Cambridge University Press.

Cameron, A. Colin and Pravin K. Trivedi. 2009. *Microeconomics Using Stata*. College Station, TX: Stata Press.

Camp, Meghan J., Timothy Johnson, Janet Rachlow, Lisa Shipley, Bonnie Woods, and D. Zeh. 2012. "When to Run and When to Hide: The Influence of Concealment, Visibility, and Proximity to Refugia on Perceptions of Risk." *Ethology* 118, 10: 1010–17.

Camp, Roderic Ai. 2016. "Democratizing Mexican Politics, 1982–2012." In William H. Beezley, ed., *Oxford Research Encyclopedia of Latin American History*. Oxford: Oxford University Press, DOI: 10.1093/acrefore/9780199366439.013.12.

Camus, Albert. 1991 [1956]. *The Rebel*. New York: Vintage International.

Caparini, Marina and Otwin Marenin. 2005. "Crime, Insecurity and Police Reform in Post-Socialist CEE." *Journal of Power Institutions in Post-Soviet Societies* 2, at https://journals.openedition.org/pipss/330.

Card, David and Alan B. Krueger. 1994. "Minimum Wages and Employment: A Case Study of the Fast-Food Industry in New Jersey and Pennsylvania." *American Economic Review* 84, 4: 772–93.

Carothers, Thomas. 1999. *Aiding Democracy Abroad: The Learning Curve*. Washington, DC: Carnegie Endowment.

Carothers, Thomas 2010. "The Continuing Backlash against Democracy Promotion." In Peter Burnell and Richard Youngs, eds, *New Challenges to Democratization*. New York: Routledge, 59–72.

Carp, Benjamin L. 2007. *Rebels Rising: Cities and the American Revolution*. Oxford: Oxford University Press.

Carter, David B., and Curtis S. Signorino. 2010. "Back to the Future: Modeling Time Dependence in Binary Data." *Political Analysis* 18, 3: 271–92.

Cassese, Antonio. 1995. *Self-Determination of Peoples: A Legal Reappraisal*. Cambridge: Cambridge University Press.

Castells, Manuel. 1983. *The City and the Grassroots: A Cross-Cultural Theory of Urban Social Movements*. Berkeley, CA: University of California Press.

Castells, Manuel. 1996. *The Rise of the Network Society*. Cambridge, MA: Blackwell.

Cave, Danielle, Samantha Hoffman, Alex Joske, Fergus Ryan, and Elise Thomas. 2019. "Mapping China's Technology Giants." International Cyber Policy Centre, Australian Strategic Policy Institute. Report No. 15 (available at https://s3-ap-southeast-2.amazonaws.com/ad-aspi/2019-05/Mapping%20China%27s%20technology%20giants.pdf?EINwiNpste_FojtgOPriHtlFSD2OD2tL).

Cederman, Lars-Erik, Andreas Wimmer, and Brian Min. 2010. "Why Do Ethnic Groups Rebel? New Data and Analysis." *World Politics* 62, 1: 87–119.

Chabris, Christopher F., and Eliot S. Hearst. 2003. "Visualization, Pattern Recognition, and Forward Search: Effects of Playing Speed and Sight of the Position on Grandmaster Chess Errors." *Cognitive Science* 27, 4: 637–48.

Chambers, Deborah. 2013. *Social Media and Personal Relationships: Online Intimacies and Networked Friendship*. London: Palgrave MacMillan.

Chandler, Tertius. 1987. *Four Thousand Years of Urban Growth: An Historical Census*. Lewiston, NY: St. David's University Press.

Channon, John. 1992. "The Peasantry in the Revolutions of 1917." In Edith Rogovin Frankel, Jonathan Frankel, and Baruch Knei-Paz, eds, *Revolution in Russia: Reassessments of 1917*. Cambridge: Cambridge University Press, 105–30.

Chazan, Naomi, ed. 1991. *Irredentism and International Politics*. Boulder, CO: Lynne Rienner Publishers.

Chenoweth, Erica. 2017. "Trends in Nonviolent Resistance and State Response: Is Violence towards Civilian-Based Movements on the Rise?" *Global Responsibility to Protect* 9, 1: 86–100.

Chenoweth, Erica and Margherita Belgioioso. 2019. "The Physics of Dissent and the Effects of Movement Momentum." *Nature Human Behaviour* 3, 10: 1088–95.

Chenoweth, Erica and Christopher Wiley Shay. 2020. "List of Campaigns in NAVCO 1.3," https://doi.org/10.7910/DVN/ON9XND, Harvard Dataverse, V1, UNF:6:GD3vspZ7XK 7H7KFdiKFICw== [fileUNF].

Chenoweth, Erica and Maria J. Stephan. 2011. *Why Civil Resistance Works: The Strategic Logic of Nonviolent Conflict*. New York: Columbia University Press.

Chenoweth, Erica and Jay Ulfelder. 2015. "Can Structural Conditions Explain the Onset of Nonviolent Uprisings?" *Journal of Conflict Resolution*, DOI: 0022002715576574.

Chikhladze, Giga and Irakli Chikhladze. 2005. "The Rose Revolution: A Chronicle." In Zurab Karumidze and James V. Wertsch, eds, *'Enough!': The Rose Revolution in the Republic of Georgia 2003*. New York: Nova Science Publishers, 1–20.

Chirot, Daniel and Charles Ragin. 1975. "The Market, Tradition, and Peasant Rebellion: The Case of Romania in 1907." *American Sociological Review* 40, 4: 428–44.

Chivers, C. J. 2005. "How Top Spies in Ukraine Changed the Nation's Path." *The New York Times*, January 17, A1.

Chomiak, Laryssa. 2014. "Architecture of Resistance in Tunisia." In Lina Khatib and Ellen Lust, eds, *Taking to the Streets: The Transformation of Arab Activism*. Baltimore: Johns Hopkins University Press, 22–51.

Chorley, Katharine. 1973. *Armies and the Art of Revolution*. Boston, MA: Beacon.

Clark, David. 1996. *Urban World/Global City*. London: Routledge.

Clarke, Killian. 2014. "Unexpected Brokers of Mobilization: Contingency and Networks in the 2011 Egyptian Uprising." *Comparative Politics* 46, 4: 379–97.

Clarke, Killian. 2018. "On the Origins and Success of Counterrevolutions, 1940–2015." Paper presented at the annual meeting of the American Political Science Association, Boston, MA.

Clarke, Killian. 2020. "Overthrowing Revolution: The Emergence and Success of Counterrevolution, 1900–2015." Unpublished paper.

Clarke, Killian and Korhan Kocak. 2020. "Launching Revolution: Social Media and the Egyptian Uprising's First Movers." *British Journal of Political Science* 50, 3: 1025–45.

Coatsworth, John H. 1988. "Patterns of Rural Rebellion in Latin America: Mexico in Comparative Perspective." In Friedrich Katz, ed., *Riot, Rebellion, and Revolution: Rural Social Conflict in Mexico*. Princeton, NJ: Princeton University Press, 21–63.

Cohen, Lenard J. 2001. *Serpent in the Bosom: The Rise and Fall of Slobodan Milošević*. Boulder, CO: Westview Press.

Colby, Frank Moore, ed. 1908. *The New International Yearbook: A Compendium of the World's Progress for the Year 1907*. New York: Dodd, Mead and Company.

Collier, Paul. 1999. "On the Economic Consequences of Civil War." *Oxford Economic Papers* 51, 1: 168–83.

Collier, Paul. 2003. *Breaking the Conflict Trap: Civil War and Development Policy*. Washington, DC: World Bank Publications.

Collier, Paul and Anke Hoeffler. 2004. "Greed and Grievance in Civil War." *Oxford Economic Papers* 56, 4: 563–95.

Collier, Paul and Anke Hoeffler. 2005. "Coup Traps: Why does Africa Have So Many Coups d'État?" Unpublished paper, Centre for the Study of African Economies, Department of Economics, University of Oxford (available at https://ora.ox.ac.uk/objects/uuid:49097086-8505-4eb2-8174-314ce1aa3ebb).

Coppedge, Michael, John Gerring, Staffan I. Lindberg, Svend-Erik Skaaning, Jan Teorell, David Altman, Michael Bernhard et al. 2016. "V-Dem [Country-Year/Country-Date] Dataset v6." Varieties of Democracy (V-Dem) Project, at https://www.v-dem.net/en/.

Coppedge, Michael, John Gerring, Carl Henrik Knutsen, Staffan I. Lindberg, Svend-Erik Skaaning, Jan Teorell, David Altman et al. 2018. "V-Dem Codebook v8." Varieties of Democracy (V-Dem) Project.

Cornelius, Wayne A. 1975. *Politics and the Migrant Poor in Mexico City*. Stanford, CA: Stanford University Press.

Courvoisier, Delphine S., Christophe Combescure, Thomas Agoritsas, Angèle Gayet-Ageron, and Thomas V Perneger. 2011. "Performance of Logistic Regression Modeling: Beyond the Number of Events per Variable, the Role of Data Structure." *Journal of Clinical Epidemiology* 64: 993–1000.

Coveney, Joseph. 2008. "FIRTHLOGIT: Stata Module to Calculate Bias Reduction in Logistic Regression. Statistical Software Components, Boston College Department of Economics.

Cox, Wendell. 2017. *World Urban Areas* (13th edition). St. Louis, MO: Demographia.

Creveld, Martin van, ed. 1996. *The Encyclopedia of Revolutions and Revolutionaries: From Anarchism to Zhou Enlai*. New York: Facts on File.

Cukierman, Alex, Sebastian Edwards, and Guido Tabellini. 1992. "Seigniorage and Political Instability." *American Economic Review* 82, 3: 537–55.

Cunningham, David E., Kristian Skrede Gleditsch, and Idean Salehyan. 2013. "Non-State Actors in Civil Wars: A New Dataset." *Conflict Management and Peace Science* 30, 5: 516–53.

Cunningham, Kathleen Gallagher and Emily Beaulieu. 2010. "Dissent, Repression, and Inconsistency." In Erica Chenoweth and Adria Lawrence, eds, *Rethinking Violence: States and Non-State Actors in Conflict*. Cambridge, MA: MIT Press, 173–95.

Cybriwsky, Roman. 2014. "Kyiv's Maidan: From Duma Square to Sacred Space." *Eurasian Geography and Economics* 55, 3: 270–85.

Dahl, Robert A. 1971. *Polyarchy: Participation and Opposition*. New Haven, CT: Yale University Press.

Dalacoura, Katerina. 2012. "The 2011 Uprisings in the Arab Middle East: Political Change and Geopolitical Implications." *International Affairs* 88: 63–79.

Daragahi, Borzou. 2013. "Egyptians Become Victims of Soaring Crime Rate." *The Financial Times*, May 1, at https://www.ft.com/content/7ffac226-adab-11e2-a2c7-00144feabdc0.

Darden, Keith. 2008. "The Integrity of Corrupt States: Graft as an Informal State Institution." *Politics & Society* 36, 1: 35–59.

Daugherty, Leo J., III 1995. "The Bear and the Scimitar: Soviet Central Asians and the War in Afghanistan, 1979–1989." *The Journal of Slavic Military Studies* 8, 1: 73–96.

Davenport, Christian. 2007. "State Repression and Political Order." *Annual Review of Political Science* 10: 1–23.

David, Roman and Ian Holliday. 2012. "International Sanctions or International Justice? Shaping Political Development in Myanmar." *Australian Journal of International Affairs* 66, 2: 121–38.
Davidson, Donald. 1980. *Essays on Actions and Events*. New York: Oxford University Press.
Davies, James C. 1962. "Toward a Theory of Revolution." *American Sociological Review* 27, 1: 5–19.
Davies, R. W. 1990. "Introduction: From Tsarism to NEP." In R. W. Davies, ed., *From Tsarism to the New Economic Policy: Continuity and Change in the Economy of the USSR*. London: Macmillan, 1–26.
Davison, Neil. 2009. *"Non-Lethal" Weapons*. New York: Palgrave Macmillan.
De Waal, Thomas. 2013. "So Long, Saakashvili: The Presidency That Lived by Spin—and Died by It." *Foreign Affairs* (October), at http://georgica.tsu.edu.ge/files/01-Politics/De%20Waal-2013.pdf.
Deaton, Clifford. 2015. "The Revolution Will Not Be Occupied: Theorizing Urban Revolutionary Movements in Tehran, Prague, and Paris." *Territory, Politics, Governance* 3, 2: 205–26.
Debray, Régis. 1968. *Revolution in the Revolution?* London: Penguin.
Decalo, Samuel. 1976. *Coups and Army Rule in Africa: Studies in Military Style*. New Haven, CT: Yale University Press.
Deininger, Klaus, Denys Nizalov, and Sudhir K. Singh. 2013. "Are Mega-Farms the Future of Global Agriculture? Exploring the Farm Size-Productivity Relationship for Large Commercial Farms in Ukraine." Kyiv School of Economics and Kyiv Economics Institute discussion paper (available at http://repec.kse.org.ua/pdf/KSE_dp49.pdf).
Deininger, Klaus, and Pedro Olinto. 1999. "Asset Distribution, Inequality, and Growth." World Bank Policy Research Working Paper No. 2375.
Della Porta, Donatella. 2016. *Where Did the Revolution Go? Contentious Politics and the Quality of Democracy*. Cambridge: Cambridge University Press.
Della Porta, Donatella and Herbert Reiter. 1998. "Introduction: The Policing of Protest in Western Democracies." In Donatella Della Porter and Herbert Reiter, eds, *Policing Protest: The Control of Mass Demonstrations in Western Democracies*. Minneapolis: University of Minnesota Press, 1–32.
Demirjian, Karoun. 2014. "Meanwhile in Russia, Putin Passes Law against Protests." *The Washington Post*, July 22, at https://www.washingtonpost.com/news/worldviews/wp/2014/07/22/meanwhile-in-russia-putin-passes-law-against-protests/?utm_term=.75710fecec53.
DeNardo, James. 1985. *Power in Numbers: The Political Strategy of Protest and Rebellion*. Princeton, NJ: Princeton University Press.
Denyer, Simon. 2018. "Beijing Bets on Facial Recognition in a Big Drive for Total Surveillance." *The Washington Post*, January 7, at https://www.washingtonpost.com/news/world/wp/2018/01/07/feature/in-china-facial-recognition-is-sharp-end-of-a-drive-for-total-surveillance/?utm_term=.8d124b251ccd.
Desai, Raj and Harry Eckstein. 1990. "Insurgency: The Transformation of Peasant Rebellion." *World Politics* 42, 4: 441–65.
Dikötter, Frank. 1997. "Crime and Punishment in Post-Liberation China: The Prisoners of a Beijing Gaol in the 1950s." *The China Quarterly* 149 (March): 147–59.
Dimitrov, Nikola D. 2007. "Streets of Anger: Opposition Protests in Belgrade and Sofia during the Winter Months of 1996–1997." In Matthias Reiss, ed., *The Street as Stage: Protest Marches and Public Rallies since the Nineteenth Century*. Oxford: Oxford University Press, 231–53.

Diuk, Nadia. 2006. "The Triumph of Civil Society." In Anders Åslund and Michael McFaul, eds, *Revolution in Orange: The Origins of Ukraine's Democratic Breakthrough*. Washington, DC: Carnegie Endowment for International Peace: 69–84.

Dix, Robert H. 1983. "The Varieties of Revolution." *Comparative Politics* 15, 3: 281–94.

Dix, Robert H. 1984. "Why Revolutions Succeed and Fail." *Polity* 16, 3: 423–46.

Djuve, Vilde Lunnan, Carl Henrik Knutsen, and Tore Wig. 2020. "Patterns of Regime Breakdown since the French Revolution." *Comparative Political Studies* 53, 6: 923–58.

Dobbs, Richard, Sven Smit, Jaana Remes, James Manyika, Charles Roxburgh, and Alejandro Restrepo. 2011. "Urban World: Mapping the Economic Power of Cities." McKinsey Global Institute report, March 1, at https://www.mckinsey.com/featured-insights/urbanization/urban-world-mapping-the-economic-power-of-cities.

Doffman, Zak. 2019. "Telegram Bug 'Exploited' by Chinese Agencies, Hong Kong Activists Claim." *Forbes*, August 25, at https://www.forbes.com/sites/zakdoffman/2019/08/25/chinese-agencies-crack-telegram-a-timely-warning-for-end-to-end-encryption/#204352af6342.

Doherty, David and Peter Schraeder. 2014. "Patterns of Participation in a Revolution and its Aftermath." Working paper (available at http://orion.luc.edu/~ddoherty/documents/Tunisia_Participation.pdf).

Dorell, Oren. 2013. "Egypt's Ailing Economy Is at the Heart of the Unrest." *USA Today*, July 2, at https://www.usatoday.com/story/news/world/2013/07/02/egypt-morsi-economy/2482971/.

Douglas, William A. 1963. "Korean Students and Politics." *Asian Survey* 3, 12: 594–95.

Douglass, Mike. 2008. "Civil Society for Itself and in the Public Sphere: Comparative Research on Globalization, Cities and Civic Space in Pacific Asia." In Mike Douglass, K. C. Ho, and Giok Ling Ooi, eds, *Globalization, the City and Civil Society in Pacific Asia: The Social Production of Civic Spaces*. London: Routledge, 27–49.

Downes, Alexander B. and Jonathan Monten. 2013. "Forced to Be Free: Why Foreign-Imposed Regime Change Rarely Leads to Democratization." *International Security* 37, 4: 90–131.

Dunn, John. 1972. *Modern Revolutions*. Cambridge: Cambridge University Press.

Dunn, John. 2008. "Understanding Revolution." In John Foran, David Lane, and Andreja Zivcovic, eds, *Revolution in the Making of the Modern World: Social Identities, Globalization, and Modernity*. New York: Routledge, 27–26.

Dyczok, Marta. 2014. "Breaking Through the Information Blockade: Election and Revolution in Ukraine in 2004." In Bohdan Harasymiv (with Oleh S. Ilnytzskyj), ed., *Aspects of the Orange Revolution II: Information and Manipulation Strategies in the 2004 Ukrainian Presidential Elections*. Stuttgart: Ibidem-Verlag, 77–106.

Earl, Jennifer. 2004. "Controlling Protest: New Directions for Research on the Social Control of Protest." In Daniel J. Myers and Daniel M. Cress, eds, *Authority in Contention*. Amsterdam: Elsevier, 55–83.

Eck, Kristine. 2009. "From Armed Conflict to War: Ethnic Mobilization and Conflict Intensification." *International Studies Quarterly* 53, 2: 369–88.

Eckstein, Susan. 1982. "The Impact of Revolution on Social Welfare in Latin America." *Theory and Society* 11, 1: 43–94.

Edelman, Robert. 2016. *Proletarian Peasants: The Revolution of 1905 in Russia's Southwest*. Ithaca, NY: Cornell University Press.

Edland, Anne and Ola Svenson. 1993. "Judgment and Decision Making under Time Pressure: Studies and Findings." In Ola Svenson and A. John Maule, eds, *Time Pressure and Stress in Human Judgment and Decision Making*. New York: Springer, 7–40.

Einsidel, Sebastian von. 2014. "Major Recent Trends in Violent Conflict." United Nations University Centre for Policy Research Occasional Paper, Tokyo, November 2014.

Eisenstadt, Shmuel Noah. 1963. *The Political Systems of Empires*. New York: The Free Press.

Eisenstein, Elizabeth I. 1986. "On Revolution and the Printed Word." In Roy Porter and Mikulas Teich, eds, *Revolution in History*. Cambridge: Cambridge University Press, 186–205.

Eisinger, Peter K. 1973. "The Conditions of Protest Behavior in American Cities." *American Political Science Review* 67, 1: 11–28.

El Chazli, Youssef, 2016. "A Geography of Revolt in Alexandria, Egypt's Second Capital." *Metropolitics*, February 23, at http://www.metropolitiques.eu/A-Geography-of-Revolt-in.html?lang=fr.

El Chazli, Youssef. 2017. "Four Scenes of the Egyptian Revolution in Alexandria: A Microhistory of January 25." *Mada*, January 25, at https://www.madamasr.com/en/2017/01/25/feature/politics/four-scenes-of-the-egyptian-revolution-in-alexandria-a-microhistory-of-january-25/.

El-Ghobashy, Mona. 2012. "The Praxis of the Egyptian Revolution." In Jeannie Sowers and Chris Toensing, eds, *The Journey to Tahrir: Revolution, Protest, and Social Change in Egypt*. London: Verso, 21–40.

El-Hamalawy, Hossam. 2001. "The 1977 Bread Intifada." MA thesis, American University in Cairo (excerpts available at https://www.scribd.com/doc/12893045/1977-Bread-Uprising).

Elias, Norbert. 1994. *The Civilizing Process: The History of Manners and State Formation and Civilization* (translated by Edmund Jephcott). Oxford: Blackwell.

El-Kouny, Nada. 2012. "Farmers' Rights Advocate Challenges Egypt's Post-Mubarak Agriculture Policy," Ahramonline, August 27, at http://english.ahram.org.eg/NewsContent/1/64/51319/Egypt/Politics-/Farmers-rights-advocate-challenges-Egypts-postMuba.aspx.

Ellsworth, Brian. 2014. "Jailed Opposition Leader Calls for More Venezuela Protests." *Reuters*, March 3, at https://www.reuters.com/article/us-venezuela-protests/jailed-opposition-leader-calls-for-more-venezuela-protests-idUSBREA221M220140303.

Elshahed, Mohamed. 2011. "Tahrir Square: Social Media, Public Space." *Places* (February), at https://placesjournal.org/article/tahrir-square-social-media-public-space/.

Eltahawy, Mona. 2018. "Seven Years after the 'Arab Spring,' Tunisia is Leading Another Revolution—on Women's Rights." *The Washington Post*, January 31, at https://www.washingtonpost.com/news/global-opinions/wp/2018/01/31/seven-years-after-the-arab-spring-tunisia-is-leading-another-revolution-on-womens-rights/?utm_term=.d880bee2f122.

Eltantawy, Nahed and Julie B. Wiest. 2011. "Social Media in the Egyptian Revolution: Reconsidering Resource Mobilization Theory." *International Journal of Communication* 5: 1207–24.

Engels, Friedrich. 1956. *The Peasant War in Germany*. Moscow: Foreign Languages Publishing House.

Epping-Jäger, Cornelia. 2011. "Hitler's Voice: The Loudspeaker under National Socialism." *Intermédialités* 17: 83–104.

Erickson, Lennart and Dietrich Vollrath. 2004. "Dimensions of Land Inequality and Economic Development." IMF Working Paper WP/04/158 (available at https://www.imf.org/external/pubs/ft/wp/2004/wp04158.pdf).

Ersoy, Can 2015. "A Place for Revolution: Urban Space in the Arab Spring." In Saïd Amir Arjomand, ed., *The Arab Revolution of 2011: A Comparative Perspective*. Albany, NY: SUNY Press, 113–31.

Esping-Andersen, Gosta. 1990. *The Three Worlds of Welfare Capitalism*. Princeton, NJ: Princeton University Press.

Farhi, Farideh. 1990. *States and Urban-Based Revolutions: Iran and Nicaragua*. Urbana, IL: University of Illinois Press.

FAO (Food and Agriculture Organization of the United Nations). 1955. *Report on the 1950 World Census of Agriculture. Census Results by Countries*. Rome: FAO.

FAO (Food and Agriculture Organization of the United Nations). 1971. *Report on the 1960 World Census of Agriculture: Analysis and International Comparison of Census Results*. Rome: FAO.

FAO (Food and Agriculture Organization of the United Nations). 1981. *1970 World Census of Agriculture, Analysis and International Comparison of Results*. Rome: FAO.

Fearon, James D. 2003. "Ethnic and Cultural Diversity by Country." *Journal of Economic Growth* 8, 2: 195–222.

Fearon, James D. and David D. Laitin. 2003. "Ethnicity, Insurgency, and Civil War." *American Political Science Review* 97, 1: 75–90.

Feenstra, Robert C., Robert Inklaar, and Marcel P. Timmer. 2015. "The Next Generation of the Penn World Table." *American Economic Review* 105, 10: 3150–82.

Feierabend, Ivo K., Rosalind L. Feierabend, and Ted Robert Gurr, eds. 1972. *Anger, Violence, and Politics: Theories and Research*. Englewood Cliffs, NJ: Prentice-Hall.

Feigenbaum, Anna. 2017a. "Tear Gas: 100 Years in the Making." *The Atlantic*, August 16, at https://www.theatlantic.com/international/archive/2014/08/100-years-of-tear-gas/378632/.

Feigenbaum, Anna. 2017b. *Tear Gas: From the Battlefields of World War I to the Streets of Today*. London: Verso Books.

Feldman, Allen. 1991. *Formations of Violence: The Narrative of the Body and Political Terror in Northern Ireland*. Chicago: University of Chicago Press.

Figes, Orlando. 1996. *A People's Tragedy: The Russian Revolution, 1891–1924*. New York: Penguin.

Figes, Orlando. 2014. *Revolutionary Russia, 1891–1991: A History*. New York: Henry Holt and Company.

Filiu, Jean-Pierre. 2011. *The Arab Revolution: Ten Lessons from the Democratic Uprising*. Oxford: Oxford University Press.

Fink, Christina. 2009. "The Moment of the Monks: Burma, 2007." In Adam Roberts and Timothy Garton Ash, eds, *Civil Resistance and Power Politics: The Experience of Non-Violent Action from Gandhi to the Present*. Oxford: Oxford University Press, 354–70.

Firth, David. 1993. "Bias Reduction of Maximum Likelihood Estimates." *Biometrika* 80, 1: 27–38.

Fischer, Claude S. 1982. *To Dwell Among Friends: Personal Networks in Town and City*. Chicago: University of Chicago Press.

Fishman, Robert M. 2011. "Democratic Practice after the Revolution: The Case of Portugal and Beyond," *Politics & Society* 39, 2: 233–67.

Florea, Adrian. 2012. "Where Do We Go from Here? Conceptual, Theoretical, and Methodological Gaps in the Large-N Civil War Research Program." *International Studies Review* 14, 1: 78–98.

Fonseca, Jaime R. S. 2008. "The Application of Mixture Modeling and Information Criteria for Discovering Patterns of Coronary Heart Disease." *Journal of Applied Quantitative Methods* 3, 4: 292–303.

Foran, John. 2005. *Taking Power: On the Origins of Third World Revolutions.* Cambridge: Cambridge University Press.

Foran, John and Jeff Goodwin. 1993. "Revolutionary Outcomes in Iran and Nicaragua: Coalition Fragmentation, War, and the Limits of Social Transformation." *Theory and Society* 22, 2: 209–47.

Ford, Matt. 2014. "A Dictator's Guide to Urban Design." *The Atlantic*, February 21, at https://www.theatlantic.com/international/archive/2014/02/a-dictators-guide-to-urban-design/283953/.

Fortna, Virginia Page and Reyko Huang. 2012. "Democratization after Civil War: A Brush-Clearing Exercise." *International Studies Quarterly* 56, 4: 801–8.

Fouquin, Michel and Jules Hugot. 2016. "Two Centuries of Bilateral Trade and Gravity Data: 1827–2014." CEPII Working Paper 2016-14, Centre d'études prospectives et d'informations internationales (CEPII).

Fournier, Anna. 2006. "Ukraine's Orange Revolution: Beyond Soviet Citizenship?" Paper presented at the Second Annual Danyliw Research Seminar in Contemporary Ukrainian Studies, Chair of Ukrainian Studies, University of Ottawa.

Foy, Michael and Brian Barton. 2011. *The Easter Rising.* Stroud: The History Press.

Francisco, Ronald A. 2004. "After the Massacre: Mobilization in the Wake of Harsh Repression," *Mobilization* 9: 107–26.

Frankema, Ewout. 2010. "The Colonial Roots of Land Inequality: Geography, Factor Endowments, or Institutions?" *The Economic History Review* 63, 2: 418–51.

Franklin, James C. 2015. "Persistent Challengers: Repression, Concessions, Challenger Strength, and Commitment in Latin America," *Mobilization* 20, 1: 61–80.

Freedom House. 2016. *Freedom in the World*, at https://freedomhouse.org/report/freedom-world/2016/niger.

French, David. 2015. *Fighting EOKA: The British Counter-Insurgency Campaign on Cyprus, 1955–1959.* Oxford: Oxford University Press.

Frère, Marie-Soleil and Pierre Englebert. 2015. "Briefing: Burkina Faso—the Fall of Blaise Compaoré." *African Affairs* 114, 455: 295–307.

Friend, Theodore. 2003. *Indonesian Destinies.* Cambridge, MA: Harvard University Press.

Fukuyama, Francis. 1992. *The End of History and the Last Man.* New York: The Free Press.

Fukuyama, Francis and Michael McFaul. 2008. "Should Democracy Be Promoted or Demoted?" *Washington Quarterly* 31, 1: 23–45.

Fung, Edmund S. K. 1980. *The Military Dimension of the Chinese Revolution: The New Army and its Role in the Revolution of 1911.* Vancouver: University of British Columbia Press.

Future Market Insights. 2019. "Riot Control Vehicle Market 2018–2028: Non-Lethal Crowd Control Systems to See Higher Demand," at https://www.futuremarketinsights.com/reports/riot-control-vehicle-market.

Gabowitsch, Mischa. 2017. *Protest in Putin's Russia.* Malden, MA: Polity Press.

Gamson, William A. 1975. *The Strategy of Social Protest.* Homewood, IL: Dorsey Press.

Gandhi, Jennifer and Adam Przeworski. 2006. "Cooperation, Cooptation, and Rebellion under Dictatorship." *Economics and Politics* 18, 1: 1–26.

Garboś, Marcel Radosław. 2018. "Revolution and the Defence of Civilization: Polish Visions of Nationhood, Property and Territory in Right-Bank Ukraine (1917–22)." *Slavonic & East European Review* 96, 3: 469–506.

Garfield, Bob. 2004. "Revolution, Inc." National Public Radio, December 3, at http://www.wnyc.org/story/129044-revolution-inc?tab=transcript.

Garriga, Ana Carolina. 2016. "Human Rights Regimes, Reputation, and Foreign Direct Investment." *International Studies Quarterly* 60, 1: 160–72.

Garton Ash, Timothy. 1990. *The Magic Lantern: The Revolution of '89 Witnessed in Warsaw, Budapest, Berlin and Prague*. New York: Vintage.

Geddes, Barbara, Joseph Wright, and Erica Frantz. 2014. "Autocratic Breakdown and Regime Transitions: A New Data Set." *Perspectives on Politics* 12, 2: 313–31.

Gehl, Jan. 2011. *Life between Buildings: Using Public Space*. Washington, DC: Island Press.

Gersovitz, Mark and Norma Kriger. 2013. "What Is a Civil War? A Critical Review of Its Definition and (Econometric) Consequences." The World Bank, at https://openknowledge.worldbank.org/bitstream/handle/10986/21428/wbro_28_2_159.pdf;sequence=1.

Ghodsee, Kristen. 2015. *The Left Side of History: World War II and the Unfulfilled Promise of Communism*. Durham, NC: Duke University Press.

Ghonim, Wael. 2012. *Revolution 2.0: The Power of the People Is Greater Than the People in Power*. Boston, MA: Houghton Mifflin Harcourt.

Giddens, Anthony. 1987. *The Nation-State and Violence*, vol. 2. Berkeley, CA: University of California Press.

Giddens, Anthony. 1990. *The Consequences of Modernity*. Cambridge: Polity Press.

Gill, Graeme 1979. *Peasants and Government in the Russian Revolution*. London: London School of Economics and Political Science.

Giugni, Marco. 1999. "How Social Movements Matter: Past Research, Present Problems, Future Developments." In Marco Giugni, Doug McAdam, and Charles Tilly, eds, *How Social Movements Matter*. Minneapolis: University of Minnesota Press, xiii–xxxiii.

Givan, Rebecca Kolins, Kenneth M. Roberts, and Sarah A. Soule, eds. 2010. *The Diffusion of Social Movements: Actors, Mechanisms, and Political Effects*. Cambridge: Cambridge University Press.

Gladwell, Malcolm. 2010. "Small Change: Why the Revolution Will Not Be Tweeted," *The New Yorker*, October 4.

Gleditsch, Kristian Skrede. 2007. "Transnational Dimensions of Civil War." *Journal of Peace Research* 44, 3: 293–309.

Gleditsch, N. P., P. Wallensteen, M. Eriksson, M. Sollenberg, and H. Strand. 2002. "Armed Conflict 1946–2001: A New Dataset," *Journal of Peace Research* 39: 615–37.

Godec, Robert F. 2009. "Troubled Tunisia: What Should We Do?" In "U.S. Embassy Cables: Tunisia—A U.S. Foreign Policy Conundrum," *The Guardian*, https://www.theguardian.com/world/us-embassy-cables-documents/217138.

Goemans, Henk E., Kristian Skrede Gleditsch, and Giacomo Chiozza. 2009. "Introducing Archigos: A Dataset of Political Leaders." *Journal of Peace Research* 46, 2: 269–83.

Goldstein, Joshua S. 2011. *Winning the War on War: The Decline of Armed Conflict Worldwide*. New York: Penguin.

Goldstone, Jack A. 1980. "Theories of Revolution: The Third Generation." *World Politics* 32, 3: 425–53.

Goldstone, Jack A. 1991. *Revolution and Rebellion in the Early Modern World*. Berkeley, CA: University of California Press.

Goldstone, Jack A. 1994. "Is Revolution Individually Rational?" *Rationality and Society* 6: 139–66.

Goldstone, Jack A. 1998a. "Social Movements or Revolutions? On the Evolution and Outcomes of Collective Action." In Marco Giugni, Doug McAdam, and Charles Tilly, eds, *From Contention to Democracy*. Lanham, MD: Rowman & Littlefield, 125–45.

Goldstone, Jack A. 1998b. *The Encyclopedia of Political Revolutions*. Washington, DC: Congressional Quarterly.

Goldstone, Jack A. 2001. "Toward a Fourth Generation of Revolutionary Theory." *Annual Review of Political Science* 4: 139–87.

Goldstone, Jack A. 2002. "Population and Security: How Demographic Change Can Lead to Violent Conflict." *Journal of International Affairs* 56, 1: 3–21.

Goldstone, Jack A. 2003. "Comparative Historical Analysis and Knowledge Accumulation in the Study of Revolutions." In James Mahoney and Dietrich Rueschemeyer, eds, *Comparative Historical Analysis in the Social Sciences*. Cambridge: Cambridge University Press, 41–90.

Goldstone, Jack A. 2013. *Revolutions: A Very Short Introduction*. Oxford: Oxford University Press.

Goldstone, Jack A., Robert H. Bates, David L. Epstein, Ted Robert Gurr, Michael B. Lustik, Monty G. Marshall, Jay Ulfelder, and Mark Woodward 2010. "A Global Model for Forecasting Political Instability." *American Journal of Political Science* 54, 1: 190–208.

Goldstone, Jack A. and Charles Tilly. 2001. "Threat (and Opportunity): Popular Action and State Response in the Dynamics of Contentious Action." In Ronald R. Aminzade, Jack A. Goldstone, Douglas McAdam, Elizabeth J. Perry, William H. Sewell, Sidney Tarrow, and Charles Tilly, eds, *Silence and Voice in the Study of Contentious Politics*. Cambridge: Cambridge University Press, 179–94.

Golovanov, V. 1989. "Garantii dlia 'neformalov,'" *Literaturnaia gazeta*, 13 September: 12.

Goodwin, Jeff. 2001. *No Other Way Out: States and Revolutionary Movements, 1945–1991*. Cambridge: Cambridge University Press.

Goodwin, Jeff. 2003. "The Renewal of Socialism and the Decline of Revolution." In John Foran, ed., *The Future of Revolutions: Rethinking Radical Change in the Era of Globalization*. London: ZED, 59–72.

Gordy, Eric D. 2000. "Serbia's Bulldozer Revolution: Conditions and Prospects." *Southeast European Politics*, 1, 2: 78–89.

Gould, Roger V. 1991. "Multiple Networks and Mobilization in the Paris Commune, 1871." *American Sociological Review* 56, 6: 716–29.

Gould, Roger V. 1995. *Insurgent Identities: Class, Community, and Protest in Paris from 1848 to the Commune*. Chicago: University of Chicago Press.

Granovetter, Mark S. 1973. "The Strength of Weak Ties." *American Journal of Sociology* 78, 6: 1360–80.

Graziano, Teresa. 2012. "The Tunisian Diaspora: Between 'Digital Riots' and Web Activism." *Social Science Information* 51, 4: 534–50.

Green, Donald P., Soo Yeon Kim, and David H. Yoon. 2001. "Dirty Pool." *International Organization* 55, 2: 441–68.

Greene, Kenneth F. 2007. *Why Dominant Parties Lose: Mexico's Democratization in Comparative Perspective*. Cambridge: Cambridge University Press.

Greene, William H. 2012. *Econometric Analysis* (7th edition). Upper Saddle River, NJ: Prentice Hall.

Greitens, Sheena Chestnut. 2019. "'Surveillance with Chinese Characteristics:' The Development and Global Export of Chinese Policing Technology." Unpublished paper.

Grewal, Sharan. 2016. "A Quiet Revolution: The Tunisian Military after Ben Ali." Carnegie Endowment for International Peace, at https://carnegieendowment.org/2016/02/24/quiet-revolution-tunisian-military-after-ben-ali-pub-62780.

Grewal, Sharan. 2019. "Military Defection during Localized Protests: The Case of Tataouine." *International Studies Quarterly* 63, 2: 259–69.

Grieb, Kenneth J. 1976. "The Guatemalan Military and the Revolution of 1944." *The Americas* 32, 4: 524–43.

Gruzd, Anatoliy and Ksenia Tsyganova. 2015. "Information Wars and Online Activism during the 2013/2014 Crisis in Ukraine: Examining the Social Structures of Pro- and Anti-Maidan Groups." *Policy & Internet* 7, 2: 121–58.

Guevara, Ernesto "Che." 1961. "Guerrilla Warfare" (available at https://mltheory.files.wordpress.com/2017/06/che_guevara_guerrilla_warfare.pdf).

Gumede, William. 2017. "The Democracy Deficit of Africa's Liberation Movements Turned Governments," *Politikon* 44, 1: 27–48.

Gunitsky, Seva. 2015. "Corrupting the Cyber-Commons: Social Media as a Tool of Autocratic Stability." *Perspectives on Politics* 13, 1: 42–54.

Gunitsky, Seva. 2017. *Aftershocks: Great Powers and Domestic Reforms in the Twentieth Century*. Princeton, NJ: Princeton University Press.

Gunning, Jeroen and Ilan Zvi Baron. 2014. *Why Occupy a Square? People, Protests and Movements in the Egyptian Revolution*. Oxford: Oxford University Press.

Gupta, Dipak K., Harinder Singh, Tom Sprague. 1993. "Government Coercion of Dissidents: Deterrence or Provocation?" *Journal of Conflict Resolution* 37, 2: 301–39.

Gurr, Ted Robert. 1970. *Why Men Rebel*. Princeton, NJ: Princeton University Press.

Gurses, Mehmet and T. David Mason. 2008. "Democracy out of Anarchy: The Prospects for Post–Civil-War Democracy." *Social Science Quarterly* 89, 2: 315–36.

Gyimah-Brempong, K. and S. Camacho. 1998. "Political Instability, Human Capital, and Economic Growth in Latin America." *Journal of Developing Areas* 32: 449–66.

Haar, Rohini J., Vincent Iacopino, Nikhil Ranadive, Madhavi Dandu, and Sheri D. Weiser. 2017. "Death, Injury, and Disability from Kinetic Impact Projectiles in Crowd-Control Settings: A Systematic Review." *BMJ Open* 7, 12: 1–9.

Haber, Stephen and Victor Menaldo. 2011. "Do Natural Resources Fuel Authoritarianism? A Reappraisal of the Resource Curse." *American Political Science Review* 105, 1: 1–26.

Hafez, Sherine. 2012. "No Longer a Bargain: Women, Masculinity, and the Egyptian Uprising." *American Ethnologist* 39, 1: 37–42.

Hafner-Burton, Emilie, and Kiyoteru Tsutsui. 2007. "Justice Lost! The Failure of International Human Rights Law to Matter Where Needed Most." *Journal of Peace Research* 44, 4: 407–25.

Hafner-Burton, Emilie, Kiyoteru Tsutsui, and John W. Meyer. 2008. "International Human Rights Law and the Politics of Legitimation: Repressive States and Human Rights Treaties." *International Sociology* 23, 1: 115–41.

Haggard, Stephan and Robert R. Kaufman. 2012. "Inequality and Regime Change: Democratic Transitions and the Stability of Democratic Rule." *American Political Science Review* 106, 3: 495–516.

Hagopian, Mark. 1974. *The Phenomenon of Revolution*. New York: Dodd and Mead.

Hall, Thomas. 1997. *Planning Europe's Capital Cities: Aspects of Nineteenth-Century Urban Development*. London: E. & F. N. Spon.

Hamacher, Adriana. 2020. "Elon Musk Offers Help to Belarus. Can His Starlink Satellites Route Around Censorship?" *Decrypt*, August 13, at https://decrypt.co/38659/elon-musk-offers-help-to-belarus-can-his-starlink-satellites-route-around-censorship.

Hamm, Michael F. 1993. *Kiev: A Portrait, 1800–1917*. Princeton, NJ: Princeton University Press.

Hammond, John L. 1998. *Fighting to Learn: Popular Education and Guerrilla War in El Savador*. New Brunswick, NJ: Rutgers University Press.

Hansen, Arve. 2017. "Public Space in the Soviet City: A Spatial Perspective on Mass Protests in Minsk." *Nordlit* 39: 33–57.

Hanson, Jonathan K. and Sigman Rachel. 2013. "Leviathan's Latent Dimensions: Measuring State Capacity for Comparative Political Research." Paper presented at the World Bank Political Economy Brown Bag Lunch Series, Washington, DC.

Hany, Sara. 2015. "It Is Just . . . the Beginning." In Asaad Al-Saleh, ed., *Voices of the Arab Spring*. New York: Columbia University Press, 67–70.

Harison, Casey. 2000. "The Rise and Decline of a Revolutionary Space: Paris' Place de Grève and the Stonemasons of Creuse, 1750–1900." *Journal of Social History* 34, 2: 403–36.

Harris, Richard Legé. 2000. *Death of a Revolutionary: Che Guevara's Last Mission*. New York: W.W. Norton & Company.

Hart, Daniel, Robert Atkins, and James Youniss. 2005. "Knowledge, Youth Bulges, and Rebellion." *Psychological Science* 16, 8: 661–62.

Hart, Gillian. 1993. "Comment on 'Losers and Winners in Economic Growth.'" *The World Bank Economic Review* 7, Supplement 1: 299–303.

Harvey, David. 1990. *The Condition of Post-Modernity*. London: Blackwell.

Harvey, David. 2003. *Paris, Capital of Modernity*. New York: Routledge.

Harvey, David. 2010. *Social Justice and the City*. Athens, GA: University of Georgia Press.

Harvey, David. 2013. *Rebel Cities: From the Right to the City to Urban Revolutions*. London: Verso.

Harwood, Richard. 1983. "Guerilla War is Overrated." *The Washington Post*, July 24, at https://www.washingtonpost.com/archive/opinions/1983/07/24/guerilla-war-is-overrated/99bc1499-018f-439c-a127-3064fc933cd5/?utm_term=.87b008e52b18.

Hasebe, Takuya. 2013. "Copula-Based Maximum-Likelihood Estimation of Sample-Selection Models." *The Stata Journal* 13, 3: 547–73.

Hasegawa, Tsuyoshi. 1981. *The February Revolution: Petrograd, 1917*. Seattle: University of Washington Press.

Hasegawa, Tsuyoshi. 2017. *Crime and Punishment in the Russian Revolution: Mob Justice and Police in Petrograd*. Cambridge, MA: Harvard University Press.

Hassanpour, Navid. 2014. "Media Disruption and Revolutionary Unrest: Evidence from Mubarak's Quasi-Experiment." *Political Communication* 31, 1: 1–24.

Hausman, Jerry A. and Daniel L. McFadden. 1984. "Specification Tests for the Multinomial Logit Model." *Econometrica* 52, 5: 1219–40.

Heckman, James J. 1979. "Sample Selection Bias as a Specification Error." *Econometrica* 47: 153–61.

Heckman, J. J., Ichimura, H., and Todd, P. E. 1997. "Matching as an Econometric Evaluation Estimator: Evidence from Evaluating a Job Training Programme." *Review of Economic Studies* 64: 605–54.

Heger, Lindsay and Idean Salehyan. 2007. "Ruthless Rulers: Coalition Size and the Severity of Civil Conflict." *International Studies Quarterly* 51, 2: 385–403.

Hegre, Havard and Nicholas Sambanis. 2006. "Sensitivity Analysis of the Empirical Literature on Civil War Onset." *Journal of Conflict Resolution* 50, 4: 508–35.

Heinze, Georg, and Michael Schemper. 2002. "A Solution to the Problem of Separation in Logistic Regression." *Statistics in Medicine* 21, 16: 2409–19.

Helvey, Robert L. 1984. *On Strategic Nonviolent Conflict: Thinking About the Fundamentals.* Boston, MA: Albert Einstein Institute.

Henisz, W. J. 2002. "The Institutional Environment for Infrastructure Investment." *Industrial and Corporate Change* 11, 2: 355–89.

Herbert, Steve. 1997. *Policing Space: Territoriality and the Los Angeles Police Department.* Minneapolis: University of Minnesota Press.

Hershkovitz, Linda. 1993. "Tiananmen Square and the Politics of Place." *Political Geography* 12, 5: 395–420.

Herzfeld, Michael. 2016. *Siege of the Spirits: Community and Polity in Bangkok.* Chicago: University of Chicago Press.

Heston, Alan, Robert Summers, and Bettina Aten. 2009. Penn World Table Version 6.3, Center for International Comparisons of Production, Income and Prices at the University of Pennsylvania.

Heywood, Anthony J. 2005. "Socialists, Liberals and the Union of Unions in Kyiv during the 1905 Revolution." In Anthony J. Heywood and Jonathan D. Smele, eds, *The Russian Revolution of 1905: Centenary Perspectives.* New York: Routledge, 177–95.

Hibbs, Douglas A. 1973. *Mass Political Violence.* New York: Wiley.

Himka, John-Paul. 1992. "Nationality Problems in the Habsburg Monarchy and the Soviet Union: The Perspective of History." In Richard L. Rudolph and David F. Good, eds, *Nationalism and Empire: The Habsburg Empire and the Soviet Union.* New York: St. Martin's Press, 79–93.

Hinthorne, Lauren. 2011. "Democratic Crisis or Crisis of Confidence? What Local Perceptual Lenses Tell Us about Madagascar's 2009 Political Crisis." *Democratization* 18, 2: 535–61.

Hinton, Carma (dir.). 1996. *The Gate of Heavenly Peace.* Boston, MA: Long Bow Group.

Hobsbawm, Eric. 1962. *The Age of Revolution, 1789–1848.* New York: Vintage.

Hobsbawm, Eric J. 1974. "Peasant Land Occupations." *Past & Present* 62: 120–52.

Hobsbawm, Eric J. 2005. "Cities and Insurrections." *Global Urban Development* 1, 1: 1–8.

Hoffman, David E. 2002. *The Oligarchs: Wealth and Power in the New Russia.* New York: PublicAffairs.

Hofheinz, Roy. 1977. *The Broken Wave: The Chinese Communist Peasant Movement, 1922–1928.* Cambridge, MA: Harvard University Press.

Holland, Alisha C. 2017. *Forbearance as Redistribution: The Politics of Informal Welfare in Latin America.* Cambridge: Cambridge University Press.

Holmes, Amy Austin. 2019. *Coups and Revolutions: Mass Mobilization, the Egyptian Military, and the United States from Mubarak to Sisi*. Oxford: Oxford University Press.

Holquist, Peter. 2002. *Making War, Forging Revolution: Russia's Continuum of Crisis, 1914–1921*. Cambridge, MA: Harvard University Press.

Honwana, Alcinda. 2013. *Youth and Revolution in Tunisia*. London: Zed Books.

Hopper, Rex D. 1950. "The Revolutionary Process: A Frame of Reference for the Study of Revolutionary Movements." *Social Forces* 28, 3: 270–79.

Hough, Jerry F. 1997. *Democratization and Revolution in the USSR*. Washington, DC: Brookings Institution Press.

House, Jonathan M. 2014. *Controlling Paris: Armed Forces and Counter-Revolution, 1789–1848*. New York: New York University Press.

Howard, Marc Morjé and Meir R. Walters. 2015. "Mass Mobilization and the Democracy Bias." *Middle East Policy* 22, 2: 145–55.

Howard, Philip N. and Muzammil M. Hussain. 2011. "The Role of Digital Media." *Journal of Democracy* 22, 3: 35–48.

Hrycak, Alexandra. 2007. "Seeing Orange: Women's Activism and Ukraine's Orange Revolution." *Women's Studies Quarterly* 35, 3/4: 208–25.

Hu, Frank B., Jack Goldberg, Donald Hedeker, Brian R. Flay, and Mary Ann Pentz. 1998. "Comparison of Population-Averaged and Subject-Specific Approaches for Analyzing Repeated Binary Outcomes." *American Journal of Epidemiology* 147, 7: 694–703.

Huang, Reyko. 2016. *The Wartime Origins of Democratization: Civil War, Rebel Governance, and Political Regimes*. Cambridge: Cambridge University Press.

Hugo, Victor. 1982 [1862]. *Les Misérables* (translated and with an introduction by Norman Denny). London: Penguin Books.

Humphreys, Macartan and Jeremy M. Weinstein. 2008. "Who Fights? The Determinants of Participation in Civil War." *American Journal of Political Science* 52, 2: 436–55.

Humphreys, Paul. 2014. *The Chances of Explanation: Causal Explanation in the Social, Medical, and Physical Sciences*. Princeton, NJ: Princeton University Press.

Hung, Wu. 1991. "Tiananmen Square: A Political History of Monument." *Representations* 35 (Summer): 84–117.

Huntington, Samuel P. 1968. *Political Order in Changing Societies*. New Haven, CT: Yale University Press.

Huntington, Samuel P. and Joan M. Nelson. 1976. *No Easy Choice: Political Participation in Developing Countries*. Cambridge, MA: Harvard University Press.

Husung, Hans-Gerhard. 1982. "Collective Violent Protest during the German *Vormärz*." In Wolfgang J. Mommsen and Gerhard Hirschfeld, eds, *Social Protest, Violence, and Terror in Nineteenth- and Twentieth-Century Europe*. New York: St. Martin's Press, 32–47.

IFAD (International Fund for Agricultural Development). 2001. *Rural Poverty Report 2001: The Challenge of Ending Rural Poverty*. Oxford: Oxford University Press.

Iliffe, John. 1967. "The Organization of the Maji Maji Rebellion." *The Journal of African History* 8, 3: 495–512.

Illugadóttir, Vera. 2013. "A History of Tahrir (+ photos)." *Your Middle East*, April 29, at http://www.yourmiddleeast.com/features/a-history-of-tahrir-photos_10643.

Imai, Kosuke, In Song Kim, and Erik Wang. 2018. "Matching Methods for Causal Inference with Time-Series Cross-Section Data." Unpublished paper (available at https://imai.princeton.edu/research/files/tscs.pdf).

Imbens, Guido W. and Jeffrey M. Wooldridge. 2009. "Recent Developments in the Econometrics of Program Evaluation." *Journal of Economic Literature* 47: 5–86.

Inclán, María de la Luz. 2009. "Repressive Threats, Procedural Concessions, and the Zapatista Cycle of Protests, 1994–2003." *Journal of Conflict Resolution* 53, 5: 794–819.

Inglehart, R., C. Haerpfer, A. Moreno, C. Welzel, K. Kizilova, J. Diez-Medrano, M. Lagos et al. 2014. World Values Survey: Round Six—Country-Pooled Datafile Version. Madrid: JD Systems Institute, at www.worldvaluessurvey.org/WVSDocumentationWV6.jsp.

Jackman, Robert W., Rosemary H. T. O'Kane, Thomas H. Johnson, Pat McGowan, and Robert O. Slater. 1986. "Explaining African Coups d'État." *American Political Science Review* 80, 1: 225–49.

Jasper, James M. 1999. "Recruiting Intimates, Recruiting Strangers: Building the Contemporary Animal Rights Movement." In Jo Freeman and Victoria Johnson, eds, *Waves of Protest: Social Movements since the Sixties*. Lanham, MD: Rowman & Littlefield, 65–82.

Jebnoun, Noureddine. 2014. "In the Shadow of Power: Civil–Military Relations and the Tunisian Popular Uprising." *The Journal of North African Studies* 19, 3: 296–316.

Jenkins, Stephen P. 1995. "Easy Estimation Methods for Discrete-Time Duration Models." *Oxford Bulletin of Economics and Statistics* 57, 1: 129–36.

Johansen, Anja. 2005. *Soldiers as Police: The French and Prussian Armies and the Policing of Popular Protest, 1889–1914*. Aldershot: Ashgate.

Johnson, Bryan. 1987. *The Four Days of Courage: The Untold Story of the People Who Brought Down Marcos*. New York: The Free Press.

Johnson, Chalmers, ed. 1970. *Change in Communist Systems*. Stanford, CA: Stanford University Press.

Johnson, Chalmers. 1982. *Revolutionary Change*. Stanford, CA: Stanford University Press.

Johnson, Kay Ann. 2009. *Women, the Family, and Peasant Revolution in China*. Chicago: University of Chicago Press.

Jong-A-Pin, Richard. 2009. "On the Measurement of Political Instability and Its Impact on Economic Growth." *European Journal of Political Economy* 25, 1: 15–29.

Jorba, Laia and Bruce Bimber. 2012. "The Impact of Digital Media on Citizenship from a Global Perspective." In Eva Anduiza, Michael J. Jensen, and Laia Jorba, eds, *Digital Media and Political Engagement Worldwide: A Comparative Study*. Cambridge: Cambridge University Press, 16–38.

Jowett, Philip and Alejandro de Quesada. 2013. *The Mexican Revolution 1910–20*. Oxford: Bloomsbury.

Kaboub, Fadhel. 2014. "The Making of the Tunisian Revolution." *Middle East Development Journal*, 5, 1: 1–21.

Kadivar, Mohammad Ali. 2018a. "Mass Mobilization and the Durability of New Democracies." *American Sociological Review* 83, 2: 390–417.

Kadivar, Mohammad Ali. 2018b. "Why Haven't Reformists Joined the Protests Sweeping Iran?" *The Washington Post*, January 5, at https://www.washingtonpost.com/news/monkey-cage

/wp/2018/01/05/why-havent-reformists-joined-the-protests-sweeping-iran/?utm_term =.901061b78347.
Kadivar, Mohammad Ali and Neil Ketchley. 2018. "Sticks, Stones, and Molotov Cocktails: Unarmed Collective Violence and Democratization." *Socius: Sociological Research for a Dynamic World* 4: 1–16.
Kalbfleisch, John D. and Ross L. Prentice. 2002. *The Statistical Analysis of Failure Time Data* (2nd edition). Hoboken, NJ: John Wiley & Sons.
Kalyvas, Stathis N. 2004. "The Urban Bias in Research on Civil Wars." *Security Studies* 13, 3: 160–90.
Kalyvas, Stathis N. 2006. *The Logic of Violence in Civil War*. Cambridge: Cambridge University Press.
Kalyvas, Stathis N. and Laia Balcells. 2010. "International System and Technologies of Rebellion: How the End of the Cold War Shaped Internal Conflict." *American Political Science Review* 104, 3: 415–29.
Kalyvas, Stathis N. and Matthew Adam Kocher. 2007. "How 'Free' is Free Riding in Civil Wars? Violence, Insurgency, and the Collective Action Problem." *World Politics* 59, 2: 177–216.
Kang, Seonjou and James Meernik. 2005. "Civil War Destruction and the Prospects for Economic Growth." *The Journal of Politics* 67, 1: 88–109.
Kapustin, Boris. 2019. "What May Be Wrong with the 'End' in the End-of-Revolution Thesis?" In Elena Namli, ed., *Future(s) of the Revolution and the Reformation*. London: Palgrave Macmillan, 121–52.
Karatnycky, Adrian. 2005. "Ukraine's Orange Revolution." *Foreign Affairs* 84, 2: 35–52.
Karatnycky, Adrian. 2006. "The Fall and Rise of Ukraine's Political Opposition: From Kuchmagate to the Orange Revolution." In Anders Åslund and Michael McFaul, eds, *Revolution in Orange: The Origins of Ukraine's Democratic Breakthrough*. Washington, DC: Carnegie Endowment for International Peace, 29–44.
Karumidze, Zurab and James V. Wertsch, eds. 2005. *Enough! The Rose Revolution in the Republic of Georgia 2003*. New York: Nova Science Publishers.
Kasfir, Nelson. 2015. "Rebel Governance—Constructing a Field of Inquiry: Definitions, Scope, Patterns, Order, Causes." In Ana Arjona, Nelson Kasfir, and Zachariah Mampilly, eds, *Rebel Governance in Civil War*. Cambridge: Cambridge University Press, 21–46.
Katsiaficas, George N. 2012. *Asia's Unknown Uprisings: South Korean Social Movements in the 20th Century*. Oakland, CA: PM Press.
Katsiaficas, George. 2013. *Asia's Unknown Uprisings: People Power in the Philippines, Burma, Tibet, China, Taiwan, Bangladesh, Nepal, Thailand, and Indonesia, 1947–2009*. Oakland, CA: PM Press.
Katz, Mark N. 1999. *Revolutions and Revolutionary Waves*. New York: St. Martin's Press.
Kavada, Anastasia and Orsalia Dimitriou, 2017. "Protest Spaces Online and Offline: The Indignant Movement in Syntagma Square." In Gavin Brown, Anna Feigenbaum, Fabian Frenzel, and Patrick McCurdy, eds, *Protest Camps in International Context: Spaces, Infrastructures and Media of Resistance*. Bristol: Policy Press: 71–90.
Keesing's World News Archive (online version). 1931–86. Bethesda, MD: Keesing's Worldwide, at http://keesings.com/index_new.php.

Kelley, Jonathan and Herbert S. Klein. 1977. "Revolution and the Rebirth of Inequality: A Theory of Stratification in Postrevolutionary Society." *American Journal of Sociology* 83, 1: 78–99.

Kennard, Matt and Claire Provost. 2015. "Burma's Bizarre Capital: A Super-Sized Slice of Post-Apocalypse Suburbia." *The Guardian*, March 19, at https://www.theguardian.com/cities/2015/mar/19/burmas-capital-naypyidaw-post-apocalypse-suburbia-highways-wifi.

Kenney, Padraic. 2003. *A Carnival of Revolution: Central Europe 1989*. Oxford: Oxford University Press.

Kerkvliet, Benedict J. 1977. *The Huk Rebellion: A Study of Peasant Revolt in the Philippines*. Berkeley, CA: University of California Press.

Ketchley, Neil. 2014. "'The Army and the People are One Hand!' Fraternization and the 25th January Egyptian Revolution." *Comparative Studies in Society and History* 56, 1: 155–86.

Ketchley, Neil. 2016. "Elite-led Protest and Authoritarian State Capture in Egypt." Paper presented at the conference "From Mobilization to Counter-Revolution: The Arab Spring in Comparative Perspective," University of Oxford.

Ketchley, Neil. 2017. *Egypt in a Time of Revolution: Contentious Politics and the Arab Spring*. Cambridge: Cambridge University Press.

Kettani, Houssain. 2010a. "Muslim Population in Africa: 1950–2020." *International Journal of Environmental Science and Development* 1, 2: 136.

Kettani, Houssain. 2010b. "Muslim Population in Asia: 1950–2020." *International Journal of Environmental Science and Development* 1, 2: 143.

Kettani, Houssain. 2010c. "Muslim Population in Europe: 1950–2020." *International Journal of Environmental Science and Development* 1, 2: 154.

Kettani, Houssain. 2010d. "Muslim Population in Oceania: 1950–2020." *International Journal of Environmental Science and Development* 1, 2: 165.

Kettani, Houssain. 2010e. "Muslim Population in the Americas: 1950–2020." *International Journal of Environmental Science and Development* 1, 2: 127.

Khalaf, Amal. 2013. "Squaring the Circle: Bahrain's Pearl Roundabout." *Middle East Critique* 22, 3: 265–80.

Khalil, Andrea. 2014. "Tunisia's Women: Partners in Revolution." *The Journal of North African Studies* 19, 2: 186–99.

Khalil, Ashraf. 2011. *Liberation Square: Inside the Egyptian Revolution and the Rebirth of a Nation*. New York: St. Martin's Press.

Khamidov, Alisher. 2002. "Kyrgyzstan's Unrest Linked to Clan Rivalries." *Eurasianet*, June 5, at https://eurasianet.org/kyrgyzstans-unrest-linked-to-clan-rivalries.

Khazanov, Anatoly M. 1998. "Post-Communist Moscow: Re-Building the 'Third Rome' in the Country of Missed Opportunities?" *City & Society* 10, 1: 269–314.

Khedhir, Yesmina. 2015. "Tunisia's Hard Times and Its Best Times." In Asaad Al-Saleh, ed., *Voices of the Arab Spring*. New York: Columbia University Press, 41–44.

Khiterer, Viktoriya. 1992. "The October 1905 Pogrom in Kiev." *East European Jewish Affairs* 22, 2: 21–23.

Kiernan, Ben. 1996. *The Pol Pot Regime: Race, Power and Genocide in Cambodia under the Khmer Rouge, 1975–1979*. New Haven, CT: Yale University Press.

Kim, Nam Kyu. 2016. "Revisiting Economic Shocks and Coups." *Journal of Conflict Resolution* 60, 1: 3–31.

Kim, Quee-Young. 1983. *The Fall of Syngman Rhee*. Berkeley, CA: Institute of East Asian Studies.

Kim, Sunhyuk. 2007. "Civil Society and Democratization in South Korea." In Charles K. Armstrong, ed., *Korean Society: Civil Society, Democracy and the State*. New York: Routledge, 92–108.

King, Gary, Christopher Lucas, and Richard A. Nielsen. 2017. "The Balance-Sample Size Frontier in Matching Methods for Causal Inference." *American Journal of Political Science* 61, 2: 473–89.

King, Gary, Jennifer Pan, and Margaret E. Roberts. 2013. "How Censorship in China Allows Government Criticism but Silences Collective Expression." *American Political Science Review* 107, 2: 326–43.

King, Gary and Langche Zeng. 2001a. "Explaining Rare Events in International Relations." *International Organization* 55, 3: 693–715.

King, Gary and Langche Zeng. 2001b. "Logistic Regression in Rare Events Data." *Political Analysis* 9: 137–63.

Kingma, Kees. 1997. "Demobilization of Combatants after Civil Wars in Africa and Their Reintegration into Civilian Life." *Policy Sciences* 30, 3: 151–65.

Kirkpatrick, David D. 2011a. "Mubarak Orders Crackdown, with Revolt Sweeping Egypt," *The New York Times*, January 29: A1 and A10.

Kirkpatrick, David D. 2011b. "Crime Wave in Egypt Has People Afraid, even the Police." *The New York Times*, May 12, at https://www.nytimes.com/2011/05/13/world/middleeast/13egypt.html.

Kisangani, Emizet F. and Jeffrey Pickering. 2008. "International Military Intervention, 1989–2005." Inter-University Consortium for Political and Social Research, Data Collection No. 21282, University of Michigan.

Klandermans, Bert. 2010. "Peace Demonstrations or Anti-Government Marches? The Political Attitudes of the Protesters." In Stefaan Walgrave and Dieter Rucht, eds, *The World Says No To War: Demonstrations Against the War on Iraq*. Minneapolis: University of Minnesota Press, 98–118.

Klooster, Wim. 2018. *Revolutions in the Atlantic World: A Comparative History*. New York: NYU Press.

Knight, Alan. 1986. *The Mexican Revolution*, 2 vols. Cambridge: Cambridge University Press.

Knutsen, Carl Henrik. 2014. "Income Growth and Revolutions." *Social Science Quarterly* 95, 4: 920–37.

Kohli, Atul. 2004. *State-Led Development: Political Power and Industrialization in the Global Periphery*. Cambridge: Cambridge University Press.

Kohn, George Childs. 1999. *Dictionary of Wars* (revised edition). New York: Facts on File.

Kongkirati, Prajak. 2012. "Thailand: The Cultural Politics of Student Resistance." In Meredith L. Weiss, ed., *Student Activism in Asia: Between Protest and Powerlessness*. Minneapolis: University of Minnesota Press, 234–41.

Koplow, David A. 2010. *Death by Moderation: The US Military's Quest for Useable Weapons*. Cambridge: Cambridge University Press.

Kornhauser, William. 1959. *The Politics of Mass Society*. Glencoe, IL: Free Press.

Koselleck, Reinhart. 2004. *Futures Past: On the Semantics of Historical Time*. New York: Columbia University Press.

Kowal, Paweł and Maciej Wapiński. 2014. "A Tale of Three Maidans." *New Eastern Europe* 11, 2: 7–12.

Kozenko, Andrei. 2007. "'Marsh nesoglasnykh' ostalsia nesoglasovannym: Pravozashchitniki ne smogli zashchitit' sami sebia," *Kommersant'*, April 10, at https://www.kommersant.ru/doc/757313.

Kubik, Jan. 1994. *Power of Symbols against the Symbols of Power: The Rise of Solidarity and the Fall of State Socialism in Poland*. University Park, PA: Pennsylvania State University Press.

Kudelia, Serhiy. 2018. "When Numbers Are Not Enough: The Strategic Use of Violence in Ukraine's 2014 Revolution." *Comparative Politics* 50, 4: 501–21.

Kukhianidze, Alexandre. 2009. "Corruption and Organized Crime in Georgia before and after the 'Rose Revolution.'" *Central Asian Survey* 28, 2: 215–34.

Kulyk, Volodymyr. 2011. "Language Identity, Linguistic Diversity and Political Cleavages: Evidence from Ukraine." *Nations and Nationalism* 17, 3: 627–48.

Kumar, Krishan. 2008. "The Future of Revolution: Imitation or Innovation?" in John Foran, David Lane, and Andreja Zivkovic, eds, *Revolution in the Making of the Modern World: Social Identities, Globalization, and Modernity*. London: Routledge, 222–35.

Kuran, Timur. 1997. *Private Truths, Public Lies: The Social Consequences of Preference Falsification*. Cambridge, MA: Harvard University Press.

Kurzman, Charles. 1996. "Structural Opportunity and Perceived Opportunity in Social-Movement Theory: The Iranian Revolution of 1979," *American Sociological Review* 61, 1: 153–70.

Kurzman, Charles. 2004. *The Unthinkable Revolution in Iran*. Cambridge, MA: Harvard University Press.

Kurzman, Charles. 2008. *Democracy Denied, 1905–1915: Intellectuals and the Fate of Democracy*. Cambridge, MA: Harvard University Press.

Kushkush, Isma'il. 2012. "In New Protests, Echoes of an Uprising That Shook Sudan." *The New York Times*, February 23, at https://www.nytimes.com/2012/02/24/world/africa/echoes-of-an-arab-revolution-that-rocked-sudan-circa-1964.html?pagewanted=all&_r=0.

Kutmanaliev, Joldon. 2015. "Public and Communal Spaces and Their Relation to the Spatial Dynamics of Ethnic Riots: Violence and Non-Violence in the City of Osh." *International Journal of Sociology and Social Policy* 35, 7/8: 449–77.

Kuzio, Taras. 2004. "Yanukovych-Gate Unfolds after Ukrainian Elections," *Eurasia Daily Monitor*, December 3, at https://jamestown.org/program/yanukovych-gate-unfolds-after-ukrainian-elections/.

Kuzio, Taras. 2005a. "Details Emerge of Second Russian Plot to Assassinate Yushchenko." *Eurasia Daily Monitor*, January 5, at https://jamestown.org/program/details-emerge-of-second-russian-plot-to-assassinate-yushchenko/.

Kuzio, Taras. 2005b. "Did Ukraine's Security Service Really Prevent Bloodshed during the Orange Revolution?" *Eurasia Daily Monitor*, January 24, at https://jamestown.org/program/did-ukraines-security-service-really-prevent-bloodshed-during-the-orange-revolution/.

Kuzio, Taras. 2010. "Nationalism, Identity and Civil Society in Ukraine: Understanding the Orange Revolution." *Communist and Post-Communist Studies* 43: 285–96.

Kuzio, Taras. 2015. "Competing Nationalisms, Euromaidan, and the Russian–Ukrainian Conflict." *Studies in Ethnicity and Nationalism* 15, 1: 157–69.

Lachapelle, Jean, Steven Levitsky, Lucan A. Way, and Adam E. Casey. 2020. "Social Revolution and Authoritarian Durability." *World Politics* 72, 4: 1–44.
Lacina, Bethany. 2006. "Explaining the Severity of Civil Wars." *Journal of Conflict Resolution* 50, 2: 276–89.
Lacina, Bethany and Nils Petter Gleditsch. 2005. "Monitoring Trends in Global Combat: A New Dataset of Battle Deaths." *European Journal of Population* 21, 2–3: 145–66.
Lacina, Bethany, Nils Petter Gleditsch, and Bruce Russett. 2006. "The Declining Risk of Death in Battle." *International Studies Quarterly* 50, 3: 673–80.
Lambini, Cosmas Kombat, Matthew Sabbi, Trung Thanh Nguyen, and Peter Narh. 2014. "Access and Investment Implication of Land Reforms: A Comparative Study of Ghana, Kenya, and Vietnam." Unpublished paper (available at https://www.researchgate.net/profile/Cosmas_Lambini/publication/275638142_Access_and_investment_implication_of_land_reforms_A_comparative_study_of_Ghana_Kenya_and_Vietnam/links/5540baa00cf2718618da8fa8.pdf).
Lan, David. 1985. *Guns and Rain: Guerrillas and Spirit Mediums in Zimbabwe*. Oxford: James Currey Publishers.
Lane, David. 2008. "The Orange Revolution: 'People's Revolution' or Revolutionary Coup?" *The British Journal of Politics and International Relations* 10, 4: 525–49.
Langer, Jonas, Seymour Wapner, and Heinz Werner. 1961. "The Effect of Danger upon the Experience of Time." *The American Journal of Psychology* 74, 1: 94–97.
Lapidus, Gail Warshofsky.1978. *Women in Soviet Society: Equality, Development, and Social Change*. Berkeley, CA: University of California Press.
Lawson, George. 2005. *Negotiated Revolutions: The Czech Republic, South Africa and Chile*. Aldershot: Ashgate.
Lawson, George. 2016. "Within and beyond the 'Fourth Generation' of Revolutionary Theory." *Sociological Theory* 34, 2: 106–27.
Lawson, George. 2019. *Anatomies of Revolution*. Cambridge: Cambridge University Press.
Le Blanc, Joerg. 2013. "The Urban Environment and Its Influences on Insurgent Campaigns." *Terrorism and Political Violence* 25, 5: 798–819.
Le Bon, Gustave. 1913. *The Psychology of Revolution*. New York: G. P. Putnam & Sons.
Lebed', Aleksandr. 1995. *Za derzhavu obidno. . . .* Moscow: Moskovskaia pravda.
Lee, John. 2009. *The Gas Attacks: Ypres 1915*. Barnsley: Pen & Sword.
Lee, L. 1978. "Unionism and Wage Rates: A Simultaneous Equations Model with Qualitative and Limited Dependent Variables." *International Economic Review* 19: 415–33.
Lee, Lung-Fei. 1983. "Generalized Econometric Models with Selectivity." *Econometrica* 51, 2: 507–12.
Lee, Nelson K. 2009. "How is a Political Public Space Made? The Birth of Tiananmen Square and the May Fourth Movement." *Political Geography* 28, 1: 32–43.
Lee, Terence. 2015. *Defect or Defend: Military Responses to Popular Protests in Authoritarian Asia*. Baltimore: Johns Hopkins University Press.
Lees, Lynn and Charles Tilly. 1972. "The People of June 1848." Center for Research on Social Organization, University of Michigan Working Paper 70 (available at https://deepblue.lib.umich.edu/bitstream/handle/2027.42/50851/70.pdf).
Lefebvre, Henri. 1991. *The Production of Space*. Oxford: Blackwell.

Lefebvre, Henri. 2003. *The Urban Revolution* (translated by Robert Bononno). Minneapolis: University of Minnesota Press.

Leibenluft, Jacob. 2008. "Purple Water Cannons: Why Would the Police Spray Protesters with Colored Water?" *Slate*, June 12, http://www.slate.com/articles/news_and_politics/explainer/2008/06/purple_water_cannons.html.

Leitgöb, Heinz. 2013. "The Problem of Modeling Rare Events in ML-based Logistic Regression." Paper presented at the European Survey Research Association, Ljubljana.

Leith, James A. 1991. *Space and Revolution: Projects for Monuments, Squares, and Public Buildings in France, 1789–1799*. Montreal: McGill-Queen's University Press.

Lemert, Charles C. and Garth Gillan. 1982. *Michel Foucault: Social Theory as Transgression*. New York: Columbia University Press.

Lenin, V. I. 1977. *Collected Works*, vol. 29. Moscow: Progress Publishers.

Lenin, V. I. 1980. *Collected Works*, vol. 35. Moscow: Progress Publishers.

Lenin, V. I. 1981. *Collected Works*, vol. 23. Moscow: Progress Publishers.

Levi, Margaret. 1981. "The Predatory Theory of Rule." *Politics & Society* 10, 4: 431–65.

Levinson, Alfred A., John J. Gurney, and Melissa B. Kirkley. 1992. "Diamond Sources and Production: Past, Present, and Future." *Gems & Gemology* (Winter): 234–54.

Levinson, Sanford. 1998. *Written in Stone: Public Monuments in Changing Societies*. Durham, NC: Duke University Press.

Levitsky, Steven and Lucan A. Way. 2010. *Competitive Authoritarianism: Hybrid Regimes after the Cold War*. Cambridge: Cambridge University Press.

Levitsky, Steven R. and Lucan A. Way. 2012. "Beyond Patronage: Violent Struggle, Ruling Party Cohesion, and Authoritarian Durability." *Perspectives on Politics* 10, 4: 869–89.

Levitsky, Steven R. and Lucan A. Way. 2022. *Social Revolution and Authoritarian Durability in the Modern World*. Princeton, NJ: Princeton University Press.

Lewin, Moshe. 1991. *The Gorbachev Phenomenon*. Berkeley, CA: University of California Press.

Lewis, Aidan. 2011. "Tracking Down the Ben Ali and Trabelsi Fortune." *BBC News*, January 31, at http://www.bbc.com/news/world-africa-12302659.

Lichbach, Mark Irving. 1987. "Deterrence or Escalation? The Puzzle of Aggregate Studies of Repression and Dissent." *Journal of Conflict Resolution* 31, 2: 266–97.

Lichbach, Mark Irving. 1998. *The Rebel's Dilemma*. Ann Arbor, MI: University of Michigan Press.

Lidegaard, Bo. 2009. *A Short History of Denmark in the 20th Century*. Copenhagen: Gyldendal.

Lieven, Anatol. 1993. *The Baltic Revolution: Estonia, Latvia, Lithuania and the Path to Independence*. New Haven, CT: Yale University Press.

Lim, Merlyna. 2002. "Cyber-Civic Space in Indonesia: From Panopticon to Pandemonium?" *International Development Planning Review* 24, 4: 383–400.

Lipset, Seymour Martin. 1960. *Political Man: The Social Bases of Politics*. Garden City, NY: Doubleday.

Lipton, Michael. 2009. *Land Reform in Developing Countries: Property Rights and Property Wrongs*. New York: Routledge.

Little, Roderick J. A. 1992. "Regression with Missing X's: A Review." *Journal of the American Statistical Association* 87, 420: 1227–37.

Little, Roderick J. A. and Donald B. Rubin. 2002. *Statistical Analysis with Missing Data* (2nd edition). New York: John Wiley & Sons.

Litvinova, Daria. 2020. "Russia Lifts Ineffective Ban on Telegram Messaging App." *Associated Press*, June 18, https://apnews.com/1da061ce00eb531291b143ace0eed1c9.

Lloyd, Nick. 2010. "The Amritsar Massacre and the Minimum Force Debate." *Small Wars & Insurgencies* 21, 2: 382–403.

Lohmann, Susanne. 1994. "The Dynamics of Informational Cascades: The Monday Demonstrations in Leipzig, East Germany, 1989–91." *World Politics* 47: 42–101.

Londregan, John B. and Keith T. Poole. 1990. "Poverty, the Coup Trap, and the Seizure of Executive Power." *World Politics* 42, 2: 151–83.

Long, J. Scott. 1997. *Regression Models for Categorical and Limited Dependent Variables*. Thousand Oaks, CA: Sage.

Long, J. Scott and Jeremy Freese. 2014. *Regression Models for Categorical Dependent Variables Using Stata* (3rd edition). College Station, TX: Stata Press.

Lowder, S. K., J. Skoet, and S. Singh. 2014. "What Do We Really Know about the Number and Distribution of Farms and Family Farms Worldwide?" Background paper for The State of Food and Agriculture 2014. ESA Working Paper No. 14–02. Rome, FAO.

Luciak, Ilja A. 2001. *After the Revolution: Gender and Democracy in El Salvador, Nicaragua, and Guatemala*. Baltimore: Johns Hopkins University Press.

Lührmann, A., V. Mechkova, and K. L. Marquardt. 2017. "Constraining Governments: New Indices of Vertical, Horizontal and Diagonal Accountability." V-Dem Working Paper Series 46, 72 (available at http://www.ssrn.com/abstract=2956464).

Lujala, Päivi, Nils Petter Gleditsch, and Elisabeth Gilmore. 2005. "A Diamond Curse? Civil War and a Lootable Resource." *Journal of Conflict Resolution* 49, 4: 538–62.

Lupu, Yonatan and Geoffrey Wallace. 2019. "Violence, Nonviolence, and the Effects of International Human Rights Law." *American Journal of Political Science* 63, 2: 411–26.

Lutterbeck, Derek. 2013. "Arab Uprisings, Armed Forces, and Civil–Military Relations." *Armed Forces & Society* 39, 1: 28–52.

Lyall, Jason, Graeme Blair, and Kosuke Imai. 2013. "Explaining Support for Combatants during Wartime: A Survey Experiment in Afghanistan." *American Political Science Review* 107, 4: 679–705.

Lyall, Jason and Isaiah Wilson III. 2009. "Rage against the Machines: Explaining Outcomes in Counterinsurgency Wars." *International Organization* 63, 1: 67–106.

Lynch, Marc. 2006. *Voices of the New Arab Public: Iraq, Al-Jazeera, and Middle East Politics Today*. New York: Columbia University Press.

Lynch, Marc. 2011. "After Egypt: The Limits and Promise of Online Challenges to the Authoritarian Arab State." *Perspectives on Politics* 9, 2: 301–10.

Lynch, Marc. 2012. *The Arab Uprising: The Unfinished Revolutions of the New Middle East*. New York: PublicAffairs.

Lysenko, Volodymyr and Kevin Desouza. 2010. "Role of Internet-Based Information Flows and Technologies in Electoral Revolutions: The Case of Ukraine's Orange Revolution." *First Monday* 15, 9, at http://uncommonculture.org/ojs/index.php/fm/article/view/2992.

Mabrouk, Mehdi. 2011. "A Revolution for Dignity and Freedom: Preliminary Observations on the Social and Cultural Background to the Tunisian Revolution." *The Journal of North African Studies* 16, 4: 625–35.

Machiavelli, Niccolò. 1952. *The Prince* (translated by Luigi Ricci). New York: The New American Library of World Literature.

Maclaren, Alexander. 1902. *The Secret of Power and Other Sermons*. New York: Funk and Wagnalls.

Madanipour, Ali. 1999. "Why Are the Design and Development of Public Spaces Significant for Cities?" *Environment and Planning B: Planning and Design* 26, 6: 879–91.

Maddala, G. S. and F. D. Nelson. 1975. "Switching Regression Models with Exogenous and Endogenous Switching." In *Proceedings of the American Statistical Association*, vol. 5. Washington, DC: Business and Economics Section, 423–26.

Maeda, Kentaro and Adam Ziegfeld. 2015. "Socioeconomic Status and Corruption Perceptions around the World." *Research and Politics* (April–June): 1–9.

Magaloni, Beatriz. 2006. *Voting for Autocracy: Hegemonic Party Survival and Its Demise in Mexico*. Cambridge: Cambridge University Press.

Magaloni, Beatriz. 2008. "Credible Power-Sharing and the Longevity of Authoritarian Rule." *Comparative Political Studies* 41, 4–5: 715–41.

Mainwaring, Scott and Aníbal Pérez-Liñán. 2007. "Why Regions of the World Are Important: Regional Specificities and Region-Wide Diffusion of Democracy." In Gerardo Luis Munck, ed., *Regimes and Democracy in Latin America: Theories and Methods*. Oxford: Oxford University Press, 199–229.

Malecki, Edward S. 1973. "Theories of Revolution and Industrialized Societies." *The Journal of Politics* 35, 4: 948–85.

Malia, Martin. 2006. *History's Locomotives: Revolutions and the Making of the Modern World*. New Haven, CT: Yale University Press.

Malpezzi, Stephen. 2006. "Cross-Country Patterns of Urban Development." In Richard J. Arnott and Daniel P. McMillen, eds, *A Companion to Urban Economics*. Oxford: Blackwell, 55–71.

Mamot, Patricio R. 1986. *People Power: Profile of Filipino Heroism*. Quezon City: New Day Publishers.

Mann, Michael. 1986. *The Sources of Social Power*, vol. 1. Cambridge: Cambridge University Press.

Manning, Willard G., and John Mullahy. 2001. "Estimating Log Models: To Transform or Not to Transform?" *Journal of Health Economics* 20, 4: 461–94.

Maréchal, Nathalie. 2018. "From Russia with Crypto: A Political History of Telegram." Paper presented at the 8th Workshop on Free and Open Communications on the Internet (available at https://www.usenix.org/conference/foci18/presentation/marechal).

Marighella, Carlos. 2011. *Minimanual of the Urban Guerrilla*. Seattle: CreateSpace Independent Publishing.

Marples, David R. and Frederick V. Mills, eds. 2014. *Ukraine's Euromaidan: Analyses of a Civil Revolution*. New York: Columbia University Press.

Marshall, Monty G. and Donna Ramsey Marshall. 2015. "Coup d'État Events, 1946–2014 Codebook." Vienna, VA: Center for Systemic Peace.

Martin, Deborah and Byron Miller. 2003. "Space and Contentious Politics." *Mobilization: An International Quarterly* 8, 2: 143–56.

Martin, Terry. 2001. *The Affirmative Action Empire: Nations and Nationalism in the Soviet Union, 1923–1939*. Ithaca, NY: Cornell University Press.

Marwell, Gerald and Pamela Oliver. 1993. *The Critical Mass in Collective Action: A Micro-Social Theory*. Cambridge: Cambridge University Press.

Marx, Karl and Friedrich Engels. 1990. *Collected Works*, vol. 27: *Engels: 1890–95, re Europe*. Chadwell Heath: Lawrence & Wishart.

Mason, T. David. 1992. "Women's Participation in Central American Revolutions: A Theoretical Perspective." *Comparative Political Studies* 25, 1: 63–89.

Massell, Gregory J. 1974. *The Surrogate Proletariat: Moslem Women and Revolutionary Strategies in Soviet Central Asia, 1919–1929*. Princeton, NJ: Princeton University Press.

Massey, Doreen. 1994. *Space, Place, and Gender*. Minneapolis: University of Minnesota Press.

Matanock, Aila M. and Miguel García-Sánchez. 2017. "Does Counterinsurgent Success Match Social Support? Evidence from a Survey Experiment in Colombia." *The Journal of Politics* 80, 3: 800–814.

Mather, F. C. 1974. "The General Strike of 1842: A Study in Leadership, Organization and the Threat of Revolution during the Plug Plot Disturbances." In R. Quinault and J. Stevenson, eds, *Popular Protest and Public Order: Six Studies in British History, 1790–1920*. London: George Allen & Unwin, 115–40.

Maung, Maung. 1999. *The 1988 Uprising in Burma*. New Haven, CT: Yale University Southeast Asia Studies.

Maunganidze, Ottilia. 2009. "Madagascar: Anatomy of a Recurrent Crisis." Institute for Security Studies, Pretoria (available at https://www.africaportal.org/publications/madagascar-anatomy-of-a-recurrent-crisis/).

Mauro, Paolo. 1995. "Corruption and Growth." *The Quarterly Journal of Economics* 110, 3: 681–712.

Mayer, Arno J. 2000. *The Furies: Violence and Terror in the French and Russian Revolutions*. Princeton, NJ: Princeton University Press.

Mazur, Kevin. 2017. "Social Networks and Sectarian Mobilization in the Syrian Uprising: The Social Bases of Conflict in Homs." Unpublished paper, University of Oxford.

Mazur, Kevin. 2021. *Revolution in Syria: Identity, Networks, and Repression*. Cambridge: Cambridge University Press.

Mbaku, John Mukum. 1994. "Military Coups as Rent-Seeking Behavior." *Journal of Political and Military Sociology* 22 (Winter): 241–84.

McAdam, Doug. 1986. "Recruitment to High-Risk Activism: The Case of Freedom Summer." *American Journal of Sociology* 92, 1: 64–90.

McAdam, Doug and Ronnelle Paulsen. 1993. "Specifying the Relationship between Social Ties and Activism." *American Journal of Sociology* 99, 3: 640–67.

McAdam, Doug, Sidney Tarrow, and Charles Tilly. 2001. *Dynamics of Contention*. Cambridge: Cambridge University Press.

McCarthy, John D. and Clark McPhail. 1998. "The Institutionalization of Protest in the United States." In David S. Meyer and Sidney Tarrow, eds, *The Social Movement Society: Contentious Politics for a New Century*. Lanham, MD: Rowman & Littlefield, 83–110.

McCarthy, John D., Clark McPhail, and Jackie Smith. 1996. "Images of Protest: Dimensions of Selection Bias in Media Coverage of Washington Demonstrations, 1982 and 1991." *American Sociological Review* 61: 478–99.

McCarthy, John D. and Mayer N. Zald. 1977. "Resource Mobilization and Social Movements: A Partial Theory." *American Journal of Sociology* 82, 6: 1212–41.

McGoogan, Cara. 2017. "Facial Recognition Fitted to 5,000 CCTV Cameras in Moscow." *The Telegraph*, September 29, at http://www.telegraph.co.uk/technology/2017/09/29/facial-recognition-fitted-5000-cctv-cameras-moscow/.

McLauchlin, Theodore. 2015. "Desertion and Collective Action in Civil Wars." *International Studies Quarterly* 59: 669–79.

McMahon, Darrin M. 1996. "The Birthplace of the Revolution: Public Space and Political Community in the Palais-Royal of Louis-Philippe-Joseph d'Orleans, 1781–1789." *French History* 10 (March): 1–29.

McNab, Chris. 2015. *Riot Control Vehicles: 1945–Present*. London: Bloomsbury Publishing.

McPeek, Mark A. 2004. "The Growth/Predation Risk Trade-Off: So What Is the Mechanism?" *The American Naturalist* 163, 5: E88–E111.

Mehra, Ajay. 2005. "Urban Villages of Delhi." In Evelin Hust and Michael Mann, eds, *Urbanization and Governance in India*. New Delhi: Manohar, 279–310.

Melander, Erik, Magnus Öberg, and Jonathan Hall. 2009. "Are 'New Wars' More Atrocious? Battle Severity, Civilians Killed and Forced Migration before and after the End of the Cold War." *European Journal of International Relations* 15, 3: 505–36.

Melson, Robert. 1992. *Revolution and Genocide: On the Origins of the Armenian Genocide and the Holocaust*. Chicago: University of Chicago Press.

Mendoza, Amado, Jr. 2009. "'People Power' in the Philippines, 1983–1986," in Adam Roberts and Timothy Garton Ash, eds, *Civil Resistance and Power Politics: The Experience of Non-Violent Action from Gandhi to the Present*. Oxford: Oxford University Press, 179–96.

Merriman, John M. 2014. *Massacre: The Life and Death of the Paris Commune*. New York: Basic Books.

Michaelsen, Marcus. 2015. "The Politics of Online Journalism in Iran." In David M. Faris and Babak Rahimi, eds, *Iran and Social Media*. Albany, NY: SUNY Press, 101–22.

Midlarsky, Manus I. 1982. "Scarcity and Inequality." *Journal of Conflict Resolution* 26: 3–38.

Migdal, Joel S. 1974. *Peasants, Politics and Revolution: Pressures toward Political and Social Change in the Third World*. Princeton, NJ: Princeton University Press.

Mill, John Stuart. 1950. *Philosophy of Scientific Method*. New York: Hafner Publishing Company.

Miller, Byron and Walter Nicholls. 2013. "Social Movements in Urban Society: The City as a Space of Politicization." *Urban Geography* 34, 4: 452–73.

Minahan, James, ed. 2002. *Encyclopedia of the Stateless Nations*. Westport, CT: Greenwood Publishing Group.

Ming, K. and P. R. Rosenbaum. 2001. "A Note on Optimal Matching with Variable Controls Using the Assignment Algorithm." *Journal of Computational and Graphical Statistics* 10: 455–63.

Minorities at Risk Project. 2009. "Minorities at Risk Dataset." Center for International Development and Conflict Management, College Park, MD (available at http://www.mar.umd.edu/).

Misiunas, Romuald J. and Rein Taagepera. 1993. *The Baltic States, Years of Dependence, 1940–1990*. Berkeley, CA: University of California Press.

Mitchell, Brian R. 2007a. *International Historical Statistics: Africa, Asia & Oceania, 1750–2005*. New York: Palgrave Macmillan.

Mitchell, Brian R. 2007b. *International Historical Statistics: Europe, 1750–2005.* New York: Palgrave Macmillan.

Mitchell, Brian R. 2007c. *International Historical Statistics: The Americas 1750–2005.* New York: Palgrave Macmillan.

Mitchell, Don and Lynn A. Staeheli. 2005. "Permitting Protest: Parsing the Fine Geography of Dissent in America." *International Journal of Urban and Regional Research* 29, 4: 796–813.

Mitchell, W.J.T. 2013. "Image, Space, Revolution: The Arts of Occupation." In W.J.T. Mitchell, Bernard E. Harcourt, and Michael Taussig, eds, *Occupy: Three Inquiries in Disobedience.* Chicago: University of Chicago Press, 93–130.

Mo, Pak Hung. 2001. "Corruption and Economic Growth." *Journal of Comparative Economics* 29, 1: 66–79.

Moeckli, Daniel. 2016. *Exclusion from Public Space: A Comparative Constitutional Analysis.* Cambridge: Cambridge University Press.

Moffitt Robert A. 1999. "Econometric Methods for Labor Market Analysis," In O. Ashenfelter and D. Card, eds, *Handbook of Labor Economics,* vol. 3A. Amsterdam: Elsevier, 1367–97.

Montgomery, Michael T. and Brian F. Farrell. 1993. "Tropical Cyclone Formation." *Journal of the Atmospheric Sciences* 50, 2: 285–310.

Moore, Barrington, Jr. 1966. *Social Origins of Dictatorship and Democracy: Lord and Peasant in the Making of the Modern World.* Boston, MA: Beacon Press.

Moore, Matthew. 2012. "Selling to Both Sides: The Effects of Major Conventional Weapons Transfers on Civil War Severity and Duration." *International Interactions* 38, 3: 325–47.

Moore, Will H. 1998. "Repression and Dissent: Substitution, Context, and Timing." *American Journal of Political Science* 42, 3: 851–73.

Morris, Tim P., Ian R. White, and Patrick Royston. 2014. "Tuning Multiple Imputation by Predictive Mean Matching and Local Residual Draws." *BMC Medical Research Methodology* 14: 75–87.

Mouzykantskii, Ilya. 2011. "In Belarus, Just Being Can Prompt an Arrest." *The New York Times,* July 30: A4.

Moyo, Sam. 2014. "Land Ownership Patterns and Income Inequality in Southern Africa." Unpublished paper (available at http://www.un.org/en/development/desa/policy/wess/wess_bg_papers/bp_wess2014_moyo.pdf).

Mueller, Lisa. 2013. "Democratic Revolutionaries or Pocketbook Protesters? The Roots of the 2009–2010 Uprisings in Niger." *African Affairs* 112, 448: 398–420.

Mumford, Lewis. 1938. *The Culture of Cities.* New York: Harcourt Brace.

Murdoch, James C. and Todd Sandler. 2002. "Economic Growth, Civil Wars, and Spatial Spillovers." *Journal of Conflict Resolution* 46, 1: 91–110.

Myoe, Maung Aung. 2008. "The Road to Naypyitaw: Making Sense of the Myanmar Government's Decision to Move its Capital." Asia Research Institute Working Paper No. 79 (available at http://www.ari.nus.edu.sg/wps/wps06_079.pdf).

Nafziger, Steven and Peter Lindert. 2013. "Russian Inequality on the Eve of Revolution." Unpublished paper (available at http://web.williams.edu/Economics/wp/Nafziger_Lindert_Inequality_Sept2013.pdf).

Naghibi, Nima. 2011. "Diasporic Disclosures: Social Networking, Neda, and the 2009 Iranian Presidential Elections." *Biography* 34, 1: 56–69.

Nagl, John A. 2006. "Forward." In David Galula, *Counterinsurgency Warfare: Theory and Practice*. Westport, CT: Praeger Security International, vii–x.

Nagl, John A., James F. Amos, Sarah Sewall, and David H. Petraeus. 2008. *The US Army/Marine Corps Counterinsurgency Field Manual*. Chicago: University of Chicago Press.

Nair, Sheila. 2007. "The Limits of Protest and Prospects for Political Reform in Malaysia." *Critical Asian Studies* 39, 3: 339–68.

National Petroleum Council. 1964. *Impact of Oil Exports from the Soviet Bloc*. Washington, DC: National Petroleum Council.

Neal, Andrew, Sven Opitz, and Chris Zebrowski. 2019. "Capturing Protest in Urban Environments: The 'Police Kettle' as a Territorial Strategy." *Environment and Planning D: Society and Space* 37, 6: 1045–63.

Nedosekina, Evgeniya. 2011. "The Buried Freedom." Strelka Institute for Media, Architecture and Design, September 13, at https://issuu.com/strelkainstitute/docs/the_buried_freedom.

Nejad, Reza Masoudi. 2013. "The Spatial Logic of the Crowd: The Effectiveness of Protest in Public Space." *International Journal of Islamic Architecture* 2, 1: 157–78.

Nel, Philip and Marjolein Righarts. 2008. "Natural Disasters and the Risk of Violent Civil Conflict." *International Studies Quarterly* 52, 1: 159–85.

Nemes, Szilard, Junmei Miao Jonasson, Anna Genell, and Gunnar Steineck. 2009. "Bias in Odds Ratios by Logistic Regression Modelling and Sample Size." *BMC Medical Research Methodology* 9, 1: 56–60.

Nepstad, Sharon Erickson. 2011. *Nonviolent Revolutions: Civil Resistance in the Late Twentieth Century*. Oxford: Oxford University Press.

Nepstad, Sharon Erickson. 2013. "Mutiny and Nonviolence in the Arab Spring: Exploring Military Defections and Loyalty in Egypt, Bahrain, and Syria." *Journal of Peace Research* 50, 3: 337–49.

Ness, Immanuel, ed. 2009. *The International Encyclopedia of Revolution and Protest (1500 to the Present)*, 8 vols. Oxford: Wiley-Blackwell.

Neuhaus, John M., John D. Kalbfleisch, and Walter W. Hauck. 1991. "A Comparison of Cluster-Specific and Population-Averaged Approaches for Analyzing Correlated Binary Data." *International Statistical Review/Revue Internationale de Statistique* 59, 1: 25–35.

Neumayer, Eric and Thomas Plümper. 2017. *Robustness Tests for Quantitative Research*. Cambridge: Cambridge University Press.

Nicholls, Walter. 2008. "The Urban Question Revisited: The Importance of Cities for Social Movements." *International Journal of Urban and Regional Research* 32: 1468–2427.

Nielsen, Richard A. 2016. "Case Selection via Matching." *Sociological Methods & Research* 45, 3: 569–97.

Nielsen, Richard A. and Beth A. Simmons. 2015. "Rewards for Ratification: Payoffs for Participating in the International Human Rights Regime?" *International Studies Quarterly* 59, 2: 197–208.

Nikolayenko, Olena. 2017. *Youth Movements and Elections in Eastern Europe*. Cambridge: Cambridge University Press.

Nodia, Ghia. 2000. "The End of Revolution?" *Journal of Democracy* 11, 1: 164–71.

Nordlinger, Eric A. 1977. *Soldiers in Politics: Military Coups and Governments*. Englewood Cliffs, NJ: Prentice Hall, 1977.

O'Connor, Francis Patrick and Leonidas Oikonomakis. 2015. "Preconflict Mobilization Strategies and Urban–Rural Transition: The Cases of the PKK and the FLN/EZLN." *Mobilization: An International Quarterly* 20, 3: 379–99.

Offe, Claus. 1985. "New Social Movements: Challenging the Boundaries of Institutional Politics." *Social Research* 52, 4: 817–68.

Oliynyk, Olena. 2015. "The Architectural Image of Kiev's Central Square as a Symbol of National Identity." *Tales of Urban Lives and Spaces: De Urbanitate* 3: 83–92.

Ollamh, G. and C. Lanthier. 2016. "Urban Protest in Bahrain: (Re)configuring Public Space." In Deen Sharp and Claire Panetta, eds, *Beyond the Square: Urbanism and the Arab Uprisings*. New York: Terreform, 143–61.

Olson, Mancur. 1971. *The Logic of Collective Action: Public Goods and the Theory of Groups* (revised edition). Cambridge, MA: Harvard University Press.

Olson, Mancur. 1982. *The Rise and Decline of Nations: Economic Growth, Stagflation, and Social Rigidities*. New Haven, CT: Yale University Press.

Olsson-Yaouzis, Nicolas. 2010. "Revolutionaries, Despots, and Rationality." *Rationality and Society* 22, 3: 283–99.

O'Mahoney, Ivan (dir.). 2006. *How to Plan a Revolution*. 2006. London: BBC.

Onuch, Olga. 2014a. *Mapping Mass Mobilizations: Understanding Revolutionary Moments in Ukraine and Argentina*. London: Palgrave.

Onuch, Olga. 2014b. "Social Networks and Social Media in Ukrainian 'Euromaidan' Protests." *The Washington Post*, January 2, https://www.washingtonpost.com/news/monkey-cage/wp/2014/01/02/social-networks-and-social-media-in-ukrainian-euromaidan-protests-2/.

Onuch, Olga and Gwendolyn Sasse. 2016. "The Maidan in Movement: Diversity and the Cycles of Protest." *Europe-Asia Studies* 68, 4: 556–87.

Opp, Karl Dieter. 1994. "Repression and Revolutionary Action: East Germany in 1989." *Rationality and Society* (January): 101–38.

Opp, Karl-Dieter and Wolfgang Roehl. 1990. "Repression, Micromobilization, and Political Protest." *Social Forces* 69, 2: 521–47.

Opp, Karl-Dieter, Peter Voss, and Christiane Gern. 1995. *Origins of a Spontaneous Revolution: East Germany, 1989*. Ann Arbor, MI: University of Michigan Press.

O'Sullivan, Patrick. 1983. "A Geographical Analysis of Guerrilla Warfare." *Political Geography Quarterly* 2, 2: 139–50.

Owen, John M., IV. 2010. *The Clash of Ideas in World Politics*. Princeton, NJ: Princeton University Press.

Pachon, Alejandro. 2014. "Loyalty and Defection: Misunderstanding Civil–Military Relations in Tunisia during the 'Arab Spring.'" *Journal of Strategic Studies* 37, 4: 508–31.

Paige, Jeffery M. 1975. *Agrarian Revolution: Social Movements and Export Agriculture in the Underdeveloped World*. New York: Free Press.

Palmer, Robert Roswell. 2014. *The Age of the Democratic Revolution: A Political History of Europe and America, 1760–1800* (updated edition). Princeton, NJ: Princeton University Press.

Palmer, Stanley H. 1988. *Police and Protest in England and Ireland, 1780–1850*. Cambridge: Cambridge University Press.

Pan, Wei. 2001. "Akaike's Information Criterion in Generalized Estimating Equations." *Biometrics* 57, 1: 120–25.

Panina, Natalya. 2005. *Ukrainian Society 1994–2005: Sociological Monitoring*. Kyiv: International Center for Policy Studies.

Paraskevas, Frederique. 2011. "Tahrir Square and Haussmann's Paris: Physical Manifestations of Political Doctrines." *Architectural Association* 30, 11, at http://www.aaschool.ac.uk/Downloads/awards/Frederique_Paraskevas.pdf.

Parkinson, John. 2012. *Democracy and Public Space: The Physical Sites of Democratic Performance*. Oxford: Oxford University Press.

Parkinson, Sarah Elizabeth. 2013. "Organizing Rebellion: Rethinking High-Risk Mobilization and Social Networks in War." *American Political Science Review* 107, 3: 418–32.

Parkman, Patricia. 1990. *Insurrectionary Civic Strikes in Latin America, 1931–1961*. Boston, MA: Albert Einstein Institution.

Parsa, Misagh. 2003. "Will Democratization and Globalization Make Revolutions Obsolete?" In John Foran, ed., *The Future of Revolutions: Rethinking Radical Change in the Era of Globalization*. London: ZED, 73–82.

Patel, David S. 2013. "Roundabouts and Revolutions: Public Squares, Coordination, and the Diffusion of the Arab Uprisings." Unpublished paper (available at http://aalims.org/uploads/Patel.pdf).

Patton, David F. 2011. "Annus Mirabilis: 1989 and German Unification." In Helmut Walser Smith, ed., *The Oxford Handbook of Modern German History*. Oxford: Oxford University Press: 753–74.

Pearlman, Wendy. 2013. "Emotions and the Microfoundations of the Arab Uprisings." *Perspectives on Politics* 11, 2: 387–409.

Pearson, Frederic S. and Robert A. Baumann. 1993. "International Military Intervention, 1946–1988." Inter-University Consortium for Political and Social Research, Data Collection No. 6035, University of Michigan.

Peduzzi, Peter, John Concato, Elizabeth Kemper, Theodore R Holford, and Alvan R. Feinstein. 1996. "A Simulation Study of the Number of Events per Variable in Logistic Regression Analysis." *Journal of Clinical Epidemiology* 49, 12: 1373–79.

Pemstein, D., K. L. Marquardt, E. Tzelgov, Y.-T. Wang, J. Krusell, and F. Miri. 2018. "The V-Dem Measurement Model: Latent Variable Analysis for Cross-National and Cross-Temporal Expert-Coded Data," V-Dem Working Paper Series 21 (available at http://www.ssrn.com/abstract=2704787).

Pepe, Margaret Sullivan. 2003. *The Statistical Evaluation of Medical Tests for Classification and Prediction*. Oxford: Oxford University Press.

Pepinsky, Thomas B. 2009. *Economic Crises and the Breakdown of Authoritarian Regimes: Indonesia and Malaysia in Comparative Perspective*. Cambridge: Cambridge University Press.

Perlmutter, Amos. 1969. "The Praetorian State and the Praetorian Army: Toward a Taxonomy of Civil–Military Relations in Developing Polities." *Comparative Politics* 1, 3: 382–404.

Petersen, Roger D. 2001. *Resistance and Rebellion: Lessons from Eastern Europe*. Cambridge: Cambridge University Press.

Pettersson, Therése and Peter Wallensteen. 2015. "Armed Conflicts, 1946–2014." *Journal of Peace Research* 52, 4: 536–50.

Phillips, Charles and Alan Axelrod. 2005. *Encyclopedia of Wars*, 3 vols. New York: Facts on File.

Pieke, Frank N. 1996. *The Ordinary and the Extraordinary: An Anthropological Study of Chinese Reform and the 1989 People's Movement in Beijing*. London: Kegan Paul International.

Pierskalla, Jan H. and Florian M. Hollenbach. 2013. "Technology and Collective Action: The Effect of Cell Phone Coverage on Political Violence in Africa." *American Political Science Review* 107, 2: 207–24.

Pierskalla, Jan, Anna Schultz, and Erik Wibbels. 2017. "Order, Distance, and Local Development over the Long-Run." *Quarterly Journal of Political Science* 12, 4: 375–404.

Pierson, Paul. 2003. "Big, Slow-Moving, and . . . Invisible: Macrosocial Processes in the Study of Comparative Politics." In James Mahoney and Dietrich Rueschemeyer, eds, *Comparative Historical Analysis in the Social Sciences*. Cambridge: Cambridge University Press, 177–207.

Pincus, Steven. 2014. *1688: The First Modern Revolution*. New Haven, CT: Yale University Press.

Pinker, Steven. 2011. *The Better Angels of Our Nature: Why Violence Has Declined*. New York: Viking.

Pipes, Richard. 1990. *The Russian Revolution*. New York: Vintage Books.

Piselli, Fortunata. 2007. "Communities, Places, and Social Networks." *American Behavioral Scientist* 50, 7: 867–78.

Piven, Frances Fox and Richard A. Cloward. 1979. *Poor People's Movements: Why They Succeed, How They Fail*. New York: Vintage.

Plümper, Thomas and Eric Neumayer. 2010. "The Level of Democracy during Interregnum Periods: Recoding the Polity2 Score." *Political Analysis* 18, 2: 206–26.

Polasky, Janet L. 2015. *Revolutions without Borders: The Call to Liberty in the Atlantic World*. New Haven, CT: Yale University Press.

Pollak, Martha D. 1991. *Turin, 1564–1680: Urban Design, Military Culture, and the Creation of the Absolutist Capital*. Chicago: University of Chicago Press.

Polletta, Francesca. 2006. *It Was Like a Fever: Storytelling in Protest and Politics*. Chicago: University of Chicago Press.

Ponticelli, Jacopo and Hans-Joachim Voth. 2012. "Austerity and Anarchy: Budget Cuts and Social Unrest in Europe, 1919–2008." Barcelona Graduate School of Economics, Paper No. 676.

Popkin, Samuel L. 1979. *The Rational Peasant: The Political Economy of Rural Society in Vietnam*. Berkeley, CA: University of California Press.

Portnov, Andriy and Tetiana Portnova. 2015. "The Ukrainian 'Eurorevolution': Dynamics and Meaning." In Viktor Stepanenko and Yaroslav Pylynsky, eds, *Ukraine after the Euromaidan: Challenges and Hopes*. Berlin: Peter Lang, 59–72.

Powell, Jonathan. 2012. "Determinants of the Attempting and Outcome of Coups d'État." *Journal of Conflict Resolution* 56, 6: 1017–40.

Powell, Jonathan and Clayton Thyne. 2011. "Global Instances of Coups from 1950–Present." *Journal of Peace Research* 48, 2: 249–59.

Pravilova, Ekaterina. 2014. *A Public Empire: Property and the Quest for the Common Good in Imperial Russia*. Princeton, NJ: Princeton University Press.

Pryor, Frederic L. 1992. *The Red and the Green: The Rise and Fall of Collectivized Agriculture in Marxist Regimes*. Princeton, NJ: Princeton University Press.

Rabea, Aly Hassan Amin. 2015. "It Happened in Egypt!" In Asaad Al-Saleh, ed., *Voices of the Arab Spring*. New York: Columbia University Press, 83–88.

Rabinowitch, Alexander. 1991. *Prelude to Revolution: The Petrograd Bolsheviks and the July 1917 Uprising*. Bloomington, IN: Indiana University Press.

Radnitz, Scott. 2006. "What Really Happened in Kyrgyzstan?" *Journal of Democracy* 17, 2: 132–46.

Rafael, Vicente L. 2003. "The Cell Phone and the Crowd: Messianic Politics in the Contemporary Philippines." *Philippine Political Science Journal* 24, 47: 3–36.

Rahaghi, John. 2012. "New Tools, Old Goals: Comparing the Role of Technology in the 1979 Iranian Revolution and the 2009 Green Movement." *Journal of Information Policy* 2: 151–82.

Rainey, Carlisle and Kelly McCaskey. 2015. "Estimating Logit Models with Small Samples." Unpublished paper (available at http://www.carlislerainey.com/papers/small.pdf).

Ranger, Terence O. 1968. "Connections between 'Primary Resistance' Movements and Modern Mass Nationalism in East and Central Africa." *The Journal of African History* 9, 3: 437–53.

Rassler, Karen. 1996. "Concessions, Repression, and Political Protest in the Iranian Revolution." *American Sociological Review* 61, 1: 132–52.

Read, Donald. 1958. *Peterloo: The "Massacre" and Its Background*. Manchester: University of Manchester Press.

Reichardt, Sven. 2007. "Fascist Marches in Italy and Germany: Squadre and SA before the Seizure of Power." In Matthias Reiss, ed., *The Street as Stage: Protest Marches and Public Rallies since the Nineteenth Century*. Oxford: Oxford University Press, 169–89.

Reicher, Stephen and Clifford Stott. 2007. "Becoming the Subjects of History: An Outline of the Psychology of Crowds." In Matthias Reiss, ed., *The Street as Stage: Protest Marches and Public Rallies since the Nineteenth Century*. Oxford, UK: Oxford University Press, 25–39.

Reid, Ben. 2001. "The Philippine Democratic Uprising and the Contradictions of Neoliberalism: EDSA II." *Third World Quarterly* 22, 5: 777–93.

Reinhart, Carmen M. and Kenneth S. Rogoff. 2009. *This Time It's Different: Eight Centuries of Financial Folly*. Princeton, NJ: Princeton University Press.

Reiss, Matthias. 2007. "Introduction." In Matthias Reiss, ed., *The Street as Stage: Protest Marches and Public Rallies since the Nineteenth Century*. Oxford: Oxford University Press, 1–21.

Retish, Aaron B. 2008. *Russia's Peasants in Revolution and Civil War: Citizenship, Identity, and the Creation of the Soviet State, 1914–1922*. Cambridge: Cambridge University Press.

Reznik, Oleksandr. 2016. "From the Orange Revolution to the Revolution of Dignity: Dynamics of the Protest Actions in Ukraine." *East European Politics and Societies* 30, 4: 750–65.

Rhoads, Christopher and Loretta Chao. 2009. "Iran's Web Spying Aided by Western Technology: European Gear Used in Vast Effort to Monitor Communications." *The Wall Street Journal*, June 22, at https://www.wsj.com/articles/SB124562668777335653.

Rhoads, Edward J. M. 1975. *China's Republican Revolution: The Case of Kwangtung, 1895–1913*. Cambridge, MA: Harvard University Press.

Richardson, R. C. 1992. "Town and Countryside in the English Revolution." In R. C. Richardson, ed., *Town and Countryside in the English Revolution*. Manchester: Manchester University Press, 1–18.

Riesenberg, Peter. 1992. *Citizenship in the Western Tradition: Plato to Rousseau*. Chapel Hill, NC: University of North Carolina Press.

Ritter, Daniel P. 2015. *The Iron Cage of Liberalism: International Politics and Unarmed Revolutions in the Middle East and North Africa*. Oxford: Oxford University Press.

Roberts, Margaret E. 2018. *Censored: Distraction and Diversion inside China's Great Firewall*. Princeton, NJ: Princeton University Press.

Robertson, Graeme B. 2009. "Managing Society: Protest, Civil Society, and Regime in Putin's Russia." *Slavic Review* 68, 3: 528–47.

Rodrik, Dani and Romain Wacziarg. 2005. "Do Democratic Transitions Produce Bad Economic Outcomes?" *American Economic Review* 95, 2: 50–55.

Rose, Carol. 1986. "The Comedy of Commons: Custom, Commerce, and Inherently Public Property." *The University of Chicago Law Review* 53, 3: 711–81.

Rosenbaum, Paul R. and Donald B. Rubin. 1983. "The Central Role of the Propensity Score in Observational Studies for Causal Effects." *Biometrika* 70, 1: 41–55.

Rosenberg, Tina. 2011. "Revolution U." *Foreign Policy*, February 17, at http://foreignpolicy.com/2011/02/17/revolution-u-2/.

Rosenfeld, Bryn. 2017. "Reevaluating the Middle Class Protest Paradigm: A Case-Control Study of Democratic Protest Coalitions in Russia." *American Political Science Review* 111, 4: 637–52.

Rosenfeld, Bryn. 2021. *The Autocratic Middle Class: How State Dependency Reduces the Demand for Democracy*. Princeton, NJ: Princeton University Press.

Rosenthal, Anton. 2000. "Spectacle, Fear, and Protest: A Guide to the History of Urban Public Space in Latin America." *Social Science History* 24, 1: 33–73.

Ross, Kristin. 1988. *The Emergence of Social Space: Rimbaud and the Paris Commune*. Minneapolis: University of Minnesota Press.

Ross, Michael L. 2001. "Does Oil Hinder Democracy?" *World Politics* 53, 3: 325–61.

Ross, Michael. 2006. "A Closer Look at Oil, Diamonds, and Civil War." *Annual Review of Political Science* 9: 265–300.

Ross, Michael and Paasha Mahdavi. 2015. "Oil and Gas Data, 1932–2014," https://doi.org/10.7910/DVN/ZTPW0Y, Harvard Dataverse, V2, UNF:6:xdrpUdF2kYUJYCgVfgMGcQ== [fileUNF].

Rotberg, Robert I. 2008. "Repressive, Aggressive, and Rogue Nation-States: How Odious, How Dangerous?" In Robert I. Rotberg. ed., *Worst of the Worst: Dealing with Repressive and Rogue Nations*. Washington, DC: Brookings Institution Press, 1–39.

Routledge, Paul. 2010. "Nineteen Days in April: Urban Protest and Democracy in Nepal." *Urban Studies* 47, 6: 1279–99.

Rubin, Donald B. 1973a. "Matching to Remove Bias in Observational Studies." *Biometrics* 29, 1: 159–83.

Rubin, Donald B. 1973b. "The Use of Matched Sampling and Regression Adjustment to Remove Bias in Observational Studies." *Biometrics* 29, 1: 184–203.

Rubin, Donald B. 1974. "Estimating Causal Effects of Treatments in Randomized and Nonrandomized Studies." *Journal of Educational Psychology* 66, 5: 688–701.

Rubin, Donald B. 2001. "Using Propensity Scores to Help Design Observational Studies: Application to the Tobacco Litigation." *Health Services and Outcomes Research Methodology* 2, 3–4: 169–88.

Rucht, Dieter. 2007. "On the Sociology of Protest Marches." In Matthias Reiss, ed., *The Street as Stage: Protest Marches and Public Rallies since the Nineteenth Century*. Oxford: Oxford University Press, 49–57.

Rudé, George. 1995. *The Crowd in History: A Study of Popular Disturbances in France and England, 1730–1848*. London: Serif.

Russett, Bruce M. 1964. "Inequality and Instability: The Relation of Land Tenure to Politics." *World Politics* 16, 3: 442–54.

Ryan, Yasmine. 2011. "How Tunisia's Revolution Began." *Al Jazeera*, January 26, at https://www.aljazeera.com/features/2011/1/26/how-tunisias-revolution-began.

Sabean, David. 1976. "The Communal Basis of Pre-1800 Peasant Uprisings in Western Europe." *Comparative Politics* 8, 3: 355–64.

Sakwa, Richard. 2001. "The Age of Paradox: The Anti-Revolutionary Revolutions of 1989–91." In Moira Donald and Tim Rees, eds, *Reinterpreting Revolution in Twentieth-Century Europe*. London: Palgrave, 159–76.

Salemink, Oscar. 1994. "The Return of the Python God: Multiple Interpretations of a Millenarian Movement in Colonial Vietnam." *History and Anthropology* 8, 1–4: 129–64.

Sambanis, Nicholas. 2004. "What is Civil War? Conceptual and Empirical Complexities of an Operational Definition." *Journal of Conflict Resolution* 48, 6: 814–58.

Samuels, David and Henry Thomson. 2019. "Lord, Peasant . . . and Tractor? Agricultural Mechanization and Moore's Thesis." Unpublished paper, presented at Princeton University, 5 April.

Samuelson, Robert J. 1968. "French Student Revolt: An Account of the Origins and Objectives." *Science* 160, 3831: 971–74.

Sarkees, Meredith Reid and Frank Wayman. 2010. *Resort to War: 1816–2007*. Washington DC: CQ Press (available at http://www.correlatesofwar.org/data-sets/COW-war).

Sarkees, Meredith, Frank Wayman, and J. David Singer. 2003. "Inter-State, Intra-State, and Extra-State Wars: A Comprehensive Look at Their Distribution over Time, 1816–1997." *International Studies Quarterly* 47, 1: 49–70.

Sassen, Saskia. 2001. *The Global City: New York, London, Tokyo*. Princeton, NJ: Princeton University Press.

Sassen, Saskia. 2011. "The Global Street: Making the Political." *Globalizations* 8, 5: 573–79.

Scharre, Paul. 2018. *Army of None: Autonomous Weapons and the Future of War*. New York: W. W. Norton & Company.

Schattschneider, E. E. 1960. *The Semi-Sovereign People: A Realist's View of Democracy in America*. New York: Holt, Rinehart & Winston.

Schock, Kurt. 2005. *Unarmed Insurrections: People Power Movements in Nondemocracies*. Minneapolis: University of Minnesota Press.

Schram, Stuart. 1966. *Mao Tse-Tung*. Baltimore: Penguin.

Schwartz, J., C. Spix, G. Touloumi, L. Bachárová, T. Barumamdzadeh, A. le Tertre, T. Piekarksi et al. 1996. "Methodological Issues in Studies of Air Pollution and Daily Counts of Deaths or Hospital Admissions." *Journal of Epidemiology and Community Health* 50 (Supplement 1): S3–S11.

Schwedler, Jillian. 2018. "Political Dissent in Amman, Jordan: Neoliberal Geographies of Protest and Policing." In Sanford F. Schram and Marianna Pavlovskaya, eds, *Rethinking Neoliberalism: Resisting the Disciplinary Regime*. New York: Routledge, 197–212.

Schwirtz, Michael. 2011. "Russia Allows Protest but Tries to Discourage Attendance." *The New York Times*, December 20: A8.

Scott, James C. 1977. *The Moral Economy of the Peasant: Rebellion and Subsistence in Southeast Asia*. New Haven, CT: Yale University Press.

Scott, James C. 1990. *Domination and the Arts of Resistance: Hidden Transcripts*. New Haven, CT: Yale University Press.

Seekins, Donald M. 2009. "'Runaway Chickens' and Myanmar Identity: Relocating Burma's Capital." *City* 13, 1: 63–70.

Selbin, Eric. 2010. *Revolution, Rebellion, Resistance: The Power of Story*. New York: ZED Books.

Selth, Andrew. 2008. "Myanmar's 'Saffron Revolution' and the Limits of International Influence." *Australian Journal of International Affairs* 62, 3: 281–97.

Sennett, Richard. 1978. *The Fall of Public Man*. New York: Vintage Books.

Seton-Watson, Hugh. 1951. "Twentieth Century Revolution." *The Political Quarterly* 22, 3: 251–65.

Sewell, William H. 1996. "Historical Events as Transformations of Structures: Inventing Revolution at the Bastille." *Theory and Society* 25, 6: 841–81.

Sewell, William H., Jr. 2001. "Space in Contentious Politics." In Ronald R. Aminzade et al., eds. *Silence and Voice in the Study of Contentious Politics*. Cambridge: Cambridge University Press, 51–88.

Seymour, James D. 1990. "Human Rights and the World Response to the 1989 Crackdown in China." *China Information* 4, 4: 1–14.

Shaiban, Baraa. 2012. "After Years of Silence." In Asaad Al-Saleh, ed., *Voices of the Arab Spring*. New York: Columbia University Press, 159–73.

Shanin, Teodor. 1986. *Russia, 1905–07: Revolution as a Moment of Truth*, vol. 2. New Haven, CT: Yale University Press.

Shapiro, Jacob N. and Nils B. Weidmann. 2015. "Is the Phone Mightier than the Sword? Cellphones and Insurgent Violence in Iraq." *International Organization* 69, 2: 247–74.

Sharp, Gene. 2012. *From Dictatorship to Democracy: A Conceptual Framework for Liberation*. New York: The New Press.

Shelton, Allison M., Szymon M. Stojek, and Patricia L. Sullivan. 2013. "What Do We Know about Civil War Outcomes?" *International Studies Review* 15, 4: 515–38.

Shen, Simon and Paul Chi-yuen Chan. 2010. "Failure of the Saffron Revolution and Aftermath: Revisiting the Transitologist Assumption." *The Journal of Comparative Asian Development* 9, 1: 31–57.

Sherwood, Harriet. 2011. "In Tahrir Square, Egyptian Protesters Think the Unthinkable—Victory." *The Guardian*, January 31, at https://www.theguardian.com/world/2011/jan/31/tahrir-square-egypt-demonstrators-think-victory.

Shoul, Simeon. 2008. "British Tear Gas Doctrine between the World Wars." *War in History* 15, 2: 168–90.

Siani-Davies, Peter. 2005. *The Romanian Revolution of December 1989*. Ithaca, NY: Cornell University Press.

Sierra, J. A. n.d. "The Landing of the Granma," at http://www.historyofcuba.com/history/granma.htm.

Sigman, Mariano, Pablo Etchemendy, Diego Fernandez Slezak, and Guillermo A. Cecchi. 2010. "Response Time Distributions in Rapid Chess: A Large-Scale Decision Making Experiment." *Frontiers in Neuroscience* 4, 60: 1–12.

Sigman, R. and Lindberg, S. I. 2015. "The Index of Egalitarian Democracy and its Components: V-Dem's Conceptualization and Measurement." V-Dem Working Paper Series 20 (available at http://www.ssrn.com/abstract=2727612).

Silver, Morris. 1974. "Political Revolution and Repression: An Economic Approach." *Public Choice* 17, 1: 63–71.

Simmons, Beth A. 2009. *Mobilizing for Human Rights: International Law in Domestic Politics*. Cambridge: Cambridge University Press.

Simpson, Erin M. 2013. "The Songs of Angry Men." *Foreign Policy*, January 4, at http://foreignpolicy.com/2013/01/04/the-songs-of-angry-men/.

Singer, D. J. and M. Small. 1994. "Correlates of War Project: International and Civil War Data, 1816–1992." Ann Arbor, MI: Inter-University Consortium for Political and Social Research.

Skocpol, Theda. 1979. *States and Social Revolutions: A Comparative Analysis of France, Russia, and China*. Cambridge: Cambridge University Press.

Skocpol, Theda. 1994. *Social Revolutions in the Modern World*. Cambridge: Cambridge University Press.

Slade, Gavin. 2012. "Georgia's War on Crime: Creating Security in a Post-Revolutionary Context." *European Security* 21, 1: 37–56.

Slater, Dan. 2009. "Revolutions, Crackdowns, and Quiescence: Communal Elites and Democratic Mobilization in Southeast Asia." *American Journal of Sociology* 115, 1: 203–54.

Slater, Dan. 2010. *Ordering Power: Contentious Politics and Authoritarian Leviathans in Southeast Asia*. Cambridge: Cambridge University Press.

Slater, Dan and Nicholas Rush Smith. 2016. "The Power of Counterrevolution: Elitist Origins of Political Order in Postcolonial Asia and Africa." *American Journal of Sociology* 121, 5: 1472–516.

Sly, Liz. 2020. "Stirrings of Unrest Around the World Could Portend Turmoil as Economies Collapse." *The Washington Post* April 19, at https://www.washingtonpost.com/world/coronavirus-protests-lebanon-india-iraq/2020/04/19/1581dde4-7e5f-11ea-84c2-0792d8591911_story.html.

Small, Kenneth A. and Cheng Hsiao. 1985. "Multinomial Logit Specification Tests." *International Economic Review* 26, 3: 619–27.

Smelser, Neil. 1963. *Theory of Collective Behavior*. New York: Free Press.

Smith, Jeffrey R. 2000. "Depth of Corruption Surfacing in Yugoslavia." *The Washington Post*, October 22, at https://www.washingtonpost.com/archive/politics/2000/10/22/depth-of-corruption-surfacing-in-yugoslavia/f2821183-fb0e-470a-a9d9-7d3394ece220/?utm_term=.5a7e75c4caff.

Smith, Matthew J. 2004. "Vive 1804! The Haitian Revolution and the Revolutionary Generation of 1946." *Caribbean Quarterly* 50, 4: 25–41.

Smith, Murray D. 2003. "Modelling Sample Selection Using Archimedean Copulas." *The Econometrics Journal* 6, 1: 99–123.

Smith, Rick. 2019. *The End of Killing: How Our Newest Technologies Can Solve Humanity's Oldest Problem*. Vancouver: Page Two Books.

Snow, Edgar. 1973. *Red Star over China* (revised and enlarged edition). New York: Grove Press.

Snyder, Robert S. 1999. "The End of Revolution?" *The Review of Politics* 61, 1: 5–28.

Soifer, Hillel, and Matthias vom Hau. 2008. "Unpacking the Strength of the State: The Utility of State Infrastructural Power." *Studies in Comparative International Development* 43, 3–4: 231–51.

Solomon, Robert L. 1969. "Saya San and the Burmese Rebellion." *Modern Asian Studies* 3, 3: 209–23.

Solov'ev, V. A. n.d. "Istoriia Manezhskoi ploshchadi." SV-Astur, at http://www.svastour.ru/articles/puteshestviya/rossiya/moskva/istoriya-manezhnoy-ploshchadi.html.

Sorokin, Pitrim A. 1925. *The Sociology of Revolution*. Philadelphia: J. P. Lippincott Company.
Soule, Sarah A. and Christian Davenport. 2009. "Velvet Glove, Iron Fist, or Even Hand? Protest Policing in the United States, 1960–1990." *Mobilization* 14, 1: 1–22.
Sperber, Jonathan. 2005. *The European Revolutions, 1848–1851*. Cambridge: Cambridge University Press.
Staniland, Paul. 2010. "Cities on Fire: Social Mobilization, State Policy, and Urban Insurgency." *Comparative Political Studies* 43, 12: 1623–49.
Staniland, Paul. 2014. *Networks of Rebellion: Explaining Insurgent Cohesion and Collapse*. Ithaca, NY: Cornell University Press.
Stepanenko, Viktor. 2005. "How Ukrainians View Their Orange Revolution: Public Opinion and the National Peculiarities of Citizenry Political Activities." *Demokratizatsiya* 13, 4: 595–616.
Stephen, Chris. 2016. "Tunisia Imposes Curfew as Unrest Grows over Lack of Jobs." *The Guardian*, January 22, at https://www.theguardian.com/world/2016/jan/22/tunisia-unrest-government-imposes-night-curfew-unemployment-protests-attacks.
Stinchcombe, Arthur L. 1999. "Ending Revolutions and Building New Governments." *Annual Review of Political Science* 2: 49–73.
Stites, Richard. 1976. "Zhenotdel: Bolshevism and Russian Women, 1917–1930." *Russian History* 3, 2: 174–93.
Stokes, Gale. 1993. *The Walls Came Tumbling Down: The Collapse of Communism in Eastern Europe*. Oxford: Oxford University Press.
Stokes, Susan C. 1991. "Politics and Latin America's Urban Poor: Reflections from a Lima Shantytown." *Latin American Research Review* 26, 2: 75–101.
Stokes, Susan. 2009. "Political Clientelism." In Carles Boix and Susan Stokes, eds, *The Oxford Handbook of Comparative Politics*. Oxford: Oxford University Press, 648–73.
Straus, Scott. 2006. *The Order of Genocide: Race, Power, and War in Rwanda*. Ithaca, NY: Cornell University Press.
Straus, Scott. 2015. *Making and Unmaking Nations: War, Leadership, and Genocide in Modern Africa*. Ithaca, NY: Cornell University Press.
Stuart, Elizabeth A. 2010. "Matching Methods for Causal Inference: A Review and a Look Forward." *Statistical Science: A Review Journal of the Institute of Mathematical Statistics* 25, 1: 1–21.
Sukhanov, Nikolai N. 1922. *Zapiski o revoliutsii*, vol. 1. Berlin: Izdatel'stvso Z. I. Grzhebina.
Sullivan, Christopher M. 2016. "Undermining Resistance: Mobilization, Repression, and the Enforcement of Political Order." *Journal of Conflict Resolution* 60, 7: 1163–90.
Sundström, Aksel, Pamela Paxton, Yi-Ting Wang, and Staffan Lindberg. 2015. "Women's Political Empowerment: A New Global Index, 1900–2012." Varieties of Democracy Institute Working Paper Series, No. 18.
Svolik, Milan W. 2012. *The Politics of Authoritarian Rule*. Cambridge: Cambridge University Press.
Sweig, Julia. 2002. *Inside the Cuban Revolution: Fidel Castro and the Urban Underground*. Cambridge, MA: Harvard University Press.
Tadros, Mariz. 2011. "Sectarianism and Its Discontents in Post-Mubarak Egypt." *Middle East Report* 41, 2: 26–31.
Tai, Hung-chao. 1974. *Land Reform and Politics: A Comparative Analysis*. Berkeley, CA: University of California Press, 1974.

Tarrow, Sidney. 1991. "'Aiming at a Moving Target': Social Science and the Recent Rebellions in Eastern Europe." *PS: Political Science and Politics* 24, 1: 12–20.

Tarrow, Sidney. 1998. *Power in Movement: Social Movements and Contentious Politics* (2nd edition). Cambridge: Cambridge University Press.

Tarrow, Sidney. 2005. *The New Transnational Activism*. Cambridge: Cambridge University Press.

Taylor, Michael. 1988. "Rationality and Revolutionary Collective Action." In Michael Taylor, ed., *Rationality and Revolution*. Cambridge: Cambridge University Press, 63–97.

Tezcür, Güneş Murat. 2016. "Ordinary People, Extraordinary Risks: Participation in an Ethnic Rebellion." *American Political Science Review* 110, 2: 247–64.

Thawnghmung, Ardeth Maung and Maung Aung Myoe. 2008. "Myanmar in 2007: A Turning Point in the Roadmap?" *Asian Survey* 48, 1: 13–19.

Thomas, Martin. 2012. *Violence and Colonial Order: Police, Workers and Protest in the European Colonial Empires, 1918–1940*. Cambridge: Cambridge University Press.

Thompson, Mark R. 2004. *Democratic Revolutions: Asia and Eastern Europe*. New York: Routledge.

Thompson, Nick. 1999. "What Makes a Revolution? Burma's Revolt of 1988 and a Comparative Analysis of the Revolutions of the Late 1980s." *Studies in Conflict and Terrorism* 22, 1: 33–52.

Thomson, Henry. 2016. "Rural Grievances, Landholding Inequality and Civil Conflict." *International Studies Quarterly* 60, 3: 511–519.

Thyne, Clayton. 2010. "Supporter of Stability or Agent of Agitation? The Effect of United States Foreign Policy on Coups in Latin America, 1960–1999." *Journal of Peace Research* 47, 4: 1–13.

Tillack, Peter and Eberhard Schulze. 2012. "Decollectivization and Restructuring of Farms," in P. Wehrheim, K. Frohberg, E. Serova, and J. von Braun, eds, *Russia's Agro-Food Sector: Towards Truly Functioning Markets*. Bonn: Kluwer, 447–70.

Tilly, Charles. 1964. *The Vendée*. Cambridge, MA: Harvard University Press.

Tilly, Charles. 1974. *An Urban World*. Boston, MA: Little, Brown and Company.

Tilly, Charles. 1978. *From Mobilization to Revolution*. New York: Random House.

Tilly, Charles. 1984. *Big Structures, Large Processes, Huge Comparisons*. New York: Russell Sage Foundation.

Tilly, Charles. 1990. *Coercion, Capital, and European States, AD 990–1990*. Cambridge, MA: Blackwell.

Tilly, Charles. 1993. *European Revolutions, 1492–1992*. Oxford: Oxford University Press.

Tilly, Charles. 1995a. "The Bourgeois Gentilshommes of Revolutionary Theory." In Nikki R. Keddie, ed., *Debating Revolutions*. New York: New York University Press, 136–41.

Tilly, Charles. 1995b. *Popular Contention in Great Britain, 1758–1834*. Cambridge, MA: Harvard University Press.

Tilly, Charles. 2000. "Spaces of Contention." *Mobilization* 5, 2: 135–59.

Tilly, Charles. 2003. *The Politics of Collective Violence*. Cambridge: Cambridge University Press.

Tilly, Charles. 2008. *Contentious Performances*. Cambridge: Cambridge University Press.

Tocqueville, Alexis de. 1969. *Democracy in America* (translated by George Lawrence). Garden City, NY: Doubleday.

Tocqueville, Alexis de. 2011. *The Ancien Regime and the French Revolution* (translated by Jon Elster and Arthur Goldhammer). Cambridge: Cambridge University Press.

Tőkés, Rudolf. 1967. *Béla Kun and the Hungarian Soviet Republic: The Origins and Role of the Communist Party of Hungary in the Revolutions of 1918–1919*. New York: F. A. Praeger.

Tonkiss, Frank. 2005. *Space, the City and Social Theory: Social Relations and Urban Forms.* Cambridge: Polity.

Topolyan, Polina 2017. "Urban Democracy." *European Politics,* July 9, at https://www.europeanpolitics.ro/index.php/2017/07/09/guest-article-urban-democracy/.

Torba, Valentyn. 2016. "The Lesson of the Revolution on the Granite." *Den',* October 4, at http://m.day.kyiv.ua/en/article/day-after-day/lesson-revolution-granite.

Traugott, Mark. 1995. "Capital Cities and Revolution." *Social Science History* 19, 1: 147–68.

Traugott, Mark. 2002. *Armies of the Poor.* New Brunswick, NJ: Transaction Publishers.

Traugott, Mark. 2010. *The Insurgent Barricade.* Berkeley, CA: University of California Press.

Trilling, Lionel. 1972. *Sincerity and Authenticity.* Cambridge, MA: Harvard University Press.

Trimberger, Ellen Kay. 1978. *Revolution from Above: Military Bureaucrats and Development in Japan, Turkey, Egypt, and Peru.* New Brunswick, NJ: Transaction.

Trotsky, Leon. 1932. *The History of the Russian Revolution,* 3 vols. New York: Simon and Schuster.

Tsebelis, George and John Sprague. 1989. "Coercion and Revolution: Variations on a Predator–Prey Model." *Mathematical and Computer Modelling* 12, 4–5: 547–59.

Tucker, Joshua A. 2007. "Enough! Electoral Fraud, Collective Action Problems, and Post-Communist Colored Revolutions." *Perspectives on Politics* 5, 3: 535–51.

Tucker, Robert C., ed. 1972. *Marx-Engels Reader.* New York: W. W. Norton.

Tufekci, Zeynep and Christopher Wilson. 2012. "Social Media and the Decision to Participate in Political Protest: Observations from Tahrir Square." *Journal of Communication* 62, 2: 363–79.

Tullock, Gordon. 1971. "The Paradox of Revolution." *Public Choice* 11, 1: 89–99.

Uitermark, Justus, Maaren Loopmans, and Walter Nicholls. 2012. "Cities and Social Movements: Theorizing Beyond the Right to the City." *Environment and Planning A* 44 (November): 2546–54.

Ulfelder, Jay. 2005. "Contentious Collective Action and the Breakdown of Authoritarian Regimes." *International Political Science Review* 26, 3: 311–34.

United Nations Center for Human Settlements (Habitat). 2001. *Cities in a Globalizing World: Global Report on Human Settlements 2001.* London: Earthscan.

United Nations Department of Economic and Social Affairs, Population Division. 2005. "The Diversity of Changing Population Age Structures in the World." UN/POP/PD/2005/1 (available at http://www.un.org/esa/population/meetings/EGMPopAge/1_UNPD_Trends.pdf).

United Nations Department of Economic and Social Affairs, Population Division. 2006. *World Urbanization Prospects: The 2005 Revision.* New York: United Nations.

United Nations Department of Economic and Social Affairs, Population Division. 2014. "World Urbanization Prospects, the 2014 revision" (available at https://esa.un.org/unpd/wup/CD-ROM/).

United Nations. 2019. *World Urbanization Prospects: The 2018 Revision.* New York: Department of Economic and Social Affairs.

United Nations. 2020. *Inequality in a Rapidly Changing World.* New York: Department of Economic and Social Affairs.

United States Institute of Peace. 2001. "Whither the Bulldozer? Nonviolent Revolution and the Transition to Democracy in Serbia." Special report, Washington, DC, August 6.

UNU-WIDER. 2017. "World Income Inequality Database (WIID3.4)," https://www.wider.unu.edu/database/world-income-inequality-database-wiid34.

Urdal, Henrik. 2006. "A Clash of Generations? Youth Bulges and Political Violence." *International Studies Quarterly* 50, 3: 607–29.

Urdal, Henrik 2008. "Population, Resources, and Political Violence: A Subnational Study of India, 1956–2002." *Journal of Conflict Resolution* 52: 590–617.

Vale, Lawrence J. 2014. "Capital Architecture and National Identity." In Michael Minkenberg, ed., *Power and Architecture: The Construction of Capitals and the Politics of Space*. New York: Berghahn Books, 31–52.

Valentino, Benjamin, Paul Huth, and Dylan Balch-Lindsay. 2004. "'Draining the Sea': Mass Killing and Guerilla Warfare." *International Organization* 58, 2: 375–407.

Valiyev, Anar M. 2006. "Parliamentary Elections in Azerbaijan: A Failed Revolution." *Problems of Postcommunism* 53, 3: 17–35.

Van Buuren, Stef. 2018. *Flexible Imputation of Missing Data* (2nd edition). Boca Raton, FL: Chapman & Hall.

Van Ginkel, Joost R., Marielle Linting, Ralph C. A. Rippe, and Anja van der Voort. 2020. "Rebutting Existing Misconceptions about Multiple Imputation as a Method for Handling Missing Data." *Journal of Personality Assessment* 102, 3: 297–308.

Van Laer, Jeroen. 2010. "Activists Online and Offline: The Internet as an Information Channel for Protest Demonstrations." *Mobilization: An International Quarterly* 15, 3: 347–66.

Van Laer, Jeroen and Peter Van Aelst. 2010. "Internet and Social Movement Action Repertoires: Opportunities and Limitations." *Information, Communication & Society* 13, 8: 1146–71.

Van Smeden, Maarten, Joris A. H. de Groot, Karel G. M. Moons, Gary S. Collins, Douglas G. Altman, Marinus J. C. Eijkemans, and Johannes B. Reitsma. 2016. "No Rationale for 1 Variable per 10 Events Criterion for Binary Logistic Regression Analysis." *BMC Medical Research Methodology* 16, DOI 10.1186/s12874-016-0267-3.

Vanhanen, Tatu. 2003. "Democratization and Power Resources 1850–2000" (computer file). FSD1216, version 1.0 (2003-03-10). Tampere, Finland: Finnish Social Science Data Archive.

Vega, Luis Mercier. 1969. *Guerrillas in Latin America: The Technique of the Counter-State*. New York: Frederick A. Praeger.

Vejvoda, Ivan. 2009. "Civil Society versus Slobodan Milosevic: Serbia, 1991–2000." In Adam Roberts and Timothy Garton Ash, eds, *Civil Resistance and Power Politics: The Experience of Non-Violent Action from Gandhi to the Present*. Oxford: Oxford University Press, 295–316.

Verba, Sidney, Kay Lehman Schlozman, and Henry E. Brady. 1995. *Voice and Equality: Civic Voluntarism in American Politics*. Cambridge, MA: Harvard University Press.

Verba, Sidney, Norman H. Nie, and Jae-on Kim. 1978. *Participation and Political Equality: A Seven-Nation Comparison*. Chicago: University of Chicago Press.

Vermunt, Jeroen K. and Jay Magidson. 2002. "Latent Class Cluster Analysis." In J. A. Hagenaars and A. L. McCutcheon, eds, *Applied Latent Class Analysis*. Cambridge: Cambridge University Press, 88–106.

Vickers, Miranda and James Pettifer. 1997. *Albania: From Anarchy to a Balkan Identity*. London: Hurst & Company.

Vilas, Carlos M. 2006. "Neoliberal Meltdown and Social Protest: Argentina 2001–2002." *Critical Sociology* 32, 1: 163–86.

Vittinghoff, Eric and Charles E. McCulloch. 2007. "Relaxing the Rule of Ten Events per Variable in Logistic and Cox Regression." *American Journal of Epidemiology* 165, 6: 710–18.

Vogler, Richard. 1991. *Reading the Riot Act: The Magistracy, the Police, and the Army in Civil Disorder*. Milton Keynes: Open University Press.

Volkov, Denis. 2012. "Protestnoe dvizhenia v Rossii v kontse 2011–2012 gg.: Istoki, dinamika, rezultaty." Levada-Tsentr, Moscow, September 2012, at https://www.hse.ru/data/2012/11/03/1249193438/movementreport.pdf.

Waddington, Philip A. J. 1987. "Towards Paramilitarism? Dilemmas in Policing Civil Disorder." *The British Journal of Criminology* 27, 1: 37–46.

Wahlström, Mattias. 2010. "Producing Spaces for Representation: Racist Marches, Counter-demonstrations, and Public-Order Policing." *Environment and Planning D: Society and Space* 28, 5: 811–27.

Walder, Andrew G. 2009. "Political Sociology and Social Movements." *Annual Review of Sociology* 35: 393–412.

Walker, Louise. 2013. *Waking from the Dream, Mexico's Middle Classes after 1968*. Stanford, CA: Stanford University Press.

Wallace, Jeremy. 2013. "Cities, Redistribution, and Authoritarian Regime Survival." *The Journal of Politics* 75, 3: 632–45.

Walt, Stephen M. 1996. *Revolution and War*. Ithaca, NY: Cornell University Press.

Wang, Vivian, Maria Abi-Habab, and Vivian Yee. 2020. "'This Government is Lucky': Coronavirus Quiets Global Protest Movements." *The New York Times*, April 23, at https://www.nytimes.com/2020/04/23/world/asia/coronavirus-protest-hong-kong-india-lebanon.html?referringSource=articleShare.

Wantchekon, Leonard and Zvika Neeman. 2002. "A Theory of Post-Civil War Democratization." *Journal of Theoretical Politics* 14, 4: 439–64.

Way, Lucan. 2005. "Kuchma's Failed Authoritarianism," *Journal of Democracy* 16, 2: 131–45.

Wayne, Leslie. 2016. "A Ukrainian Kleptocrat Wants His Money and U.S. Asylum." *The New York Times*, July 6, at https://www.nytimes.com/2016/07/07/business/international/a-ukrainian-kleptocrat-wants-his-money-and-us-asylum.html.

Weber, Max. 1958. *The City*. New York: The Free Press.

Wedeen, Lisa. 2019. *Authoritarian Apprehensions: Ideology, Judgment, and Mourning in Syria*. Chicago: University of Chicago Press.

Weede, Erich and Edward N. Muller. 1997. "Consequences of Revolutions." *Rationality and Society* 9, 3: 327–50.

Weinstein, Jeremy M. 2006. *Inside Rebellion: The Politics of Insurgent Violence*. Cambridge: Cambridge University Press.

Weiss, Meredith L. 2006. *Protest and Possibilities: Civil Society and Coalitions for Political Change in Malaysia*. Stanford, CA: Stanford University Press.

Westad, Odd Arne. 2005. *The Global Cold War: Third World Interventions and the Making of Our Times*. Cambridge: Cambridge University Press.

Weyland, Kurt. 2009. "The Diffusion of Revolution: '1848' in Europe and Latin America." *International Organization* 63, 3: 391–423.

Weyland, Kurt. 2012. "The Arab Spring: Why the Surprising Similarities with the Revolutionary Wave of 1848?" *Perspectives on Politics* 10, 4: 917–34.

Weyland, Kurt. 2014. *Making Waves: Democratic Contention in Europe and Latin America since the Revolutions of 1848*. Cambridge: Cambridge University Press.

Wheaton, Bernard and Zdenek Kavan. 1992. *The Velvet Revolution: Czechoslovakia, 1988–1991*. Boulder, CO: Westview Press.

White, Ian R. and John B. Carlin. 2010. "Bias and Efficiency of Multiple Imputation Compared with Complete-Case Analysis for Missing Covariate Values." *Statistics in Medicine* 29, 28: 2920–31.

White, Ian R., Patrick Royston, and Angela M. Wood. 2011. "Multiple Imputation Using Chained Equations: Issues and Guidance for Practice." *Statistics in Medicine* 30, 4: 377–99.

White, Robert and Terry White Falkenberg. 1991. "Revolutionaries in the City: On the Resources of Urban Guerrillas." *Terrorism and Political Violence* 3, 4: 100–132.

White, Stephen and Ian McAllister. 2009. "Rethinking the 'Orange Revolution.'" *Journal of Communist Studies and Transition Politics* 25, 2: 227–54.

Wibbels, Erik. 2019. "Seeing the State: Measuring State Capacity across Geography," at https://sites.duke.edu/statecapacity/files/2019/04/Wibbels-2019-Measuring-State-Capacity.pdf.

Wickham-Crowley, Timothy P. 1992. *Guerrillas and Revolution in Latin America: A Comparative Study of Insurgents and Regimes since 1956*. Princeton, NJ: Princeton University Press.

Williams, Kieran. 2009. "Civil Resistance in the 'Velvet Revolution,' 1968–1989." In Adam Roberts and Timothy Garton Ash, eds, *Civil Resistance and Power Politics*. Oxford: Oxford University Press, 110–26.

Wilson, Andrew. 2005. *Ukraine's Orange Revolution*. New Haven, CT: Yale University Press.

Wilson, Andrew. 2014. *Ukraine Crisis: What It Means for the West*. New Haven, CT: Yale University Press.

Wimmer, Andreas. 2012. *Waves of War: Nationalism, State Formation, and Ethnic Exclusion in the Modern World*. Cambridge: Cambridge University Press.

Wimmer, Andreas, Lars-Erik Cederman, and Brian Min. 2009. "Ethnic Politics and Armed Conflict: A Configurational Analysis of a New Global Dataset." *American Sociological Review* 74, 2: 316–37.

Wimmer, Andreas and Brian Min. 2006. "From Empire to Nation-State: Explaining Wars in the Modern World, 1816–2001." *American Sociological Review* 71, 6: 867–97.

Wirth, Louis. 1969. "Urbanism as a Way of Life." In Richard Sennett, ed., *Classic Essays on the Culture of Cities*. Englewood Cliffs, NJ: Prentice-Hall, 143–64.

Wolf, Eric R. 1969. *Peasant Wars of the Twentieth Century*. New York: Harper & Row.

Wood, Elisabeth Jean. 2000. *Forging Democracy from Below: Insurgent Transitions in South Africa and El Salvador*. Cambridge: Cambridge University Press.

Wood, Elisabeth Jean. 2003. *Insurgent Collective Action and Civil War in El Salvador*. Cambridge: Cambridge University Press.

Wood, Elisabeth Jean. 2009. "Ethnographic Research in the Shadow of Civil War." In Edward Schatz, ed., *Political Ethnography: What Immersion Contributes to the Study of Power*. Chicago: University of Chicago Press, 119–42.

Wood, Lesley J. 2014. *Crisis and Control: The Militarization of Protest Policing*. London: Pluto Press.

World Almanac. 1905. New York: Press Publishing.

Wright, Erik Olin. 1980. "Class and Occupation," *Theory and Society* 9, 1: 177–214.

Wright, Joseph. 2009. "How Foreign Aid Can Foster Democratization in Authoritarian Regimes." *American Journal of Political Science* 53, 3: 552–71.

Wright, Joseph and Abel Escribà-Folch. 2012. "Authoritarian Institutions and Regime Survival: Transitions to Democracy and Subsequent Autocracy." *British Journal of Political Science* 42, 2: 283–309.

Wright, Joseph, Erica Frantz, and Barbara Geddes. 2015. "Oil and Autocratic Regime Survival." *British Journal of Political Science* 45, 2: 287–306.

Xu, Xu. 2020. "To Repress or to Co-opt? Authoritarian Control in the Age of Digital Surveillance." *American Journal of Political Science*, at https://doi.org/10.1111/ajps.12514.

Yaka, Özge and Serhat Karakayali. 2017. "Emergent Infrastructures: Solidarity, Spontaneity and Encounter at Istanbul's Gezi Park Uprising." In Gavin Brown, Anna Feigenbaum, Fabian Frenzel, and Patrick McCurdy, eds, *Protest Camps in International Context: Spaces, Infrastructures and Media of Resistance*. Bristol: Policy Press, 53–70.

Yarwood, Richard and Till Paasche. 2015. "The Relational Geographies of Policing and Security." *Geography Compass* 9, 6: 362–70.

Yom, Sean L. and F. Gregory Gause III. 2012. "Resilient Royals: How Arab Monarchies Hang On." *Journal of Democracy* 23, 4: 74–88.

York, Steve (dir.). 2007. *Orange Revolution* (DVD). Washington, DC: York/Zimmerman Films.

Zakay, Dan. 1993. "The Impact of Time Perception Processes on Decision Making under Time Stress." In Ola Svenson and A. John Maule, eds, *Time Pressure and Stress in Human Judgment and Decision Making*. New York: Springer, 59–72.

Zamiatin, Evgenii. 1967. *My*. New York: Mezhdunarodnoe literaturnoe sodruzhestvo.

Zhao, Dingxin. 2004. *The Power of Tiananmen: State–Society Relations and the 1989 Beijing Student Movement*. Chicago: University of Chicago Press.

Zhukovsky, Arkadii. 2008a. "Khreshchatyk." In Roman Senkus, ed., *Internet Encyclopedia of Ukraine*. Toronto: Canadian Institute of Ukrainian Studies, at http://www.encyclopediaofukraine.com/display.asp?linkpath=pages%5CK%5CH%5CKhreshchatyk.htm.

Zhukovsky, Arkadii. 2008b. "The Struggle for Independence." In Roman Senkus, ed., *Internet Encyclopedia of Ukraine*. Toronto: Canadian Institute of Ukrainian Studies, at http://www.encyclopediaofukraine.com/display.asp?linkpath=pages%5CS%5CT%5CStruggleforIndependence1917hD720.htm.

Zimmermann, Ekkart. 1990. "On the Outcomes of Revolutions: Some Preliminary Considerations." *Sociological Theory* 8, 1: 33–47.

Zimmermann, Matilde. 2001. *Sandinista: Carlos Fonseca and the Nicaraguan Revolution*. Durham, NC: Duke University Press.

Žižek, Slavoj. 2011. "For Egypt, This Is the Miracle of Tahrir Square." *The Guardian*, February 10, at https://www.theguardian.com/global/2011/feb/10/egypt-miracle-tahrir-square.

Zunes, Stephen. 1994. "Unarmed Insurrections against Authoritarian Governments in the Third World: A New Kind of Revolution?" *Third World Quarterly* 15, 3: 403–26.

INDEX

Note: Page numbers in italic type indicate figures or tables.

agency, revolutionary role of, 35–37, 106–8, 198, 224
age of revolutionary participants, 290–92, *290*. *See also* youth, revolutionary participation of
Agha-Soltan, Neda, 100
agrarian-bureaucratic society, 6, 15, 34, 57, 65–71, 420
Albania, 142–43, 426
Albertus, Michael, 69
Alexandria (Egypt): in Egyptian Revolution, 218, 228, 269; public space and revolutionary mobilization in, 253–54, *255*
Algeria, 67, 339n45, 346, 374, 426
Algerian Revolution (1954–62), 319, 327
Aliyev, Ilham, 163, 166
Al Jazeera, 310, 312
Amann, Peter, 47n80
American Revolution, 22, 25, 85
Amritsar massacre (1919), 348
Angolan War for Independence, 204
Anti-Chavez Revolt (Venezuela, 2002), 30n34
anti-colonial revolutions, 57, 61n6, 73, 83, 89–90, 167n40, 351
APRA Rebellion (Peru, 1932), 63, 324
April Revolution (South Korea, 1960), 162, 209, 216–17, 233, 259, 274, 351, 360, 412
April 6 Youth Movement (Egypt), 291, 300, 311
Aquino, Corazon (Cory), 140, 222–23, 234
Aquino, Ninoy, 140
Arab Barometer surveys, 280–84, 280n, 288, 303, 311, 312

Arab Spring: catalysts of, 11; cultural divisions within, 300–301; democratic values and, 273, 304, 307; digital technologies and, 310–11; gender of participants in, 289; media use within, 310; military's role in, 164; nationalism as factor in, 300; regime type as factor in, 110; as revolutionary wave, 58, 168–69; role of squares in, 253; secondary cities in, 259n83. *See also* Bahrain; Egyptian Revolution (2011); February 20 Movement (Morocco); Libya; Syria; Tunisian Revolution (2010); Yemeni Revolution (2011).
Arel, Dominique, 212
Arendt, Hannah, 24, 94, 319
Argentina, 74n34, 99
Aristotle, 236
armed rebellion: in cities, 5, 21, 43, 52, 75–81, 184–85, 192, 246–47, 209, 260–61, 321, 335, 345–46; and civil war, 323–24; in the countryside, 5, 21, 42–43, 52, 74–75, 78–79, 183, 185–87, 209, 260, 335; and social revolution, 79; 157; urban civic repertoire vs., 13, 43, 81, 152, 338. *See also* civil war; violence
Armenia: color revolution attempt in (2008), 112, 155n5; revolution in 2018, 426, 433
Armenian Genocide (1915–16), 319
Ashworth, Gregory, 75
Asian financial crisis (1997), 99, 138–39, 147
August Uprising (Georgia, 1924), 339n
Aung San Suu Kyi, 130

547

Aya, Rod, 362
Azerbaijan: Black January (1990) in, 324; economy after failed color revolution, 387; failed color revolution (2005) in, 155, 160, 163–64, 166; police force in, 166; resources/wealth of, 163–64

backlash mobilization, 17, 21, 43, 81, 134, 136, 137, 139, 160, 220, 347, 349, 351, 357, 423
Bahrain: cultural divisions within, 133; government repression of revolution in, 262–63; public space in, 248–49, 262, 263; shooting into crowds in, 354; social networks in, 85–86
Balbas, Braulio, 231
Barany, Zoltan, 164
Baron, Ilan Zvi, 244
barricades, 5, 75, 76, 233, 246, 261, 272, 346, 351, 352
Basic Principles on the Use of Force and Firearms by Law Enforcement Officials, 355
Basque Separatist Movement, 74n34
Batista, Fulgencio, 49
batons, 211, 350
Bayat, Asef, 11, 252, 253
Belarus: absence of symbolic public space in, 250n48; failed color revolution in (2006), 155n5; failed revolution attempt in (2020), 427, 428n21, 433; government repression in, 268–69, 429
Bellamy, Alex, 346
Bellin, Eva, 164
Ben Ali, Zine El Abidine, 124–26, 164n34, 224n92, 277, 311
Beninese Revolution (1989), 29, 111, 114
Bennett, Lance, 312, 315–17
Berridge, W. J., 256
Biden, Joe, 430
Bill of Rights (United States), 265
biographical availability, 287
Black January (Azerbaijan, 1990), 324
Black Power Revolution (Trinidad, 1970), 74
Boldin, Valery, 221

Bolivia, 91
Bolshevik Revolution (Russia, 1917). See October Revolution (Russia, 1917)
bomb cyclone analogy, 105, 139, 150
Bouazizi, Mohamed, 125–26, 277
Boudreau, Julie-Anne, 206
bourgeoisie, 10, 10n33, 31, 419
Box, George, 48
Braunfels, Wolfgang, 242
Brinton, Crane, 31–32, 361
Brown, Wendy, 418n6
Bulgarian partisans, 204
Bulldozer Revolution (Serbia, 2000), 23, 29, 96, 114, 126–28, 132, 155n5, 201, 229, 412
bullets, wooden, rubber, or plastic, 352–53
Burjanadze, Nino, 212
Burkina Faso, 30
Burma. See Myanmar
Burma Socialist Program Party, 129

Calderon, Felipe, 145n
Calhoun, Craig, 215, 217–18, 226–27, 233
Cairo: public space and revolutionary mobilization in, 251–52, 254, 255, 257
Calvino, Italo, 19
Cambodian Genocide (1975–79), 319, 404
Camus, Albert, 271
capital cities, 4–5, 17, 79–80, 241–42, 259, 260, 262–63
Capitol Riot (United States, 2020), 430n
Cárdenas, Cuauhtémoc, 146
Carnation Revolution (Portugal, 1974), 8, 96, 361–62, 364
Carothers, Thomas, 97
Carter, Jimmy, 95
Casey, William, 222
Castro, Fidel, 49, 76, 206–7
Cavalry (use of, for repression), 251, 261, 344, 348–49, 350, 351
Ceaușescu, Nicolae, 202, 224–26
Cedar Revolution (Lebanon, 2005), 28
Charter 77, 136
Cheka, 377–78
chemical weapons, 345, 351

Chenoweth, Erica, 176, 181–82, 185–87
Chiang Kai-shek, 203
Chiapas Rebellion (Mexico, 1994), 4n6, 79, 144, 146
Chile, 426n14
Chilean Revolution (1931), 72n
China: economy after Tiananmen repressions, 387; hyperinflation after revolution, 393; international role of, 430; post-revolutionary crime in, 378; post-revolutionary violence in, 404; public space in, 242, 249–50; shooting into crowds in, 353, 356; surveillance in, 429; Tiananmen Uprising (1989) in, 133, 160, 214–15, 217–218, 226–228, 233
Chinese Revolution (1949), 22, 35n53, 78, 78n51, 112, 249, 319, 327, 393, 405
Christian X, King of Denmark, 141–42
Chun Doo Hwan, 135
Chung-hee, Park, 360
cities: concentration of people, power, and wealth in, 3–6, 14, 18, 21, 30, 43, 57, 257–59, 262–63, 418, 420, 425, 427–28; defined, 38; design of, 81–82, 241–42, 251–59; digital technologies in, 89, 276, 308–17, 331, 421, 428–29; globalization centered on, 6, 98, 421; growth and concentration of people, power, and wealth in, 6, 9, 14, 15, 17, 21, 43, 56–57, 67–68, 71, 79–80, 85–86, 152–53, 180–81, 185, 193, 331, 339, 358, 421–22, 425, 432; nineteenth-century and early twentieth-century revolutions in, 5, 20, 30–31, 246, 419; outcomes of armed revolts in, 5, 21; populations of, 79–80, 259, *260*, 421; as sites of revolution, 4–7, 9–10, 13–14, 15, 20, 30–38, 93, 259, 425; social networks in, 85–88; social revolutions in, 73–76, 78; state presence in, 4–5, 10, 14–17, 20, 38–39, 38n65, 42, 241–42, 244, 257–59, *258*, 262–63; visibility of opposition in, 44, 82, 89, 99–100, 102, 152, 193, 241, 248, 252–53, 257, 266, 268, 270, 321, 331, 340, 358, 422. *See also* armed rebellion: in cities; capital cities; public space in revolutionary contention; urban civic revolutions; urban revolutions

citizenship, 9, 299–300
Civic Forum (Czechoslovakia), 136
civil liberties, after social and urban civic revolutions, 406–8, *407*, *408*
civil society: defined, 308n94, 308n95; regime position toward, 370, 372; and revolutionary mobilization, 96–97, 126, 132, 276, 307–12, 316; urban context for, 86; women's participation in, 403. *See also* social networks
civil war: defined, 52, 165n36, 323, 323n10; development of revolution into, 333–38; ethnic, 332–33, 338; external aid provided for, 61, 328; military's role in, 165–66; mortality in, 322–38, *326*; rural revolutions and, 52, 74–75, 77; rural vs. urban locations for, 331–32, 335, 339; temporal factors in, 324, 328; weaponry used in, 344–45. *See also* armed rebellion
clandestine revolutionary movements, 76–79, 188, 272
clapping protests (Belarus), 268
class: after social revolutions, 383, 396–98, 401; after urban civic revolutions, 401; changing revolutionary participation over time by, 82–83, *83*, 112,; growing global inequalities in, 432; among participants in urban civic revolutionary contention, 7, 10–11, 17, 84, 107, 112, 187, 275, 292–98, *293*, *295*, *296*; social revolutions and, 3–4, 5, 22–23, 33, 53, 63–64, 66, 107, 112, 149, 157, 251, 335;. *See also* intellectuals/intelligentsia; middle class; peasants; workers
Clinton, Bill, 96
closed regimes: and revolutions, 42, 93, 108, 109, 158–61, *158*. *See also* Polity scale; regimes; regime type
coalitional leaderships: fragility of, 18, 24, 302, 363, 389, 415; liberation movements compared to, 189–90; maximization of participation aided by, 45, 189, 302, 423; negative quality of, 13, 45, 275, 302, 307,

coalitional leaderships (*continued*) 318, 373; outcomes of revolutions linked to, 188–89; and political beliefs of revolution participants, 275, 302–7, *303*; in urban civic revolutions, 13, 18, 45,153, 275, 302–7, 317–18, 389, 395, 423. *See also* negative coalitions

Code of Conduct for Law Enforcement Officials, 355

Cold War: military coups during, 62; mortality in revolutions during and after, 321, 322, 327–38, *329–30*; patterns of revolutionary onset during, 57–64, 95; revolutionary participation by youth during and after, 69, 82; risk of revolution during and after, 119, 123–24, 126, 129–30, 132, 134, 136–37, 139, 141–44, 147; rural context of revolutionary activity during, 5, 33, 69, 73; social revolutions during, 64; success of revolutions during and after, 155; urban context of revolutionary activity after, 65, 69, 71–72, 74, 95, 97, 115, 119, 123–24, 248

Colombia, 352

color revolutions, 58, 97, 130, 155n5, 160, 163, 267, 273

Colosio, Luis Donaldo, 146

communication technologies: international impact of, 100–101; revolutionary diffusion via, 101; in urban settings, 80; in urban vs. rural settings, 87–89, *87*. *See also* digital technologies; mobile phones; print media; radio; social media; television

Communist Party (China), 78

communist regimes: collapse of, in eastern Europe, 23, 95–96, 136, 142, 160, 234, 377; post-revolutionary outcomes of, 370. *See also* Soviet Union, collapse of

Compaoré, Blaise, 30

concessions, 162, 219–21

confusion in urban revolutionary processes, 217, 222, 234

Connolly, James, 77

consequences of revolutions, 359–416; aftermaths vs. legacies, 363–64; analysis of, 363–68; attitudes toward, 359; challenges for, 361, 363, 373–74, 415; civil liberties as, 406–8, *407*, *408*; comparison of successful vs. failed revolutions, 364, 380–87; counterrevolutionary outcomes, 374; crime as, 377–78; in economic sphere, 378–95; equality vs. inequality as, 396–403; government accountability as, 410–13, *413*, *414*; regime durability as, 9, 18, 24–25, 46, 359–60, 363, 369–78, 423–24; rule of law as, 409–10, *411*, *412*; scholarship on, 360–62; social revolutions, 18, 362–63, 369–70, 374–78, 382–85, *383*, *384*, 388, 392–416; trajectories of development, 364; urban civic revolutions, 18, 363, 369–70, 373–74, 378, *385*, 386–90, *386*, 393–416, 423–24. *See also* substantive success; success of revolutions

Constitutional Revolution (Persia, 1905), 81n62

consumption, revolutionary participation by, 294–96, *295*

contained revolutionary contention: defined, 322; mortality in, 322, 325, 339–44, *340*, *341–42*

contingency and error: in onset of revolutions, 36–37, 104–5; in regime-opposition interactions, 213–17; in rural revolutions, 206–8, 235; time as factor in, 21, 41–42; in urban revolutions, 16, 21, 41–42, 198, 208–19, 235. *See also* agency, revolutionary role of; information problems; process of revolutionary contention; time

corruption: as feature of regimes susceptible to urban civic revolts, 9–12, 93, 107, 111–12, 122; as grievance among urban civic revolutionary participants, 275, 304, 307; after successful urban civic revolutions, 9, 18, 363, 389–90, *391*, 392

counterinsurgency strategies, 44–45, 159, 182n62, 259–69, 346, 426–28

counterrevolution, 95, 279–87, *280*, *282*, 310, 371, 374, 430

coupvolutions, 29–30, 30n34, 53, 426. *See also* military coups

Cox proportional hazards model, 369
crime, after social and urban civic revolutions, 377–78
critical mass theory, 86, 115
Cuba, 67, 108
Cuban Revolution (1933), 72n
Cuban Revolution (1953–1959), 49, 52, 72, 206–7
cultural division: in aftermath of successful social and urban civic revolutions, 401–2; as factor in urban civic revolutionary onset, 133; as factor in urban civic revolutionary participation, 12, 298–301, 299
Cultural Revolution (China, 1966–76), 29, 404
Cyprus Emergency (1955–59), 353
Czechoslovakia, 136–37, 137

Daoud Khan, Mohammed, 202n10
Davies, James, 32
death. *See* mortality in revolutions
Deaton, Clifford, 249
debt, after social and urban civic revolutions, 393–94
De la Rúa, Fernando, 99
democracy: crisis of, 430–31; electoral, compared to post–revolutionary urban civic governments, 18, 363, 405–11, 413–14, 416, 424; revolutionary success against, 159; U.S. promotion of, as contributor to urban civic revolutions, 95–97, 421, 430; urban civic revolution participants' commitments to, 17, 273–74, 275, 307, 406
demonstrations, as revolutionary tactic, 184–85, 248, 266
Deng Xiaoping, 214
Denmark, 141–42, 257
Dervish Rebellion (Somalia, 1899), 48n85
difference-in-difference research design, 364–68
diffusion, revolutionary, 44, 57–58, 101, 107, 130, 134, 142, 154, 167–169, 173n49, 193, 368, 430
digital technologies: identities associated with, 316–17; as information source in urban civic revolutions, 88–89, 312, 313n113, 314–316, 315; prevalence of, 308–9; revolutionary commitment linked to use of, 313–14; social networks and use of, 313–14; surveillance using, 428–29; as technology of revolt, 13, 88–89, 308–17, 313n113, 428. *See also* mobile phones; social media
Djibouti, 133
doctrine of necessity, 346, 348, 349, 354–56
Doe, Samuel K., 202n10
Downes, Alexander B., 47
Dunn, John, 3, 424
durability of post-revolutionary governments, 18, 24–25, 46, 359–60, 363, 369–78, 423–24
Durov, Nikolai and Pavel, 428
Dyer, Reginald, 348

earthquake analogy, 103–5, 149
Easter Crisis (Denmark, 1920), 81n62, 141–42
eastern European revolutions (1989), 23, 96, 136, 142, 160, 234, 377
Easter Uprising (Ireland, 1916), 77, 344
East German Revolution (1989), 27, 111, 162, 209, 259
East Germany, 109, 111
economic growth and development: corruption as influence on, 389–90; after failed vs. successful revolutions, 380–87, 380, 381, 383–86; and mortality in revolutions, 343, 388; post-revolutionary, 378–95; in social revolutions, 112, 113, 114; social revolutions' effect on, 382–85, 383, 384, 388, 392–95; in urban civic revolutions, 10–11, 112–14, 113, 114; urban civic revolutions' effect on, 385, 386–90, 386, 393–95
EDSA 2 Revolution (Philippines, 2001), 140–41
education, urban civic revolutionary participation by, 296–98, 297, 431
Egypt: age structure of, 290; autocratic regime in, 109; civil society in, 308, 311–12, 312; class and employment in, 292; corruption in, 112; counterrevolution in, 360; digital technology use in, 310–12, 314; economic factors in, 112; leader longevity in, 111;

Egypt (*continued*)
    post-revolutionary crime in, 377; post-revolutionary economy in, 395; public space and protest in, 244, 251–55, 257, 269; regime counterinsurgency strategies in, 230; regime-opposition interactions in, 232–33; revolutionary participation in, 281, 282, 288, 289–92, 294–302, 304, 308, 314–15, *315*; shooting into crowds in, 354
Egyptian Counter-Revolution (2013), 30n34, 360
Egyptian Revolution (1919), 251
Egyptian Revolution (2011), 45, 49, 54, 111, 160, 162, 185n65, 204, 210–11, 218–19, 228, 230, 232–33, 234, 255, 273n7, 274–75, 277, 280–82, 281n30, 282, 284–85, 288, 289–316, *315*, 360, 374, 377, 402, 412
1848 revolutions, 5, 167, 247, 261, 345
8888 Uprising (Myanmar, 1988), 114, 128–30, 160, 262, 345, 347, 357
electoral turnovers in authoritarian regimes, 25, 28, 29, 47–48
El Salvador, 204, 339n45
emotions in revolutionary processes, 35, 77, 134, 199, 204, 216–19, 221, 244n23
endogenous switching model, 325, 328, 331, 334, 339
Engels, Friedrich, 5, 403
English Civil War, 4n7
Enrile, Juan Ponce, 140, 223
Erdogan, Recep, 249
error. *See* contingency and error
Estrada, Joseph, 141
Ethiopia, 268, 426n14
ethnic civil wars, 332–33, 338
Euromaidan Revolution (Ukraine, 2013), 54, 99, 132–33, 134, 201, 239, 255, 268, 269, 274–75, 277, 279–80, 280, 284–85, 287, 289–316, 376, 402, 427
European Union, 133, 277
evolutionary biology, 40, 41, 419, 425, 428
exogenous events: influence on post-revolutionary developments, 365; regime repression and, 219; as trigger for revolution, 132, 134–39

Facebook, 13, 211, 218, 309, 310–12
facial recognition software, 41, 429
failed revolutions, 4, 53, 63, 154–55, 160, 181, 258, 276–77, 362, 364, 366–67, 374, 379–81, 384–85, 387, 389, 390, 393n77, 394–95, 401, 407n104, 408n106, 409n107, 426
fascism, 256, 360, 430
February Revolution (Russia, 1917), 13, 205, 213–14, 222, 230–31, 237, 246, 349, 377.
February 20 Movement (Morocco), 28
Finland, 108
first-generation theories of revolution, 31–32
Fischer, Claude, 86
Fishman, Robert, 361, 364
FLN/EZLN, 78–79
Foran, John, 373n33
Ford, Matt, 253, 257
foreign invasion, 25, 28, 47–48, 53, 323, 324n15
Foucault, Michel, 3
fourth-generation theories of revolution, 35–38
France, 74n34, 82, 85, 100, 272, 308, 312, 347, 349, 350, 351, 352, 353, 356
Frantz, Erica, 48, 110, 161
fraternization, 167, 231–33, 233n126, 346
Freedom House, 96
freedoms, in post-revolutionary society, 406–8, *407–10*
French Revolution, 22–25, 35, 30, 35, 246, 247n34, 361
Fukuyama, Francis, 96

Gaddafi, Muammar, 202, 357
Gamson, William, 175, 187–88
Garton Ash, Timothy, 29n29
Geddes, Barbara, 48, 110, 161
Gediminas, 249
gender of urban civic revolutionary participants, 289–90, *289*. *See also* women
Geneva conventions, 355
genocide: and revolution, 319–20, 320n4, 403–4
geopolitics, influence of on revolutions, 14, 16, 18, 30n34, 37, 41, 61, 62, 64, 95–97, 102, 321, 326, 338, 357–58, 428, 429–30

Georgia: corruption on the eve of the Rose Revolution, 112; networks in, 189; police's role in Rose Revolution in, 166; public space and the 1989 Tbilisi massacres, 220–21, 257
German Peasants' War (1525), 27
Germany, 108, 324, 349–50, 352
Gezi Park protests, 249
Ghonim, Wael, 185n65, 210, 213, 300
Giddens, Anthony, 9, 97
Giugni, Marco, 182
globalization: cities as centers of, 6, 98, 421; defined, 97; features of, 98; revolutions affected by, 97–100. *See also* international system
Glorious Revolution, 22
goals of revolution, 24, 50, 53, 157, 361; and revolutionary mortality, 335, 343; in rural revolutions, 90–91, 209; success of revolutions linked to, 182, 185, 187–88, 190, 362, 363, 383, 396n82, 403; for urban civic revolutions, 8–13, 10n33, 20–21, 53, 93, 209–10, 415
Goldstone, Jack, 35, 68, 86, 103–4, 221, 320, 414
Gongadze, Georgy, 131–32
Goodwin, Jeff, 25n12, 159, 359, 373n33
Gorbachev, Mikhail, 221, 227, 264
Gould, Roger, 85
government accountability, after social and urban civic revolutions, 410–13, *413*, 414
Granovetter, Mark, 86–87
Great Purge (Soviet Union, 1936–38), 404
Guatemala, 324n13, 426
Guatemalan Revolution (1944), 30
guerrilla warfare, 49, 52n92, 73, 76, 76n47, 78, 182, 203, 204, 207
Guevara, Che, 6, 76, 78, 91, 182, 203, 207
Gulf Cooperation Council, 263
Gunning, Jeroen, 244
Gurr, Ted Robert, 32
Gypsies, attitudes toward among revolutionary participants in Ukraine, 307

Habyarimana, Juvénal, 202n10
Haiti, 163, 426
Haitian Revolution (1791), 4n7

Haitian Revolution (1946), 163
Hasegawa, Tsyuoshi, 213–14, 222
Haussman, Georges-Eugène, and Haussmanization, 81–82, 251, 263
Havel, Václav, 136
Heckman selection model, 325
Henisz, Witold, 389
Herbert, Steve, 259–60
Herfindahl index, 302, 302n82, 316
Hitler, Adolf, 430
Hobsbawm, Eric, 80n59, 245
Holmes, Amy Austin, 29n29
Honecker, Erich, 111, 162
Horthy, Miklós, 360
House, Jonathan, 260–61, 272
Houthi Rebellion (Yemen, 2004), 28n
Hugo, Victor, 151
Huk Rebellion (Philippines), 204
human rights, 95, 130, 140, 265, 267, 354–57, 430
Hungarian Revolution (1919), 360
Hungarian Revolution (1956), 324
Huntington, Samuel, 32–33, 62, 73
hurricane analogy, 16, 105–6, 149–50
Hussein, Saddam, 339n
Hu Yao Bang, 214

Ibrahim, Anwar, 148
Ilinden Revolt (Macedonia, 1903), 78n51
IMF. *See* International Monetary Fund
income: urban civic revolutionary participation by, 294–96, *295*, 432
Independence Square (Maidan) in Kyiv, 1–3, 236–40
India, 85, 108, 348
Indignados Movement (Spain, 2011), 28
Indonesia: corruption on eve of Indonesian Revolution (1998), 112; influence of exogenous events on, 99, 137–39, 147–48; leader longevity in, 111, 162; probability of urban civic revolutionary onset in, 137–39, *138*
Indonesian Revolution (1998), 99, 114, 137–39, 148, 162, 243, 248, 365
inequality, after social and urban civic revolutions, 396–403, *399, 400*, 432

inflation, after social and urban civic revolutions, 390–92
information problems: consequences of, 16, 42, 199, 234–35; rumors as instance of, 207, 208, 217–18, 223–24, 235; in rural revolutions, 199, 207; in urban revolutions, 16, 21, 41–42, 199, 423
Institute of Sociology of the Ukrainian Academy of Sciences, 277
Institutional Revolutionary Party (Mexico, PRI), 146
intellectuals/intelligentsia, 7, 31, 32, 78, 82, 83, 227, 292, 293
interactions, regime-opposition. See regime-opposition interactions
International Covenant on Civil and Political Rights, 355
International Criminal Court, 357
international law, and revolutionary contention, 354–57, 354n99
International Monetary Fund (IMF), 99, 138
international system: communication technologies and, 100–101; revolutions affected by, 57, 95–101; urban revolutions more exposed to, 44; transnational waves of revolution in, 44, 101, 134, 167–69, 169n44. See also geopolitics, influence of on revolutions; globalization
internet. See digital technologies; social media
investment, after social and urban civic revolutions, 387, 390–92
Iran: autocratic regime on eve of 2011 protests, 109, 160; communication technologies of diaspora groups from, 100–1; control over public space in, 261; digital technology use in, 315–16, 428; durability of post-revolutionary regime, 370; electoral protests in, 155n5, 160, 261, 315–16; geopolitics and civil wars, 358; White Revolution in, 29
Iranian Revolution (1979), 35n53, 63, 63n10, 74, 217n67
Irish Republican Brotherhood, 77
Islam, as factor of revolutionary participation in Egypt and Tunisia, 301–2, 301

Ismail, Pasha, 251
Istanbul, 249

James II, King of England, 22
Jangal Rebellion (Iran, 1915), 78n51
Jasper, James M., 44n70
Jews, attitudes toward among revolutionary participants in Ukraine, 307
Johansen, Anja, 349
Johnson, Bryan, 216, 223, 231n121
Johnson, Chalmers, 32
Jordan, 244
June Uprising (Paris, 1848), 345–46
June Uprising (South Korea, 1987), 29, 113, 134–36, 160
JVP Insurrection (Sri Lanka, 1971), 74

Kalinin, Mikhail, 237
Kalyvas, Stathis, 181, 328n24, 331
Kampang Buluh Uprising (Malaysia, 1928), 324
Károlyi, Mihály, 360
Kazakhstan, 387
Kérékou, Mathieu, 111
Ketchley, Neil, 231–32
Khalil, Ashraf, 230
Khomeini, Ayatollah, 100
Kim, Quee-Young, 233
Kinakh, Anatoliy, 302
Kmara, 96
Kocher, Matthew, 181
Kollontai, Alexandra, 13
Kornhauser, William, 32
Kuchma, Leonid, 96, 131–32, 180, 201, 212–13, 229, 277
Kumar, Krishan, 418n3
Kun, Béla, 360
Kuran, Timur, 36, 104–5, 199, 208, 209
Kurdish Rebellion (Iraq, 1979), 28n
Kurzman, Charles, 234
Kyiv: during Euromaidan Revolution (2013) in, 277; public space in, 236–39, 250–51, 255; Orange Revolution (2004) in; 2–3, 13–14, 212–13, 277; Revolution of 1905 in, 1–2, 13–14.

Kyiv International Institute of Sociology (KIIS) survey, 283–86
Kyrgyz Revolution (2010), 402
Kyrgyzstan, 85n76, 163, 354, 402

La Matanza (El Salvador, 1932), 339n
landed elites, 10n33, 34, 67, 70, 91, 102, 107, 245, 354, 379, 420
land inequality, 6, 10, 66–70, 66, 421
land seizures/occupations, 245–46
language use, as factor in revolutionary participation in Ukraine, 298–99, 299
latent class cluster analysis, 304, 304n88
Lazorenko, Pavlo, 131
leaders: age of, 161–62; fate of, after revolutions, 202, 202nn9–12; longevity of, as factor in urban civic revolutionary onset, 110–11, 111, 161
Lebed, Aleksandr, 164–65
Le Blanc, Joerg, 77
Le Bon, Gustave, 31–32, 31n39
Lefebvre, Henri, 198, 244
Leith, James, 241
Lenin, Vladimir, 12–13, 201, 205, 238, 264, 375; *What is to Be Done*, 12
Lépine, Louis, 350
Lescot, Élie, 163
lethality of weapons, 17, 321, 327, 327n22, 344–53
Levinson, Sanford, 244n21
Levitsky, Steven, 370–72
liberation movements, 188, 189–90
Libya, 125, 202, 354, 357, 358
Life in Transitional Societies II (LITS II) survey, 308
Limonov, Eduard, 267
linear strategies of revolt, 252–56
Li Peng, 227–28
literacy, and revolution, 88, 181, 204, 331
Lithuania, 249, 354
Long March, of Mao Zedong, 203
López Obrador, Andrés Manuel, 145n
Lukashenko, Alexander, 250n48, 268–69, 428n21
Luzhkov, Yuri, 264

Machiavelli, Niccolò, 359
MacLaren, Alexander, 56
Madagascar: cultural divisions and revolution in, 133; economic inequality and revolution in, 99; electoral revolution in, 29, 413; leader longevity and revolution in, 111; shooting into crowds in, 354
Maduro, Nicolás, 114, 268
Magaloni, Beatriz, 146
Mahfouz, Asmaa, 300
Malaysia, 147–49, 147, 324
Mali, 354, 433
Malia, Martin, 14n44
Mao Zedong, 29, 78, 182, 203–4, 249–50
Maoist revolutions, 29, 75, 144n93
marches and processions: and militarization of revolt, 246; spatial dimensions of, 252–56. *See also* linear strategies of revolt
Marcos, Ferdinand, 111, 140, 202n11, 216, 222–24, 231, 248, 333
Marcos, Imelda, 333
Marighella, Carlos, 76, 76n47
Martin, Terry, 402
Marx, Karl, 20, 30–31
Marxism, 10n33, 33
Marxism-Leninism, 95
Masol, Vitalii, 239
Mather, F. C., 26n18
May 1968 (France), 74n34, 353
Mayer, Arno, 354
May Fourth Movement (China, 1919), 249
McAdam, Doug, 46
McFaul, Michael, 96
Medvedev, Dmitry, 267
Meiji Restoration, 29n25
Mexican Revolution (1910), 22, 63, 78n51, 162, 245, 319, 327, 405
Mexico: FLN/EZLN in, 78–79; land inequality in, 67; probability of urban civic revolutionary onset in, 144–47, 145
Michaelsen, Marcus, 100

middle class: corruption as grievance of, 11–12, 148; defined, 10; growth of, 12, 32–33, 113, 146, 148, 292, 418; and neoliberal development, 11, 99, 113, 125, 247, 421; and social revolutions, 49, 79; urban civic revolutionary participation of, 7, 11, 17, 84, 112–14, 273, 275, 294, 421, 430; in urban revolutions, 84

migration, as source of urban growth, 68, 86

military: in aftermath of social and. urban civic revolutions, 375–76; defection of, 29–30, 81–82, 164–67, 189, 228, 229, 232, 233, 346; opportunities in urban revolutions for interactions with the opposition, 75, 77, 167, 186, 200, 221–22, 229–33, 262–63; pay and supply of, 164–66, *165*; policing functions of, 164–67, 346, 349–50; professionalization of, 164–67, 349; role of, in outcomes of revolution, 47, 91, 164–67, 373–74; and urban armed rebellions, 5, 43n67, 75–76, 186, 187; and violent engagement with citizens, 81, 216, 219, 224, 230–31, 233, 262, 347–49, 353–57, 427. *See also* coupvolutions, fraternization; military coups; police; soldiers, revolutionary participation of

military coups: in Cold War era, 62; frequency of, 47–48, 62–63; revolutionary episodes compared to, 16, 25, 28, 29, 47–48, 62–63, *62*, 107, 119, *120–21*, *122–23*, 378–79; success of, 47–48, 63n9; after urban civic revolutions, 412. *See also* coupvolutions; military; soldiers, revolutionary participation of

military regimes, 109–10, 119, 129, 130, 135, 160–61, 250

Mill, John Stuart, 106, 108, 198

Miller, Byron, 189

Milošević, Slobodan, 23, 96, 126–28, 201, 229, 256

mistakes. *See* contingency and error

MNR Revolution (Bolivia, 1952), 324

mobile phones, 41, 181, 308–10, 312n111. *See also* communication technologies; digital technologies; social media

mobilization of revolutionary participants: challenges of, 272–73; civil society as factor in, 309–10; communication technologies as factor in, 13, 80, 88–89, 102, 308–9, 312–17, 428; life circumstances as factor in, 287; network ties as factor in, 86–87, 313–14; social media as factor in, 89, 315–16; success of revolutions linked to, 153, 176, 180, 181–85, *183*, 185n65; urban design as factor in, 239, 241, 252–54; urbanization as factor in, 13–14, 15, 21, 43–44, 80, 85, 152, 153, 180–82, 185, 248, 270, 317, 419, 422

Mohamad, Mahathir, 147–48

Moldovan Peasant Revolt (1907), 27

momentum, revolutionary, 230

Monitoring surveys, 277–79, 283–88, 302, 304, 307

Montagnard Rebellion (1964), 28n

Monten, Jonathan, 47

Montoneros Rebellion (Argentina), 74n34

monumental space, 45, 241, 242, 244, 263

Moore, Barrington, 70

Moroz, Oleksandr, 302

Morsi, Mohamed, 360, 395

mortality in revolutions: civil war linked to, 322–44; in contained episodes, 322, 325, 339–44, *340*, *341–42*; decline of, 17, 320–21, 339, 351–53, 357–58, 423; in early urban revolutions, 345–49; economic factors in, 343; figures on, 321–22, *322*; geopolitics as factor in, 321, 322, 327–38, *329–30*, 338, 357–58; government reputation as factor in, 346, 354; highest incidences of, 319, 327, 339n; international norms affecting, 354–57; moral unease about, 43, 346–47, 423; from 1900 to present, 321–44; post-revolutionary economy affected by, 388; regime vs. opposition victory as factor in, 332; in rural revolutions, 17, 186–87, 331; in social revolutions, 319–20, 332–33; success of revolutions in relation to, 185–87, 320, 343–44; technological factors in, 344–53; urbanization as factor in, 17, 321, 331, 339, 340, 343, 355; variation in, 319–20. *See also* violence

Movement of People for Progress (Burkina Faso), 30
Mubarak, Hosni, 111, 162, 210–11, 218, 230, 244, 252, 255, 257, 269, 277, 311, 377
Mugabe, Robert, 426
Mumford, Lewis, 38
Musk, Elon, 428n21
Muslim Brotherhood, 302, 308
Mussolini, Benito, 256, 430
Myanmar: autocratic regime and urban civic revolution in, 109; government repression in, 357; probability of urban civic revolutionary onset in, 128–30, *128*; relocation of capital city in, 262–63; shooting into crowds in, 353, 354. *See also* 8888 Uprising; Saffron Revolution

Napoleon, 24
Nasser, Gamal Abdel, 252
National Action Party (Mexico, PAN), 146
National Democratic Front (Mexico, FDN), 146
National Democratic Institute (U.S.), 96
National Endowment for Democracy (U.S.), 96
nationalism, 45, 250, 275, 298–300, 305, 317, 402, 431
NATO. *See* North Atlantic Treaty Organization
Naypyitaw (Myanmar), 258n81, 262–63
Nazis, 80, 237–38
necessity. *See* doctrine of necessity
negative coalitions, 45, 275, 302–307, 317–18, 373, 395, 423. *See also* coalitional leaderships: negative quality of
Nejad, Reza, 257
neoliberalism: economic effects of, 292, 394, 421, 432; and frequency of strikes as revolutionary tactic, 247; in Mexico, 144; and middle class, 11, 99, 113, 125, 247, 421; revolutions in the era of, 10, 12, 57, 94, 98–99, 102, 113–14, 418, 421; in Tunisia, 125, 292
Nepal: capital city insulated from effects of civil war in, 75; economic development and social revolution in, 112; peasant participation in urban civic revolution in, 7; regime type and urban civic revolution in, 108; social revolutionary contention in, 4n6

Ne Win, 129
newspapers. *See* print media
New York Times (newspaper), 432
Nicaragua: failed urban civic revolt (2018) in, 426; land inequality in, 67; 1963 failed social revolution attempt in, 207; post-revolutionary economy in, 382; regime on eve of social revolution in, 108; social revolution in, 4.
Nicholas II, Tsar of Russia, 1, 202, 214, 346, 354
Nichols, Walter, 189
Niger, 142
Niger Constitutional Crisis (2009), 142
1991 Uprising (Iraq), 339n
nongovernmental organizations (NGOs), 96–97
non-revolutionary sieges of government, 28
North Atlantic Treaty Organization (NATO), 304n87, 305, 357

occupation of squares, 243, 247–49, 252–53, 254, 255
Occupy Wall Street Movement, 27
October Revolution (Russia, 1917), 22, 27, 29, 35, 35n53, 52, 72, 164n31, 201, 205, 238, 245, 319, 327, 365, 377, 383, 393, 401, 402–3, 405, 417, 430
October Revolution (Sudan, 1964), 256, 412
oil production: as factor affecting outcomes of revolutionary contention, 162, 173; as factor in urban civic revolutionary onset, 115, 119; in military coups and social revolutions, 122;
Olson, Mancur, 379
Omel'chenko, Aleksandr, 185n65
onset of revolutions, 16, 35, 42; frequency of, 57–59, *58*, *59*, 62, 64–65, *64*; patterns in, 57–58, *58*; probabilistic structural approach to, 106–8; of social revolutionary episodes, 62–63, 66–67, 119–123; and state independence, 89–90; transnational waves as

onset of revolutions (*continued*)
context for, 44, 101, 134, 167–69, 169n44; of urban and rural revolutionary episodes, 72–74, 93; of urban civic revolutionary episodes, 64–65, 93, 103–123; and youth bulges, 69

open regimes, 108–9, 157–60, *158*. *See also* Polity scale; regime type; regimes

opposition success, 4, 5, 19, 47–48, 53, 151–97; abruptness of, in urban revolutions, 228; defined, 16, 46, 151; increased probability of, 24, 44, 152, 153–57, *155*, 194–95, 426; incumbent regime characteristics as factor in, 169, *170–72*, 173–75, 194–95; opposition goals, capacities, and tactics as factors in, 175–92, *177–79*, 194–95; regime strengths and weaknesses as factors in, 157–75; in social revolutions, 62–64, 66–67, 76; transnational waves and, 154; in urban civic revolutions, 44–45, 82, 157; in urban and rural revolutions, 76, 87, 153, 156–157, 228. *See also* substantive success; success of revolutions

Orange Revolution (Ukraine, 2004), 2–3, 8, 11, 12, 13, 24, 29, 54, 96, 113, 132, 164, 176, 185n65, 201, 204, 229, 239, 272n5, 274–80, *280*, 283–316, 360, 412, 427

organizational forms of revolutionary opposition: durability of post-revolutionary regimes and, 370–73; mobilization of revolutionary participants affected by, 13, 80, 188–89; opposition success linked to, 187–90; for urban civic revolutions, 13–14, 80, 188–89. *See also* coalitional leaderships; liberation movements; clandestine revolutionary movements; vanguard parties

Orwell, George, 263
O'Sullivan, Patrick, 74–75
Otpor, 96, 127–28, 201
Owen, John M., IV, 47n82

pacification of revolution. *See* mortality in revolutions; violence
Paige, Jeffrey, 33

pandemic, 432
parallel trends assumption, 366
Paris, public space in, 4–5, 81–82, 247n34, 251, 261
Paris Commune (1871), 346
Parisian National Guard, 85
Parkinson, John, 243, 252, 253
participation in urban civic revolutions, 271–318; age and, 290–92, *290*; class and, 292–98, *293*, *295*, *296*; experiences of, 218–19; gender and, 289–90, *289*; identities and characteristics associated with, 17, 271–302; information sources and, 312, 313n113, 314, *315*; and minimalist goals, 187–88; modes and degrees of involvement of, 278–86, *280*, *282*; motives for, 8, 208–9, 211, 272–74, 272n5, 303–4, 406, 423; numbers and, 176, 180–85, *180*, *183*, 185n65, 211, 248; participation in rural revolutions compared to, 271–73; public employees and, 273, 273n7; public opinion surveys of, 54, 274–88; revolutionary tactics and, 8, 13, 15, 17, 21, 43, 79–81, 180–81, 250; scaling up of, 86–89, 102, 181, 250, 270, 276, 308–9; social demographics of, 288–302; social networks and, 84–88. *See also* mobilization of revolutionary participants

Patel, David, 253
Pearlman, Wendy, 168
peasants, 1–2, 5, 7, 32–33, 34, 35, 57, 66–68, 70, 72, 78, 82–84, 144, 245–46, 420
People Power Revolution (Philippines, 1986), 30n34, 111, 114, 135–36, 139–41, 160, 204, 216, 217, 222–24, 231, 234, 248, 250, 333
People Power revolutions (East Asia), 96
People's Daily (newspaper), 215
pepper spray, 351
personalist regimes: and urban civic revolutions 110–11; and revolutionary outcomes, 161
Peterloo Massacre (Manchester, 1819), 80, 348–49
Petersen, Roger, 84, 278
Philippine–American War (1899), 48n85

Philippines: corruption in, 112; leader longevity in, 111; probability of urban civic revolutionary onset in, 139–41, *140*; mistakes in revolutionary contention, 222–24; regime type in, 108, 109

Phillips, Wendell, 34, 103

PKK, 78–79

plastic bullets, 352–53

police: defection of, 152; international guidelines for, 355–56; opportunities in urban revolutions for interactions with the opposition, 75, 77, 186, 200, 221–22, 229–33, 230–31; pay and supply of, 152, 166; regime deployment of, 125–26, 129, 136, 164, 211, 215–18, 224–26, 267, 311, 350–53, 427; social control strategies of, 259–60, 265, 350–53, 355–56; social media exposure of brutality by, 310; as target of revolutionary violence, 255, 256; usefulness of, in urban environments, 166. *See also* military

political beliefs, of urban civic revolution participants, 275, 302–7, *303*

Political Instability Task Force, 320

political opportunities, 42, 93–94, 97, 128, 144, 421

politicide, 320, 320n4

Polity scale, 93, 108–9, *108*, 122, 158–60, *158*. *See also* closed regimes; open regimes

population size, as factor in revolution, 115

populism, 430–31

Pora, 132, 309

poverty. *See* urban poor

Powell, Jonathan, 47

power of numbers: in highly closed regimes, 160; and international law, 355; and post-revolutionary governance, 374; in rural rebellions, 43; and social media, 89; and urban civic repertoire, 8, 13, 56, 373, 422; urbanization and, 15, 18, 21, 43, 45, 80, 152, 180–81, 193, 270, 335; and violence, 187, 338, 358

praetorian model of coups, 62

Pravyi Sektor (Right Sector), 315

preference falsification, 234, 276, 282–85, 294n62

pressurized water (for crowd control), 352

print media, as communications technology in revolution, 12–13, 80, 87–88

probabilistic structural approach, 37–38, 106–50; case examples of predictability using, 123–49; discussion of the model, 115–19; explanation of, 106–8

processions. *See* linear strategies of revolt; marches and processions

process of revolutionary contention, 16, 198–235; dynamism of, 199; momentum in, 230; moves and countermoves in, 219–28; sports game analogy for, 200–208, 219–33; surprises in, 208–19; temporal factors in, 203–6, 208; in urban vs. rural settings, 199, 203–4. *See also* agency, revolutionary role of; public space in revolutionary contention; regime-opposition interactions; revolutionary episodes; urban civic repertoire

proximity dilemma in revolution: defined, 5, 15, 20, 39; diagram of repression-disruption trade-off within, 39; evolutionary biology analogy for, 40, 419; globalization's effect on repression-disruption trade-off as part of, 100; process of revolutionary contention affected by, 199, 419; significance of, 40, 41–42, 239; spatial relocation for managing, 39–40; structural changes affecting, 41; tactical choices affecting, 40–41, 42–43, 185; and technological change, 13, 14, 15, 18, 37, 41, 81, 88, 98, 100, 308–11, 321, 327 328n24, 344–53, 419, 428–29; and temporal dimension of revolution, 21, 41–42; urban context for, 15, 20, 38–45, 75–82, 152, 185. *See also* public space in revolutionary contention; repression-disruption trade-off

public space in urban civic revolutionary contention, 17, 236–70; comparisons of Kyiv demonstrations, 236–37; as consequence of urban design, 81–82, 241–42; opposition tactics enabled by, 44–45, 82, 239, 241, 251–59, 422; regime tactics concerning, 45, 241, 259–69; significance of, 239, 241, 244, 249–51, 422–23; social media contrasted with, 243; types of, 248–50

public sphere, 243
Putin, Vladimir, 26, 267, 428, 430

quasi-revolutionary protests, 26, 28, 142n88, 145n94, 148, 254n65, 256, 313n113, 314, 316, 426n14
Qurayshi, Ahmad al-, 256

radio, as communications technology in revolution, 80, 87–88, 139, 223
Ramos, Fidel, 223
ranged weapons, 231–32
rational choice analysis, 35–36
Ratsiraka, Didier, 111
Ravalomanana, Marc, 99, 413
Reagan, Ronald, 95
Receiver Operating Characteristic (ROC) curve, 173, 174, 175, 191, 192
regime-opposition interactions: case examples of, 213–17, 222–33; in fourth-generation theories of revolution, 36–37; negotiations in, 229; onset of revolutions linked to, 134–39, 144, 149–50; regime repertoire in, 219–22; speed and unpredictability of, 200, 206, 213–17; in urban revolutions, 219–28
regimes: corruption as feature of, 9–12, 18, 111–12; and modes of regime-change, 3, 14, 20, 25–30, 47–48, 62–63, 96–7, 104, 119–123, 275, 284–86, 298, 418; options of, in response to revolutionary challenges, 219–22; strengths and weaknesses of, in face of revolutionary challenges, 157–75. See also closed regimes; open regimes; Polity scale; regime-opposition interactions; regime type
regime type: location of revolutions in relation to, 42; urban civic vs. social revolutionary contention compared by, 93, 108–10, 109; vulnerability to overthrow by revolution by, 157–61, 158. See also closed regimes; open regimes; Polity scale; regimes

religion: evoked in revolution, 234, 250; as factor in revolutionary participation, 299–302, 301
repression-disruption trade-off, 15, 21, 38–43, 74–82, 96, 100, 151–53, 174–75, 185, 192–93, 197, 270, 272, 419–20, 422, 427, 429. See also proximity dilemma
revolution: cities as sites of, 4–7, 9–10, 13–14, 15, 20–21, 30–38, 93, 259, 425; comparison of factors in, 120–21; defining, 3, 21–30; divine explanations for, 234; early meanings and uses of the term, 22; evolution and adaptation of, 18, 23, 37, 37n63, 418–19, 425, 427–28, 433; future of, 18, 425–33; methods of studying, 48–49, 54–55, 106–8; number of participants as feature of, 4n6; organization and technology of, 12–14; other modes of politics compared to, 25–29, 28, 47–48; prevalence of, 19, 47–48, 107, 418; structural conditions for, 34–35, 103–4; sports game analogy for, 200–208, 219–33; temporal factors in, 47, 205–6; theories of, 19–21, 31–38, 53–54, 65–66, 91, 94–95, 103–4, 107, 122–23, 418–19; variety of goals of, 23, 51, 53. See also armed rebellion; goals of revolution; mortality in revolutions; process of revolutionary contention; revolutionary episodes; social revolutions; success of revolutions; urban civic revolutions
revolutionary episodes: defined, 46–47; duration of, 60, 60; sports game analogy for, 200–208, 219–33; goals of, 50, 53; identifying beginnings and ends of, 47; locations of, 49, 51, 52, 71–74, 72, 73; military coups compared to, 47–48, 62–63, 62, 120–21, 122; onset of, 57–62, 58; outcomes of, 51, 53; tactics of, 50, 52–53; temporal factors in, 47, 205; territorial risk of experiencing, 61–62, 61; as unit of analysis, 46–54. See also onset of revolutions; process of revolutionary contention
Revolution of 1830 (France), 347

Revolution of 1848 (France), 347
revolutions-from-above, 29
Rhee, Syngman, 162, 202, 209, 217, 233, 259, 274, 351
right of rebellion, 354, 354n99
right to assembly, 265
"right to the city," 20, 243
right-wing populism, 430–31, 430n
Riot Act (England, 1714), 347–48
riot-control vehicles, 352
riot shields, 353
riots, revolutionary, 8, 29, 52, 58, 80n59, 81, 152, 185, 246–47, 345, 419, 427, 433
risk attendant on revolution: essential nature of, 24; mitigation of, 17; opposition vs. regime attitudes toward, 203; participants' willingness for, 359; social ties as factor in considering, 84–87; in unarmed revolt, 14. *See also* proximity dilemma
Ritter, Daniel P., 37n63, 97n118
ROC curve. *See* Receiver Operating Characteristic (ROC) curve
Roh Tae-woo, 135
Rojas Pinilla, Gustavo, 352
Romania, 8, 218, 202, 224–26, 354
Romanian Revolution (1989), 8, 218, 324–26
Rosenfeld, Bryn, 11, 273
Rose Revolution (Georgia, 2003), 96, 113, 132, 152, 189, 205, 209, 212, 378, 413
Ross, Kristin, 244
rubber bullets, 353
Rubin causal model, 365
Rudé, George, 246, 345
Ruhr Uprising (Germany, 1920), 324
rule of law, after social and urban civic revolutions, 409–10, *411*, *412*
rumors, 207, 208, 217–18, 223–24, 235
rural revolutions: advantages of, 5, 21, 43, 74–75, 78–79; between-battle behavior during, 204; challenges for, 75; contingency and error in, 206–8, 235; counterinsurgency strategies in, 260; decline of, 56; goals of, 90–91, 209; growth of social revolutions as, 73–74, 78–79, 78n51, 420; information problems in, 199, 207; numbers of participants in, 182–84; organizational cohesion in, 271–72; probability of success of, 157–92; proximity dilemma for, 39; spatial politics in, 244–45; temporal factors in, 42, 77–78, 199, 203–4, 228–29; urban revolutions compared to, 21, 33, 38–39, 57; violence and mortality in, 17, 186–87, 331; weak states favorable to, 42, 57, 74, 91
Russia: autocratic regime in, 108; economic factors in, 112; electoral protests of 2011–12 in, 26, 313n113, 314, 316; international role of, 430; land inequality in, 67; military defection in, 164–65; post-revolutionary crime in, 377–78; post-revolutionary economy in, 382–83, 393; post-revolutionary violence in, 403–4; public space in, 264–68; shooting into crowds in, 354; social inequality in, 401–3; surveillance in, 429
Russian Revolution (1905), 1, 5, 201, 339n, 346
Russian Revolution (1917). *See* February Revolution; October Revolution
Rwandan Genocide (1994), 319

Saakashvili, Mikheil, 378, 413
safe zones, 5, 75, 91, 260, 270
Saffron Revolution (Myanmar, 2007), 128–30, 134, 160, 262
Said, Khaled, 311
Salinas, Carlos, 146
Sandinista National Liberation Front (FSLN), 4, 207
Sassen, Saskia, 9, 251, 331
scaling up, of revolutionary mobilization, 86–89, 102, 181, 250, 270, 276, 308–9
Scott, James, 244n21
second-generation theories of revolution, 32–33, 66
Segerberg, Alexandra, 312, 315, 317
Sein Lwin, 129
Serbia: probability of urban civic revolutionary onset in, 126–28, *127*; protest tactics in, 256; 2018 protests in, 426. *See also* Bulldozer Revolution (Serbia, 2000)

Setif Uprising (Algeria, 1945), 339n
Seton-Watson, Hugh, 14, 425
Sewell, William, 4–5, 20, 20n5, 46
Shafiq, Ahmed, 377
Shanin, Teodor, 235
Sharp Eyes, 429
Shevardnadze, Eduard, 166, 189, 209
siege, 25–27
Simmons, Beth, 356
Sin, Jaime, 141, 248
Singing Revolution (Estonia, 1987–91), 29, 402
Sisi, Abdel Fattah el-, 360
Skocpol, Theda, 3, 5–6, 7, 23, 34–35, 35n53, 53, 57, 67, 91, 94, 103, 107, 123, 418, 420
Slater, Dan, 147–48, 374
smart cities, 429
Smeshko, Ihor, 229
Smith, Nicholas Rush, 374
social class. *See* class
social inequality, after social and urban civic revolutions, 396–403, 432
social media: physical spaces contrasted with, 243; revolutionary commitment associated with use of, 314; revolutionary role of, 88–89, 100–101, 276, 310–11, 315–16
social movements, 28, 29
social movement theory, 35
social networks, 84–88, 313–14. *See also* civil society
social revolutions: in cities, 73–76, 78; civil liberties following, 406–8, *407*, *409*; corruption following, 390, *391*; decline of, 3–4, 6, 15–16, 56, 63–64, 69–71, 101–2, 420; crime following, 377–78; defined, 3; duration of revolutionary contention in and regime survival following, 372–73; economics as catalyst in, 112; government accountability following, 410–13, *413*; grievances of, 10; land inequality and, 66–70, *66*; onset of, 63–64, *63*, *66*; outcomes of, 18, 362–63, 369–70, 374–78, 382–85, *383*, *384*, 388, 392–416; as paradigm in the study of revolution, 21–23; regime type and, 108, *109*, 110; role of rural context in, 33–35, 73, 78–79, 78n51, 420; rule of law following, 409–10, *411*; social formation of agrarian-bureaucratic society underpinning, 5–6, 34, 67, 91, 420; social inequality following, 396–403, *397*, *399*; success rate of, 157; theories of, 33–35, 65, 91, 94–95, 101–2, 104–5; urban civic revolutions compared to, 4, 7, 16, 18, 22, 56–57, 65–66, 107–8, 149–50, 362–63, 369–70, 372–78, 383–416; urban vs. rural location of, 4–5, 20–21, 33–35, 78–79; violence and mortality in, 319–20, 332–33, 403–4, *404*. *See also* urban social revolutions
soldiers, revolutionary participation of, 83–84. *See also* military coups
Solidarity uprising (Poland, 1980), 8
Somoza, Anastasio, 4
Somoza Debayle, Anastasio, 202n10, 207
Soros Foundation, 96
South Korea: economy on eve of urban civic contention, 112; probability of urban civic revolutionary onset in, 134–36, *135*; regime-opposition interactions in, 233; role of exogenous events in, 134–36. *See also* April Revolution; June Uprising
sovereignty, 9, 20, 27, 89, 209, 244, 253, 430
Soviet Union, collapse of, 95, 160, 205, 221, 264, 417
space, as factor in revolution, 20–21, 38–46. *See also* public space in revolutionary contention
Spartacist Uprising (Germany 1919), 324
Sri Lanka, 108
Stalin, Joseph, 29, 237, 264
Starlink, 428n21
state: cultural divisions in relation to, 12; despotic and predatory potential of 10, 11, 12, 17, 40, 57, 93, 107, 318, 422, 425, 431; increasing number of, 89–91; infrastructural power of, 38n65, 42, 57, 91, 93–4, 175, 421; repressive capacity of, 5, 38–39, 43, 74–82, 93, 219–22 (*see also* military; police); resources/wealth of, 162–64; thickened presence of, in cities, 4–5, 10, 14–17, 20, 38–39, 38n65,

42, 241–42, 244, 257–59, 258, 262–63; weakness of, 42, 57, 74, 91, 93. *See also* proximity dilemma; regime-opposition interactions; regimes; state capacity

state capacity: effects of social and urban civic revolutions on, 374–77; location of revolutions linked to, 91–93, 92; types of revolution linked to, 91–93, 92. *See also* state: repressive capacity of; state: weakness of

Stephan, Maria, 176, 181–82, 185–87

Stetskiv, Taras, 212–13

Stinchcombe, Arthur, 361

Stolypin, Piotr, 237

strikes, 8, 52, 81, 183, 185, 209, 247

strong network ties, 84–86, 313–14

structural adjustment programs, 99, 138

students, as revolution participants, 7, 82–83, 293–94, 422

substantive success, 151

suburbanization, 85

success of revolutions, 16, 19; comparison of successful and failed revolutions, 364, 369, 379–80, 380, 381, 383–86, 384–95, 391, 392, 397–400, 404–5, 407–14; criteria of, 24–25, 151, 362; factors in, 44, 156–92; fragility of, 9, 18, 24–25, 46, 359–60, 363, 369–78, 423–24; likelihood of, 152–57; location and type as factor in, 156–92, 156, 158; maximalist criterion of, 151; military's role in, 164–67; minimalist criterion of, 151; mortality in relation to, 320, 343–44; patterns of, 153–54, 154, 155; probability of, 193, 194–95, 196–97, 426; proximity to state power as factor in, 257–58, 258; regime type as factor in, 157–61; in social vs. urban civic revolutions, 369–70; urban civic repertoire's effect on, 18, 44, 82, 152, 157, 159–60, 190, 192–93, 248, 422; during waves of revolution, 167–69, 169n44. *See also* failed revolutions; military coups: success of; opposition success; substantive success

Sudan, 2018 revolution in, 426

Sudanese Revolution (1985), 30n34

Suharto, 99, 111, 137–39, 162, 248

Sukarno, 248

Sukhanov, Nikolai, 222

Sunflower Student Movement (Taiwan, 2014), 28

surveillance, digital, 428–29

Svolik, Milan W., 48n84

Syria: diffusion of Arab Spring to, 168; shooting into crowds in, 354; social networks in, 85–86

Tandja, Mamadou, 142

Tarrow, Sidney, 46, 93–94

Tbilisi massacres, 220–21, 257

tear gas, 351–52

technological change and revolution, 13, 14, 15, 18, 37, 41, 81, 88, 98, 100, 308–11, 321, 327 328n24, 344–53, 419, 428–29

Telegram, 428

television, 13, 80, 87–88, 100, 101, 181, 243, 255, 309–12, 313n113

terrorist movements, 77

Thai Democracy Movement (1973), 82–83, 102, 250, 412

Thailand, 354

Than Shwe, 130

Thermidor, as metaphor for post-revolutionary change, 361

thickened history, 200, 205, 218

third-generation theories of revolution, 33–35, 37–38, 65–66, 71, 101–4, 144

Thomas, Martin, 348, 352

Thyne, Clayton, 47

Tiananmen Uprising (China, 1989), 113, 160, 214–18, 226–28, 233, 249–50, 356, 387

Tilly, Charles, xvii, 25n12, 27, 46, 89, 103, 151, 221, 252, 269

time: in civil wars, 324, 328; decision making affected by pressures of, 206, 221; and momentum, 230; outcomes affected by duration of revolution, 371–73, 371; of revolutionary episodes, 47, 205; in rural revolutions, 42, 77–78, 199, 203–4, 228–29; thickened history as aspect of, 200, 205, 218; in urban revolutions, 21, 41–42, 77–78, 200, 204–6, 208, 213, 228–30, 423

Timoshenko, Yulia, 302
Tocqueville, Alexis de, 20, 30, 418
Togo, 133
Trabelsi, Leila, 125
trade-off, repression-disruption. *See* proximity dilemma; repression-disruption trade-off
Traugott, Mark, 43n67, 246–47
Trimberger, Ellen Kay, 29n25
Trimech, Abdesslem, 125
Trotsky, Leon, 3, 27, 29–30, 164, 205, 230, 418
Trujillo, Rafael, 163
Trump, Donald, 141n80, 430, 430n
truncheons, 350
Tulip Revolution (Kyrgyzstan, 2005), 85n76, 163
Tunisia: age structure of, 290; autocratic regime in, 109; civil society in, 308, 312; class and employment in, 292; digital technology use in, 310–12; economic factors in revolution in, 112; military role in revolution in, 164n34; post-revolutionary economy in, 386–87; probability of urban civic revolutionary onset in, 123–26, *124*; shooting into crowds in, 354
Tunisian Revolution (2010), 13, 45, 54, 114, 123–26, 204, 218, 224n92, 259, 273n7, 274–75, 277, 280–82, *282*, 284–85, 289–316, *315*
Tupamaros, 74n34
Turkish War of Independence, 29n25
Twelve Demands, 27
Twitter, 13, 243, 309, 310, 315
228 Uprising (Taiwan, 1947), 339n

Ubico, Jorge, 30
Ukraine: age structure of, 290; civil society in, 307–8; class and employment in, 292; corruption in, 112; cultural division as factor in, 133; digital technology use in, 309–10; economic factors in revolutions in, 99, 112; electoral protests in, 212–13; number of revolutionary participants in, 176, 180; probability of urban civic revolutionary onset in, 130–33, *131*; public space in, 1–3, 13–14, 236–40, 269; shooting into crowds in, 354. *See also* Euromaidan Revolution; Orange Revolution
"Ukraine without Kuchma" campaign, 132, 201, 212, 239
unarmed revolts: changing prevalence of, 81; deaths in, 81; and geopolitics, 97n118; and international law, 354–56; as mass siege of government, 25–26; vs. "nonviolent" revolution, 52n91; number of participants as factor in, 8, 13, 43, 79, 325, 419; organization and technology affecting, 80–81; as part of urban civic repertoire, 153, 190, 343, 347–353, 422; risks of, 14, 80–81, 321, 427; in rural settings, 43, 52; in urban settings, 14, 19, 21, 43, 81, 185. *See also* urban civic repertoire.
Uniates, 299, 310
United Nations, 6, 355–56, 425
United Nations General Assembly, 355
United Russia Party, 26
United States: international power of, 96, 358, 421, 429–30; role of, in revolutions, 95–97, 99, 140, 357, 421, 430. *See also* American Revolution
Universal Declaration of Human Rights, 265, 355
urban civic repertoire: configuration of public space as factor in, 251–59; declining mortality in revolutions linked to, 321, 343, 352, 355; digital technologies' effect on, 13, 89, 205, 276, 308–16; elements of, 43–44, 81, 152–53, 247–48; emergence of, 13, 15, 20–21; future of, 425–32; success of, 18, 43, 82, 152–53, 157, 159–60, 190, 192–93, 248, 422; urban armed revolt vs., 13, 43, 81, 152, 321; urbanization and proliferation of, 13, 15, 21, 43, 152, 180–81, 184–85, 250, 422. *See also* process of revolutionary contention; urban civic revolutions
urban civic revolutions: capital cities as sites for, 259, 262–63; challenges for, 5, 21, 43, 75–77, 152, 235; civil liberties following, 406–8, *408*, *410*; coalitional character of, 13, 18, 24, 45, 188–89, 275, 302–7, 318, 363,

415, 423; corruption as catalyst for, 9–12, 111–12; corruption following, 389–90, 392; crime following, 377–78; defined, 7–8, 107; "democratic" label applied to, 8–9, 17, 275, 304, 307, 318, 406; economics as factor in, 10–11; exogenous events as catalysts for, 134–39; failures and disappointments of, 18, 363, 373, 388–90, 403, 411–16, 424, 431; frequency of, 8, 14, 15, 19, 56, 58–59, *58*, *59*, 62, 64–65, 426; future of, 18, 425–33; geopolitics as factor in, 95–97. 429–30; goals and targets of, 8–13, 10n33, 20–21, 53, 93, 153, 157, 188, 190, 209–10, 244, 275, 343, 363, 373, 415, 422, 423, 430–31; government accountability following, 410–13, *414*; hurricane analogy for, 16, 105–6, 149–50; international aspect of, 44; military coups compared to, 122; military's role in, 166; opportunities for interactions with military or police in, 75, 77, 167, 186, 200, 221–22, 229–33; organization and technology of, 13–14, 276, 302–17; other urban revolutions compared to, *64*, 184; predictability of, 123–49; post-revolutionary outcomes of, 18, 363, 369–70, 373–74, 378, *385*, 386–90, *386*, 393–416, 423–24; public space as site for, 242–59; regime-opposition interactions in, 134–39, 144, 213–17, 219–28; regime type as factor in, 93, 108–10, *109*; right-wing populism compared to, 430–31; rule of law following, 409–10, *412*; rural revolutions compared to, 21, 38–39, 57; success of, 152, 153, 156–57, 184–85, 190–91; social inequality following, 396–403, *398*, *400*, 432; social revolutions compared to, 4, 7, 16, 18, 22, 56–57, 65–66, 107–8, 149–50, 362–63, 369–70, 372–78, 383–416; social structure as factor in, 288–302; spatial strategies against, 259–69; structural conditions for, 102, 105–8, 123–50, 198, 208, 421, 427–28; tactics of (*see* urban civic repertoire); temporal factors in, 21, 41–42, 77–78, 200, 204–6, 208, 213, 228–30, 372–73, 423; violence in, 187, *405*, 427 (*see*

also mortality in revolutions); waves of, 44, 101, 134, 167–69. *See also* cities; onset of urban civic revolutions; participants in urban civic revolutions; process of revolutionary contention; proximity dilemma; public space in revolutionary contention; success of revolutions; urban civic repertoire; urban revolutions

urban revolutions: contingency and error in, 16, 21, 41–42, 198–200, 208–19, 222–28, 235; definition, 49, 52; factors affecting outcomes within, 173–75, 183–85, 191, 193; fraternization within, 231–33; globalization and, 97–101; growth of, 4, 15–16, 56–57, 64–65, 72–74; information problems in, 16, 21, 41–42, 199; and political regimes, 21, 42, 92–94; speed of, 16, 21, 200, 206, 213–17, 221; and proximity dilemma, 15, 21, 41–42, 75–82; public space and, 17, 246–48, 251–55, 260–61; study of, 21, 30–33, 35, 36–37; surprises in, 200, 208–19, 234; violence within, 187, 321, 324, 331, 335, 340, 345–49, 350–53 *See also* cities; public space in revolutionary contention; urban civic revolutions; urbanization

urbanization: demographics of, 68; geographical spread of, 67–68, 420, 432; growth of, 67–68; mortality in revolutions linked to, 17, 321, 331, 339–40, 343, 355; processes involved in, 85–86; revolutionary episodes associated with, 71–72, *71*, *74*; revolutionary role of, 15, 43–44; revolutionary tactics affected by, 180–81, 420–22; success of revolutions linked to, 156–57

urban poor, revolutionary participation of, 84, 432

Uruguay, 74n34

Valasco coup (Peru), 29n25
Vale, Lawrence, 242
vanguard parties: and individual participation in revolutions, 271; and post-revolutionary regime durability, 370; and revolutionary success, 188; and social revolutions, 12–13

Vanhanen, Tatu, 66–70
Velvet Revolution (Czechoslovakia, 1989), 136–37
Venezuela: corruption in, 112; economic contraction and revolutionary contention in, 114; public space in, 268; shooting into crowds in, 354; surveillance in, 429
Vietnam, 67
Vietnamese Revolution (1954–62), 327
Villaroel, Gualberto, 202
violence: in Euromaidan Revolution, 255, 277, 284, 289–90, 296, 298, 427; as feature of revolution, 23–24, 319, 358; gender of revolutionary participants linked to, 289–90; military–citizen, 81, 216, 224, 230–31, 233, 262, 347–49, 353–57, 427; outcomes of revolutions in relation to, 175–76, 182, 185–87, *186*; perpetrators of largescale, 320; police–citizen, 125–26, 129, 136, 164, 211, 215–18, 224–26, 267, 311, 350–51, 427; in social revolutions, 319–20, 332–33, 403–4, *404*; tactics in relation to, 255; in urban civic revolutions, 187, *405*, 427. *See also* mortality in revolutions
Vkontakte, 428

Wallace, Jeremy, 87
war, as cause/effect of revolution, 94–95. *See also* civil war
water cannons, 352
Way, Lucan, 370–72
weak network ties, 86–87
Weber, Max, 24

Weyland, Kurt, 167, 168
White Revolution (Iran), 29
Wickham-Crowley, Timothy, 78
wildfire analogy, 104–5, 149
women, post-revolutionary status of, 402–3. *See also* gender of revolutionary participants
wooden bullets, 352–53
workers, 5, 7, 10, 12, 23, 31, 32, 35n53, 82–83, 135, 163, 213–14, 225, 227, 246, 251, 252, 292–94, 352n84, 419, 421
World Bank, 125
Wright, Joseph, 48, 110, 161

Xinhai Revolution (China, 1911), 30, 339n

Yanukovych, Viktor, 2, 99, 132–33, 202, 229, 269, 277–79, 286, 360, 427
Yeltsin, Boris, 164, 264, 267
Yemen, 354
Yemeni Revolution (2011), 254
youth, revolutionary participation of, 68–69, 82–83, 290–92
youth bulge theories, 68–69
Yushchenko, Viktor, 2, 180, 212, 229, 278, 283–84, 286, 302, 360

Žižek, Slavoj, 234
Zamiatin, Yevgenii, 417, 433
Zedillo, Ernesto, 146
zeitnot (time trouble), 206
Zhao Ziyang, 227
Zhvania, Zurab, 205, 209
Zimbabwe, 204, 429

A NOTE ON THE TYPE

This book has been composed in Arno, an Old-style serif typeface in the classic Venetian tradition, designed by Robert Slimbach at Adobe.

Milton Keynes UK
Ingram Content Group UK Ltd.
UKHW012004131023
430518UK00003B/119